ESSENTIALS OF RISK MANAGEMENT AND INSURANCE

SECOND EDITION

EMMETT J. VAUGHAN
University of Iowa

THERESE M. VAUGHAN
Drake University

JOHN WILEY & SONS, INC.

NEW YORK   CHICHESTER   WEINHEIM   BRISBANE   TORONTO   SINGAPORE

Publisher: Susan Elbe
Acquisitions Editor: Leslie Kraham
Executive Marketing Manager: Ilse Wolf
Editorial Assistant: Cynthia Snyder
Senior Production Editor: Patricia McFadden
Senior Designer: Harry Nolan
Illustration Editor: Gene Aiello
Production Management Services: Ingrao Associates

This book was set in New Baskerville by Nesbitt Graphics and printed and bound by R.R. Donnelly & Sons.
The cover was printed by Lehigh Press.
This book is printed on acid-free paper. ∞

ISBN 0-471-33183-X

Printed in the United States of America

10 9 8 7 6 5 4 3 2

ABOUT THE AUTHORS

Emmett J. Vaughan holds the Partington Professorship in Insurance at the University of Iowa, where he is Dean of the Division of Continuing Education. Professor Vaughan received his undergraduate degree in economics from Creighton University and his M.A. and Ph.D. in economics and insurance from the University of Nebraska.

Therese M. Vaughan is currently Commissioner of Insurance for the State of Iowa. She has held faculty positions at Temple University and Drake University. Commissioner Vaughan received her undergraduate degree in economics and insurance from the University of Iowa and her Ph.D. in insurance from the Wharton School of Business.

To Brooke, Cale, Cate, Jillian, Kevin, Rachel Ann, and Shane

PREFACE

As its title indicates, this book covers the essentials of risk management and insurance. It evolved from the sixth edition of *Fundamentals of Risk and Insurance,* an advanced-level general insurance text that has been used by college and university students for more than nearly three decades. Over the years, some users of *Fundamentals of Risk and Insurance* had asked for a briefer version of the book, which admittedly tends to be somewhat encyclopedic. In response to these requests, in 1995, we created a brief edition of *Fundamentals* by eliminating some of the detail in the book that did not seem to us to be essential. The result was the first edition of *Essentials of Insurance.* In this second edition, in response to the recommendations of users, we have expanded the discussion of risk management, while retaining the original emphasis on the insurance product and the use of insurance within the risk management framework. To reflect the increased emphasis on risk management, we have changed the title to *Essentials of Risk Management and Insurance.* As this title indicates, this second edition is about *risk management* and it is about *insurance.* Although one can study risk management with little more than a passing reference to insurance and while generations of students studied insurance before the concept of risk management was introduced, we believe that it makes sense to combine the study of the two fields, especially when the student is likely to take a single course that deals with the risk financing problem. As an introduction to

the subject, it is intended for students who have had little or no prior education in risk management or insurance. It may serve as the basis for more advanced texts for those students who intend to specialize in the field of insurance, and at the same time it constitutes a compendium of the things an informed citizen and consumer should know about the subject.

Why Study Risk Management and Insurance?

The reasons for studying risk management and insurance are varied. For some, the study is undertaken in preparation for a career in the field. Others study to improve their knowledge of the subject to become more knowledgeable consumers. The average individual will spend a significant percentage of his or her disposable income on insurance over a lifetime, and one of the logical reasons for studying insurance is to learn how it can be used in personal financial planning. Still others study insurance as a part of the discipline of risk management, the managerial function that aims at preserving the operating effectiveness of the organization.

Although each of these reasons is adequate justification for the study of insurance, whether the study of insurance should be considered *essential* for business students depends on the approach and the specifics of what is studied. Although some have argued that the study of insurance per se is a narrow specialty, the broader discipline of risk management—of which insurance buying is only a part—is clearly a function that all future managers should understand. A proper understanding of the methods of dealing with exposures to loss is essential to organizational managers. Although insurance is only one of the techniques that can be used to deal with pure risks, risk management decisions presuppose an understanding of the nature and functions of insurance.

We believe that insurance and risk management is a subject that needs to be taught in colleges and universities. Far from the narrow specialty as it is sometimes characterized, the field has a breadth that few disciplines equal. As you progress through the book, you will encounter applications from economics, statistics, finance, accounting, law, decision theory, and ethics.

Because the study of risk management and insurance draws on these different disciplines, it is sometimes considered a subset of one of them. Thus, in many colleges and universities, insurance and risk management are a part of the finance curriculum, reflecting the financial nature of the risk management function. In other schools, it is considered a part of economics, while in still other schools it is located in another department. This organizational ambiguity reflects the confusion concerning what the study of risk management and insurance entails.

In fact, the field of risk management and insurance is a separate and distinct discipline, which draws on and integrates the knowledge from a number of other business fields. In a micro sense, it is a discipline in which various methodologies are brought to bear on a significant problem.

Viewed from a macro perspective, the study of insurance addresses a variety of important issues facing society today: the high cost of medical care, crime, the tort system, pollution and the environment, and the broad subject of ethics. Indeed, it is not an exaggeration to say that the debates in the insurance arena address questions of what kind of society we will have and who will pay for what within that society. Debates over the cost of insurance and the way in which insurance prices should be determined have intensified over the past two decades. The current debate over health insurance illustrates how central to the core of our society is the insurance mechanism and how we, as consumers, are all affected by the way in which insurance operates.

Finally, the study of risk management and insurance is a fertile field for considering the subject of ethics in business and in society. Indeed, the ubiquitous presence of ethical problems in the field of insurance transactions raises an important question: Is ethics something to be studied and learned, or is it something innate in the individual? Although practices within the insurance industry provide one venue for exploring the subject of ethics, personal insurance buying provides an even better one. Insurance buyers face ethical issues that provide a personal backdrop for the examination of ethics in personal conduct. We have attempted to provide a framework for exploring ethical issues in the Questions for Discussion at the end of several chapters.

Organization of the book

The book is divided into three major sections. In the first section, we examine the concept of risk, the nature of the insurance device, and the principles of risk management. This section also provides an overview of the insurance industry and the manner in which it operates.

The second section examines the traditional fields of life and health insurance as solutions to the risks connected with the loss of income. The Social Security system, workers compensation, and other social insurance coverages are discussed in this section to permit the student to integrate the coverage under these programs in planning income protection.

The final section of the book deals with the risks associated with the ownership of property and legal liability. The major emphasis in this section is on coverages applicable to the individual or family (although commercial insurance coverages are also treated briefly).

The book is designed to fit a one-semester or two-quarter course. We have composed what we consider to be a logical sequence for the subject matter, but the book can be used flexibly. Sections Two and Three in particular may be taken in different order. In addition, several of the chapters in Section One can be eliminated or deferred until after Sections Two and Three have been discussed.

Changes in the Second Edition

In addition to the updating of material to reflect the changes in the field since 1995, when the first edition was published, there are several changes in the second edition, virtually all of which have been prompted by suggestions from users of the first edition and users of *Fundamentals of Risk and Insurance,* on which this book is based. The major change is a significant expansion of the discussion of risk management in the first section of the book. To accommodate the expansion of the discussion of risk management, we have deleted or condensed some of the detail relating to specific types of life insurance policies that was included in the first edition. We have also added a chapter on employee benefits and business uses of life and health insurance. To accommodate this material, we condensed the chapters on special life insurance policies and managing the retirement risk in the first edition and relocated this material to other chapters.

In Section Three, we have continued the emphasis on insurance coverages for the individual and family. We continue to believe that the complexities of the commercial insurance field are inappropriate for an introductory course in insurance.

Users of the first edition will notice that the policy forms that were printed in a separate booklet with the first edition are now included as ap-

pendices in the text. A number of users of the *Fundamentals* book had suggested the separate booklet for policy forms, but the response from most users persuaded us to return to the original format in which the policy forms are included in the text.

Another feature of this edition is the listing of Web sites of interest at the end of each chapter. Most students will not need to be told about the significant impact that the Internet and World Wide Web have had on education. There are numerous insurance-related Web sites and the number continues to grow. These Web sites can be a valuable source of information on the changes that continue to occur both in government-sponsored programs and in the insurance industry. Although the authors have visited each of the sites listed, Web sites tend to come and go and the URLs may change over time. Despite these impediments, the Web sites listed at the end of each chapter are a useful point of departure for exploring this valuable resource.

Acknowledgments

We have been supported and encouraged in this revision by many people. First and foremost are the members of our families, all of whom sacrificed much to assist us. We thank them all for their help, but more importantly for their understanding.

In addition, we owe much to our teachers, whose influence left an indelible mark on us and on this book. Among these, we include our colleague, Professor Michael Murray, who has shared his insights with us over the years and whose influence on our ideas has been significant. We also acknowledge a debt to Professor Sajjad A. Hashmi, whose review of the first edition in the *Journal of Risk and Insurance* provided valuable guidance in preparing the second edition. We also offer thanks to all of our former students. Their many comments and intelligent questions contributed to the design of the book and to the examples and illustrations used. Finally, we thank Jan Koopman, who assisted in the preparation of the manuscript.

From the teachers who will use this book as a text, we will be grateful to receive advice concerning any errors that should be corrected and any material that should be added or omitted when it is again revised. To the students who will be compelled to read it, we extend the hope that the material presented will seem as exciting and interesting as it has seemed to us.

Emmett J. Vaughan
Iowa City, Iowa

Therese M. Vaughan
Des Moines, Iowa
January 2000

CONTENTS

24 Commercial Property and Liability Coverages 477

25 Insurance in the Future 501

SECTION ONE

RISK, RISK MANAGEMENT, AND INSURANCE

CHAPTER 1

The Problem of Risk

Risk is a combination of hazards and is measured by probability.
—Irving Pfeffer
Insurance and Economic Theory

CHAPTER OBJECTIVES

When you have finished this chapter, you should be able to

- Define and explain the meaning of the term "risk"

- Distinguish among the terms "risk," "peril," and "hazard"

- Identify and explain the classes of hazards

- Differentiate between pure risk and speculative risk

- Differentiate between fundamental and particular risk

- Describe the categories into which pure risk may be subdivided

- Identify and explain the principal methods of handling risk

You see the mangled metal of two cars that have collided on an interstate highway. A fire engine with its siren screaming roars down the street. A building in your neighborhood burns or you see an ambulance racing to the hospital. All these tragic events arouse your interest and emotions. After the noise and excitement have died down, you are grateful that the loss did not happen to you, and you may even feel sorry for whoever suffered the loss. But you're glad that it wasn't you. Losses like these happen to some people, while others go along happily, free from misfortune. The fact that these losses or similar events could happen to you and the fact that you can't tell for sure whether or not they will, is a condition we call risk. Risk is a pervasive condition of human existence.

While our instinctive understanding of the concept of risk is clear enough, terms that have a simple meaning in everyday usage sometimes have a special meaning when used in a particular field of study. In this chapter we will examine the concept of "risk" as the fundamental problem with which insurance deals. In addition, we will also examine several related concepts.

The Concept of Risk

It would seem on the surface that the term risk is a simple enough notion. When someone states that there is risk in a particular situation, the listener understands what is meant: that in the given situation, there is uncertainty about the outcome and the possibility exists that the outcome will be unfavorable. This intuitive notion of risk, which implies a lack of knowledge about the future and the possibility of some adverse consequence, is satisfactory for conversational usage, but for our purpose a somewhat more rigid definition is desirable.

Economists, statisticians, decision theorists, and insurance theorists have long discussed the concepts of "risk" and "uncertainty" in an attempt to construct a definition of risk that is useful for analysis in each field of study. Thus far, they have not been able to agree on a single definition that can be used in each field. A definition of risk that is suitable for the economist or statistician may be worthless as an analytic tool for the insurance theorist. The fact that each group treats a different body of subject matter requires the use of different concepts. Although the statistician, the decision theorist, and the insurance theorist all use the term risk, they may each mean something entirely different.

To compound the problem, the term risk is used by people in the insurance business to mean either a peril insured against (e.g., fire is a risk to which most property is exposed) or a person or property protected by insurance (e.g., many insurance companies feel that young drivers are not good risks). In this text, however, we will use the term in its general meaning, to indicate a situation where an exposure to loss exists.

Current Definitions of Risk

If we were to survey the best-known insurance textbooks used in colleges and universities today, we would find a general lack of agreement concerning the definition of risk.[1] Although the insurance theorists have not agreed on a universal definition, there are common elements in all the definitions: indeterminacy and loss.

- The notion of an indeterminate outcome is implicit in all definitions of risk: the outcome must be in question. When risk is said to exist, there must always be at least two possible outcomes. If we know for certain that a loss will occur, there is no risk. Investment in a capital asset, for example, usually involves a realization that the asset is subject to physical depreciation and that its value will decline. Here the outcome is certain and so there is no risk.

- At least one of the possible outcomes is undesirable. This may be a loss in the generally accepted sense, in which something the individual possesses is lost, or it may be a gain smaller than the gain that was possible. For example, the investor who fails to take advantage of an opportunity "loses" the gain that might have been made. The investor faced with the choice between two stocks may be said to "lose" if he or she chooses the one that increases in value less than the alternative.

Our Definition of Risk

Our definition of risk defines risk as a condition of the real world in which there is an exposure to adversity. More specifically, we define risk as follows:

> Risk is a condition in which there is a possibility of an adverse deviation from a desired outcome that is expected or hoped for.

---

[1] The term "risk" is variously defined as (1) the chance of loss, (2) the possibility of loss, (3) uncertainty, (4) the dispersion of actual from expected results, or (5) the probability of any outcome different from the one expected.

Note first that in this definition risk is a condition of the real world; it is a combination of circumstances in the external environment. Note also that in this combination of circumstances, there is a *possibility* of loss. When we say that an event is possible, we mean that it has a probability between zero and one; it is neither impossible nor definite. Note also that there is no requirement that the possibility be measurable; only that it must exist. We may or may not be able to measure the degree of risk, but the probability of the adverse outcome must be between zero and one.

The undesirable event is described as "an adverse deviation from a desired outcome that is *expected* or *hoped for.*" The reference to a desired outcome that is either expected or hoped for contemplates both individual and aggregate loss exposures. The individual hopes that adversity will not occur, and it is the possibility that this hope will not be met that constitutes risk. If you own a house, you hope that it will not catch fire. When you make a wager, you hope that the outcome will be favorable. The fact that the outcome in either event may be something other than what you hope constitutes the possibility of loss or risk. In the case of an insurer, actuaries predict some specified number and amount of losses and charge a premium based on this expectation. The amount of predicted losses is the desired outcome that is expected by the insurer. For the insurer, risk is the possibility that losses will deviate adversely from what is expected.

Uncertainty and Its Relationship to Risk

Because the term "uncertainty" is often used in connection with the term "risk" (sometimes even interchangeably), it seems appropriate to explain the relationship between the two terms.

The most widely held meaning of *uncertainty* refers to a state of mind characterized by doubt, based on a lack of knowledge about what will or will not happen in the future. It is the opposite of certainty, which is a conviction or certitude about a particular situation. A student says "I am certain I will get an A in this course," which means the same as "I am positive I will get an A in this course." Both statements reflect a conviction about the outcome. Uncertainty, on the other hand, is the opposite mental state. If one says "I am uncertain what grade I am going to get in this course," the statement reflects a lack of knowledge about the outcome. Uncertainty, then, is simply a psychological reaction to the absence of knowledge about the future.[2] The existence of

---

[2]In addition to its meaning as a psychological phenomenon, a second possible meaning of the term uncertainty relates to probability and is contrasted with a second meaning of certainty: a situation in which the probability of an event is 100 percent. An event may be said to be impossible (probability = 0), certain (probability = 1), or uncertain. Used in reference to the likelihood of an event, uncertain simply means that the probability is judged to be between 0 and 1.

Tidbits, Vignettes, and Conundrums 1.1

Fate, Luck, Predestination, and Prayer

Why do good things happen to some people and bad things happen to other people? Philosophers, theologians, economists, and even physicists have debated the subject for centuries. The debate involves disagreement about fate, luck, predestination, determinism, and divine providence. Do we live in a deterministic world where things are predestined or are events the result of random chance? When we say someone is lucky, is it a reference to past good fortune or does it imply the likelihood of good fortune in the future?

risk—a condition or combination of circumstances in which there is a possibility of loss—creates uncertainty on the part of individuals when that risk is recognized.

The individual's conviction or lack thereof (certainty or uncertainty) about a specific fact situation may or may not coincide with the conditions of the real world. The student who says "I am certain I will get an A in this course" may actually get a B, a C, a D, or even an F. Uncertainty varies with the knowledge and attitudes of the person.

Different attitudes are possible for different individuals under identical conditions of the real world. It is possible, for example, for a person to experience uncertainty in a situation in which he or she imagines that there is a chance of loss, but where no chance of loss exists. Similarly, it is possible for an individual to feel no uncertainty regarding a particular risk when the exposure to loss is not recognized. Whether or not a risk is recognized, however, does not alter its existence. When there is a possibility of loss, risk exists whether or not the person exposed to loss is aware of the risk.[3]

The Degree of Risk

It is intuitively obvious that there are some situations in which the risk is greater than other situations. Just as we should agree on what we mean when we use the term risk, we should agree on the way(s) in which risk can be measured. Precisely what is meant when we say that one alternative involves "more risk" or "less risk" than another?

It would seem that the most commonly accepted meaning of "degree of risk" is related to the likelihood of occurrence. We intuitively consider those events with a high probability of loss to be "riskier" than those with a low probability. This intuitive notion of the degree of risk is consistent with our definition of risk. When risk is defined as the possibility of an adverse deviation from a desired outcome that is expected or hoped for, the degree of risk is measured by the probability of the adverse deviation. In the case of the individual, the hope is that no loss will occur, so that the probability of a deviation from what is hoped for (which is the measure of risk) varies directly with the probability that a loss will occur. In the case of the individual, we measure risk in terms of the probability of an adverse deviation from what is hoped for. Actuarial tables tell us, for example, that the probability of death at age 52 is approximately 1 percent and that at age 79 it is about 10 percent. At age 97, the probability of death increases to nearly 50 percent. Using the probability of an adverse deviation from the outcome that is hoped for, we view the risk of death at age 79 as greater than that at age 52, but less than that at age 97. The higher the probability that an event will occur, the greater is the likelihood of a deviation from the outcome that is hoped for and the greater the risk, as long as the probability of loss is less than 1.

In the game of Russian roulette, there is more risk when there are two bullets in a revolver's six chambers than when there is one bullet. Adding a third bullet increases the risk, as does adding the fourth bullet and the fifth bullet. Adding the fourth and fifth bullets increases the probability of a deviation from the hoped-for outcome. If a sixth bullet is added, the player can no longer expect or even hope that the outcome will be favorable. The sixth bullet makes the outcome certain, and risk no longer exists. If the probability of loss is 1.0, there is no chance of an outcome other

---

[3]Some authors equate our notion of uncertainty with subjective risk, which is a person's perception of risk. An individual may perceive risk where it does not exist. (Navigators in Columbus's day perceived a risk of falling off the edge of the world.) They may also fail to perceive risk when it does exist. The distinction between objective risk and subjective risk (i.e., between risk and uncertainty) is important because subjective risk affects the decisions people make. Better information reduces uncertainty (improves subjective risk estimates) and leads to better decisions.

than that which is expected and, therefore, no hope of a favorable result. Similarly, when the probability of loss is zero, there is no possibility of loss and therefore no risk.

In the case of a large number of exposure units, estimates can be made about the likelihood that a given number of losses will occur, and predictions can be made on the basis of these estimates. Here the expectation is that the predicted number of losses will occur. In the case of aggregate exposures, the degree of risk is not the probability of a single occurrence or loss; it is the probability of some outcome different from that predicted or expected. Insurance companies make predictions about losses that are expected to occur and charge a premium based on this prediction. For the insurance company, then, the risk is that its prediction will not be accurate. Suppose that based on past experience, an insurer estimates that 1 out of 1000 houses will burn. If the company insures 100,000 houses, it might predict that 100 houses will burn out of the 100,000 insured, but it is highly unlikely that 100, and only 100, houses will burn. The actual experience will undoubtedly deviate from the expectation, and insofar as this deviation is unfavorable, the insurance company faces risk. Therefore, the insurance company makes a prediction not only with respect to the number of houses that will burn, but also estimates the range of error. The prediction might be that 100 losses will occur and that the range of possible deviation will be plus or minus 10. Some number of houses between 90 and 110 are expected to burn, and the possibility that the number will be more than 100 is the insurer's risk. Students who have studied statistics will note that when one of the standard measures of dispersion (such as the standard deviation) is used, risk is measurable, and we can say that more risk or less risk exists in a given situation, depending on the standard deviation.

At times we use the terms *more risk* and *less risk* to indicate a measure of the possible size of the loss. Many people would say that there is more risk involved in a possible loss of $1000 than in

that of $1, even though the probability of loss is the same in both cases. The probability that a loss may occur and the potential severity of the loss if it does occur contribute to the intensity of one's reaction to risk. It seems, therefore, that a measurement of risk should recognize the magnitude of the potential loss. Given two situations, one involving a $1000 exposure and the other a $1 exposure, and assuming the same probability in each case, it seems appropriate to state that there is a greater risk in the case of the possible loss of $1000. This is consistent with our definition of risk, since the loss of $1000 is a greater deviation from what is hoped for (that is, no loss) than is the loss of $1. On the other hand, given two situations where the amount exposed is the same (for example, $1000), there is more risk in the situation with the greater probability of loss.

While it may be difficult to relate the size of the potential loss and the probability of that loss in the measurement of risk, the concept of expected value may be used to relate these two facets of a given risk situation. The expected value of a loss in a given situation is the probability of that loss multiplied by the amount of the potential loss. If the amount at risk is $10 and the probability of loss is 0.10, the expected value of the loss is $1. If the amount at risk is $100 and the probability is 0.01, the expected value is also $1. This is a very useful concept, as we shall see later.

Risk × %(Probab of loss) = Expected Value of Loss

Risk Distinguished from Peril and Hazard

It is not uncommon for the terms *peril* and *hazard* to be used interchangeably with each other and with "risk." However, to be precise, it is important to distinguish these terms. A peril is a cause of a loss. We speak of the peril of "fire" or "windstorm," or "hail" or "theft." Each of these is the cause of the loss that occurs. A hazard, on the other hand, is a condition that may create or increase the chance of a loss arising from a given peril. It is possible for something to be both a peril and a hazard. For instance, sickness is a peril causing economic loss, but it is also a hazard that increases the chance of loss from the peril of premature death. Hazards are normally classified into three categories:

- *Physical hazards* consist of those physical properties that increase the chance of loss from the various perils. Examples of physical hazards that increase the possibility of loss from the peril of fire are the type of construction, the location of the property, and the occupancy of the building.

- *Moral hazard* refers to the increase in the probability of loss that results from dishonest tendencies in the character of the insured person. More simply, it is the dishonest tendencies on the part of an insured that may induce that person to attempt to defraud the insurance company. A dishonest person, in the hope of collecting from the insurance company, may intentionally cause a loss or may exaggerate the amount of a loss in an attempt to collect more than the amount to which he or she is entitled. Fraud is a significant problem for insurance companies and increases the cost of insurance.

- *Morale hazard,* not to be confused with moral hazard, acts to increase losses where insurance exists, not necessarily because of dishonesty, but because of a different attitude toward losses that will be paid by insurance. When people have purchased insurance, they may have a more careless attitude toward preventing losses or may have a different attitude toward the cost of restoring damage. Morale hazard is also reflected in the attitude of persons who are not insureds. The tendency of physicians to provide more expensive levels of care when costs are covered by insurance is a part of the morale hazard. Similarly, the inclination of juries to make larger awards when the loss is covered by insurance—the so-

called "deep pocket" syndrome—is another example of morale hazard. In short, morale hazard acts to increase both the frequency and severity of losses when such losses are covered by insurance.

In addition to these three traditional types of hazard, a fourth hazard—the legal hazard—should be recognized. *Legal hazard* refers to the increase in the frequency and severity of loss that arises from legal doctrines enacted by legislatures and created by the courts. Jurisdictions in which legal doctrines favor a plaintiff represent a hazard to persons or organizations who are sued at tort. Although legal hazard is greatest in the field of legal liability, it also exists in the case of property exposures. In a jurisdiction where the law imposes obligations on property owners to clean up debris from property losses or demolish damaged buildings, the exposure to loss is increased.

Classifications of Risk

Risks may be classified in many ways; however, there are certain distinctions that are particularly important for our purposes. These include the following.

Financial and Nonfinancial Risks

In its broadest context, the term *risk* includes all situations in which there is an exposure to adversity. In some cases this adversity involves financial loss, while in others it does not. There is some element of risk in every aspect of human endeavor, and many of these risks have no (or only incidental) financial consequences. In this text we are concerned with those risks that involve a financial loss.

Financial risk involves the relationship between an individual (or an organization) and an asset or expectation of income that may be lost or damaged. Thus, financial risk involves three elements: (1) the individual or organization who is exposed to loss, (2) the asset or income whose destruction or dispossession will cause financial loss, and (3) a peril that can cause the loss.

The first element in financial risk is that *someone* will be affected by the occurrence of an event. During the devastating floods in the Midwest in 1993, millions of acres of farmland were damaged by flood waters, causing billions of dollars in financial loss to owners. In addition, according to the game commissions in the affected states, the effect of the flood on wildlife in the area was severe. Although the loss of wildlife may, in some sense, have diminished the quality of life for residents of the area, there was no financial loss resulting from the destruction of the wildlife and fauna.

The second and third elements are the thing of value and the peril that can cause the loss of the thing of value. The individual who owns nothing of value and who has no prospects for improving that situation faces no financial risk. Further, if nothing could happen to the individual's assets or expected income, there is no risk.

Static and Dynamic Risks

A second important distinction is between static and dynamic risks.[4] Dynamic risks are those resulting from changes in the economy. Changes in the price level, consumer tastes, income and output, and technology may cause financial loss to members of the economy. These dynamic risks normally benefit society over the long run, since they are the result of adjustments to misallocation of resources. Although these dynamic risks may affect a large number of individuals, they are generally considered less predictable than static risks, since they do not occur with any precise degree of regularity.

Static risks involve those losses that would occur even if there were no changes in the economy. If we could hold consumer tastes, output and income, and the level of technology constant, some individuals would still suffer financial loss. These losses arise from causes other than the changes in the economy, such as the perils of nature and the dishonesty of other individuals. Unlike dynamic risks, static risks are not a source of gain to society. Static losses involve either the destruction of the asset or a change in its possession as a result of dishonesty or human failure. Static losses tend to occur with a degree of regularity over time and, as a result, are generally predictable. Because they are predictable, static risks are more suited to treatment by insurance than are dynamic risks.

Fundamental and Particular Risks

The distinction between fundamental and particular risks is based on the difference in the origin and consequences of the losses.[5] *Fundamental risks* involve losses that are impersonal in origin and consequence. They are group risks, caused for the most part by economic, social, and political phenomena, although they may also result from physical occurrences. They affect large segments or even all of the population. *Particular risks* involve losses that arise out of individual events and are felt by individuals rather than by the entire group. They may be static or dynamic. Unemployment, war, inflation, earthquakes, and floods are all fundamental risks. The burning of a house and the robbery of a bank are particular risks.

Since fundamental risks are caused by conditions more or less beyond the control of the individuals who suffer the losses and since they are not the fault of anyone in particular, it is held that

---

[4]The dynamic-static distinction was made by Willett. See Alan H. Willett, *The Economic Theory of Risk and Insurance* (Philadelphia: University of Pennsylvania Press, 1951), pp. 14–19.

[5]The distinction between fundamental and particular risks is based on C.A. Kulp's discussion of risk (which he referred to as "hazard"). See C.A. Kulp, *Casualty Insurance*, 3rd ed. (New York: Ronald Press, 1956), pp. 3, 4.

society rather than the individual has a responsibility to deal with them. Although some fundamental risks are dealt with through private insurance,[6] it is an inappropriate tool for dealing with most fundamental risks. Usually, some form of social insurance or other government transfer program is used to deal with fundamental risks. Unemployment and occupational disabilities are fundamental risks treated through social insurance. Flood damage or earthquakes make a district a disaster area eligible for federal funds.

Particular risks are considered to be the individual's own responsibility, inappropriate subjects for action by society as a whole. They are dealt with by the individual through the use of insurance, loss prevention, or some other technique.

Pure and Speculative Risks

One of the most useful distinctions is that between pure risk and speculative risk.[7] *Speculative risk* describes a situation where there is a possibility of loss, but also a possibility of gain. Gambling is a good example of a speculative risk. In a gambling situation, risk is deliberately created in the hope of gain. The student wagering $10 on the outcome of Saturday's game faces the possibility of loss, but this is accompanied by the possibility of gain. The entrepreneur or capitalist faces speculative risk in the quest for profit. The investment made may be lost if the product is not accepted by the market at a price sufficient to cover costs, but this risk is borne in return for the possibility of profit. The term *pure risk,* in contrast, is used to designate those situations that involve only the

chance of loss or no loss. One of the best examples of pure risk is the possibility of loss surrounding the ownership of property. The person who buys an automobile, for example, immediately faces the possibility that something may happen to damage or destroy the automobile. The possible outcomes are loss or no loss.

The distinction between pure and speculative risks is an important one, because normally only pure risks are insurable. Insurance is not concerned with the protection of individuals against those losses arising out of speculative risks. Speculative risk is voluntarily accepted because of its two-dimensional nature, which includes the possibility of gain. Not all pure risks are insurable, and a further distinction between insurable and uninsurable pure risks may also be made. A discussion of this difference will be delayed until Chapter 3.

Classifications of Pure Risk

While it would be impossible in this book to list all the risks confronting an individual or business, we can briefly outline the nature of the various pure risks that we face. For the most part, these are also static risks. Pure risks that exist for individuals and business firms can be classified under one of the following:

1. *Personal Risks.* These consist of the possibility of loss of income or assets as a result of the loss of the ability to earn income. In general, earning power is subject to four perils: (a) premature death, (b) dependent old age, (c) sickness or disability, and (d) unemployment. The significance of these risks has increased with economic development and advances in the standard of living. As productivity has increased, personal incomes have risen. Although this is clearly a positive development, it also means that we have more to lose. As one's earning power increases over time, the loss of that earning power becomes greater. The higher one's standard of

---

[6]For example, earthquake insurance is available from private insurers in most parts of the country, and flood insurance is frequently included in contracts covering movable personal property. Flood insurance on real property is available through private insurers only on a limited basis.

[7]Although the distinction between pure and speculative risk had been introduced earlier, Albert H. Mowbray formalized the distinction. See Albert H. Mowbray and Ralph H. Blanchard, *Insurance, Its Theory and Practice in the United States*, 5th ed. (New York: McGraw-Hill, 1961), pp. 6, 7.

living, the greater the severity of loss when the income that supports that standard of living is impaired.

2. *Property risks.* Anyone who owns property faces property risks simply because such possessions can be destroyed or stolen. Property risks embrace two distinct types of loss: direct loss and indirect or "consequential" loss. Direct loss is the simplest to understand: if a house is destroyed by fire, the owner loses the value of the house. This is a direct loss. However, in addition to losing the value of the building itself, the property owner no longer has a place to live, and during the time required to rebuild the house, it is likely that the owner will incur additional expenses living somewhere else. This loss of use of the destroyed asset is an "indirect," or "consequential," loss. An even better example is the case of a business firm. When a firm's facilities are destroyed, it loses not only the value of those facilities but also the income that would have been earned through their use. Property risks, then, can involve two types of losses: (a) the loss of the property and (b) loss of use of the property resulting in lost income or additional expenses.

Property risks are defined by three parameters: the individual's or organization's ownership (or a similar relationship) of an asset, the asset itself, and the peril that can cause damage. Originally, the perils that threatened property consisted of the perils of nature (windstorms, earthquakes, lightning, floods, landslides) and the actions of people (negligence and intentional damage). With advances in technology, new perils and hazards have emerged. Fire, steam, electricity, and nuclear power have all produced new types of losses. The advent of the information age and our dependence on computers continues the trend. As society advances and technology becomes more complex, there are simply more things that can go wrong.

3. *Liability risks.* The basic peril in the liability risk is the unintentional injury of other persons or damage to their property through negligence or carelessness; however, liability may also result from intentional injuries or damage. Under our legal system, the laws provide that one who has injured another, or damaged another's property through negligence or otherwise, can be held responsible for the harm caused. Liability risks therefore involve the possibility of loss of present assets or future income as a result of damages assessed or legal liability arising out of either intentional or unintentional torts, or invasion of the rights of others.

4. *Risks arising from failure of others.* When another person agrees to perform a service for you, he or she undertakes an obligation that you hope will be met. When the person's failure to meet this obligation would result in your financial loss, risk exists. Examples of risks in this category would include failure of a contractor to complete a construction project as scheduled, or failure of debtors to make payments as expected.

Risks of the Modern Environment

From the dawn of civilization, humans have faced the possibility of loss. While many of the risks that threatened our earliest ancestors have disappeared, they have been replaced by new risks that accompanied advancing technology. Many of the risks facing business today were unknown a generation ago. Some of these new risks arise from changes in the legal environment. They include potential liability for a profusion of new transgressions: environmental damage, discrimination in employment, sexual harassment, and violence in the workplace. Other risks accompanied the emergence of the age of information technology: interruptions of business resulting from computer failures, privacy issues, and computer fraud. The bandits and pirates that threatened early traders have been replaced by hackers who commit vandalism and electronic larceny. Daily newspapers indicate the simultaneous threat of new-age hazards and age-old perils of nature. The hazards posed by the nuclear age were demonstrated by the incident at the Three Mile Island nuclear facility in Pennsylvania in 1979 and the accident at the Soviet Union's Chernobyl plant in April 1987. The ravages that can be wreaked by nature are evidenced by Hurricane Andrew's $22 billion-plus in damages, by the floods of near-biblical proportions that ravaged the Midwest United States in 1993 and by earthquakes in California and Kobi, Japan in 1993 and 1994. The bombing of the World Trade Center in 1993 and the Oklahoma Federal Building in 1995 serve as reminders that it is not just nature that can cause death and destruction, but people as well. Although other losses are less spectacular, it is only because they affect a single individual or a single firm. For the party who suffers the loss, they are no less devastating.

Increasing Severity of Losses

As might be expected, with the increasing array of risks, the dollar amount of losses arising from accidents has also increased. Interestingly, however, the increasing dollar amount of losses is not solely a function of the increasing number of risks. Even those losses that arise from the perils of nature—windstorms, earthquakes, and floods—have exhibited an increasing severity. Nor is the increasing severity merely a reflection of inflation; the dollar total from these losses continues to increase even when adjusted for inflation. Although the number of earthquakes, floods, and windstorms occur at essentially the same rate as in the past, each new catastrophe seems to exceed previous losses. The reason, of course, is that there is simply more

wealth, more investment, and more assets exposed to loss. As business has become more capital intensive, as the technology of production equipment becomes more costly, capital investment increases. With the growth in capital investment, the risk of financial loss also increases.

The Burden of Risk

Regardless of the manner in which risk is defined, the greatest burden in connection with risk is that some losses will actually occur. When a house is destroyed by fire, or money is stolen, or a wage earner dies, there is a financial loss. When someone is negligent and that negligence results in injury to a person or damage to property, there is a financial loss. These losses are the primary burden of risk and the primary reason that individuals attempt to avoid risk or alleviate its impact.

In addition to the losses themselves, there are other detrimental aspects of risk. The uncertainty as to whether the loss will occur requires the prudent individual to prepare for its possible occurrence. In the absence of insurance, one way this can be done is to accumulate a reserve fund to meet the losses if they do occur. Accumulation of such a reserve fund carries an opportunity cost, for funds must be available at the time of the loss and must therefore be held in a highly liquid state. The return on such funds will presumably be less than if they were put to alternate uses. If each property owner accumulates his or her own fund, the amount of funds held in such reserves will be greater than if the funds are amassed collectively.

Furthermore, the existence of risk may have a deterrent effect on economic growth and capital accumulation. Progress in the economy is determined to a large extent by the rate of capital accumulation, but the investment of capital involves risk that is distasteful. Investors as a class will incur the risks of a new undertaking only if the return on the investment is sufficiently high to compensate for both the dynamic and static risks. The cost of capital is higher in those situations where

Tidbits, Vignettes, and Conundrums 1.2

Increasing Loss Severity

The San Francisco earthquake of 1906 caused an estimated $24 million in direct earthquake damage, followed by $500 million in fire damage. The cost in 1998 dollars would have been about $9 billion. Damage from an earthquake of the same intensity as the 1906 quake would likely exceed $100 billion; San Francisco today is a dramatically different place from the San Francisco of 1906. Buildings are taller and more expensive to build, and there are more of them. There are more people, more cars, and more "stuff" today than in 1906. As population and wealth increase, the exposure to loss is magnified. The richer we become as a society, the more wealth is exposed to loss.

the risk is greater, and the consumer must pay the resulting higher cost of the goods and services or they will not be forthcoming.

Finally, the uncertainty connected with risk usually produces a feeling of frustration and mental unrest. This is particularly true in the case of pure risk. Speculative risk is attractive to many individuals. The gambler obviously enjoys the uncertainty connected with wagering more than the certainty of not gambling—otherwise he or she would not gamble. But here it is the possibility of gain or profit, which exists only in the speculative risk category, that is attractive. In the case of pure risk, where there is no compensating chance of gain, risk is distasteful. Most people hope that misfortunes will not befall them and that their present state of well being will continue. While they hope that no misfortune will occur, people are nevertheless likely to worry about possible mishaps. This worry, which induces a feeling of less well-being, is an additional burden of risk.

Managing Risk

There is no escape from the presence of risk, and humanity must accordingly seek ways of dealing with it. Some risks—generally of a fundamental nature—are met through the collective efforts of society and government. Municipal police and fire departments are good examples of the collectively financed approaches to dealing with risk, but there are countless others that might be suggested. Although society and government can help to alleviate the burden of risks in many areas, there are some risks that are considered to be the responsibility of the individual.

Given the vast array of risks faced by individuals and businesses, and the variety of possible ways to deal with them, a systematic process is needed to make decisions. In Chapter 2, we will begin our discussion of risk management and consider a systematic approach for dealing with pure risks faced by individuals and firms.

Important Concepts to Remember

risk
uncertainty
possibility of loss
degree of risk
probability of loss
expected value
peril
hazard

physical hazard
moral hazard
morale hazard
static risk
dynamic risk
liability risk
fundamental risk
particular risk

pure risk
speculative risk
personal risk
property risk
direct loss
indirect loss
liability risk

Questions for Review

1. Define risk. In your definition, state the relationship between risk and uncertainty.

2. Risk may be subclassified in several ways. List the three principal ways in which risk may be categorized, and explain the distinguishing characteristics of each class.

3. The distinction between "pure risk" and "speculative risk" is important because only pure risks are normally insurable. Why is the distinction between "fundamental risk" and "particular risk" important?

4. Explain how pure risk has an adverse effect on economic activity.

5. List the four types of pure risk facing an individual or an organization and give an example of each.

6. Distinguish between direct and indirect property losses.

7. The text discusses the "burden of risk." What are the two principal ways in which the impact of risk may be felt by an individual or an organization?

8. Distinguish between "perils" and "hazards" and give two specific examples of each.

9. Briefly distinguish among the three categories into which hazards may be divided and give an example of each.

10. With respect to each of the following, indicate whether you would classify the event or condition as a peril or a hazard: an earthquake, sickness, worry, a careless act, an economic depression.

Questions for Discussion

1. Two 9-year-old boys are watching a televised replay of a boxing match between Muhummad Ali and Joe Frazier on a program called "Great Fights of the Century." Since the fight took place before they were old enough to remember the outcome, neither knows who won and they bet on the outcome. Tom bets on Ali and Tim bets on Frazier. Does risk exist in this situation? For Tim? For Tom?

2. Mike says, "The possibility that my house may burn is a pure risk for me, but if I buy insurance, it is a speculative risk for the insurance company." Do you agree? Why or why not?

3. If risk is distasteful, how do you account for the existence of gambling, a pastime in which the participants indicate that they obviously prefer the risk involved to the security of not gambling?

4. Some risks facing the individual result from choices regarding lifestyle. Risky sports such as skydiving, bungee jumping, and mountain climbing and behavior such as smoking, binge drinking, and driving at excessive speed represent choices that expose one to risk. Would you classify such risks as pure or speculative risks?

5. Both the probability of loss and its potential severity affect the intensity with which risk is felt by an individual. Would you find a 50% chance of losing $100 or a 5% chance of losing $1000 more distasteful? Why?

Suggestions for Additional Reading

Berenstein, Peter L. *Against the Gods—The Remarkable Story of Risk*. New York: John Wiley & Sons, 1996.
Kulp, C. A., and John W. Hall. *Casualty Insurance*, 4th ed. New York: Ronald Press, 1968. Chapter 1.
Mowbray, A. H., R. H. Blanchard, and C. Arthur Williams. *Insurance*, 6th ed. New York: McGraw-Hill, 1969. Chapter 1.
Pfeffer, I. *Insurance and Economic Theory*. Homewood, IL: Richard D. Irwin, 1956.

Willet, A. *The Economic Theory of Risk and Insurance.* Philadelphia: University of Pennsylvania Press, 1951.

Wood, Oliver G., Jr. "Evolution of the Concept of Risk." *Journal of Risk and Insurance,* 31, 1 (March 1964).

Websites to Explore

Gamma Iota Sigma: http://connectyou.com/ic/gamma.htm

Insurance News Network: http://www.insure.com/

RISKWeb: http://www.RISKWeb.com/

CHAPTER 2

Introduction to Risk Management

*It is, generally speaking, all measures conferring security upon the
undertaking and requisite peace of mind upon the personnel.*
—Henri Fayol

CHAPTER OBJECTIVES

When you have finished this chapter, you should be able to

- Describe the evolution of modern risk management and identify the developments that led to the transition from insurance management to risk management

- Define and explain what is meant by the term "risk management"

- Identify the various reporting relationships that the risk management function may assume in an organization

- Identify the two broad approaches to dealing with risk that are recognized by modern risk management theory

- Identify the five techniques that are used in managing risk

- Describe risk management's contribution to the organization

- Distinguish risk management from insurance management and general management

Risk management is a scientific approach to the problem of pure risk, which has as its objective the reduction and elimination of pure risks facing the business firm. Risk management evolved from the field of corporate insurance buying, and is now recognized as a distinct and important function for all businesses and organizations. Many business firms have highly trained individuals who specialize in dealing with pure risk. In some cases this is a full-time job for one person, or even for an entire department within the company. Those who are responsible for the entire program of pure risk management (of which insurance buying is only a part) are risk managers. Although the term *risk management* is a recent phenomenon, the actual practice of risk management is as old as civilization itself. In the broad sense of the term, risk management is the process of protecting one's person and assets. In the narrower sense, it is a managerial function of business, which uses a scientific approach to dealing with risks. As such, it is based on a specific philosophy and follows a well-defined sequence of steps. In this chapter, we will examine the distinguishing features of risk management.

The History of Modern Risk Management

Although the term "risk management" may have been used earlier in the special sense in which it is used here, the general trend in its current usage began in the early 1950s. One of the earliest references to the concept of risk management in literature appeared in the *Harvard Business Review* in 1956.[1] In that article, the author proposed what, for the time, seemed a revolutionary idea— that someone within the organization should be responsible for "managing" the organization's pure risks. At the time the term "risk manager" was suggested, many large corporations already had a staff position referred to as the "Insurance Manager." This was an apt title, since in most cases, the position entailed procuring, maintaining, and paying for a portfolio of insurance policies obtained for the benefit of the company. The earliest insurance managers were employed by the first of the giant corporations, the railroads and steel companies, which employed insurance managers as early as the turn of the century. As the capital investment in other industries grew, insurance came to be a more and more significant

[1]See Russell B. Gallagher, "Risk Management: A New Phase of Cost Control," *Harvard Business Review*, (September–October), 1956.

item in the budget of firms. Gradually, the insurance-buying function was assigned as a specific responsibility to in-house specialists.

Although risk management has its roots in corporate insurance buying, the transition from insurance buying to risk management was not an inevitable evolutionary process. The emergence of risk management was a revolution that signaled a dramatic shift in philosophy. It occurred when the attitude toward insurance changed and insurance lost its traditional status as the standard approach for dealing with a corporation's risk. For the insurance manager, insurance had always been the standard accepted approach to dealing with risks. Although insurance management included techniques other than insurance (such as non-insurance or retention and loss prevention and control), these techniques had always been considered primarily as supplements to insurance.

The preeminence of insurance as a method for dealing with pure risks by corporate insurance buyers is probably understandable. Many of the earliest insurance buyers were skilled insurance technicians, often hired from an insurance agency or brokerage firm. They understood the principles of insurance and applied their knowledge to obtain the best coverage for the premium dollars spent. Traditional insurance textbooks had always preached against the dollar-trading practices that characterized some lines of insurance and most insurance buyers knew that economies could be achieved through the judicial use of deductibles. Despite these precursors of the risk management philosophy, the notion persisted that insurance was the preferred approach for dealing with risk. When insurance was generally agreed to be the standard approach to dealing with pure risks, the decision not to insure was courageous indeed. If an uninsured loss occurred, the risk manager would surely have been criticized for the decision not to insure. The problem was that not much consideration was given to whether insurance was the most appropriate solution to the organization's risk. The insurance managers' function was to buy insurance and they could hardly be criticized for doing so. After all, that was their job.

What caused the change in attitude toward insurance and the shift to the risk management philosophy? Although there is room for disagreement, it can be argued that the risk management philosophy had to wait for the development and growth of decision theory, with its emphasis on cost-benefit analysis, expected value, and the other tools of scientific decision making.

Whether it was an accident of timing or cause and effect, the risk management movement in the business community coincided with a revision of the curriculum in business colleges throughout the United States. The most significant changes in the curriculum were the introduction of *operations research* and *management science*, with a shift in focus from descriptive courses to normative decision theory.[2] Where previous courses described *how* and *why* people chose among options, new courses in decision theory focused on how choices *should* be made.

As time passed, a few of the more sophisticated corporate managers came to realize that there might be more cost-efficient ways of dealing with risk. It occurred to them that perhaps the most effective approach would be to prevent losses from happening in the first place, and to minimize the economic consequences of the losses they were unable to prevent. From this simple beginning came the discipline of risk management, which is based on the notion that management, having identified and evaluated the risks to which it is exposed, can plan to avoid the occurrence of certain losses and minimize the impact of others. This led to the conclusion that the cost of risk can be *managed*, and held to the lowest levels possible.

The risk management philosophy made sense, and it spread from organization to organization.

When the insurance buyer's professional association decided to change its name to the Risk and Insurance Management Society (RIMS) in 1975, the change signaled a transition that was well underway. The Risk and Insurance Management Society publishes a magazine called *Risk Management* and the Insurance Division of the American Management Association publishes a wide range of reports and studies to assist risk managers. In addition, the Insurance Institute of America developed an education program in risk management with a series of examinations leading to a diploma in risk management. The curriculum for this program was revised in 1973, and a professional designation, Associate in Risk Management (ARM), was instituted.

As it exists today, risk management represents the merging of three specialties: decision theory, risk financing, and risk control. Decision theory has its roots in operations research and management science. The risk financing specialty came from the disciplines of finance and insurance, and the risk control specialty represents the merger of traditional safety management and loss prevention, as developed by the insurance industry, and systems safety from the military and aerospace industry.

✓ Risk Management Defined

As a relatively new discipline, risk management has been defined in a variety of ways by different writers and users of the term. Although they differ in detail, most definitions offered thus far stress two points: first, that risk management is principally concerned with pure risk, and second, that it is a process or function that involves managing those risks. We propose the following definition of risk management.

> Risk management is a scientific approach to dealing with pure risks by anticipating possible accidental losses and designing and im-

---

[2]Decision theory is a branch of *management science*, a broad discipline that includes all rational approaches to decision making that are based on the application of scientific methodology. Decision theory is applied to complex problems in which the outcomes of the various choices are uncertain, including situations in which the probabilities of outcomes are unknown.

plementing procedures that minimize the occurrence of loss or the financial impact of the losses that do occur.

Note first that risk management is described as a "scientific approach" to the problem of pure risks. Although risk management seeks to proceed in a scientific manner, it must be admitted that risk management is not a science in the same sense as are the physical sciences, any more than management itself is a science. As the term is generally understood, a "science" is a body of knowledge based on laws and principles that can be used to predict outcomes. Scientists seek to discover and test the laws of the science through laboratory experiments aimed at discovering the laws that govern or control the events being studied. The standard method of physical sciences, for example, is the controlled experiment, but risk managers cannot use this method. Instead, risk management derives its rules (laws) from the general knowledge of experience, through deduction, and from precepts drawn from other disciplines, particularly decision theory. Although risk management is not a science, it uses a scientific approach to the problem of pure risk. This scientific approach that distinguishes risk management from earlier approaches to risk decisions can be illustrated by contrasting it with those earlier approaches.

Humans have always found ways to deal with risks, and have reacted to adversity in a variety of ways. At the personal level, the natural instinct for self-preservation dictates an instinctive reaction to danger and hazards. Like most creatures, we react automatically to danger, taking whatever measures are available to avoid injury or loss. These instinctive reactions to risk situations are not decisions, but the innate self-preservation instinct.

In addition to our instinctive reactions to danger, much of what one might classify as personal risk management is a learned behavior. "Don't play with matches," "Don't tease the dog," "Don't run with scissors," are all axioms of risk management that are instilled in the individual from an early age. Individuals acquire a body of principles that dictate patterns of action that are designed to protect and preserve. They become innate standards for behavior that, while sometimes violated, represent rules for personal loss prevention and control.

Another part of human behavior in responding to risk is institutionalized. Many insurance-buying decisions are dictated by legal, contractual, or societal conventions. The youthful driver does not really want to buy automobile insurance. He or she wants to drive a car. Most states require that if you drive, you must have insurance. Similarly, while there are probably some consumers who must decide whether to purchase homeowners insurance, for the overwhelming majority, there is really little choice. Unless the individual can purchase the home for cash, there will be a mortgage, and the lender will insist on insurance. In short, many risk management and insurance decisions at the personal level are dictated by convention.

Often, the same institutional, legal, and societal pressures dictate risk management and insurance decisions in the business world. Business managers have found themselves responsible for the management of a firm's risks without any notion of how to go about the process. Bewildered by the confusing array of insurance coverages available, many business managers turned the problem of what to buy over to an outside party, such as an insurance agent. More often than not, the decision to delegate the management of risk to an outside party is based on the misperception that insurance buying involves complicated decisions that the business manager is incapable of making. And because the agent does not want to be in a defensive position when a loss occurs, he or she recommends more rather than less insurance. The result is often dissatisfaction on the part of the buyer over "the high cost of insurance."

Risk management, by approaching the decisions related to pure risk scientifically, is a solution to the challenges in dealing with pure risks. In fact, the distinguishing feature of risk management is the way in which it approaches the decision-making process. Risk management seeks to make the "best" decision about how to deal with a particular risk. In the next chapter, we will see how this is done.

Risk Management Tools

Our definition of risk management states that it deals with risk by designing and implementing procedures that minimize the occurrence of loss or the financial impact of the losses that do occur. This indicates the two broad techniques that are used in risk management for dealing with risks. In the terminology of modern risk management, the techniques for dealing with risk are grouped into two broad approaches: risk control and risk financing. Risk control focuses on minimizing the risk of loss to which the firm is exposed, and includes the techniques of *avoidance* and *reduction.* Risk financing concentrates on arranging the availability of funds to meet losses arising from the risks that remain after the application of risk control techniques, and includes the tools of *retention* and *transfer.*[3]

Risk Control

Broadly defined, *risk control* consists of those techniques that are designed to minimize, at the least possible costs, those risks to which the organization is exposed. Risk control methods include risk avoidance, and the various approaches at reducing risk through loss prevention and control efforts.

Risk Avoidance

Technically, avoidance takes place when decisions are made that prevent a risk from even coming into existence. Risks are avoided when the organization refuses to accept the risk even for an in-

stant. The high incidence of medical malpractice claims in some fields has resulted in a shortage of practitioners in these areas. This is risk avoidance.

The classic example of risk avoidance by a business firm is a decision not to manufacture a particularly dangerous product because of the inherent risk. Given the potential for liability claims that may result if a consumer is injured by a product, some firms judge that the risk is not worth the potential gain.

Risk avoidance should be used in those instances in which the exposure has catastrophic potential and the risk cannot be reduced or transferred. Generally, these conditions will exist in the case of risks for which both the frequency and the severity are high and neither can be reduced.

While avoidance is the only alternative for dealing with some risks, it is a negative rather than a positive approach. Personal advancement of the individual and progress in the economy both require risk taking. If avoidance is used extensively, the firm may not be able to achieve its primary objectives. A manufacturer cannot avoid the risk of product liability and still stay in business. For this reason, avoidance is, in a sense, the last resort in dealing with risk. It is used when there is no other alternative.

Risk Reduction

Risk reduction consists of all techniques that are designed to reduce the likelihood of loss, or the potential severity of those losses that do occur. It is common to distinguish between those efforts aimed at preventing losses from occurring and those efforts aimed at minimizing the severity of loss if it should occur, referring to them respectively as "loss prevention" and "loss control." As the designation implies, the emphasis of "loss prevention" is on preventing the occurrence of loss, that is, on controlling the frequency. Examples of loss prevention techniques include steps to reduce the number of employee injuries by installing protective devices around machinery. Machine guards aim at reducing the frequency of loss. Other risk reduction techniques aim at re-

---

[3]Risk control and risk financing are discussed in greater detail in Chapter 5.

ducing the severity of those losses that actually do occur, such as, for example, the installation of sprinkler systems. These are loss control measures. Other methods of controlling severity include segregation or dispersion of assets and salvage efforts. Dispersion of assets will not reduce the number of fires or explosions that may occur, but it can limit the potential severity of the losses that do occur. Salvage operations after a loss has occurred can minimize the resulting costs of the loss.

Risk Financing

Risk financing, in contrast with risk control, consists of those techniques that focus on arrangements designed to guarantee the availability of funds to meet those losses that do occur. Fundamentally, risk financing takes the form of retention or transfer. All risks that cannot be avoided or reduced must, by definition, be transferred or retained. Frequently, transfer and retention are used in combination for a particular risk, with a portion of the risk retained and a part transferred.

Risk Retention

The forms that risk-financing techniques may assume can also vary considerably. Retention, for example, may be accompanied by specific budgetary allocations to meet uninsured losses and may involve the accumulation of a fund to meet deviations from expected losses. On the other hand, retention may be less formal, without any form of specific funding. A larger firm may use a loss-sensitive rating program (in which the premium varies directly with losses), various forms of self-insured retention plans, or even a captive insurer. The small organization uses deductibles, noninsurance, and various other forms of retention techniques. The specific programs may differ, but the approach is the same.

Risk retention may be conscious or unconscious (that is, intentional or unintentional). Be-

cause risk retention is the "residual" or "default" risk management technique, any exposures that are not avoided, reduced, or transferred are retained. This means that when nothing is done about a particular exposure, the risk is retained. Unintentional (unconscious) retention occurs when a risk is not recognized. The firm unwittingly and unintentionally retains the risk of loss arising out of the exposure. Unintentional retention can also occur in those instances in which the risk has been recognized, but when the measures designed to deal with it are improperly implemented. If, for example, the risk manager recognizes the possibility of loss in connection with a particular exposure and intends to transfer that exposure through insurance, but then acquires an insurance policy that does not fully cover the loss, the risk is retained.

Unintentional risk retention is always undesirable. Because the risk is not perceived, the risk manager is never afforded the opportunity to make the decision concerning what should be done about it on a rational basis. Also, when the unintentional retention occurs as a result of improper implementation of the technique that was designed to deal with the exposure, the resulting retention is contrary to the intent of the risk manager.

Risk retention may be voluntary or involuntary. Voluntary retention results from a decision to retain risk rather than to avoid or transfer it. Involuntary retention occurs when it is not possible to avoid, reduce, or transfer the exposure to an insurance company. Uninsurable exposures are an example of involuntary retention.

Some forms of voluntary retention occur by default. When an organization purchases insurance that does not adequately cover the exposure, it retains the risk of loss for that part of the exposure that is inadequately insured. When a $5 million building is insured for $4 million, the organization retains a $1 million risk of loss. Similarly, in the case of liability insurance, an organization retains the risk of loss in excess of the limits of coverage that it carries. A business that carries a $5 million umbrella, for example, tacitly assumes

---

Tidbits, Vignettes, and Conundrums 2.1

The Psychic Hotline

History reveals that in addition to the instinctive reactions to risk and the efforts to avoid exposure to adversity, humankind has attempted in various ways to predict or change the future. The earliest efforts at *predicting* the future included astrology and divination—the attempt to discover the future by interpreting signs, such as the entrails of sacrificed animals. Early efforts to *change* the future included rituals and magic to keep lightning away, placate volcanoes, or otherwise prevent injury. It is not clear whether these efforts were intended to achieve results directly, or merely to ask for intervention from a higher force; in either case, the intent was to prevent the occurrence of undesirable events.

---

the risk of all losses in excess of this limit. Although the risk manager may explicitly consider the decision in this context, selecting the $5 million limit is a decision to retain risks in excess of that limit.

A final distinction that may be drawn is between funded retention and unfunded retention. In a funded retention program, the firm earmarks assets and holds them in some liquid or semiliquid form against the possible losses that are retained. The need for segregated assets to fund the retention program will depend on the firm's cash flow and the size of the losses that may result from the retained exposure.

Risk Transfer

Transfer may be accomplished in a variety of ways. Transfer of risk through the purchase of insurance contracts is, of course, a primary approach to risk transfer. In consideration of a specific payment (the premium) by one party, the second party contracts to indemnify the first party up to a certain limit for the specified loss that may or may not occur.

Another example of risk transfer is the process of hedging, where an individual guards against the risk of price changes in one asset by buying or selling another asset whose price changes in an offsetting direction. For example, futures markets have been created to allow farmers to protect themselves against changes in the price of their crop between planting and harvesting. A farmer sells a futures contract, which is actually a promise to deliver at a fixed price in the future. If the value of the farmer's crop declines, the value of the farmer's future position goes up to offset the loss.[4]

Risk transfer may also take the form of contractual arrangements such as *hold-harmless agreements,* in which one individual assumes another's possibility of loss.[5] For example, a tenant may agree under the terms of a lease to pay any judgments against the landlord that arise out of the use of the premises. Risk transfer may also involve subcontracting certain activities, or it may take the form of surety bonds.

---

[4]Hedging operations are made possible by speculators who buy and sell futures contracts in the hope of making a profit as a result of a change in price. The speculator attempts to predict the prices months in advance of delivery and buys and sells on the basis of these estimates. It is the speculator's willingness to buy and sell futures that makes possible the hedging process, and it is to the speculator that the risk is transferred.

[5]Although risk transfer by means of insurance constitutes risk financing, some transfers (such as hold-harmless agreements or other contractual transfers) are a form of risk control.

Risk Sharing

While avoidance, reduction, retention, and transfer are the primary tools for dealing with risk, a fifth tool—*risk sharing*—is sometimes cited as a way of dealing with risk. Risk is shared when there is some type of arrangement to share losses. For example, a business may enter into a joint venture with another business, agreeing to share the profits and losses from the venture. Another noteworthy example of risk sharing is the corporation. Under this form of business, the investments of a large number of persons are pooled, and each investor bears only a portion of the risk that the enterprise may fail.

Risk sharing may be viewed as a special case of risk transfer and risk retention. It is a form of transfer, because the risk of the individual is transferred to the group. It may also be viewed as a form of retention, in which the risks of a number of individuals are retained collectively.[6] As we shall see, insurance may be viewed as a form of risk sharing. One basic characteristic of the insurance device is the sharing of risk by the members of the group.

Risk Management as a Business Function

As noted earlier, risk management is a merger of the disciplines of decision theory, finance, insurance theory, and loss prevention and control specialties. Because risk management draws on these different disciplines, it is sometimes considered a subset of one of them. In many colleges and universities, insurance and risk management are a part of the finance curriculum while in other schools it is located in another department. In fact, the study of risk management is a separate

and distinct discipline, which draws on and integrates the knowledge from a variety of other business fields. The same ambiguity about the nature of risk management is reflected in the view of risk management within many organizations. In some organizations, it is viewed as a part of finance, while in other organizations it may be considered a part of the safety organization. In the organization, as in the academic environment, risk management is a distinct and separate function of business.

The famous French management authority, Henri Fayol, writing in 1916, divided all activities of industrial undertakings into six broad functions, including one (which Fayol called "security") that is essentially equivalent to what we now call risk management. The six broad functions into which Fayol divided industrial undertaking were *technical activities* (such as production and manufacturing), *commercial activities* (buying and selling), *financial activities* (finding sources of capital and managing capital flows), *accounting activities* (recording and analyzing financial information), *managerial activities* (organizing, planning, command, coordination, and control), and *security activities* (protecting the property and persons of the enterprise).[7]

While the other functions described by Fayol all developed as well-defined academic disciplines, and became divisions in the corporate structure headed by a vice president, "security" somehow got lost in the shuffle, and it was not until the 1950s that Fayol's six-function division of business activities was resurrected.

Distinguishing Characteristics of Risk Management

A better understanding of the risk management function and its place in the organization can be

---

[6]Sharing may also be viewed as either risk transfer or retention. In a pooling operation, when the parties agree to share risks, it is transfer if it works, and retention if it does not work.

[7]Henri Fayol, *General and Industrial Management* (New York: Pitman Publishing Corporation, 1949), p. 4. This is an English translation of the book originally published in French in 1916.

gained by distinguishing risk management from general management and from insurance management.

Risk Management Distinguished from General Management

Initially, risk management should be distinguished from general management. Risk management differs from general management in its scope. Risk management deals with risk, but so too does general management. The difference, of course, is in the type of risks with which general management and risk management deal. General management is responsible for dealing with *all* risks facing the organization, including both speculative and pure risks.

The risk manager's area of responsibility is narrower in scope, and is limited primarily to pure risks. General managers, who have stewardship of assets and income of the firm, are concerned with losses arising from both pure and speculative risks. They delegate to risk managers the duties associated with pure risks, and the risk manager becomes responsible for conserving the assets and the income of the organization from losses associated with pure risks. Thus, while the responsibility of "general" management is to conserve the assets of the organization and maximize profit, the risk manager is responsible for a part of this general responsibility. More specifically, the risk manager is responsible for that segment of general management's mission that relates to pure risks.

Risk Management Distinguished from Insurance Management

In addition to its relationship to general management, risk management should also be distinguished from insurance management. Risk management is broader than insurance management, in that it deals with both insurable and uninsurable risks, and the choice of the appropriate techniques for dealing with these risks. Because risk management evolved from insurance management, the focus of some risk managers has been primarily on *insurable* risk. Properly, the focus should include all *pure* risk, insurable and uninsurable. In other words, the risk manager cannot ignore those pure risks that are not insurable. A good example is shoplifting losses. Although shoplifting losses represent a pure risk exposure, it is not generally insurable on an economical basis.

Risk management also differs from insurance management in philosophy. The insurance manager views insurance as the accepted norm or standard approach to dealing with risk, and retention is viewed as an exception to this standard. The insurance manager contemplates his or her insurance program and asks "Are there any risks that I should retain?" "How much will I save in insurance costs if I retain them?" In viewing loss prevention measures, the insurance manager asks "How much will this measure reduce my insurance costs?" "How long will it take for a new sprinkler system to pay for itself in reduced fire insurance premiums?" The risk manager, in contrast, views insurance as simply one of several approaches to dealing with pure risks. Rather than asking "Which risks should I retain?" the risk manager asks "Which risks must I insure?"

The difference is obviously one of emphasis. The insurance-management philosophy views insurance as the accepted norm, and retention or non-insurance must be justified by a premium reduction that is, in some sense or another, "big enough." Under the risk management philosophy, it is insurance that must be justified. Since the cost of insurance must generally exceed the average losses of those who are insured, the risk manager believes that insurance is a last resort, and should be used only when necessary.

Risk management then, is something more than insurance management, in that it deals with both insurable and uninsurable risks, but it is something less than general management, since it does not deal (except incidentally) with business risk.

Risk Management's Contribution to the Organization

Risk management can contribute to the organization's general goals in several ways. The first and most important way is in guaranteeing, as far as possible, that the organization will not be prevented from pursuing its other goals as a result of losses associated with pure risks. If risk management made no contributions other than guaranteeing survival, this alone would seem to justify its existence. But risk management can contribute to corporate and organizational goals in other ways.

Risk management can contribute directly to profit by controlling the cost of risk for the organization, that is, by achieving the goal of economy. Since profits depend on the level of expenses relative to income, to the extent that risk management activities reduce expenses, they directly increase profits. There are several ways in which risk management activities can directly affect the level of costs. One, of course, is in the area of insurance buying. To the extent that the risk manager is able to achieve economies in the purchase of insurance, the reduced cost will increase profits. In choosing between transfer and retention, the risk manager will select the most cost-effective approach. This means that expenses for risk transfer will generally be lower in organizations where the choice between transfer and retention considers the relative cost of each approach.

Risk management can also reduce expenses through risk control measures. To the extent that the cost of loss prevention and control measures is less than the dollar amount of losses that are prevented, the expense of uninsured loss is reduced. In addition, since loss prevention and control measures can also reduce the cost of insurance, risk control has a dual effect on expenses. Risk control measures that reduce the cost of losses include those measures that prevent losses from occurring as well as those that reduce the amount of loss when a loss does occur.

In addition to the reduction in expenses associated with losses, risk management can, in some instances, increase income. It can also be argued that when the pure risks facing an organization are minimized—through appropriate control and financing techniques—the firm has greater latitude in the speculative risks it can undertake. Although it is useful to distinguish between pure and speculative risks with respect to the manner in which they are addressed and the responsibility for dealing with them, there are inevitable trade-offs between pure and speculative risk in the overall risk portfolio of an organization. It has been argued that the total amount of risk that an organization faces is important, since firms with higher total risk are more likely to find themselves in financial distress than firms with lower total risk. When the organization faces significant pure risks that cannot be (or simply are not) reduced or transferred, its ability to bear speculative risk is reduced. By managing the amount of pure risk with which the organization must contend, risk management increases the firm's ability to engage in speculative risks.

Risk management can also permit an organization to engage in activities that involve speculative risk by minimizing the pure risks associated with such ventures. Consider, for example, the organization contemplating an entry into international markets. This decision will create both pure and speculative risks for the organization. If the combination of pure and speculative risks exceeds the risk threshold that management is willing to accept, the international venture may be abandoned. If, on the other hand, the risk manager can reduce the level of pure risk, the aggregate pure and speculative risk may be reduced to a level that management finds acceptable. To illustrate, suppose the corporation's top management is considering setting up a subsidiary in a politically troubled country. The threat of expropriation may appear to be too great and might cause management to reject the opportunity in favor of a safer but less profitable alternative. However, if the risk manager reports that political risk insurance is available and reasonably priced, management may decide in favor of the opportunity and thereby generate an increased revenue and profits. The risk manager, who theoretically is responsible for managing all pure risks and can choose from many alternative risk treatment methods, is also in a position to contribute substantially to the operating results of the corporation.[8]

The Risk Manager's Job

The term "risk manager" can be used in a functional sense to mean anyone who performs the risk management job, regardless of whether that person is an employee of the organization, an outside consultant, or an agent or broker. As the term will be used here, however, it will refer to an individual employed by the organization who is responsible for the risk management function.

Even when viewed from this perspective, every organization has a risk manager. The individual may not recognize that he or she is performing the risk management function, but in every organization someone must make decisions that relate to the pure risks facing the organization. In a large corporation the risk manager is (or should be) a well-paid professional who has a specific title and job description that relates to the management of risks. In a small company he or she may be the president or managing partner. In a moderate-sized company, he may be the chief financial officer or someone on an intermediate staff level.

The scope of the risk manager's job differs across organizations. In the broadest case, the risk manager has overall responsibility for all risk control and risk financing activities, including the organization's employee benefit plan. Periodic surveys conducted by the Risk and Insurance Management Society reveal that the responsibilities and duties of risk managers vary with the size of the organization. In some instances, the risk managers are also responsible for the firm's employee benefit plans, while in other cases, their responsibility is limited to those risks that threaten the firm itself.

About one-fourth of risk managers reported having responsibility for some loss prevention activities within their organizations. A higher percentage reported more responsibility for safety and fire engineering, however, than for security, which seems to indicate some fragmentation in responsibility for loss prevention in organizations.

Position in the Organization

In general, one usually finds risk managers in one of three corporate departments, depending on the history and development of risk management in the particular firm. In some organizations, the risk manager evolved from the insurance manager, who has traditionally been located in the finance division or under the comptroller. In these companies, risk management is viewed as a financial function and reports to the finance department. In companies where the risk manager evolved from the employee benefits manager, the risk manager may be in the personnel division. Finally, in some companies the risk manager will have developed from the safety function. Here, the risk manager will generally be located in the division that traditionally housed the safety director, usually the production division.

Most risk managers have a financial orientation, reporting to a vice president of finance, treasurer, or comptroller, although there is a growing school of thought that says he or she should be in a less specialized department, reporting to an executive vice president or even the president to illustrate the companywide scope of risk management activities.

---

[8]See Marshall W. Reavis, "The Corporate Risk Manager's Contribution to Profit," *Journal of Risk and Insurance*, XXXVI, No. 4 (September 1969), pp. 473–479.

Risk Management and Speculative Risks

The term risk management is increasingly used to describe the management of speculative risk, particularly by persons in the field of finance. The U.S. Department of Agriculture, for example, uses the term risk management in reference to risks related to commodity market prices and the management of these risks by hedging, futures, options, and derivatives.[9] Similarly, banks and other financial institutions define the term *risk management* to include the management of such financial risks as interest rate risk and credit risk. To preserve the distinction between risk management in its original sense (as an approach for dealing with pure risk) and the management of financial risk, the term *financial risk management* is often used for the latter.

In recent years, there has been considerable discussion about the potential shift toward *enterprise risk management*, which would bring together the management of all risks—financial, operational, strategic, and traditionally insured hazards—into a single portfolio. Those who advocate a transition to enterprise risk management include some risk managers (and risk management scholars) who believe that the traditional focus of risk management on pure risk has been too narrow. They conclude that the convergence of responsibility for managing pure risks and other risks is a foregone conclusion and that the responsibility of risk managers should be expanded to include other risks, especially those relating to other facets of finance. "Risk is risk," they argue, "and the distinction between pure risk and speculative risk is an artificial one created and perpetuated by academics." Corporate managers are concerned (or should be) about the total risk portfolio of the firm and attempt to manage risks,

regardless of the source. They buy insurance to protect against losses that may arise from pure risks, and they use commodity and financial futures to hedge against fluctuations in interest rates and foreign exchange rates. In most cases, the decisions about how the organization will deal with the various risks it faces have been made independently; one person (or department) deals with pure risks, another deals with the risk of interest rates and fluctuations in foreign exchange, and others deal with production and market risks. Critics make the case that since the separate decisions collectively affect the total risk of the firm, they should be integrated into a single framework that will determine the totality of risk, including both pure and speculative.

The counterargument is that whether the distinction between pure and speculative risk is real or artificial, the techniques used to address some types of risks differ significantly from those used to address others. Despite the arguments of those who would like to expand the concept of risk management, other authorities see clear and unequivocal distinctions among risks and have no problem in delineating pure risks from speculative risks. The reason that decisions about different risks have been made separately is not that the risks arise from different sources, but because the techniques that are used to deal with them are different. Corporate treasurers who deal with interest rate and currency risks refer to their activities as *risk management*, as indeed it is. But the expertise required for managing these risks is different from the expertise required for managing pure risks. Although some risk managers have the expertise to deal in the arena of hedging, futures, options, and derivatives, there are others who feel sufficiently challenged by their existing responsibilities. For the foreseeable future, these risk managers will comprise the overwhelming majority of the profession.

Thus far, the concept of enterprise risk management is more theoretical than a reflection of practice. What remains unclear is who will have ultimate responsibility for managing a company's

---

[9]Derivatives are financial instruments (investments) whose value is derived from the value of other assets, such as commodities or financial indexes.

Tidbits, Vignettes, and Conundrums 2.2

Career Opportunity

In the November 1, 1999 issue of *U.S. News & World Report*, "Risk Manager" was listed as one of 21 "Hot Jobs for the Year 2000." The article stated, "Progressive firms are relying on risk managers, previously the worriers who recommended safety plans and disaster insurance, to plan the future." The indicated salary ranges for the career were $90,000 to $150,000 annually for VPs and $50,000 to $78,000 for associative VPs.

---

enterprise risk portfolio. The disagreement is not about whether financial risks susceptible to treatment by derivatives, futures, and options should be managed, but whether they should be managed by the same person who manages the risks of fires, explosions, embezzlements, and legal liability. Nor is there disagreement that someone needs to manage the organization's total risk portfolio. The dispute is over whether this overall management of enterprise risk should be done by the risk manager. Skeptics who question whether the transition to enterprise risk management will actually occur argue that there is already an authority with the overall responsibility for managing enterprise risk, the CEO (chief executive officer).

Misconceptions About Risk Management

While risk management has become a popular topic of discussion, some of what is discussed reflects a misunderstanding of risk management. Some of these misconceptions reflect a misreading of the literature, while others reflect defects in the literature itself. The first misconception is that the risk management concept is principally applicable to large organizations. The second is that the risk management approach to dealing with pure risks seeks to minimize the role of insurance.

Universal Applicability

If one were to judge on the basis of much of the literature dealing with the concept of risk management, it would be easy to conclude that risk management has no useful application except with respect to the problems facing a large industrial complex. This misconception can easily result from the fact that many of the techniques with which writers have been preoccupied (e.g., self-insurance plans, captive insurers, etc.) *do* apply primarily to giant organizations. Most of the articles on risk management have been written by practicing professional risk managers. It is natural that they would write about the techniques they use in their own companies, and virtually all professional risk managers are employed by large organizations. But it cannot be overemphasized that the risk management philosophy and approach applies to organizations of all sizes (and to individuals as well for that matter), even though some of the more esoteric techniques may have limited application in the case of the average organization.

As the risk manager's position has increased within the corporate framework and "risk management" has become a recognized term in business jargon, the interest in risk management has increased in businesses of all sizes. While it is obvious that the small firm cannot afford a full-time professional risk manager, the principles of risk management are as applicable to the small organization as to the giant international firm. As the discussion in this text will illustrate, the principles of risk management are nothing more than common sense applied to the management of pure risks facing an individual or organization. The principles are applicable to organizations of all sizes, as well as to individuals and families. While the techniques may differ in scope and complexity, the same risk management tools are used in either case.

Anti-Insurance Bias?

The second misconception about risk management—that it is anti-insurance in its orientation and that it seeks to minimize the role of insurance in dealing with risk—also stems from risk management literature. Much of the literature on risk management has also been preoccupied with topics related to risk retention, self-insurance programs, and captive insurance companies. Indeed, if one were to ask practitioners in the insurance field to describe the essence of risk management—that is, its philosophy—many would respond that the major emphasis of risk management is on the retention of risk and on the use of deductibles. While it is true that retention is an important technique for dealing with risks, it is not what risk management is all about.

The essence of risk management is *not* in the retention of exposures. Rather it is in dealing with risks by whatever mechanism is most appropriate. In many instances, commercial insurance will be the only acceptable approach. While the risk management philosophy suggests that there are some risks that should be retained, it also dictates

that there are some risks that must be transferred. The primary focus of the risk manager should be on the identification of the risks that must be transferred to achieve the primary risk management objective. Only after this determination has been made does the question of which risks should be retained arise. More often than not, determining which risks should be transferred also determines which risks will be retained: the residual class that does not need to be transferred.

Risk Management and the Individual

Risk management evolved formally as a function of business. Insurance managers became risk managers, and with the transition certain principles of scientific insurance buying, which had always been used to some extent, were formalized. For the most part these principles are common sense applications of the cost-benefit principle, and they are equally applicable to the insurance-buying decisions of the individual or the family unit. Like the business firm, the individual or family unit has a limited number of dollars that can be allocated toward the protection of assets and income against loss. Personal risk management is concerned with the allocation of these dollars in some optimal manner, and makes use of the same techniques as does business risk management. In order to achieve maximum protection against static losses, the individual must select from among the risk management tools of retention, reduction, and transfer.

Important Concepts to Remember

risk management	loss control	Henri Fayol
risk control	risk financing	security function
risk avoidance	risk retention	insurance management
risk reduction	risk transfer	insurable risk
loss prevention	risk sharing	

Questions for Review

1. Identify the two broad approaches to dealing with risk that are recognized by modern risk management theory.

2. Identify and briefly describe the four basic techniques available to the risk manager for dealing with the pure risks facing the firm. Give an example of each technique.

3. The text states that the emergence of risk management was a revolution that signaled a dramatic shift in philosophy. What was this change in philosophy?

4. Briefly describe the development of risk management as a function of business in the United States. What, in your opinion, were the primary motivating forces and the strategic factors that led to the development of risk management?

5. Describe the responsibility of the risk manager and the risk manager's position within the organization.

6. What is the relationship between risk management and insurance management? In your answer you should demonstrate an understanding of the difference between the two fields.

7. Describe the relationship between risk management and general management. In what ways does a risk manager become involved in the overall supervision of the firm?

8. Identify two common misconceptions about risk management, and explain why these misconceptions developed.

9. Distinguish between risk management, financial risk management, and enterprise risk management.

10. Describe the conditions in which risk avoidance should be used and explain why it is used in these circumstances.

Questions for Discussion

1. In some sense, a risk manager must be a "jack of all trades," because of the breadth of his or her activities. Identify several areas in which a risk manager should be knowledgeable, and explain why this would be useful for the risk manager. What type of educational background should a risk manager have?

2. In a large, multidivision company, risk management may be centralized or decentralized. Which approach, in your opinion, is likely to produce the greatest benefits? Why?

3. The American Risk and Insurance Association has argued that risk management should be added to the required core of knowledge in business administration. To what extent do you agree or disagree that risk management should be a required course in a business curriculum?

4. Describe risk management's direct contribution to profit.

5. In your opinion, should the corporate risk manager's responsibility be expanded to include financial risk management?

Suggestions for Additional Reading

Doherty, Neil A. *Corporate Risk Management: A Financial Exposition.* New York: McGraw-Hill, 1985.
Fayol, Henri. *General and Industrial Management.* New York: Pitman Publishing Corporation, 1949.

Gallagher, Russel B. "Risk Management: A New Phase of Cost Control." *Harvard Business Review* (Sept.–Oct. 1956).

Harrington, Scott E., and Gregory R. Niehaus. *Risk Management and Insurance*. New York: McGraw-Hill, 1998.

Head, George L., and Stephen Horn II. *Essentials of Risk Management*, 3rd ed., vols. 1 and 2. Malvern, PA: Insurance Institute of America, 1997.

Mehr, R. I., and B. A. Hedges. *Risk Management in the Business Enterprise*. Homewood, IL: Richard D. Irwin, 1963. Chapters 5–9.

Mehr, R. I., and B. A. Hedges. *Risk Management: Concepts and Applications*. Homewood, IL: Richard D. Irwin, 1974. Chapters 7–12.

Reavis, Marshall W. "The Corporate Risk Manager's Contribution to Profit." *Journal of Risk and Insurance*, 36, 3 (Sept. 1969).

Skipper, Harold D. Jr. *International Risk and Insurance: An Environmental-Managerial Approach*. Irwin, NY: McGraw-Hill, 1998.

Vaughan, Emmett J. *Risk Management*. New York: John Wiley & Sons, 1997.

Williams, C. Arthur, Peter C. Young, and Michael Smith. *Risk Management and Insurance*, 8th ed. New York: McGraw-Hill, 1998.

Websites to Explore

International Risk Management Institute, Inc.: http://irmi.com

Nonprofit Risk Management Center: http://www.nonprofitrisk.org

Practical Risk Management: http://www.pracrisk.com/

Public Agency Risk Managers Association (PARMA): http://www.parma.com

Risk and Insurance Management Society, Inc.: http://www.rims.org

RiskINFO: http://www.riskinfo.com/

Ultimate Insurance Links: http://www.barryklein.com/

CHAPTER 3

The Insurance Device

Bear ye one another's burden.
New Testament, Gal. 6:2

CHAPTER OBJECTIVES

When you have finished this chapter, you should be able to

- Define insurance from the viewpoint of the individual and of society

- Identify and explain the two essential features in the operation of insurance

- Explain how the law of large numbers supports the operation of the insurance mechanism

- Identify and explain the desirable elements of an insurable risk

- Explain what is meant by adverse selection and why it is a problem for insurers

- Explain the economic contributions of insurance

- Describe the three broad fields into which insurance may be classified, citing the distinguishing features of each

- Distinguish between social insurance and private insurance

- Identify the major classes of private insurance

- Identify the most important social insurance programs

- Explain the nature and operations of public guarantee insurance programs

The Nature and Functions of Insurance

As we have seen, there are a number of ways of dealing with risk. In this book we are primarily concerned with the most formal of these various approaches. We turn now to an examination of the insurance device, focusing on its nature and the manner in which it deals with risk.

Risk Sharing and Risk Transfer

Insurance is a complicated and intricate mechanism, and it is consequently difficult to define. However, in its simplest aspect, it has two fundamental characteristics:

- Transferring or shifting risk from one individual to a group

- Sharing losses, on some equitable basis, by all members of the group

To illustrate the way in which insurance works, let us assume that there are 1000 dwellings in a given community and, for simplicity, that the value of each house is $100,000. Each owner faces the risk that his or her house may catch on fire. If a fire occurs, a financial loss of up to $100,000 could result. Some houses will undoubtedly burn, but the probability that all will is remote. Now, let us assume that the owners of these dwellings enter into an agreement to share the cost of losses as they occur, so that no single individual will be forced to bear an entire loss of $100,000. Whenever a house burns, each of the 1000 owners contributes his or her proportionate share of the amount of the loss. If the house is a total loss, each of the 1000 owners will pay $100 and the owner of the destroyed house will be indemnified for the $100,000 loss. Those who suffer losses are indemnified by those who do not. Those who escape loss are willing to pay those who do not because by doing so they help to eliminate the possibility that they themselves might suffer a $100,000 loss.

Through the agreement to share the losses, the economic burden of the losses is spread throughout the group. This is essentially the way insurance works, for what we have described is a pure assessment mutual insurance operation.

There are some potential difficulties with the operation of such a plan, the most obvious being the possibility that some members of the group might refuse to pay their assessment at the time of a loss. This problem can be overcome by requiring payment in advance. To require payment in advance for the losses that may take place, it will be necessary to have some idea as to the amount of those losses. This may be calculated on the basis of past experience. Let us now assume that on the basis of past experience, we are able to predict with reasonable accuracy that 2 of the 1000 houses will burn. We could charge each member of the group $200, making a total of $200,000. In addition to the cost of the losses, there would no doubt be some expenses in the operation of the program. Also there is a possibility that our predictions might not be entirely accurate. We might, therefore, charge each member of the group $300 instead of $200, thereby providing for the payment of expenses and also providing a cushion against deviations from our expectations. Each of the 1000 homeowners will incur a small certain cost of $300 in exchange for a promise of indemnification in the amount of $100,000 if his or her house burns down. This $300 premium is, in effect, the individual's share of the total losses and expenses of the group.

Insurance Defined from the Viewpoint of the Individual

Based on the preceding description, we may define insurance from the individual's viewpoint as follows:

From an individual point of view, insurance is an economic device whereby the individual substitutes a small certain cost (the premium) for a large uncertain financial loss (the contingency insured against) that would exist if it were not for the insurance.

The primary function of insurance is the creation of the counterpart of risk, which is security. Insurance does not decrease the uncertainty for the individual as to whether the event will occur, nor does it alter the probability of occurrence, but it does reduce the probability of financial loss connected with the event. From the individual's point of view, the purchase of an adequate amount of insurance on a house eliminates the uncertainty regarding a financial loss in the event that the house should burn down.

Some people seem to believe that they have somehow wasted their money in purchasing insurance if a loss does not occur and indemnity is not received. Some even feel that if they have not had a loss during the policy term, their premium should be returned. Relative to the first, we know that even if a loss does not occur during the policy term, the insured has received something for the premium: the promise of indemnification if a loss had occurred. With respect to the second, the insurance principle is based on the contributions of the many paying the losses of the unfortunate few. If the premiums were returned to the many who did not have losses, there would be no funds available to pay for the losses of the few who did. Basically, then, the insurance device is a method of loss distribution. What would be a devastating loss to an individual is spread in an equitable manner to all members of the group, and it is on this basis that insurance can exist.

Risk Reduction Through Pooling

In addition to eliminating risk at the level of the individual through transfer, the insurance mechanism reduces risk (and the uncertainty related to risk) for society as a whole. The risk the insurance company faces is not merely a summation of the risks transferred to it by individuals; the insurance company is able to do something that

the individual cannot, and that is to predict within rather narrow limits the amount of losses that will actually occur. If the insurer could predict future losses with absolute precision, it would face no possibility of loss. It would collect each individual's share of the total losses and expenses of operation and use these funds to pay the losses and expenses as they occur. If the predictions are not accurate, the premiums that the insurer has charged may be inadequate. The accuracy of the insurer's predictions is based on the law of large numbers. By combining a large number of homogeneous exposure units, the insurer is able to make predictions for the group as a whole. This is accomplished through the theory of probability.

Probability Theory and the Law of Large Numbers

Probability theory is the body of knowledge concerned with measuring the likelihood that something will happen and making predictions on the basis of this likelihood. It deals with random events and is based on the premise that, while some events appear to be a matter of chance, they actually occur with regularity over a large number of trials. The likelihood of an event is assigned a numerical value between 0 and 1, with those that are impossible assigned a value of 0 and those that are inevitable assigned a value of 1. Events that may or may not happen are assigned a value between 0 and 1, with higher values assigned to those estimated to have a greater likelihood or "probability" of occurring.

At this point, it may be useful to distinguish between two interpretations of probability:

- *The relative frequency interpretation.* The probability assigned to an event signifies the relative frequency of its occurrence that would be expected, given a large number of separate independent trials. In this interpretation, only events that may be repeated for a "long run" may be governed by probabilities.

- *The subjective interpretation.* The probability of an event is measured by the degree of belief in the likelihood of the given incident's occurrence. For example, the coach of a football team may state that his team has a 70 percent chance of winning the conference title, a student may state that he has a 50:50 chance of getting a B in a course, or the weather forecaster may state that there is a 90 percent chance of rain.

Both of these interpretations are used in the insurance industry, but for the moment let us concentrate on the relative frequency interpretation.

Determining the Probability of an Event

To obtain an estimate of the probability of an event in the relative frequency interpretation, one of two methods can be used. The first is to examine the underlying conditions that cause the event. For example, if we say that the probability of getting a "head" when tossing a coin is 0.5 or 1/2, we have assumed or determined that the coin is perfectly balanced and that there is no interference on the part of the "tosser." If we ignore the absurd suggestion that the coin might land on its edge, there are only two possible outcomes, and these are equally likely. Therefore, we know that the probability is 0.5. In the same manner, we know that the probability of rolling a six with a single die is 1/6 or that the probability of drawing the ace of spades from a complete and well-shuffled deck is 1/52. These probabilities are deducible or obvious from the nature of the event. Because they are determined before an experiment in this manner (i.e., on the basis of causality), they are called *a priori* probabilities.

These *a priori* probabilities are not of great significance for us except insofar as they can be used to illustrate the operation of the law of large numbers. Even though we know that the probability of flipping a head is 0.5, we also know that we cannot use this knowledge to predict whether a given flip will result in a head or a tail. We know that the probability has little relevance for a single trial.

Given a sufficient number of flips, however, we would expect the result to approach one-half heads and one-half tails. We feel that this is true even though we may not have the inclination to test it. This common sense notion that the probability is meaningful only over a large number of trials is an intuitive recognition of the *law of large numbers*, which in its simplest form states that

> The observed frequency of an event more nearly approaches the underlying probability of the population as the number of trials approaches infinity.

In other words, for the probability to work itself out, a large number of flips or tosses is necessary. The greater the number of trials or flips, the more nearly the observed result will approach the underlying probability of 0.5.

Clearly, this *a priori* method of determining the probability of an event is the preferred method, but except in the most elementary situations, determining causality is not practical. Therefore, another approach is employed. When we do not know the underlying probability of an event and cannot deduce it from the nature of the event, we can estimate it on the basis of past experience. Suppose that we are told that the probability that a 21-year-old male will die before reaching age 22 is 0.00191. What does this mean? It means that someone has examined mortality statistics and discovered that, in the past, 191 men out of every 100,000 alive at age 21 have died before reaching age 22. It also means that, barring changes in the causes of these deaths, we can expect approximately the same proportion of 21-year-olds to die in the future.

Here, the probability is interpreted as the relative frequency resulting from a long series of trials or observations, and it is estimated after observation of the past rather than from the nature of the event as in the case of *a priori* probabilities. These probabilities, computed after a study of past experience, are called *a posteriori* or empirical probabilities. They differ from *a priori* probabilities, such as those observed in flipping a coin, in the

---

Tidbits, Vignettes, and Conundrums 3.1

Misrepresentations, Post-Claim Underwriting, and Risk Transfer

An insurer who specializes in marketing life insurance to low-income persons was sued in a class action suit alleging that the company's agents engaged in cleansheeting when assisting prospects, some of whom could not read or write, in completing applications for life insurance. (Cleansheeting is the practice of omitting material facts from an application or making an untrue, false, deceptive, or misleading statement in order to obtain the policy.) The agents entered false statements on the applications, which were then signed by the applicant. The insurer later used these false statements as the basis for denial of claims by insureds who died during the policy's contestable period (the first two years after the policy's inception during which an insurer can contest the policy because of misstatements by the insured). A class action suit was brought against the insurer on behalf of the insureds, arguing that the agents' actions combined with the post-claim underwriting process made all policies worthless during the first two years. The insurer argued that only those persons who had actually died suffered a loss. What principle is involved in this disagreement?

---

method by which they are determined, but not in their interpretation. In addition, while the probability computed prior to the flipping of a coin can be considered to be exact, those computed on the basis of past experience are only estimates of the true probability.

The law of large numbers, which tells us that *a priori* estimates are meaningful only over a large number of trials, is the basis for the *a posteriori* estimates. Since the observed frequency of an event approaches the underlying probability of the population as the number of trials increases, we can obtain a notion of the underlying probability by observing events that have occurred. After observing the proportion of the time that the various outcomes have occurred over a long period of time under essentially the same conditions, we construct an index of the relative frequency of the occurrence of each possible outcome. This index of the relative frequency of each of all possible outcomes is called a *probability distribution,* and the probability assigned to the event is the *average rate at which the outcome is expected to occur.*

In making probability estimates on the basis of past experience or historical data, we use the techniques of statistical inference, which is to say

that we make inferences about the population based on sample data. It is not usually possible to examine the entire population, so we must be content with a sample. We take a sample to draw a conclusion about some measure of the population (referred to as a parameter) based on a sample value (called a sample statistic). In attempting to estimate the probability of an event, the parameter of the population in which we are interested is the mean or average frequency of occurrence, and we attempt to estimate this value based on our sample. Because only partial information is available, there is the possibility that our estimate of the mean of the population (the probability) will be wrong.

We know that the observed frequency of an event will approach the underlying probability as the number of trials increases. It therefore follows that the larger the sample upon which our estimate of the probability is based, the more closely our estimate should approximate the true probability.

Unfortunately, it is seldom possible to take as large a sample as we would like. Instead, we make an estimate (called a point estimate) of the mean of the population based on the mean of the sample and then estimate the probability that the mean of the population falls within a certain range of this point estimate. Put somewhat differently, we estimate the population mean on the basis of the sample, and then we allow a margin for error. The extent of the margin for error will depend on the concentration of the values that make up the mean and the size of the sample. The greater the dispersion of the individual values from the mean (i.e., the greater the variation in data upon which the sample mean is based), the less certain we can be that our point estimate approximates the true mean of the population.

To illustrate this principle,[1] let us assume that an insurance company that has insured 1000 houses each year for the past five years examines its records and finds the following losses:

Year	Houses That Burn
1	7
2	11
3	10
4	9
5	13

Over the five-year period, a total of 50 houses have burned, or an average of 10 houses per year. Since the number of houses insured each year was 1000, we estimate the chance of loss to be 1/100 or 0.01. In so doing, we are simply saying, "The average number of losses in our sample was 10 houses per 1000. If the mean of our sample approximates the mean of the entire population (all houses), the probability of loss is 0.01, and we predict that 10 houses will burn the sixth year if 1000 houses are again insured." But we cannot be certain that we are correct in our estimate of the probability. The mean of our sample (our esti-

---

[1]This example is not intended as an illustration of the way insurance companies actually compute rates. As a matter of fact, industry ratemaking practices bear little resemblance to the process described here. The example merely serves to show how the law of large numbers is the basis for the insurance mechanism.

mate of the probability) may not be the same as the mean of the universe (the true probability). The confidence we can place in our estimate of the probability will vary with the dispersion or variation in the values that make up the mean of the sample. Compare this second set of losses with the preceding set:

Year	Houses That Burn
1	16
2	4
3	10
4	12
5	8

The total number of losses over the five-year period is again 50, and the average or mean losses per year is again 10. However, there is a greater variation in the number of losses from year to year. Even though the mean is the same in both groups, we would expect the mean of the first set of data to correspond more closely with the mean of the population. The greater the variation in the data upon which our estimate of the probability is based, the greater is likely to be the variation between our estimate of the probability and the true probability. Since there is a relationship between the variation in the values that make up the sample mean and the likelihood that the sample mean approximates the population mean, it is useful to be able to measure the variation in these values.

Measures of Dispersion and the Probability Estimate

Statisticians have developed several measures of the dispersion in a group of values. For example, in the case of the first set of losses (7, 11, 10, 9, 13), the number of losses in any given year varied from 7 to 13; in the second set of losses (16, 4, 10, 12, 8), the number of losses varied from 4 to 16. This variation from the smallest number to the largest number is called the range, which is the simplest of the measures of dispersion. Another measure is the *variance*, which is computed by squaring the annual deviations of the values from the mean and then taking an average of these squared differences. For example, the variance of the two sets of losses under discussion here would be computed as follows:

Year	Average Losses	Actual Losses	Difference	Difference Squared
1	10	7	3	9
2	10	11	1	1
3	10	10	0	0
4	10	9	1	1
5	10	13	3	29
				20

$$\frac{\text{Summation of differences squared}}{\text{Number of years}} = \frac{20}{5} = 4$$

Year	Average Losses	Actual Losses	Difference	Difference Squared
1	10	16	6	36
2	10	4	6	36
3	10	10	0	0
4	10	12	2	4
5	10	8	2	24
				80

$$\frac{\text{Summation of differences squared}}{\text{Number of years}} = \frac{80}{5} = 16$$

The variance of the first set of losses is 4, and that of the second set is 16. The larger variance of the second set is simply an indication of the greater variation in the data that compose the mean.

The square root of the variance is called the *standard deviation*, which is the most widely used and perhaps the most useful of all measures of dispersion. Since the variance of the first group of losses is 4, the standard deviation of that group is 2. In the case of the second set, where the variance is 16, the standard deviation is 4. Like the variance, the standard deviation is simply a number that measures the concentration of the values

about their mean. The smaller the standard deviation relative to the mean, the less the dispersion and the more uniform the values. To return to the question of the accuracy of our point estimate of the probability based on the sample mean, the standard deviation is particularly useful in making estimates about the probable accuracy of this point estimate. In a sample with a lower standard deviation, we can be more confident in our estimate of the population mean.

Even if we knew with certainty, however, that the population mean is 10 houses burning next year, it does not mean that 10 houses will in fact burn. In a normal distribution, 68.27 percent of the cases will fall within the range of the mean plus or minus one standard deviation. The mean plus or minus two standard deviations will describe the range within which 95.45 percent of the cases will lie, and the range of three standard deviations above and below the mean will include 99.73 percent of the values in the distribution. Using the sample mean as our point estimate of the probability, we can estimate the probability that the number of houses burning next year will be within a certain range of the sample mean, provided that we know the standard deviation of the distribution. In the case of the first set of losses, where the standard deviation was calculated to be 2, there is a 68.27 percent probability that the number of houses burning next year will be between 8 and 12 (i.e., 10 ± 2), a 95.45 percent probability that the number burning will be between 6 and 14 (10 ± [2 × 2]), and a 99.73 percent probability that the number will be between 4 and 16 (10 ± [3 × 2]). In the case of the second set of data, where the values were more dispersed and the standard deviation was calculated to be 4, there is a 68.27 percent probability that the number of houses burning will be between 6 and 14, a 95.45 percent probability that it will be between 2 and 18, and a 99.73 percent probability that it will be between 0 and 22.

Exactly what does all this mean? It means that there is uncertainty inherent in our predictions. During the past five years, the average number of losses per 1000 dwellings has been 10, and on the basis of our estimate of the probability, we might predict 10 losses if 1000 houses are insured the sixth year, but we cannot be certain that our estimate of the probability is correct. Even if our estimate of the probability is correct, a different number of houses may burn next year. As a matter of fact, in the case of our first sample, our computations indicate that at best we can be 99 percent certain only that the true probability lies somewhere in the range of 4 to 16 losses per 1000 houses. The number of houses that may be expected to burn next year, other things being equal, is some number between 4 and 16. This means that actual results may be expected to deviate by as much as 6 from the predicted 10. This represents a possible deviation of 60 percent (6/10) from the expected value.

Other things being equal, the larger our sample, the more closely we will expect the mean of the sample to coincide with the mean of the population and the smaller will be the margin we must allow for error. This is reflected by the fact (which can be demonstrated mathematically) that the standard deviation of a distribution is inversely proportional to the square root of the number of items in the sample. For example, let us assume that we are able to increase the number of houses in our sample from 1000 to 100,000 per year and that we observe a 100-fold increase in losses.[2] The average number of losses observed per year will increase from 10 to 1000. The standard deviation will also have increased, but, and this is the critical point, it will not have increased proportionately, for the standard deviation increases only by the square root of the increase in the size of the sample. Observed losses increase 100-fold with a 100-fold increase in exposures, but the standard deviation will increase only 10-fold. Thus the standard deviation, which is calculated to be 2 at the 1000 exposure level, will increase to

only 20 at the level of 100,000 houses. The new mean is 1000, and the mean plus or minus three standard deviations is now 1000 ± 60 and not 1000 ± 600. We can predict 1000 losses next year if 100,000 houses are insured, and we can feel 99 percent confident that the expected number of losses will fall somewhere between 940 and 1060. This represents a potential deviation of only 6 percent (60/1000) from the expected value. The area of uncertainty has decreased, because the size of the sample has increased. Note that in our example, neither the probability nor our estimate of it has changed. The number of losses expected per 1000 houses is the same, but we are more confident that our estimate approximates the true probability.

Dual Application of the Law of Large Numbers

Based on the preceding discussion, it should be apparent that the law of large numbers is important in insurance for two reasons. First, a large sample will improve our estimate of the underlying probability. Even when we have estimated the probability on the basis of the sample of 100,000 houses per year, we cannot expect the narrower range of possible deviation if our estimate is applied to 1000 houses. As we have seen, even in the case of *a priori* probabilities where the probability is known, it must be applied to a large number of trials if we expect actual results to approximate the true probability. Therefore, in the case of empirical probabilities, the requirement of a large number has dual application:

- To estimate the underlying probability accurately, the insurance company must have a sufficiently large sample. The larger the sample, the more accurate will be the estimate of the probability.

- Once the estimate of the probability has been made, it must be applied to a sufficiently large number of exposure units to permit the underlying probability to work itself out.

---

[2]It is entirely possible that this larger sample might indicate a different number of losses per 1000 houses than the smaller sample, simply because our estimate based on the sample of 1000 was a poorer estimate of the true probability than that based on a sample of 100,000. For the purpose of simplification, we have assumed that the number of observed losses per 1000 does not change.

In this sense, to the insurance company, the law of large numbers means that the larger the number of cases examined in the sampling process, the better the chance of making a good estimate of the probability; the larger the number of exposure units to which the estimate is applied, the better the chance that actual experience will approximate a good estimate of the probability.

In making predictions on the basis of historical data, the insurance company implicitly says: "If things continue to happen in the future as they have happened in the past, and if our estimate of what has happened in the past is accurate, this is what we may expect." But things may not happen in the future as they have in the past. As a matter of fact, it is likely that the probability involved is constantly changing. In addition, we may not have a good estimate of the probability. All of this means that things may not turn out as expected. Since the insurance company bases its rates on its expectation of future losses, it must be concerned with the extent to which actual experience is likely to deviate from predicted results. For the insurance company, risk (or the possibility of financial loss) is measured by the potential deviation of actual from predicted results, and the accuracy of prediction is enhanced when the predictions are based on and are applied to a large number of exposure units. If the insurance company's actuaries could be absolutely certain that their predictions would be 100 percent accurate, there would be no possibility of loss for the insurance company, because premium income would always be sufficient to pay losses and expenses. Insofar as actual events may differ from predictions, risk exists for the insurer. To the extent that accuracy in prediction is attained, risk is reduced.

As a final point, it should be noted that although probability theory plays an important role in the operation of insurance, insurance does not always depend on probabilities and predictions. Insurance arrangements can exist in which the participants agree to share losses and to determine each party's share of the costs on a post-loss basis. It is only when insurance is to be operated on an advance premium basis, with the partici-pants paying their share of losses in advance, that probability theory and predictions are important.

Insurance Defined from the Viewpoint of Society

In addition to eliminating risk for the individual through transfer, the insurance device reduces the aggregate amount of risk in the economy by substituting certain costs for uncertain losses. These costs are assessed on the basis of the predictions made through the use of the law of large numbers. We may now formulate a second definition of insurance:

> From the social point of view, insurance is an economic device for reducing and elimi-nating risk through the process of combin-ing a sufficient number of homogeneous exposures into a group to make the losses predictable for the group as a whole.

Insurance does not prevent losses,[3] nor does it reduce the cost of losses to the economy as a whole. As a matter of fact, it may very well have the opposite effect of causing losses and increasing the cost of losses for the economy as a whole. The existence of insurance encourages some losses for the purpose of defrauding the insurer. In addition, people are less careful and may exert less effort to prevent losses than they might if the insurance did not exist. Also, the economy incurs certain additional costs in the operation of the insurance mechanism. Not only must the cost of the losses be borne, but the expense of distributing the losses on some equitable basis adds to this cost.

---

[3]In many forms of property and casualty insurance, loss-prevention efforts are a major feature, but these loss-prevention activities are not essentially a part of the operation of the insurance principle. Insurance could exist without them, and they could and do exist without insurance. Insurance in and of itself does not favorably alter the probability of loss.

The Economic Contribution of Insurance

Property that is destroyed by an insured contingency is not replaced through the existence of an insurance contract. True, the funds from the insurance company may be used to replace the property, but when a house or building burns, society has lost a want-satisfying good. Insurance as an economic device is justified because it creates certainty about the financial burden of losses and because it spreads the losses that do occur. In providing a mechanism through which losses can be shared and uncertainty reduced, insurance brings peace of mind to society's members and makes costs more certain.

Insurance also provides for a more optimal utilization of capital. Without the possibility of insurance, individuals and businesses would have to maintain relatively large reserve funds to meet the risks that they must assume. These funds would be in the form of idle cash, or would be invested in safe, liquid, and low-interest-bearing securities. This would be an inefficient use of capital. When the risk is transferred to the professional risk bearer, the deviations from expected results are minimized. As a consequence, insurers are obligated to keep much smaller reserves than would be the case if insurance did not exist. The released funds are then available for investment in more productive pursuits, resulting in a much greater productivity of capital.

Insurance and Gambling

Perhaps we should make one final distinction regarding the nature of insurance. It is often claimed that insurance is a form of gambling. "You bet that you will die and the insurance company bets that you won't" or "I bet the insurance company $300 against $100,000 that my house will burn." The fallacy of these statements should be obvious. In the case of a wager, there is no chance of loss, and hence no risk, before the wa-

ger. In the case of insurance, the chance of loss exists whether or not there is an insurance contract in effect. In other words, the basic distinction between insurance and gambling is that gambling creates a risk, while insurance provides for the transfer of existing risk.

Elements of an Insurable Risk

While it is theoretically possible to insure all possibilities of loss, some are not insurable at a reasonable price. For practical reasons, insurers are not willing to accept all the risks that others may wish to transfer to them. To be considered a proper subject for insurance, certain characteristics should be present. The four features listed next represent the "ideal" elements of an insurable risk. Although it is desirable that the risk have these characteristics, it is possible for certain risks that do not have them to be insured.

1. *There must be a sufficiently large number of homogeneous exposure units to make the losses reasonably predictable.* Insurance, as we have seen, is based on the operation of the law of large numbers. A large number of exposure units enhances the operation of an insurance plan by making estimates of future losses more accurate.

2. *The loss produced by the risk must be definite and measurable.* It must be a type of loss that is relatively difficult to counterfeit, and it must be capable of financial measurement. In other words, we must be able to tell when a loss has taken place, and we must be able to set some value on the extent of it.

3. *The loss must be fortuitous or accidental.* It must be something that may or may not happen. Further, the loss should be beyond the control of the insured. Since we assume that past experience was a result of chance happening, the predictions concerning the future will be valid only if

future happenings are also a result of chance.

4. *The loss must not be catastrophic.* It must be unlikely to produce loss to a large percentage of the exposure units at the same time. The insurance principle is based on a notion of sharing losses, and inherent in this idea is the assumption that only a small percentage of the group will suffer loss at any one time. Damage that results from enemy attack would be catastrophic in nature. There are additional perils, such as floods, which, while they would not affect everyone in the society, would affect only those who had purchased insurance. The principle of randomness in selection is closely related to the requirement that the loss must not be catastrophic.

Randomness

The future experience of the group to which we apply our predictions will approximate the experience of the group upon which the predictions are based only if both have approximately the same characteristics. There must be a proportion of good and bad risks in the first group equal to the proportion of good and bad risks of the group on whose experience the prediction is made. Yet, human nature acts to interfere with the randomness necessary to permit random composition of the current group. The losses that are predicted are based on the average experience of the older group, but there are always some individuals who are, and who realize that they are, worse than average risks. Because the chance of loss for these risks is greater than that for the other members of society, they have a tendency to desire insurance coverage to a greater extent than the remainder of the group. This tendency results in what is known as *adverse selection.* Adverse selection is the tendency of the persons whose exposure to loss is higher than average to purchase or continue insurance to a greater extent than those whose exposure is less than average. Unless some provision is made to prevent adverse selection, predictions based on past experience would be useless in foretelling future experience. Adverse selection works in the direction of accumulating bad risks. Since the predictions of future losses are based on the average loss of the past (in which both good and poor exposures were involved), if the experience of the future is based on the experience of a larger proportion of bad risks, it will be worse than that of the past, and the predictions will be invalid.

Adverse selection long caused private insurers to avoid the field of flood insurance. The adverse selection inherent in insuring fixed properties against the peril of flood is obvious. Only those individuals who feel that they are exposed to loss by flood are interested in flood insurance, and yet in the event of a flood, there is a likelihood that all these individuals would suffer loss. The element of the sharing of the losses of a few by the many who suffered no loss would not exist. Although some insurers have written coverage against flood on fixed properties, the coverage has not generally been available from private insurers for those who need it most.[4]

The "war-risk exclusion" that life insurance companies insert in their contracts during wartime is another example of the adverse selection principle. The war-risk exclusion is inserted in policies during wartime to prevent soldiers who would not otherwise have purchased insurance from doing so when they are exposed to a greater chance of loss. Policies that are sold before the war begins (and do not have the war-risk exclusion) cover deaths that result from war. If the policies purchased during the war were based on the same randomness as those sold in peacetime, the war-risk exclusion would not be necessary, but in

---

[4]After decades of agitation for the government to "do something" about flood exposure, a federal flood insurance program was enacted in 1968. This program is discussed in greater detail in Chapter 19.

Tidbits, Vignettes, and Conundrums 3.2

Billion-Dollar Body

Early in 2000, the tabloid *British Sun* published a report that singer Jennifer Lopez had insured her body with Lloyds for $1 billion. Other papers and magazines picked up and repeated the story, which was later denied by Ms. Lopez. The widespread acceptance of the story is attributable to Lloyds' willingness to provide such insurance in the past. In the 1940s, Betty Grable insured her legs with Lloyds' for $1 million. Lloyds has insured Dolly Parton's breasts for $600,000, and Bruce Springsteen's voice for $6 million.

While these exposures do not meet the desirable element of an insurable risk that there be a large number of exposures, the transactions are still insurance. The underwriters at Lloyds substitute mass underwriting (where a single risk is spread among many insurers) for the mass of exposures. In addition, the premiums charged for such coverages are heavily loaded, that is, higher than probability requires.

---

the absence of such a provision, the randomness would not exist and the company would be selected against.

Economic Feasibility

Sometimes, an additional attribute is listed as a requirement of an insurable risk—that the cost of the insurance must not be high in relation to the possible loss or that the insurance must be economically feasible. We can hardly call this a requirement of an insurable risk in view of the fact that the principle is widely violated in the insurance industry today. The four elements of an insurable risk are characteristics of certain risks that permit the successful operation of the insurance principle. If a given risk lacks one of these elements, the operation of the insurance mechanism is impeded. The principle of "economically feasible insurability" is not really an impediment to the operation of the insurance principle, but rather a violation of the principles of risk management and common sense.

Self-insurance

The term *self-insurance* has become a well-established part of the terminology of the insurance field, despite disagreement as to whether such a mechanism is possible.[5] From a purely semantic point of view, the term self-insurance represents a definitional impossibility. The insurance mechanism consists of transfer of risk or pooling of exposure units, and since one cannot pool with or transfer to himself or herself, it can be argued that self-insurance is impossible. However, the term is widely used, and we ought therefore to establish an acceptable operational definition, semantically incorrect though it may be.

Under some circumstances, it is possible for a business firm or other organization to engage in the same types of activities as a commercial insurer dealing with its own risks. When these activities involve the operation of the law of large numbers and predictions regarding future losses, they are

---

[5]For example, see Matthew Lenz, Jr., "Self-insurance, Semantics, and Other Hang-ups," *CPCU Annals*, XXVIII (June 1975).

commonly referred to as "self-insurance."[6] To be operationally dependable, such programs should have the following characteristics:

- The organization should be large enough to permit the combination of a sufficiently large number of exposure units to make losses predictable. The program should generally be based on the operation of the law of large numbers.

- The plan must be financially dependable. In most cases, this will require the accumulation of funds to meet losses that occur, with a sufficient accumulation to safeguard against unexpected deviations from predicted losses.

- The individual units exposed to loss must be distributed geographically in such a manner as to prevent a catastrophe. A loss affecting enough units to result in severe financial loss should be impossible.

Even apart from its semantic shortcomings, self-insurance is an overworked term. Few companies or organizations are large enough to engage in a sound program meeting the requirements outlined here. In the majority of cases, risks are simply retained without attempting to make estimates of future losses. In many cases, no fund is maintained to pay for losses. Furthermore, until the fund reaches the size where it is adequate to pay the largest loss possible, the possibility of loss is not eliminated for the individual exposure units.

The Fields of Insurance

Insurance is a broad, generic term, embracing the entire array of institutions that deal with risk through the device of sharing and transfer of risks. Insurance may be divided and subdivided into classifications based on the perils insured against or the fundamental nature of the particular program. The primary distinction is between private insurance and social insurance. In addition to these two classes, there is a third class of quasi-social insurance coverages called *public benefit guarantee programs* that are sometimes classified as social insurance.

Private (Voluntary) Insurance

Private insurance is insurance that is characterized by contractual transfers of risk from individuals and organizations to professional risk bearers. It is usually (but not always) voluntary, and generally (but not always) based on market-determined prices. Although most private insurance is voluntary, some coverages are compulsory for particular individuals (such as auto liability insurance in most states). Furthermore, although most private insurance is sold by private firms, in some cases, it is offered by the government.[7] Private insurance in the United States may be classified into three broad categories: life insurance, health insurance, and property and liability insurance.

Life Insurance

Life insurance is designed to provide protection against two distinct risks: premature death and superannuation. As a matter of personal preference, death at any age is probably premature, and superannuation (living too long) does not normally strike one as an undesirable contingency.

---

[6]Technically, such programs are retention programs that employ insurance techniques. In spite of its semantic shortcomings, the term *self-insurance* is a convenient way of distinguishing the retention programs that utilize insurance techniques from those that do not.

[7]Examples of some types of private insurance sold by the government include life insurance, available through the Veterans Administration, federal crop insurance, and federal flood insurance.

From a practical point of view, however, a person can, and sometimes does, die before adequate preparation has been made for the future financial requirements of dependents. In the same way, a person can, and often does, outlive income-earning ability. Life insurance, endowments, and annuities protect the individual and his or her dependents against the undesirable financial consequences of premature death and superannuation.

Health Insurance

Health insurance (also sometimes called "accident and health insurance") is insurance against loss by sickness or accidental bodily injury. The loss may be the loss of wages caused by the sickness or accident, or it may be expenses for doctor bills, hospital bills, medicine, and so forth. Included within this category are forms of insurance that provide lump-sum or periodic payments in the event of loss occasioned by sickness or accident, such as disability income insurance and accidental death and dismemberment insurance.

Property and Liability Insurance

Property and liability insurance consists of those forms of insurance designed to protect against losses resulting from damage to or loss of property and losses arising from legal liability.[8] It includes the following types of insurance:

Fire insurance

Ocean marine

Inland marine

Boiler and machinery insurance

Crime insurance

---

[8]Historically, property and liability insurance was referred to as *fire and casualty* (or sometimes *property and casualty*) insurance. The evolution of property and liability insurance is discussed in Chapter 6.

Workers compensation insurance

Liability insurance

Automobile insurance

Accident and health insurance

Fidelity and Surety Bonds

Bonding is divided into two classes: fidelity bonds and surety bonds. Fidelity bonds protect against dishonesty by employees and are commonly called "employee dishonesty insurance." In most respects they resemble insurance more closely than do surety bonds, and most authorities consider them to be a form of casualty insurance.

Surety bonds represent a special class of risk transfer device, and opinions differ as to whether surety bonds should be classified as insurance. There are basic differences between a surety bond and an insurance policy, and, strictly speaking, it can be argued that surety bonds are not contracts of insurance. In general terms, a surety bond is an agreement by one party, the "surety," to answer to a third person, called the "obligee," for the debt or default of another party, called the "principal." The surety guarantees a certain type of conduct on the part of the principal, and if the principal fails to behave in the manner guaranteed, the surety will be responsible to the obligee. In a sense, the surety is analogous to the cosigner of a note and like a cosigner, becomes responsible for the obligation in the event of the principal's default. The primary obligation to perform rests with the principal, but if the principal is unable to meet the commitment after exhausting all his or her resources, the surety must provide funds to pay for the loss. In this event the surety may take possession of the principal's assets and convert them into cash to reimburse itself for the loss paid. Most surety bonds are issued for persons doing contract construction, those connected with court actions, and those seeking licenses and permits.

Although surety bonds are not a form of insurance, insurance regulators normally include them within the framework of the contracts they regulate. Furthermore, property and liability insurers sell these bonds, and suretyship is normally considered to be a part of the property and liability insurance business.

Social Insurance

Social insurance differs from private insurance in a number of respects. In the case of social insurance, we use the insurance mechanism for transferring and sharing risk, but we do so on a somewhat qualified basis. Social insurance provides compulsory protection for personal risks—those that involve the possible loss of income or assets because of premature death, dependent old age, sickness or disability, or unemployment. Social insurance seeks to provide a "floor of protection" to persons who would not individually be able to cope with certain fundamental risks. It does this by providing benefits not only to those in need, but to others as well.

Modern social insurance originated in Germany in the 1880s under chancellor Otto von Bismarck. Over the period from 1884 through 1889, Germany constructed a model social insurance program composed of three elements. The first was *sickness insurance* for practically all employed persons, a nineteenth-century universal health insurance program. The second element was *accident insurance*, for work-related injuries—in effect, the first workers compensation program. The final element in the program was *insurance for invalidity and old age*, the equivalent of our Social Security system.[9] From Germany, the idea of social

insurance spread to other European nations and eventually to the United States.

In the United States, the first social insurance program was the workers compensation system, which was adopted by the individual states during the early 1900s. A quarter of a century later, the Social Security Act of 1935 established the Old-Age, Survivors, and Disability Insurance Program, better known as the Social Security system. The Social Security Act also encouraged the states to enact unemployment insurance laws, which every state has done. In 1965, Medicare was added to the Social Security system, providing health insurance for persons over age 65. Finally, six jurisdictions (California, Hawaii, New Jersey, New York, Rhode Island, and Puerto Rico) have enacted *compulsory temporary disability laws*, which require insurance against loss of income from nonoccupational disabilities. Thus, social insurance programs in the United States exist at both the state and federal level. State programs include workers compensation and unemployment insurance in all states and compulsory temporary disability insurance in six states. Federal programs include the Old-Age, Survivors, and Disability Insurance Program and Medicare.

Social Insurance Defined

Any definition of social insurance must, by its very nature, be rather complex. The following definition of social insurance has been proposed:[10]

> Social insurance is a device for the pooling of risks by their transfer to an organization, usually governmental, that is required by law to provide pecuniary or service benefits to or on behalf of covered persons upon the

---

[9]Interestingly, Bismark's support for these programs was not motivated by an inclination toward social engineering. Rather, it was a shrewd political move designed to counter the rapid growth of socialism in Germany. One of the central themes of the social democrats' agenda was the promise of old-age benefits for workers. In effect, Bismark simply outbid the socialists at their own game.

[10]The Commission on Insurance Terminology of the American Risk and Insurance Association.

occurrence of certain predesignated losses under all the following conditions:

1. Coverage is compulsory by law in virtually all instances.
2. Eligibility for benefits is derived, in fact or in effect, from contributions having been made to the program by or in respect of the claimant or the person as to whom the claimant is dependent: there is no requirement that the individual demonstrate inadequate financial resources, although a dependency status may need to be established.
3. The method of determining benefits is prescribed by law.
4. The benefits for any individual are not directly related to contributions made by or in respect to him or her, but instead usually redistribute income so as to favor certain groups such as those with low former wages or large numbers of dependents.
5. There is a definite plan for financing the benefits that is designed to be adequate in terms of long-range considerations.
6. The cost is borne primarily by contributions that are usually made by covered persons, their employers, or both.
7. The plan is administered or at least supervised by the government.
8. The plan is not established by the government solely for its present or former employees.

Certain elements in the definition require clarification. First, the mere fact that a specific type of insurance is compulsory does not make it a social insurance program. Compulsory automobile insurance, for example, does not meet other conditions listed and, therefore, is not social insurance. Furthermore, although the government is usually the transferor in a social insurance plan, this is not a prerequisite. Workers compensation insurance is a social insurance coverage that is sold by commercial insurers.

The second of the conditions listed in the definition distinguishes social insurance from public assistance or welfare programs, in which eligibility for benefits is based on need. Because of the contributions made by or on behalf of the insureds under a social insurance program, the right to benefits is essentially a statutory right and is not based on "need" or a "means test."

More than any of the others, the fourth element in the definition distinguishes social insurance from private insurance. In private insurance, insurers attempt to distribute the loss costs equitably, in proportion to the loss-producing characteristics of the insureds. It would be considered inequitable, for example, to charge a 25-year-old person the same premium for life insurance as that charged to a 65-year-old person. In social insurance, individual equity is secondary in importance to the social adequacy of the benefits. Benefits are weighted in favor of certain groups so that all persons will be provided a minimum floor of protection. In the federal Social Security program, for example, the benefits are weighted in favor of the low-income groups, and persons with large families. Although benefits under social insurance programs are not directly proportional to contributions, they are at least loosely related to the earnings of the individual. Therefore, even though social adequacy rather than individual equity is stressed, there is at least a loose relationship between earnings and benefits.

The fifth condition, that there be a definite plan for financing the benefits that is designed to satisfy long-range considerations, merely requires that there be some sort of long-range planning. It does not demand that the obligations under the program be fully funded. In private insurance, insurers are required to maintain reserves to fund the future obligations they incur. In social insurance, the future obligations are rarely funded in full, but depend on the future taxing power of the government.

The sixth principle is known as the *self-supporting contributory principle*. This means that the costs are not financed from the general revenues of the Treasury, but are paid for primarily by those who expect to benefit from the programs. In most instances the support is derived from contributions by employees, employers, and the self-employed. This method of financing is unique to American social insurance programs, because in most other countries with extensive programs, a part or all of the financing comes from general government revenues.

Public Guarantee Insurance Programs

In addition to private insurance and social insurance coverages, there are some insurance programs that do not fit precisely into either field. This third class of insurance programs consists of government-operated, compulsory, quasi-social insurance programs, mainly in connection with financial institutions holding assets belonging to the public. We call these *public guarantee insurance programs*. Under these programs, government-funded agencies use the insurance principle to provide protection to lenders, depositors, or investors against loss arising from the collapse of a financial institution or some other type of fiduciary holding deposits of the public. Usually, the insurance is allied with the function of regulation.

The modern prototype for this form of insurance, the Federal Deposit Insurance Corporation (FDIC), is a public corporation created by the federal government in 1933 to insure deposits in banks and protect depositors against loss in case of bank failure. The FDIC currently insures accounts of any one depositor up to $100,000. The FDIC was originally funded by an appropriation from general government revenues; its income is now derived from a 1/12 of 1 percent annual assessment on the deposits of the banks covered.[11]

Other federal public guarantee insurance programs include the National Credit Union Administration (NCUA), which provides deposit insurance for members of credit unions, the Securities Investor Protection Corporation, which provides custodial account protection up to $500,000 for investors who allow their brokers to keep their securities for safety and trading convenience, and the Pension Benefit Guaranty Corporation, which offers insurance guaranteeing employees covered by private pension plans that they will receive their vested benefits up to a specified maximum if the plan is terminated.

Similarities in the Various Fields of Insurance

As we have seen in this chapter, the term "insurance" encompasses a wide variety of approaches used by society for sharing risks. While attempting to distinguish among the various classes of insurance, we have focused on the differences. In closing, we should also note some of the similarities, lest the emphasis on differences obscure the common elements. Although the actual details of operation may vary, all three types of insurance use some form of pooling of the exposure units exposed to risk. In every instance the possibility of loss is transferred from the individual to the group, where losses are shared on some prescribed basis. Each program calls for specific contributions made by the participants and designed to meet the costs of the system. The basic concepts of pooling and sharing of losses and the individual's substitution of a small, certain cost for a large, uncertain loss are fundamental to all the programs.

---

[11]A similar federal instrumentality, the Federal Savings and Loan Insurance Corporation (FSLIC) ended in 1989 in the face of massive savings and loan failures of 1987, 1988, and 1989. Legislation enacted by Congress in 1988 as a part of the savings and loan "bailout" consolidated deposit insurance for savings and loan associations with that for commercial banks in the FDIC. The Government Accounting Office has estimated the cost of the savings and loan bailout to be $257 billion by 2021.

Important Concepts to Remember

insurance defined from the view-point of the individual
randomness
insurance defined from the view-point of society
economic feasibility
a priori probabilities
statistical probabilities
a posteriori probabilities
law of large numbers
dispersion

adverse selection
standard deviation
relative frequency interpretation
subjective interpretation
sample
variance
elements of an insurable risk
self-insurance
private insurance
social insurance
public benefit guarantee program

ocean marine insurance
inland marine insurance
fire insurance
health insurance
casualty insurance
property insurance
liability insurance
surety bonds
surety
principal
obligee

Questions for Review

1. List and explain each of the desirable elements of an insurable risk.

2. Explain the dual application of the law of large numbers as it pertains to the operation of insurance.

3. Identify and explain the chief economic contributions of insurance.

4. What is the effect of an increase in the number of observations in a sampling technique on:
   a. the underlying probability of the event
   b. our estimate of the probability
   c. the standard deviation

5. Identify the two fundamental functions involved in the operation of the insurance mechanism.

6. Why is the term self-insurance a misnomer?

7. How does insurance substitute certainty from the standpoint of the insured?

8. Give examples of three uninsurable exposures and indicate why each is uninsurable.

9. Describe the characteristics that distinguish private insurance, social insurance, and public benefit guarantee programs.

10. Briefly describe the three general categories into which private or voluntary insurance may be divided.

Questions for Discussion

1. There are many strikes in the United States, bringing financial suffering to both employers and workers. Would you expect a commercial insurer to provide insurance protection to either the workers or the employers to cover losses resulting from these strikes? Why or why not?

2. Suppose that the members of your class enter into an agreement under whose terms all would chip in to pay for the damage to any automobile owned by a class member that was damaged in a collision. Explain if this is insurance and whether you would be willing to participate.

3. A friend tells you about a plan for the formation of an insurance company which will issue insurance policies to protect a person who buys stock against a decline in the value of that stock. Explain why you believe the scheme will or will not work.

4. "Other things being equal, one should prefer to purchase insurance from the largest insurance company possible." On what basis does the author of this statement probably base this conclusion?

5. "In view of the operation of the law of large numbers, the most beneficial and logical development in the insurance industry would be the emergence of a monopolistic insurer." Do you agree? Why or why not?

Suggestions for Additional Reading

Denenberg, Herbert S. "The Legal Definition of Insurance." *Journal of Risk and Insurance*, 30, 3 (Sept. 1963).

Faulkner, E. J., ed. *Man's Quest for Security*. Lincoln, NE: University of Nebraska Press, 1966.

Kulp, C. A., and John W. Hall. *Casualty Insurance*, 4th ed. New York: Ronald Press, 1968. Chapter 1.

Lenz, Matthew, Jr. "Self-insurance, Semantics, and Other Hang-Ups." *CPCU Annals*, 28 (June 1975).

Mowbray, A. H., R. H. Blanchard, and C. Arthur Williams. *Insurance*, 6th ed. New York: McGraw-Hill, 1969. Chapters 5, 6.

Rejda, George E. *Social Insurance and Economic Security*, 6th ed. Englewood Cliffs, NJ: Prentice Hall, 1998.

Smith, Barry D. *How Insurance Works: An Introduction to Property and Liability Insurance*, 2nd ed. Malvern, PA: Insurance Institute of America, 1994.

Websites to Explore

Automation Management Group Links of Interest: http://www.taan.com/inssites.htm

Gamma Iota Sigma: http://connectyou.com/ic/gamma.htm

Insurance News Network: http://www.insure.com/

RISKWeb: http://www.RISKWeb.com/

Ultimate insurance links: http://www.barryklein.com/

CHAPTER 4

The Risk Management Process

Things which matter most
must never be at the mercy of things which matter least.
—Goethe

CHAPTER OBJECTIVES

When you have finished this chapter, you should be able to

- Identify the steps in the risk management process

- Explain the importance of risk management objectives

- Identify the contributions that insurers have made to the practice of risk identification

- Identify and briefly describe the major tools that are used in the risk identification process

- Identify two decision models from the field of decision theory that may be used in risk management decision making and explain the circumstances in which each is applicable

- Identify the three rules of risk management and explain how they relate to the management science decision models

- Explain why evaluation and review is an essential step in the risk management process

The Risk Management Process

The risk management process can be divided into a series of individual steps that must be accomplished in managing risks. Identifying these individual steps helps to guarantee that important phases in the process will not be overlooked. While it is useful for the purpose of analysis to discuss each of these steps separately, it should be understood that in actual practice the steps tend to merge with one another. The six steps in the risk management process are:

1. Determination of objectives
2. Identification of the risks
3. Evaluation of the risks
4. Considering alternatives and selecting the risk treatment device
5. Implementing the decision
6. Evaluation and review

Determination of Objectives

The first step in the risk management process is the determination of the objectives of the risk management program—deciding precisely what it is that the organization would like its risk management program to do. Despite its importance, determining the objectives of the program is the step in the risk management process that is most likely to be overlooked. As a consequence, the risk management efforts of many firms are fragmented and inconsistent. Many of the defects in risk management programs stem from an ambiguity regarding the objectives of the program.

Mehr and Hedges, in their classic *Risk Management in the Business Enterprise*, suggest that risk management has a variety of objectives, which they classify into two categories, pre-loss objec-

tives and post-loss objectives, and suggest the following objectives in each category:[1]

Post-Loss Objectives	Pre-Loss Objectives
Survival	Economy
Continuity of operations	Reduction in anxiety
Earning stability	Meeting externally
Continued growth	imposed obligations
Social responsibility	Social responsibility

Although all of the pre-loss and post-loss objectives suggested by Mehr and Hedges have relevance in the risk management effort, multiple objectives such as these naturally raise the question as to which is primary.

Value Maximization Objectives

One eminent scholar has argued that the ultimate goal of risk management is the same as the ultimate goal of the other functions in a business—to maximize the value of the organization.[2] Modern financial theory suggests that this value that is to be maximized is reflected in the market value of the organization's common stock. According to this view, risk management decisions should be appraised against the standard of whether or not they contribute to value maximization. It is a view with which it is difficult to disagree. It is also a view that is not inconsistent with the objectives suggested by Mehr and Hedges. With limited exceptions, all of the Mehr and Hedges objectives do, in one way or another, contribute to value maximization. Value maximization is the ultimate goal of the organization, and is a reasonable standard for appraising corporate decisions in a consistent manner. At the

---

[1]Robert I. Mehr and Bob A. Hedges, *Risk Management: Concepts and Applications* (Homewood, IL: Richard D. Irwin, 1974), p. 4.
[2]Neil A. Doherty, *Corporate Risk Management* (New York: McGraw-Hill, 1985), Chapters 1 and 2.

same time, the value maximization objective has some limitations for risk management. The most important is that it is relevant primarily to the business sector. For other organizations—nonprofit organizations and government bodies—value maximization is not particularly relevant.

The Primary Objective of Risk Management

The first objective of risk management, like the first law of nature, is survival; to guarantee the continuing existence of the organization as an operating entity in the economy. The primary goal of risk management is not to contribute directly to the other goals of the organization—whatever they may be. Rather it is to guarantee that the attainment of these other goals will not be prevented by losses that might arise out of pure risks. This means that the most important objective is not to minimize costs, or to contribute to the profit of the organization. Nor is it to comply with legal requirements or to meet some nebulous responsibility related to social responsibility of the firm. It can and does do all of these things, but they are not the principle reason for its existence. The principle objective of risk management is to preserve the operating effectiveness of the organization. We propose the following primary objective for the risk management function:

> The primary objective of risk management is to preserve the operating effectiveness of the organization, that is, to guarantee that the organization is not prevented from achieving its other objectives by the losses that might arise out of pure risk.

The risk management objective must reflect the uncertainty inherent in the risk management situation. Since one cannot know what losses will occur and what the amount of such losses will be, the arrangements made to guarantee survival in the event of loss must reflect the worst possible combination of outcomes. If a loss occurs and, as a result, the organization is prevented from pursuing its other objectives, it is clear that the risk management objective has not been achieved. While not immediately obvious, it is equally true that the risk management objective has not been achieved when there are unprotected loss exposures that could prevent the organization from pursuing its other objectives should the loss occur, even if the loss does not occur. For this reason, the objective refers to losses that *might* arise out of pure risks. The question is not only whether the organization survives, but whether it would have survived under a different combination of circumstances.

The Risk Management Policy

Major policy decisions related to insurance should be made by the highest policy-making body in the organization—such as the board of directors—since these decisions are likely to involve large financial considerations, either in terms of premiums paid over the long term, or risks assumed if hazards are not insured. In addition, it is the board of directors and the professional managers of the firm, after all, who are responsible for the preservation of the organization's assets. Once the objectives have been identified, they should be formally recognized in a risk management policy. A formal risk management policy statement provides a basis for achieving a logical and consistent program by providing guidance for those responsible for programming and buying the firm's insurance. Figure 4.1 is a sample of a corporate risk management policy.

Identifying Risk Exposures

Obviously, before anything can be done about the risks an organization faces, someone must be aware of them. In one way or another, someone

Risk Management Policy

1. It shall be the policy of Iowa Pork Packers, Inc. to avoid, reduce, or transfer the risk of loss arising out of property damage, legal liability, and dishonesty in all cases in which the exposure could result in loss that would bankrupt or seriously impair the operating efficiency of the firm.
2. It shall be the policy of Iowa Pork Packers, Inc. to assume the risk of loss arising out of property damage, legal liability, and dishonesty in all cases in which the exposure is so small or dispersed that a loss would not significantly affect the operations or the financial position of the firm.
3. It shall be the policy of Iowa Pork Packers, Inc. to provide safe working conditions for its employees. Under no circumstances will the risk of serious injury or death of employees be considered an acceptable risk.
4. Insurance will be purchased against all major loss exposures which might result in loss in excess of $100,000 or 10 percent of the projected annual working capital through the purchase of appropriate forms of property and liability insurance against the widest range of perils and hazards available.
5. Insurance will not be purchased to cover loss exposures below the amount of $10,000 unless such insurance is required by law or by contract, or in those instances in which it is desirable to obtain special services such as inspection or claim adjustment in connection with the insurance.
6. The administration of the risk management program will be under the direction of the Insurance Administrator, such responsibility to include placement of insurance coverages, maintenance of property appraisals and inventory valuations, processing of claims and maintenance of loss records, and supervision of loss prevention activities.
7. Safety and loss prevention recommendations by OSHA officials and insurance company loss prevention personnel will be given serious consideration and implemented whenever feasible. In those instances in which such recommendations are not implemented, a written justification for nonimplementation will be filed with the Board of Directors by the company officer making the decision.
8. Insurance will be placed only in insurance companies rated A+ or A in *Best's Policyholders Ratings*. Insurance placed in any other companies will require a written report of the particulars, such report to be filed with the Board of Directors by the Insurance Administrator.

Figure 4.1 Sample Risk Management Policy

must dig into the operations of the company and discover the risks to which the firm is exposed. In one sense, risk identification is the most difficult step in the risk management process. It is difficult because it is a continual process and because it is virtually impossible to know when it has been done completely.

It is difficult to generalize about the risks that a given organization is likely to face, because differences in operations and conditions give rise to varying risks. Some risks are relatively obvious, while there are many that can be, and often are, overlooked. In order to reduce the possibility of failure to discover important risks facing the firm, most risk managers use some systematic approach to the problem of risk identification.

Risk Identification Techniques

The first step in risk identification is to gain as thorough a knowledge as possible of the organization and its operations. The risk manager needs a general knowledge of the goals and functions of the organization—what it does and where it does it. This knowledge can be gained through inspections, interviews with appropriate persons within and outside the organization, and by an examination of internal records and documents.

Analysis of Documents

The history of the organization and its current operations are recorded in a variety of records. These records represent a basic source of information required for risk analysis and exposure identification. These documents include the organization's financial statements, leases and other contracts, asset schedules, inventory records, appraisals and valuation reports, buy-sell agreements, and countless other documents.

Analysis of the firm's financial statements, in particular, can aid in the process of risk identification. The asset listing in the balance sheet may alert the risk manager to the existence of assets that might otherwise be overlooked. The income

and expense classification in the income statement may likewise indicate areas of operation of which the risk manager was unaware.[3]

Flow Charts

Another tool that is useful in risk identification is a flow chart. A flow chart of an organization's internal operations views the firm as a processing unit and seeks to discover all the contingencies that could interrupt its processes. These might include damage to a strategic asset located in a *bottleneck* within the firm's operations or the loss of the services of a key individual or group through disability, death, or resignation. When extended to include the flow of goods and services to and from customers and suppliers, the flow chart approach to risk identification can highlight potential accidents that can disrupt the firm's activities and its profits.[4]

Internal Communication System

To identify new risks, the risk manager needs a far-reaching information system that yields current information on new developments that may give rise to risk. Among the various activities that have relevance to the risk management function, some of the more important are new construction, remodeling, or renovation of the firm's properties; the introduction of new programs, products, activities, or operations; and other similar changes in the organization's activities.

---

[3]The "financial statement method" of risk analysis was proposed by the risk manager of a national corporation and has become a more or less standard approach to the risk identification problem. See A. Hawthorne Criddle, "A Theory of Risk Discovery," *National Insurance Buyer,* vol. 6, no. 1 (January 1959).

[4]The use of flow charts in risk analysis was suggested in the early 1960s. See A. J. Ingley, "Problems of Risk Analysis," *The Growing Job of Risk Management,* AMA Management Report no. 70 (New York: American Management Association, 1962), pp. 137–138.

Tools of Risk Identification

Exposure identification is an essential phase of both risk management and insurance management. Because insurance management is the older field, the technique of identifying insurable exposures was already highly developed when the risk management movement began. Insurance companies developed insurance policy checklists, which identify the various risks for which they offered coverage. They also developed extensive application forms for various types of insurance that elicited information about hazards that need to be reflected in rating and underwriting decisions. Although these tools naturally focused on the perils and hazards against which insurers offered protection, they provided a base upon which risk identification methods could be constructed. Many of the tools that had been used by insurance agents and insurance managers to identify insurable exposures were expanded and adapted to aid in the identification of other risks for which the risk manager is responsible.

A few of the more important tools used in risk identification include risk analysis questionnaires, exposure checklists, and insurance policy checklists. These, combined with a vivid imagination and a thorough understanding of the organization's operations, can help to guarantee that important exposures are not overlooked.

Risk Analysis Questionnaires

Risk analysis questionnaires, also sometimes called "fact finders," are designed to assist in identifying risks facing an organization. They do this by leading the user through a series of penetrating questions, the answers to which indicate hazards and conditions that give rise to risk. Originally, such questionnaires were generic and were intended for use by a wide range of businesses. As a result they did not address unusual exposures or identify loss areas that might be unique to a given firm. Today, risk analysis questionnaires are available for a wide range of specific industries.

Exposure Checklists

A second important aid in risk identification and one of the most common tools for risk analysis is a risk exposure checklist, which is simply a listing of common exposures. Obviously, a checklist cannot include all possible exposures to which an organization may be subject; the nature and operations of different organizations vary too widely for that. However, it can be effectively used in conjunction with other risk identification tools as a final check to reduce the chance of overlooking a serious exposure.

Insurance Policy Checklists

Insurance policy checklists are available from insurance companies and from publishers specializing in insurance-related publications. Typically, such lists include a catalogue of the various policies or types of insurance that a given business might need. The risk manager simply consults such a list, picking out those policies applicable to the firm. A principal defect in using insurance policy checklists for risk identification is that such checklists concentrate on insurable risks only, ignoring the uninsurable pure risks.[5]

Expert Systems

With the advances in computer technology, many of the tools and techniques used in risk identification have been consolidated in computer software to create expert systems. An expert system used in risk identification incorporates the features of risk analysis questionnaires, exposure checklists, and insurance policy checklists in a single tool. The most sophisticated risk management expert systems include detailed, industry-specific risk questionnaires and exposure checklists. These detailed survey questionnaires assist in the identification not only of common expo-

---

[5]One of the most widely used policy checklists is a publication entitled *Coverages Applicable,* published by Rough Notes Co. of Indianapolis.

sures, but of those that might be unique to the specific industry.[6]

Combination Approach Required

The preferred approach to risk identification consists of a combination approach, in which all of the tools listed above are brought to bear on the problem. In a sense, each of these tools can provide a part of the puzzle, and combined they can be of considerable assistance to the risk manager. But no individual approach or combination of these tools can replace the diligence and imagination of the risk manager in discovering the risks to which the firm is exposed.

Evaluating Risks

Once the risks have been identified, the risk manager must evaluate them. "Evaluation" implies some ranking in terms of importance, and ranking suggests measuring some aspect of the factors to be ranked. In the case of loss exposures, there are two facets that must be considered; the possible severity of loss, and the possible frequency or probability of loss. Evaluation involves measuring the potential size of the loss and the probability that the loss is likely to occur.

A Priority Ranking Based on Severity

One of the techniques used by scientists and engineers in the U.S. space program was *criticality analysis*—an attempt to distinguish the truly important things from the overwhelming mass of

[6]An expert system is a computer program for decision making that uses knowledge and analytical rules defined by experts in the field. Expert systems originated in the 1960s and are now used in a wide range of fields, including medicine, finance, insurance, and risk management.

unimportant things. Given the wide range of losses that can occur, from the minute to the catastrophic, it seems logical that exposures be ranked according to their criticality. Certain risks, because of the severity of the possible loss, will demand attention prior to others, and in most instances there will be a number of exposures that are equally demanding.

Any exposure that involves a loss that would represent a financial catastrophe ranks in the same category, and there is no distinction among risks in this class. It makes little difference if bankruptcy results from a liability loss, a flood, or an uninsured fire loss. The net effect is the same. Therefore, rather than ranking exposures in some order of importance such as "1, 2, 3, . . . etc.," it is more appropriate to rank them into general classifications such as critical, important, and unimportant. One set of criteria that may be used in establishing such a priority ranking focuses on the financial impact that the loss would have on the firm. For example:

- *Critical risks* include all exposures to loss in which the possible losses are of a magnitude that would result in bankruptcy.

- *Important risks* include those exposures in which the possible losses would not result in bankruptcy, but would require the firm to borrow in order to continue operations.

- *Unimportant risks* include those exposures in which the possible losses could be met out of the existing assets or current income of the firm without imposing undue financial strain.

Assignment of individual exposures into one of these three categories requires determination of the amount of financial loss that might result from a given exposure and also requires determination of the ability of the firm to absorb such losses. Determining the ability to absorb the losses involves measuring the level of uninsured loss that could be borne without resorting to credit, and determining the maximum credit capacity of the firm.

The Prouty Measures of Severity

The risk manager of a large national corporation has suggested a classification for measuring loss severity, based on a system used by insurance underwriters. Richard Prouty suggested that for each potential loss, the risk manager should estimate two measures of loss: the *maximum possible loss* (MPL) and the *probable maximum loss* (PML).[7] The maximum possible loss is the worst loss that could occur, given the worst possible combination of circumstances. The probable maximum loss, on the other hand, is the loss that is likely, given the most likely combination of circumstances.

The distinction between the MPL and the PML is derived from the art of the underwriter. In assessing exposures being considered for insurance, property insurance underwriters attempt to estimate the PML for each property. Although the underwriter recognizes that it is conceivable that a ten-story building to be insured could burn to the ground, he or she also realizes that this is highly unlikely. Therefore, rather than focusing on the total value of the structure, the underwriter attempts to determine how large is the *most likely* loss. Given the underwriter's spread of risk and the numerous properties in his or her risk portfolio, this is a reasonable strategy. It may also be a reasonable strategy for the risk manager with a large number of properties. For the risk manager with a single structure, or a limited number of properties, however, the important measure of severity is the *maximum possible loss*.

The Loss Unit Concept

One of the most relevant measures of severity, which unfortunately has not been widely discussed, is the *loss unit*. The loss unit is the total of all financial losses that can result from a single event, taking into consideration the various exposures. It includes the loss for direct damage to property, the loss of income, and the liabilities that can result from a single occurrence. Computing the loss unit requires calculation of the maximum possible loss for each of these exposures and then aggregating the totals. The significance of the loss unit lies in the fact that whereas an organization might be able to retain certain of the exposures individually, there is no guarantee that losses will occur individually. The loss unit is an attempt to alert management to the potential catastrophe that could result from the worst possible conditions.

Probability and Priority Rankings

Although the potential severity is the most important factor in ranking exposures, an estimate of the probability may also be useful in differentiating among exposures with relatively equal potential severity. Other things being equal, exposures characterized by high frequency should receive attention before exposures in which the loss frequency is low. Exposures that exhibit a high loss frequency are often susceptible to improvement through risk control measures. Having some notion of the loss frequency for different exposures can help determine where control efforts should be directed. Even broad generalizations about the likelihood of loss may be useful. One suggested approach is to classify probability as *almost nil* (meaning that, in the opinion of the risk manager, the event is probably not going to happen), *slight* (meaning that while the event is possible, it has not happened and is unlikely to occur in the future), *moderate* (meaning that the event has occasionally happened and will probably happen again), and *definite* (meaning that the event has happened regularly in the past and is expected to occur regularly in the future).[8] Although probability estimates such as these may be of some help in risk management decisions, when the appropriate data are available more precise mathemati-

---

[7]Richard Prouty, *Industrial Insurance: A Formal Approach to Risk Analysis and Evaluation* (Washington, D.C.: Machinery and Allied Products Institute, January 19, 1960).

[8]See Richard Prouty, *Industrial Insurance: A Formal Approach to Risk Analysis and Evaluation* (Washington, D.C.: Machinery and Allied Products Institute, 1960).

cal estimates of the probabilities will be useful. Some organizations, by virtue of their size and the scope of their operations, may be able to use probability estimates in risk financing decisions.

Consideration of Alternatives and Selection of the Risk Treatment Device

Once the risks have been identified and evaluated, the next step is the consideration of the techniques that should be used to deal with each risk. This phase of the risk management process is primarily a problem in decision making: more precisely, it is deciding which of the available techniques should be used in dealing with each risk. Numerous strategies have been suggested for this phase of the risk management process. Some have proven to be more productive than others.

Utility Theory and Risk Management Decisions

Some theorists have suggested that utility theory be used as an approach to risk management decisions, especially in regard to retention and transfer.[9] They would use the expected value concept to compare an individual's preferences (utility) for different states of uncertainty (e.g., "Which would you prefer, a 10% chance of losing $1000 or a 1% chance of losing $10,000?"). Once the individual's preference for different states of uncertainty (his or her "utility function") has been derived, it is used in a calculation that multiplies utility units by the probability that each level of loss might occur. This calculation is made for each decision being considered and the decision that produces the lowest expected loss of utility is

selected. We will not discuss the process by which the utility function is derived primarily because we do not believe that it is a useful tool for risk management decisions.

The theory of marginal utility was constructed by economists in an attempt to explain *why* people make the consumer choices they do. It does not and is not intended to provide guidance on the decisions people *should* make.[10] Using a utility function (real or hypothetical) as the basis for risk-related decisions could conceivably lead to more consistent decisions, but there is no reason to believe that those decisions would be good. They might be consistent, but consistently bad decisions.

Decision Theory and Risk Management Decisions

The most appropriate approaches to risk management decisions are drawn from decision theory and operations research. The types of problems addressed by the decision theory approach to decision making are those for which there is not an obvious solution, the situation that characterizes many risk management decisions. The decision theory approach aims at identifying the *best* decision or solution to the problem.

Cost-Benefit Analysis

In theory, each of the techniques of risk management should be used when it is the most effective technique for dealing with a particular risk. Further, each technique should be used up to the

---

[9]For example, see Mark R. Greene and Oscar N. Serbein, *Risk Management: Text and Cases* (Reston, VA: Reston Publishing, 1983), p. 52.

[10]The seminal article on utility and choices involving risk was written to provide a theoretical explanation for the apparent inconsistencies in human behavior with respect to risk. Some people will purchase insurance, indicating a distaste for uncertainty, while other people gamble, indicating that they prefer risk to certainty. To explain this anomaly, Friedman and Savage hypothesized that people who buy insurance have a different utility curve from that of gamblers. See Milton Friedman and L. J. Savage, "Utility Analysis of Choices Involving Risk," *Journal of Political Economy*, LVI (August 1948), pp. 279–304.

Tidbits, Vignettes, and Conundrums 4.1

Good Decisions and Bad Decisions

Suppose that you and I wager a dollar on the flip of a coin. As you flip the coin, you say "call it" and I say "heads." Is my choice of *heads* a good decision or a bad decision? Knowing the probabilities—that *heads* is as likely as *tails*—the decision is as good a decision as I can make. (*Tails* would, of course, have been an equally good decision.) Now suppose that as a result of the toss, the coin ended up tails and I lose my dollar. I made a good decision, but the outcome was not what I had hoped it would be.

Now let us change the scenario. Suppose that I offer to wager $50,000 on the flip of the same coin ($50,000 which, by the way, I don't have). You accept and flip the coin. The outcome in this case is, as I predicted, a head (and I win your $50,000). One can argue that this second decision was a bad one, even though the outcome was favorable. There is an incongruity between decisions that are good or bad and those that turn out right or wrong.

---

point at which each dollar spent on the measure will produce a dollar in saving through reduction in losses. This is simply cost-benefit analysis, which attempts to measure the benefit of any course of action against its costs.

Applying marginal-benefit/marginal-cost analysis to the risk management problem is complicated by several factors. The first is that the costs associated with different choices may be unknown. When future costs are uncertain, one can estimate expected costs from the potential payoffs and the probabilities of various outcomes.

Expected Value

Decision theory literature suggests three classes of decision-making situations, based on the knowledge the decision-maker has about the possible outcomes or results (called *states of nature*). The first is *decision making under certainty*, which defines the situation in which the outcomes that result from each choice are known (and therefore, when cost-benefit analysis is appropriate). The second is *decision making under risk*, in which the outcomes are uncertain but where probability

estimates are available for the various outcomes. Finally, *decision making under uncertainty* means that the probability of occurrence of each outcome is not known.

In decision making under risk, where the probability of different outcomes can be predicted with reasonable precision, expected values can be computed to determine the most promising choice. For example, a blackjack player with a count of 16 who "stands" against the dealer's ten will lose 78.8 percent of the time and win 21.2 percent of the time, for an expected value of -0.576. If the player "hits" the 16 against the dealer's ten, he or she will lose 77.9 percent of the time and will win 22.1 percent of the time, for an expected value of -0.557. Thus, the expected value is higher if the player hits 16 against the dealer's ten than if he or she stands.

In some situations, the expected value criterion that is used in decision making under risk can be used as a strategy for risk management decisions, such as the choice between retention and the purchase of insurance. A decision or choice is described in terms of a payoff matrix, a rectangular array whose rows represent alternative courses of action and whose columns represent the outcomes or states of nature. The expected value for a particular decision is the sum of the weighted payoffs for that decision. The weight for each payoff is the probability that the payoff occurs multiplied by the value.

For the purpose of illustration, assume a loss exposure of $100,000, for which the probability is estimated to be .01. Assume further that insurance against loss from this exposure will cost $1,500 annually. The expected value for the two possible choices (Insure and Retain), given the two possible states of nature (No Loss and Loss Occurs), would be computed as follows:

	State 1 No Loss	State 2 Loss Occurs	Expected Value
Insure	−$1,500 × .99	−$1,500 × .01	−$1,500
Retain	$0 × .99	−$100,000 × .01	−$1,000

Applying the expected value criterion, the decision to retain is the most attractive. Adding the expected values for the two possible outcomes (state 1 and state 2) for the decision *Insure,* the expected value of the decision is −$1,500: (−$1,500 × .01 + −$1,500 × .99). For the decision *Retain,* the expected value is −$1,000. If the decision is made on the basis of expected value, retention would be selected as the appropriate decision, since −$1,000 is less than −$1,500. It may be noted parenthetically that, given an accurate estimate of probabilities, the expected value criterion will always suggest retention over transfer through insurance. This is because the premium for insurance includes not only the expected value of the loss, but the cost of operating the insurance mechanism as well. Assuming that the insurer has an accurate estimate of probability, the cost of insurance is *always* greater than the expected value of a loss.

There are two problems with the expected value model for risk management decisions. The first is that the expected value model requires that the decision-maker have accurate information on the probabilities, which is not available as often as desired. Second, and more important, even when accurate probability estimates are available, actual experience will deviate from the expected value. Although the *long-run* expected value of the retention strategy is −$1,000, a loss of $100,000 *could* occur. If a $100,000 loss is unacceptable to management, the long-run expected value is irrelevant. There is little consolation following the bankruptcy that results from the uninsured $100,000 loss in the fact that the retention strategy would have been the cost-effective strategy in the long run if the firm had survived.

Pascal's Wager

The defects in the expected value strategy suggested the need for a different strategy in some situations. Blaise Pascal, a seventeenth-century mathematician, considered the situation in which the probability of an outcome is not known, and in which there is a significant difference in the possible outcomes. The question about which Pascal was concerned was the existence of God. For our purposes, the importance of Pascal's analysis of this question is not the question itself, but the logic of the analysis and its implications for risk management. The analysis led Pascal to what one author has cited as the beginning of the theory of decision making.[11]

According to Pascal, there is no way to estimate the probability or likelihood that God exists. One believes in God or one does not. The decision, therefore, is not whether to believe in God, but rather whether to act as if God exists or does not exist. The choice, in Pascal's view, is, in effect, a bet on whether or not God exists. According to Pascal's wager, if one bets that God exists, he or she will lead a good life. A person who chooses to lead an evil life is wagering that God does not exist. If God does not exist, whether you lead a good life or a bad one is immaterial. But suppose, says Pascal, that God does exist. If you bet against the existence of God (by refusing to lead a good life) you run the risk of eternal damnation, while the

---

[11]Ian Hacking, *The Emergency of Probability: A Philosophical Study of Early Ideas about Probability, Induction, and Statistical Inherence* (London: Cambridge University Press), p. 62.

winner of the bet that God exists has the possibility of salvation. Because salvation is preferable to damnation, for Pascal the correct decision is to act as if God exists.

"Pascal's wager" introduces two significant principles for decision-making. The first is that there are some situations in which the consequence (magnitude of the potential loss) rather than the probability should be the first consideration. Put somewhat differently, there are some situations in which one of the outcomes is so undesirable that its possibility is unacceptable. The second is that even when dependable estimates of the probability are not available, decisions made under conditions of uncertainty can be made on a rational basis.[12]

Minimax Regret Strategy

In modern decision theory, the equivalent of Pascal's strategy is known as minimax (for minimize maximum regret). In the minimax regret strategy, the decision-maker attempts to minimize the maximum loss or maximum regret. For problems such as those in the area of risk management, in which payoffs such as costs are to be minimized, the maximum cost of each decision for each of the possible outcomes is listed and the minimum of the maximums is selected as the appropriate choice, which gives rise to the term *minimax*. Returning to the $100,000 building with the $1,500 insurance premium, an uninsured $100,000 loss represents the greater maximum loss and the choice Insure will minimize the maximum cost.

	State 1 No Loss	State 2 Loss Occurs	Maximum Loss
Insure	−$1,500	−$1,500	−$1,500
Retain	$0	−$100,000	−$100,000

In risk management, the premise on which the minimax cost or minimax regret strategies are based is Pascal's contention that when the probability of loss cannot be determined, one should chose the option in which the potential for regret is the lowest. The minimax cost or minimax regret strategies are appropriate when the maximum cost associated with one of the possible states of nature is unacceptable to management. This would be the case, for example, when the potential loss that might arise is beyond the firm's ability to bear; the situation in which one of the states of nature would result in bankruptcy and would result in failure to achieve the risk management objective.

It should be noted that while the expected value strategy will always suggest retention as the preferred approach, a minimax strategy will always suggest transfer. The obvious key, then, is to determine the situations in which each strategy should be applied.

The Rules of Risk Management

Both the expected value strategy and the minimax strategy have application in risk management decisions. Because the decisions recommended by these strategies are diametrically opposed (the expected value strategy will always suggest retention as the preferred approach and the minimax strategy will always suggest transfer), the obvious key is to determine the situations in which each strategy should be applied. This question was addressed in the first textbook on the subject of risk management. One of the earliest contributions to the risk management field was the development of a set of "rules of risk management."[13] These rules are simply common-sense principles applied to risk situations:

---

[12]This discussion of Pascal's wager is based on a discussion in Peter L. Bernstein, *Against the Gods—The Remarkable Story of Risk* (New York: Wiley, 1998), pp. 69–71.

[13]These rules appeared in the first edition of Robert I. Mehr and Bob A. Hedges, *Risk Management in the Business Enterprise* (Homewood, IL.: Richard D. Irwin, 1963), pp. 16–26.

1. Don't risk more than you can afford to lose.
2. Consider the odds.
3. Don't risk a lot for a little.

Simple as they appear, these three rules provide a basic framework within which risk management decisions can be made. Unfortunately, they are sometimes misunderstood and are often neglected.

Don't Risk More Than You Can Afford to Lose

The first of the three rules—"don't risk more than you can afford to lose"—is the most important. Although it does not necessarily tell us *what* should be done about a given risk, it does identify the risks about which *something* must be done. If we begin with the recognition that when nothing is done about a particular risk that risk is retained, identifying the risks about which something must be done resolves into determining which risks cannot be retained. The answer is explicitly stated in the first rule.

The most important consideration in determining which risks require some specific action is the maximum potential loss that might result from the risk. If the maximum potential loss from a given exposure is so large that it would result in an unbearable loss, retention is not realistic. The possible severity must be reduced to a manageable level or the risk must be transferred. If severity cannot be reduced and the risk cannot be transferred, it must be avoided. In decision theory terms, "don't risk more than you can afford to lose" identifies the decisions for which either the minimax cost or minimax regret strategy is appropriate.

Consider the Odds

If an individual can determine the probability that a loss may occur, he or she is in a better posi-

tion to deal with the risk than would be the case without such information. However, it is possible to attach undue significance to such probabilities, since the probability that a loss may or may not occur is less important than the possible severity if it does occur. Even when the probability of loss is low, the primary consideration is the potential severity.

This is not to say that the probability associated with a given exposure is not a consideration in determining what to do about that risk. Just as the potential severity indicates the risk about which something must be done (that is, the risks that cannot be retained), knowing whether the probability that a loss will occur is slight, moderate, or quite high can assist the risk manager in deciding what should be done about a given risk (although not in the way that most people think).

A high probability is an indication that insurance is probably not an economical way of dealing with the risk. This is because insurance operates on the basis of averages. Based on past experience, the insurer estimates the amount that it must collect in premiums to cover the losses that will occur. In addition to covering the losses, the premium must cover the insurer's other expenses. Therefore, paradoxical though it may seem, the best buys in insurance involve those losses that are least likely to happen. The higher the probability of loss, the less suitable is insurance as a device for dealing with the exposure.

The best buys in insurance are those in which the probability is low and the possible severity is high. The worst buys are those in which the size of the potential loss is low and the probability of loss is high. The most effective way to deal with those exposures in which the probability of loss is high is through loss prevention measures aimed at reducing the probability of loss.

The second rule of risk management, "consider the odds," suggests that the likelihood or probability of loss may be an important factor in deciding what to do about a particular risk—but which risks? Logically, consideration of the odds is limited to those situations in which the first rule, "don't risk more than you can afford to lose," does not apply. For decisions in which one of the possible states of nature is ruin, the minimax cost or minimax regret strategies are appropriate.

Having limited our application of probability to situations in which ruin is not one of the possible outcomes or states of nature, it should be noted that even in this limited set of decisions, situations in which probability theory is useful abound. Among the more fertile fields for analysis are the selection of deductibles, and the decision to insure or retain moderate losses.

Don't Risk a Lot for a Little

Whereas the first rule provides guidance for those risks that should be transferred (those involving catastrophic losses in which the potential severity cannot be reduced) and the second rule provides guidance for those that should not be insured (those in which the probability of loss is very high), they leave a residual class of risks for which another rule is needed.

The third rule dictates that there should be a reasonable relationship between the cost of transferring risk and the value that accrues to the transferor. It provides guidance in two directions. First, risks should not be retained when the possible loss is large (a lot) relative to the premiums saved through retention (a little). On the other hand, there are instances in which the premium that is required to insure a risk is disproportionately high relative to the risk transferred. In these cases, the premiums represent "a lot" while the possible loss is "a little."

Whereas the rule "don't risk more than you can afford to lose" imposes a maximum level on the risks that should be retained, the rule "don't risk a lot for a little" suggests that some risks below this maximum retention level should also be transferred. While the maximum retention level should be the same for all risks, the actual retention level for some exposures may be less than this maximum.

Risk Characteristics as Determinants of the Tool

From the foregoing discussion, it is clear that there are some risks that should be transferred and some that should be retained. It is also clear that both transfer and retention are unsatisfactory in other cases, and that avoidance or reduction is necessary. What determines when a given approach should be used?

It is the characteristic of the risk itself that determines which of the four tools of risk management is most appropriate in a given situation. Under what circumstances is each of the tools appropriate?

Based on the foregoing discussion, it is possible at this point to summarize a few general guidelines with respect to the relationship of the various tools and particular risks. The matrix below categorizes risks into four classes, based on the combination of frequency (probability) and severity of each risk. Although real-world risks are not divided so conveniently, most exposures can be classified according to their frequency and potential severity.

	High Frequency	Low Frequency
High Severity	retain	reduce retain
Low Severity	transfer reduce	Avoid reduce

When the possible severity of loss is high, retention is not realistic and some other technique is necessary. However, we have also noted that when the probability of loss is high, insurance becomes too costly. Through a process of elimination, we conclude that the appropriate tools for dealing with risks characterized by high severity and high frequency are avoidance and reduction. Reduction may be used when it is possible to reduce either the severity or the frequency to a manageable level. Otherwise, the risk should be avoided.

Risks characterized by high severity and low frequency are best dealt with through insurance.

The high severity implies a catastrophic impact if the loss should occur, and the low probability implies a low expected value and a low cost of transfer.

Risks characterized by low severity and high frequency are most appropriately dealt with through retention and reduction: retention because the high frequency implies that transfer will be costly, and reduction to reduce the aggregate amount of losses that must be borne.

Finally, those risks characterized by low severity and low frequency are best handled through retention. They seldom occur, and when they do happen, the financial impact is inconsequential.

Although not all risks will fit precisely into the categories in the matrix, most exposures can be classified according to their frequency and potential severity. In those instances in which the probability or severity is not high or low the principles may be modified by judgment.

The Special Case of Risk Reduction

From a theoretical perspective, decisions regarding the application of risk management techniques should be made on the basis of a marginal-benefit/marginal-cost rule. This means that from the viewpoint of minimizing costs, each of the techniques for dealing with risk should be utilized when that particular technique represents the lowest-cost approach to the risk in question. Also, a given technique should be used only up to that point at which the last dollar spent achieves a dollar reduction in the cost of losses or risk and no further. However, this basic principle must sometimes be modified in the case of loss prevention and control methods. Humanitarian considerations and legal requirements sometimes dictate that loss prevention and control measures go beyond the optimal marginal-cost/marginal-benefit point. For example, the federal Occupational Safety and Health Act requires employers to incur expenses for job safety loss prevention and control

measures that might not be justified on a pure cost-benefit basis.[14]

Risk Management Information Systems

The basic risk management function is decision making, and information is the raw material of good decisions. To support the decision-making function, the risk manager needs accurate and timely information on various facets of the organization's operations. Much of the information required for risk management decisions exists within the organization, but in a scattered and unstructured form. The information becomes more useful when it is combined into a useful database that facilitates analysis, that is, when it is integrated in a *risk management information system* (RMIS). By consolidating quantitative aspects of the risk management function in a relational database, coded by organizational unit, the RMIS provides the raw material for risk management decisions. Among other things, the RMIS will include information on losses, premiums, and other risk-related expenditures. Some of this information is available from internal sources and some is provided by the organization's insurers.

---

[14]Decisions with respect to loss prevention in connection with employee injuries have been greatly affected by OSHA. The Williams-Steiger Act, better known as the Occupational Safety and Health Act (OSHA) of 1970 established a new agency within the U.S. Department of Labor, the Occupational Safety and Health Administration, which is empowered to set and enforce health and safety standards for almost all private employers in the nation. There are mandatory penalties under the law up to $1,000 for each violation and optional penalties up to $1,000 for nonserious violations. Penalties may be assessed for every day that an employer fails to correct a violation during a period set in a citation from OSHA. In addition, an employer who willfully or repeatedly breaks the law is subject to penalties up to $10,000 for each violation. Any willful violation of standards resulting in an employee's death, upon conviction, is punishable by a fine of up to six months' imprisonment or $10,000. The maximum penalty under the law is life imprisonment for killing an OSHA inspector.

There are a number of vendors that sell prepackaged risk management information system software, but many organizations have developed their own in-house systems.

Implementing the Decision

The decision is made to retain a risk. This may be accomplished with or without a reserve and with or without a fund. If the decision is made to include the accumulation of a fund, the administrative procedure must be inaugurated to implement the decision. If the decision is made to use loss prevention to deal with a particular risk, the proper loss prevention program must be designed and implemented. The decision to transfer the risk through insurance must be followed by the selection of an insurer, and negotiations for and placement of the insurance.

Evaluation and Review

Evaluation and review must be included in the program for two reasons. First, the risk management process does not take place in a vacuum. Things change: new risks arise and old risks disappear. The techniques that were appropriate last year may not be the most advisable this year, and constant attention is required. Second, mistakes are sometimes made. Evaluation and review of the risk management program permits the risk manager to review his or her decisions and discover any mistakes before they become costly.

How does one review a risk management program? Basically, it is by repeating each of the steps in the risk management process to determine whether past decisions were proper in the light of existing conditions and whether they were properly executed. The risk manager reevaluates the program's objectives, repeats the identification process to assure, insofar as possible, that it was performed correctly, and then evaluates

the risks that have been identified and verifies that the decision on how to address each risk was proper. Finally, the implementation of the decisions must be verified to make sure they were executed as intended.

Evaluation and Review as Managerial Control

The evaluation and review phase of the risk management process is the managerial control phase of the risk management process. The purpose of controlling is to verify that operations are going according to plans. Control requires (1) setting standards or objectives to be achieved; (2) measuring performance against those standards and objectives; and (3) taking corrective action when actual results differ from the intended results. In this context, it should be recognized that a disastrous loss need not occur for performance to deviate from what is intended. Because risk management deals with decisions under conditions of uncertainty, adequate performance is measured not only based on whether the organization has survived, but whether it would have survived under a different set of more adverse circumstances. The existence of an inadequately addressed exposure with catastrophic potential represents a deviation from the intended objective. It is this type of deviation from objectives that the risk management control process is intended to address.

Quantitative Performance Standards

Ideally, standards should be quantified whenever possible. One quantifiable measure of risk management performance that is frequently suggested is the *cost of risk*, which is the total expenditures for risk management, including insurance premiums paid and retained losses, expressed as a percentage of revenues. RIMS publishes annual studies on the *cost of risk*, which makes it convenient for the risk manager to compare the risk management costs of the organization with other firms in the same industry. Although the cost of risk varies from industry to industry, it generally averages something in the neighborhood of 1 percent of revenues. Although the cost of risk may fluctuate because of factors over which the risk manager has no control, it is a useful standard when properly interpreted.

Quantitative performance standards are more prevalent in the area of risk control than for risk financing functions. Standard injury rates reflecting frequency and severity are available as benchmarks for measuring performance in the area of employee safety. Similarly, motor vehicle accident rates and other frequency and severity rates are useful benchmarks in measuring risk control measures.

Risk Management Audits

Although evaluation and review is an ongoing process that is performed without interruption, the risk management program should periodically be subjected to a comprehensive review called a *risk management audit*. Most people are familiar with the term *audit* as it is used in the accounting field, where it refers to a formal examination of financial records by public accountants to verify the accuracy, fairness, and integrity of the accounting records. The term audit has a second meaning, which is any thorough examination and evaluation of a problem, and it is this second meaning that is implied in the risk management audit. A risk management audit is a detailed and systematic review of a risk management program, designed to determine whether the objectives of the program are appropriate to the needs of the organization, whether the measures designed to achieve those objectives are suitable, and whether the measures have been properly implemented.

Whereas risk management audits *may* be conducted by an external party, they may also be performed internally. When the risk management department has the required in-house expertise, it may establish a system for internal audits of the risk management function on a regularly scheduled basis. Although internal audits may lack the objectivity of external audits and are not substitutes for external audits, they can provide many of the same benefits. The benefits of internal audits will be maximized to the extent that they are conducted in the same way as an external audit.

Important Concepts to Remember

risk management process
determination of objectives
identification of the risks
evaluation of the risks
considering alternatives and selecting the risk treatment device
implementing the decision
evaluation and review
insurance policy checklists
risk analysis questionnaires
flow process charts
critical risks
important risks
unimportant risks
risk management policy
tools of risk management
cost-benefit analysis

utility theory
decision making under certainty
decision making under risk
decision making under uncertainty
expected value
minimax regret
rules of risk management
don't risk more than you can afford to lose
consider the odds
don't risk a lot for a little
frequency
severity
Occupational Safety and Health Act (OSHA)
expert system
post-loss objectives

pre-loss objectives
survival
cost of risk
risk management policy
maximum retention limit
uninsured loss reserve fund
aggregate loss retention level
minimum retention level
risk analysis questionnaires
fact finders
exposure checklists
insurance policy checklists
financial statement method
flow charts
risk management information systems

Questions for Review

1. List and briefly describe the six steps in the risk management process.

2. Describe the criteria that the text suggests be used in prioritizing risks in terms of their importance.

3. Describe the two strategies that may be employed in risk management decisions and explain the situation in which each is appropriate.

4. Three rules of risk management proposed by Mehr and Hedges are discussed in this chapter. List these rules and explain the implications of each in determining what should be done about individual exposures facing a business firm.

5. Why are loss prevention and control measures subject to different considerations than the choice with respect to other techniques for dealing with risk?

6. Explain how knowing the frequency and severity of loss for a given exposure to loss is helpful in determining what should be done about that exposure.

7. Explain the importance of the evaluation and review phase in risk management.

8. Identify the primary risk management objective and explain why it is preeminent.

9. Describe the general nature of a corporate risk management policy.

10. Explain why risk identification is generally considered to be the most difficult step in the risk management process.

Questions for Discussion

1. Which of the six steps in the risk management process do you believe is the most difficult for the risk manager? Which would you suspect is the most frequently overlooked or neglected?

2. The principles and rules of risk management appear to be just plain common sense. In view of this fact, how do you account for the widespread violation of these rules in insurance buying today?

3. Explain the relationship, if any, among the statements: "Don't risk more than you can afford to lose," "These people who need insurance most are those who can least afford it," and "Insurance should be considered as a last resort."

4. In an effort to reduce insurance costs, the risk manager of a medium-sized manufacturing firm canceled the property insurance on the firm's $8.5 million plant and equipment, for which the annual premium was about $265,000. Two years later when the action was discovered, the risk manager was called on the carpet by a horrified vice president of finance. "What were you thinking of?" demanded the VP. "What if we had had a loss?" "But," responded the risk manager, "we didn't have a loss. The fact that I saved the firm over half a million dollars in the past two years is proof that the decision was the right one." If you agree with the risk manager, help him convince the vice president that he is right. If you disagree, help the VP convince the risk manager that he is wrong.

5. Explain the purpose and intent of each of the provisions in the sample risk management policy in Figure 4.1.

Suggestions for Additional Reading

Doherty, Neil A. *Corporate Risk Management: A Financial Exposition.* New York: McGraw-Hill, 1985.

Harrington, Scott E., and Gregory R. Niehaus. *Risk Management and Insurance.* New York: McGraw-Hill, 1998.

Head, George L., and Stephen Horn II. *Essentials of Risk Management,* 3rd ed., vols. 1 and 2. Malvern, PA: Insurance Institute of America, 1997.

Mehr, R. I., and B. A. Hedges. *Risk Management in the Business Enterprise.* Homewood, IL: Richard D. Irwin, 1963. Chapters 5–9.

Ralston, August R., ed. *Risk Management Manual,* vol. 3, section 14. Santa Monica, CA: Merritt Co. (loose-leaf service with monthly supplements).

Vaughan, Emmett J. *Risk Management.* New York: Wiley, 1997.

Williams, C. Arthur, Peter C. Young, and Michael Smith. *Risk Management and Insurance,* 8th ed. New York: McGraw-Hill, 1998.

Websites to Explore

International Risk Management Institute, Inc.: http://irmi.com

Nonprofit Risk Management Center: http://www.nonprofitrisk.org

Occupational Safety and Health Administration (OSHA): http://www.osha.gov/

Practical Risk Management: http://www.pracrisk.com/

Warren, McVeigh & Griffin Consultants: http://www.griffincom.com/

Public Agency Risk Managers Association (PARMA): http://www.parma.com

Risk and Insurance Management Society, Inc.: http://www.rims.org

RiskINFO: http://www.riskinfo.com/

Self Insurance Institute of America: http://www.siia.org

CHAPTER 5

Risk Management Applications

*When a great company, or even a great merchant, has twenty or thirty ships at
sea, they may, as it were, insure one another. The premium saved upon them
all, may more than compensate such losses as they are likely to meet within the
common course of chances.*
—Adam Smith, *The Wealth of Nations, 1776*

CHAPTER OBJECTIVES

When you have finished this chapter, you should be able to

- Explain how a business might use risk avoidance in dealing with risk and why avoidance is subject to limitations in its application by businesses

- Distinguish between loss prevention and loss control measures

- Explain the difference in philosophy between the domino theory and energy release theory of accident causation

- Describe the nature and purpose of disaster planning

In this chapter, we turn to a more detailed examination of the techniques of risk management, risk control and risk finance, examining the ways in which risk control and risk financing decisions are implemented. This chapter is intended to provide an overview of risk control and risk financing techniques. With respect to risk control, specifically, the chapter is not intended as a crash course in loss prevention and control. The loss prevention and control measures that are appropriate for the variety of hazards that can produce losses differ from hazard to hazard. They encompass fire prevention engineering and industrial safety, security measures, legal analysis,

and a variety of engineering applications. These are highly sophisticated disciplines, for which people prepare through years of education and training. It would be presumptuous to suggest that we can summarize these disciplines in a few pages. However, the discussion will provide an introduction to the broad area of risk control that should give the reader an appreciation of the contribution that risk control makes to achieving the risk management objectives. With respect to risk financing, much of the rest of the text focuses on the specific insurance coverages that are used to implement risk transfer decisions. In this chapter, we will examine some of the specialized approaches to retention and the process of insurance buying generally.

Risk Control

Historical Neglect of Risk Control

Although the situation has changed dramatically with the growth of risk management, there was a time when risk control was a relatively neglected function. This was true for several reasons. First, the timing of the expenditures for loss control and for the benefits from reduced losses are different. Loss prevention costs must be incurred here and now. The benefits they will generate are all in the future. Furthermore, the benefits are more elusive, requiring measurement of something that does not happen (losses). Because the benefits of loss prevention and control efforts are difficult to measure, expenditures in this area are sometimes difficult to justify on a cost-benefit basis, and as a result lose in competition with other funding needs.

Another factor was that, until recently, state and federal regulations were less stringent. Consumerism, government regulations, and the tort system have created a new environment, and have gotten the attention of the business world with a vengeance. Due partly to the growth of risk management but more to state and federal mandates and tort liability, risk control programs are an important facet of every organization's efforts to deal with risk.

Government Standards and Risk Control

One factor that has encouraged advances in risk control throughout the business world has been government standards and regulations. The theory behind government regulations related to safety is that businesses will not implement risk control measures unless they are compelled to do so, primarily because businesses underestimate the benefits of such measures. Once adopted, the statutory standard becomes mandatory for all individuals and businesses covered by the law. The Occupational Safety and Health Administration (OSHA) regulations are perhaps the best example of statutory loss control standards. OSHA was a legislative recognition of the fact that businesses must sometimes be compelled to make loss prevention expenditures. If the employers could not find justification for employee safety expenditures on a cost-benefit basis, Congress would give them the incentive by imposing penalties for failure to do so. State and local building and fire codes represent another example of government mandates for loss prevention and control measures. Although these standards typify the effect of government intervention, standards and regulations exist in a variety of areas, including employee safety, consumer products, environmental damage, fire safety, and other areas.

Voluntary Standards

In addition to the statutory standards, nongovernment groups have adopted voluntary or consensual standards that provide guidance on loss control. Although these standards are not legally binding, they have an important influence on the safety efforts. The standards promulgated by the Underwriters Laboratories (UL) are a good example. The UL tests a variety of products for conformance with its own safety standards, most of which have as their primary objective the personal safety of users of the tested products. Although UL certification of a product is voluntary on the part of the manufacturer, most commercial insurance companies will provide product liability insurance only to manufacturers who use UL approved materials or whose products bear the UL label.

Areas of Risk Control

Many organizations have a safety director who is responsible for the organization's industrial safety (employee injury) program. Some organizations might also have a security organization and others might have a property protection program. Depending on the nature and scope of the organization's operations, risk control efforts may involve many or all of the following:

Employee safety

Employment practices liability

Nonemployee crime control

Internal controls (employee dishonesty)

Computer security

Transit exposures

Property exposures—direct loss

Property exposures—indirect loss

Liability risk control

Motor vehicle safety

Antiterrorism

Disaster planning

This abbreviated inventory of loss prevention and control specialties indicates the challenge in attempting to describe the specific risk control measures that may be a part of the risk management effort. It also suggests the differences in the types of expertise required for risk control. Most techniques used in loss prevention and control are specific to one area or another. Preventing employee injuries calls for a different kind of expertise than reducing the risk of employee dishonesty. Few organizations will have all types of such expertise in-house, which means that assistance must often be obtained from outside the organization.

The appropriate expertise is often available in connection with insurance coverage or in connection with other professional services. Insurance companies provide assistance in employee safety, fire prevention and control, and fleet safety. Assistance in establishing effective internal controls, which are the heart of an employee dishonesty prevention program, is likely to be available from the firm's public accountants. Local police and security specialists can provide assistance in the area of nonemployee crime.

The Risk Manager and Risk Control

The success of a corporate risk control program depends on the quality of management it receives. It can be argued that risk control requires an advocate within the organization—someone who is responsible for the overall coordination of the risk control function, regardless of the particular area of loss involved. There are many authorities who feel that responsibility and authority for the development of a total loss prevention and control program should be vested in a single person. The risk manager, by virtue of his or her familiarity with the exposures of the organization and the costs arising from such exposures, is a logical person to whom such responsibility might be assigned. Although the risk manager will rarely possess the wide range of skills required for a comprehensive loss prevention and control effort, he or she is in a position to recognize the need for risk control and the contacts to access persons who have the needed skills.

In many organizations, responsibility for risk control for different exposures is distributed throughout the organization. Regardless of where responsibility for risk control is assigned within the organization, the risk control efforts are directly relevant to the risk management process and the risk manager has a vested interest in the effectiveness of these efforts. Risk control measures support both transfer and retention. Companies that insure all or part of their risk find that loss experience is their most valuable negotiating point with respect to availability, coverage, and premium costs. Poor or escalating loss experience is usually met by restricted availability of coverage and higher premiums. The organization with good loss experience is likely to find that insurance markets for its risks are readily available.

Even when the risk manager does not have direct responsibility for risk control efforts, he or she has an implied responsibility for monitoring the effectiveness of risk control efforts. Because the effectiveness of risk control directly affects the cost of risk, when risk control is ineffective or substandard, the risk manager is in a position to measure the effectiveness of risk control efforts. When the risk manager does not have direct responsibility for the design and execution of risk control programs, he or she can serve in a monitoring role.

Theories of Accident Causation

Some accidental losses result from the forces of nature, such as windstorms, lightning, and earthquakes. Others result from the careless acts of individuals. Still others result from willful and malicious or criminal acts of humans. Understanding why losses happen can be useful in designing programs for their prevention. To date, no one has developed a dominant general theory of accident causation. There are, however, two general theories that have some explanatory value: the *domino theory* developed by H. W. Heinrich, a safety engineer and pioneer in the field of industrial accident safety, and the *energy release theory*, developed by Dr. William Haddon, Jr. of the Insurance Institute for Highway Safety. Although these authors were concerned with different types of loss (Heinrich with industrial accidents and employee injuries, and Haddon with highway safety), both are general theories, in the sense that they have application across the entire range of loss prevention and control activities.

Heinrich's Domino Theory

According to Heinrich, an "accident" is one factor in a sequence that can lead to an injury. The factors can be visualized as a series of dominoes standing on edge; when one falls, a chain reaction results in an accident. Each domino is dependent on the preceding factor (see Figure 5.1). In Heinrich's theory, a personal injury (the final domino) occurs only as a result of an accident (the preceding domino). Heinrich defined an *accident* as any unplanned and uncontrolled event in which the action or reaction of an object, substance, person, or radiation *could* result in per-

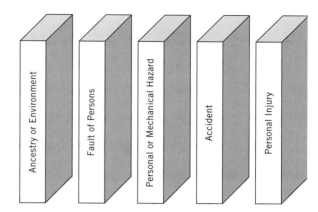

Figure 5.1   Heinrich's Domino Theory

sonal injury or property damage. In this context, an accident need not actually result in injury or property damage. If a person slips and falls, an injury may or may not result, but for Heinrich, an accident has taken place. Accidents are the result of personal or mechanical hazards (the third domino). Personal or mechanical hazards result from faults of persons (the second domino), which in turn result from ancestry or environment (the first domino).

When an injury or property damage occurs, all five factors are involved. If one of the factors in the sequence leading to an accident can be removed, the loss can be prevented. Heinrich believes that we should be interested in all five factors, but be concerned primarily with accidents and the proximate causes of those accidents. For Heinrich, the major cause of accidents—and losses—is an unsafe human act.

William Haddon's Energy Release Theory

Instead of concentrating on human behavior, Haddon treats accidents as a physical engineering problem. Accidents result when energy that is out of control puts more stress on a structure (property or person) than that structure can tolerate without damage. The model is generic, and situations in which "energy is out of control" can include fire losses, accidents, industrial injuries, and virtually any other situation in which injury or damage can result. Hitting your thumb with a hammer, burning your body in a scalding shower, or getting a shock from an electric outlet are all examples of excessive energy. So too is the destruction of a building by a hurricane or an explosion or a collision on the freeway. In Haddon's model, losses can be prevented and their effects minimized by controlling the amount of energy that is released and by changing the structures that the energy could damage—in other words, through engineering.

The strategies Haddon proposed to address the problem of energy out of control include preventing the creation of the hazard in the first place and controlling the amount of hazard that is created. When the hazard cannot be prevented or limited, Haddon would separate (by time or by space) the hazard at the property or person to be protected. When property or people cannot be separated from the hazard, they should be made more resistant to damage from the hazard. Finally, when damage has occurred, measures should be taken to repair the damage caused by the hazard.

The Two Theories and Approaches to Risk Control

The difference between the Heinrich and Haddon theories can be viewed as a difference in emphasis. Both theories explain a sequence that leads to damage or injury. Unlike Heinrich, who places most of the blame for accidents on human behavior that leads to mechanical or physical hazards, Haddon concentrates on the physical engineering aspects of the conditions that give rise to accidents. This difference in emphasis in the two theories is reflected in the two broad approaches to risk control that have emerged. Some loss prevention measures focus on the individual, and seek to modify human behavior. This is the *human behavior approach*. Other prevention efforts are aimed at mechanical and environmental fac-

tors, and seek to eliminate hazards. This is referred to as the *engineering approach*.

Human Behavior Approach The human behavior approach stresses safety education and the motivation of persons. Proponents of this approach to loss prevention argue that most accidents are committed by unsafe acts, and that the greatest gains in safety and loss prevention can be achieved through efforts aimed at modifying human behavior. The efforts aimed at modifying human behavior include *education* and *enforcement*.

Education serves two important functions in risk control efforts. First, it alerts those exposed to loss to the existence of the hazards and impresses on them the consequences of the losses to which they are exposed. Hopefully, it creates a heightened sense of concern over the individual's own safety. In addition, education can also provide guidance on the "safer way" of performing certain functions. Safety education, safety posters, safety committees, and safety rules are all examples of the education facet of the human behavior approach to loss prevention.

The other part of the human behavior approach to risk control is *enforcement*. For some unknown reason, many people feel exempt from the rules governing safety and loss prevention. Because individuals must be motivated to follow rules, a system must be devised for enforcement. Traffic laws, municipal building codes, plant safety rules, and fire safety all need to be enforced and this enforcement is the second aspect of the human behavior emphasis in loss control. The penalties associated with enforcement procedures act as deterrents to undesirable behavior.

Engineering Approach The engineering approach to loss prevention and control emphasizes the elimination of unsafe physical conditions by such measures as fire-resistive construction, burglary-resistant safes, boiler inspections, machine guards, and safer cars. The basic premise in the engineering approach is that the environment can be engineered to protect people and property. The engineering approach views accidents and losses as inevitable consequences of the inter-action of people and their environment—unless measures are taken to modify that environment.

One version of the engineering approach to risk control—systems safety—is a branch of and developed from systems engineering, which deals with the design and creation of complex systems. As the name indicates, systems safety views a process, a situation, a problem, a machine, or any other entity as a *system*, rather than as just a process, situation, problem, or machine. An accident occurs when a human or a mechanical component of a system fails to function when it should. The objective of systems safety is to identify these failures before they occur and either eliminate them or minimize their effects.

Systems safety is not a single methodology, but a variety of techniques designed to analyze systems and identify potential system failures. The common theme in these methodologies is the attempt to identify system failures before they occur through an examination of all accidents and "near misses" to discern patterns that might indicate causality.[1]

Control Measures and Time of Application

Haddon proposed a classification for risk control measures that can be useful in considering risk control measures generally. Control measures are classified first, according to their time of application. They are also classified according to whether they are directed toward the person, the machinery and equipment, or the environment.

With respect to timing, risk control measures are classified according to whether they are applied before the accident, at the time of the accident, or after the accident (i.e., pre-event actions, simultaneous-with-event actions, and post-event actions). Pre-event risk control measures aim at preventing losses from occurring. They include the wide range of protective devices and procedures that are designed to eliminate accidents and other types of losses. In general, pre-event measures focus on the elimination of hazards. These include such diverse measures as constructing fire- and earthquake-resistant buildings, the design and testing of products, and the selection and training of drivers. Pre-event control measures also include measures such as the separation of assets to control severity. During World War II, for example, the risk of loss arising out of the manufacture of munitions was reduced by establishing numerous small plants, rather than a few large ones. Loss control for employee dishonesty uses separation of assets and separation of responsibilities to minimize both the likelihood and the amount of loss. *Redundancy* is another pre-event risk control measure. Stand-by generating facilities for power outages and alternate sources of materials and supplies are examples of redundancy as a loss control measure.

Simultaneous-with-event control measures are designed to minimize the amount of loss or damage that occurs when an accident is not prevented. Thus, seat belts and airbags do not prevent one from having an accident, but may reduce the amount of injury that occurs. Similarly, a sprinkler system does not prevent fire, but will help to limit the damage that results when a fire does occur.

Post-event loss control measures focus on minimizing the amount of damage or loss that results from the occurrence of a loss. In the case of property exposures, post-event control measures include salvage operations, which are designed to maximize the value of undamaged property or property that is only partially damaged.[2] For employee injuries, post-event control measures include rehabilitation of the injured worker. In the area of legal liability, post-event risk control measures include an aggressive defense, negotiated settlements with injured parties, alternative dis-

---

[1]For an interesting perspective on the history of systems safety see Vernon L. Grose, *Managing Risk: Systematic Loss Prevention for Executives* (Englewood Cliffs, NJ: Prentice-Hall, 1987).

[2]Salvage efforts include efforts to protect property from further damage and arranging for the sale or other disposition of undamaged property at the highest price.

pute resolution procedures (e.g., arbitration), and structured settlements.[3]

Besides the classification in terms of the time of application, risk control measures may be divided according to whether they are directed at persons, mechanical devices or mechanisms, or the environment. Drivers' education and licensing, for example, focuses on the person. Automobile safety features, such as seat belts and airbags, focus on the machine. Road signs, stoplights, and intersection control focus on the environment.

When the time of application and the mechanism toward which the loss control measure is directed are combined, we can construct a matrix that summarizes the possible combinations of loss prevention and control techniques (see Figure 5.2). Thus, there are nine possible combinations of timing and mechanisms toward which the loss prevention measures may be directed. This provides a useful way in which to consider risk control measures for virtually any exposure.

	Prior to Event	*At Time of Event*	*After Event*
Individual			
Machinery			
Environment			

Figure 5.2 Timing and Targets of Control Measures

Sources of Assistance for Risk Control

There are numerous organizations in our society dedicated to promoting safety and loss prevention. Many of these organizations have direct ties with the insurance industry. Indeed, many of the major advancements in risk control have come directly from the efforts of insurance companies, both individually and collectively. For example, much of our current knowledge about industrial safety and the protection of employees from the hazards of the workplace originated from the efforts of the insurers writing workers compensation insurance. The first researchers to address the problems associated with injury in the workplace were insurance company employees, and their studies have provided much of the knowledge still used in loss prevention programs today.

Loss Control Services Available from Insurers

Given the historical emphasis of insurers on loss prevention and control efforts, it is not surprising that insurance companies remain one of the most widely used sources of loss prevention and control assistance. In some lines of insurance, such as boiler and machinery insurance, the loss prevention and inspection services are perhaps the major reason that the coverage is purchased. Insurers conduct loss control activities both for their own benefit and as a service to their insureds. The major benefit to the insurer is in making accounts more profitable by reducing the amount of losses. Equally important, an insurer's loss control specialists can sometimes devise ways to improve loss experience to an extent that allows the insurer to write an account that would otherwise be unacceptable.

Other Sources of Assistance

In addition to the assistance available from insurance companies, assistance for various types of loss exposures is available from a variety of sources. A number of organizations provide consulting services on such diverse areas as the design of industrial safety and motor vehicle safety programs, environmental compliance, employment practices, computer security, and other specialties.

Although it is not common to think of lawyers as loss prevention and control specialists, it is

---

[3]A structured settlement is a negotiated settlement of a bodily injury claim in which the plaintiff is offered an income payable for life, rather than a lump sum. If the plaintiff accepts the offer, an annuity is generally purchased from a life insurer to provide the promised benefits.

clear that in the post-loss phase of liability loss control, they are the major players. Once an event has occurred that could give rise to a lawsuit and to legal liability, the engineering and human behavior approaches are replaced by the legal efforts at loss control. Defense attorneys who specialize in defending and negotiating settlements for bodily injury and property damage are loss control specialists in the same sense as a sprinkler system is a mechanism for controlling the damage caused by fire.

The accountant is a major loss prevention and control specialist in the field of employee crime. By designing and implementing internal controls in the organization's financial recordkeeping system, the accountant seeks to minimize the potential for dishonesty on the part of the organization's employees. Auditing is a loss prevention tool for employee dishonesty and is effective in controlling both the frequency and the severity of loss.

Disaster Planning

At the time of a disaster, normal operating procedures, the chain of command, and communication links may be interrupted. Confusion and chaotic conditions can prevent normally effective executives from taking the steps that are required to reduce the severity of the losses resulting from the disaster, whatever it may be. The objective of a disaster plan is to allow those responsible for the enterprise during an emergency to focus on the solution of major problems. To accomplish this objective, the disaster plan establishes an emergency organization designed to perform specific tasks before, during, and after a disaster. It also establishes priorities for the use of resources available at the time of the disaster and thereafter.

An initial step in developing the disaster plan is to establish priorities that will be followed in resolving conflicts when developing the plan. Although every organization must set its own priorities, the following is illustrative of the types of priorities that might be included and their ranking.

- The first priority will be to protect human life.
- The second priority will be to prevent or minimize personal injury.
- The third priority will be to prevent and minimize the potential damage to physical assets.
- The fourth priority will be to restore normal operations as quickly as possible.

With these priorities established, measures aimed at achieving the priorities can then be identified. Measures to protect human life and prevent injuries will include plans for evacuation of personnel and the provision of required shelter, strategies designed to protect persons who must remain in threatened areas, and measures to provide medical assistance for persons who may be injured. Measures aimed at minimizing property damage will include plans for the removal of threatened property when time allows, maintenance of critical records at alternate sites, and common-sense measures designed to protect and preserve property at the time of and after the disaster. Measures to restore normal operations quickly may include advance arrangements to relocate certain functions (such as computer operations), identification of alternate facilities, and provision for resupply of materials and replacement of equipment.[4]

Risk Financing

General Considerations

The choice between the risk financing alternatives—retention and transfer—is sometimes dictated by the first rule of risk management. When a risk exceeds the organization's risk bearing capacity, it must be reduced or transferred. In other

[4]The Federal Emergency Management Agency (FEMA) Web site includes a wealth of information on disaster planning. See http://www.fema.gov/impact/im_bustip.htm.

Tidbits, Vignettes, and Conundrums 5.1

Family Disaster Plans

Although disaster planning is recognized as an essential part of the risk management program of a commercial enterprise, the value of disaster planning is less well recognized by individuals and families. The Federal Emergency Management Agency (FEMA) Web site includes a model family disaster plan. See http://www.fema.gov/pte/displan.htm.

---

cases, however, where the organization could afford the loss, there may still be advantages in transfer. It may be desirable, for example, to obtain the services of an insurance company for the investigation and settlement of liability losses or the inspection services that are offered in connection with boiler and machinery insurance. In addition, there are some instances in which risk transfer will produce economies despite the fact that the cost of insurance exceeds expected value. Two considerations in particular may affect the transfer-retention decision: the cost of financing risk and the tax treatment of insurance premiums and retained losses.

The Cost of Financing Risk

The choice between transfer and retention and the way in which retention and transfer should be combined should recognize the distinction between the cost of financing losses and cost of financing risk. A review of terminology may be helpful. A loss is a decline in or disappearance of value due to a contingency. Not all losses involve risk, which is the possibility of a deviation from what is expected or hoped for.

Consider a firm that owns buildings worth $1,000,000. Insurance on the buildings will cost $30,000. Assuming a loss ratio of about 65 or 66 percent, the expected loss (that is, the average loss per insured) is roughly $20,000. In fact, let us also assume that the manufacturer's past losses have been about average, or $20,000 a year. If expected losses are $20,000 a year, but could be as much as $1,000,000, the risk is $980,000 ($1,000,000 minus $20,000). The $20,000 represents a predictable loss, while the remaining $980,000 represents "risk," which, like the cost of losses, can be transferred or retained.

If the firm decides to retain the entire risk of loss, it will presumably continue to incur $20,000 in losses annually. In addition, to protect against the possibility of a total $1,000,000 loss, it must maintain a liquid reserve of $980,000. The cost of the retention program will be the $20,000 in annual losses that must be paid plus the opportunity cost on the $980,000 reserve. This opportunity cost is measured as the difference between the return that will be earned on the reserve (which must be kept in a semiliquid form), and the return that could be realized if the $980,000 were applied to the firm's operations. If the average return on funds applied to operations is say, 15 percent and the interest that can be earned on the invested reserve is 6 percent, the opportunity cost is $88,200 ([15% − 6%] × 980,000). Thus, the cost of insuring is $30,000, while the cost of retention is $108,200 ($20,000 in losses plus the $88,200 opportunity cost).[5] A more complete analysis would consider the effect of taxes on

---

[5]If the firm decides that it will not maintain a reserve, but will borrow the required $980,000 if a total loss occurs, the net effect is the same, since it will need to maintain $980,000 of its line of credit free for use in the event of a loss. The opportunity cost is the same in either case.

both costs. Assuming a combined state and federal marginal tax rate of 50 percent, the cost of insurance would be $15,000 and the cost of retention would be $54,100.

Tax Considerations In Risk Financing Decisions

One element that should be considered in the choice of the approach to risk financing for a particular risk is the impact that taxes may have on insurance costs and losses. In the case of a business firm, for instance, property and liability insurance premiums are a deductible business expense, as are uninsured losses. However, contributions to a *funded retention program* are not deductible. The inability to deduct contributions to a reserve fund does not eliminate the tax deductibility of self-insured losses—it only forces companies to wait until they actually incur a loss before taking the deduction. The decision to purchase insurance may be influenced by the fact that uninsured losses are deductible in the year in which they occur only to the extent of profit during that year and that the tax deduction resulting from the uninsured loss may be reduced by low profits in the year in which it occurs.[6]

Tax Treatment of Property Loss Insurance Recoveries

Under current tax law, a business is allowed a deduction for the book value of property that is destroyed by an accident, such as a fire or windstorm. If the book value of the asset is the same as the insurance recovery, the deduction for the damaged property offsets the insurance proceeds. When there is a difference between the actual value of an asset and its book value, insurance recovery can exceed the book value of an asset that has been destroyed. Suppose, for example, that the XYZ Corporation owns a building that it has insured for its replacement cost value of $10 million. The book value of the asset—the original cost less accumulated depreciation—is $5 million. If a total loss occurs, XYZ's deduction for the building is limited to its depreciated basis of $5 million. The insurance recovery of $10 million therefore exceeds the deductible basis by $5 million, and XYZ realizes a taxable gain. This type of loss and recovery is termed an *involuntary conversion* and is subject to special tax treatment under *Internal Revenue Code* Section 1033(a). For an involuntary conversion, the taxpayer has the option of recognizing (and paying taxes on) the gain, or deferring taxation of the gain. XYZ can recognize the $5 million in taxable gain, pay the appropriate tax, and enter the new building built with the insurance proceeds in its books with a $10 million basis. If XYZ elects to defer taxation of the gain, the new $10 million building will be entered in the books at the same basis ($5 million) as the building that was destroyed.

Risk Retention

Risk retention encompasses a variety of risk financing techniques. In its simplest form, retained losses are simply paid as an operating expense like any other costs. At the most complex level, it can involve the formation of a captive insurance company to serve as a vehicle for funding the retained losses.

The use of formal risk retention programs has grown over the years for a number of reasons. In some cases, such as self-insurance of employer-provided health expense benefits, commercial insurance alternatives are available, but employers have found that they can achieve economies through self-insurance. In other cases, retention resulted from a perceived failure of the commercial insurance market. Faced with escalating insurance costs and, in some instances, the inability

---

[6]Unlike the case of the business firm, insurance premiums are not a tax-deductible expenditure for the individual. In addition, casualty losses sustained by an individual are deductible only to the extent that each loss exceeds $100 and the aggregate for all excess losses exceeds 10 percent of the individual's adjusted gross income.

to obtain certain types of liability insurance, some organizations opted to self-insure or simply "go bare," paying claims directly out of their income. Other organizations banded together to form group-owned captives or risk-retention pools.

Funding the Retention Program

In the preceding chapter, we examined the decisions regarding which risks should be transferred and which should be retained. Given formulation of a rationally conceived retention program, there remains the problem of providing for the losses that arise from retained risk and guaranteeing the availability of funds to meet the losses that occur. Often this will require that the retention program be supported through some form of tangible reserves. When an organization elects to retain some of its risks it may be logical to budget for the uninsured losses that will probably take place. Whether the retention program should be supported by a formal funding program—the segregation of specific assets to cover losses—depends on the size of the potential losses, the variability in losses from year to year, and the availability of assets in the absence of a fund.

Self-Insurance

In Chapter 3 we noted that while self-insurance is technically a definitional impossibility, the term has found widespread acceptance in the business world.[7] Although there are theoretical defects in the term self-insurance, it is a convenient way of distinguishing retention programs that utilize insurance techniques from those that do not. Self-insurance programs are distinguished from other retention programs mainly in the formality of the arrangement. In some instances this means ob-

taining approval from a state regulatory agency to retain risks, under specifically defined conditions. In other cases, it means the formal trappings of an insurance program, including funding measures based on actuarial calculations and the contractual definitions of the exposures. When the self-insurance involves third parties (such as employees in an employer-sponsored health insurance program), there is a need for the other insurance formalities, such as certificates of coverage and premiums. It is in this limited sense that the term self-insurance is used in this section.

Reasons for Self-Insurance

The main reason that organizations elect to self-insure certain exposures is that they believe it will be cheaper to do so in the long run. This is particularly true in cases in which there is no need for the financial protection furnished by insurance.

1. Self-insurance avoids certain expenses associated with traditional commercial insurance. These include, among other things, insurer overhead and profit, agents' commissions, and the premium taxes paid by insurers.

2. The organization may believe that its loss experience is significantly better than the average experience upon which rates are made, or that the rating system does not accurately reflect the hazards associated with the exposure.

3. Insurance companies collect large sums of money that they can invest until the funds are needed for payment of losses. In some instances, the actual payments are not made until long after the premiums are collected. Some corporate financial managers believe that the investment income from these reserves is not adequately reflected in rates, and that they can reduce the cost of their insurance by capturing these investable funds through self-insurance.

---

[7]Many state laws, for example, refer to the "self-insurance" of the workers compensation exposure, usually under conditions that do not conform to a textbook definition of self-insurance.

4. Finally, self-insurers can sometimes avoid the "social load" in insurance rates that results from statutory mandates that insurers cover some insureds on a subsidized basis. The underwriting losses the insurers incur are passed on to other insureds in the form of higher premiums than their hazards justify.

Disadvantages of Self-Insurance

Offsetting the perceived advantages of self-insurance, there are certain disadvantages.

1. Self-insurance can leave the organization exposed to catastrophic loss. This disadvantage can be eliminated if the self-insurer purchases insurance for potentially catastrophic losses, much in the same way as do insurers.

2. There may be greater variation of costs from year to year. When this variation is great, the firm may lose the tax deduction for the losses that occur in years when there are no profits from which to deduct the losses.

3. Self-insurance of some exposures can create adverse employee and public relations. There may be advantages to the organization in having its claims handled by an insurer (as opposed to the staff of the employer organization).

4. Self-insurance may involve the loss of ancillary services provided by an insurer. Most of these relate to loss prevention and claims handling. These services can be purchased separately from an insurer (under an arrangement called "unbundling") or from specialty firms. The cost of obtaining these services must be included in the cost of the self-insurance when a comparison is made with commercial insurance.

As self-insurance became more popular among large corporations, insurers developed loss-sensitive rating programs and retention programs to compete with self-insurance. These include programs with large deductibles, experience rating (in which the insured's own loss experience is a major factor in the cost of the insurance), and "cash-flow" plans (in which the premium payment arrangement allows the insured to retain premiums for investment until the funds are required for payment of losses).

Captive Insurance Companies

Captive insurance companies represent a special case of risk retention and, in some instances, risk transfer. A *captive insurance company* is an entity created and controlled by a parent, whose main purpose is to provide insurance to its corporate owner. Under this definition, two types of organizations may be considered: pure captives and association or group captives.

A pure captive is an insurance company established by a noninsurance organization solely for the purpose of underwriting risks of the parent and its affiliates. Although the term "captive" has sometimes been loosely applied to include other affiliated insurers, as used here the term *captive* does not include insurance subsidiaries whose purpose is to write insurance for the general public.[8]

An association or group captive is an insurance company established by a group of companies to underwrite their own collective risks. These captives are also sometimes referred to as "trade association insurance companies" (TAICs) and also as "risk-retention groups." The term *risk-retention group* was added to the terminology of the captive field by the Risk Retention Acts of 1981 and 1986 (discussed below).

---

[8]Under this definition, J. C. Penney Casualty Insurance, a subsidiary of J. C. Penney Company, Inc., would not be considered a captive, since it was not organized for the purpose of underwriting the exposures of its parent. Some pure captives have broadened into writing business of others and eventually moved from captives to ordinary insurance subsidiaries.

Captive Domiciles

Captives have traditionally been classified as on-shore or offshore. An onshore captive is incorporated and conducts business as a licensed insurer under one of the laws of the states. Although a limited number of states have special legislation related to the formation of captives,[9] most U.S. captives have been domiciled offshore (in Bermuda or one of the other jurisdictions whose legal system encourages the location of captives). The main reason for organizing a captive off-shore is to take advantage of the lower capital and surplus requirements and the less rigorous regulations that exist in these jurisdictions.

Growth of Captives

There has been a steady growth in the number of captives, from a few hundred or so in the late 1950s to an estimated 4000 by 1999. Captives were conceived because they offered an alternative to the commercial market and because it was believed that certain tax benefits were available through captives that could not be attained through an internal retention program. Although the hoped-for tax advantages did not materialize, captives have been continued for other reasons.

Tax Treatment of Captives

One of the original rationales for captives was the hope that the parent company would be permitted to deduct premiums paid to the captive that would not be deductible as contributions to a self-insurance reserve. With the exception of group captives, the IRS has rejected this strategy. The IRS argues that with a captive, there is no shifting of risk and no loss of control of the premiums. Therefore, the premiums paid to a single-parent captive are viewed as nondeductible contributions to a self-insurance reserve.[10]

The situation is different in the case of group captives, for which the IRS has allowed the deduction of premiums. The IRS position on group captives is that a large number of insureds creates a true element of insurance through spreading of risk. The IRS has also indicated that a captive's assumption of outside risks is a factor in the taxpayer's favor and may permit a deduction of premiums paid by the parent when there is a true pooling of exposures.

Captives themselves are also subject to taxation. In addition to state premium taxes and "excess and surplus lines" taxes that apply to traditional insurers, a federal excise tax may apply to premiums of a captive insurer domiciled outside the U.S.[11]

Risk Retention Act of 1986

The most recent wave of captives followed enactment of the federal Risk Retention Act of 1986 (RRA–86), which exempted group captives formed to insure liability risks from much of state regulation. This 1986 act expanded a 1981 act, which had applied to product liability only. The 1986 law expanded the provisions of the law to apply to most liability coverages except workers compensation and employers liability. Like its predecessor, the Risk Retention Act of 1986 authorized two mechanisms for group treatment of

---

[9]Colorado was the first state to enact legislation (in 1972) designed to encourage the formation of captives, reducing some of the stringent requirements normally applied to insurers in such areas as capitalization, rating, pool participation, and surplus. Since Colorado's legislation authorizing captives, Delaware, Florida, Hawaii, Illinois, Maine, New York, Tennessee, Vermont, and Virginia have also passed laws that encourage the formation of captives, and all have experienced some success. Vermont has been the most successful by far in attracting captives.

[10]The IRS formalized this position in Revenue Ruling 77-316 and was upheld by the courts in *Carnation Company v. Commissioner of Internal Revenue,* 71 T.C., no. 39, December 16, 1978; and *Clougherty Packing Co. v. Commissioner of Internal Revenue,* U.S.C.A., 9th, no. 85-7707, March 3, 1987.

[11]*Internal Revenue Code* Section 4371 assesses a 4 percent tax on premiums (except life insurance) written directly with a foreign insurer and a 1 percent tax on reinsurance premiums placed with a foreign insurer.

liability risks: risk retention groups and insurance purchasing groups.

A risk-retention group is essentially a group-owned insurer whose primary function is assuming and spreading the liability risks of its members. As their name implies, risk-retention groups are formed for the purpose of retaining or pooling risk. The members must have a community of interest (i.e., similar risks), and once organized, they can offer "memberships" to others with similar needs on a nationwide basis. The jurisdiction in which it is chartered regulates the formation and operation of the risk retention group. Once it is chartered in its state of domicile, the risk-retention group may then operate in any other state simply by filing notice of its intent with the respective state insurance department.

In addition to risk-retention groups, the Risk Retention Act of 1986 also authorized insurance-purchasing groups. Insurance-purchasing groups are not insurers and do not retain risk. Rather, they purchase insurance on a group basis for their members. The coverage is purchased in the conventional insurance market, and state laws that prohibit the group purchase of property and liability insurance are nullified with respect to qualified purchasing groups.

Risk-Sharing Pools

Risk-sharing pools are mechanisms that are closely related to and sometimes confused with association or group captives, but they actually constitute a separate technique. A group of entities may elect to pool their exposures, sharing the losses that occur, without creating a formal corporate insurance structure.[12] A separate corporate insurer is not created, but the risks are nevertheless "insured" by the pooling mechanism.

---

[12] The laws in virtually all states currently permit public bodies such as municipalities and counties to form self-insurance or risk-sharing pools. The pools are generally deemed not to be insurance companies and are not subject to the provisions of the state's insurance laws, except as specifically provided by the statutes under which they are organized.

Viewed from one perspective, pooling may be considered a form of transfer, in the sense that the risks of the pooling members are transferred from the individuals to the group. Viewed from a different perspective, pooling is a form of retention, in which the entity's risks are retained along with those of the other pooling members. This dual nature of pooling stems from the sometimes-forgotten fact that in a pooling arrangement, members are both insureds and insurers.

Risk Transfer: Buying Insurance

Although insurance is only one of the techniques available for dealing with the pure risks that the individual or the firm faces, many of the risk management decisions culminate in a choice between insurance and noninsurance. Thus, it is useful to examine the application of some basic principles of risk management to the area of insurance buying.

Common Errors in Buying Insurance

In general, the mistakes that most organizations make when buying insurance fall into two categories: buying too little and buying too much. The first, which is potentially the more costly, consists of the failure to purchase essential coverages, which can leave the individual or organization exposed to unbearable financial loss. On the other hand, it is possible to purchase too much insurance, buying protection against losses that could more economically be retained. The difficulty in buying the right amount of insurance is compounded by the fact that it is possible to make both mistakes at the same time. Although most firms and individuals spend enough to provide an adequate insurance program, critical risks are sometimes ignored, leaving gaps in the overall pattern of protection, while unimportant risks are insured, using valuable premium dollars that would be more effectively spent elsewhere.

The Need for a Plan

To obtain maximum benefit from the premium dollars spent, some sort of plan is needed. Otherwise, there is a tendency to view the purchase of insurance as a series of individual isolated decisions, rather than a single problem, and there are no guidelines to provide for a logical consistency in dealing with the various risks faced.

A Priority Ranking for Insurance Expenditures

A plan can be constructed to set priorities for the allocation of premium dollars based on the previously discussed classification of risks into *critical*, *important*, and *unimportant*, with insurance coverages designed to protect against these risks classified as *essential*, *important*, and *optional*.

1. *Essential* insurance coverages include those that are designed to protect against losses that could result in bankruptcy. Insurance coverage required by law or by contract is also essential.

2. *Important* insurance coverages include those that protect against losses that would force the insured to borrow or resort to credit.

3. *Optional* insurance coverages include those that protect against losses that could be met out of existing assets or current income.

The Large Loss Principle—Essential Coverages First   The primary emphasis on essential coverages follows the first rule of risk management and the axiom that the probability that a loss may or may not occur is less important than the possible size of the loss. Since the organization must of necessity assume some risks and transfer others, it seems only rational to begin by transferring those that it could not afford to bear. The need for insurance is dictated by the inability to withstand the loss in question if the insurance is not purchased. In determining whether to purchase insurance in a particular situation, the important question is not "can I afford it?" but rather "can I afford to be without it?"

When the available dollars cannot provide all of the essential and important coverages the individual or organization wants to carry, the question becomes where to cut. One approach is to assume a part of the loss in connection with these coverages through higher deductibles. If coverage for small losses is eliminated through deductibles, the premium credits granted may permit the purchase of other important coverages.

Insurance as a Last Resort—Optional Coverages   As we have seen, insurance always costs more than the expected value of the loss. This is because, in addition to the expected value of the loss (the pure premium), the cost of operating the insurance mechanism must also be borne by the policyholders. For this reason, insurance should be considered a last resort, to be used only when absolutely necessary.

There is nothing intrinsically wrong with optional coverages. They are just not a very good way to spend the limited number of dollars that are available for the purchase of insurance. The real problem with respect to such coverages is that the individual who insures against small losses often does so at the expense of exposures that involve losses that would be financially catastrophic. While it may be expected that an individual or business firm might desire to purchase some optional coverages, such coverages should not be purchased until all important coverages have been purchased, and, of course, all essential coverages should be purchased before premiums are spent on the less critical important coverages.

Selecting the Agent

While the selection of an insurance company is an important aspect of the insurance-buying process, so too is the selection of the agent. When an insurance policy is purchased, a part of the pre-

Tidbits, Vignettes, and Conundrums 5.2

Adam Smith on Lotteries

In what sense is the following passage relevant to the discussion of the principles of insurance buying?

The world neither saw, nor ever will see, a perfectly fair lottery; or one in which the whole gain compensated the whole loss; because the undertaker could make nothing by it. . . . In order to have a better chance for some of the great prizes, some people purchase several tickets, and others, small shares in a still greater number. There is not, however, a more certain proposition in mathematics, than that the more tickets you adventure upon, the more likely you are to be a loser. Adventure upon all the tickets in the lottery, and you lose for certain; and the greater the number of your tickets, the nearer you approach to this certainty.
—Adam Smith, *The Wealth of Nations.*

mium goes to the insurance company to pay for the protection. A second part is compensation to the agent for the service he or she provides to the insured. The most important part of this service consists of the advice the agent gives. From the insured's perspective, the primary qualifications of a good agent are knowledge of the insurance field and an interest in the needs of the client. One indicator of a knowledgeable and professional agent is a professional designation; the Chartered Property and Casualty Underwriter (CPCU) designation and the Chartered Life Underwriter (CLU) designation both indicate that the agent is sufficiently motivated to work in a formal educational program for professional development. However, there are many competent and knowledgeable agents who do not have these designations.

Selecting the Company

The insured may receive assistance from the agent in selecting an insurer if the agent represents several companies. However, in the case of those agents who represent a single company, the selection of the agent will automatically include the selection of the company. In choosing a company, the major consideration should be its financial stability. In addition, certain aspects of the company's operation, such as its attitude toward claims and cancellation of policyholders' protection, are important. Finally, cost is a consideration, as is the insurer's ability to deliver ancillary services desired by the insured, such as loss control advice.

Data on the financial stability of insurance companies are available from several sources that specialize in providing information on the companies' financial strength, the efficiency of their operation, and the caliber of management. For many years, the principal rating agency for both property and liability insurers and life insurers was Alfred M. Best Company. Recently, four other firms have entered the insurance company–rating field. They are Standard and Poor's Corporation, Moody's Investors Service, Inc., Duff & Phelps/MCM Investment Research Company, and Weiss Ratings, Inc. Each of the rating services uses a slightly different classification system, and the categories have slightly different designations. All rating services, however, distinguish between insurers whose financial condition is deemed adequate and insurers that are classified as vulnerable or weak.[13]

When properly used, the ratings assigned by rating services can be effective tools for avoiding delinquent insurance companies. In utilizing the

[13]The rating services can be accessed at their Web sites listed at the end of the chapter.

ratings for both property and liability insurers and life insurers, the ratings should be checked for a period of years. If there has been a downward trend in the rating, further investigation into the cause of the change is warranted. For many years, the suggested standard was an A+ rating from A. M. Best Company for a period of at least six years.[14] A current authority recommends that one should select a life insurance company that has very high ratings from at least two of the four rating firms other than Best.[15]

In addition to reviewing financial ratings, the insured will want information on a company's attitude toward claims and other business practices. Although this information is more difficult to obtain, there are some sources a consumer can look to. In the business world, trade associations can often provide information on specialty insurers that provide particular types of coverage. In addition, most state insurance departments will provide information on the number and types of complaints against specific insurers, as well as other comparative information.

[14]See Herbert S. Denenberg, "Is 'A Plus' Really a Passing Grade?" *Journal of Risk and Insurance*, vol. 34 (September 1967).

[15]Joseph M. Belth, "Financial Strength Ratings of Life-Health Insurance Companies," *Insurance Forum*, vol. 21, nos. 3 and 4 (March/April 1994), p. 15.

Important Concepts to Remember

government standards
domino theory
energy-release theory
human-behavior approach
engineering approach
systems safety
pre-event action

simultaneous-with-event action
post-event action
separation of assets
salvage
rehabilitation
redundancy
disaster plan

essential insurance coverages
important insurance coverages
optional insurance coverages
large loss principle
insurance as a last resort

Questions for Review

1. Explain what is meant by government standards and explain in what way(s) they affect the risk management function of an organization.

2. Describe the general thesis of Heinrich's domino theory.

3. Describe the general thesis of Haddon's energy release theory.

4. Describe the two general approaches to loss prevention and control.

5. Explain the classification of loss prevention and control measures according to their time of application.

6. Identify the classification of loss prevention and control measures based on the object toward which the measure is directed.

7. Distinguish between the cost of financing risk and the cost of financing losses.

8. Identify the reasons for self-insurance and the disadvantages of self-insurance.

9. Distinguish between pure captives and group association captives.

10. Identify three categories into which insurance coverages may be priority ranked, indicating the nature of the exposures or risks to which each applies.

Questions for Discussion

1. To what can the historical neglect of the risk control function be attributed?

2. Explain how each of the following represents an approach to risk control:
   a. separation of assets
   b. salvage
   c. rehabilitation
   d. redundancy

3. Identify the priorities for a disaster plan described in the text. Do you agree or disagree with the priorities?

4. While it is generally agreed that both the human behavior and engineering approach have application in risk control, which of the two approaches do you believe holds the greatest potential for preventing and reducing loss?

5. The IRS does not generally permit a parent company to deduct premiums paid to a pure captive, but may permit it if the captive assumes outside risk. What is the basis for this position? Do you agree or disagree with it?

Suggestions for Additional Reading

Barrese, James, and Jack Nelson. "The Tax Treatment of Captives," *CPCU Journal*, vol. 43, no. 2 (June 1990).

Bird, Frank E., and Frank J. Loftus. *Loss Control Management*. Logamille, GA: International Loss Control Institute, 1976.

Denenberg, Herbert S. "Is 'A-Plus' Really a Passing Grade?" *Journal of Risk and Insurance*, vol. 34, no. 3 (Sept. 1967).

Grose, Vernon L. *Managing Risk: Systematic Loss Prevention for Executives*. Englewood Cliffs, NJ: Prentice-Hall, 1987.

Harrington, Scott E., and Gregory R. Niehaus. *Risk Management and Insurance*. New York: McGraw-Hill, 1998.

Head, George L., and Stephen Horn II. *Essentials of Risk Management*, 3rd ed., vols. 1 and 2. Malvern, PA: Insurance Institute of America, 1997.

Vaughan, Emmett J. *Risk Management*. New York: Wiley, 1997.

Websites to Explore

A. M. Best Company: http://www.ambest.com

American Society of Safety Engineers: http://www.asse.org/

Captive Insurance Companies Association: http://www.captive.com

Duff & Phelps Credit Rating Co.: http://www.dcrco.com/

Federal Emergency Management Agency: http://www.fema.gov/

International Risk Management Institute, Inc.: http://irmi.com

Moody's Investors Service: http://www.moodys.com

Nonprofit Risk Management Center: http://www.nonprofitrisk.org

Occupational Safety and Health Administration (OSHA): http://www.osha.gov/

Practical Risk Management: http://www.pracrisk.com/

Public Agency Risk Managers Association (PARMA): http://www.parma.com

Risk and Insurance Management Society, Inc.: http://www.rims.org

RiskINFO: http://www.riskinfo.com/

Self Insurance Institute of America: http://www.siia.org

Standard and Poor's Insurance Rating Services: http://www.standardandpoors.com/

Underwriters Laboratory: http://www.ul.com/

Weiss Ratings, Inc.: http://www.weissratings.com/

CHAPTER 6

The Private Insurance Industry

*The trade of insurance gives great security to the fortunes of private people,
and by dividing among a great many that loss which would ruin an
individual, makes it fall light and easy upon the whole society.*
—Adam Smith, *The Wealth of Nations*

CHAPTER OBJECTIVES

When you have finished this chapter, you should be able to

- Identify the categories of insurer by type of product

- Identify the major categories of insurers by form of ownership

- Identify and describe the distinguishing characteristics of the different categories of insurers by form of ownership

- Identify the different distribution systems that are used in property and liability insurance and life insurance

- Describe the ways in which insurers compete

- Describe the evidences that indicate the extent of competition in the insurance industry

- Identify and describe the major areas in which insurers cooperate

Despite the benefits that accrue to society through operation of the insurance mechanism, it is self-evident that such a complicated and intricate device does not come into existence by itself. Someone must estimate the probability of loss, collect the funds necessary to compensate those who suffer loss, make payments for the losses that do occur, and provide for the general administration of the program. These are the functions performed by insurers. In addition, insurance is a product; it must be sold. Individuals must be made aware of their need for insurance. This is the task of insurance agents.

Measured by any one of a number of standards, insurance in the United States is a large industry. There are over 6200 insurance companies operating in this country. These firms employ more than 2.2 million persons and administer assets of more than $4 trillion. Premiums written by the private insurance industry total more than $1 trillion, or slightly more than 11.4 percent of the gross national product. Of this total, approximately $345 billion was life insurance and annuity premiums, about $375 billion went for health insurance, and roughly $287 billion was for property and liability insurance.[1] In addition to the private insurance indicated by these totals, state and federal government agencies sell some forms of private or voluntary insurance.

We begin our examination of the insurance industry with a brief look at the development of insurance as a business. Although we are primarily concerned with insurance in this country, since insurance has its roots in the Old World, we will consider its development prior to the formation of the United States as well.

A Brief History of Private Insurance

Because the historical development of insurance as a field of business helps to explain the division among the various lines of insurance, it may be helpful to take a brief look at the historical development of insurance as an institution.

Insurance in Antiquity

There is evidence of practices resembling insurance in the ancient world. As early as 3000 B.C., Chinese merchants used the technique of sharing risk. These merchants shipped their goods by boat down river, and because of treacherous rapids, not all the boats made it safely. To reduce the impact of losses on any one individual, the merchants devised the plan of distributing their goods on each other's boats. When a boat was dashed to pieces on the rocks, the loss was shared by all rather than falling upon a single individual.

About 500 years later the famous *Great Code of Hammurabi* provided for the transfer of the risk of loss from merchants to moneylenders. A trader whose goods were lost to bandits was relieved of the debt to the moneylender who had loaned the money to buy the goods. Babylonian moneylenders undoubtedly loaded their interest charges to compensate for this transfer of risk. This innovation was adapted to the risks of sea trade by Phoenicians and then by the Greeks. Loans were made to ship owners and merchants engaged in trade, with the ship or cargo pledged as collateral. The borrower was offered an option whereby, for a somewhat higher interest charge, the lender agreed to cancel the loan if the ship or cargo were lost at sea.[2] In this way, the risk of loss was transferred from the owner of the boat or cargo to the lender. These contracts were referred to as *bottomry* contracts in those cases where the ship was pledged and *respondentia* contracts when the cargo was the security.

The first evidence of anything resembling life insurance evolved from ancient benevolent societies, whose members contributed to a fund to aid less fortunate members of the group. As early as 2500 B.C., Egyptian stonemasons organized a club to provide funds for the burial of members. Later, around the third century B.C., Greek burial societies, funded by contributions of members, were common devices for meeting the expenses of burial and the needs of widows and orphans. Roman burial and benevolent societies known as the *Collegia* performed the same function. Although these examples indicate some features of

---

[1]Insurance Information Institute, *Insurance Facts* (New York: III, 1994), and American Council of Life Insurance, *Life Insurance Fact Book* (Washington, D.C.: ACLI, 1994).

[2]The additional interest on such loans was called a "premium," and the term has become a part of insurance terminology, indicating the payment made by the insured.

insurance, the modern insurance business has its roots in the commercial revolution in Europe following the Crusades.

Origins of the Modern Insurance Business

Marine insurance, the oldest of the modern branches of insurance, appears to have been started in Italy sometime in the thirteenth century. From there it spread to the other countries on the continent and then to England through the Lombard merchants, who came to dominate British commerce and finance during the fifteenth century. This early marine insurance was written by individuals rather than by insurance companies as we know them. A ship owner or merchant who wanted protection for the ship or cargo prepared and circulated a sheet with information describing the ship, its cargo, its destination, and other pertinent information. Those who agreed to accept a part of the risk wrote their names under the description of the risk and the terms of the agreement. This practice of "writing under" the agreement gave rise to the term *underwriter,* which has retained its meaning as one who selects and rejects risks. Ship owners seeking insurance and the individuals who organized themselves into groups of underwriters found the coffee houses of London convenient meeting places. One of the coffee houses, owned by Edward Lloyd, became the main meeting place because its proprietor made available paper and pens and information regarding shipping. This coffee house eventually became Lloyds' of London.

The second of the modern branches of insurance was life insurance. In 1536, a group of marine underwriters in London issued what appears to have been the first modern life insurance policy to a certain William Gybbons. The policy was a one-year term policy in the amount of £400. As an interesting footnote to history, Gybbons died within the year and the underwriters paid the

£400. Other attempts similar to this were tried from time to time (although probably not by the underwriters who had insured Gybbons).

Although Edmund Halley (of Halley's comet fame) had prepared a mortality table as early as 1693, it was not until nearly 100 years later that any degree of accuracy was achieved in predicting mortality. The first modern life insurance company, the Society for the Assurance of Widows and Orphans, a London company founded in 1699, charged all insureds the same premium. It and several companies that followed it were unsuccessful. Then, in 1762, the Equitable Society for the Assurance of Life and Survivorship introduced the innovation of premiums that varied with the age of the insured and became immediately successful.

Fire insurance in the modern era dates from 1666, when the Great Fire of London occurred. The fire raged for five days, virtually destroying the city, and providing the impetus for modern fire insurance. An English physician named Nicholas Barbon (who had been relatively unsuccessful in medicine) entered the construction business during the rebuilding of the city and at the same time started the business of insuring the newly built houses against loss by fire. Other entrepreneurs soon followed his lead.

Insurance in the United States

During the Colonial period, most insurance in the United States was marine insurance, placed with British insurers. The first successful insurer actually located in this country was a mutual fire insurance company founded in 1752 by Benjamin Franklin and a group of his associates, called the Philadelphia Contributionship for the Insurance of Houses from Loss by Fire.[3] The first capital

---

[3]A company founded in Charleston, South Carolina, in 1735, the Friendly Society for Mutual Insuring of Houses, preceded the Philadelphia Contributionship. However, it lasted only a few years and very little is known about it.

stock insurance company in the United States was the Insurance Company of North America, which was founded as an association in 1792 and incorporated in 1794. Its charter gave it broad underwriting powers that permitted it to engage in all lines of insurance but it limited its writings to fire and marine insurance.

The first life insurance company in America was founded in 1759. It was a stock company called The Corporation for Relief of Poor and Distressed Presbyterian Ministers and the Poor and Distressed Widows and Children of Presbyterian Ministers. This company is still in operation and is the oldest active life insurance company in the world. Between 1759 and 1835, several other stock companies were formed, but none survived. The first mutual life insurance company was New England Life, founded in 1835. It was followed by a dozen more companies that have survived to the present day.

In the mid-1800s, a new type of insurance called *casualty insurance* appeared. The earliest form of casualty insurance was accident insurance, and, like fire, marine, and life insurance, it originated in the Old World. The British Parliament chartered a company in 1848 to sell insurance against accidents to railroad passengers. A company formed in the United States to sell this type of insurance to travelers, the Travelers Insurance Company, wrote its first policy in 1864. The next type of insurance for accidents was boiler explosion coverage, which appeared in 1886. Boiler insurance was followed by employers liability insurance in 1886 and then elevator and public liability insurance in 1889. The first auto liability policy in the United States was written in 1898, and workers compensation insurance followed in 1910. As these new types of insurance appeared, they were offered by specialty companies that did not write fire, marine, or life. The new forms of insurance (which generally covered losses arising from various types of accidents or casualties) came to be called *casualty insurance* and the companies that wrote them were called *casualty insurers.*

Monoline Organization in the United States

Initially, insurers elected to specialize in a particular type of insurance. Then, as more and more states began to regulate insurance, state limitations on the companies' underwriting powers became common. The industry became organized on a monoline basis, with companies restricted by law to the writing of a single line of insurance. Under this system, three distinct classes of insurance developed: life insurers, fire insurers, and casualty insurers.

A company that wrote fire insurance was not permitted to write casualty insurance and a casualty company could not write fire insurance. Neither fire insurance companies nor casualty insurance companies could write life insurance, and life insurance companies were permitted to write only life insurance and health insurance. This form of operation was unique to the United States. British and European companies usually received charters that authorized them to sell insurance of all kinds anywhere in the world.

There were three reasons for the compartmentalization of the American system. First, it was supposed that the monoline system would allow insurers to specialize in a particular field of insurance and develop greater proficiency in that field. Second, it was felt that the segregation of insurance by class would permit a more accurate appraisal of the financial qualification required for each type of insurance, and that regulatory requirements could be established to fit each class. Finally, insurance regulators feared that there was a danger in combining fire insurance, which seemed more subject to catastrophes, with life insurance. The various conflagrations, such as the New York fire of 1835, helped to reinforce this opinion.[4]

---

[4]During the early years of the property insurance industry in the United States, catastrophic losses wiped out many companies. The most well known of these losses were the great New York City fire of 1835, which wiped out 23 of the 26 New York companies and almost wiped out New York; the 1871 Chicago fire, which made Mrs. O'Leary's cow famous; and the fire that accompanied the 1906 San Francisco earthquake.

The Multiple-Line Transition

In the late 1940s, individual states began to change their laws to allow multiple-line operations, permitting property and casualty insurers to cross the barriers that had separated them and write both property and casualty coverages. Insurers began a transition to *multiple-line underwriting*, the combination of property and casualty insurance in a single company. This allowed insurers to offer *package policies* that combine property and liability coverages.

Multiple-line legislation did not end underwriting compartmentalization. It merely permitted the companies in the property and casualty insurance fields to cross the traditional barriers when an insurer met the capital and surplus requirements of each line. It did not, in most cases, end the barrier between life insurance and property and casualty insurance.

Classification of Private Insurers

Insurers may be classified according to the type of insurance they sell, their licensing status, their legal form of ownership, or the marketing system they employ.

Classification by Type of Product

We can distinguish among three types of insurers based on their product. Life insurance companies sell life contracts and annuities and, in addition, write health insurance. Property and liability insurance companies market all forms of property and liability insurance (including health insurance) but do not write life insurance. Health insurers are a class of specialty insurers, concentrating on their one area of risk. While there are other specialty insurers that write only a single line of property or liability insurance, these may be classed as property and liability companies.

Many insurance companies operate in groups, often called *fleets,* which consist of a number of insurance companies under common ownership and often under common management. Insurance company groups developed during the monoline era and were designed to permit the writing of both property and casualty coverages by insurers under a common management. Since a fire company could not write casualty coverages and a casualty company was forbidden to issue fire coverage, the logical solution was to form two companies and operate them in tandem. Although this reason for company fleets no longer exists, the form of operation persists, and much of the insurance written in the United States is written by insurers that operate as members of "groups" or "fleets." Initially, insurance company fleets limited their operations to the property and liability field, but eventually property and liability insurers acquired life insurers and life insurers have acquired property and liability insurance companies. In many cases, the operating insurance companies are owned by a holding company.

Classification By Place of Incorporation and Licensing

A *domestic* insurer within any given state is an insurer that is incorporated in that state, or, if it is not incorporated, was formed under the laws of that state. A *foreign* insurer is one that is incorporated in another state of the United States or formed under the laws of another state. *Alien* insurers are incorporated or formed in another country.

A licensed (or *admitted*) insurer with regard to any particular state is an insurer that has been granted a license to operate in that state. An unlicensed (or *nonadmitted*) insurer is one that has not been granted a license. As a general rule, insurance agents are licensed to place insurance only with admitted insurers.[5]

Classification by Legal Form of Ownership

Broadly speaking, insurers can be classified into six categories based on their form of ownership.

1. Capital stock insurance companies
2. Mutual insurance companies
3. Reciprocals or interinsurance exchanges
4. Lloyd's associations
5. Health expense associations
6. Government insurers

Capital Stock Insurance Companies

Capital stock insurance companies are organized as profit-making ventures, with the stockholders assuming the risk that is transferred by the individual insureds. If the actuarial predictions prove accurate, the premiums collected are sufficient to pay losses and operating expenses while returning a profit to the stockholders. The capital invested by the stockholders provides funds to run the company until premium income is sufficient to pay losses and operating expense. In addition, it provides a cushion to guarantee that obligations to policyholders will be met. The distinguishing characteristics of a capital stock company are (1) the premium charged by the company is final—there is no form of contingent liability for policyholders; (2) the board of directors is elected by the stockholders; and (3) earnings are distributed to shareholders as dividends on their stock.

[5]When a prospective buyer cannot obtain required coverage from insurers who are licensed to do business in the state, state *excess and surplus lines laws* permit coverage to be placed in a nonadmitted insurer. In most states, only agents who hold a special license may place insurance in a nonadmitted insurer.

Mutual Insurance Companies

In contrast to a stock company, a *mutual insurance company* is owned by its policyholders. Normally, a mutual company is incorporated, and in many states this is a legal requirement. The distinguishing characteristics of a mutual insurer are its lack of capital stock and the distribution of earnings. Unlike the capital stock company, the mutual company has no paid-in capital as a guarantee of solvency in the event of adverse experience. For this reason, mutual insurers need to accumulate a surplus to protect against such adverse contingencies as heavy losses or a decline in investment return. Any money left after paying all costs of operation is returned to the policyholders in the form of dividends. Included in the concept of "costs" that must be paid is the addition to the surplus of the company.

A limited number of mutual insurers issue assessable policies, in which the insured has a contingent liability and is subject to assessment if losses exceed advance premiums.[6] However, all states permit mutual insurers to issue nonassessable policies when they have attained the same financial strength required of a capital stock company writing the same type of business. The advance premium that is collected is intended to be sufficient to cover all losses and expenses. If it is not, the additional costs are paid out of the accumulated surplus. All the larger mutual insurers in the United States operate on this basis. Unlike capital stock companies, the premium of a mutual insurer is not fixed, and the excess of premium income over costs may be returned to policyholders as dividends.

In the final analysis, there are few practical differences between a mutual company operating on

[6]Some mutual insurers operate on a post-loss assessment basis, in which premiums are payable after a loss occurs. The nuclear energy industry operates a post-loss assessment mutual to provide liability insurance for losses arising out of nuclear incidents. In addition, some mutuals charge an advance premium, but reserve the right to levy additional assessments if losses exceed the advance premiums collected. *County mutuals* authorized by the insurance laws of many states usually operate as advance premium assessable mutuals.

an advance premium basis with nonassessable policies and a capital stock company. Although the policyholders own the mutual company in theory, there are no vested rights of ownership for these policyholders except in the case of liquidation. Policyholders acquire their ownership interest when they purchase a policy from the mutual insurer. They abandon that ownership when they nonrenew their insurance or are canceled by the insurer. Furthermore, while the policyholders theoretically control the company, this is on a basis equivalent to the theoretical control of the stockholders over the management in a large corporation with many individual stockholders.

Demutualization and Mutual Insurance Holding Companies In recent years, a number of mutual insurance companies have demutualized. Demutualization refers to the process by which a mutual insurance company changes its organization structure, converting from the mutual form to a capital stock or modified capital stock form. Although there are several motivations for demutualization, the most important have been the need to access capital and the desire for diversification.

Mutual insurance companies have limited ways of raising capital. Whereas a stock insurer can issue shares of stock to acquire capital, a mutual insurer must generate it internally, from profits. Although mutual insurers can raise limited amounts of capital through subordinated loans (called surplus notes), they do not have access to equity funding. Increasingly, competition within the insurance industry has led to a greater emphasis on capital strength and the inability to access capital markets can limit an insurer's growth and restrict its marketing strategies. In response to the need for increased flexibility, a number of mutual insurance companies have *demutualized,* which is to say that they have converted into stock corporations. Because a mutual insurance company is owned by its policyholders, demutualization involves insuring stock to policyholders. As a general rule, policyholders have been offered a choice between stock in the new corporation or cash. Some

policyholders have accepted stock while others have taken the cash.

In addition to total demutualization, some insurers have opted for a different approach, a mutual insurance holding company. About half of the states have adopted mutual insurance holding company laws, under which a mutual insurer converts to a stock insurer that is owned by a mutual holding company. The policyholders own the mutual holding company (similar to the way in which they owned the mutual insurer), while their contractual rights as insureds remain in the stock insurance company. This structure is more flexible. The holding company can hold other subsidiaries, and may raise capital by issuing stock in the subsidiaries. State law generally requires that voting control remain with the holding company.

Fraternal Insurers Fraternal societies are specialized forms of mutual insurers. Basically, fraternal societies are nonprofit organizations that operate on the basis of "lodges" with a representative form of government. Fraternals have primarily concentrated their activity in the field of life insurance, although they sometimes sell sickness and accident insurance. Since fraternals are considered to be charitable institutions, they do not pay federal income tax or state premium tax.

Reciprocals

The *reciprocal exchange* (also called an *interinsurance* exchange) is a particularly American innovation, and while reciprocals are only a small segment of the insurance industry (there are about 50 in existence), they are significant. A *reciprocal* is an unincorporated group of individuals, called subscribers, who exchange insurance risks. Each member (or subscriber) is both an insured and an insurer: as a member of the group, the individual is insured by each of the other members and, in turn, insures each of them. Reciprocal exchanges are sometimes confused with mutual insurers, and while there is a similarity, there is also

---

Tidbits, Vignettes, and Conundrums 6.1

Demutualization and Mutual Holding Companies

Some mutual insurers have "demutualized" by changing from the mutual form of ownership to capital stock companies. In such cases, the mutual ownership is converted into stock ownership or a cash equivalent of the stock. In a mutual holding company conversion, the mutual ownership remains with the policyholders, and a new group of owners who purchases stock becomes joint owners with the policyholders. The mutual holding company approach to reorganization has been criticized as detrimental to policyholders. Do policyholders lose something when a mutual insurer converts to a mutual holding company? If so, what, and to whom do they lose it?

---

a fundamental difference. Unlike a mutual insurer, in which members of the group assume their liability collectively; in a reciprocal exchange, each subscriber assumes his or her liability inidividually and not as a member of the group. This means that another member cannot be called upon to assume the liability of a defaulting member.

The distinguishing characteristic of a reciprocal is the administrator, who is called the *attorney-in-fact*. This official derives authority through a power of attorney granted by each of the subscribers, which is used to commit the members as insurers of each other's property. The attorney-in-fact receives some percentage of the premiums paid by the subscribers (usually about 25 percent) to cover the expenses of operating the program. Reciprocals confine their operations to the property and casualty fields. The portion of the total premiums written through interinsurance exchanges is relatively small. In 1999, only about 6 percent of all property and casualty premiums were written through reciprocals.

Lloyd's Associations

Lloyd's associations are yet another source of insurance coverage, although strictly speaking, these organizations do not themselves underwrite insurance. Lloyd's associations include Lloyd's of London and American Lloyd's.

Lloyd's of London Lloyd's of London is the oldest and perhaps the most famous insurance organization in the world. Generally speaking, Lloyd's is a corporation for marketing the services of a group of individuals. The organization itself does not issue insurance policies or provide insurance protection. The actual insurance is underwritten by individual underwriting members, referred to as *Names*, usually operating through syndicates. Technically, each Name is a separate "insurance company," insuring risks separately or collectively with other members. In a sense, Lloyd's is similar to the New York Stock Exchange, in which the physical facilities are owned by the stock exchange and are made available to members for the transaction of business. Lloyd's is governed by a group known as the Committee of Lloyd's, which establishes standards with which members must comply. Normally, policies written through Lloyd's are issued by a number of the individual underwriters, and each underwriter assumes a fraction of the risk. The Lloyd's policy contains the statement, "Each for his own part and not for one another," indicating that the underwriters assume liability individually and that each underwriter is liable only for his or her own commitments.

Originally, each underwriter at Lloyd's conducted business as an individual proprietor or as a member of a syndicate. No corporations or other limitations on liability were permitted, and

Tidbits, Vignettes, and Conundrums 6.2

To the Last Collar Button

Historically, the financial integrity of Lloyd's has been based on the unlimited liability of the Names (as individual underwriters at Lloyd's are known) who, as the saying went, pledged their personal fortunes "to the last collar button." In the face of huge losses relating to asbestos liability that were sustained in the period from 1988 to 1992, about 30 Names committed suicide. Despite the 1995 reorganization, in 2000, litigation against Lloyd's by 230 former Names (including 24 citizens of the United States) continued. The claimants, who were seeking $237 million in damages, allege that they were misled by Lloyd's insiders concerning the growing level of asbestos claims at the time they joined Lloyd's.

every member of Lloyd's exposed his or her entire personal fortune in addition to their business assets. In 1995, in response to internal conflicts and litigation, Lloyds' adopted a complex *Reconstruction and Renewal Plan,* one part of which established new financial standards for membership. Corporate entities with limited liability were authorized and the financial requirements for individuals were increased. By 1999, corporate capital accounted for the majority of underwriting capacity at Lloyd's, although some individual Names with unlimited liability still participate.[7] Although Lloyd's of London is famous throughout the United States, it is licensed in only two states, Illinois and Kentucky.[8]

American Lloyd's Associations The *American Lloyd's associations* are an attempt to copy the success of (and capitalize on the fame of) Lloyd's of London. An American Lloyd's is simply a group of individuals who operate an insurance mechanism using the same principles of individual liability of insurers as Lloyd's of London. Following the practice at Lloyd's of London, each underwriter assumes a part of a risk and is liable only for his or her portion of the risk. Individual underwriters have no obligation to cover losses for which a defaulting member is responsible. Although this is essentially the same system used by Lloyd's of London, many American Lloyd's associations lack the strict regulation that the original Lloyd's imposes on its members. Most states have laws prohibiting the organization or licensing of American Lloyd's. American Lloyd's associations that do exist operate almost exclusively in the property insurance field.

Insurance Exchanges In 1979, the states of Florida, Illinois, and New York enacted legislation authorizing the formation of "insurance exchanges," patterned after the method of operation used at Lloyds, in which a number of underwriters participate in providing insurance under a single contract. The exchanges were created to insure large, unusual, or hard-to-insure exposures. The Florida and New York exchanges encountered financial difficulties and both closed in 1988. The Illinois exchange continues to operate successfully.

---

[7]For an interesting perspective on the difficulties at Lloyd's, see Adam Raphael, *Ultimate Risk: The Inside Story of the Lloyd's Catastrophe* (New York: Four Walls Eight Windows, 1995), and Elizabeth Luessenhop and Martin Mayer, *Risky Business: An Insider's Account of the Disaster at Lloyd's of London* (New York: Scribner, 1995). See also Lloyd's Web site at http://www.lloydsoflondon.co.uk/.

[8]Despite the fact that Lloyd's is licensed in only two states, it provides insurance in other states as well, under the provisions of state *excess and surplus line laws* noted earlier in the chapter.

Health Expense Associations

Health Expense Associations are unique to the field of health insurance. They include Blue Cross and Blue Shield associations and managed care organizations. The Blue Cross and Blue Shield plans originated as nonprofit associations, usually organized under special state enabling legislation to provide for prepayment of hospital and surgical expenses. Managed care organizations include *health maintenance organizations* (HMOs) and *provider-sponsored organizations* (PSOs).[9] The insurance element in the operation of HMOs and PSOs derives from the manner in which they charge for their services, which is called "*capitation.*" Under the capitation approach, individual subscribers pay an annual fee and in return receive a wide range of health care services that is provided by the HMO or PSO. HMOs and PSOs differ from commercial insurers in the fact that they are also health care providers. They are similar to commercial insurers in the fact that, by providing their services to enrollees for a fixed prepayment (capitation), they make possible the transfer and sharing of risk.

Government Insurers

In addition to the social insurance programs they operate, federal and state governments also offer some forms of private (voluntary) insurance. The private insurance programs of government have developed for diverse reasons. In some cases, the risks they cover do not lend themselves to private insurance, because either the hazards were too great or the private insurers were subject to adverse selection. In other instances, they originated because of the inability or reluctance of private insurers to meet society's needs for some form of private insurance. In some cases, government private insurance programs have been established as tools of social change and are designed to provide a subsidy to particular segments of society or to help solve social ills afflicting individual classes of citizens. Finally, government insurance programs have sometimes been founded on the mistaken notion that such programs could somehow repeal the law of averages and provide insurance at a lower cost than would be charged by private insurers.

Federal Private (Voluntary) Insurance Programs
Over the years, the federal government has engaged in a number of private insurance fields. In some programs, the government cooperates with private insurers, providing reinsurance or other forms of subsidy in meeting risks that the private insurance industry could not meet alone. The following are the federal programs that offer forms of private insurance.

1. *Post Office insurance coverages.* The U.S. Post Office sells insurance on registered mail and parcel post. The program is a convenience to occasional customers who desire insurance on property in the mail.

2. *Federal crop insurance.* Federal crop insurance has existed in one form or another since 1938. The current program dates from the Federal Crop Insurance Act of 1980, which established a new federal "multi-peril" crop insurance program.

3. *Mortgage loan insurance.* The federal government provides mortgage loan insurance through five agencies: the FHA, the VA, the Federal Home Loan Mortgage Corporation, the Federal Home Loan Bank Board, and the Farmers Home Administration. The coverage protects pri-

[9]A *provider-sponsored organization* (PSO) is essentially an HMO that is organized by a partnership of health care providers, such as hospitals and a group of physicians. The terminology for provider-sponsored organizations has been revised several times, as health care reformers reinvent the concept. At various times and in different proposals, provider-sponsored organizations have been called *physician-hospital organizations* (PHOs) and *organized delivery systems* (ODSs). The PSO designation is used in the Tax Reform Act of 1997 in connection with new Medicare options and is likely to become the standard designation for these organizations.

vate financial institutions against loss from the borrower's default on a mortgage loan.[10]

4. *National Flood Insurance Program.* The 1968 Housing and Urban Development (HUD) Act established a National Flood Insurance Program that is conducted as a partnership between the federal government and the private insurance industry.

5. *SBA surety bond program.* Congress established the Small Business Administration (SBA) Surety Bond Guarantee Program in 1971. Under this plan the SBA reinsures private sureties that issue bonds to small contractors who would be unable to obtain a bond without this government backing.

6. *Export-Import Bank.* The U.S. Export-Import Bank, in cooperation with a group of private insurers known as the Foreign Credit Insurance Association (FCIA), offers U.S. exporters protection against *political risks,* such as expropriation or inconvertibility of the foreign currency into dollars, and credit losses resulting from war, insurrection, or revolution.

7. *Overseas Private Investor Corporation.* The Overseas Private Investor Corporation (OPIC) is a U.S. government agency organized to insure Americans who invest in foreign countries against loss by political risks such as war, revolution, insurrection, expropriation, or inconvertibility of foreign currency into dollars.

8. *Servicemen's and veterans' life insurance.* The U.S. Veterans Administration (VA) operates five separate life insurance programs, under which the government itself serves

as the insurer. Only one program (Service Disabled Veterans Insurance) is still open to new issues.

Other forms of private insurance that have been offered by the federal government in the past but that have been discontinued include war-risk insurance (during World Wars I and II), the Federal Riot Reinsurance Program (1968–1983), and the Federal Crime Insurance Program (1971–1997). No new federal private insurance programs have been introduced since 1971.[11]

State Private (Voluntary) Insurance Programs Like the federal government, a number of individual states offer private or voluntary insurance, but the number and variety of state programs is far more limited. The state programs that do exist more often than not compete with those of the private insurance industry. About half the states sell workers compensation insurance.[12] In addition, the State of Wisconsin operates a state life insurance fund and Maryland operates a state automobile insurance fund. Finally, the states of California, Florida, and Hawaii have created state catastrophe funds to provide direct insurance and reinsurance for hurricane and earthquake losses.

Classification According to Marketing System

Through a process of evolution, several marketing forms have developed, each of which has as its goal the attainment of efficiency in distribution and service. These marketing systems are based

---

[10]Mortgage loan insurance is also available from private insurers, and it is estimated that they insure a greater dollar volume of loans than does the FHA. See Joseph E. Johnson and George B. Flanigan, "Private Mortgage Insurance," *CPCU Annals,* vol. 26, no. 4 (December 1973), and "Regulation of Private Mortgage Insurance," *ibid.,* vol. 27, no. 2 (June 1974).

[11]Although no new federal insurance programs have been introduced in the past two decades, serious attention is now focused on the proposal to create a federal earthquake reinsurance program, primarily as a result of the California earthquakes of 1989 and 1993 and Hurricane Andrew in 1992.

[12]State workers compensation funds are discussed in Chapter 12.

on differing relationships between the insurance company and the agents or sales representatives through which they market.

The Agent

With few exceptions, marketing in the insurance industry revolves around the agent; however, his or her role varies in different lines of insurance. In the field of property and liability insurance, the *agent* is "an individual authorized to create, terminate, and modify contracts of insurance." In life insurance the agent's power is more limited. Life insurance agents are appointed with the authorization to solicit and deliver contracts of insurance; however, they cannot, as can the property and liability agent, "bind" the insurance company to risk.[13]

The insurance agent is first and foremost the representative of the insurance company. An insurance *broker*, on the other hand, is a representative of the insured. Although the broker represents the insured, he or she normally receives compensation in the form of a commission from the company. The fact that the broker is not an agent of the insurer means that he or she does not have the power to *bind* the company. The broker merely solicits business from clients and then places the business with an insurer. Brokers represent an important segment of the insurance marketing mechanism, particularly in large cities, where they control large segments of the market.

Life Insurance Distribution System

With the exception of a small amount of life insurance that is sold through the mail, most life insurance is sold by agents or brokers. Most agents are independent contractors, but they may also be employees of the general agency or insurer. Life insurance companies originally insisted that

individual agents represent them exclusively, but there is an increasing trend toward multiple-company representation and brokerage of life insurance. The agent may work through a general agency, a branch office, or a personal producing general agent's office.

General agents are independent businesspeople, appointed by the company they represent to sell life insurance in specified territories and to appoint subagents. The general agency receives an overriding commission on all business written by its subagents, out of which it pays agency expenses. Most general agents also receive some sort of financial assistance from their companies in the form of a contribution toward the general agency expense. The fact that the general agent hires, trains, and compensates subagents makes the general agency a relatively inexpensive and riskless manner of starting in a new area.

In the branch office system, the sales force is supervised by a branch manager who, in contrast to the general agent, is a salaried employee of the insurance company. Expenses of the branch office are paid by the home office, because the branch office is simply an extension of the home office. The agents assigned to a branch office may be employees of the insurer or independent contractors.

Personal producing general agents (PPGAs) are agents who have established a record of successful production and who are granted a contract that gives them greater compensation than they received as agents. Like the general agent, the PPGAs absorb all their own expenses, including office facilities, clerical staff, and other overhead expenses. Although most PPGAs have the authority to employ or appoint their own agents and use independent brokers, such appointments are usually limited, since personal production is the PPGA's prime purpose.

Property and Liability Distribution Systems

In the field of property and liability insurance, companies may be classified into two groups

---

[13]"Binding" refers to the authority of an agent to commit his or her insurance company to a contract for the insurance. The authority of agents is discussed in Chapter 9.

based on their distribution system: (1) those who operate through the American Agency System and (2) the "direct writers." The agents who operate through the American Agency System are known as independent agents, while those who represent direct writers are called captive agents.

The American Agency System Independent agents normally represent several companies, dividing the policies they sell among those companies according to their choice. Independent agents are said to "own their expirations," which means that they may place the renewals of policies they have sold with some other insurer if they choose to do so. One implication of the ownership of renewals by independent agents is that it prevents the insurance company from paying a lower commission on renewal business.

Direct Writers Direct writers operate through salaried representatives (as in the case of the Liberty Mutual Insurance Company) or through exclusive or captive agents (as in the case of Nationwide, State Farm, and Allstate).[14] The compensation of the salesperson may be in the form of a salary, or it may be a commission. In the case of the exclusive agent, it is normally commission. The important point is that the agent or the salaried employee does not own the expirations and has no choice regarding where the policy is renewed. Since the agent cannot transfer business to another insurer, the direct-writing company can pay a small renewal commission or none at all.

The ownership of renewals is the most important difference between the two types of agents, and from this difference arise other distinctions in the method of operation. Since the direct-writing agent receives little or no commission on re-

newals, the production of new business is of crucial importance. In a sense, the life insurance agent is in the same position, because the renewal commission on life insurance is quite low. Because renewal commissions are low for direct-writing agents, the agent's income depends on the generation of new business. The independent agent, on the other hand, places greater emphasis on the retention of accounts presently serviced.

Direct Response Distribution of Insurance

Life insurance, health insurance, and property and liability insurance are all sold by insurers operating under a "direct response" system. These insurers do not use agents, but promote the sale of insurance by mass media advertising and by direct mail and, more recently, via the Internet. Historically, the direct response system has accounted for a small portion of the total insurance sold in this country, but this could change with the expansion of marketing over the World Wide Web.

Consultants and Financial Planners

In addition to insurance agents and brokers, there are a growing number of risk management and insurance consultants who do not represent insurers or sell insurance, but offer their services on a fee basis. Many states regulate the activities of these consultants and require that they be licensed.

In the personal lines field, there has been a rapid growth in the financial planning profession, which focuses on the broad spectrum of an individual's or family's economic goals. It includes budgeting, planned accumulation of wealth, risk management, and tax minimization. Because protection of assets is a cornerstone of a financial plan, financial planners have become an important source of advice on personal risk management and insurance, especially for wealthy members of society. Although anyone can call himself or herself a financial planner, only persons who have met certain educational standards may use

---

[14]Technically, companies that operate through exclusive agents are not "direct writers" but rather "exclusive-agent companies." However, the term direct writer is commonly used in reference both to companies operating through salaried representatives and those operating through exclusive agents.

one of the financial planning industry's professional designations.[15]

Cooperation in the Insurance Industry

Insurance by its very nature is cooperative. Despite the fact that insurance companies and agents compete vigorously with each other, there are many areas in which both companies and agents cooperate. In some cases, this arises out of economic necessity. Many cooperative organizations are formed and supported by groups of insurance companies to perform functions that would mean a duplication of effort if each company carried them out individually. In other instances, the cooperation is designed to spread risk among insurers, by sharing losses. In still other cases, the objective of the cooperation is improved public relations and personnel education. The following are a few of the more important cooperative efforts that occur within the insurance industry.

Distressed and Residual Risk Pools

One of the most socially significant areas of cooperation among insurers is found in the techniques used to deal with certain classes of insureds that are unprofitable but that, for various reasons, must be insured. Property and liability insurers in all states are required to participate in shared markets, a euphemism for the involuntary markets in which insurance is provided to applicants that do not meet normal underwriting standards. In some instances, applicants are shared on some predetermined basis. In others, losses are shared. The following are a few of the more important programs that have been designed to deal with the problem of the high-risk insured.

1. *The automobile shared market.* Some drivers, because of their past records and the likelihood of future losses that those records indicate, are unacceptable to insurers in the normal course of business. Because it is deemed socially undesirable to permit such drivers on the road without insurance, the insurance industry has established special mechanisms to provide the necessary coverage. The most widely used approach is the Automobile Insurance Plan (formerly called Assigned Risk Plan), which is currently used in 42 states. This plan functions by sharing applicants, with each auto insurer operating in a state accepting a share of the undesirable drivers, based on the percentage of the state's total auto insurance that it writes. The remaining 8 states use other plans to achieve the same result.[16]

2. *Workers compensation assigned-risk pools.* Shared-market plans also exist in the field of workers compensation insurance. Here, employers who are not acceptable to insurers in the standard market are assigned to insurers, based on each insurer's percentage of the standard market.

3. *Medical malpractice pools.* In the mid-1970s, many insurers withdrew from the medical malpractice insurance field, creating a "malpractice crisis," in which many physicians found that they were unable to obtain professional liability insurance at any price. In many states, a part of the response was the formation of reinsurance pools, in

---

[15]The Certified Financial Planner (CFP) designation is awarded by the College for Financial Planning, and requires successful completion of 6 three-hour examinations covering all elements of the financial planning process. The Chartered Financial Consultant (ChFC) designation is awarded by the American College to individuals who have passed 13 two-hour examinations. The ChFC designation is often held in conjunction with the CLU designation.

[16]The operation of these programs is discussed in greater detail in Chapter 23.

which all liability insurers in the state share in the premiums and losses associated with medical malpractice insurance.

4. *FAIR plans.* FAIR plans are insurance industry pools that provide insurance to property owners in inner-city and other high-risk areas who are unable to obtain insurance through normal market channels because of location or other factors over which they have no control. Property owners who cannot obtain insurance through normal markets apply to the state FAIR plan for coverage. After inspecting the property, the FAIR plan assigns the property to an insurer or informs the owner what physical hazards must be corrected before the property will be insured.[17]

5. *Beach and windstorm pools.* Special beach and windstorm plans exist in seven states along the Atlantic and Gulf coasts where vulnerability to hurricanes and severe windstorm damage is especially high.[18] The beach and windstorm pools operate in essentially the same way as state FAIR plans.

6. *State health insurance plans.* A number of states have created state health insurance pools for persons who cannot obtain cov-

erage in the normal market. Persons who are not eligible for Medicare or Medicaid and who cannot buy private health insurance obtain coverage from the pools, usually at a subsidized rate.[19]

Educational Organizations

The field of insurance requires continuing education of a scale that is matched by few professions. Several educational organizations exist for agents and agency or company employees who wish to improve their knowledge and increase their professionalism. The American Institute for Property and Liability Underwriters is the leading educational organization in the field of property and liability insurance. It sponsors the course of instruction leading to the professional designation Chartered Property and Casualty Underwriter (CPCU). This designation is a symbol of professional attainment that relatively few individuals achieve. A companion organization, the Insurance Institute of America, offers basic courses called the "IIA" program that are a preparation for the rigorous requirements of the CPCU study program. In the life insurance field, the American College of Life Underwriters is the equivalent of the American Institute and sponsors a course of instruction that leads to the life insurance designation Chartered Life Underwriter (CLU).

Underwriting Syndicates

In addition to the other forms of cooperation, insurers sometimes join together in underwriting syndicates for the purpose of handling risks that

---

[17]The term FAIR is an acronym for Fair Access to Insurance Requirements. State FAIR plans currently exist in California, Connecticut, Delaware, Georgia, Illinois, Indiana, Iowa, Kansas, Kentucky, Louisiana, Maryland, Massachusetts, Michigan, Minnesota, Missouri, New Jersey, New Mexico, New York, North Carolina, Ohio, Oregon, Pennsylvania, Rhode Island, Virginia, Washington, and Wisconsin. The FAIR plans were created as an adjunct to a federal riot reinsurance program created by Congress in the aftermath of an epidemic of urban riots in the summer of 1967. The reinsurance program, which ended in 1983, protected the private insurers against catastrophic losses from civil disorders. Participation in the reinsurance program was optional on a state-by-state basis, but if a state chose to participate, all property insurers operating in the state were required to join the state-supervised FAIR plan.
[18]Alabama, Florida, Louisiana, Mississippi, North Carolina, South Carolina, and Texas.

[19]By 1999, the following 23 states had created such pools: California, Colorado, Connecticut, Florida, Georgia, Illinois, Indiana, Iowa, Maine, Minnesota, Montana, Louisiana, Nebraska, New Mexico, North Dakota, Oregon, South Carolina, Tennessee, Texas, Utah, Washington, Wisconsin, and Wyoming.

would be beyond the capacity of an individual company. In these syndicates, which are found primarily in the property and liability field, insurers make use of the basic insurance principle of spreading risk and sharing losses. The most prominent syndicates include the Associated Factory Mutual Insurance companies, the Industrial-Risk Insurers, and the Improved-Risk Mutuals, all of which write insurance on large concentrations of values and offer extensive loss-prevention services in connection with the insurance. Properties insured by these syndicates are generally classed as "highly protected risks." Other syndicates deal with the specialized exposures or concentrations of values that characterize the insurance needs of particular industries. Insurance for liability arising out of nuclear accidents is provided by an insurance industry pool, American Nuclear Insurers. Two syndicates, the Associated Aviation Underwriters and the United States Aircraft Insurance Group, offer insurance for aviation risks and the American Hull Insurance Syndicate specializes in coverage for ocean-going ships of American registry.

Competition in the Insurance Industry

Competition in the insurance industry today is intense, perhaps more so than at any time in history. Competition occurs in both price and product quality.

Price Competition

Price competition in the insurance industry occurs primarily at the company level where rates are set. Insurance companies compete on the basis of price by attempting to offer a lower-priced product than do other companies dealing in the same line of insurance. The agent does not (except in isolated cases) participate in setting the price of the product. Exceptions exist in the case of extremely large accounts on which the commission is negotiated, and the final commission agreed upon is a factor in the final premium. In general, the pricing of the product by his or her companies is a factor outside of the control of the agent. Price competition between agencies does, of course, take place, but it is based on the price competition between the companies that the agencies represent. There are differences in price among companies, and in the selection of the companies that he or she will represent the agent has control over the price of the contracts the agency sells. Agencies that want to compete on a price basis do so by entering into contracts with insurers whose marketing strategy also emphasizes price.

The price of insurance, like most prices, is a function of the cost of production, and to the extent that companies are successful in reducing their costs, they can also reduce their prices. The following costs are common to all insurance companies:

1. Losses and loss adjustment expense
2. Acquisition expense
3. Administrative expense (company overhead)
4. Taxes
5. Profit and contingencies

The first of the costs listed can be an area of considerable difference among companies. Some companies, through selective underwriting, have achieved significantly lower loss costs. It should be recognized, however, that lower premiums achieved by selective underwriting reflect a different "product." The unique nature of price competition in insurance rests on the little-understood fact that the individual to whom an insurance policy is sold is, in a sense, the "product" that the insurer sells. It is the combination of hazards and loss-producing characteristics that the individual brings to the insured group that represents the risk transferred to the insurer. This means that two insurers selling policies to different individuals may be selling dramatically different products. If an insurer succeeds in selecting customers with lower-than-average probabilities of loss, it sells a product whose cost is lower and for which a lower premium may be charged.

In addition to differences in loss costs, differences in other costs can allow an insurer to offer lower prices for its products. Acquisition expense, in particular, can reflect substantial premium savings. The major part of the production costs have traditionally been agents' commissions. Some companies, especially the direct writers, have been able to reduce premium costs by reducing or eliminating agents' commissions. Even in life insurance where the agent's commission is usually a significant cost only in the first years, lower commission scales may permit lower premiums. Differences in administrative expenses and profit can also produce different aggregate costs. Although taxes represent only a small percentage of the total premium, the state premium tax is levied as a percentage of the total premiums and therefore tends to magnify the differences among companies in the other costs.

The differences that can exist in the common costs of insurers help to explain the differences in the premiums charged by insurers. If a company is successful in reducing any of its costs below those of its competitors, it is able to offer coverage at a lower price or derive a higher profit on its operations. Insurers whose costs are excessive find it difficult to maintain an adequate market share.

Product Competition

Product differentiation occurs both at the company and at the agency level. Companies offer different forms of policies, with broader insuring agreements or additional provisions that are beneficial to the insured. Product competition among insurers also occurs in the area of service, where some insurers excel in providing loss prevention and inspection services to their clients. Assistance in industrial safety, loss prevention, rehabilitation of injured workers, and similar services are an important part of a bundle of services that represent

the total insurance product purchased by corporate insureds.

Agencies also compete with one another in the product they offer to their clients. Basically, the agent's product consists of advice in the selection of the proper coverage to meet the client's needs, selection of the appropriate insurer, and assistance at the time of a loss. This means that quality competition at the agency level is based on the technical competence of the personnel employed by the agency or brokerage firm.

Is the Insurance Industry Really Competitive?

The decades of the 1980s and 1990s witnessed a fierce debate over the question of whether or not the insurance industry is competitive. Industry critics base their attack that the industry is not competitive on the industry's partial exemption from the federal antitrust laws, which were enacted by Congress in 1945. But this criticism ignores the fact that the industry is regulated by the states. We will defer our discussion of the regulation of insurance until Chapter 8. For the present, let us consider the debate by examining whether the industry exhibits the characteristics of a competitive industry.

Insurance Industry Market Structure

Economists traditionally focus on market structure and market conduct as measures of competition in an industry. Important factors in the market structure include the number of competitors and the percentage of the market controlled by the largest firms. Market conduct is reflected by the ease of entry into the market and by changes in market share over time. So how does the insurance industry stack up?

- There are numerous competitors in each of the three major sectors in the insurance industry. Each field is highly decentralized, with no firm controlling as much as 10 percent of the market nationally. Consumers have a wide range of sellers from which to choose, offering differentiated products at different prices.

- Not only is the number of insurers operating in each field of insurance large, the number has grown over time, indicating freedom of entry into and exit from the market. There are few barriers to entry by new competitors—not only is it easy to form a new company or expand an existing one, but insurers face competition from alternatives to the traditional insurance market (e.g., risk retention groups).

- Concurrent with the growth in the number of insurers, major shifts in market segments have occurred. In the property and liability field, the direct-writing companies have captured a significant share of the market previously controlled by agency companies. In life insurance, the shift has been from companies selling traditional forms of coverage to companies marketing newer forms, such as universal life and variable life insurance. In health insurance, the shift in market share has been from traditional health insurers to HMOs and other capitating health care providers.

Based on the number of competitors, freedom of entry into the market, and changes in market share over time, one would conclude that all three segments of the insurance industry exhibit the structure of a highly competitive industry.

Evidence of Intensity of the Competition

In addition to the market structure, three additional factors indicate a highly competitive market and attest to the intensity of the competition in the property and liability field and, to a lesser extent, in the life and health insurance fields:

1. The industry is highly cyclical, a hallmark of a competitive industry, evidencing the inability of insurers to control output, prices, or profits.

2. Profits in recent years have consistently been below those for most other industries.

3. Insurer insolvencies occur on a regular basis.

The Insurance Cycle

The property and liability industry is highly cyclical, and goes through periods of underwriting profit, followed by periods of losses; the insurance market is characterized as "hard" or "soft," depending on the phase of the cycle. During periods when insurers are earning underwriting profits, the market is said to be soft, as insurers engage in price-cutting to increase their market share. The price-cutting includes not only reduction in the absolute level of rates, but the loosening of underwriting standards. This has the natural result of generating losses, resulting in a hard market, during which insurers increase prices and tighten underwriting standards. This cyclical pattern is precisely the conduct one would expect in a highly competitive market, and is convincing evidence of the absence of collusion.

Although it is sometimes suggested that the underwriting cycle results from mismanagement within the insurance industry, this criticism ignores the fact that in a competitive market, competitors do not set the market price. Competitors accept the price that is set by the interaction of market forces. The pricing decisions of insurance companies are a response to the cycle, not a cause. Insurers cut prices not because they want to, but because they are required to by the pressure of market forces.

Industry Profitability

Because the property and liability insurance industry has been the most widely criticized, it has

Table 6.1   Insurer Insolvencies 1980–1999

Year	Life and Health Insurer Insolvencies	Property and Liability Insurer Insolvencies
1980	9	5
1981	8	9
1982	10	8
1983	20	11
1984	11	27
1985	9	52
1986	14	32
1987	20	25
1988	19	42
1989	42	52
1990	41	43
1991	58	47
1992	32	59
1993	22	24
1994	11	22
1995	3	10
1996	6	9
1997	7	27
1998	17	8
1999	19	6

Sources: A. M. Best and National Association of Insurance Commissioners.

attracted the greatest interest from scholars. Numerous studies over the past two decades have examined the structure of the property and liability insurance industry. These studies were conducted by scholars from the academic world, by government commissions, by federal agencies, and by the U.S. Government Accounting Office. Using different methodologies and different models, the researchers independently reached the same conclusion: that the industry is competitively structured, that there is no evidence of excessive profits, and that the rate of return to firms in the industry is generally less than that for other industries with the same risk.[20]

Insurer Insolvencies

Table 6.1 indicates the number of insurer insolvencies during the period since 1980 in both the life and health and property and liability fields. Although insolvencies do not, in themselves, provide conclusive evidence of competition, the insolvencies that chronically occur in the insurance industry do support the other evidence of the intensity of competition in the industry.

Although the insolvency rate in the insurance field is significantly below that in the field of banking or other financial institutions, the growing number of insolvencies stands in mute testimony to the demands of a competitive marketplace. It also provides a convenient point of departure for our next chapter, which deals with the regulation of insurance.

---

[20]A 1989 Government Accounting Office study, entitled *Insurance: Profitability of the Automobile Lines of the Insurance Industry*, concluded that the after-tax earnings on auto insurance over the period 1978 through 1987 produced an average 10.4 percent return on surplus. This is lower than the average rate of return on banks, utilities, and transportation for the same period.

Important Concepts to Remember

domestic insurer
foreign insurer
alien insurer
admitted insurer
nonadmitted insurer
mutual insurance company
capital stock insurance company
reciprocals
Lloyd's association

assessment mutual
advance premium mutual
assessable policy
attorney-in-fact
Blue Cross
Blue Shield
health maintenance organization
agent
broker

American Agency System
direct writer
independent agent
captive agent
ownership of renewals
fraternal insurer
company groups
fleets
CPCU

CLU

residual risk pool

Automobile Insurance Plan

FAIR Plan

insurance exchange

mortgage loan insurance

National Flood Insurance Program

SBA Surety Bond Guarantee Program

Export-Import Bank

Overseas Private Investor Corporation

post-insolvency assessment fund

Questions for Review

1. Identify the classes into which insurers can be classified according to product and according to the place of incorporation and licensing.

2. List the types of insurers as classified by legal form of ownership, and briefly describe the distinguishing characteristics of each type.

3. Distinguish between an insurance agent and an insurance broker. What is the significance of the distinction from the insured's viewpoint?

4. What is meant by the expression that independent agents "own their expirations?" Why is this important?

5. How does the authority of a life insurance agent differ from that of a property and liability insurance agent?

6. What are the general methods of operation of Lloyd's of London, and why does it receive such wide publicity?

7. Identify the various costs that are common to all insurers and explain the extent to which these costs may differ from one insurer to another.

8. How do you account for the fact that two insurers may charge significantly different premiums for identical coverage?

9. How does the insurance industry fund the losses associated with shared markets such as FAIR plans and Automobile Insurance Plans?

10. What evidence exists that the insurance industry is competitive?

Questions for Discussion

1. "When an insurer is successful in its efforts to select insureds from the better than average classes, the gain in its competitive position is magnified by the impact of this success on its competitors." Explain what is meant by this statement.

2. Do you agree with the assertion in the chapter that the insurance industry is highly competitive? Why or why not? What evidence exists that the industry is not competitive?

3. Critics have argued that demutualization is detrimental to the policyholders of a mutual

insurance company. Why would this be the case?

4. Independent insurance agents often represent insurers with different prices for the same coverage. In what way does this pose a dilemma for the agent? How can the dilemma be resolved?

5. What, in your opinion, is the potential for marketing life insurance via the World Wide Web? What is the potential for marketing automobile and homeowners insurance via the World Wide Web?

Suggestions for Additional Reading

American Council of Life Insurance. *Life Insurance Fact Book.* Washington, D.C.: American Council of Life Insurance, annual.

Black, Kenneth, Jr., and Harold D. Skipper, Jr. *Life Insurance,* 13th ed. Englewood Cliffs, NJ: Prentice Hall, 2000. Chapter 3.

Gibbs, D. E. W. *Lloyd's of London: A Study of Individualism.* New York: St. Martin's Press, 1975.

Health Insurance Institute. *Source Book of Health Insurance Data.* New York: Health Insurance Institute, annual.

Huebner, S. S., Kenneth Black, Jr., and Bernard L. Webb. *Property and Liability Insurance,* 4th ed. Englewood Cliffs, NJ: Prentice Hall, 1995. Chapters 34 and 35.

Insurance Information Institute. *Insurance Facts, Property-Liability-Inland Marine-Surety.* New York: Insurance Information Institute, annual.

Nelli, H. O., and R. A. Marshall. *The Private Insurance Business in the United States,* Research Paper 48. Atlanta, GA: Bureau of Business and Economic Research, Georgia State College, June 1969.

Pfeffer, I. "The Early History of Insurance," *CPCU Annals,* vol. 29, nos. 11, 19, 23 (Summer 1966).

Websites to Explore

Alliance of American Insurers: http://www.allianceai.org

American Insurance Association: http://www.aiadc.com

American Insurance Services Group: http://www.aisg.org/

Best's Review: http://www.ambest.com/review/

Factory Mutual System: http://www.factorymutual.com/

Federal Emergency Management Agency (FEMA): http://www.fema.gov/

Independent Insurance Agents of America, Inc.: http://www.iiaa.org

Insurance Information Institute: http://www.iii.org

Insurance Institute of America, Inc.: http://www.aicpcu.org

Lloyd's of London: http://www.lloydsoflondon.co.uk/

National Association of Independent Insurers: http://www.naii.org

National Association of Insurance & Financial Advisors: http://www.naifa.org/

National Association of Mutual Insurance Companies: http://www.namic.org

National Association of Professional Insurance Agents: http://www.pianet.com/

National Underwriter Company: http://www.nuco.com/

Surety Association of America: http://www.surety.org

Ultimate insurance links: http://www.barryklein.com/

CHAPTER 7

Functions of Insurers

What I advise is that each contentedly practice the trade he understands.
—Horace, *Epistles*

CHAPTER OBJECTIVES

When you have finished this chapter, you should be able to

- Identify and differentiate between the two broad approaches to ratemaking

- Explain the purpose of underwriting and describe the underwriting process

- Identify the principal sources of information on which an underwriter may rely

- Identify and differentiate among the various types of adjusters

- Explain the nature of insurance company reserves

- Explain the effect of statutory accounting requirements on the indicated profitability of insurers

- Describe the types of reinsurance and discuss the purposes of reinsurance

- Explain what is meant by the securitization of insurable risk and how it functions as an alternative to reinsurance

- Explain the way in which insurance companies are taxed

As a part of our study of the insurance mechanism and the way in which it works, it will be helpful to examine some unique aspects of insurance company operations that are required by the insurance transaction. In addition, we will examine some of the financial aspects of insurers' operations.

Although there are operational differences between life insurance companies and property and liability insurers, the major activities of all insurers may be classified as follows:

1. Ratemaking
2. Production
3. Underwriting
4. Loss adjustment
5. Investment

In addition to these, there are, of course, other activities common to most business firms such as accounting, personnel management, market research, and so on.

Ratemaking

An insurance rate is the price per unit of insurance. Like any other price, it depends on the cost of production. However, in insurance, unlike other industries, the cost of production is not known when the contract is sold, and it will not be known until sometime in the future, when the policy has expired. One basic difference between insurance pricing and the pricing function in other industries is that the price for insurance must be based on a prediction. The process of predicting future losses and future expenses and allocating these costs among the various classes of insureds is called *ratemaking*.

The ratemaking function in a life insurance company is performed by the actuarial department, or in smaller companies, by an actuarial

consulting firm.[1] In the property and liability field, rates are developed from trended loss statistics provided by an advisory organization or accumulated by the individual insurer. In the field of marine insurance and inland marine insurance, rates are often made by the underwriter on a judgment basis.

In addition to the statutory requirements that insurance rates must be adequate, not excessive, and not unfairly discriminatory, certain other characteristics are considered desirable. To the extent possible, for example, rates should be relatively stable over time, so that the public is not subjected to wide variations in cost from year to year. At the same time, rates should be sufficiently responsive to changing conditions to avoid inadequacies in the event of deteriorating loss experience. Finally, whenever possible, it is also desirable that the rate provide some incentive for the insured to prevent loss.

Some Basic Concepts

A rate is the price charged for each unit of protection or exposure and should be distinguished from a premium, which is determined by multiplying the rate by the number of units of protection purchased. The unit of protection to which a rate applies differs for various lines of insurance. In life insurance, for example, rates are computed for each $1000 in protection; in fire insurance, the rate applies to each $100 of coverage. In workers compensation the rate is applied to each $100 of the insured's payroll.

Regardless of the type of insurance, the premium income of the insurer must be sufficient to cover losses and expenses. To obtain this premium income, the insurer must predict the claims and expenses, and then allocate these anticipated

---

[1]Much of the discussion of ratemaking in this chapter pertains to property and liability insurance. Because of the long-term nature of life insurance contracts, special complications mark the life insurance ratemaking process.

costs among the various classes of policyholders. The final premium that the insured pays is called the "gross premium" and is based on a gross rate. The gross rate is composed of two parts, one designed to provide for the payment of losses and a second, called a loading, to cover the expenses of operation. That part of the rate that is intended to cover losses is called the pure premium when expressed in dollars and cents, and the expected loss ratio when expressed as a percentage. The part of the rate or premium intended to cover expenses is called the expense ratio.[2]

Although some differences exist among different lines of insurance, in general, the pure premium is determined by dividing expected losses by the number of exposure units. For example, if 100,000 automobiles generate $30,000,000 in losses, the pure premium is $300:

$$\frac{\text{Losses}}{\text{Exposure units}} = \frac{\$30,000,000}{100,000} = \$300$$

The process of converting the pure premium into a gross rate requires addition of the loading, which is intended to cover the expenses that will be required in the production and servicing of the insurance. The various classes of expenses for which provision must be made normally include commissions and other acquisition costs, general administrative expense, premium taxes, and an allowance for profit and contingencies. In converting the pure premium into a gross rate, these expenses are usually treated as a percentage of the final rate, on the assumption that they will increase proportionately with premiums. Since most of the expenses do actually vary with premiums, the assumption is reasonably realistic.

The final gross rate is derived by dividing the pure premium by a *permissible loss ratio.* The permissible loss ratio is the percentage of the premium (and so the rate) that will be available to pay losses after provision for expenses. The conversion is made by the formula

$$\text{Gross rate} = \frac{\text{Pure premium}}{1 - \text{Expense ratio}}$$

Using the $300 pure premium computed in our previous example, and assuming an expense ratio of 0.40,

$$\text{Gross rate} = \frac{\$300}{1 - 0.40} = \frac{\$300}{0.60} = \$500$$

While the pure premium varies with the loss experience for the particular line of insurance, the expense ratio also varies from one line to another, depending on the commissions and the other expenses involved.

Advisory Organizations

As we have seen, the accuracy of an insurer's predictions increases with the number of exposures on which they are based. In the property and liability field, insurers pool loss statistics to increase the accuracy of the rate-making process. By pooling their loss statistics, insurers support *advisory organizations* (also called *rating bureaus*) that use these statistics as the raw material for computing trended loss costs (i.e., pure premiums). Some larger insurers maintain their own loss statistics and compute their own loss costs.[3] In either case, the insurer then adds a loading, which reflects its unique expenses, to the loss costs to derive a final rate. Some of the more important advisory organizations are the following:

1. *The Insurance Services Office* (ISO). The Insurance Services Office provides a wide

---

[2]The expected loss ratio and expense ratio refer to components of a rate. The actual loss ratio and expense ratio describe the relationship between incurred losses and expenses over some period of time. The expense ratio plus the loss ratio are called the combined ratio. If an insurer collects $100 million in premiums on a group of policies and incurs $70 million in losses and $35 million in expenses on those policies, it would have a 70 percent loss ratio, a 35 percent expense ratio, and a 105 percent combined ratio.

[3]There are no rating bureaus in the life insurance field. The ratemaking function in a life insurance company is performed by the actuarial department or, in smaller companies, by an actuarial consulting firm. The Society of Actuaries, a voluntary association of actuaries, holds periodic meetings for the exchange of information with the goal of improving premium determination.

range of advisory, rating, and actuarial services relating to property and casualty insurance, including the development of policy forms, loss information, and related services for multiple-line coverages. It computes and publishes trended loss data for most property and liability insurance lines other than workers compensation. The ISO was originally owned and controlled by insurance companies. In 1994, ISO members approved a new structure in which ISO's board consists of seven noninsurers and four industry representatives.

2. *The American Association of Insurance Services* (AAIS). The American Association of Insurance Services performs approximately the same functions for its subscribers as does the ISO.

3. *The National Council on Compensation Insurance.* The National Council on Compensation Insurance develops and administers rating plans and systems for workers compensation insurance.

At one time, rating bureaus used the loss statistics reported by their members to compute final advisory rates, which the bureaus then filed with state insurance departments on behalf of their members. Nonbureau companies either maintained their own loss statistics and filed their rates independently, or used the bureau rate as a point of departure, modifying it to reflect their own experience and expenses. Because insurers that used rates filed by bureaus charged the same rates for coverage, industry critics argued that the activities of rating bureaus constituted a form of "price-fixing" and that these activities permitted the industry to operate as a "cartel."[4] In 1989, the ISO announced its decision to stop providing advisory rates to its members. Instead, it now provides insurers with trended loss costs only. Insurers develop and add their own factors for expenses, profits, and contingencies. In 1990, the National Council of Compensation Insurance and the Surety Association of America announced that they would follow the same practice.

Types of Rates

The approach to setting rates is quite similar in most instances, but it is possible to distinguish between two different types of rates: class and individual.

Class Rates

The term *class rating* refers to the practice of computing a price per unit of insurance that applies to all applicants possessing a given set of characteristics. For example, a class rate might apply to all types of dwelling of a given type of construction in a specific city. Rates that apply to all individuals of a given age and sex are also examples of class rates. The advantage of the class-rating system is that it permits the insurer to apply a single rate to a large number of insureds, simplifying the process of determining their premiums. In establishing rating classes, the ratemaker must compromise between a large class, which will include a greater number of exposures and thereby increase the credibility of predictions, and one sufficiently narrow to permit homogeneity. Class rating is the most common approach in use by the insurance industry today and is used in life insurance and most property and liability fields.

Individual Rates

There are some instances in which the characteristics of the units to be insured vary so widely that it is necessary to determine rates on a basis that measures the loss-producing characteristics of each individual exposure unit. There are four approaches to individual rating: judgment rating, schedule rating, experience rating, and retrospective rating.

[4]The accusation that advisory rates constituted a system of price-fixing ignores the fact that insurers were free to participate in bureaus or file their rates independently, thereby precluding the price-fixing and market-sharing activities of a cartel. As a matter of fact, a significant portion of the market is controlled by nonbureau companies, which develop their own rates and price their products individually.

Judgment Rating   In some lines of insurance, the rate is determined for each individual risk on a judgment basis. Here the processes of underwriting and ratemaking merge, and the underwriter decides whether the exposure is to be accepted and at what rate. Judgment rating is used when credible statistics are lacking, or when the exposure units are so varied that it is impossible to construct a class. This technique is most frequently applied in the ocean marine field, although it is also used in other lines of insurance.

Schedule Rating   Schedule rating, as its name implies, makes rates by applying a schedule of charges and credits to some base rate to determine the appropriate rate for an individual exposure unit. In commercial fire insurance, for example, the rates for many buildings are determined by adding debits and subtracting credits from a base rate, which represents a standard building. The debits and credits represent those features of the particular building's construction, occupancy, fire protection, and neighborhood that deviate from the standard. Through the application of these debits and credits, the physical characteristics of each schedule-rated building determine that building's rate.

Experience Rating   In experience rating, the insured's own past loss experience enters into the determination of the final premium. Experience rating is superimposed on a class-rating system and adjusts the insured's premium upward or downward, depending on the extent to which his or her experience has deviated from the average experience of the class. It is most frequently used in the fields of workers compensation, general liability, and group life and health insurance. Generally, experience rating is used only when the insured generates a premium large enough to be considered statistically credible.

Retrospective Rating   A retrospective-rating plan is a self-rated program under which the ac-

tual losses during the policy period determine the final premium for the coverage, subject to a maximum and a minimum. A deposit premium is charged at the inception of the policy and then adjusted after the policy period has expired, to reflect actual losses incurred. In a sense, a "retro" plan is like a cost-plus contract, the major difference being that it is subject to a maximum and a minimum. Retrospective rating is used in the field of workers compensation, general liability, automobile, and group health insurance. However, only very large insureds will usually elect these plans.

Adjusting the Level of Rates

Once policies have been written and the loss experience on those policies emerges, the experience becomes the basis for adjusting the level of rates. The change in rate levels indicated by raw data is usually tempered by a credibility factor, which reflects the degree of confidence the ratemakers believe should be given to past losses as predictors of future losses. The credibility assigned to a particular body of loss experience is determined primarily by the size of the body of experience. To obtain a sufficiently large body of experience for credibility, the ratemaker must sometimes include several years of experience. Experience of the most recent years may be weighted more heavily than that of the earlier years or the data may be adjusted by a trend factor. A trend factor is a multiplier calculated from the changes in average claim payments, changes in a price index, or some similar series of data. The trend indicated by past experience is usually extended to the midpoint of the period for which the rates will be used.

Production

The production department of an insurance company, sometimes called the agency department, is its sales or marketing division. This department supervises the external portion of the sales effort, which is conducted by the agents or salaried representatives of the company. The various marketing systems under which the outside salespeople operate were discussed in Chapter 6. The internal portion of the production function is carried on by the production (or agency) department. It is the responsibility of this department to select and appoint agents and to assist in sales. In general, it renders assistance to agents in technical matters. Special agents, or marketing representatives, assist the agent directly in marketing problems. The special agent is a technician who calls on agents, acting as an intermediary between the production department and the agent. This person renders assistance when needed on rating and programming insurance coverages and also attempts to encourage the producers.

Underwriting

Underwriting is the process of selecting and classifying exposures. It is an essential element in the operation of any insurance program, because unless the company selects from among its applicants, the inevitable result will be adverse selection. The primary objective of underwriting is to guard against adverse selection. There must be the same mix of good and bad risks in the group insured as there were in the group from which the rates were taken. The tendency of the poorer-than-average risks to seek insurance to a greater extent than do the average or better-than-average risks must be blocked.

It is important to understand that the goal of underwriting is not the selection of risks that will not have losses. It is to avoid a disproportionate number of bad risks, thereby equalizing the actual losses with the expected ones. In addition to this goal, there are certain other objectives. While attempting to avoid adverse selection through rejection of undesirable risks, the underwriter must secure an adequate volume of exposures in each

class. In addition, he or she must guard against congestion or concentration of exposures that might result in a catastrophe.

The importance of the underwriting function rests on its relationship to the adequacy of rates. The actuaries compute rates based on past experience. The underwriter must determine into which of the classes, if any, each exposure unit should go. Poor underwriting can wipe out the efforts of the actuary, rendering a good rate inadequate. For this reason, those who perform the underwriting function must develop a keen sense of judgment and a thorough knowledge of the hazards associated with various types of coverage.

The Underwriting Process

Underwriting begins with the formulation of the company's underwriting policy, which is generally established by the officers in charge of underwriting. The underwriting policy establishes the framework within which the *desk underwriter* (the individual who applies underwriting policy to applicants) makes decisions. This policy specifies the lines of insurance that will be written as well as prohibited exposures, the amount of coverage to be permitted on various types of exposure, the areas of the country in which each line will be written, and similar restrictions. The desk underwriter is usually not involved in the formation of the company underwriting policy.

The desk underwriter's job is to evaluate applications for insurance, accepting some and rejecting others that do not meet the company's underwriting requirements. When a risk is rejected, it is because the underwriter feels that the hazards connected with it are excessive in relation to the rate. There are five sources from which the underwriter obtains information regarding the hazards inherent in an exposure:

1. *Application.* The basic source of underwriting information is the application, which varies for each line of insurance and for each type of coverage. The broader and

more liberal the contract, usually the more detailed the information required in the application. The questions on the application are designed to give the underwriter the information needed to decide if he or she will accept the exposure, reject it, or seek additional information.

2. *Information from the agent or broker.* In many cases the underwriter places much weight on the recommendations of the agent or broker. This varies with the experience the underwriter has had with the particular agent. In certain cases the underwriter will agree to accept an exposure that does not meet the underwriting requirement of the company. Such exposures are referred to as *accommodation risks,* because they are accepted to accommodate a valued client or agent.

3. *Credit reports.* In some cases the underwriter will request a report from a credit report provider, a company that specializes in the practice of assembling or evaluating consumer credit information or other information on consumers for the purpose of furnishing consumer reports to third parties. Credit reports may include information on a wide range of personal characteristics of the individual, including financial status, occupation, character, and the extent to which he or she uses alcoholic beverages (or to which neighbors say he or she uses them). These reports provide additional information the underwriter can use in evaluating the exposure.

4. *Information bureaus.* In addition to the inspection report, the underwriter may seek information from one of the cooperative information bureaus the industry supports. The best example of this is the Medical Information Bureau (MIB), which maintains centralized files on the physical condition of applicants who have applied for life insurance in member companies.

In automobile insurance, the company may obtain a copy of the applicant's motor vehicle record with a list of violations from the state department of motor vehicles.

5. *Physical examinations or inspections.* In life insurance, the primary focus is on the health of the applicant. One of the most critical pieces of information in underwriting is the report of the physician. Physicians selected by the insurance company supply the insurer with medical reports after a physical examination; these reports are a very important source of underwriting information. In the field of property and liability insurance, the equivalent of the physical examination in life insurance is the inspection of the premises. Although such inspections are not always conducted, the practice is increasing.

Postselection Underwriting

In some lines of insurance, the insurance company has the opportunity periodically to reevaluate its insureds. When the coverage in question is cancelable or optionally renewable,[5] the underwriting process may include postselection (or renewal) underwriting, in which the insurer decides whether the insurance should be continued.

When a review of the experience with a particular policy or account indicates that the losses have been excessive, the underwriter may insist on a higher deductible at renewal. In other instances, the underwriter may decide that the coverage should not be continued and will decline to renew it, or even cancel it outright. Insurance companies differ in the extent to which they exercise their renewal underwriting options. In some fields, such as auto insurance, some insurers are very selective and show little hesitation in re-

---

[5]Cancellation is the process of terminating coverage prior to the normal expiration date.

Tidbits, Vignettes, and Conundrums 7.1

Credit Scoring

For some time, insurance companies have used *credit scoring* as a tool for underwriting auto insurance. Credit scoring is an allegedly scientific means of determining a person's creditworthiness, based on statistical correlation between factors such as marital status, type of job, length of employment, amount of income, and past payment history and the record of credit payments by groups of individuals. Initially, it was used by lenders to judge the level of risk in extending credit to applicants for mortgages, car loans, and credit cards. It is now also used by insurance companies in underwriting automobile insurance. Critics argue that use of credit scoring for insurance underwriting decisions is totally inappropriate and that a person's credit history and driving are unrelated.

Despite the criticism, an increasing number of insurers are using credit scores in underwriting, sometimes weighting the credit score more heavily than the person's actual driving record. Applicants with a poor driving record may be rejected even if they have a high credit score, but exceptions are rarely made for persons with a clean driving record but a low credit score.

In 1997, the National Association of Insurance Commissioners issued a white paper, *Credit Reports and Insurance Underwriting,* which addresses some of the regulatory issues relating to unfair discrimination that may arise in the use of credit reports and credit scoring in insurance underwriting.

---

fusing to renew or in canceling an insured who has demonstrated unsatisfactory loss experience.

Restrictions on Postselection Underwriting

Because cancellation or the refusal of the insurer to renew some forms of insurance can work an undue hardship on the insured, many states have enacted statutes or have imposed regulations that restrict the insurer's right to exercise these options. Some of the laws merely require the insurer to give advance notice of its intent to refuse renewal. Other laws prohibit midterm cancellation, except for certain specified reasons, after the policy has been in effect for a designated period of time, such as 60 days. Finally, the laws of many states prohibit insurers from canceling or refusing to renew coverage because of an insured's age, sex, occupation, race, or place of residence. These laws require the insurer to furnish an explanation of the reason for cancellation or declination.

While the restrictions on the right of a company to cancel or refuse to renew have been beneficial in many areas, they have also made it harder to obtain insurance. When legislative restraints are imposed on the insurers' ability to engage in postselection underwriting, insurers typically become increasingly selective before issuing a policy in the first place.

Loss Adjustment

One basic purpose of insurance is to provide for the indemnification of those members of the group who suffer losses. This is accomplished in the loss-settlement process, but it is sometimes a great deal more complicated than just passing out money. The payment of losses that have occurred is the function of the claims department. Life insurance companies refer to employees who settle losses as claim representatives or benefit representatives. The nature of the difficulties frequently encountered in the property and liability field is evidenced by the fact that employees of the claims department in this field are called "adjusters."

Adjusters

Broadly speaking, an adjuster is an individual who investigates losses. He or she determines whether a loss is covered and if so, the amount of payment to be made. The *adjusters* used by a particular company may include insurance agents, staff adjusters, or independent adjusters. Agents frequently act as adjusters in the case of small property losses. Many agents have "draft authority," which means that they are authorized to issue company checks in payment of losses up to some stipulated amount. Even in cases where the amount of the loss exceeds the draft authority, the agent may handle the settlement of the loss.

Most insurers employ *staff adjusters* who are salaried representatives of the company. The use of a company staff adjuster in a given area is dictated by the amount of work available. In a locality where the company has a large volume of claims, it will use a staff adjuster. If the volume of claims is too small to support a full-time adjuster, the company will contract for adjusting service with an *independent adjuster,* a firm that offers its services to insurance companies and bills each company directly for the expense of adjustment.[6]

The *public adjuster* is quite different from the other types discussed. Unlike the other adjusters, all of whom represent the insurance company, the public adjuster represents the policyholder. A public adjuster is a specialist available to the insured who does not feel able to handle his or her own claim. The most common method of compensation for public adjusters is a contingency fee basis, under which the adjuster collects a percentage of the settlement; the usual fee is 10 percent of the amount recovered from the insurance company. In return for his fee, the public adjuster performs the actions normally required of the insured such as preparing estimates of the loss, presenting the amount of the claim to the insurance company, and negotiating the final settlement. A limited number of public adjusters hold one of two professional designations granted by the National Association of Public Insurance Adjusters. The Certified Professional Public Adjuster (CPPA) designation and the Senior Professional Public Adjuster (SPPA) designation are granted to public adjusters who pass a rigorous examination.

Courses of Action in Claim Settlement

It is obviously important that the insurance company pay its claims fairly and promptly, but it is equally important that the company resist unjust claims and avoid overpayment of losses. The view is rapidly increasing among insurers that prompt, courteous, and fair claim service is one of the most effective competitive tools available to a company.

There are two basic courses open to the company when confronted with a claim: pay or contest. In most cases there is little question concerning coverage, and payment of the loss is the most common procedure. In those instances where the company feels that a claim should not be paid, it will deny liability and thereby contest the claim. There are two grounds on which an insurer might deny payment: either because the

---

[6]At one time, insurance companies joined together to support *adjustment bureaus,* which they organized to settle fire losses, but which eventually came to handle other types of claims as well. The largest of these bureaus was the General Adjustment Bureau (GAB), organized in 1896. Following an investigation by the U.S. Department of Justice in 1970, the companies that owned the GAB agreed to divest themselves of their stock in the company. GAB now operates as an independent adjuster.

loss did not occur or because the policy does not cover the loss. A loss might not be covered under the policy because it does not fall within the scope of the insuring agreement, because it is excluded, because it happened when the policy was not in force, or because the insured has violated a policy condition.

It is inevitable that there will be disagreements regarding loss settlements. In some cases, the insured will mistakenly feel that a loss should have been covered under the policy when in fact it is not. Adjusters, being human, also err, and there are occasions when a legitimate claim is denied. In addition to the question of whether the loss is covered, the amount of the loss can be a source of disagreement. Value is often a matter of opinion, and we should therefore not be surprised that the insured and the adjuster may differ regarding the amount of the loss.

On the surface, it would appear that the insured is relatively powerless against the insurance company in the event of a dispute. This, however, is not the case. In those instances where the disagreement is over the amount of the loss, most policies provide for compulsory arbitration on the request of either party. In the case of a denial based on an alleged lack of coverage, the insured who feels unfairly treated may appeal to the state insurance commissioner, who is responsible for protecting consumers' interests. Finally, the insured has recourse through the courts. In some instances, the only alternative remaining to the insured is to bring suit against the company.

Miscellaneous Functions

In addition to those already discussed, there are various other functions necessary for the successful operation of an insurance company. Among these are the legal function, accounting, and engineering. The legal department and the accounting department perform functions similar to those provided by these departments in other industries. The legal department furnishes legal advice of a general corporate nature to the company. In addition, it counsels on such matters as policy forms, relations with agents, compliance of the company with state statutes, and the legality of agreements. It may or may not render assistance to the claims department in connection with claim settlements. Many companies have a separate legal staff as a part of the claims department, which is independent from the legal department.

The engineering department, which is unique to the property and liability insurers, is charged with the responsibility of inspecting premises to be insured to determine their acceptability and with assisting insureds with their loss control efforts. In addition, the engineering department benefits the company's insured by making loss-prevention recommendations.

Financial Aspects of Insurer Operations

Although the functions just described constitute the technical or "insurance" aspects of insurer operations, our discussion of insurer operations would not be complete without a brief mention of the financial aspects of insurer operations. These include the investment function, which accounts for most or all of the profits achieved by insurers, insurance company accounting, reinsurance, and the taxation of insurers.

The Investment Function

As a result of their operations, insurance companies accumulate large amounts of money for the payment of claims in the future. When these are added to the funds of the companies themselves, the assets total over $1.7 trillion. It would be a costly waste to permit these funds to remain idle, and it is the responsibility of the finance department or a finance committee of the company to see that they are properly invested. Because a portion of their invested funds must go to meet future claims, the primary requisite of insurance company investments is safety of principal. In addition, the return earned on investment is an important factor in rates. Life insurance companies assume some minimum rate of interest earning in their premium computations. Even where property and liability insurers are not required to include investment income explicitly in their rate calculations, the investment income that is earned subsidizes the underwriting experience and is therefore a factor in ratemaking in this field as well.

Life Insurance Company Investments

In the field of life insurance, the contracts are typically long term in nature. For this reason, life insurance companies put their funds primarily in long-term investments, with approximately two-thirds of their total assets invested in corporate bonds and mortgages. Common stocks account for less than 5 percent of the total investments of life insurers, and government bonds about 18 percent. The percentage composition of the investments of all life insurers is indicated in Table 7.1.

Property and Liability Insurer Investments

Unlike life insurance contracts, the obligations of property and liability companies are generally short term. Property and liability insurers hold about one-fifth of their invested assets in corporate stocks. About three-fourths of their investments are in bonds, of which approximately 75 percent consists of government and special revenue bonds. Investments in mortgages and real estate are insignificant. The composition of property and liability insurers' investments is also listed in Table 7.1.

Table 7.1 Percentage Composition of Insurer Investments

Type of Investment	Life Insurers	Property and Liability Insurers
Corporate stocks	31.10%	24.08%
Corporate bonds	38.70	19.56
Government bonds	11.99	39.78
Mortgages	7.38	0.22
Real estate	1.60	
Policy loans	3.22	
Miscellaneous	6.01	16.35
	100.00	100.00

Source: American Council of Life Insurance, *Insurance Fact Book* (Washington, DC: ACLI, 1999), and A. M. Best and Company, *Best's Aggregates and Averages* (Morristown, NJ: Best, annual).

Cash Flow Underwriting

It has been said—only half in jest—that property and liability insurers are not so much insurance companies as investment companies that raise the money for their investments by selling insurance. This observation was undoubtedly prompted by the size of the industry's investment portfolio and the importance of investment income in the overall operating profit of property and liability insurers. For the past three decades, property and liability insurers have about broken even or even lost money on underwriting, but investment income has provided an overall operating profit. The dependence on insurance premiums as funds for investment led to a phenomenon known as *cash flow underwriting.* As the term is generally understood, cash flow underwriting refers to the pricing practice aimed at maximizing written premium income rather than underwriting profit. In cash flow underwriting, insurers price their products below the amount needed to cover losses and expenses to compete for premium dollars that can be invested. The rationale is that the investment income earned on written premiums will more than offset any underwriting loss that may be incurred. Insurers compete for dollars that can be invested at a higher rate than the cost of those funds. An insurer with a combined ratio of, say, 106 percent is, in effect, paying the policyholders 6 percent for the use of their money. If those funds can be invested at some rate greater than 6 percent, the leveraged investment will increase the return to stockholders.

Insurance Company Accounting

The set of accounting procedures used by insurance companies is referred to as statutory accounting, because it is required by the statutes of the various states.[7] Basically, the statutory system is a combination of a cash and an accrual method and differs from generally accepted accounting principles (GAAP) in a number of ways. Because the principal emphasis in statutory accounting is on the ability of the insurer to fulfill its obligations under the contracts it issues, statutory accounting is, in most areas, ultraconservative. While all insurance companies are required to file financial statements using statutory accounting principles, some companies also have statements that use GAAP. GAAP statements are required by the SEC if the company is publicly traded.

The Equity Section of the Balance Sheet

The equity section of the balance sheet for any business consists of the excess of asset values over the liabilities of the firm. In the case of stock companies, it consists of the capital stock and surplus, which represent amounts paid in by stockholders

and any retained earnings of the company. Because there is no capital stock in mutual insurance companies, the total of the equity section of a mutual insurer is called surplus. In both stock and mutual companies, this is referred to as *policyholders' surplus*, indicating that this is the amount available, over and above the liabilities, to meet obligations to the company's policyholders.

Balance Sheet Assets

While most noninsurance companies recognize all assets, insurance companies recognize only those that are readily convertible into cash. These are called *admitted assets*. Assets such as supplies, furniture and fixtures, office machines and equipment, and premiums past due 90 days or more are *nonadmitted assets* and do not appear on the balance sheet. The elimination of these nonadmitted assets, whose liquidity is questionable, tends to understate the equity section of the balance sheet.

Statutory accounting also differs from GAAP in the valuation of certain assets. Stocks are carried at market value, as determined by the Security Valuation Office of the NAIC based on market values at the end of the year. Bonds not in default of interest or principal payments are carried at their amortized value. (Bonds in default are carried at market value.) Changes in the market value of stocks held by insurers directly influence the equity section of the balance sheet, while changes in the market value of bonds do not. Unrealized capital gains or losses on stocks under the statutory system are reported directly as changes in equity, but are not realized until the sale is made. Unrealized gains are usually not recognized under GAAP.

Balance Sheet Liabilities

The major liabilities of insurance companies are debts to policyholders and claimants called "reserves." In insurance accounting and insurance

---

[7]Statutory accounting is geared to the National Association of Insurance Commissioners (NAIC) Annual Statement Blank—a standardized reporting format developed by the NAIC by which each company must file an annual statement with the insurance department of its home state and with every other state in which it is licensed to do business. There are two versions of the Annual Statement Blank, one for property and liability insurers and one for life insurers. With minor exceptions, the required information and the manner in which it is to be submitted are the same for all states.

terminology generally, the term reserve is almost synonymous with "liability." The most important reserves of a property and liability insurer are the unearned premium reserve and loss reserves. In life insurance, the most important reserve is the policy reserve.

The Unearned Premium Reserve Insurers collect in advance for protection that will be provided over some period of future time. If the insurer were permitted to use premiums currently being collected for future protection to meet obligations on policies that were sold in the past, it would be perpetrating a fraud on current purchasers. The safest way in which the advance premium form of operation can be conducted is to require that insurance company financial statements specifically recognize the fact that the premiums being collected represent payment for coverage over a specified time in the future. In property and liability insurance, this is done in two ways. First, insurers are permitted to include premiums as income only as the premiums become earned—that is, only as the time for which protection is provided passes. In addition, the insurer is required to establish a deferred income account called the *unearned premium reserve* as a liability in the balance sheet. It represents the premiums that insureds have paid in advance for the unexpired terms of their outstanding policies and the amount that would be refunded in the event of cancellation. For each policy, the unearned premium reserve at the inception of the policy period is equal to the full premium that the insured has paid. During the policy period, the unearned premium reserve for that policy declines steadily to zero by a straight mathematical formula.

Unearned premium reserves also arise in life insurance, but here they are called policy reserves. During the early years of some life insurance policies, the insured premium is higher than necessary to cover mortality costs. The excess is retained as a policy reserve to offset higher mortality costs at advanced ages.

Loss Reserves. There is generally a delay between the time a loss occurs and the time when it is actually paid. In some lines of insurance, the delay may be substantial. Statutory accounting requires insurers to recognize their liability for losses that have occurred by establishing loss reserves. Statutory accounting makes a distinction between "incurred" losses and "paid" losses. Incurred losses refer to those losses actually taking place during the period under consideration, regardless of when they are actually paid. Paid losses refers to losses paid during a particular period without regard to the time that the loss actually occurred. Recognition of the difference between paid and incurred losses is made through liability accounts called "loss" or "claim" reserves.

There are two major classes of loss reserves: a reserve for losses reported but not yet paid and a reserve for incurred but not reported (IBNR) losses. Reserves for losses reported but not yet paid can be established by an examination of each claim and an estimate of its ultimate cost. The reserve for IBNR losses is usually estimated on the basis of the past experience of the insurer. Loss reserves are not significant in life insurance.

Statutory Underwriting Profit or Loss

As noted, an insurer is allowed to count premiums as income only as the time for which protection has been provided passes. Most expenses, on the other hand, must be paid when the policy is written. Because insurers are required to establish unearned premium reserve without a deduction for expenses incurred, there is a mismatching of revenues and expenses that creates distortions in the indicated underwriting results. A property and liability insurer appears less profitable than is actually the case when premiums are increasing and more profitable than it is during periods of declining business.

Theoretically, if an insurer's premium volume were stable, the understatement of profit for the current year would be offset by an overstatement of profit in subsequent years. As a practical matter, however, premiums written are rarely stable. When premiums are increasing, the increase in the unearned premium reserve (which includes an allowance for expenses that have already been paid) is greater than necessary to cover anticipated losses. This excess is called the "redundancy" in the unearned premium reserve. As premiums are earned, the excess reserve will be released, and a part of it, representing prepaid expenses, will not be needed to pay losses and will indicate a statutory underwriting gain. Persons familiar with the property and liability insurance industry are aware of the distortions in the figures on operations indicated by statutory accounting conventions and make allowances for these distortions.

The surplus of a life insurance company is subject to a drain during periods of increasing sales similar to that of a property and liability insurer. Life insurance companies pay very high first-year commissions, sometimes more than 100 percent of the first-year premium. As a result, the sale of a new policy generally results in a reduction in surplus. Unlike the problem in the property and liability field, state statutes have recognized this problem and permit life insurers to compensate for high first-year policy expenses through a modified reserving system. Under these modified reserving systems, the insurer is permitted to compensate for some of the initial expenses associated with the policy by deferring the establishment of the first-year reserve, thereby freeing the bulk of the initial premium for the payment of expenses.

Investment Results

Investment income is shown separately from the results of underwriting in the insurer's Summary of Operations. The investment income of a property and liability insurer is composed basically of interest on bonds, dividends on stocks, and interest on collateral loans and bank deposits. It also includes realized capital gains and losses. Statutory investment income does not include unrealized capital gains or losses, which are recorded as direct changes in the insurer's balance sheet.

Reinsurance

Reinsurance is a device whereby an insurance company may avoid the catastrophe hazard in the operation of the insurance mechanism. As the term indicates, reinsurance is insurance for insurers. It is based on the same principles of sharing and transfer as insurance itself. In a reinsurance transaction the insurer seeking reinsurance is known as the "direct writer" or the ceding company, while the company assuming part of the risk is known simply as the "reinsurer." That portion of a risk that the direct writer retains is called the "net line" or the net retention. The act of transferring a part of the risk to the reinsurance company is called "ceding," and that portion of the risk passed on to the reinsurer is called the "cession."

Reinsurance had a very simple beginning. When a risk that was too large for the company to handle safely was presented to an insurer, it began to shop around for another insurance company that was willing to take a portion of the risk in return for a portion of the premium. A few current reinsurance operations are still conducted in this manner, but the ever-present danger that a devastating loss might occur before the reinsurance becomes effective led to the development of modern reinsurance treaties. Reinsurance may provide protection against a comparatively large single loss or a large number of small losses caused by a single occurrence.

Types of Reinsurance Treaties

There are two types of reinsurance treaties: facultative and automatic. Under a facultative treaty, each risk is submitted by the direct writer to the reinsurer for acceptance or rejection. Although the terms under which reinsurance will take place are spelled out, the direct writer is not obliged to submit a risk to the reinsurer and the reinsurer may accept or reject risks that are submitted. Until the risk has been submitted and accepted, the direct writer carries the entire risk. Under the terms of an automatic treaty, the reinsurer agrees—in advance—to accept a portion of certain risks that meet the reinsurance underwriting rules of the reinsurer. The direct writer is obligated to cede a portion of the risk to which the automatic treaty applies.

Reinsurance in Property and Liability Insurance

There are two essential ways in which risk is shared under reinsurance agreements in the field of property and liability insurance. The reinsurance agreement may require the reinsurer to share in every loss that occurs to a reinsured risk, or it may require the reinsurer to pay only after a loss reaches a certain size. The first arrangement is called *proportional reinsurance* and includes *quota share* and *surplus line* reinsurance. The second approach is called *excess loss reinsurance*. In the case of proportional reinsurance, the direct writer pays the reinsurer a proportionate share of the premium (less an allowance for expenses) based on the percentage of the risk the reinsurer assumes. The reinsurer then becomes responsible for a portion of the unearned premium reserve and the payment of losses based on the division of the risk between the parties. In excess reinsurance, the direct writer, in effect, purchases insurance with a high deductible. The premium for excess loss reinsurance is a small fraction of the direct writer's premium.

Another method of reinsurance is pooling. Under one pooling arrangement, each member assumes a percentage of every risk written by a member of the pool. This pooling arrangement is a form of proportional reinsurance. On the other hand, the pool may share only in large losses, as is the case with the Workers' Compensation Reinsurance Bureau. After a member of the pool has suffered a loss in excess of a specified amount (e.g., $100,000 as a result of one disaster), the other members of the pool share the remainder of the loss.

Reinsurance in Life Insurance

In the field of life insurance, reinsurance may take one of two forms: the term insurance approach and the coinsurance approach. Under the term insurance approach, the direct writer purchases yearly renewable term insurance equal to the difference between the face value of the policy and the reserve, which is the amount at risk for the company. The coinsurance approach to reinsurance in life insurance is similar to the quota share approach in property and liability insurance; the ceding company transfers some portion of the face amount of the policy to the reinsurer, and the reinsurer becomes liable for its proportional share of the death claim. In addition, the reinsurer becomes responsible for maintaining the policy reserve on its share of the policy.

Functions of Reinsurance

Reinsurance actually serves two important purposes. The first, which is fairly obvious, is the spreading of risk. Insurance companies are able to avoid catastrophe losses by passing on a portion of any risk too large to handle. In addition, through excess-loss reinsurance arrangements, a company may protect itself against a single occurrence of catastrophic scope. Smaller companies are permitted to insure exposures they could not otherwise handle within the bounds of safety.

The second function reinsurance performs is not as immediately obvious: it is a financial function. As we have seen, when the premium volume of an insurer is expanding, the result will be a drain on surplus. With an expanding premium volume, the insurer's surplus is reduced and its ability to write new business can be restricted. In the absence of some other alternative, a company could expand only to a certain point and would then be required to stop and wait for the premiums to become earned, freeing surplus.

Reinsurance provides a solution to this dilemma. When an insurer reinsures a portion of the business it has written using proportional reinsurance, it pays a part of the premium to the reinsurer. The reinsurer then establishes the unearned premium reserves or policy reserves required, and the direct writer is relieved of the obligation to maintain such reserves. In this way, excess capacity of one insurer may be transferred to another insurer through reinsurance.

The Catastrophe Risk Exchange (CATEX)

The Catastrophe Risk Exchange, Inc. (CATEX) is a computer-based electronic market for the exchange of insurance risks by insurance companies and reinsurers that was founded in 1995. CATEX does not function in any way as a risk-bearer and does not represent any of the parties to an exchange. It limits its activities to organizing and operating the mechanism for the efficient exchange of risks. This is accomplished through a highly secure electronic system on which participants can advertise risks they want to exchange with other parties who have risks in different geographic locations. A typical swap, for example, could involve several units of Florida windstorm exposures for California earthquake exposures. Although CATEX has been in existence for a short time, the operation has been highly successful.

Risk Financing Alternatives to Reinsurance

Our discussion of insurance company financial operations would not be complete without at least a brief mention of one of the most recent developments in insurance finance. This is the *securitization of insurable risk* through *insurance derivatives*. Derivatives are financial instruments that embody futures or options in security, commodity, and financial markets. They have a price that is derived (hence the name) from the value of commodity prices, interest rates, stock market prices, foreign exchange rates, and now insurance indexes.

Like reinsurance, insurance derivatives are designed to transfer a part of an insurer's underwriting risk to another party. Derivatives differ from reinsurance as an approach to risk financing in their function of securitizing insurance risk—that is, in linking it to securities. Instead of transferring specific portfolios of risks, insurers make what, in a sense, is a side bet with another party—an investor or speculator—on whether a catastrophe loss will occur. These side bets take the form of securities traded in a market or, in some cases, private placements. The securitization of insurable risk through derivatives involves two types of instruments: catastrophe insurance options traded on the Chicago Board of Trade (and more recently, at the Bermuda Commodities Exchange), and the private placement of *catastrophe bonds.*

Catastrophe Futures and Options

Since 1995, the Chicago Board of Trade (CBOT) has offered a market in catastrophe insurance *options* known as PCS options (because they are based on a benchmark of catastrophe loss estimates, provided by the firm *Property Claim Services*). The value of a catastrophe insurance option is directly linked to the industry's losses from natural disasters in a particular area over a specified period of time. The greater the losses, the higher will be the value of the cash settlement if the option is exercised. By acquiring call options—the right to buy futures contracts whose price is pegged to disaster losses—an insurer can earn a trading profit and thereby arrange a source of funds to pay claims for catastrophe losses. By taking the other side of the trade, investors can collect a favorable return during periods of favorable loss experience.

If this sounds like a win-lose situation, that is because it is. Like stock index futures, catastrophe insurance options are a zero-sum game. For every winner, there is a loser. When an insurer buys an insurance future in anticipation of increasing losses, the other half of the contract is filled by a speculator who is betting against the occurrence of a catastrophe. Although the volume of trades on the CBOT remains modest, it is growing.[8]

Catastrophe Bonds

Catastrophe bonds (known as *cat bonds* and sometimes as *act of God bonds*) are issued by an insurance company with the repayment terms linked to the company's losses from disasters, or acts of God. A loss exceeding a certain size automatically produces changes in the bonds' structure designed to protect the issuing insurer's capital base. Typically, some or all of the principal is forgiven or subject to deferred payment if the issuing insurer suffers a disaster of above a specified amount.

As in the case of futures options, investors who purchase cat bonds are speculating that during a particular period, a catastrophe loss will not affect the regions covered by the bonds. If good weather prevails during the bond period, the investor wins. If a disaster strikes, he or she loses. Again, it is the willingness of the speculator to make a "side bet" that is the essential requirement for cat bonds.

The future of insurance derivatives remains to be seen. Although Illinois, New York, and California have approved the use of futures by insurers licensed in those states, most states have not addressed the regulatory issues related to catastrophe insurance options or catastrophe bonds. Given its long history, reinsurance is well understood from a regulatory, legal, and accounting basis, while insurance derivatives are new and untested. Equally important, based on the transactions that have been made thus far, there do not seem to be any particular economies in derivatives compared with traditional reinsurance.

---

[8]In 1997, a second exchange began trading insurance futures contracts and options, the Bermuda Commodities Exchange, which was incorporated in 1996.

Taxation of Insurance Companies

Insurance companies, like all business corporations, are subject to federal, state, and local taxes. At the federal level, insurers are subject to the federal income tax. At the state level, they pay property taxes like other businesses and, in addition, are liable for a number of special taxes levied on insurers, the most important of which is the premium tax.

State Premium Tax

Taxation of insurance companies by the states grew out of the states' need for revenue and a desire to protect domestic insurers by a tariff on out-of-state companies. As time went by, most states came to levy the premium tax on the premium income of both domestic and foreign insurers. Currently, every state imposes a premium tax on insurers operating within its borders. In essence, this tax is a sales tax on the premiums for all policies sold by an insurer within the state. The amount of the tax varies among the states; the maximum in any state is 4 percent, with the most typical amount being 2 percent. The tax paid by the insurer is, of course, added to the cost of the insurance contract and is passed on to the policyholder. Most states tax all companies alike, but some states still apply the tax only to out-of-state companies, or they tax domestic companies at a preferential rate.[9]

---

[9]Most states have reciprocal or retaliatory premium tax laws. Under a retaliatory law, the state imposes the same tax on the admitted companies of another state as that state imposes on the companies of the initial state doing business in the foreign state. For example, if Iowa taxes all companies doing business within its borders at the rate of 2 percent and Illinois taxes the companies organized in Iowa at the rate of 3 percent, companies from Illinois that are admitted to Iowa would be taxed 3 percent.

Federal Income Taxes

For the purpose of taxation under the *Internal Revenue Code*, insurance companies are classified into three categories: life insurance companies, nonlife mutual insurance companies, and insurance companies other than life or mutual. In general, all three classes are subject to the same tax rates as are other corporations. However, they differ from other corporations, and from each other,

in the manner in which taxable income is determined. These differences reflect the prepayment of expenses by insurers and the manner in which loss reserves are calculated.

Although the preceding discussion of insurer functions and insurer finance provides only a cursory treatment of these subjects, understanding even these general notions of the ways in which insurers operate will make the material in the following chapters easier to understand.

Important Concepts to Remember

rate	loss reserves	statutory profit (loss)
premium	combined ratio	policy reserves
gross rate	class rating	Medical Information Bureau (MIB)
loading	individual rating	staff adjuster
pure premium	judgment rating	independent adjuster
expected loss ratio	schedule rating	public adjuster
loss ratio	experience rating	Annual Statement Blank
expense ratio	retrospective rating	statutory accounting
nonadmitted assets	special agent	admitted assets
incurred losses	unearned premium reserves	reinsurance
paid losses	policyholders' surplus	premium tax

Questions for Review

1. List and briefly explain the steps in the underwriting process.

2. Sales representatives of property and liability insurance companies sometimes refer to the "sales prevention department." What department of the company are they referring to? Explain.

3. List and briefly explain the steps in the loss-adjustment process.

4. List several reasons for which a claim might be completely denied.

5. Name the various types of adjusters used by property and liability insurers.

6. What characteristics of the insurance business make reserves necessary?

7. Define the unearned premium reserve and briefly explain how it is calculated. Why is the unearned premium reserve often referred to as the "reinsurance reserve?"

8. The XYZ Insurance Company had an unearned premium reserve of $20 million at the end of 1999. During 2000 it wrote $25 million in annual premiums. At the end of 2000, its unearned premium reserve was $23 million. What were earned premiums during 2000?

9. The XYZ Insurance Company had loss reserves of $7 million at the end of 1999. During 2000, it paid $7 million in losses, and had loss reserves in the amount of $6 million at the end of 2000. What were the incurred losses for 2000?

10. Give two specific reasons for reinsurance. Distinguish between "facultative" and "treaty" reinsurance.

Questions for Discussion

1. Do you agree with legislation imposing restrictions on the right of an insurance company to engage in postselection underwriting?

2. At one time it was suggested that the problem of providing insurance protection against loss by flood be met by providing coverage against the flood peril as a mandatory part of the Standard Fire Policy. Do you agree with this solution? Why or why not?

3. "Pricing is much more difficult in insurance than in other business fields, because the cost of production is not known until after the product has been delivered." To what extent is this statement true and to what extent false?

4. The primary emphasis in statutory accounting is supposedly on financial conservatism.

However, some statutory techniques violate this principle. Discuss three ways in which statutory accounting is ultraconservative, and two areas where the principle of conservatism is violated.

5. In 1999, an Illinois jury awarded $1.2 billion to plaintiffs in a class action suit against State Farm, the nation's largest insurer, for their use of competitive or non-OEM parts (i.e., auto parts that were not manufactured by the original automobile manufacturer). Almost immediately, a class action suit was instituted against seven more of the nation's top insurers by the same attorneys and in the same state. Had you been a member of the jury, how would you have voted in this case?

Suggestions for Additional Reading

Black, Kenneth, Jr., and Harold D. Skipper, Jr. *Life Insurance*, 13th ed. Englewood Cliffs, NJ: Prentice Hall, 1994. Chapters 23–25, 32–33.

Gart, Alan, and David J. Nye. *Insurance Company Finance and Investments*, 3rd ed. Malvern, PA: Insurance Institute of America, 1994.

Huebner, S. S., Kenneth Black, Jr., and Bernard L. Webb. *Property and Liability Insurance*, 4th ed. Englewood Cliffs, NJ: Prentice Hall, 1995. Chapters 36–38.

Launie, J. J., J. Finley Lee, and Norman A. Baglini. *Principles of Property and Liability Underwriting*, 3rd ed. Malvern, Pa: Insurance Institute of America, 1986.

Markham, James J., ed. *Property Loss Adjusting*, Vols. I and II. Malvern, PA: Insurance Institute of America, 1990.

Mooney, Sean, and Larry Cohen. *Basic Concepts of Accounting and Taxation of Property/Casualty Insurance Companies*. New York: Insurance Information Institute, 1995.

Reinarz, Robert C., Janice O. Schloss, Gary S. Patrik, and Peter R. Kensicki. *Reinsurance Practices*, Vols. I and II. Malvern, PA: Insurance Institute of America, 1990.

Troxel, Terrie E., and George E. Bouchie. *Property-Liability Insurance Accounting and Finance*, 3rd ed. Malvern, PA: American Institute for Property and Liability Underwriters, 1990.

Webb, Bernard L., Howard N. Anderson, John A. Cookman, and Peter R. Kensicki. *Principles of Reinsurance*, Vols. I and II. Malvern, PA: Insurance Institute of America, 1990.

Zolkos, Rodd. "Catastrophe Bonds Take Risk Financing by Storm," *Business Insurance* (December 22, 1997), p. 18.

Websites to Explore

Bermuda Commodities Exchange: http://www.bcoe.bm/

Casualty Actuarial Society: http://www.casact.org

CATEX: http://www.catex.com/

Chicago Board of Trade: http://CBOT.com

Claims magazine: http://www.claimsmag.com/

Hedge Financial Products: http://www.hedgefin.com/

Independent Reinsurance Underwriters Association, Inc.: http://www.captive.com

Insurance Accounting and Systems Association: http://www.connectyou.com/ins/index.htm

Insurance Services Office, Inc.: http://www.iso.com

Medical Information Bureau: http://www.mib.com/

National Association of Public Insurance Adjusters: http://www.napia.com/

National Underwriter Company: http://www.nuco.com/

Property Loss Research Bureau: http://homepage.interaccess.com/~plrb/

Reinsurance Association of America: http://www.raanet.org

Society of Actuaries: http://www.soa.org/

CHAPTER 8

Regulation of the Insurance Industry

The safety of the people shall be the highest law.
—Cicero

CHAPTER OBJECTIVES

When you have finished this chapter, you should be able to

- Identify and explain the reasons that insurance is subject to regulation

- Identify the major areas of insurer operations that are regulated

- Trace the history of insurance regulation and identify the landmark cases and laws that led to the current regulatory environment

- Identify and explain the statutory requirements that exist with respect to insurance rates

- Describe the different approaches the states have taken toward the regulation of insurance rates

- Identify the arguments favoring state or federal regulation of insurance

The Why of Government Regulation of Insurance

Before turning to the subject of the manner in which the insurance industry is regulated, it is appropriate that we examine the rationale for that regulation. Many of the original reasons for the regulation of the insurance industry are now being challenged, and new regulatory goals are being proposed. For the discussion that follows, it will be helpful if the reader is familiar with the reasons for regulation generally, which is the basis for insurance regulation.

The Why of Regulation Generally

As a starting point, it should be made clear that there are important differences of opinion among economists on the subject of government regulation, and much of the controversy concerning insurance regulation reflects these differences. While there is little disagreement in principle on the need for some form of government control of business, there is serious disagreement on the form that this control should take.

Some economists believe in an efficient market and maintain that competition will generally produce the greatest benefits to society. While economists of this school agree that some form of government control is necessary, they would like the principal role of government to be that of maintaining competition. Other economists distrust the market, or at least have less confidence in its operation. They believe the lesson of history to be that regulation is often needed to prevent abuse of consumers and that regulations should be imposed wherever there is a likelihood of market failure. A market failure occurs when the "market" cannot, for some reason, produce the benefits that are usually associated with competition.

Approaches to Government Control of Business

Broadly speaking, government control of business takes one of two forms, paralleling the two economic philosophies just noted: antitrust and regulation. Antitrust concentrates on maintaining competition, while regulation involves the application of specific performance standards to the firms in an industry. The principal thrust of antitrust is to curtail monopoly power. It focuses on preventing collusion, opposing mergers that lead to excessive concentration, and abating market power. The theory of antitrust is that if the government prevents monopoly and unfair competition, competition will result in the public welfare.

Regulation, in contrast to antitrust, represents a more direct involvement of government in the affairs of business. It usually consists of two types of actions by government: restricting entry into the market (usually because competition is thought to be infeasible, but sometimes on other grounds) and controlling prices to guarantee that the firms in an industry do not obtain excessive profits. Regulation is adopted as an alternative to antitrust in those instances in which competition is considered infeasible or in the case of industries that, because of monopolistic tendencies, must be subject to control. Natural monopolies, for example, are licensed and their pricing decisions controlled to protect the consumer from exploitation. Cartelized industries are regulated for the same reasons. Here, regulation is required because of a lack of competition, and it seeks to generate results similar to those that would exist in a competitive industry. Regulation may also be deemed necessary when there is a tendency toward destructive competition. Still another reason is a lack of safety or security for consumers in financial markets or industries of a fiduciary nature. The role of regulation, then, is to restrict the actions of firms in an industry, forcing them to behave in a way that will produce results as near as possible to those that would occur in a competitive market.

Rationale for Regulation of the Insurance Industry

In insurance, the problem of monopoly is not significant, but there are still reasons for government restraint. The rationale for regulation of insurance differs from that of monopolized or cartelized industries because the potential "market failures" are also different. The first of the potential market failures in insurance stems from the fiduciary nature of insurer operations; the second stems from the uncertainties inherent in the insurance-pricing process.

Vested in the Public Interest Rationale

The first rationale for the regulation of insurance is that it is an industry that is vested in the public interest. The courts have long held that insurance, like banking, is pervasive in its influence and that failures in this field can affect persons other than those directly involved in the transaction.[1] Individuals purchase insurance to protect themselves against financial loss at a later time, and it is important to the public welfare that the insurer promising to indemnify insureds for future losses fulfill its promises.

Classical economists held that competition serves the consumer by forcing inefficient firms out of the market. Contrary to this classical model, which held that the failure of some firms from time to time was a wholesome phenomenon, the public interest is not served by the failure of insurers, because of the resulting losses to policyholders and claimants. The "vested in the public interest" rationale for regulation of the insurance industry holds that the insurance industry, like any other business holding vast sums of money in trust for the public, should be subject to government regulation because of its fiduciary nature.

Although the public interest rationale has a relationship to the area of pricing and competition, its implications are much broader. It implies a need for regulation of insurance in many areas, of which pricing is only one. The fiduciary nature of insurer operations and the extensive influence of insurance on members of society require regulation of entry into the market (i.e., the licensing of companies), the investment practices of insurers, and similar areas related to insurer solvency. In addition, the complexity of the insurance product requires regulatory scrutiny of contracts and the licensing of practitioners to insure their competence. All this means that because insurance is "vested in the public interest," the industry would require regulation even if it were not for the second rationale for regulation, discussed next.

Destructive Competition Rationale

The second rationale for the regulation of insurance (currently being challenged by some parties) is that competition in some fields of insurance, if left unregulated, could become excessive. While regulation in many other industries aims at enforcing competition and preventing artificially high prices, insurance regulation was designed—at least initially—for the opposite reason: to prevent excessive competition and inadequate prices. It was argued that in the absence of regulation, the natural tendency in the insurance industry would be toward the keenest sort of cutthroat competition. There is considerable disagreement on this point, and many question the validity of the argument. Nevertheless, those who argue that insurance regulation must be aimed at preventing too much competition maintain that the basic danger in the insurance industry is the possibility that in vying for business, companies may underestimate future losses and, as a result, fail.

Goals of Insurance Regulation

Originally, the goals of insurance regulation were clearly understood and generally agreed upon by all concerned. The function of insurance regulation was to promote the welfare of the public by ensuring fair contracts at fair prices from financially strong companies. The "market failures" that insurance regulation was intended to correct were insolvencies (no matter what their source) and unfair treatment of insureds by insurers. In short, the dual goals of regulation were solvency and equity.[2]

---

[1]The U.S. Supreme Court ruled that insurance is a business "affected with the public interest" in 1914. See *German Alliance Insurance Company v. Lewis,* 233 U.S. 380 (1914).

[2]These goals were articulated by Professor Spencer L. Kimball, who referred to them as the principles of "solidity" and *aequum et bonum.* See Spencer L. Kimball, *Essays in Insurance Regulation* (Ann Arbor, MI: The Author, 1966), pp. 3–10.

Although the original goals still dominate the regulatory philosophy, new goals—still emerging—focus on the availability and affordability of insurance. Public dissatisfaction with the increasing cost of insurance, the inability of some consumers to obtain insurance at a price they are willing and able to pay, and a growing philosophy of entitlement have created pressure from some quarters for regulatory programs designed to guarantee the availability of insurance to all who desire it at affordable rates. Increasingly, those who cannot obtain insurance at a price they feel they can afford are demanding a subsidy from the rest of society. The traditional approach to this subsidy has been a residual risk pool, such as the Automobile Insurance Plans, the FAIR plans, and the medical malpractice insurance pools. Here, insurers are compelled to write coverages at rates below those that would be required to cover losses and expenses. The losses sustained are passed on to other insureds as higher premiums. More recently, the availability–affordability demands have focused on a new issue: the manner in which insurance rates should be determined and the extent to which each insured's costs should reflect the hazards he or she brings to the pool of insured persons.[3]

A Brief History of Insurance Regulation

The earliest forms of insurance regulation related to the premium taxes imposed by the states on out-of-state insurers and grew out of the registration and reporting requirements imposed for the purpose of determining insurers' tax liabilities. Although statutes dealing with insurance had been enacted by the states as early as the beginning of the nineteenth century, the history of modern insurance regulation begins shortly before the Civil War, when several states established bodies to supervise insurance operations within their borders. The New Hampshire Board of Insurance Commissioners, established in 1851, was the first of these bodies. Massachusetts followed shortly thereafter, and New York created its board in 1859.

Paul v. Virginia

The case of *Paul v. Virginia* focused on the preeminence of the right of the states or federal government to regulate insurance. The U.S. Constitution gives the federal government the right to regulate interstate commerce, and the issue in *Paul v. Virginia* was whether insurance is interstate commerce. Samuel Paul was a native of Virginia who represented New York insurance companies in his home state. Paul challenged the right of the state to regulate insurance by selling policies without obtaining a state license. The state denied Paul a license, because his insurer would not comply with the demand of the state of Virginia for a security deposit. Likewise, a license for the insurer was denied on the same grounds. When Paul continued to sell insurance without a license, he was arrested and fined $50. The case was carried to the U.S. Supreme Court, where it was finally decided in 1869. In its decision, the Supreme Court ruled that insurance was not interstate commerce.[4] The decision of the U.S. Supreme Court that insurance was not interstate commerce and, therefore, was not subject to regulation by the federal government stood for 75 years.

Regulation from 1869 to 1944

During the 75 years following the *Paul v. Virginia* decision, the insurance industry was regulated by

---

[3]The issues in the availability/affordability debate are discussed in the chapter appendix.

[4]*Paul v. Virginia,* 231 U.S. 495 (1869).

the individual states. This was a period of rapid development and expansion for the entire economy, and the insurance industry was no exception. The quality of regulation varied from state to state, and it was inevitable that abuses would creep into the operation of the insurance business. In the period following the Civil War, for example, many life insurance companies were operated in a precarious manner. Unsound business practices were common, and advertising claims were greatly inflated. During a depression in the 1870s, many of these poorly managed firms failed.

Shortly after the turn of the century, big business was being condemned and investigated, and the rapid growth of the life insurance industry plus these abuses attracted attention. In 1905, the New York State legislature appointed a committee to investigate the abuses in the life insurance industry. The committee was named after its chairman, Senator William W. Armstrong. The Armstrong Investigation identified many abuses, and legislation was enacted in New York to correct these abuses.

In 1910, a second committee was appointed in New York, this time to investigate the property insurance industry. Like the Armstrong Committee, the Merritt Committee Investigation proved to be a significant event in the development of the industry. Although they were state inquiries, the fact that many states patterned their laws after those of New York State made their effect pervasive.

South-Eastern Underwriters Association Case

After a period of 75 years, another test of the authority of the federal government to regulate insurance was made. In 1942, the attorney general of the United States filed a brief under the Sherman Act against the South-Eastern Underwriters Association (SEUA), a cooperative rating bureau, alleging that the bureau constituted a combination in restraint of trade. In its decision of the SEUA case in 1944, the Supreme Court reversed its decision of *Paul v. Virginia*, stating that insurance is interstate commerce and, as such, is subject to regulation by the federal government.[5] This decision stands today.

Public Law 15

While the SEUA case was being decided and appealed, the insurance industry viewed with considerable alarm the prospect that the court might overturn *Paul v. Virginia*. The insurance industry arranged to have bills introduced into Congress that would have exempted it from the federal antitrust laws, but these bills were all defeated. Finally, the National Association of Insurance Commissioners drafted a law that could be passed. This was *Public Law 15*, or the *McCarran–Ferguson Act*, which became law on March 9, 1945.

In the *McCarran–Ferguson Act*, Congress reaffirmed the right of the federal government to regulate insurance, but agreed that it would not exercise this right as long as the industry was adequately regulated by the states. The law declared a moratorium on the regulation of insurance by the federal government, stating that the federal government would not regulate the industry until January 1, 1948, when the federal antitrust laws would be "applicable to the business of insurance to the extent that such business is not regulated by the states." In effect, the law explicitly grants to the states the power to regulate the insurance business—a power that the Supreme Court in the SEUA case had concluded was vested in Congress under the Commerce Clause of the Constitution. The exemption from federal law was not complete, however. The act provided that the Sherman Act would continue to apply to boycott, coercion, or intimidation.

Following enactment of *Public Law 15*, the states moved to put their regulatory houses in order, passing rating laws, defining unfair trade practices, and extending licensing and solvency requirements.

---

[5] *United States v. South-Eastern Underwriters Association*, 322 U.S. 533 (1944).

Regulation Today

Insurance is presently regulated by the several states through the three basic branches of our state governments: legislative, judicial, and executive.

Regulation by the Legislative Branch

Each state enacts laws that govern the conduct of the insurance industry within its boundaries. These laws spell out the requirements that must be met by persons wishing to organize a domestic insurance company in the state and also define the standards that foreign insurers must meet to obtain a license to do business in the state. In addition, the insurance code sets forth the standards of solvency that are to be enforced and provides for the regulation of rates and investments. It also provides for the licensing of agents.

Regulation by the Judicial Branch

The judicial branch exercises control over the insurance industry through the courts by rendering decisions on the meaning of policy terms and ruling on the constitutionality of the state insurance laws and the actions of those administering the law.

Regulation by the Executive Branch: The Commissioner of Insurance

The central figure in the regulation of the insurance industry in each state is the commissioner of insurance.[6] In most states this official is appointed by the governor of the state and is

charged with the administration of the insurance laws and the general supervision of the business. Although a part of the executive branch of the state government, the commissioner frequently makes rulings that have the binding force of law and exercises judicial power in interpreting and enforcing the insurance code.

National Association of Insurance Commissioners

The National Association of Insurance Commissioners (NAIC) has been an active force in the regulation of insurance since it was founded in 1871. Although it has no legal power over insurance regulation, it is an important force. Through it, the 50 state commissioners exchange information and ideas and coordinate regulatory activities. Based on the information exchanged at its four annual meetings, the NAIC makes recommendations for legislation and policy. The individual commissioners are free to accept or reject these recommendations, but in the past most commissioners have seen fit to accept the recommendations appropriate for their particular states.

Areas Regulated

It is common to distinguish between two broad, but interrelated, areas of insurance regulation: solvency regulation and market regulation.

Solvency Regulation

Clearly, a primary focus of insurance regulation is on insurer solvency. Indeed, it has been argued that this should be the primary function of regulation. Regulatory interest in insurer solvency is concerned with the early detection of potential insolvencies and prevention of consumer suffering when insolvencies occur.

---

[6]Although the title "commissioner of insurance" is the most common, in some states the chief insurance regulator is referred to as the "director of insurance" or the "superintendent of insurance."

Licensing of Companies

The power to license insurance companies allows the insurance department to control the formation of new companies. It also permits the state to control which companies will be allowed to do business in the state. In effect, when a company is licensed, the commissioner certifies the company with regard to its financial stability and soundness of methods of operation. Before licensing a firm to conduct business in the state, the commissioner must be satisfied that the company to be licensed meets the capital and surplus requirements specified in the insurance code of the state. These requirements vary from state to state, and depend on the type of business the insurer will conduct and whether the company is a stock or mutual insurer.

In the 1990s, the NAIC developed risk-based capital (RBC) standards for life insurers (1992), property-liability insurers (1993), and health insurers (1997). The NAIC's RBC models have been adopted widely across the country. Under the RBC standards, the amount of capital required for an insurer varies, based on the specific risks facing the insurer, including risks associated with underwriting, the insurer's investment portfolio, and other risks not reflected by these factors.

Besides the capital and surplus requirement, the commissioner normally reviews the personal characteristics of the organizers, promoters, and incorporators of the company to determine their competence and experience. The commissioner may deny the application for a license if the company's founders seem unworthy of public trust.

Reporting and Financial Analysis

It has long been recognized that the key to protecting policyholders from insurer insolvencies lies in detecting potential failures before they occur. Insurance regulators rely on analysis of various insurer reports and financial examinations to detect potentially troubled companies.

Insurers are subject to significant regulatory reporting requirements. The insurance code requires every licensed insurer to submit annual and quarterly reports to the commissioner of insurance. These reports include information about the assets and liabilities of the company; its investments; its income, loss payments, and expenses; and any other information desired by the commissioner. Actuaries must sign opinions attesting to the adequacy of reserves. Insurers must calculate and report their risk-based capital requirements annually. All of this information, along with other publicly available information about the company, is analyzed by state insurance departments on an ongoing basis.

The NAIC serves an important role in the financial analysis process. It maintains a database of financial information filed by insurers and automated tools to assist with financial analysis. In 1974, the NAIC adopted the Insurance Regulatory Information System (IRIS) to assist regulators in identifying potentially troubled insurers. Under IRIS, an insurer's performance on a series of financial tests is examined. Deviations from expected norms are taken as an indication that closer scrutiny of the insurer is needed. Currently, IRIS consists of 11 tests for property-liability insurers and 12 tests for life and health insurers. In the early 1990s, IRIS was expanded and enhanced to create the Financial Analysis Solvency Tracking System (FAST). Under FAST, a score is assigned to each company, based on its performance on a series of ratios and other financial indicators. The specific financial tests used and the company scores are kept confidential by the NAIC. Today, FAST is widely used by state regulators when prioritizing companies for further review. In addition to the many tools made available to states, the NAIC has created the Financial Analysis Division (FAD) to monitor the financial performance of "nationally significant companies." This Division reports potential problems to the Financial Analysis Working Group of the NAIC, which coordinates with the commissioner in the company's state of domicile to resolve concerns.

Examination of Companies

In addition to the annual report, a periodic inspection of each company conducting business in the state is made by the commissioner's office. The insurance commissioner may examine or inquire into the affairs of any company transacting business in the state at any time, but the insurance code normally requires a comprehensive examination at least once every three to five years. It is a detailed procedure, often lasting an extended period, during which the examiners scrutinize every aspect of the firm's operation. Targeted exams may be done more frequently and focus on a particular area of concern.

To eliminate duplication of effort, the insurance department of each state takes responsibility for examining those companies that are domiciled in the state. The state calling the exam invites participation from the other zones in which the company does business. (The NAIC is divided into four zones.) Other states in which the insurer does business typically accept the examination results, eliminating the need for separate exams of foreign insurers.

Regulation of Reserves

As explained in the preceding chapter, insurance companies are required to establish liabilities called "reserves" to explicitly recognize their obligations to policyholders and claimants. Life insurers are required to maintain "policy reserves" on outstanding policies and to reflect these reserves as liabilities in their financial statements. In the property and liability field, insurers are permitted to include premiums as income only as the premiums become earned—that is, only as the time for which protection is provided passes. In addition, the insurer is required to establish a deferred income account as a liability, called the unearned premium reserve, the primary purpose of which is to place a claim against assets that will presumably be required to pay losses occurring in the future. In addition to the unearned premium reserve and policy reserves, property and liability insurers are required to maintain loss reserves. These include a reserve for losses reported but not yet paid and a reserve for losses that have occurred but have not yet been reported to the insurer because of a lag in claim reporting.

The insurance code of most states specifies the manner in which the reserves must be computed. In addition, the code requires the insurance company to deposit cash or securities with the commissioner of insurance, based on the amount of the reserves.

The critical importance of the reserves in the financial stability and solvency of an insurer is apparent when we recognize that the reserves are true liabilities. They are an actuarial measurement of the company's liabilities to its policyholders and claimants that must be offset by assets. If the reserves are understated, the net worth of the company is overstated.

Investments

To the extent that an insurer's promises depend on the value of its investments, those investments must be sound. For this reason, the insurance code of each state spells out the particular investments permitted to each type of insurance company in the state. The investments permitted are usually U.S. government obligations; state, municipal, and territorial bonds; Canadian bonds; mortgage loans; certain high-grade corporate bonds; and, subject to limitations, preferred and common stocks. In general, property and liability insurers are granted greater latitude in their investments than are life insurers. Life insurers are generally allowed to invest only a small percentage of their assets in common stocks. Consequently, common stocks account for less than 10 percent of the total investment holdings of life insurance companies, while approximately one-third of the assets of property and liability companies are in common stocks. Insurers must file their investments with the NAIC's Securities Valuation Office (SVO), which rates the credit quality of the securities and establishes rules for valuing them.

Dealing with Insolvencies

Although the principal thrust of insurance regulation is to avoid insolvencies, on occasion they do occur, and in such instances the commissioner of insurance must institute the necessary proceedings to have the insurer's assets taken over by an official liquidator. Usually, liquidation is a last resort, and the commissioner will often take steps to rehabilitate a company when an examination suggests that it is impaired or in a hazardous condition. In attempting to rehabilitate a company, the commissioner may direct that substantial portions of the firm's business be reinsured with other companies. Sometimes, the shaky firm may be merged with a stronger insurer. Often, the public is unaware that the company was threatened by insolvency.

When these efforts fail or when the company's position is too hazardous to attempt rehabilitation, the Insurance Department of the state in which the company is domiciled handles the liquidation. In such cases, the commissioner may apply to a district court for permission to take possession of the company to conduct or close its business.

State Insolvency Funds

Insolvency guarantee funds designed to compensate members of the public who suffer loss because of failure of property and liability insurers or life and health insurers exist in all states.[7] Generally, each claim is subject to a deductible (e.g., $100), and there is a cap on the amount that will be paid, requiring the policyholders and claimants to bear a part of the loss themselves. Most funds operate on a postinsolvency basis, in which insurers operating in the state are assessed their proportionate share of losses after an insolvency occurs. The New York plan for property and liability insurers is based on a preinsolvency assessment. In

some states, the assessments are allowed as tax offsets, permitting solvent insurers that have paid assessments to recoup these losses by reducing their premium taxes.

NAIC Accreditation Program

In 1990, in an effort to address certain deficiencies in state regulation, the NAIC created the accreditation program, a system for certifying state insurance departments that meet minimum standards in the area of solvency regulation. As a result, many states have significantly strengthened their financial analysis and examinations processes in the last decade. The measures that must be adopted by a state to be accredited by the NAIC include 18 laws and regulations addressing such areas as examination processes, accounting standards, investment regulation, insurance holding companies, managing general agents, reinsurance intermediaries, and credit for reinsurance. In addition, states must meet standards dealing with how financial analysis and examinations are conducted. By the end of 1999, insurance departments in 48 states and the District of Columbia were accredited.

Market regulation

A second major focus of insurance regulation is the fair treatment of policyholders. An insurer might be financially sound and yet indulge in practices that are detrimental to the public, such as unfairly discriminating against an insured or engaging in sharp claim practices. The commissioner attempts to control such activities. Market regulation encompasses such areas as advertising and other marketing issues, claims payment, underwriting, content of insurance policies, and rates charged.

Unfair Practices

All states have Unfair Trade Practices Acts prohibiting an insurer from using unfair methods of competition or other unfair or deceptive acts or

---

[7]Most of the property and liability insolvency guarantee funds date from the early 1970s when they were established to forestall the formation of a federal agency, which had been proposed to perform the same function.

practices. These laws prohibit unfair discrimination in underwriting, misrepresentation and false advertising, and twisting and rebating. Rebating consists of directly or indirectly giving or offering to give any portion of the premium or any other consideration to an insurance buyer as an inducement to purchase insurance. An example of unlawful rebating would be an offer by an insurance agent to give a part of his or her commission to a prospective insured.[8] Twisting is the practice of inducing a policyholder to lapse or cancel a policy of one insurer to replace it with the policy of another insurer in a way that would prejudice the interest of the policyholder. Although there are a surprising number of cases in which replacement of a contract would clearly benefit the policyholder, there have also been cases in which agents have taken advantage of uninformed consumers in the replacement process. States have also adopted laws governing claims settlement and prohibiting unfair claims settlement practices.

Policy Forms

Since the insurance product is a contract, by its very nature it is technical. In most cases, consumers are asked to purchase a product in which they become a party to a contract that they have not read nor would understand if it was read. Because insurance contracts are complicated, they must be approved by the regulatory authorities to ensure that the insurance-buying public will not be mistreated as a result of unfair provisions. In addition, the solvency of the insurers must be protected against unreasonable commitments they might make under stress of competition. In some states, new policy forms and endorsements need only be filed with the commissioner's office before they are put into use; if the commissioner does not approve of the form, it is then withdrawn. In most states, however, the law requires the approval of a form before it is adopted.

---

[8]Although antirebating laws have been accepted without much question for about 70 years, they are now being challenged as anticompetitive in effect.

Competence of Agents

Because of the technical complications in the insurance product, it is particularly important that those selling insurance understand the contracts they propose to sell. Most states require applicants for a license to demonstrate by examination that they understand the contracts they propose to offer to the public and the laws under which they will operate and to meet continuing education requirements. Also, the agents must be respected and responsible residents of their individual communities.

Consumer Complaints and Assistance

All state insurance departments offer assistance to consumers in resolving disputes with insurers and insurance agents. During 1998, the states handled over 400,000 consumer complaints. In addition, most states have consumer information programs that provide educational brochures and other useful information.

Regulation of Rates

The original rationale for regulation of insurance rates was that such regulation was needed to achieve the dual goals of regulation (solvency and equity). To the extent that the insurer's promise depends on the price it charges for these promises, it was felt that these rates must be subject to government control. All states (with the exception of Illinois, which does not currently have a rating law) provide for the regulation of insurance rates, requiring that the rates must be adequate, not excessive, and not unfairly discriminatory.

Adequacy is the primary requirement. The rates, with interest income from investments, must be sufficient to pay all losses as they occur and all expenses connected with the production and servicing of the business.

In addition to being adequate, the insurance rates must not be excessive. Insurance has be-

---

Tidbits, Vignettes, and Conundrums 8.1

A Consumer Complaint

In 1997, the NAIC created a Holocaust Insurance Issues Working Group to facilitate payment of insurance claims due to Holocaust survivors and their heirs. This working group led to the NAIC's participation in the International Holocaust Commission, which includes European insurance regulators, representatives of the NAIC, the World Jewish Congress, World Jewish Restitution Organization, and representatives of European insurance companies. Through the advocacy of the International Holocaust Commission, coupled with the threat of sanctions against Swiss and German insurance companies and banks by U.S. regulators, holocaust survivors are increasingly receiving payment of claims due for over half a century as European insurance companies honor previously denied claims. European companies that will make payments for these claims include Allianz of Germany, Axa of France, Generali of Italy, Zurich Financial Services Group, Winterhur Swiss Insurance Co., and Baloise Insurance Group of Switzerland.

---

come regarded as a product that is essential to the well being of society's members, and insurers may not take advantage of this need to realize unreasonable returns.

Finally, insurance rates must not discriminate unfairly. The emphasis in this requirement is on unfairly, since the very nature of insurance rates requires some degree of discrimination. By not being unfairly discriminatory, we mean that the insurance company may not charge a significantly different rate for two clients with approximately the same degree of risk. Any variation in rates charged must have an actuarial basis.

While all states have legislation requiring that rates must be reasonable, adequate, and not unfairly discriminatory, the manner in which these requirements are enforced varies with different lines of insurance and also varies, sometimes, from state to state.

Regulation of Life Insurance Rates

Apart from making certain that the companies do not engage in price discrimination, most states do not exercise any form of direct control over the level of life insurance rates.[9] However, life insurance rates are regulated indirectly. Regulation of dividends and mutual insurers' accumulation of surplus represents an indirect control on maximum rates. In addition, legal limits on the expense portion of the premium help to control the cost of life insurance in those states that impose such limits.[10] Finally, state laws prescribe the mortality tables and interest assumptions that must be

---

[9]Credit insurance rates represent an exception. In most states, the sale of credit insurance is subject to special regulation, resulting from past abuses in the field characterized by a phenomenon called "reverse competition." Credit insurance is sold through lenders to a captive market. Prior to the regulation of credit rates, competition tended to increase rates and keep them high, because of the insurance companies' practice of bidding for the lenders' business through the payment of excessive commissions whose cost was passed on to the consumer. Most states regulate credit life rates under the terms of the NAIC Model Credit Life and Credit Accident and Health Act.

[10]New York, for example, limits the amount of commission payable to a soliciting agent in the first year of an ordinary life policy to 55 percent of the premium. Different limitations apply to other types of policies. Companies not licensed to sell in New York sometimes pay commissions as high as 125 percent of the first-year premium.

used in computing policy reserves, which means that the adequacy of life insurance rates is also indirectly regulated. If the insurer's rate structure is too low, premium income will be insufficient to generate the assets required to meet the required reserves.

Although these indirect forms of rate regulation do exist, they represent an extremely limited form of control. Most expenses are not controlled, and there are no limits set on profits (other than that imposed on mutual insurers in accumulating surplus).

Regulation of Property and Liability Rates

There is considerable diversity in the approaches taken by the states in the regulation of property and liability rates. Although there are other systems, we will discuss the four most common approaches: prior approval, open competition or no file, file and use, and use and file.[11] In addition, we will briefly note the newest system, known as "flex rating."

Prior-Approval System   Most states follow the "prior-approval" approach, patterned after the All-Industry Model Rating Law, developed by the NAIC in 1946 following the SEUA case. Under this system, the insurance company must obtain approval of its intended rates from the commissioner before they may be used, and the commissioner retains the right to disapprove the rates after they become effective. Statistical data in the form of trended loss experience and projected expenses are filed as supporting data with requests for approval of rates.[12] An insurer may au-

thorize an advisory organization to file loss costs on its behalf, or it may accumulate and file its own loss statistics. Advisory organizations compute trended loss costs based on the experience of a large number of insurers. Insurers using these loss costs then add an allowance for their expenses and profit. Because smaller insurers do not usually have a sufficiently large number of exposures to devise credible rates, only larger insurers usually make independent filings.

Open Competition   While the most common approach to the regulation of property and liability rates remains the prior-approval approach, pressure mounts from time to time for replacement of this system with so-called open-competition laws, which are more accurately described as no-file laws.[13] The no-file approach follows the pattern of a California law, which existed from 1947 until it was repealed in 1987. Open-competition laws are based on the premise that competition, not government authority, is the preferred governor of rates. Barring the existence of an anticompetitive situation or practice, the commissioner does not regulate rates as such. Insurance companies are not required to file their rates for approval, but can use whatever rates their experience or that of a bureau dictates. In effect, the position of property and liability insurers under such a law is much the same as life insurers, which, as we have noted, are subject only to indirect control of their rates.[14]

File and Use   A third system of rate regulation, file-and-use laws, represents something of a com-

---

[11]In addition to these four systems, there are at least two other systems: state-made rates and mandatory bureau rates. State-made automobile rates are used in Massachusetts. Mandatory bureau rates are used in the District of Columbia, Louisiana, and Mississippi for fire insurance and in North Carolina for fire and automobile insurance.

[12]It is difficult to classify states with respect to their system of rate regulation because many states follow more than one system. A given state may use the prior-approval system for some lines and file and use or use and file for others.

[13]The use of the term "open-competition" to identify this type of law has proven to be an unfortunate choice, for it has been interpreted by some to imply an absence of competition in states using the prior-approval system. Because prior-approval rate regulation is often used in other industries as an alternative to competition, some observers assume that this is also the case with insurance. In fact, the industry is highly price competitive not only in states with open-competition laws but in the prior-approval states as well.

[14]States using the open-competition system in 1999 were Hawaii (auto), Idaho, Kentucky, and Wyoming.

promise between the prior-approval system patterned after the All-Industry Model Rating Law and the no-file system. Under the file-and-use approach, the insurer must file proposed rate changes, but may use the new rates immediately or after a brief waiting period (e.g., 30 days). However, the rates may subsequently be disapproved by the commissioner. The chief advantage of the file-and-use system is that there is a shorter delay between the time a rate adjustment is needed and the time it becomes effective.[15]

Use and File The fourth system, use-and-file, is considered by many authorities to be virtually identical in effect to the open-competition approach. Rates may be used without regulatory approval, but they are filed with the regulator for information purposes.[16]

Flex Rating Flex rating combines elements of both the prior-approval system and the open-competition system. Under the flex-rating system, a range is established for insurance rates. Insurers are permitted to change their rates both up and down within the established range in response to market conditions and without prior approval. Increases above or decreases below the established range require prior approval. Although flex rating is controversial, it is argued that flex rating can improve both the open-competition and the prior-approval systems.

Diversity as a Reflection of State Preference

While it may be surprising that the states have taken such diverse approaches to the regulation

of property and liability insurance rates, the truth is that there is still considerable difference of opinion about the proper role of regulation with respect to rates. The question is clearly one upon which reasonable men and women disagree.

Commercial Lines Deregulation

In 1998, the National Association of Insurance Commissioners endorsed deregulation of rates and forms for some segments of the property and liability commercial lines insurance market. The NAIC's recommendations recognize a new class of insureds, intended to capture those insureds that are more sophisticated, understand insurance markets, and are unlikely to need regulatory protection. These are known as exempt commercial policyholders (ECPs).[17] Policies sold to ECPs would be exempt from rate and form regulation. In addition to easing the requirements for policies sold to ECPs, the NAIC endorsed a move toward more competitive rating systems in the commercial lines market generally.

State versus Federal Regulation

The prospect of federal regulation of the insurance industry has loomed since the SEUA case in 1944. While the McCarran–Ferguson Act left regulation in the hands of the states, it did so with the implicit condition that the federal government would not regulate insurance as long as the states did a good job.

---

[15]The file-and-use system encompasses a wide range of rate regulatory systems, some of which are similar to the prior-approval system, with others that, in effect, operate like the open-competition system.

[16]In 1999, the use-and-file system was used by Florida (except workers compensation), Iowa (personal auto and homeowners), Kentucky (personal auto, homeowners, workers compensation), New Jersey (commercial lines), Tennessee (commercial lines), Utah, Vermont, and Wisconsin (except workers compensation and personal auto).

[17]The NAIC defined ECPs to include companies that meet two or more of the following criteria: a net worth of more than $50 million; net revenue/sales of more than $100 million; employ more than 500 people; use a risk manager; aggregate premiums of more than $500 million; nonprofit or public with an annual budget or assets of at least $45 million; municipality with a population exceeding 50,000.

Pressure for Repeal of McCarran–Ferguson

Bills to repeal or otherwise modify McCarran–Ferguson have been introduced in virtually every session of Congress during the past three decades. Some bills would make the insurance industry subject to federal antitrust laws without exception. Others would grant a partial exemption from the antitrust laws, allowing insurers to engage in limited cooperation in ratemaking, primarily through exchange of loss data and in joint preparation and filing of policy forms. Still others would create a separate federal insurance regulator as an alternative to state insurance regulation. In 1999, market developments led to increased pressure to amend McCarran-Ferguson. Since the 1930s, national banks had been prohibited by federal banking law from affiliating with insurance companies. In 1999, Congress enacted S. 900, the Financial Services Modernization Act, which permitted bank–insurer affiliations. Many experts were predicting a wave of such affiliations in the next several years. To the extent banks affiliate with insurers, there may be pressure to modify the state system.

Large national banks are accustomed to a dual regulatory system. State banking regulators coexist with national banking regulators, and banks have some freedom to elect the system they prefer. Many national banks have openly expressed their preference for a dual regulatory system over the current state-based insurance regulatory system. At a minimum, the states will be encouraged to eliminate redundancies and unnecessary differences across states, fostering a more consistent national system of regulation.

Arguments Favoring Federal Regulation

Those who advocate repeal of the McCarran–Ferguson Act may be divided into two broad groups, diametrically opposed in their philosophies, but unanimous in their agreement that the law should be repealed.

The first group consists of those who argue that the states have done an inadequate job of regulating the industry. While these critics admit that some states have done a good job in regulating insurance, they point out that the quality of regulation nationwide has been uneven. The result in some cases has been the failure of companies and public suffering. These advocates of federal regulation argue that the lack of consistency among the states has caused inconvenience, duplication of effort, and waste. A single federal system of regulation, it is argued, would provide uniformity and better quality regulation. In essence, it is argued that since insurance is interstate commerce, there should be one body to provide for uniform nationwide regulation.

The second group advocating the repeal of McCarran–Ferguson argue for its repeal on completely different grounds. A 1977 U.S. Department of Justice study, for example, argued that regulation of rates is unnecessary and that the repeal of McCarran–Ferguson is desirable because it would subject insurers to the Sherman Act and other federal antitrust statutes. Some who advocate repeal of McCarran–Ferguson believe that the spread of open-competition laws has been too slow and that repeal of the law is desirable for the purpose of ending the prior-approval approach to rate regulation.[18]

Interestingly, those who have suggested a change from state regulation to a federal system often see this shift in different terms. Some who favor the change do so because they feel that state regulation has been ineffective. Clearly, these advocates of federal regulation expect more, rather than less, regulation under a federal system. Other advocates of change, such as the Department of Justice, favor the shift because of a philosophical predisposition in favor of antitrust. Still others are concerned about consumer issues re-

[18]U.S. Department of Justice, *The Pricing and Marketing of Insurance* (Washington, D.C.: U.S. Government Printing Office, 1977).

lating to availability and affordability and see a shift to a federal system of regulation as a solution to these contradictory goals. Finally, there are some people within the insurance industry who view the prospect of the repeal of McCarran–Ferguson as an escape from the burdensome requirements of state regulation.

Arguments Favoring State Regulation

The opponents of federal regulation argue that the individual states have the experience and expertise necessary to meet and solve the critical issues, and that state regulatory authorities, being more familiar with location conditions and problems, are more responsive to local needs. They also argue that a federal system of regulation would of necessity be superimposed on the state system.

Perhaps the most impressive argument against federal regulation is the same as the one generally raised in favor of federal regulation—that a federal system would substitute a uniform system for the existing diversity under the states. While the differences in approach to regulation taken by the states are often condemned as a defect of state regulation, "uniformity" is a neutral term, implying neither goodness nor badness. Given the performance of some regulatory agencies (both at the state and federal level), the uniformity that it is claimed would exist under a federal system might be viewed as a defect rather than a benefit. State regulation provides the ability and freedom to innovate, experiment, and emulate. If a mistake is made in state regulation, it is limited to one jurisdiction and does not become national in scope. Federal regulation, with its uniformity, would eliminate the localized expressions of preference regarding the manner in which the industry should be regulated. To argue that there is something fundamentally wrong with differences in regulation among the various states is to quarrel with the entire concept of federalism and the legitimacy of individual states having independent powers and responsibilities.

The controversy between the proponents of state regulation and those who advocate federal control will no doubt continue. The eventual result may well be a dual system of regulation, but even if this takes place, the debate regarding the superiority of one system over the other will not end.

CHAPTER APPENDIX
Availability and Affordability

One of the newest areas of government concern, and also one of the most significant issues facing the insurance industry today, is the availability of insurance and the difficulty that some classes have experienced in obtaining insurance at affordable rates. Although there are many products that some members of our society cannot afford, it has been argued that insurance is fundamentally different from other products and that the insurance industry has a responsibility to make insurance "available" at "affordable" rates to all who want and need it. The issues in this debate are far reaching and touch such questions as the type of society we will have, and who will pay what in that society. In this appendix, we will examine some ways in which the demand for availability and affordability affects the insurance market and consider the implications of this debate.

The Essence of the Debate

From a regulatory perspective, the key issue in the debate over availability and affordability is whether availability and affordability problems that arise in insurance represent market failures that should be addressed by regulation.

"Availability" and "affordability" are concepts that economists know as supply and demand. Availability is a synonym for "supply," and like the economist's idea of supply, goods and services are "available" when the seller can obtain a price that will cover the cost of production.

"Affordability" refers to the ability of the consumer to pay for the insurance products that he or she requires. This is synonymous with the economist's definition of "effective demand," defined as the willingness and the ability to pay.

This means that there is an inevitable conflict between the goals of availability and affordability. When the cost of losses for a given group is low, it is clear that insurance will be available and affordable. Conversely, when the cost of losses for a given group is high, insurers will offer coverage to

that group only at a high premium, which means that it may not be affordable, absent some type of subsidy. This brings us to the real issue in the debate. In the final analysis, the debate over availability and affordability is a thinly veiled demand for cross-subsidies in the insurance market.

Existing Subsidies in the Insurance Market

Subsidies in the insurance market are not a new phenomenon. They have existed for many years. Insurance subsidies are provided in four different ways: the shared markets, mandated underwriting losses, government programs, and social pricing.

Shared Markets

The most common approach to subsidizing high-risk insureds in the past has been the shared markets, a euphemism for the distressed-risk pools noted in Chapter 6. Property and liability insurers in all states are required to participate in this residual market through automobile insurance plans (assigned-risk plans), FAIR plans, and, more recently, joint underwriting associations established to provide medical malpractice insurance to physicians. Under each of these programs, unwanted insureds are assigned to insurers or are insured by an industrywide loss-sharing pool. Almost without exception, losses and expenses incurred in the shared market exceed premiums by a substantial margin, and insurers pass the losses they sustain in the shared market on to other insurance buyers in the form of higher premiums.

Mandated Underwriting Losses

A second approach to cross-subsidies in insurance arises when insurers are required to write a particular line of insurance at a loss, generally on the grounds that their overall operating results are satisfactory. Although cross-subsidies of this type are sometimes the unintended result of inaccuracies in the rating process, they also occur because of regulatory fiat. The question is whether insurers should overcharge buyers of homeowners insurance to subsidize the cost of automobile insurance, or whether premiums for fire and marine insurance should be loaded to cover losses under malpractice and product liability insurance.

Government Insurance Programs

Government-operated insurance plans represent still another approach to subsidies in insurance. When applicants who are not insurable through normal market channels are insured under a government program at a loss, a subsidy is provided from taxpayers through the general revenues of the government body or through a special tax on some members of society. Subsidies of this type are expected in social insurance programs, but they also exist in private insurance programs operated by state and federal government.

A Related Issue: Social Pricing

The debate over availability and affordability shifted to a different plane in the 1970s, with the introduction of the idea of social rating. The new disagreement was over what constitutes "equity" in insurance pricing. The protagonists in this debate were those who believe that the price of insurance should be based on the cost of production and that each segment of the insurance-buying public should pay the cost of losses for that segment, and those who argue that the rating system should not permit certain factors to be used in defining the segments. The net effect of legally banning the use of these rating factors is to create subsidies to some segments of the insurance market.

To appreciate the significance of the issue, it is necessary to understand how social pricing differs from the traditional cost-based approach. Under the traditional approach, insurers group insureds into reasonably homogeneous classes to predict the losses of the group and to charge all members of a given class the same price per unit of insurance. The criteria used to assign insureds to the respective rate classes are those that actuaries believe are related to claim frequency and severity. In automobile insurance, for example, these criteria have normally included age, sex, and marital status of the principal operator; the use of the auto; anticipated mileage; and the area in which the automobile is principally garaged. Thus, since young, unmarried males as a group have tended to have more auto losses per capita than do other policyholders, they are charged higher premiums. Policyholders living in heavily urbanized areas generally have higher losses than do drivers living in other areas, and they too have been charged higher premiums. The philosophy of the system is based on the use of classification criteria that are demonstrably related to losses, and the premiums to be charged each class are a reflection of the losses of that class.

The proponents of social rating argue that it is unfair for insurance costs to vary because of group distinctions such as age, sex, or other factors "over which the individual has no control." These critics would like to change the system, maintaining that it is unfair for a particular young, unmarried male driver, for example, to pay more for automobile insurance than other motorists, even though statistics show that these drivers, on average, have far more accidents than do other groups in the population.

Gender-Neutral Rating   The debate over social pricing is complicated by the fact that some parties who favor social pricing are motivated by ideals other than availability and affordability. The issue in the debate over gender-neutral (unisex) rating, for example, is fundamentally different from the debate over availability and affordability. While most advocates of social pricing are clearly arguing for a system of cross-subsidies, cost is not the primary consideration for many who support gender-neutral rating. In fact, women would actually pay more for their insurance in some cases, but the advocates of gender-neutral rating view the changes in the distribution of costs as being of secondary importance. The arguments for gender-neutral rating stem from a philosophical premise: that there are some rating factors that are unacceptable from a public policy perspective. Implicit in their arguments is the notion that if you allow differentiation between men and women in insurance rating, the differentiation becomes manifest in other areas.

Those who oppose social rating (including gender-neutral rating) also argue from a fundamental principle. The question in their view is whether market intervention should be used. Should prices be determined by the market, or should they be determined by regulatory fiat? They argue that once the principle of market intervention is considered acceptable, it can be justified for disparate reasons.

The debate between the advocates of cost-based pricing and social pricing is far from academic. The traditional rating factors upon which automobile insurance rates have been based in the past have been modified or eliminated in the states of California, Hawaii, Massachusetts, Michigan, Montana, North Carolina, and Pennsylvania and are being challenged in other states. Montana enacted a full-scale unisex law in 1983, which became effective in 1985.

Income-Redistribution Effects of Subsidies in Insurance

When the insurers in a given jurisdiction are required to write insurance at a loss for classes that would otherwise be unacceptable, the losses must be passed on to other policyholders in the form of higher rates. This is true whether the losses are incurred in the shared market, through mandated underwriting losses, or through the rate structure. In these situations, the insurance industry serves as a tax-gathering, benefit-dispensing system that redistributes income among members of society.

The use of private insurers as a tax-gathering and income-redistribution mechanism is not something that was planned or rationally conceived. The industry moved into the system over time, accepting cross-subsidization as a solution first for one class, and then for another. The first rate-subsidy mechanisms were the automobile assigned-risk plans, which were voluntarily established by insurers out of the fear that if the private insurance industry did not provide the insurance, the government would, and because there was no reason to believe that if the government entered the insurance market it would limit its writings to the undesirable risks.

Although the main issue for some people today is still the method we should use to provide the subsidy to those who demand availability and affordability, the entire debate has prompted a reappraisal of the systems that have been used in the past to subsidize some buyers. Increasingly, some observers are suggesting that the distinctions among the approaches to subsidization are artificial and that it makes little difference if the subsidy is granted through an industry pool, through the tax system, or through the rating system. In each case, one group in society pays a part of the costs that would—absent government interference—fall on a different group. For many, the question is no longer how we should provide the subsidy, but whether it should be provided at all. To address the question of whether subsidies in the insurance market are wise, we should look more closely at the reasons that availability and affordability problems sometimes exist in the insurance market.

Causes of Availability Problems

Insurance availability problems arise for three reasons. The first is that the absolute supply of insurance is limited. Insurers are limited in the aggregate amount of insurance they may write by regulatory standards that dictate the relationship between premiums written and insurers' surplus. Because insurers are limited in the volume of insurance they can write, they must select from among the risks offered to them. An underwriter who must accept some risks and reject others will accept those that have the greatest likelihood of yielding a profit.

Besides the finite supply of insurance, availability problems arise when the price at which the insurance may be sold is less than the costs that will be incurred by selling it. Even if insurers had unlimited surplus, there would still be some classes of insurance that they would reject. There are some lines of insurance that are demonstrably unprofitable for insurers. The reason that some lines of insurance are unprofitable is that the anticipated losses and expenses of providing the insurance exceed the premium the insurer can charge for the coverage. Usually, this occurs in markets where regulatory restrictions on insurer prices are somewhat inflexible. Given the choice between insuring exposures on which they are almost guaranteed to lose money and those on which they can reasonably expect to earn a profit, insurance companies logically choose the latter.

Finally, the cyclical nature of the insurance industry creates periodic shortages of insurance. The insurance cycle results in changes in insurers' surplus and profits. When surplus falls, the supply of insurance is reduced. The reduction in insurer profits that results from the soft phase of the cycle makes insurers more restrictive in their underwriting, further restricting availability.

Industry critics have suggested that availability problems in insurance indicate that the mechanism is somehow defective, and that it is not working properly. In fact, availability problems are simply an indication that the insurance marketplace is highly competitive. It reflects the pressures on insurers to operate at a point of efficiency and the absence of excess profits that might permit insurers to offer coverage in areas where they would expect to lose money.

Causes of Affordability Problems

"Affordability" refers to the consumer's ability to pay for the insurance product he or she requires. What is "affordable" is determined by (1) the cost of the insurance and (2) the income of the buyer. Insurance is deemed not affordable when its cost is too high. But "high" is a relative term. The important question from a policy perspective is whether the premium is high only in relation to persons with low income, or if it is high because it reflects an excessive hazard. To express the equation as a truism, some affordability problems arise because the insurance premium is too high, and some arise because the buyer's income is too low.

The first "affordability" problem results not from the absolute level of the insurance premium itself, but from the price of insurance relative to the low income of the buyer. A premium that is affordable to a consumer with one income level may be unaffordable to another consumer with a lower income level. This "affordability" problem is the same problem the poor face with respect to the affordability of food, housing, reasonable health care, education, and a wide range of other goods and services. It is an income-distribution problem, not a flaw in the insurance mechanism.

The second "affordability" problem results from the absolute level of the insurance premium itself, which, in turn, results from the hazards associated with the risk for which insurance is sought. Here, the premium is too high and the insurance is unaffordable even for the consumer who is not in the low-income class. There are some groups who, because of the hazards they represent, find insurance "unaffordable" because the potential costs they represent to the insurer require a premium that they are unable or unwilling to pay. In this case, the insurance is unaffordable not because the consumer's income is too low, but because the cost of the insurance is considered too high. These affordability problems are a signal that there is a societal problem that ought to be addressed.

The insurance mechanism provides a service to society when it prices protection based on hazard. Insurance is a mirror of society, and through its process of spreading losses helps to identify activities and exposures that are greater than the price society is willing to pay.

Two decades ago, trampoline centers dotted the national landscape. For a dollar or so, consumers could bounce on a trampoline until their hearts were content, or until they injured themselves. Trampoline centers have disappeared, primarily because the insurance mechanism, through the free-market pricing process, said that these trampoline centers imposed costs on society that were too great for the benefits.

When the affordability problem results from excessive hazard rather than low income, providing a subsidy may make the insurance affordable, but it hides the problem that the premium reflects. By hiding problems, it eliminates societal pressures to do something about them. Subsidies that make insurance affordable in those cases in which the unaffordability is a function of the high hazards are counterproductive.

Affordability problems that result from income distribution may be an appropriate realm for subsidies. There are some members of our society who cannot afford insurance they need to purchase. Like the other necessities of life that the unfortunate require but cannot afford, there are many who feel that we, as a society, have an obligation to help them to obtain insurance or otherwise satisfy this need. The important question is the manner in which a subsidy should be provided. A second question is how those entitled to a subsidy can be identified.

The subsidy could, of course, be made available through the pricing system. But this is enormously complicated. It requires compulsion and a complex regulatory structure to ensure compliance. Also, there is no mechanism in the insurance-pricing system for identifying affordability problems or for distinguishing affordability problems that result from low income from those that result from excessive hazard.

Most important, attempts to provide subsidies through the pricing system create distortions in the market that diminish the benefits of competition. Cross-subsidies in insurance pricing can result in a misallocation of resources, a luxury that the nation's economy can ill afford.

Finally, there is an additional objection to providing subsidies through the insurance-pricing system, even more compelling from the perspective of those who advocate subsidies for humanitarian reasons. It is that cross-subsidies in the insurance-pricing system are likely to fail in achieving the intended results. There is no guarantee that use of the insurance-pricing system to effect subsidies will result in a more equitable burden of the insurance cost.

Although cross-subsidies in insurance are designed to provide an income transfer from one segment of society to another, they differ from most other income-redistribution programs in one critical respect. There is a basic assumption—unstated perhaps, but assumed—that the cost of insurance coverage is beyond the means of the beneficiary of the subsidy and that cross-subsidization is necessary in order for them to obtain this modern necessity. This is obviously unproven. Indeed, the reverse may be true. It is entirely conceivable that those persons accepted at standard rates, but who are required to subsidize the high-risk insureds, are those to whom social equity would dictate that income be redistributed.

Cross-subsidies that operate through the pricing system are just as likely to take a dollar from a person in need and give it to an affluent person as to take a dollar from the rich person and give it to the poor one. The assumption that persons whose exposures justify high premiums are by definition deserving or in need of a subsidy is unwarranted.

Many observers believe that if members of society require a subsidy for the purchase of insurance, the subsidy should be provided through the tax system, in the same way that subsidies to the needy are provided for food, housing, and medical care. The tax system is designed to achieve income-redistribution objectives, and the insurance mechanism is not. Under the tax system, mechanisms are already in place that determine whether a subsidy is needed. Also, the progressive tax structure helps to ensure that those who provide the subsidy are those who are able to provide it.

This is not to suggest that availability and affordability of insurance are not appropriate goals for society. It merely expresses the truism that availability and affordability are mathematically incompatible and inconsistent with a competitive market. It suggests, second, that not all instances in which insurance is not affordable are appropriate subjects for subsidies. Finally, it suggests that if a subsidy is to be provided, it should not be provided through the insurance-pricing system.

Important Concepts to Remember

antitrust
regulation
market failure theory
vested in the public interest
destructive competition
   rationale
Paul v. Virginia
Armstrong Investigation
Merritt Investigation
SEUA case
McCarran–Ferguson Act

Public Law 15
National Association of Insurance
   Commissioners
solvency regulation
financial analysis
financial examinations
insolvency guarantee funds
market regulation
unfair trade practices
rebating
twisting

legal requirements of insurance
   rates
prior approval approach
use-and-file approach
file-and-use approach
competitive rating law
no-file approach
flex rating
shared markets
social pricing
gender-neutral rating

Questions for Review

1. Explain why the field of insurance has been regarded as a type of business that requires government regulation.

2. Precisely what is meant by the statement that insurance is an industry that is "vested in the public interest?"

3. Identify the landmark decisions and statutes that led to the present status of insurance as respects the federal antitrust laws.

4. Briefly outline the provisions of Public Law 15.

5. Distinguish between solvency regulation and market regulation and identify the major elements of each.

6. Describe the four principal approaches to rate regulation in the property and liability field.

7. List and briefly explain the statutory requirements with respect to insurance rates.

8. Describe the operation of the state insolvency funds. To what types of insurers do they apply?

9. Briefly describe the arguments for and against federal regulation of insurance.

10. What arguments would probably be advanced by those opposing a change from a prior-approval rating law to an open-competition law? What arguments would be advanced by those who favored the change?

Questions for Discussion

1. In most states, the office of commissioner of insurance is an appointed office. Do you feel that it would be better if it were elective? Why or why not?

2. Why is it necessary for insurance agents and brokers in many states to pass qualification examinations? Do you feel that these exami-

nations in your state are too hard or too easy?

3. While it is generally agreed that unrestricted price competition among insurers could be detrimental to the public, some people argue that antirebating laws represent an unnecessary restriction on price competition among

insurance agents, and that such laws should be repealed. What is your opinion?

4. "Competition can be depended upon to keep rates from being excessive, and good management will keep them from being inadequate; regulation of rates is an infringement on the right of management to make business

decisions." Do you agree or disagree with this statement? Why?

5. What, in your opinion, are the major factors that should be considered in evaluating state regulation of insurance as opposed to federal regulation? What advantages do you see in each system?

Suggestions for Additional Reading

Black, Kenneth, Jr., and Harold D. Skipper, Jr. *Life Insurance*, 13th ed. Englewood Cliffs, NJ: Prentice Hall, 2000. Chapter 35.

Huebner, S. S., Kenneth Black, Jr., and Bernard L. Webb. *Property and Liability Insurance*, 4th ed. Englewood Cliffs, NJ: Prentice Hall, 1995. Chapters 39 and 40.

Keeton, Robert E., and Alan I. Widiss. *Insurance Law—Student Edition*. St. Paul, MN: West Publishing, 1988. Chapter 8.

Kimball, S. L. *Insurance and Public Policy*. Madison, WI: University of Wisconsin Press, 1960.

National Association of Insurance Commissioners. *Issues 1999*. Kansas City, MO: National Association of Insurance Commissioners, 1999.

Patterson, Edwin W. *The Insurance Commissioner in the United States: A Study in Administrative Law and Practice*. Cambridge, MA: Harvard University Press, 1927.

Vaughan, Emmett J. "Economic Implications of the Repeal of the McCarran–Ferguson Act," *State Solutions for State Problems*. Tallahassee, FL: The Last Manifesto, 1980.

———, and Therese M. Vaughan. "Proposition 103: Repealing the Law of Supply," *CPCU Journal,* vol. 43, no. 1 (March 1990).

Websites to Explore

Insurance Information Institute: http://www.iii.org/

Insurance News Network: http://www.insure.com/

Insurance Services Office, Inc.: http://www.iso.com

Journal of Insurance Regulation: http://www.naic.org/finance/research/jir/jirinfo.htm

National Association of Insurance Commissioners: http://www.naic.org

National Conference of Insurance Guaranty Funds: http://www.ncigf.org

National Council on Compensation Insurance: http://www.ncci.com

National Underwriter Company: http://www.nuco.com/

CHAPTER 9

The Legal Framework

Even lawyers were children once.
—Charles Lamb

CHAPTER OBJECTIVES

When you have finished this chapter, you should be able to

- Identify and explain the essential elements of a contract

- Explain how the general law of contracts applies to insurance contracts

- Explain why the principle of indemnity is important to the operation of the insurance mechanism

- Explain the ways in which the principle of indemnity is enforced in insurance contracts

- Explain what is meant by the statements that insurance contracts are contracts of adhesion, aleatory contracts, conditional contracts, unilateral contracts, and contracts of utmost good faith

- Define and explain the nature of waiver and estoppel

- Explain the application of the doctrines of concealment and misrepresentation in the insurance transaction

The transfer of risk from the individual to the insurer is accomplished by means of a contract between the insured and the insurance company. A contract is a binding agreement that is enforceable by the courts. Much of the law that has shaped the formal structure of insurance and influenced its content derives from the general law of contracts. But because of the many unique aspects of the insurance transaction, the general law has been modified to fit the needs of insurance. Our discussion will consider a combination of both the general contract law and its modifications relative to insurance, but with particular emphasis on those principles that are peculiar to insurance.

Insurance and the Law of Contracts

We begin our consideration of the legal aspects of insurance with a brief discussion of the general laws of contracts and the manner in which this special branch of law applies to the insurance transaction.

General Requirements of an Enforceable Contract

Insurance policies, as is the case with all contracts, must contain certain elements to be binding legally. These elements of a contract are the following:

1. Offer and acceptance
2. Consideration
3. Legal object
4. Competent parties
5. Legal form

Offer and Acceptance

To have a legally enforceable contract, there must be a definite, unqualified offer by one party, and the other party must accept this offer in its exact terms. In the case of insurance, the offer is normally made by the prospect when applying for insurance. The acceptance takes place when the agent binds coverage or when the policy is issued. There is no requirement that the contract be in writing.

Under the Statute of Frauds, an agreement that by its terms is not to be performed within one year from its effect date must be in writing. This provision has been interpreted to apply only to agreements that cannot possibly be performed within one year. Since the insurer's promise may be required to be fulfilled within one year, or even within one day, from the issue date of the policy, an insurance contract falls outside the statute. Hence, it may be said that in the absence of specific legislation to the contrary, an insurance contract can be oral in nature.[1] However, most insurance contracts are written, and only rarely is an oral contract used.

An oral contract is just as binding on both parties as is a written one. However, the difficulty of proving the terms of an oral contract, or even its existence, makes it advisable whenever possible to use written agreements. In certain instances, however, the situation may arise in which an oral contract of insurance may be necessary. When a prospective insured requests coverage from a property and liability agent, the agent may effect a contract orally, accepting the offer of the prospect. In such instances, coverage begins immediately. If a loss occurs before a written binder is issued,[2] or before the policy is issued, the company that the agent bound to the risk will be liable for the loss. However, the courts have ruled that if the agent represents more than one company, he or she must specify the company with which coverage is bound. The life insurance agent cannot bind the insurance company to a risk.

Agents' Authority   It is appropriate here to review the role of the insurance agent in the creation of a contract. In the property and liability field, in particular, the agent often acts for the insurer in accepting the insured's offer, thereby creating a contract. In addition to the power to

---

[1] The states have the power to require that insurance contracts be in writing, and some states have done so. For example, the state of Georgia requires all contracts of insurance to be in writing. Other jurisdictions prohibit oral contracts in the fields of life, health, and, occasionally, property and liability insurance. In the absence of legislation specifying that an insurance contract be in writing, such contracts may be oral.

[2] A "binder" is a temporary contract, normally issued for 30 days, that an agent uses as evidence of accepting the offer of the prospect. The binder issued by the company is accepted by the insured with the understanding that it provides the same coverage as the policy form in use by the company.

"bind" the company to a risk by acceptance, the agent often acts on behalf of the insurer in other matters. Basically, the agent's authority to act on behalf of an insurer takes three forms, each derived from a somewhat different source: the authority of the agent may be *express authority, implied authority*, or *apparent authority*.

Express authority, also sometimes called *stipulated authority*, is authority that is specifically granted to the agent. Agents are given express authority to represent a particular insurance company in an agency contract or agreement.

Implied authority is the incidental authority required or reasonably necessary to execute the express authority. Although the agency contract may not specifically authorize the agent to advertise or to collect premiums from insureds, these are acts that are reasonably necessary to the duties expressly authorized.

Apparent authority (also sometimes called *ostensible authority*) is derived from court decisions that have ruled that agents have those powers that the public has come to expect them to have. Because it is accepted by the public that property and liability agents can bind their company to a risk, they have this power, in spite of the fact that the company may not have granted it expressly. Suppose, for example, that the insurance company has told its agents not to sell any insurance on match factories, but the agent binds coverage on such an establishment. Despite the company's forbidding the agent to bind such coverage, it would be liable for any loss that occurred. As far as the public is concerned, an act by the agent is an act by the insurance company. He or she acts on behalf of the company in the insurance transaction, and under the laws of agency, these acts are deemed to be those of the company. If the agent binds the company to a risk, it is bound to that risk until such time as it effects cancellation of the contract.

Consideration

The binding force in any contract is the consideration, which is the thing of value that each party gives to the other. The consideration of the insurance company is the promises that make up the contract, such as the promise to pay if a loss should occur. The consideration on the part of the insured is the payment of the premium or the promise to pay it, plus an agreement to abide by the conditions of the contract. The promise to pay the premium is normally sufficient consideration for a legally binding contract in property and liability insurance. However, in life insurance, the first premium must be paid before the contract will take effect. And in a life insurance contract, only the first premium constitutes the consideration. This means that premiums subsequent to the first are not part of the legal consideration, since otherwise the contract could not come into existence until all the premiums were paid. The subsequent premiums, however, are conditions precedent to the continuance of the contract.

Legal Object

A contract must be legal in its purpose. A contract in which one party agreed to commit murder for a specified amount would be unenforceable in court because its object is not legal. Similarly, an insurance policy that promised to assume the consequences of the insured's criminal activity (e.g., by paying fines imposed as punishment) would be contrary to public policy. Perhaps the most common example of an insurance contract lacking a legal object is one in which an insurable interest does not exist, which the courts have generally refused to enforce. Insurance on goods illegally held would not be valid in favor of the illegal holder. With the exception of these cases and a few similar situations, insurance is considered to be a legal object.

Competent Parties

The parties to the agreement must be capable of entering into a contract in the eyes of the law. In most cases, the rules of competency are concerned with minors and the mentally incompetent. The basic principle is that some parties are not capable of understanding the contract they would enter into; therefore the courts have ruled that they are not bound by such agreements.

In the absence of a statute to the contrary, a minor is considered to be a person under the age of 21, although some states have passed laws lowering the age to 18 in recent years. In addition, the marriage of a person also creates full contractual competence under the law. The legal rule respecting a contract with a minor is that, except for contracts involving a reasonable value of necessities of life, the contract is voidable at the option of the minor. Since insurance is not considered a necessity of life by the courts, minors are not bound to the terms of insurance contracts into which they enter. Several states, however, have enacted statutes conferring on minors of a specified age or over the legal capacity to enter into valid and enforceable life insurance contracts. The age limit varies from $14\frac{1}{2}$ to 18. But in the absence of such a statute, a minor could, for example, purchase a life insurance policy at age 15 and pay the premiums until age 20, then repudiate the contract, and receive a return of all the premiums paid. Most courts would probably not permit the insurance company even to make a deduction for the cost of the pure life insurance protection received while the contract was in force. Or a minor could purchase automobile insurance for a period of a year, and just before the expiration of the policy could repudiate the contract and receive a return of premium despite having had the protection while the contract was in existence.

Legal Form

We have already noted that there is no requirement that the contract be in writing, but in many instances the form and content of a contract are carefully governed by state law. In some instances, a standard policy form may be required. In other cases, the state may prescribe mandatory provisions for particular types of policies. In addition to the use of standard contracts and provisions, states require that all types of policies be filed with, and approved by, the state regulatory authorities before the policy may be sold in the state. This, of course, is to determine whether the policy meets the requirements of the law, and to protect the policyholders from an unscrupulous insurance company that otherwise would take advantage of the public. To be in legal form, then, the insurance contract must have the same wording as the legal standard policy, or must contain, in substance, the intent of the standard provisions. It must also follow the proper legal procedure of being filed and accepted by the state regulatory authority.

Void and Voidable

The terms void and voidable are sometimes incorrectly used interchangeably. Actually, to speak of a "void contract" is a contradiction in itself. A contract that is void is not a contract at all, but rather an agreement without legal effect. In essence, it lacks one of the requirements specified by law for a valid contract. A void contract cannot be enforced by either party. For example, a contract having an illegal object is void, and neither of the parties to the contract can enforce it. A voidable contract, on the other hand, is an agreement that, for a reason satisfactory to the court, may be set aside by one of the parties. It is binding unless the party with the right to void it wishes to do so. For example, let us say that the insured has failed to comply with a condition of the agreement. The company may elect, if it chooses to do so, to fulfill its part of the contract, or it may elect to avoid it and revoke coverage. Or, let us say that a 13-year-old purchases a life insurance contract. While this contract would be binding on the insurer, in most cases it would be voidable at the option of the insured. A contract may be deemed voidable for a number of legal reasons. If one party were forced into the contract under duress, or if there were an element of fraud involved, the contract may be voided.

Special Legal Characteristics of Insurance Contracts

In addition to those principles that apply to all contracts, there are certain legal characteristics that are unique to insurance covenants.

Insurance Is a Contract of Indemnity

In many forms of insurance, particularly in property and liability, the contract is one of indemnity. This means that the insured is entitled to payment from the insurance company only if he or she has suffered a loss and only to the extent of the financial loss sustained. In simple terms, the principle of indemnity maintains that an individual should not be permitted to profit from the existence of an insurance contract but should be restored to the same financial condition that existed prior to the occurrence of the loss. Human nature being what it is, the ability to profit from the existence of an insurance policy could lead to the destruction of property, as well as to other more serious crimes. The principle of indemnity is enforced through legal doctrines and policy provisions designed to limit the amount the insured can collect to the amount of the loss. The four most important of these are the doctrine of *insurable interest,* the concept of *actual cash value,* and the "other insurance" and "subrogation" provisions of insurance contracts.

Insurable Interest

The most important legal doctrine giving substance and support to the principle of indemnity is that of insurable interest. An insurance contract is legally binding only if the insured has an interest in the subject matter of the insurance and this interest is insurable. In most instances, an insurable interest exists only if the insured would suffer a financial loss in the event of damage to, or destruction of, the subject matter of the insurance. In property and liability insurance, this rela-tionship requires a pecuniary (monetary) interest, and insurable interest is limited to the extent of that pecuniary interest. In life insurance, it is broad enough to recognize a sentimental interest or one based on love and affection.

The doctrine of insurable interest was developed to ensure that insurance would not be used for wagering purposes and also to mitigate the moral hazard. It should be obvious that if Smith can purchase insurance on Brown's house and collect if the house is damaged or destroyed, Smith would be profiting from the insurance. Smith might even be inclined to cause the damage. The doctrine is used in life insurance as a means to control wagering with human lives. It is also intended to reduce the threat of murder just as it is used in property insurance to reduce the threat of willful destruction of property. If the class of persons who can legally insure the life of another is restricted to those who are closely related to the insured by blood or marriage, or who possess such a financial relationship to the insured that they stand to gain more by his or her continued life than by death, the temptation to murder the insured will be greatly curtailed.[3] There is even a requirement in a few states that the person whose life is to be insured by another must give consent to the transaction.

Insurable Interest in Property Insurance   Ownership of an asset, such as a dwelling or an automobile, constitutes an obvious example of insurable interest. Insurable interest may also exist when an asset has been pledged as security for a loan, as in the case of a mortgage.[4] A bailee who is legally liable for the property of others in his or

---

[3]Murder, of course, may still exist. Murder of the insured by the beneficiary will not relieve the insurance company of its obligation to pay the proceeds of the policy. The proceeds will not be paid to the murderer-beneficiary, obviously, but will be paid to a contingent beneficiary or to the estate of the insured.

[4]However, the insurable interest of the mortgagee or the lienholder does not extend to the full value of the property used as collateral, but only to the extent of the indebtedness. The financial loss of a creditor would be limited to the balance of the debt, including unpaid interest.

her care has an insurable interest in such property. Other situations in which someone other than the owner of property would suffer financial loss as a result of the destruction of that property can also give rise to an insurable interest. As long as there is a relationship in which a financial loss would arise, it is a proper subject for a legally binding insurance contract.

In property insurance, the insurable interest need not exist at the inception of the policy, but the contract is valid only if an insurable interest exists at the time of a loss. At one time, it was required that an insurable interest exist at the inception of the contract in property insurance. However, this proved burdensome in commercial transactions where goods were being bought and sold and the transfer of title to the goods depended on the terms of sale. Today, insurance can be arranged prior to the acquisition of an asset, but will be valid only if an insurable interest exists at the time of the loss.

Insurable Interest in Life Insurance In life insurance, an individual has an unlimited insurable interest in his or her own life. As a general proposition, members of the person's immediate family may also have an insurable interest in his or her life. Here, a sentimental interest or one based on love and affection is sufficient to satisfy the requirement, even though a financial loss would not necessarily be involved. The family relationship of husband and wife is universally conceded, in and of itself, to satisfy the requirement. A number of courts, although perhaps a minority, have recognized the relationship of parent and child, of brother and sister, of grandparent and grandchild, and the like, as sufficient. But more remote kinships, such as cousins, have generally been rejected as insufficient unless a monetary loss would be involved.

In other relationships, particularly those of a business nature, the death of the insured must give rise to the definite and measurable financial loss if insurable interest is to exist. Examples of the latter include the interest of a theatrical producer in the life of an actor, a professional base-

ball club in the lives of outstanding players, a corporation in the lives of key employees, a partner in the lives of the other partners, and creditors in the lives of debtors. In these situations, the beneficiary must possess an insurable interest and the amount of the insurance must bear a relationship to the extent of the interest. For example, in most jurisdictions, the insurance procured by a creditor on the life of a debtor must not be disproportionate to the amount of the debt as it existed at the time the policy was issued or as it was reasonably expected to be thereafter. Again, the purpose of this requirement is to prevent the use of a debt as a cloak for a wagering transaction.

In life insurance, the reason for requiring an insurable interest is primarily to prevent speculation or wagering on life and death. For this reason, an insurable interest is required only at the inception of the policy—not when death occurs. For example, a creditor who purchases a life insurance policy on the debtor may legally continue to carry the policy after the debt has been paid.

Actual Cash Value

The second doctrine that is used to enforce the principle of indemnity is the concept of *actual cash value*. No matter how much insurance an individual purchases, the amount one may recover is limited to the amount of the actual loss. If Mr. Smith owns property worth $50,000 and insures it for $100,000, in the event of a loss, he will be permitted to collect only the actual value of the property. Generally speaking, if persons were permitted to collect the face amount of their insurance contracts, regardless of the extent of the financial loss involved, this again would make the operation of the insurance principle impossible. Overinsurance would be common and would lead to willful destruction of property. As a result, it would upset any possibility of predicting losses with any reasonable degree of accuracy. Both results would be socially and economically undesirable.

The basis of measuring the financial loss of the insured varies with the type of contract and the circumstances surrounding the loss. In most types of property and liability insurance contracts, the measure is called actual cash value. This term, however, does not have a hard-and-fast meaning, and what constitutes actual cash value can vary from one situation to another. Perhaps the most frequently used definition is "replacement cost less depreciation." For example, if your apartment is burglarized and your stereo is stolen, the insurer will make payment for the depreciated value of the property, based on its current replacement cost. Assume that the original cost of the stereo, five years ago, was $600. Owing to inflation, the cost of a replacement is $900. If the stereo is judged to have depreciated 50 percent over the ten years you have owned it, the insurer will pay $450 for the loss.

Although actual cash value is the basic measure of the financial loss of the insured in most types of property and liability insurance contracts, it is not the only measure used. Under most modern property forms, coverage is available on a "replacement-cost" basis, under which payment is made without a deduction for depreciation, provided that the insured maintains coverage equal to the full undepreciated value of the property.[5] In business interruption and in rent insurance, the measure of financial loss is the insured's loss of income that arises because of inability to use and occupy the premises because of physical damage to the property. In extra-expense insurance, the measure is the amount of abnormal expense incurred to make possible the continued operation of a business in the event its premises have been damaged or destroyed by certain specified perils. In liability insurance, it would be the amount of damages the insured is obligated to pay a third party in cases in which the negligence of the insured caused injuries of the third party. But regardless of the method used in measuring the loss, the principle of indemnity is applicable. The insurance company will pay only if a loss has occurred and only to the extent of the financial loss of the insured, not exceeding the limits of coverage purchased.

Valued Policies Valued policies are an exception to the principle of indemnity. Under a valued policy, the insurer agrees with the insured on the value of the property at the time the contract begins, and in the event of a total loss must pay the face amount of the policy. This type of contract is characteristic of ocean marine insurance and insurance on fine arts.

In ocean marine insurance, the valued policy is more an historical consequence than a modern necessity. Many years ago, if a ship were lost at sea, it could be many months before the loss became known, and in many cases it would be virtually impossible to determine exactly where the loss occurred. As a consequence, the disagreements arising from the attempts to determine the value of the destroyed property at the time and place of the loss were insurmountable. The practical alternative to actual cash value was the use of an agreed value for insurance purposes. The principle of insuring on the basis of an agreed value was developed in ocean marine insurance in early times, and it is still used today.

In those cases where it would be difficult or impossible to determine the amount of the loss after it has taken place (as in the case of a rare or valuable work of art), the valued policy is used. Under these contracts, the face amount of the policy is paid in the event of a total loss, regardless of the actual amount of financial loss.

Valued Policy Laws In addition to its use in marine insurance, the valued policy principle has been enacted into law in some form or other in about half of the states.[6] The Nebraska law is an example:

---

[5]Replacement cost coverage is discussed in greater detail in Chapter 18.

[6]Valued policy laws exist in Arkansas, California, Georgia, Kansas, Minnesota, Mississippi, Missouri, Montana, Nebraska, New Hampshire, North Dakota, Ohio, South Carolina, South Dakota, Texas, and West Virginia.

Whenever any policy of insurance shall be written to insure any real property in this state against loss by fire, tornado, or lightning, and the property insured shall be wholly destroyed, without criminal fault on the part of the insured or his assignee, the amount of the insurance written in such policy shall be taken conclusively to be the true value of the property insured and the true amount of loss and measure of damages.

This is an ill-conceived law and has little, if any, justification. Valued policy laws are based on a mistaken concept of equity; if the insured pays for a certain amount of insurance, this is the amount that should be collected if a total loss occurs. If an insured owns property with an actual cash value of $20,000 and purchases $30,000 coverage and the dwelling is totally destroyed by fire, the insurer will be obligated to pay the $30,000, even though this will yield the insured a profit of $10,000 and even though the contract promises to pay only the actual cash value of the destroyed property.[7] To permit the insured to profit through the existence of the insurance contract is in direct contradiction to the principle of indemnity and is contrary to public policy. Nevertheless, most valued policy laws have been in existence for many decades.

Cash Payment Policies The principle of indemnity has limited application in life and health insurance. In life insurance and some forms of health insurance, the insurance company contracts to pay a stated sum of money in the event of a designated occurence and this sum is payable without reference to the amount of financial loss. Such policies are referred to as *cash payment policies*. Unlike valued policies, there is no agreement regarding value, but simply an agreement to pay a specified amount. The principle is universally applied in life insurance. In health insurance, some policies are cash payment policies, while others attempt to enforce the principle of indemnity.

Other Insurance Provisions

Most insurance contracts, other than life and in most instances health, contain some clause relating to coverage by other insurance; the primary purpose of the restriction is that of preventing the insured from collecting for the same loss under two policies, and thereby profiting from the existence of duplicate insurance.

One of the most common of the other insurance clauses is one that is known as a pro rata clause. The provision in the basic fire insurance contract may be used as an illustration:

This Company shall not be liable for a greater proportion of any loss that the amount hereby insured shall bear to the whole insurance covering the property against the peril involved, whether collectible or not.

An example will clarify the meaning. Let us assume that X has a dwelling with an actual cash value of $100,000. She purchases $100,000 fire insurance coverage from Company A and $100,000 from Company B, and then suffers a fire loss of $25,000. If X could collect $25,000 from each insurance company, which she has every intention of doing, she would obviously profit from the existence of the insurance. But under the provisions of the pro rata clause in each policy, each insurer will be obligated to pay only that proportion of the loss that its insurance bears to the total fire insurance on the property. Each company will pay $12,500. This will rather effectively prevent the insured from profiting from the existence of duplicate insurance.

Another common type of other insurance clause is one that makes the insurance excess over other valid and collectible insurance. A partial

---

[7]The student is perhaps aware of the fact that, if there is a conflict between the provisions of a contract and a statute, the provisions of the statute will prevail.

statement of the other insurance clause in an inland marine personal property floater is as follows:

> If at the time of the loss or damage, there is other valid and collectible insurance which would attach . . . had this policy not been effected, then this insurance shall apply as excess over all such other insurance and in no event as contributing insurance.

This clause is typical of inland marine insurance contracts and is also found to some extent in other property and liability insurance contracts. The excess other insurance clause is a method of distributing the insurance in those instances where more than one policy covers a specific loss, and, similar in purpose with that of the pro rata clause, it prevents the insured from profiting through the existence of the insurance contract.

Another approach to other insurance is a provision in some contracts that makes the insurance inapplicable to property that is covered by other insurance. A common provision of this type states:

> We do not cover articles separately described and specifically insured by other insurance.

Provisions of this type are referred to as exculpatory clauses, since they relieve the insurer of liability for loss.

Subrogation

Another contractual provision designed to prevent the insured from making a profit is the subrogation clause. Here, if the insured collects indemnity under the policy and the loss has been caused by the negligence of some third party, the right to collect damages from the negligent party must be relinquished to the insurance carrier. However, relinquishment is required only to the extent of the amount paid by the insurance company. The right of subrogation is based on the principle that if it did not exist, the insured would be permitted to collect twice for the loss, once

from the insurance company and once from the negligent party. This, of course, would be profiting from the existence of the insurance contract.

The doctrine of subrogation is applicable only in the fields of property and liability insurance and health insurance. It is never applied in life insurance. For example, the survivors of a person who is killed by a negligent driver can collect the proceeds of life insurance policies covering the deceased and in addition sue and recover damages from the negligent driver. The insurance company has no right to reimbursement from the negligent party. The inapplicability of the doctrine is based on the principle that in life insurance the policy is not a contract of indemnity.

Originally, health insurance policies did not include a subrogation provision. Increasingly, however, medical expenses policies include a subrogation provision. Generally, disability income policies do not include a subrogation provision and the disability insurer has no right to assume the insured's recovery rights against a third party.

Insurance Is a Personal Contract

Although insurance coverage may apply to property, the risk is transferred to the company from an individual. While we speak of "insuring a house" or some other piece of property, the contract is between the company and a specifically named insured. If the insured should sell the property that is "insured," the protection is not binding in favor of the new owner of the property. Since the company has a right to decide with whom it will and will not do business, the insured cannot transfer the contract to someone else without the written consent of the insurer. The personal characteristics of the insured and the circumstances surrounding the subject matter of the coverage are important to the insurance company in determining whether it will issue the policy.

One important aspect of the application of the personal contract rule to insurance policies is the right of the insured to assign an insurance policy to another person. Since the general rule states that one cannot be forced to contract against one's will, the right of the insured to assign the policy must require the consent of the insurance company. Otherwise, the company could be legally bound on a contract with an individual to whom it would never have issued a policy originally, and on one in which the nature of the risk is altered substantially. For example, suppose an automobile owner decided to sell his or her car to a 17-year-old boy. If it were possible to assign the insurance policy to the boy without the consent of the insurer, the company would then be in the position of contracting with a person with whom originally it would not have dealt. The insured has the right to assign his or her policy, but in most contracts the assigned policy will be legally binding only with the written consent of the insurance company.

The requirement of written consent of the insurance company in the event of an assignment of the policy is not applicable to all insurance contracts. Life insurance policies are freely assignable without permission. Although no restrictions are placed on the right of the insured to assign a life insurance policy, the policy provides that the insurance company will not be bound by any assignment until it has received written notice of the assignment. This is simply for the protection of the company. An owner might, for example, assign the policy, and the company, not being aware of the fact, might make payment to someone other than the person to whom the policy was assigned. To avoid litigation and eliminate the possibility of being required to make a double payment, the company requires written notice of any assignment and is not bound by the assignment until the notice is received.

The difference in the application of the rule of assignment in life insurance as contrasted with its application in the property and liability field may be explained largely by the fact that an assignment of a life insurance policy does not alter the nature of the risk to the insurer, but merely changes the ownership of the contract. The person whose life is insured is still the person insured, and the assignment should have no appreciable effect upon the possibility of the insured's death. In property insurance, however, the assignment could have a substantial effect on the possibility of the occurrence of a loss.

Insurance Is a Unilateral Contract

By unilateral is meant that only one party to the contract is legally bound to do anything. This is in contrast with the more common bilateral contract, in which both parties to an agreement make binding promises. The insured makes no promises that can be legally enforced. For example, although most policies require the insured to file a proof of loss with the insurer in the event of loss, the insured is under no legal obligation to do so. As noted below, however, failure to abide by the conditions of the contract may prevent the insured from collecting in the event of loss.

Insurance Is a Conditional Contract

An insurance contract is said to be a conditional contract, which means that the conditions of the contract are considered to be a part of the consideration by the insured. The insurer is obligated to fulfill its promises only if the insured has fulfilled his or her promises. Because an insurance policy is a unilateral contract, the insured cannot be legally required to meet policy conditions. At the same time, if the conditions are not met, he or she may be prevented from collecting in the event of a loss. Although policy conditions are not obligations that the insured can be required to keep, they are requisites to recovery under the policy.

Insurance Is a Contract of Adhesion

A contract of adhesion is one prepared by one of the parties (the company) and accepted or rejected by the other (the insured). It is not drawn up through negotiation; the insured who does not particularly like the terms of the contract may choose not to purchase it, but if he or she does purchase it, it must be accepted as it is.

Because the insurance company has the right to draw up the contract, the courts have held that any ambiguity in the contract should be interpreted in favor of the insured. It is somewhat like the case of two small children and the device commonly adopted to settle the dispute as to which of the two gets the biggest piece of pie. "One child cuts and the other gets first pick." The company draws up the contract and the insured gets the benefit of any ambiguity.

The fact that the insurance policy is a contract of adhesion and the insured must accept or reject the terms as they are written makes the doctrine of "presumption of intent" rather important in the area of insurance. Under this doctrine, the courts have ruled that a person is bound by the terms of a written contract that he or she signs or accepts, whether he or she reads the contract or not. In other words, the court assumes that the insured reads the contract and agrees with the terms thereof.

Insurance Is an Aleatory Contract

Briefly, the term *aleatory* means that the outcome is affected by chance and that the number of dollars given up by the contracting parties will be un-

equal. The insured pays the required premium, and if no loss occurs, the insurance company pays nothing. If a loss does occur, the insured's premium is small in relation to the amount the insurer will be required to pay. In the sense that it is aleatory, an insurance contract is like a gambling contract.

Insurance Is a Contract of Utmost Good Faith

Partly due to the fact that the contract is aleatory, the insurer and the insured enter into an agreement where mutual faith is of paramount importance. The legal principle of *uberrimae fidei* (utmost good faith) has deep historical roots in its application to insurance. In the early days of marine insurance, an underwriter was often called upon to insure a ship that was halfway around the world and had to accept the word of the applicant that the ship was still afloat. The practical effect of the principle of utmost good faith today lies in the requirement that the applicant for insurance must make full and fair disclosure of the risk to the agent and the company. The risk that the company thinks it is assuming must be the same risk that the insured transfers. Any information about the risk that is known to one party should be known to the other. If the insured intention-

---

Tidbits, Vignettes, and Conundrums 9.1

"It Depends on What the Meaning of 'is' is."

Sometimes, ambiguity in an insurance contract involves issues as minute as the article that modifies a term. In the Commercial General Liability Coverage Form, for example, the policy excludes "bodily injury to an employee of the insured arising out of and in the course of employment by the insured." For corporations, the definition of insured includes not only the corporation, but its executive officers. In the case in which an employee was injured on the job and sued the president of the corporation, the exclusion was held inapplicable to the loss. Although the injured person was an employee of *an* insured, he was not an employee of *the* insured (i.e., the particular insured who was being sued).

ally fails to inform the insurer of any facts that would influence the issue of the policy or the rate at which it would be issued, the insurer may have grounds for avoiding coverage. The courts have given meaning to the principle of "utmost good faith" through the evolution of the doctrines of misrepresentation, warranty, and concealment.

Misrepresentation

A representation is an oral or written statement made by the applicant prior to, or contemporaneously with, the formation of the contract. It constitutes an inducement for the insurer to enter into the contract. Normally, the representations are the answers to certain questions that are given by the applicant concerning the subject matter of the insurance. For example, in the negotiation of a life insurance contract, if the prospect states in answer to a question that he or she has never had tuberculosis, this statement is a representation. If the statement is false, a misrepresentation exists that may provide grounds for the insurer's avoidance of the contract later on. However, a misrepresentation is grounds for voidance of a contract only if it involves what is known as a "material fact." A material fact is information that, had it been known, would have caused the insurance company to reject the application or issue the policy on substantially different terms.

The doctrine of misrepresentation is applied with varying degrees of strictness. Since frequently in ocean marine insurance there is little chance for the insurer to inspect the subject matter of the insurance, the company must place greater reliance on the information supplied by the applicant than would be the case in domestic insurance. Therefore, it has always been a rule in ocean marine insurance that a misrepresentation of a material fact, even though there was no bad faith on the part of the insured, is grounds for voiding the contract.

In most other forms of insurance, the misrepresentation must be made with fraudulent intent before the insurer can use it as grounds for voiding the contract. This application of the principle

is based on the assumption that the insurance company can inspect the subject matter of the insurance. The insurer is not obligated to depend strictly on the information provided by the insured, and therefore cannot have grounds for voidance of a contract unless it can prove a willful intent to defraud the company.

In some states there is a statutory requirement that the misrepresented or concealed material fact contribute to the loss before it can give grounds for voiding a policy. For example, in a nonmedical life insurance contract, the insured could misrepresent the fact that he has a serious heart impairment. If the insurer had known this fact, it would not have issued the policy. If the insured dies as a result of an automobile accident, and not because of the heart impairment, the company will be obligated to pay the proceeds of the policy because the misrepresented fact did not contribute to the loss. Such legislation seems to put a premium on fraud or at least make contracts based on fraudulent intent much more feasible. The rule followed in most states, that is, the possibility of voidance whether the misrepresented or concealed fact contributes to the loss or not, places the insurance contract on a much more logical and justifiable basis.

Some of the best examples of the operation of the doctrine of misrepresentation are found in automobile insurance. As a rule, the applicant for auto insurance is required to complete and sign an application that includes representations by the insured concerning such facts as the number of moving traffic violations of the insured and members of his or her household in the previous three years, the ages of the operators in the household, previous cancellations of automobile insurance, and the like. Since the answers to these questions are representations of the insured, it is revealing to note how far the courts have gone in permitting automobile insurers to void policies because of misrepresentations in the application.

In *Safeco Insurance Company v. Gonacha*, the Colorado Supreme Court held a policy to be void because of a misrepresentation by the insured that he had not had a previous cancellation or had not previously been refused insurance.[8] The court considered the false information to be material and grounds for voiding the policy, even though the application was not attached to and made a part of the policy. In other recent cases, it was held that a misstatement of age is material to the risk and so grounds for voiding the policy[9] and that a representation that the automobile would be principally garaged in a community that took a lower premium than the large city where it actually was located would also give grounds for voiding the contract.[10] In *Pittman v. West American Insurance Company*,[11] the court held that a misrepresentation in the application concerning previous accidents and major traffic convictions constituted material misrepresentations and could thus give grounds for voiding the policy. Here, the applicant stated that he had not had any accidents in the three years preceding the date of the application. However, shortly before applying for the insurance, he had an accident as a result of which he was fined for careless driving.

These cases emphasize the importance of the doctrine of misrepresentation and the necessity of providing complete and accurate information to the insurance company. Although a misrepresentation that goes undetected may produce a premium saving, if detected at the time of a loss, it can result in the loss of coverage.

Warranties

When a representation is made a part of the insurance contract, usually by physical attachment of the application to the policy, the statements of the insured then become warranties. Warranties, by definition, also include promises of the insured that are set forth in the policy. The promise to maintain certain protective devices, such as burglar alarms, in proper working order at all times would be an example. A breach of warranty may give grounds for voiding a policy without regard to the materiality of the statement or promise. Therefore, whether the insurer was prejudiced by the untruth or nonfulfillment of the promise is not a consideration. The mere breach of warranty will provide grounds for voiding the contract. The warranty, therefore, differs from a representation in that (1) the warranty need not be material and (2) the warranty must be a part of the contract.

A breach of warranty as a means of avoiding a contract is in general much too harsh a doctrine to be applied to insurance contracts. As a consequence, its unqualified use is found only in ocean marine insurance. However, in other forms of insurance, the use of the doctrine has been modified substantially. Courts have generally refused to apply the doctrine strictly. In most instances, the courts have modified the doctrine by requiring that the breach of warranty materially increase the risk before it may be used to avoid an insurance contract. There have also been some statutory modifications of the use of the doctrine. For example, in life insurance, the statements of the insured, regardless of the fact that they are part of the contract, can have the legal effect only of representations. This means that the breach of warranty must involve a material fact. Other statutory modifications provide that the breach of warranty will prevent recovery by the insured only if it increased the risk of loss, or only if it contributed to the loss. The disfavor into which warranties have fallen and the difficulties of enforcing their use is gradually leading to their abandonment except in ocean marine contracts. Instead of a promise in the form of a warranty, such as one requiring the insured to maintain certain protective equipment (e.g., burglar alarms) in proper working order at all times, the policy may provide an exclusion to the effect that the insurance coverage is not applicable while the equipment is in disrepair.

---

[8]350 Pac. (2nd) 189. Incorrect statements concerning previous cancellations have been held in other cases to be grounds for voiding coverage. *Dragosovich v. Allstate Insurance Company*, 118 N. E. (2nd) 57, is typical.

[9]*State Farm Mutual Automobile Insurance Company v. Mossey*, 195 Fed. (2nd) 56.

[10]*Purcell v. Pacific Automobile Insurance Company*, 64 Pac. (2nd) 1114.

[11]25 C. C. H. (Auto 2nd) 349.

Concealment

The disclosure of proper and accurate information is not all that is required if the knowledge of both parties of the material facts is to be equal. The applicant also has the obligation of voluntarily disclosing material facts concerning the subject matter of the insurance that the company could not be expected to know about. The failure of the insured to disclose such facts constitutes a concealment, and a willful concealment of a material fact will give grounds for voiding the policy.[12] Since the insurance company cannot be expected to inquire about everything that may be material to the subject matter of the insurance, the insured has an obligation to disclose extraordinary facts within the scope of his or her knowledge.

Legislatures have also tampered with this doctrine, and, as is the case with representations, some states require that the fact concealed contribute to the loss before it will give grounds for voiding the policy. So if faulty wiring in the attic, rather than the still, were the cause of the loss, the policy would be valid. There are many other possibilities of concealments, yet this example should be sufficient for the student to recognize that any extraordinary fact related to the subject matter of the insurance, which the insurance company could not be expected to know, requires a disclosure of such fact to the insurance company.

Waiver and Estoppel

Directly linked to the doctrines of concealment and misrepresentation are those of waiver and estoppel. These also relate directly to the law of agency and to the power of the agent. Waiver is the intentional relinquishment of a known right. If the agent issues a contract, knowing that the conditions are being violated, that agent is deemed to have waived the violation. For example, let us assume that a man takes out an auto-mobile liability policy, and in the application he states that no male drivers under 25 years of age will be operating the car, when the truth of the matter is that his 17-year-old son operates the car almost exclusively (probably in stock car races). Let us assume further that the agent knows full well that this is the case. Since the knowledge of the agent is presumed to be knowledge of the company, the agent is deemed to have waived this violation when issuing the policy. Estoppel prevents a person from alleging or denying a fact the contrary of which, by his own previous action, he has admitted. The waiving of a violation of the contract by the agent estops the company from denying liability on the basis of this violation at some time in the future. The powers of the life insurance agent, as we have said before, are somewhat more limited than are those of the property and liability agent. For the property and liability agent, however, make no mistake: the powers are extremely broad, and the power of waiver on the part of the agent has been extended by court decision. Although some property and liability contracts incorporate a provision stating that no permission affecting the insurance or changes in the policy provision are valid unless expressed in writing, some courts have ruled that the agent can waive the quoted clause along with any other clauses in the contract. In other words, the power of the agent is so strong that he or she can waive the very clause that prohibits waiver of contract provisions!

The Insurance Contract as a Contract

When members of society who have entered into a contract disagree about the terms of the contract, or one of the parties questions the very existence of the contract, either party has recourse to the courts. The court will decide the issue in question and the decision will become a part of the body of common law. Common law is sometimes termed unwritten law to contrast it with statutory or written law, which consists of statutes and codes enacted by legislatures. Common law is

---

[12]In ocean marine insurance the concealment does not have to be willful. In other forms of insurance, however, the material fact concealed must be with the intent to defraud.

unwritten in the sense that it can be found only in the various decisions of the courts. Under the doctrine of *stare decisis,* the courts, in attempting to decide an issue, look at previous decisions by other courts on the same point. If there is no precedent available, the court must decide the issue, and in doing so, it creates a precedent. At times the courts may deviate from previous precedents on the grounds that the circumstances are different, or that such deviation is necessary to serve the ends of justice.[13] The courts play an important role in the operation of private insurance. Court decisions are important in the individual case because they decide the issue. More important from our point of view, they set precedents that are applied in future instances. Court interpretations of insurance policies make policy interpretation difficult in one sense, in that there is always the distinct possibility that the court will construe a contract in a way that the insurer had not considered. On the other hand, past decisions are useful in interpreting contracts, for they indicate the court's view of the policy's meaning. Since the insurer has the option of changing future contracts, court decisions often influence the drawing of insurance contracts.

Reasonable Expectation

We have already noted that, with respect to insurance contracts, any ambiguity is interpreted against the insurer. There is a second doctrine of policy interpretation with which the reader should be familiar, the doctrine of reasonable expectation. The doctrine of the insured's reasonable expectations represents an extension of the general rule that ambiguities are to be interpreted against the insurer. Under this doctrine, the courts interpret an insurance policy to mean what a reasonable buyer would expect it to mean. When it is applied, the "reasonable expectations" of the insured determine the coverage of the pol-

icy, even though policy provisions may deny those expectations. An important corollary of this doctrine is that policy language is to be interpreted as a layperson would understand it, and not as it might be interpreted by a lawyer or other person skilled in the law of insurance.[14]

Complexity of Insurance Contracts

The complicated nature of the insurance contract has made it the butt of many jokes. "Why," people often ask, "doesn't the insurance company make the policy language simple enough for the layperson to understand?" "Why not cut out some of the excess wordage?" The answer to both questions is that the companies are in fact attempting to do precisely that. There is a trend within the industry toward simplified policy language, and much progress has been made in this area. However, it is a difficult task. As a contract enforceable by law, the insurance policy must set forth as clearly and as unambiguously as possible every condition and obligation of both parties. In addition, the insurer must attempt to define as precisely as possible the particular event against which protection is provided, while at the same time attempt to protect itself against misinterpretation by the courts. In spite of the fact that companies are attempting to simplify policy wording, the task is complicated by the stern realities of the law and the possibility that any ambiguity will be interpreted against the insurer.

Policy Construction

In the chapters that follow, we will examine a number of insurance contracts, and while all are different, they are similar in that they are all composed of four basic parts:

1. Declarations
2. Insuring agreements

---

[13]The common law of this country is based to a large extent on English common law. The term *common* was originally applied to distinguish those doctrines that were common to all of England from those applied only on a local basis.

[14]See Robert E. Keeton, *Basic Text on Insurance Law* (St. Paul, MN: West, 1971), p. 357.

3. Exclusions

4. Conditions

Declarations p·584

The declarations section contains the statements made by the insured. As we have seen, these are usually considered to be representations by the courts. Also included in this section is information about the location of the property insured, the name of the policyholder, and other matters relating to the identification of the person or property insured.

Insuring Agreements p·592

In this section, the company promises to pay for loss that falls within the scope of the insuring agreement. The promise may be narrow and specific or broad and comprehensive. In property insurance, for example, coverage is provided in one of two principal ways. Under the first approach, called *named-peril* coverage, the specific perils against which protection is provided are listed in the policy, and coverage applies only for damage arising out of the listed perils. Under the second approach, called *open-peril* coverage, the policy lists the perils for which coverage is not provided, and loss from any peril not excluded is covered.[15] Obviously, the open-peril approach is superior.

---

[15]This latter approach was formerly referred to as "all-risk" coverage, and you may still hear it referred to as such. There is a concerted effort to avoid the term "all risk," however, because it was frequently misunderstood by insurance buyers. The term "open-peril" coverage is gradually replacing the term "all risk."

Under a named-peril contract, the insured is obligated to prove that the damage was caused by an insured peril. Under an open-peril contract, the burden of proof is shifted, and the insurer must prove that the loss was caused by an excluded cause of loss.

Exclusions p·595

In this section, the insurance company states what losses are not covered. The number of exclusions has a direct relationship to the breadth or narrowness of the insuring agreement. For example, if the policy is written on a named-peril basis, the exclusions may be few. On the other hand, open-peril policies require more exclusions to eliminate coverage for those perils that are uninsurable. The exclusions are a basic part of the contract and a complete knowledge of them is essential to a thorough understanding of the agreement. Certain perils must be excluded from insurance contracts either because they are not insurable, or because the basic premium does not contemplate the exposure and the coverage must be obtained through the payment of an additional premium or under another more specialized contract.

Conditions p·597

This section spells out in detail the duties and rights of both parties. Most of the clauses contained in it are fairly standard; they relate to the duties of the insured in the event of loss and protect the insurance company from adverse loss experience through increases in the hazard within the control of the insured.

Important Concepts to Remember

requirements of an enforceable contract
offer and acceptance
consideration
legal object

legal form
competent parties
binder
voidable contract
contract of indemnity

insurable interest
actual cash value
valued policies
cash payment policies
valued policy law

pro rata clause
subrogation
personal contract
unilateral contract
contract of adhesion
conditional contract

aleatory contract
utmost good faith
uberrimae fidei
misrepresentation
material fact
breach of warranty

concealment
waiver
estoppel
reasonable expectation

Questions for Review

1. We have noted several instances in which the principle of indemnity is not enforced in the various fields of insurance. List the exceptions to the principle of indemnity with which you are now familiar and explain why each is permitted.

2. Your roommate and you have automobile insurance policies written by the same insurance company, and with identical coverage. As a matter of fact, you both drive the same year and model car, but his premium is $220 less than yours. He tells you that he was able to obtain the insurance cheaper by having the automobile registered in his father's name and having his father purchase the insurance. Advise him.

3. What is meant by the expression, "The policyholder gets the benefit of the doubt," in connection with interpretation of the provisions of the life insurance policy?

4. The principles of insurable interest, subrogation, actual cash value, and pro rata apportionment all stem from the broader principle of indemnity. Explain what is meant by the principle of indemnity, and indicate specifically in what way each of the four principles

mentioned above helps to enforce the principle of indemnity.

5. In what ways have the doctrines of warranty and misrepresentation been modified in their application to the field of insurance in the United States?

6. What is the key factor in determining whether a fact is "material" in the application of the doctrines of misrepresentation and concealment?

7. Insurance contracts are said to be aleatory. What important additional feature of insurance contracts follows from this characteristic?

8. In what sense is an insurance contract conditional? In what sense is it unilateral?

9. Strictly speaking, life insurance is not a contract of indemnity. Nevertheless, there are certain applications of the principle of indemnity in this field. To what extent does the principle of indemnity apply to life insurance?

10. Identify and briefly describe the four basic sections of insurance contracts.

Questions for Discussion

1. It was said that some people carried life insurance policies on the czar of Russia as a form of speculation. Although there was no insurable interest, presumably none of those carrying the insurance were in a position to

cause intentional injury to the czar. Do you feel this form of speculation should have been considered objectionable?

2. Fred Schwartz is from Keokuk, Iowa. He is currently attending college at the College of

Insurance in New York City. However, he purchases his automobile insurance from his hometown agent, giving his hometown address. Do you believe that the insurer could successfully deny liability in the event of an accident? On what grounds?

3. Rosie LaRue calls her insurance agent at 3:00 A.M. and asks the agent to increase the coverage on her house from $60,000 to $80,000. He agrees to do so. During the night the house burns to the ground, and the company denies liability for the additional $20,000 in coverage. On what grounds do you think the denial is based? Should the company be obligated to pay the original $60,000?

4. The subrogation provision enforces the principle of indemnity by preventing the insured from profiting from the existence of the insurance contract. What other beneficial effect might it have?

5. Jones tells the insurance company that his building is equipped with a sprinkler system and that a guard is on duty inside the premises when they are closed. Neither statement is true. The building is destroyed by a windstorm. Do you believe that an intentional misrepresentation by an applicant for insurance should permit the insurer to deny coverage for a loss even if the misrepresented fact had no relationship to the loss? Why?

Suggestions for Additional Reading

Black, Kenneth, Jr., and Harold D. Skipper, Jr. *Life Insurance*, 13th ed. Englewood Cliffs, NJ: Prentice Hall, 2000. Chapter 9.

Crawford, Murial L. *Life and Health Insurance Law*, LOMA ed. New York: McGraw-Hill, 1997.

Grieder, J. E., and W. H. Beadles. *Law and the Life Insurance Contract*, 4th ed. Homewood, IL: Richard D. Irwin, 1979.

Keeton, Robert E., and Alan I. Widiss. *Insurance Law—Student Edition*. St. Paul, MN.: West Publishing, 1988.

Lorimer, James J., et al. *The Legal Environment of Insurance*, 4th ed., vol. 1. Malvern, PA: American Institute for Property and Liability Underwriters, 1993.

McGill, D. M. *Legal Aspects of Life Insurance*. Homewood, IL: Richard D. Irwin, 1959.

Vance, W. R., and B. M. Anderson. *Handbook on the Law of Insurance*, 5th ed. St. Paul, MN: West Publishing, 1951.

Websites to Explore

Law Links on the World Wide Web: http://www.kahane.com/links.html

Law of Contracts (Cornell Law School): http://www.law.cornell.edu/topics/contracts.html

Legal Information Institute (Cornell Law School): http://www.law.cornell.edu/

SECTION TWO

LIFE AND HEALTH INSURANCE

CHAPTER 10

Managing Personal Risks

Were it not for human life values there would be no property values at all.
—S. S. Huebner

CHAPTER OBJECTIVES

When you have finished this chapter, you should be able to

- Identify the exposures that arise in connection with an individual's income

- Explain the concept of present value and why it is important in measuring life values

- Explain the human life value concept

- Describe how various lifestyles affect the risk of loss from premature death

- Explain the process of needs analysis

- Identify the sources of protection that may be available to an individual as protection in the event of premature death

- Explain how the risk of disability differs from the risk of premature death

- Explain the relationship between the risk of premature death and superannuation

In this chapter, we turn to the study of personal risks and insurance coverages designed to deal with them. As explained in Chapter 1, personal risks relate to the loss of the ability to earn income and include premature death, dependent old age (or superannuation), sickness or disability, and unemployment. A well-ordered personal insurance program should begin with protection of the individual's most valuable asset, income-earning ability. It is foolish to insure the property a person owns while neglecting to insure the asset that produces the property.

When designing a program to meet personal risks, individuals may already have some protection from a number of sources. Social insurance programs, discussed in the next chapter, may provide an income in the case of death or disability. Many individuals also receive benefits from their employers. These may include employer-provided life insurance, pension plans, disability income plans, and medical expense insurance. Where government programs or employee benefits do not meet needs, the individual must make other arrangements, either through personal savings, insurance, or some combination.

This chapter will examine the exposures faced by the individual and family. The next chapter considers the social insurance programs that may provide some resources when an individual dies or becomes disabled or unemployed. In the following chapters, we will look at insurance products designed to deal with these risks.

We begin by focusing on those risks that arise from uncertainty concerning the time of death. The individual faces two mutually exclusive risks that arise from the uncertainty concerning the time of death: premature death and superannuation. Premature death occurs when the death takes place while others remain dependent on the individual's income. Superannuation is the risk of outliving one's income, that is, the risk of retiring without adequate assets to cover living expenses during the period of retirement.

Objectives in Managing Personal Risks

As in the case of risk management generally, the first step in managing personal risks is to establish objectives. Because personal risks involve the potential loss of income, the objectives in this area logically relate to the income that would be lost.

The first objective in managing personal risks is to avoid the deprivation of the individual and those dependent on him or her in the event of a loss that causes the termination of income. Achieving this objective generally means making arrangements to replace the income that would be lost as a result of death, retirement, disability, or unemployment. Life insurance, annuities, and disability income insurance are common approaches to replacing such income.

Besides this risk management objective, there may be other objectives derived from personal financial planning that are fundamentally different from the goal of protecting dependents from deprivation. One such objective is sometimes the goal of transferring the maximum wealth possible to dependents. Note that this second objective is fundamentally different from the goal of providing for those who are dependent and who would suffer deprivation if the income on which they are dependent were terminated. Eventually, offspring reach a point at which they are no longer dependent on their parents. The parents' concern for their children, however, may not end at this point. Usually, parents want to transfer wealth to their children (or other heirs) regardless of the children's need. To achieve this goal, they want to avoid the shrinkage that can occur as assets pass from generation to generation. Fortunately, there are measures that can minimize the shrinkage of the estate. These measures are generally referred to as estate planning.

Finally, in addition to the objectives of protecting dependents from deprivation that would result from income producer's premature death and maximizing the wealth that is transferred to heirs, the individual may have other goals. These goals relate to the individual's plans for the future and things he or she hopes to achieve. They may include the education of children or grandchildren, charitable gifts, and other personal aspirations that might be frustrated by premature death.

Other Steps in Managing Personal Risks

The remaining steps in managing personal risks are the same as those discussed in Chapter 4: identifying the risks, measuring and evaluating those risks, selecting the risk management technique that will be used to address the risk, designing and implementing a plan to implement the decision, and evaluation and review. Because the risks relating to the loss of income may differ depending on the peril that threatens income, we will discuss the remaining steps in dealing with personal risks separately for each of the perils that threaten income.

Managing Risks Associated with Premature Death

Premature death is a source of loss in two ways. The first is in triggering the expenses associated with death itself. These consist primarily of funeral costs, payment of debts owed by the individual, and death transfer costs such as the cost of probate and estate taxes. The second loss occasioned by death is the loss of income that would have been earned by the deceased.

Identifying Risks Associated with Premature Death

On first consideration, it might seem that the risk of income loss resulting from premature death is universal. After all, no one lives forever. But death does not automatically result in financial loss. The individual who dies does not suffer financial loss; the financial loss is sustained by others who are dependent on the income earned by the individual. The key feature in the risk of income loss due to premature death is the existence of someone who would suffer deprivation as a result of the individual's death. The first step in determining whether the risk of lost income exists, then, is to determine whether anyone will suffer deprivation as a result of the death. When no one will be deprived of income as a result of death, there is no risk of financial loss due to premature death.

The expenses that arise directly from an individual's death, such as burial expenses, can be funded out of assets owned by the individual at the time of death. If the deceased had no assets at the time of death, burial costs must be paid by

---

Tidbits, Vignettes, and Conundrums 10.1

Retention and Personal Risks

Retaining risks that relate to personal income, like retention of other risks, requires a strategy for financing losses that occur. Financial planners generally recommend that an individual or family maintain an emergency cash reserve that can be accessed quickly and easily in time of need. Having a cash reserve reduces the need to liquidate investments in a crisis, such as a job loss or other unexpected calamity. Generally, a reserve equal to from three to six months' income is recommended. Although a near-cash emergency fund is recommended, a personal line of credit can serve as an acceptable substitute. Using a line of credit rather than a cash reserve simply means that if the occasion arises in which it must be accessed, it will need to be repaid. Obviously, it makes sense to secure the line of credit before it is needed.

survivors or by the state. Overall, however, the costs created by death—the so-called last expenses—are usually modest and seldom require significant measures.[1] The loss of income that results from the individual's death may be significantly greater, and it is the loss of one's income-earning ability that is the major risk-management problem with which most people must deal.

Measuring Risks Associated with Premature Death

Two approaches have been suggested to evaluate the risk of premature death: human life value and needs analysis. The human life value concept focuses on the earnings of the individual that would have been lost in cases of premature death. Needs analysis, on the other hand, focuses on the income and cash needs that must be met following an individual's premature death and compares those needs to resources already available.[2]

The Human Life Value

The application of the concept of *human life value* to insurance purchase decisions is generally credited to S. S. Huebner.[3] Simply stated, the human life value is based on the individual's income-earning ability; it is the present value of the income lost by dependents as a result of the person's death. Any attempt to measure the human life value must consider present value, a concept that will be familiar to students who have studied finance. Because an understanding of this con-

cept is essential to a meaningful measurement of income flows, we will pause in our discussion to review the concept for those readers who have not encountered it in their previous studies. (The student who is familiar with the concept of present value and the time value of money can flip forward through the pages to the point where we resume our discussion.)

Time Value of Money and Present Value The term *time value of money* refers to the fact that $1 today is worth more than $1 a year from now (or at some other time in the future).[4] This is because $1 now can be invested at some positive rate of return and will be worth more in the future. If $1 can be invested at 6 percent, $1.06 is the future value of a present dollar in one year at 6 percent. If we assume that the $1.06 is reinvested at 6 percent, the future value of $1 invested at 6 percent for two years is $1.00 times 1.06 times 1.06 or, $1.1236. Continuing the computation, we can determine the future value of $1 invested for any number of years; this is called *compounding*, reflecting the fact that interest is paid on the interest earned in previous periods.

Just as it is sometimes useful to know the future value of a present dollar, we sometimes want to know the *present value* of a *future dollar*. The present value of a future dollar is simply the amount that will be required, invested at a specified rate of interest, to equal a dollar in a specified number of years. The present value of a future dollar one year from now is computed by dividing the present value of a present dollar ($1) by the future value of a dollar at the specified rate of interest. For example, $1 invested at 6 percent for a year will be worth $1.06 at the end of the year. How much must we have now, so that if we invest it at 6 percent it will equal $1 at the end of the year?

$$\frac{\$1.00}{\$1.06} = \$0.943396$$

---

[1] Debts owed by the individual at the time of death represent a unique exposure. If an individual dies with debts that exceed assets, the loss falls on the creditors. Some people may feel a moral obligation to provide funds for payment of debts that exist at the time of their death, but there is no legal obligation.

[2] We cannot place a value on human life. What we attempt to measure is the income-producing capacity of the individual, which is something entirely different.

[3] S. S. Huebner, *The Economics of Life Insurance*, 3rd ed. (New York: Appleton-Century-Crofts, 1959), p. 5.

[4] The expression "A bird in the hand is worth two in the bush" expresses the time value of birds, and suggests a discount rate of 0.5 as the present value of a future bird. Here we are doing the same thing with money.

This $0.943396 is the *present value of a future dollar* or the *discount factor.* If we invest $0.943396 at 6 percent, it will equal $1 at the end of a year. We can divide the present value of a dollar in one year by the future value of a future dollar in one year to determine the present value of a dollar now in two years:

$$\frac{\$0.943396}{\$1.06} = \$0.889962$$

Present value tables are available that indicate the present value of a future dollar for various numbers of years and at various rates. Table 10.1 indicates the present value of a future dollar at various interest rates from 1 to 40 years. It indicates the value of $1 to be received at the end of some specified number of years at various discount rates. It tells how much an individual would have to invest at a given rate of interest to receive $1 at some time in the future. Reading down the table, we can see that one must invest about $0.31 at 6 percent to have $1 at the end of 20 years.

Discounted Income Flows One of the most useful applications of the concept of present value is in discounting a flow of income to determine its present value. We can estimate the human life value by discounting the expected stream of income that would accrue to the dependents as a result of their breadwinner's continued employment. If we deduct the amount of the income that would be consumed by the producer personally and discount the remainder, we have a notion of the present value of the stream of income that would be lost.

Human Life Value Illustrated For the purpose of illustration, consider a 25-year-old person, who we will assume plans to work until age 65. If we estimate that his or her average earnings will be $60,000 annually and that two-thirds of the income will be consumed by dependents, the individual's economic value to dependents is $40,000 a year for 40 years. However, the life value at age 25 is not measured by this total figure, but by the amount that, invested at some conservative rate of interest, would yield an income of $40,000 per

year for 40 years. We could compute this amount by discounting the $40,000 in each year by the appropriate discount rate for that year. Alternately, we can consult a table such as Table 10.2, which indicates the present value of $1 each year for different numbers of years. Table 10.2 indicates that a present investment of $15.046 will yield an income of $1 per year for 40 years. By multiplying $40,000 times $15.046, we obtain the sum that will yield $40,000 a year for 40 years, $601,840.[5]

Other things being equal, the economic value of the individual generally decreases over time and eventually disappears at retirement age. Table 10.3 indicates the declining economic value at different assumed rates of interest associated with an average annual income to dependents of $10,000. This table also illustrates the impact of the discount rate selected on the value indicated.

It should be obvious that this method of calculating the economic value of a life is loaded with difficulties, the chief of which is estimating future changes in income as the individual progresses in his or her career. Estimates of future earnings can at best be little more than a projection based on present earnings in the person's occupation. Furthermore, as noted, the human life value will change if future earnings are discounted at a different rate.[6]

Finally, the fact that the present value of an individual's income-producing ability is a given amount does not necessarily mean that this is the sum for which it should be insured. The impact of the income loss caused by premature death depends on the circumstances. These circumstances include how important the income is to the survivors and whether it can be replaced

---

[5]The calculation can be performed on many calculators that include financial functions.

[6]The difficulties involved in the calculation do not, however, invalidate the concept. Even though considerable guesswork is required, this is still the most acceptable method of calculating the economic value of a human life. Although it is probably a defective technique for determining the amount of life insurance that should be purchased, it is widely used in determining the amount of damages payable in wrongful death and injury cases.

Table 10.1   Present Value of $1 in N Years at Various Discount Rates

Year	1%	2%	3%	4%	5%	6%	7%	8%	9%	10%	11%	12%	13%	14%	15%
1	0.99010	0.98039	0.97087	0.96154	0.95238	0.94340	0.93458	0.92593	0.91743	0.90909	0.90090	0.89286	0.88496	0.87719	0.86957
2	0.98030	0.96117	0.94260	0.92456	0.90703	0.89000	0.87344	0.85734	0.84168	0.82645	0.81162	0.79719	0.78315	0.76947	0.75614
3	0.97059	0.94232	0.91514	0.88900	0.86384	0.83962	0.81630	0.79383	0.77218	0.75131	0.73119	0.71178	0.69305	0.67497	0.65752
4	0.96098	0.92385	0.88849	0.85480	0.82270	0.79209	0.76290	0.73503	0.70843	0.68301	0.65873	0.63552	0.61332	0.59208	0.57175
5	0.95147	0.90573	0.86261	0.82193	0.78353	0.74726	0.71299	0.68058	0.64993	0.62092	0.59345	0.56743	0.54276	0.51937	0.49718
6	0.94205	0.88797	0.83748	0.79031	0.74622	0.70496	0.66634	0.63017	0.59627	0.56447	0.53464	0.50663	0.48032	0.45559	0.43233
7	0.93272	0.87056	0.81309	0.75992	0.71068	0.66506	0.62275	0.58349	0.54703	0.51316	0.48166	0.45235	0.42506	0.39964	0.37594
8	0.92348	0.85349	0.78941	0.73069	0.67684	0.62741	0.58201	0.54027	0.50187	0.46651	0.43393	0.40388	0.37616	0.35056	0.32690
9	0.91434	0.83676	0.76642	0.70259	0.64461	0.59190	0.54393	0.50025	0.46043	0.42410	0.39092	0.36061	0.33288	0.30751	0.28426
10	0.90529	0.82035	0.74409	0.67556	0.61391	0.55839	0.50835	0.46319	0.42241	0.38554	0.35218	0.32197	0.29459	0.26974	0.24718
11	0.89632	0.80426	0.72242	0.64958	0.58468	0.52679	0.47509	0.42888	0.38753	0.35049	0.31728	0.28748	0.26070	0.23662	0.21494
12	0.88745	0.78849	0.70138	0.62460	0.55684	0.49697	0.44401	0.39711	0.35553	0.31863	0.28584	0.25668	0.23071	0.20756	0.18691
13	0.87866	0.77303	0.68095	0.60057	0.53032	0.46884	0.41496	0.36770	0.32618	0.28966	0.25751	0.22917	0.20416	0.18207	0.16253
14	0.86996	0.75788	0.66112	0.57748	0.50507	0.44230	0.38782	0.34046	0.29925	0.26333	0.23199	0.20462	0.18068	0.15971	0.14133
15	0.86135	0.74301	0.64186	0.55526	0.48102	0.41727	0.36245	0.31524	0.27454	0.23939	0.20900	0.18270	0.15989	0.14010	0.12289
16	0.85282	0.72845	0.62317	0.53391	0.45811	0.39365	0.33873	0.29189	0.25187	0.21763	0.18829	0.16312	0.14150	0.12289	0.10686
17	0.84438	0.71416	0.60502	0.51337	0.43630	0.37136	0.31657	0.27027	0.23107	0.19784	0.16963	0.14564	0.12522	0.10780	0.09293
18	0.83602	0.70016	0.58739	0.49363	0.41552	0.35034	0.29586	0.25025	0.21199	0.17986	0.15282	0.13004	0.11081	0.09456	0.08081
19	0.82774	0.68643	0.57029	0.47464	0.39573	0.33051	0.27651	0.23171	0.19449	0.16351	0.13768	0.11611	0.09806	0.08295	0.07027
20	0.81954	0.67297	0.55368	0.45639	0.37689	0.31180	0.25842	0.21455	0.17843	0.14864	0.12403	0.10367	0.08678	0.07276	0.06110
21	0.81143	0.65978	0.53755	0.43883	0.35894	0.29416	0.24151	0.19866	0.16370	0.13513	0.11174	0.09256	0.07680	0.06383	0.05313
22	0.80340	0.64684	0.52189	0.42196	0.34185	0.27751	0.22571	0.18394	0.15018	0.12285	0.10067	0.08264	0.06796	0.05599	0.04620
23	0.79544	0.63416	0.50669	0.40573	0.32557	0.26180	0.21095	0.17032	0.13778	0.11168	0.09069	0.07379	0.06014	0.04911	0.04017
24	0.78757	0.62172	0.49193	0.39012	0.31007	0.24698	0.19715	0.15770	0.12640	0.10153	0.08170	0.06588	0.05323	0.04308	0.03493
25	0.77977	0.60953	0.47761	0.37512	0.29530	0.23300	0.18425	0.14602	0.11597	0.09230	0.07361	0.05882	0.04710	0.03779	0.03038
26	0.77205	0.59758	0.46369	0.36069	0.28124	0.21981	0.17220	0.13520	0.10639	0.08391	0.06631	0.05252	0.04168	0.03315	0.02642
27	0.76440	0.58586	0.45019	0.34682	0.26785	0.20737	0.16093	0.12519	0.09761	0.07628	0.05974	0.04689	0.03689	0.02908	0.02297
28	0.75684	0.57437	0.43708	0.33348	0.25509	0.19563	0.15040	0.11591	0.08955	0.06934	0.05382	0.04187	0.03264	0.02551	0.01997
29	0.74934	0.56311	0.42435	0.32065	0.24295	0.18456	0.14056	0.10733	0.08215	0.06304	0.04849	0.03738	0.02889	0.02237	0.01737
30	0.74192	0.55207	0.41199	0.30832	0.23138	0.17411	0.13137	0.09938	0.07537	0.05731	0.04368	0.03338	0.02557	0.01963	0.01510
31	0.73458	0.54125	0.39999	0.29646	0.22036	0.16425	0.12277	0.09202	0.06915	0.05210	0.03935	0.02980	0.02262	0.01722	0.01313
32	0.72730	0.53063	0.38834	0.28506	0.20987	0.15496	0.11474	0.08520	0.06344	0.04736	0.03545	0.02661	0.02002	0.01510	0.01142
33	0.72010	0.52023	0.37703	0.27409	0.19987	0.14619	0.10723	0.07889	0.05820	0.04306	0.03194	0.02376	0.01772	0.01325	0.00993
34	0.71297	0.51003	0.36604	0.26355	0.19035	0.13791	0.10022	0.07305	0.05339	0.03914	0.02878	0.02121	0.01568	0.01162	0.00864
35	0.70591	0.50003	0.35538	0.25342	0.18129	0.13011	0.09366	0.06763	0.04899	0.03558	0.02592	0.01894	0.01388	0.01019	0.00751
36	0.69892	0.49022	0.34503	0.24367	0.17266	0.12274	0.08754	0.06262	0.04494	0.03235	0.02335	0.01691	0.01228	0.00894	0.00653
37	0.69200	0.48061	0.33498	0.23430	0.16444	0.11579	0.08181	0.05799	0.04123	0.02941	0.02104	0.01510	0.01087	0.00784	0.00568
38	0.68515	0.47119	0.32523	0.22529	0.15661	0.10924	0.07646	0.05369	0.03783	0.02673	0.01896	0.01348	0.00962	0.00688	0.00494
39	0.67837	0.46195	0.31575	0.21662	0.14915	0.10306	0.07146	0.04971	0.03470	0.02430	0.01708	0.01204	0.00851	0.00604	0.00429
40	0.67165	0.45289	0.30656	0.20829	0.14205	0.09722	0.06678	0.04603	0.03184	0.02209	0.01538	0.01075	0.00753	0.00529	0.00373

Table 10.2   Present Value of $1 Annually for N Years at Various Rates

Year	1%	2%	3%	4%	5%	6%	7%	8%	9%	10%	11%	12%	13%	14%	15%
1	0.99010	0.98039	0.97087	0.96154	0.95238	0.94340	0.93458	0.92593	0.91743	0.90909	0.90090	0.89286	0.88496	0.87719	0.86957
2	1.97040	1.94156	1.91347	1.88609	1.85941	1.83339	1.80802	1.78326	1.75911	1.73554	1.71252	1.69005	1.66810	1.64666	1.62571
3	2.94099	2.88388	2.82861	2.77509	2.72325	2.67301	2.62432	2.57710	2.53129	2.48685	2.44371	2.40183	2.36115	2.32163	2.28323
4	3.90197	3.80773	3.71710	3.62990	3.54595	3.46511	3.38721	3.31213	3.23972	3.16987	3.10245	3.03735	2.97447	2.91371	2.85498
5	4.85343	4.71346	4.57971	4.45182	4.32948	4.21236	4.10020	3.99271	3.88965	3.79079	3.69590	3.60478	3.51723	3.43308	3.35216
6	5.79548	5.60143	5.41719	5.24214	5.07569	4.91732	4.76654	4.62288	4.48592	4.35526	4.23054	4.11141	3.99755	3.88867	3.78448
7	6.72819	6.47199	6.23028	6.00205	5.78637	5.58238	5.38929	5.20637	5.03295	4.86842	4.71220	4.56376	4.42261	4.28830	4.16042
8	7.65168	7.32548	7.01969	6.73274	6.46321	6.20979	5.97130	5.74664	5.53482	5.33493	5.14612	4.96764	4.79877	4.63886	4.48732
9	8.56602	8.16224	7.78611	7.43533	7.10782	6.80169	6.51523	6.24689	5.99525	5.75902	5.53705	5.32825	5.13166	4.94637	4.77158
10	9.47130	8.98259	8.53020	8.11090	7.72173	7.36009	7.02358	6.71008	6.41766	6.14457	5.88923	5.65022	5.42624	5.21612	5.01877
11	10.36763	9.78685	9.25262	8.76048	8.30641	7.88687	7.49867	7.13896	6.80519	6.49506	6.20652	5.93770	5.68694	5.45273	5.23371
12	11.25508	10.57534	9.95400	9.38507	8.86325	8.38384	7.94269	7.53608	7.16073	6.81369	6.49236	6.19437	5.91765	5.66029	5.42062
13	12.13374	11.34837	10.63496	9.98565	9.39357	8.85268	8.35765	7.90378	7.48690	7.10336	6.74987	6.42355	6.12181	5.84236	5.58315
14	13.00370	12.10625	11.29607	10.56312	9.89864	9.29498	8.74547	8.24424	7.78615	7.36669	6.98187	6.62817	6.30249	6.00207	5.72448
15	13.86505	12.84926	11.93794	11.11839	10.37966	9.71225	9.10791	8.55948	8.06069	7.60608	7.19087	6.81086	6.46238	6.14217	5.84737
16	14.71787	13.57771	12.56110	11.65230	10.83777	10.10590	9.44665	8.85137	8.31256	7.82371	7.37916	6.97399	6.60388	6.26506	5.95423
17	15.56225	14.29187	13.16612	12.16567	11.27407	10.47726	9.76322	9.12164	8.54363	8.02155	7.54879	7.11963	6.72909	6.37286	6.04716
18	16.39827	14.99203	13.75351	12.65930	11.68959	10.82760	10.05909	9.37189	8.75563	8.20141	7.70162	7.24967	6.83991	6.46742	6.12797
19	17.22601	15.67846	14.32380	13.13394	12.08532	11.15812	10.33560	9.60360	8.95011	8.36492	7.83929	7.36578	6.93797	6.55037	6.19823
20	18.04555	16.35143	14.87747	13.59033	12.46221	11.46992	10.59401	9.81815	9.12855	8.51356	7.96333	7.46944	7.02475	6.62313	6.25933
21	18.85698	17.01121	15.41502	14.02916	12.82115	11.76408	10.83553	10.01680	9.29224	8.64869	8.07507	7.56200	7.10155	6.68696	6.31246
22	19.66038	17.65805	15.93692	14.45112	13.16300	12.04158	11.06124	10.20074	9.44243	8.77154	8.17574	7.64465	7.16951	6.74294	6.35866
23	20.45582	18.29220	16.44361	14.85684	13.48857	12.30338	11.27219	10.37106	9.58021	8.88322	8.26643	7.71843	7.22966	6.79206	6.39884
24	21.24339	18.91393	16.93554	15.24696	13.79864	12.55036	11.46933	10.52876	9.70661	8.98474	8.34814	7.78432	7.28288	6.83514	6.43377
25	22.02316	19.52346	17.41315	15.62208	14.09394	12.78336	11.65358	10.67478	9.82258	9.07704	8.42174	7.84314	7.32998	6.87293	6.46415
26	22.79520	20.12104	17.87684	15.98277	14.37519	13.00317	11.82578	10.80998	9.92897	9.16095	8.48806	7.89566	7.37167	6.90608	6.49056
27	23.55961	20.70690	18.32703	16.32959	14.64303	13.21053	11.98671	10.93516	10.02658	9.23722	8.54780	7.94255	7.40856	6.93515	6.51353
28	24.31644	21.28127	18.76411	16.66306	14.89813	13.40616	12.13711	11.05108	10.11613	9.30657	8.60162	7.98442	7.44120	6.96066	6.53351
29	25.06579	21.84438	19.18845	16.98371	15.14107	13.59072	12.27767	11.15841	10.19828	9.36961	8.65011	8.02181	7.47009	6.98304	6.55088
30	25.80771	22.39646	19.60044	17.29203	15.37245	13.76483	12.40904	11.25778	10.27365	9.42691	8.69379	8.05518	7.49565	7.00266	6.56598
31	26.54229	22.93770	20.00043	17.58849	15.59281	13.92909	12.53181	11.34980	10.34280	9.47901	8.73315	8.08499	7.51828	7.01988	6.57911
32	27.26959	23.46833	20.38877	17.87355	15.80268	14.08404	12.64656	11.43500	10.40624	9.52638	8.76860	8.11159	7.53830	7.03498	6.59053
33	27.98969	23.98856	20.76579	18.14765	16.00255	14.23023	12.75379	11.51389	10.46444	9.56943	8.80054	8.13535	7.55602	7.04823	6.60046
34	28.70267	24.49859	21.13184	18.41120	16.19290	14.36814	12.85401	11.58693	10.51784	9.60857	8.82932	8.15656	7.57170	7.05985	6.60910
35	29.40858	24.99862	21.48722	18.66461	16.37419	14.49825	12.94767	11.65457	10.56682	9.64416	8.85524	8.17550	7.58557	7.07005	6.61661
36	30.10751	25.48884	21.83225	18.90828	16.54685	14.62099	13.03521	11.71719	10.61176	9.67651	8.87859	8.19241	7.59785	7.07899	6.62314
37	30.79951	25.96945	22.16724	19.14258	16.71129	14.73678	13.11702	11.77518	10.65299	9.70592	8.89963	8.20751	7.60872	7.08683	6.62881
38	31.48466	26.44064	22.49246	19.36786	16.86789	14.84602	13.19347	11.82887	10.69082	9.73265	8.91859	8.22099	7.61833	7.09371	6.63375
39	32.16303	26.90259	22.80822	19.58448	17.01704	14.94907	13.26493	11.87858	10.72552	9.75696	8.93567	8.23303	7.62684	7.09975	6.63805
40	32.83469	27.35548	23.11477	19.79277	17.15909	15.04630	13.33171	11.92461	10.75736	9.77905	8.95105	8.24378	7.63438	7.10504	6.64178

Table 10.3   Economic Value of $10,000 Annual Income to Dependents

Age	Years Until Retirement	Present Value of $10,000 Per Year			
		At 5%	At 6%	At 7%	At 8%
20	45	177,740	154,588	136,055	121,084
25	40	171,590	150,462	133,317	119,246
30	35	163,741	144,982	129,476	116,545
35	30	153,724	137,648	124,090	112,577
40	25	140,939	127,833	116,535	106,747
45	20	124,622	124,622	114,699	105,940
50	15	103,796	97,122	91,079	85,594
55	10	77,217	73,600	70,235	67,100
60	5	43,294	42,123	41,001	39,927

from other sources. If survivors are not employed at the time of the income producer's death, they may be able to find employment to replace the lost income. If the income is not replaced, the survivors' standard of living may decline. The primary reason for the purchase of life insurance is to prevent a decline in the standard of living of dependents, and to permit the dependents to live in a manner that is close to the style they would have enjoyed if the income producer had not died. Where the loss of the individual's income would deprive no one, insurance is unnecessary. In addition, a part of the income lost through the person's death may be replaced by other sources, such as Social Security or life insurance available under a group insurance program in connection with employment.

The amount of life insurance that an individual should purchase is properly determined by the so-called *needs approach*, which determines the amount of life insurance required based on analysis of the needs that would have to be met by dependents should the income producer die.

Needs Analysis

The needs approach attempts to determine the amount of life insurance that should be purchased based on analysis of the needs of those who would suffer financial loss. *Needs analysis* has three basic steps. The first step is to identify the needs that would arise or continue to exist following the death of the individual. Second, resources already available to meet those needs must be identified. Potential resources at death might include savings, employer-provided life insurance, and various social insurance programs. Finally, the difference between needs and available resources represents unmet needs, and life insurance is one tool that may be used to meet this remaining need.

Although the concepts are different, there is a relationship between the human life value idea and the needs approach to determining the amount of insurance needed in a particular situation. In summarizing the needs that would exist if the wage earner should die, we are merely looking at the other side of the income-expenditure equation. While the life value concept focuses on the income that would be lost, the needs approach attempts to identify the allocation of that income and determine the purposes for which it would have been used. In addition, the needs approach attempts to recognize unusual or irregular expenditures that may result from the death of the individual and additional expenses that may accompany the period of readjustment following a wage earner's death.

Lifestyles and the Needs Approach

One way to illustrate the difference between the human life value approach and the needs approach to life insurance is to consider how different lifestyles affect the need for life insurance.

Single Individual

The single individual without dependents usually has little need for death protection. Unless there are parents (or others) who are dependent on a single person, there is no need for a flow of income to replace the income that might stop. Enough life insurance to cover any indebtedness and a fund for last expenses really constitutes the extent of the need. However, a young single person may still want to purchase life insurance because he or she may become uninsurable.

There are, of course, many single individuals who have dependents. These include widowed and divorced persons with children, single persons who support their parents, and single persons with other dependents. For these individuals, the need for death protection parallels that of the married couple with children.

Childless Couple

Like the unmarried person, the need of a childless couple for death protection is modest, particularly if both are employed. When both spouses are employed outside the home, the need for death protection on the part of either is usually limited to an amount needed to meet any indebtedness and to cover final expenses. However, if the childless state is a temporary one and the couple intends to have children, they may need to buy life insurance to guarantee future insurability.

Persons with Children

When children enter the picture, the problem becomes somewhat more complicated. Both parents may be employed outside the home, or one parent may act as homemaker while the other produces income. In the first case, where both parents earn income, the standard of living may be threatened if either income is lost. Unless there is a willingness to reduce the family's standard of living in the event of a reduction in family

income, the income of both spouses may have to be insured. When one parent works outside the home and the other acts as homemaker, the principal focus will be on insurance for the income-producing partner. The amount of insurance required in this case will depend, in part, on the ability and inclination of the homemaker spouse to obtain employment in the event of the income producer's death.

It is also important to recognize the contribution of the homemaking spouse. Clearly, such a spouse makes an economic contribution to the family, and the loss of the services he or she provides would create a financial burden for the family. When funds are available, this exposure should be insured, but such coverage ranks below coverage on an income-producing spouse.[7]

In the case of a single parent with children, the situation is essentially the same as for the family with a single working spouse but without the "cushion" of a potentially employable surviving spouse. In addition, some plan should exist for the guardianship and care of the surviving children.

Classification of Needs

There are two approaches to estimating income needs. The first is to deduct from current expenditures the portion of family income that is consumed by the wage earner. The remainder is the amount that the family will require should the wage earner die. This approach, however, ignores the changes in expenditures that may occur as a result of the wage earner's death. The second approach, which seems more logical, is to construct a household or family budget summarizing the expenditures that will be required. For those individuals who do not currently budget, constructing a needs-oriented insurance program may be

---

[7]In addition to the loss of homemaking and child care services provided by the homemaking spouse, other losses result from his or her death. One seldom-recognized loss is the increase in income taxes to the surviving spouse resulting from the inability to use the joint return in filing federal income taxes.

the first attempt at budgeting. While a family budget is the starting point for determining needs, there are various ways in which needs may be classified; the traditional approach includes the following:

Cash Needs	**Income Needs**
Fund for last expenses and debts	Funds for readjustment
Emergency funds	Dependency period income
Mortgage payment funds	Life income for spouse
Educational funds	

The first group, cash needs, represents those needs for which a lump-sum amount is desirable at death. The nature of the *fund for last expenses*, also called the *cleanup fund*, is relatively obvious. Death may be accompanied by high medical expenses, funeral costs, and other unplanned outlays, and the fund for last expenses is intended to cover these. Overall, the costs created by death—the so-called "last expenses"—are usually modest and seldom require significant measures. Ideally, medical expenses will be covered by a well-planned health insurance program. Whether specific funds should be provided for the payment of debts depends on the circumstances, but the planner should consider whether such funds should be provided as a part of the life insurance proceeds.

The purpose of emergency funds is to provide the survivors with a cushion for unexpected expenses that may arise as the family makes its transition to life without the deceased and thereafter. Although the selection of the amount for an emergency fund is somewhat arbitrary in any case, a typical allowance is $5000 to $10,000.

The mortgage payment fund may be an effective way of reducing the income needed during the dependency period. If the mortgage permits prepayment without penalty, future interest can be saved by paying off the loan at the death of the income producer. If the mortgage is not paid off, the mortgage expense can be met by providing a higher monthly income during the term of the mortgage.

Although educational needs are usually listed as a separate need, this is arbitrary and parents may differ in attitude regarding the obligation to help finance a child's college education. If the parents plan to assist their children with college expenses, a lump sum can be provided to help defray the cost of college, or the income of the dependency period can be extended to provide income during the college years.

The remaining three needs represent *income needs* and reflect different needs for three periods. First, many experts recommend a higher level of income during a readjustment period following the death of the wage earner. They believe that the family will have certain nonrecurring expenditures as it adjusts to a new way of life immediately following the death. Where the family will suffer a decline in standard of living following the death of an income earner, the readjustment period provides some time to accomplish that readjustment.

Income needs during the *dependency period* are the largest in most programs and consist of income required during the period for which others—generally children—would be dependent on the wage earner. The provision required for the dependency period income will depend on the number of children, their ages, and the relative contribution of the income producer to total family income. When both spouses are employed outside the home, the contribution of each income to family needs and the needs that will continue will dictate whether both incomes, or a part of both, should be insured. When one spouse produces all family income, it will usually be necessary to insure a high percentage of that income. As we will see in the next chapter, the children and surviving spouse may be eligible for Social Security benefits following the death of the wage earner. (Generally, children are eligible for benefits as long as they are under age 18, and the surviving spouse is eligible until the youngest child reaches age 16.) By themselves, however, Social Security benefits are rarely sufficient to allow the family to maintain its previous standard of living.

The ability of a homemaker spouse to obtain employment in the event of the death of the income-producing spouse is also a factor. However, the net gain from such employment is generally much less than the wages earned. First, the earnings will be subject to taxes, including Social Security and income taxes. Second, the working spouse may lose part or all of the Social Security benefits that would otherwise be payable, because earnings can reduce Social Security benefits.[8] Finally, there are the costs incurred by working, including clothing, transportation, lunches, and childcare. If life insurance provides adequate income, the surviving spouse may elect to work outside the home. Without it, he or she may be compelled to do so.

Once children are grown, the surviving spouse may still need to replace a part of the wage earner's income. This is particularly true if the surviving spouse is not employed outside the home and would have few employment opportunities if the income-producing spouse should die. Based on the structure of Social Security benefits, the spouse's life income may be divided into two parts. The first starts when the youngest child reaches 16, at which time Social Security benefits cease, and continues until the spouse's Social Security benefits resume again at age 60 or 62. Because the spouse receives no Social Security benefits during this time, it is sometimes called the *blackout period*. During this period, the entire income must come from life insurance, employment, savings, or some other source. After the blackout period, Social Security benefits will resume, and a lesser amount of supplementary income will again be necessary.

Under the needs approach, these income requirements of the family are usually listed on a month-by-month basis over time. The presenta-

tion indicates the amount of income needed, the amount available from Social Security and other sources, and the extent of the unfilled need. This information may be summarized in graphic form, as shown in Figure 10.1. The chief benefit of this graphic analysis is that it helps the individual to visualize the amounts needed as a flow of income.

The perceptive student will note, however, that the needs presented in the chart are measured in constant dollars. Because actual needs will increase with inflation, a better approach is one in which the effects of inflation can be recognized. Today, with financial calculators and microcomputer spreadsheets, factoring inflation into the measurement of future income needs is much easier.

Determining future income needs combines the processes of compounding and discounting. First, to estimate future income needs, present needs are projected at an estimated inflation rate. Social Security benefits, which are subject to automatic adjustment for inflation, are projected at the same rate of inflation. If the spouse is employed, his or her income is also projected at an assumed rate for wage increases. The difference between the inflation-adjusted gross need and the inflation-adjusted sources of income represents the unfilled need. To determine the present value of this unfilled need, we discount the projected deficiency using a discount rate that represents the anticipated earnings on the funds that will be purchased to meet the unfilled need. Table 10.4 illustrates this process.

The current value of the remaining unmet needs in Table 10.4 is $153,768. This $153,768 amount summarizes the difference between projected income needs and the projected sources of funds to meet these needs. It is the present value of the difference between needs and available resources. To determine the portion of this amount that must be insured, existing resources should be considered. For example, if the person in the illustration has say, $50,000 in life insurance available from his or her employer and savings of $20,000, the remaining unmet need is $83,768 ($153,768

---

[8]The exact amount of Social Security benefits that would be lost depends on the circumstances. Loss of Social Security benefits is discussed in the next chapter.

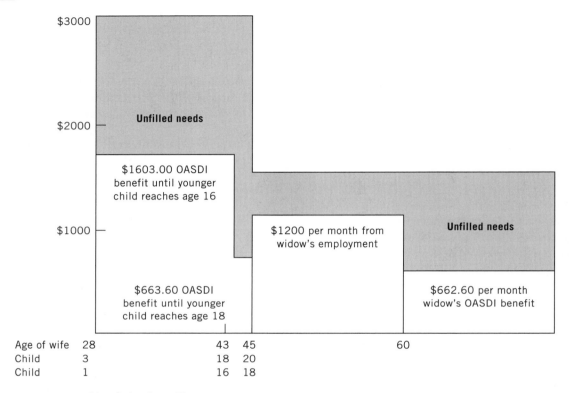

Figure 10.1 Needs Analysis Chart

minus $70,000). This is the need to be covered by the purchase of additional life insurance.[9]

Capital Liquidation versus Capital Conservation

There are two strategies regarding the amount required to fund the income needs of survivors; *capital conservation* and *capital liquidation.* The preceding illustration, which assumes that the principal will be used in meeting projected income needs, uses a capital liquidation approach.

[9]There are a variety of assumptions in our calculations, any one or all of which may not be fulfilled. It should be recognized that despite the illusion of precision implied by the multidecimal calculations of our computers, the projections are a guess.

Under the capital conservation approach (also called *capital needs analysis*) the goal is to meet income needs solely from investment income, without using the principal. The capital conservation approach requires a greater amount of capital than the capital liquidation approach. How much more will be required depends on the period for which the income stream must be provided and the return that will be earned on the capital. The longer the period and the higher the investment return, the smaller is the difference in the principal required under the capital conservation and capital liquidation approaches.[10]

[10]For a discussion of the *capital needs analysis* concept, see Thomas J. Wolff, *Capital Needs Analysis—Basic Sales Manual* (Vernon, CT: Vernon Publishing Services, 1977).

Table 10.4   Present Value of Inflation Adjusted Future Income Needs

		Age		Income Needs Projected at 3%	OASDHI Benefits Projected at 3%	Income From Mary's Employment at 4%	Projected Income Deficit	6% Discount Factor	Present Value of Projected Deficit
Year	Tom	Mary	Junior	Francesca					
1	25	25	3	1	$40,000	$16,800	$20,000	$3,200	0.94340	$3,019
2	26	26	4	2	41,200	17,304	20,800	3,096	0.89000	2,755
3	27	27	5	3	42,436	17,823	21,623	2,981	0.83962	2,503
4	28	28	6	4	43,709	18,358	22,497	2,854	0.79209	2,261
5	29	29	7	5	45,020	18,909	23,397	2,715	0.74726	2,029
6	30	30	8	6	46,371	19,476	24,333	2,562	0.70496	1,806
7	31	31	9	7	47,762	20,060	25,306	2,396	0.66506	1,593
8	32	32	10	8	49,195	20,662	26,319	2,214	0.62741	1,389
9	33	33	11	9	50,671	21,282	27,371	2,018	0.59190	1,194
10	34	34	12	10	52,191	21,920	28,466	1,805	0.55839	1,008
11	35	35	13	11	53,757	22,578	29,605	1,574	0.52679	829
12	36	36	14	12	55,369	23,255	30,789	1,325	0.49697	659
13	37	37	15	13	57,030	23,953	32,021	1,057	0.46884	496
14	38	38	16	14	58,741	24,671	33,301	769	0.44230	340
15	39	39	17	15	60,504	25,412	34,634	459	0.41727	191
16	40	40	18	16	62,319	16,772	36,019	9,528	0.39365	3,751
17	41	41	19	17	64,188	17,275	37,460	9,454	0.37136	3,511
18	42	42		18	66,114	0	38,958	27,156	0.35034	9,514
19	43	43			68,097	0	40,516	27,581	0.33051	9,116
20	44	44			70,140	0	42,137	28,003	0.31180	8,732
21	45	45			72,244	0	43,822	28,422	0.29416	8,360
22	46	46			74,412	0	45,575	28,836	0.27751	8,002
23	47	47			76,644	0	47,398	29,246	0.26180	7,656
24	48	48			78,943	0	49,294	29,649	0.24698	7,323
25	49	49			81,312	0	51,266	30,046	0.23300	7,001
26	50	50			83,751	0	53,317	30,434	0.21981	6,690
27	51	51			86,264	0	55,449	30,814	0.20737	6,390
28	52	52			88,852	0	57,667	31,184	0.19563	6,101
29	53	53			91,517	0	59,974	31,543	0.18456	5,821
30	54	54			94,263	0	62,373	31,890	0.17411	5,552
31	55	55			97,090	0	64,868	32,223	0.16425	5,293
32	56	56			100,003	0	67,463	32,541	0.15496	5,042
33	57	57			103,003	0	70,161	32,842	0.14619	4,801
34	58	58			106,093	0	72,968	33,126	0.13791	4,568
35	59	59			109,276	0	75,886	33,390	0.13011	4,344
36	60	60			112,554	0	78,922	33,633	0.12274	4,128
										153,768

The choice between the capital liquidation and capital conservation strategies relates to objectives. The capital liquidation approach is designed to meet the single risk management strategy of protecting dependents against deprivation. The capital conservation strategy seeks to also meet the personal financial planning objective of transferring wealth to heirs.

A Continuing Task

The principal defect of both the life value and the needs approaches as they are generally used is that they rely on static analysis, measuring the need for insurance at a specific point in time. This results in the purchase of an amount of insurance that may be correct at that time, but that may be incorrect as time passes. The needs of each individual will vary, depending on the age, the number of children, and financial assets. In addition, the wants of the individual may change over time, because during each period of life different needs seem more important.

The Estate Liquidity Need

One of the objectives in managing the risk of premature death may be the goal of transferring the maximum wealth possible to dependents. One of the impediments to achieving this objective arises from the fact that estates shrink as they pass from one individual to another. The major causes of estate shrinkage are probate and administration costs, which generally amount to between 4 and 5 percent of the estate and taxes, and the federal estate tax and the state inheritance tax.[11] Although risk-control measures such as estate planning can reduce the amount of these costs, the need for liquidity in the estate to meet death costs that cannot be reduced represents a need that can be met with life insurance.

[11]Estate planning is discussed in Chapter 14.

Managing the Retirement Risk

For the average college student, who has yet to begin a career, the time at which that career is likely to come to an end seems beyond the span of relevance. It is difficult to imagine the time at which the working years will eventually come to an end. It is even harder to imagine that at the time they end, there might be too few assets to live comfortably for the remainder of one's lifetime. But this is the essence of the retirement risk.

The retirement risk is the complement of the risk of premature death. If the individual dies prematurely, he or she will have no need for funds that were being accumulated for retirement. If the individual lives until retirement, provision made for premature death will not be used, but there is a need for retirement funds. Because there is a possibility of either outcome, the individual must make provision for both contingencies.

Risks Associated With Superannuation

Many people consider age 65 the "normal" retirement age, but this is a relatively recent notion in human history. In earlier periods people usually worked until they died, or until they became physically incapable of working. Today, retirement is a significant event in a person's life. Indeed, it may be said that people spend their entire lives preparing for retirement. As in the case of the biblical famine of ancient Egypt, resources are accumulated during the *income-fat* years to be consumed during the *income-lean* years. The amount that must be accumulated during the income-fat years depends on a variety of circumstances, and is influenced by the standard of living the individual wishes to maintain after retirement and the rate of inflation. It is also a function of the time for which one will live in retirement.

As a society, our current population tends to live longer after retirement than any previous generation. In 1935, a woman who reached age 65 in good health could plan on living another 13 years; for a man the life expectancy was about 12 years. By 2000, a 65-year-old woman in good health had a life expectancy of 19 years and her male counterpart had an expectancy of 16 years. For the current college-age population, life expectancies are even longer.

At the same time people are living longer, they are retiring earlier. People have quit working at earlier ages for several reasons. One is the advent of financial planning and the fact that more people are financially able to retire. In addition, many business firms are offering their employees attractive early retirement packages to make room for younger (and less expensive) workers. Many of today's college students will live 25 to 30 percent of their life span after they retire.

Two Risks Associated with Retirement

Although they are closely related, there are two distinguishable risks associated with retirement. The first is the possibility that insufficient assets will have been accumulated by the time the individual reaches retirement age. The second is the possibility that the individual may outlive the assets that have been accumulated. Given the accumulation of sufficient assets to provide an adequate standard of living after retirement, there is the question of how much of the accumulation should be consumed each year so that the accumulation will last for the individual's entire lifetime. This second problem is the easier of the two to address. The annuity principle, in which a principal sum is liquidated based on life expectancies, can be used to convert an accumulation into an income the individual cannot outlive. In Chapter 12, we will discuss the specifics of different types of annuities. For the present, it is sufficient to note that annuities are essential tools in managing the retirement risk and that they provide a convenient solution to the second problem associated with retirement, the possibility of outliving the retirement accumulation.

Approaches to the Retirement Risk

Some people attempt to avoid the risk of outliving their income by the simple expedient of not retiring. There are many who continue working beyond the normal retirement age by preference or out of necessity. People who elect not to retire do not, however, totally avoid the risk that they may outlive their income. The probability of disability increases significantly beyond age 65 and disability income insurance does not cover disabilities that commence after age 65. The individual may be forced into involuntary retirement by disability. Although continued employment at retirement age does not avoid the risk of outliving one's income, it clearly reduces the risk.

Transfer is also used as a technique for dealing with the retirement risk. Annuities can transfer the risk of outliving an accumulated sum to an insurer. In addition, some people transfer the retirement risk to their children or to society, by the simple expedient of not preparing for retirement.

Although the provision for one's retirement may combine the techniques of avoidance, reduction, and transfer, the primary technique for dealing with the retirement risk is retention. As in the case of other retention strategies, this requires the accumulation or identification of the funds that will be required to meet the loss when it occurs.

The Retirement Planning Process

Retirement planning more or less parallels the process we discussed in connection with the risk of premature death. The first step is to estimate the future income need. The amount that will be required for a comfortable retirement will depend on the rate of inflation and the life-style to which one aspires after inflation. Most retirement advisers suggest that an individual will need between 60 and 80 percent of the preretirement income to maintain a satisfactory standard of living. Although it is traditional to assume that postretirement income needs will be less than the need during the working years, it is conceivable that for some people the need may be greater. This is particularly true in the case of persons who plan to travel and engage in a variety of recreational activities during retirement.

Once the income needs at and after retirement have been identified, the next step is to identify the resources that will be available to meet those needs. These include Social Security, employer-provided pensions, and personal savings, which are referred to as "the three legs of retirement planning." For most people, the first source of retirement income will be Social Security. For many, Social Security will be supplemented by the second layer of protection, a pension provided by the employer. Beyond these two sources of retirement income, the individual will need to accumulate funds through savings that are generated during the individual's income-earning years. The portion of the retirement funding that must be accumulated by this third leg of retirement funding varies inversely with the generosity of the qualified retirement funding and the level of Social Security benefits.

Once the required monthly retirement need has been determined and the resources that will be available to meet that need have been estimated, the difference represents the monthly income need that must be met by the retirement accumulation. This monthly income need can be converted into a lump sum by computing the cost of a life annuity for the required monthly income. For a male at age 65, the cost of a $10 monthly benefit is about $1100. For a female, it is about $1350. The cost of an annuity that will provide the required monthly amount is computed by dividing the monthly requirement by $10, to determine the number of $10 per month units that must be purchased. If the monthly need is, say, $1500, the purchase price of an annuity that will provide $1500 per month to a 65-year-old female is $202,500, that is, $1500/$10 = 150 × $1350 = $202,500. The annual or monthly contribution that will be required to accumulate this amount by retirement age will depend on the period of

time for which contributions can be made and the return that can be earned on the accumulating fund. Present value tables tell us that $1 contributed each year for 40 years at 6 percent interest is $164.05. To accumulate $202,500 in 40 years, Jones must contribute $1234 a year, or about $103 a month, that is, $202,500/$164.05 = $1234.38.[12]

Table 10.5 indicates the impact that both time and rate of return can have on an accumulation fund. Obviously, the sooner one begins to accumulate funds for retirement, the greater the amount set aside, and the higher the return on the accumulating fund, the greater will be the accumulation at retirement.

Managing the Accumulation

An obvious question that arises in connection with the funds accumulated for retirement concerns the form in which these funds should be held. There are a variety of options, including life insurance and annuities, government bonds, corporate bonds, stocks, mutual funds, limited partnerships, and real estate. Financial planners have identified a number of criteria that should be considered in selecting the long-term investments that will be used in accumulating the personal savings component of one's retirement income. These include the rate of return, vulnerability to inflation, tax treatment, and safety.

Hedge Against Inflation

One approach to the problem of inflation is to invest in instruments that increase at the same or greater rate than inflation. Although there are no guarantees, a diversified portfolio of common stocks may be expected to increase in value with

---

[12]Microcomputer software programs are available that perform the retirement planning calculations. Among the more popular programs (all available only for IBM-compatible PCs) are Vanguard's Retirement Planner, Version 2.0, Harvest Time, Fidelity's Retirement Planning Thinkware, and T. Rowe Price's Retirement Planning Kit.

Table 10.5   Accumulation of $1,000 Annual Investment

Rate	*Number of Years*							
	5	10	15	20	25	30	35	40
5%	5,802	13,207	20,579	34,719	50,113	69,761	94,836	126,840
6%	5,975	13,972	22,276	38,993	58,156	83,802	118,121	164,048
7%	6,153	14,783	26,888	43,865	67,676	101,072	147,913	213,610
8%	6,335	15,645	29,324	49,422	78,954	122,345	186,102	279,781
9%	6,523	16,560	32,003	55,764	92,324	148,574	235,125	368,292
10%	6,715	17,531	34,949	63,002	108,181	180,942	298,127	486,852
11%	6,912	18,561	38,189	71,265	126,998	220,912	379,164	645,827
12%	7,115	19,654	41,753	80,698	149,333	270,292	483,463	859,142
13%	7,322	20,814	45,671	91,469	175,850	331,314	617,749	1,145,486
14%	7,535	22,044	49,980	103,768	207,332	409,736	790,673	1,529,909
15%	7,753	23,349	54,717	117,810	244,712	499,956	1,013,346	2,045,954

the price level, and many financial planners recommend that equities comprise a significant portion of the retirement fund. Although equities represent an aggressive investment strategy, the greater the time until retirement, the more aggressive one may be.

Tax Treatment

The importance of the tax treatment of investments for the retirement accumulation stems from the effect that the rate of return has on the rate at which the retirement fund will grow. Obviously, if a part of the investment income cannot be reinvested because it must go to pay taxes, the realized rate of return will be lower. Investments on which the investment income accumulates tax free, or on which the taxation of the investment return is deferred, will accumulate more rapidly and provide a greater terminal value than when the increments are subject to current taxation.[13]

[13]For example, a $1000 annual contribution on which an 8 percent return accumulates tax-free over 30 years will generate a terminal fund of $279,781. If the earnings are then taxed at 31 percent, the after-tax accumulation is $205,449. If, instead, earnings are taxed each year at the 31 percent rate, the accumulated fund falls to $144,863.

Diversification

Most informed authorities warn against putting all your eggs in one basket. A diversified portfolio composed of complementary investments is the usual recommendation. This means that a part of the portfolio should provide protection against inflation and should probably be invested in some type of equities, such as stocks or mutual funds. Another part should be invested in fixed-dollar instruments, such as certificates of deposit, bonds, life insurance, or annuities. Further, each part of the program should be diversified.

Managing the Distribution

The final step in managing the retirement risk is managing the distribution. The major decisions in this phase generally relate to the uncertainty regarding life expectancy of the retirees. They include the issue of a capital retention versus a capital liquidation strategy, the provision that would be made for inflation that occurs after retirement, and the provision that should be made in the distribution for a spouse or other dependents. Decisions in this phase of planning may require adjustments in the earlier steps as the assumptions concerning needs and funding are tested against the assumptions in the distribution plan.

Capital Retention versus Capital Liquidation Strategies

If the individual can accumulate sufficient capital so that the investment income alone will provide the required income during retirement, the capital conservation strategy is an option. In measuring whether a capital retention strategy is feasible, however, the requirements of the *Internal Revenue Code* concerning required distributions must be considered. For most persons, the accumulated principal in a retirement program will include some untaxed contributions to the retirement program, plus the untaxed earnings on those contributions. Because neither the contributions that created the accumulation nor the investment income have been taxed, the *IRC* requires that the accumulation be distributed so they can be taxed as income to the participant. One can defer distribution until age $70\frac{1}{2}$, or in some cases until actual retirement if later. When the distribution is made, it must be made over a period no longer than the life expectancy of the individual or the individual and a designated beneficiary. The longer the distribution is delayed, the shorter life expectancy over which it must be distributed.

Dealing with Inflation After Retirement

Another decision relates to the provision that will be made for inflation that will occur after retirement begins. Over a period of 20 to 30 years, inflation can severely erode the purchasing power of annuity payments and some provision should be made for this possibility. There are several approaches to this problem, including the use of a variable annuity during the annuity payout period or a graded distribution for a fixed dollar annuity, under which insurers provide payments that are lower initially, but that increase over time.

Single or Joint Life Annuity

A second major decision relates to the provision, if any, that will be made for a surviving spouse. Although some annuities make payments over the lifetime for two annuitants, there is a cost; payments during the joint lives of spouses are lower than under a straight life annuity on a single person.

Risks Associated with Disability

In discussing the need for life insurance, we noted that there may be instances in which no one would suffer financial deprivation in the event of a person's death and there is no need for life insurance. The disability income need is fundamentally different. In the case of the disability exposure, the absence of dependents does not eliminate the need for income, since the disabled person will need income during a period of disability. As a matter of fact, the income need may be greater in the case of an individual without a spouse. When a disabled person has a spouse, the domestic partner may be able to provide some income for the couple. In addition, the nondisabled spouse will serve as a care provider. The single individual does not have the cushion of a spouse's income and will generally have to hire a care provider. This means that the percentage of a single person's income that must be replaced in the event of disability may be higher than that of a person with a spouse.[14]

For the individual with dependents, the family's income needs if the wage-earner becomes disabled are certainly as great as they would be if he or she died. In fact, they would probably be greater. As in the case of life insurance, the needs

[14]In this sense, marriage represents a risk-sharing technique and the treatment of risk by combining a very small number of exposure units.

vary with the number of children in the family and with other responsibilities the insured may have. Also, as in the case of death, benefits available under employer-provided and social insurance plans should be considered in determining the need for other protection.

Some authorities argue that loss-of-income protection should come even before life insurance. When a wage earner is disabled, his or her earnings stop just as surely as if death had occurred. This "living death" of disability can be economically more severe than actual death. If the breadwinner of the family dies, the family's income stops; if he or she is disabled, not only does the income stop but expenses remain the same and usually increase. Because a disabled person— by definition—is one whose ability to work is impaired, he or she must depend on sources other than employment for income. When persons other than the disabled individual were also supported by the lost income, the problem is worse.

In addition to the fact that disability can be more burdensome financially to the individual and dependents than is usually supposed, the chance of loss at most ages is greater than the chance of death. Table 10.6 indicates the probability of death and disability at various ages.

As indicated by the data in the table, the probability of disability of at least 90 days is signifi-

cantly higher at every age during the individual's working years than is the probability of death. Nearly half the people who reach age 35 will be disabled for at least three months before reaching age 65, and the average length of the disability will be more than five years.

Needs Analysis for the Disability Risk

A needs analysis for the *disability risk* is much like the needs analysis for premature death. First, income needs for each year are projected by examining the amount required to maintain the family in the event of disability. Usually the income needs of the family will not diminish much if the wage earner is disabled. There may be a modest reduction in some expenses associated with employment, such as the cost of commuting, business lunches, and perhaps a part of the clothing budget, but the reduction will probably be small. While there may be an increase in medical expenses, adequate medical expense insurance should be available to meet the increased medical care costs.

In determining disability income needs, careful consideration must be given to the need to continue to plan for the retirement years. In our discussion of disability income contracts, we will see that most insurers will provide coverage for disability arising out of accident for the individual's entire lifetime, but limit coverage for disability arising out of sickness until age 65. How, one may ask, do we provide for income beyond age 65 for the individual who is disabled as a result of sickness? The answer is that the income need after age 65 is treated as a part of the individual's retirement needs. The need for income after age 65 will exist whether or not the person is disabled, and prudent individuals accumulate funds to supplement Social Security benefits. Since insurers do not offer lifetime disability coverage for illness, a disability protection program should provide benefits in an amount that will permit the disabled person to continue making contributions to

Table 10.6   Probability of Death and Disability at Various Ages

Age	Probability of Death Before Age 65	Probability of 90 Day Disability Before Age 65
25	24%	54%
30	23%	52%
35	22%	50%
40	21%	48%
45	20%	44%
50	18%	39%
55	15%	32%
60	9%	9%

Sources: Based on 1980 CSO Mortality Table, 1985 Commissioners Disability Table, and *McGill's Life Insurance*, ed. Edward E. Graves (Bryn Mawr, PA: American College, 1994).

his or her retirement program. In this way, the accumulation of funds intended for retirement will be there at age 65 whether or not the individual is disabled.

Resources Available to Meet the Disability Risk

After determining the needs, the next step is to identify any benefits available from existing sources. Several sources may provide protection against lost income during disability. For disability that arises out of and in the course of employment, most injured workers are entitled to benefits under their state workers compensation law. The amount of these benefits depends on the worker's earnings at the time of the injury and is defined by law. Workers in California, Hawaii, New Jersey, New York, Rhode Island, and Puerto Rico are covered for nonoccupational disabilities by compulsory programs, under which the benefits are also prescribed by law. Finally, workers

who are totally and permanently disabled and who meet special eligibility requirements qualify for disability benefits under the Social Security program. The eligibility requirements under this program are strict, and benefits are payable only if the individual is unable to engage in any substantially gainful employment.[15]

Besides these government-sponsored or supervised programs, the most common source of recovery is through group or individual disability income policies. In some instances, employers self-insure a program of disability benefits for their employees, providing either cash benefits or paid sick leave. In others, the paid sick leave plans are integrated with disability income insurance purchased from commercial insurers.

---

[15]Eligibility requirements for Social Security disability income benefits and workers compensation are discussed in Chapter 11.

Tidbits, Vignettes, and Conundrums 10.2

Managing the Risk of Unemployment

Although much has been written in insurance and financial planning books on managing the risks of premature death, superannuation, and disability, the fourth peril that threatens income—unemployment—has been relatively neglected. This is perhaps understandable, because it is the exposure for which the risk management strategies are the most limited. State unemployment insurance programs exist in all states, and most individuals will have some protection from this source. This protection, however, is limited, both in duration and in amount. Although unemployment insurance is

available on a limited basis in connection with installment credit, it is vastly overpriced. For most people, the alternatives for managing the risk of unemployment are retention and reduction. An emergency fund provides a cushion against the risk of unexpected short-term unemployment. For the longer-term exposure, a comprehensive education and specialized work skills are still the most effective loss-prevention measures against the peril of involuntary unemployment. For students, this means selecting a career that is relatively immune to fluctuations in employment.

Addressing Unmet Disability Income Needs

Unmet needs are determined by subtracting available resources from the needs that have been identified. Disability insurance may then be purchased to cover the unmet needs. The most important disability income need is long-term disability coverage for both occupational and nonoccupational disabilities to supplement Social Security and workers compensation coverage. For occupational disabilities, the disability income coverage should supplement workers compensation benefits so that the combined benefits provide the same level of coverage as for nonoccupational disabilities. Disability insurance is discussed in more detail in Chapter 15.

Evaluating the Medical Expense Exposure

No personal risk management program is complete without some protection against medical expenses. The major consideration in the area of medical expense coverage should be protection against the catastrophic loss. A variety of plans are available, ranging from plans covering a specific class of medical expenses with a small deductible to plans covering a broad array of expenses with a larger annual deductible. Because of the variety of plans available and the fact that most individuals are covered for these expenses under employer-provided plans, we defer discussion to Chapter 16.

Important Concepts to Remember

premature death
superannuation
human life value
time value of money
present value
discounting
needs approach
capital needs
analysis
insurance programming
fund for last expenses
cleanup fund

emergency fund
dependency period
capital liquidation strategy
capital conservation strategy
readjustment expense fund
premarital period
pre-child years of marriage
child-raising years
years approaching retirement
blackout period
estate planning
intestate

federal estate and gift tax rates
incidents of ownership
gross estate
taxable estate
trust
living trust
life insurance trust agreement
life annuity
retirement risk
disability risk
unemployment risk

Questions for Review

1. Briefly explain how the human life value approach differs from the needs approach in determining the amount of life insurance an individual should purchase. What is the relationship between the two approaches?

2. What, if any, are the defects in using the human life value concept in determining the amount of life insurance an individual should purchase?

3. The need for life insurance varies with the individual's lifestyle. How does this need differ for single individuals, childless couples, and persons with children?

4. Identify the "needs" that are traditionally considered in determining the amount of life insurance required for a family.

5. Identify the sources other than life insurance that might provide resources to meet needs in the case of premature death.

6. One tool for dealing with the risk of outliving one's income is a life annuity. Briefly explain how a life annuity is able to do this.

7. Identify the resources that might be available to address the retirement risk.

8. Explain why the disability needs for a particular individual are likely to be even greater than the needs in the case of premature death.

9. How should one deal with the dilemma created by the fact that disability resulting from sickness may extend beyond age 65, but insurers are generally unwilling to provide coverage for such disabilities beyond age 65?

10. Identify the resources that may be available for an individual who experiences a disability.

Questions for Discussion

1. The changing lifestyles of many Americans have modified some of the traditional principles of insurance buying. With an increase in the number of two-income families, do you think that the overall need for life insurance has (a) increased or (b) decreased? Why?

2. It is often stated that one of the most neglected areas in the life insurance field is that of insurance on the homemaker spouse. In facing the risk-management decision regarding life insurance for the family, where do you think that life insurance on a spouse who is not employed outside the home should fit?

3. What reasons can you suggest for providing a lifetime income to a spouse after any children

have been raised? Under what circumstances would you recommend against providing such a lifetime income?

4. "On first consideration, it might seem that the risk of income loss resulting from premature death is universal. After all, no one lives forever. But death does not automatically result in financial loss." Explain why you agree or disagree with this statement.

5. "The effect of the income loss occasioned by premature death depends on the circumstances." Describe a combination of circumstances in which the effect of income loss occasioned by premature death is insignificant.

Suggestions for Additional Reading

Aponte, J. B., and Herbert S. Denenberg. "A New Concept of the Economics of Life Value and the Human Life." *Journal of Risk and Insurance*, vol. 35, no. 3 (Sept. 1968).

Black, Kenneth, Jr., and Harold D. Skipper, Jr. *Life Insurance*, 13th ed. Englewood Cliffs, NJ: Prentice Hall, 2000. Chapters 1, 2, 13, 14.

Crowe, Robert M., and Charles E. Hughes, eds. *Fundamentals of Financial Planning*, 2nd ed. Bryn Mawr, PA: American College, 1993.

Hallman, G. Victor, and Karen L. Hamilton. *Personal Insurance: Life, Health & Retirement*. Malvern, PA: American Institute for CPCU, 1994. Chapters 3 and 6.

Hofflander, A. E. "The Human Life Value: A Historical Perspective." *Journal of Risk and Insurance*, vol. 33, no. 3 (Sept. 1966).

Wolff, Thomas J. *Capital Needs Analysis—Basic Sales Manual.* Vernon, CT: Vernon Publishing Services, 1977.

Websites to Explore

American College: http://www.amercoll.edu/

American Council of Life Insurance: http://www.acli.com/

American Society of CLU & ChFC: http://www.agents-online.com/ASCLU/web/index.html

Free Advice-Estate Planning: http://freeadvice.com/law/536us.htm

Institute of Certified Financial Planners: http://www.icfp.org/

Insurance News Network: http://www.insure.com/

Internal Revenue Service: http://www.irs.ustreas.gov/

International Association for Financial Planning: http://www.iafp.org/

Life Insurance Marketing and Research Association, Inc.: http://www.limra.com

Life Office Management Association (LOMA): http://www.loma.org/

S.S. Huebner Foundation for Insurance Education: http://rider.wharton.upenn.edu/~sshuebne/

Gift and Estate Tax Law: http://www.law.cornell.edu/topics/estate—gift-tax.html

CHAPTER 11

Social Insurance Programs

*The essence of social insurance is bringing
the magic of averages to the rescue of millions.*
—Winston Churchill

CHAPTER OBJECTIVES

When you have finished this chapter, you should be able to

- Identify and describe the major classes of benefits in the Old-Age, Survivors', Disability, and Health Insurance Program (OASDHI)

- Identify the persons who are eligible for benefits under the Old-Age, Survivors', and Disability Insurance (OASDI) program and how eligibility for benefits is derived

- Explain how benefits under the OASDI program are financed

- Explain how the amount of benefits received under OASDI is determined and the circumstances that can lead to a loss of benefits

- Evaluate the financial soundness of the Social Security system and identify the proposals that have been suggested to improve that soundness

- Explain the rationale for workers compensation laws and outline the principles on which the workers compensation system is based

- Describe the operation of the workers compensation system, including the types of injuries covered and the types of benefits

- Describe the nature of state unemployment compensation laws and describe the way in which the federal government encouraged states to adopt such laws

- Describe generally how coverage under state unemployment compensation laws is determined and how benefits are determined

In this chapter, we turn to social insurance programs that contribute to the security of the individual that were introduced in Chapter 3. We study these social insurance programs to acquire tools that may be used in dealing with the risks to income facing the individual. Although our examination will be brief, it will be sufficient to allow us to relate the benefits under these programs to the overall risk management problem facing the individual.

Old-Age, Survivors', Disability, and Health Insurance

The Old-Age, Survivors', Disability, and Health Insurance Program (commonly known as *Social Security*) protects eligible workers and their dependents against the financial losses associated with death, disability, superannuation, and sickness in old age. The benefits available under the program to the dependents of a deceased worker or to a disabled worker and his or her dependents are an important part of an individual's income protection program. The retirement benefits are also a fundamental element in the individual's retirement program. There are four classes of benefits.

1. *Old-age benefits.* The old-age part of OASDHI provides a lifetime pension beginning at age 65 (or a reduced benefit as early as age 62) to each eligible worker and certain eligible dependents. The amount of this pension is based on the worker's average earnings during some period in the working years.

2. *Survivors' benefits.* Although the Social Security Act originally provided only retirement benefits, complaints that the system was unfair to workers who died before retirement (or after retirement) induced Congress to expand the program, extend-

ing benefits to the dependents of a deceased worker or retiree. The survivors' portion of the program provides covered workers with a form of life insurance, the proceeds of which are payable to their dependent children and, under some conditions, surviving spouses.

3. *Disability benefits.* Disability benefits were added to the program in 1956 and applied to workers who became disabled between the ages of 50 and 64. In 1960, this coverage was broadened to all workers who meet certain eligibility requirements. A qualified worker who becomes totally and permanently disabled is treated as if he or she had reached retirement age and the worker and dependents become eligible for the benefits that would otherwise be payable at age 65.

4. *Medicare benefits.* The Medicare portion of the system was added in 1965. It offers people over 65 and certain disabled persons protection against the high cost of hospitalization and certain other kinds of medical care. In addition, it provides an option by which those eligible for the basic benefits under the medical program may purchase subsidized medical insurance to help pay for doctors' services and other expenses not covered by the basic plan.[1]

All income benefits are subject to automatic adjustments for increases in the cost of living. Benefits for all recipients are increased automatically each January if the Consumer Price Index (CPI) shows a rise in the cost of living during the preceding year. Congress retains the right to legislate increases in benefit levels, and there is no automatic increase in any year for which Congress has legislated one.

---

[1]The original income-protection elements of Social Security (Old-Age, Survivors', and Disability Insurance) are referred to as OASDI. The expanded system, which includes Medicare, is OASDHI. Medicare benefits are discussed in Chapter 16.

Eligibility and Qualification Requirements

Today, more than 95 percent of the labor force is covered by the Social Security system, most on a compulsory basis. Most of those not covered are state, local, or federal employees. To qualify for benefits, an individual must have credit for a certain amount of work under Social Security. Insured status is measured by *quarters of coverage*, and individuals earn these quarters by paying taxes on their wages. Some benefits are payable only if the worker has enough quarters of coverage to be considered *fully insured*, whereas other benefits are payable if the worker is merely *currently insured*.

Quarter of Coverage

For most employment before 1978, an individual earned one quarter of coverage for each calendar quarter in which he or she paid the Federal Insurance Contribution Act (FICA) tax on $50 or more in wages. Since 1978, the level of earnings on which FICA taxes must be paid for a quarter of coverage is adjusted annually, based on increases in average total wages for all workers. By 2000, one quarter of coverage was granted for each $780 of earnings, up to a maximum of four quarters per year. Further increases will take place as the average total wages for all workers increase.

Fully Insured Status

Fully insured status is required for retirement benefits. To be fully insured the worker must have one quarter of coverage for each year starting with the year in which he or she reaches age 22, up to, but not including, the year in which the worker reaches age 62, becomes disabled, or dies. For most people, this means 40 quarters of coverage. No worker can achieve fully insured status with fewer than 6 quarters of covered employment, and no worker needs more than 40 quar-

ters. Once a worker has 40 quarters of coverage, he or she is fully insured permanently.

Currently Insured Status

To be currently insured, a worker needs 6 quarters of coverage during the 13-quarter period ending with the quarter of death, entitlement to retirement benefits, or disability. Currently insured status entitles children of a deceased worker (and the children's mother or father) to survivors' benefits and provides a lump-sum benefit in the event of the worker's death.

Financing

The OASDHI program is administered by the Social Security Administration.[2] It is financed through a system of payroll and self-employment taxes paid by covered workers and their employers. For wage earners, a tax is paid on wages up to a specified maximum by both employers and the employee. In the original act of 1935, a tax rate of 1 percent applied to the first $3000 of an employee's wages, and the employer and employee were each liable for the tax up to a $30 annual maximum. Both the tax rate and taxable wage base to which it applies have increased over time as the program has expanded. When the Medicare program was added in 1965, a separate *Hospital Insurance tax* was added, which is combined with the Old-Age, Survivors', and Disability tax to make up the total FICA tax. The most recent change in the tax rate occurred in 1990, when the *Old-Age, Survivors', and Disability tax* was increased to 6.2 percent and the Hospital Insur-

---

[2]The Social Security Administration maintains an exceptionally useful Web page at http://www.ssa.gov/. The site provides current detailed information on all facets of the OASDI program with a link to the Health Care Financing Administration (HCFA), which administers Medicare. The HCFA Web site is http://www.hcfa.gov/.

ance tax was increased to 1.45 percent, making a combined rate of 7.65 percent, payable by the employee and matched by the employer.

The FICA tax applies to a taxable wage base that automatically increases in the year following an automatic benefit increase. Like the automatic increases in benefit levels, congressional changes in the taxable wage base override the automatic adjustment provisions. With legislated changes and automatic adjustments, the taxable wage base had increased to $72,800 by 2000 and will continue to increase in the future. Originally, the Medicare tax applied only up to the maximum taxable wage base but since 1993 has applied to total earned income without limit.

Self-employed persons pay a tax rate that is equal to the combined employer-employee contribution (i.e., 15.3 percent). Self-employed persons are allowed a deduction against income taxes equal to half the self-employment taxes paid for the year.

Amount of Benefits

Most OASDHI benefits are based on a benefit called the *primary insurance amount* (PIA), which is the retirement benefit payable to a worker who retires at the normal retirement age. Until 2000, the normal retirement age was age 65, but legislation enacted in 1983 increases the normal retirement age for persons born in 1938 and later. For each year after 1937 the person was born, the normal retirement age is increased by two months. The full retirement age for persons born in 1960 and later will be 67.

The PIA is computed from the individual's *average indexed monthly earnings* (AIME), which is the worker's average monthly wages or other earnings during his or her computation years, indexed to current wage levels. After indexing prior earnings, some years with low earnings may be dropped before the earnings are averaged. For retirement benefits, up to five years of low earnings may be dropped, but a minimum of 35 years must

be used in calculating the AIME. An individual who works longer than 40 years may be able to exclude some additional years of low earnings. Fewer years may be included if the PIA is being calculated for a worker who has died or become disabled.

The AIME is converted to the PIA using a formula prescribed by law. The formula used in converting the AIME to the PIA provides for a higher percentage of the average indexed earnings at lower income levels than at higher income levels.[3]

The Social Security Administration provides personalized benefit estimates to workers on request. In addition, in October 1999, the Social Security Administration (SSA) began mailing annual statements to all covered workers providing estimates of each worker's retirement, disability, and survivors' benefits. Workers automatically receive their statements about three months before their birth month.

Classes of Benefits

Retirement Benefits

Workers who retire at their normal retirement age receive a benefit equal to their PIA for life. A worker can retire as early as age 62, but with an actuarially-reduced benefit. The reduction depends on the worker's normal retirement age and the number of months before that date that the worker retires. For persons whose normal retirement age is 65, the benefit is reduced $\frac{5}{9}$ of 1 percent for each month prior to age 65 the worker retires. This amounts to approximately a 20 percent reduction at age 62. For persons whose normal retirement age is 67, the reduction for retire-

---

[3]For workers reaching age 65 in 1999, the PIA was computed on the basis of the following formula: 90 percent of the first $505 of AIME, plus 32 percent of the AIME from $505 to $3043, plus 15 percent of the AIME above $3043. The dollar amounts in the formula, known as *bend points*, are subject to adjustment based on changes in the national average monthly wages.

ment at age 62 will be 30 percent. Workers who delay retirement receive an increase in their PIA for each month between the ages of 65 and 72 that they delay retirement. The increase in benefits for delayed retirement will gradually rise from 5 percent per year for persons whose normal retirement age is 65 to 8 percent per year delay for persons born in 1943 and later.

In addition to the benefits received by the worker at retirement, certain dependents may receive benefits if the worker was fully insured. Total benefits received by the family, however, are subject to an overall maximum family benefit.

Spouse's Benefit The spouse of the retired worker (or a spouse divorced after 10 years of marriage) is entitled to a retirement benefit at age 65 equal to 50 percent of the worker's PIA. Like the retired worker, the spouse may choose a permanently reduced benefit as early as age 62.[4]

Children's Benefit The benefit for children of a retired worker is payable to three classes of dependent children: (1) unmarried children under age 18; (2) unmarried children age 18 or over who are disabled, provided that they were disabled before reaching age 22; and (3) unmarried children under age 19 who are full-time students in an elementary or secondary school. The benefit to each eligible child of a retired worker is 50 percent of the worker's benefit.

Mother's or Father's Benefit A retired worker's spouse who has not yet reached age 62 may still be entitled to a benefit, if he or she has care of a child who is receiving a benefit. A *mother's benefit* or *father's benefit* is payable to the spouse of a re-

tired worker if either has care of a child under 16 or a disabled child who is receiving a benefit. This benefit is 50 percent of the worker's PIA.

Family Maximum All income benefits payable to a worker and his or her dependents are subject to a family maximum. The family maximum is based on a formula applied to the PIA.[5] If total family benefits are greater than the family maximum, each individual's benefit, except the retired worker's, is reduced.

Survivors' Benefits

Benefits are payable to certain dependents of a deceased worker, provided that the worker had insured status, which varies for the different classes of survivors' benefits. Once again, total benefits are subject to an overall maximum family benefit. Survivors' benefits include the following:

Lump-Sum Death Benefit A $255 lump-sum death benefit is payable to the surviving spouse or children of the deceased worker.

Children's Benefit The *children's benefit* is payable to dependent children of a deceased worker in any of the three classes noted earlier. The benefit to each eligible child of a deceased worker is 75 percent of the worker's PIA.

Mother's or Father's Benefit A *mother's or father's benefit* is payable to the widow or widower of a deceased worker who has care of a child under 16 (or a disabled child over 16) who is receiving benefits. This benefit is 75 percent of the worker's PIA.

Widow's or Widower's Benefit The widow or widower of a deceased worker (or a worker's divorced spouse of 10 years of marriage) is entitled to a retirement benefit at age 65 equal to 100 per-

---

[4]A divorced spouse can receive benefits based on a former husband's or wife's Social Security earnings if the marriage lasted at least 10 years. The divorced spouse must be 62 or older and unmarried. If the spouse has been divorced at least two years, he or she can get benefits, even if the worker is not retired, provided the worker has enough credits to qualify for benefits and is age 62 or older. The amount of benefits a divorced spouse gets has no effect on the amount of benefits a current spouse receives.

[5]This formula, like the PIA formula, includes dollar *bend points* that are subject to adjustment based on increases in the average total wages of all workers.

cent of the worker's PIA. The widow or widower may elect to receive a permanently scaled-down benefit as early as age 60, when the benefit is 71.5 percent of the PIA. The *widow's or widower's benefit* is also payable to the spouse of a deceased worker who becomes disabled after age 50 and not more than 7 years after the death of the worker or the end of his or her entitlement to a mother's or father's benefit.

Parents' Benefit The *parents' benefit* is payable to a deceased worker's parents who are over age 62, if they were dependent on the worker for support at the time of death. One parent is entitled to a retirement benefit at age 62 equal to 82.5 percent of the worker's PIA. The maximum benefit for two dependent parents is 150 percent of the worker's PIA (75 percent each).

Required Insured Status Under the survivor benefit program, the children's benefit, mother's or father's benefit, and lump-sum death benefit are paid if the worker is either fully or currently insured. All other benefits are payable only if the worker was fully insured.

Disability Benefits

Disability benefits are payable to a worker and eligible dependents when a worker who meets special eligibility requirements is disabled within the meaning of that term under the law. Disability is defined as a "mental or physical impairment that prevents the worker from engaging in any substantial gainful employment." The disability must have lasted for 6 months and must be expected to last for at least 12 months or be expected to result in the prior death of the worker. Persons who apply for Social Security benefits are referred to the state agencies called *disability determination services* (DDSs) to evaluate the disability. If the state agency is satisfied that the worker is disabled as defined by the Social Security Act, the individual is certified as such and benefits are paid. However, benefits do not start until the worker has been disabled for five full calendar months.

Qualification requirements for disability benefits depend on the worker's age. Workers who become disabled before reaching age 24 qualify if they have 6 quarters out of the 12 quarters ending when the disability began. Workers who became disabled between ages 24 and 31 must have 1 quarter of coverage for each 2 quarters beginning at age 21 and ending with the onset of disability. Workers over age 31 must be fully insured, and must have 20 out of the last 40 quarters in covered employment.

In general, disability benefits are payable to the same categories of persons and in the same amounts as retirement benefits, but subject to a special family maximum benefit. Total monthly payments for a disabled worker with one or more dependents are limited to the lower of 85 percent of the worker's AIME or 150 percent of the worker's disability benefit (but not less than 100 percent of the worker's PIA).[6]

Summary of Qualification Requirements

Although the qualification requirements seem complicated, there is a basic principle. The survivors' benefits payable to children and mother's or father's benefits require only that the worker have been fully or currently insured. To be eligible for any retirement benefits, the worker must have been fully insured. Table 11.1 summarizes the qualification requirements for the various categories of benefits under OASDHI.

Table 11.2 lists the actual dollar amount of benefits in effect in 2000. The PIAs are adjusted automatically each January (upward only) to match increases in the CPI. This means that the

---

[6]Disability benefits may be reduced if the individual also receives workers compensation benefits. The law limits combined benefits to 80 percent of the disabled person's recent earnings. Some states have reverse offset plans, under which workers compensation benefits are reduced if the worker is entitled to Social Security benefits.

Table 11.1   Insured Status Required for OASDI Benefits

Benefit	*Insured Status Required of Workers*
Survivor benefits	
Children's benefits	Fully or currently insured
Mother's or father's benefit	Fully or currently insured
Dependent parent's benefit	Fully insured
Widow or widower age 60 or over	Fully insured
Lump-sum death benefit	Fully or currently insured
Retirement benefits	
Retired worker	Fully insured
Spouse of retired worker	Fully insured
Child of retired worker	Fully insured
Mother's or father's benefit	Fully insured
Disability benefits	
Disabled worker	20 or last 40 quarters fully insured or
Dependent of disabled worker	6 of last 12 quarters if under age 24
	1 of every 2 quarters since age 21 if between 23 and 31

benefits shown in the table will be adjusted in January 2001, depending on the increase in the CPI from the first quarter of 1999 to the first quarter of 2000.

Loss of Benefits—The OASDHI Program

A person receiving benefits may lose eligibility for benefits in several ways. The most common causes of disqualification are a change in dependency status and disqualifying income.[7]

Change in Dependency Status

Dependents of a retired or disabled worker or the survivors of a deceased worker may lose their benefits as a result of a change in their dependency status. Such changes may occur as a result of di-

vorce, adoption, marriage, or a child reaching adulthood. For example, the spouse of a retired worker who is receiving a benefit based on the qualification of that worker loses the right to the benefit after divorce, unless he or she was married to the worker for 10 years or longer. Similarly, if a child who is receiving a benefit is adopted by anyone except a stepparent, grandparent, aunt, or uncle, the payment to the child stops.

Dependency status can also be terminated by marriage, although the rules in this area are complex. As a rule, if a person receiving a monthly benefit as a dependent or survivor marries someone who is not also a beneficiary, his or her payment stops. Where both parties in the marriage are OASDI beneficiaries, payments may continue. For example, a widow receiving mother's benefits (because of a child under 16) will not lose her benefits if she marries an individual receiving retirement or disability benefits, but would lose her benefit if she married otherwise.[8]

---

[7]In addition to a change in dependency status and disqualifying income, benefits may also be lost because of conviction of treason, sabotage, or subversive activity; deportation; work in foreign countries, unless that work is also covered under OASDI; and the refusal of rehabilitation by a disabled beneficiary.

[8]Children under 18 lose their benefits if they marry, regardless of who they marry. Widows, widowers, and surviving divorced spouses lose their benefits based on the deceased worker's earnings if they remarry before age 60. Benefits to a surviving spouse or a divorced surviving spouse are not terminated if he or she remarries after age 60.

Table 11.2   Old-Age, Survivors, and Disability Benefits–2000

	Percent of PIA	Low Earnings	Average Earnings	High Earnings	Maximum Earnings
AIME		$940.00	$2090.00	$3186.00	$4161.00
PIA	100.00%	597.90	987.60	1278.90	1433.90
Retired Worker—Age 65	100.00%	597.90	987.60	1278.90	1433.90
Retired Worker—Age 62	80.00%	478.32	790.08	1023.12	1147.12
Disabled Worker Under 65	100.00%	597.90	987.60	1278.90	1433.90
Spouse of Retired Worker at 65	50.00%	298.95	493.80	639.45	716.95
Spouse of Retired Worker at 62	37.50%	224.21	370.35	479.59	537.71
Child of Retired or Disabled Worker	50.00%	298.95	493.80	639.45	716.95
Spouse Under 65 with One Child	50.00%	298.95	493.80	639.45	716.95
Widow or Widower at Age 65	100.00%	597.90	987.60	1278.90	1433.90
Widow or Widower at Age 60	71.50%	427.50	706.13	914.41	1025.24
Disabled Widow or Widower at Age 50	71.50%	427.50	706.13	914.41	1025.24
One Surviving Child	75.00%	448.43	740.70	959.18	1075.43
Widow or Widower with One Child	125.00%	747.38	1234.50	1598.63	1792.38
Family Maximum	Bend points	896.85	1847.404	2237.746	2509.365

Source: Social Security Administration (see Illustrative Benefit Tables at http//:www.ssa.gov/OACT/COLA/IllusTables.html).

Finally, benefits payable to the child of a retired, disabled, or deceased worker terminate when the child reaches adulthood, as defined by the statute. The child's benefit stops automatically when the child reaches age 18, unless the child is still in high school, in which case the benefit is payable until age 19. When the child reaches age 16, the mother's or father's benefit stops even though the child continues to receive a benefit.

Disqualifying income

For 65 years, from its inception in 1935 until 2000, the Social Security system enforced an "earnings test," under which benefits payable to beneficiaries could be reduced if the beneficiary had earned income. In 2000, faced with what most people agreed was a growing crisis in the system, Congress decided to eliminate the Social Security earnings test for persons over age 65. This means that a worker can now continue to work full-time and draw his or her full Social Security Retirement benefit.

For beneficiaries under age 65, the earnings test remains and Social Security benefits are re-

duced if the individual's earned income exceeds exempt amounts. The annual exempt amount of earnings increases each year, based on increases in national earnings. In 2000, the exempt earnings amount for persons under age 65 was $10,800. For earnings in excess of the exempt amount, $1 in benefits will be withheld for each $2 in earnings in excess of the exempt amount.

The types of income that do not count as disqualifying income and that therefore do not affect benefits are (1) pensions and retirement pay, (2) insurance annuities, (3) dividends from stock (unless the person is a dealer in stock), (4) interest on savings, (5) gifts or inheritances of money or property, (6) gain from the sale of capital assets, and (7) rental income (unless the person is a real estate dealer or participating farm landlord).

Taxation of Benefits

Social Security benefits were originally exempt from taxes. Since 1984, however, beneficiaries who have significant income in addition to the Social Security benefits must pay taxes on a portion of their Social Security benefits. The amount of the benefits subject to tax depends on the "combined income" and the filing status of the individuals. "Combined income" is the sum of adjusted gross income, tax-exempt interest, and one-half of the Social Security benefits. If combined income for an individual is between $25,000 and $34,000, up to 50 percent of benefits may be taxed. For combined income above $34,000, up to 85 percent of benefits may be taxed. For those filing joint returns, the respective break points are $32,000 and $44,000. Revenues from the taxation of Social Security benefits are transferred to the Medicare Hospital Insurance (HI) trust fund.

Soundness of the Program

One of the central issues in the debate over passage of the Social Security Act was the system's financing. Some authorities proposed that the federal government support the program out of general revenues; others maintained that it should be financed solely by the contributions of the workers and their employers. The decision was eventually reached that only revenues provided by Social Security taxes would be used to pay benefits. The bases for this decision were complex, but one of the primary reasons was to give the participants a legal and moral right to the benefits.[9]

Once the issue of a self-supporting program was settled, there was disagreement over whether to fund the program with a reserve similar to those used in private insurance or whether to operate it on a *pay-as-you-go* basis. The proponents of

[9]As Franklin D. Roosevelt aptly put it, "Those taxes were never a problem of economics. They are politics all the way through. We put those payroll contributions there so as to give the contributors a legal, moral, and political right to collect their pensions and their unemployment benefits. With those taxes in there, no damn politician can ever scrap my social security program." Quoted in Arthur M. Schlesinger, Jr., *The Coming of the New Deal* (Boston: Houghton Mifflin, 1959), pp. 308ff.

a pay-as-you-go approach eventually prevailed, creating the system currently in use.

Pay-as-You-Go System

There is a common misconception on the part of many workers that their Social Security tax contributions are held in interest-bearing accounts earmarked for their own future retirement needs. Social Security is actually an intergenerational compact—the Social Security taxes paid by today's workers and their employers go mostly to fund benefit payments for today's retirees. In turn, today's workers will receive benefits after retirement from funds that are paid by the labor force at that time. The money collected is allocated to trust funds, from which the benefits are paid. There are separate trust funds for the Old-Age and Survivors' program, the Disability program, the Hospital Insurance program of Medicare, and the Supplementary Medical Insurance program. The trust funds were conceived as a contingency reserve to cover periodic fluctuations in income, but not to fund liabilities to future recipients.

The rationale for the pay-as-you-go system seemed logical in 1935. Given a stable system with a high ratio of taxpayers to beneficiaries, modest tax rates can support generous benefits. When current workers retire, their retirement benefits are funded by a new generation of taxpayers (presumably a larger one, if there is population growth). Moreover, the new taxpayers will make contributions based on higher earnings as a result of improved national productivity. In theory, this results in an ever-increasing level of benefits.

Difficulties arise, however, when the relationship between the number of beneficiaries and the number of taxpayers changes adversely. If there are fewer taxpayers to support the benefits, tax rates must rise. That is, in fact, what has happened. During the 65 years of the program's existence, the combined employee-employer tax has increased from $60 to $11,659 for workers earning $76,200 in 2000. This increase in the FICA tax (and the financial difficulties now facing the system) stem from two causes: the increasing number of beneficiaries under the program and the increasing level of benefits. In 1950, when only retired persons and survivors were eligible for benefits, for every Social Security beneficiary, there were slightly more than 13 workers paying FICA taxes. With the expansion of the program to include disabled workers and their dependents, coupled with the changing age structure of the population, the ratio of beneficiaries to taxpayers had increased to about 1 to 3.3 by 2000. Over the next 30 years, as the large post–World War II baby boom reaches age 65, the ratio will become even worse. In 2030, when the last baby boomers reach age 65, it is projected that there will be 2.1 taxpayers for each beneficiary.

At the same time the ratio of workers to beneficiaries has been dropping, the level of benefits has been increasing. The percentage of preretirement income replaced by Social Security has risen, from a replacement rate of about 31 percent in 1970 to more than 42 percent by 2000.

"Saving Social Security"

With the growth in the number of recipients and the increasing level of benefits, the system reached a critical point in the late 1970s. In 1977, Congress enacted a Social Security *bailout plan* to save the system from impending bankruptcy. It included the largest peacetime tax increase in the history of the United States up to that time. In signing the 1977 amendments, President Carter stated, "Now this legislation will guarantee that from 1980 to the year 2030, the Social Security funds will be sound." Four years later, in 1981, the system's Board of Trustees warned that even under the most optimistic assumptions, the OASDI trust fund would be bankrupt by the end of 1982. In 1983, Congress again acted to "save Social Security." The 1983 legislation included massive tax increases in 1988 and 1990, an increase in the retirement age beginning in the year 2000, and taxation of Social Security benefits.

The 1983 changes have produced a surplus since that time. The Social Security trust funds in-

creased from modest contingency funds totaling about $45 billion in 1982 to more than $850 billion in 2000. The trust fund is expected to grow to about $4 trillion over the next twenty years. After 2014, benefit payments will exceed taxes and the trust funds will be exhausted in 2034. Thereafter, unless a solution is found, Social Security will be able to pay only about 70 percent of the benefits owed.[10]

The dramatic growth in the trust funds that will occur over the next 25 years has led to a new concern over how those funds are invested. By law, the trust funds are invested in U.S. government bonds. In effect, the federal government is borrowing money from the trust funds to cover current operations and issuing IOUs to the funds. Of course, in the next century, these bonds will have to be redeemed as the trust fund balances are depleted. This leaves the question: Where will the money come from to redeem the bonds? Presumably, it will come from taxpayers at that time. In that case, the Social Security funding problem hasn't been resolved. Rather, it has been replaced by a massive new tax problem.

Under the pay-as-you-go system, the growth in the labor force and the 3000-plus percentage increase in taxes since 1935 has permitted the system to pay retirees significantly more in benefits than those retirees had paid in taxes during their working years. For current workers, and for those who will be entering the labor force, Social Security tax rates will have to increase to balance the aging of the population and the increasing number of retirees relative to those who are working.[11] Meeting the obligations for benefits promised to workers entering the work force today will require higher payroll tax rates for employers and em-

---

[10] *1999 Annual Report of the Board of Trustees of the Old-Age and Survivors Insurance (OASI) and Disability Insurance (DI) Trust Funds.*

[11] An average worker born in 1915 and retiring at age 65 in 1980 could expect to collect about $60,000 more in benefits than the worker had paid into the system (adjusted for inflation and interest). Persons born in 1936 will about break even. Persons born after 1960 can expect to pay at least $30,000 more in payroll taxes than they will ever receive in benefits.

ployees, of up to 40 percent, compared to the current 15 percent.

Proposals for Change

In the face of these prospective difficulties, a number of proposals have been made for changes in the system. Some suggest a revision in the financing of the system; others call for a reevaluation of benefit levels.

Proposals for Changes in Financing The proposals for changes in financing the system have been many and varied. One approach suggests that the increased costs of the system be financed through higher taxes rather than through raising the earnings base. Proponents of this position argue that benefit increases should not be financed by the "painless" process of simply increasing the tax base. Higher tax rates would require all covered workers to share in the increased cost, thereby making the desirability of the increased benefits an issue to be considered by all.

Other proposals for changes in the system's funding take a directly opposite position, maintaining that the system is already highly regressive (most burdensome on low-income groups) and that the tax base should be eliminated completely, with Social Security taxes applying to all income earned. Others of this school have suggested that the system should be financed out of general revenues rather than through a separate tax.

Proposals for Changes in Benefit Levels The Social Security system was intended to provide a *floor of protection*, meaning an amount sufficient to maintain a minimum standard of living. This floor of protection was then to be supplemented by the individual through private insurance or other devices. Some critics believe that the system currently provides benefits to recipients far in excess of this floor of protection level. They have suggested that the level of benefits be limited.

A second proposal for changing the benefits structure focuses on the age for receiving full retirement benefits. When the Social Security Act was passed in 1935, the normal retirement age for benefits was 65. The 1983 amendments have instituted a gradual increase in this age to 67 years by the year 2022. Critics argue that this compromise did not go far enough, and that there should be a significant and faster increase in the normal retirement age. They base this argument on the dramatic improvements in life expectancy since 1935, resulting in a much longer period of retirement for current retirees.[12]

Privatizing Social Security The most dramatic proposal for addressing the financial problems affecting Social Security is that it be privatized, with a change from the current pay-as-you-go system to a program with advance funding, in which contributions by workers and their employers are invested in the private sector. At one time, this would have been unthinkable. As long as Social Security was a "good deal" for participants and provided benefits that were substantially greater than the contributions they had made, a fundamental reform such as privatization was politically impossible. The current crisis in the system and the increasing imbalance between participant contributions and benefits has opened consideration to a variety of alternatives, including privatization, an idea that is gaining support.

There are two versions of the privatization strategy. Under one, workers would be allowed to invest a part of what they now pay in FICA taxes through a system of credits for contributions to private retirement programs, such as individual retirement accounts (IRAs).[13] Under the second version, FICA taxes received by the trust funds would be invested in the private sector rather than in government bonds, as is now the case.[14]

---

[12]According to Hardy and Hardy, *Social Insecurity*, in 1935, the remaining life expectancy for a man retiring at age 65 was 11.9 years. (For a woman it was 13.2 years.) Today, the life expectancy of a 65-year-old is 16 years for a male and 19.2 years for a female.

[13]Peter J. Ferrara, *Social Security: The Inherent Contradiction* (Washington, DC: Cato Institute, 1984), and *Social Security: Averting the Crisis* (Washington, DC: Cato Institute, 1984).

[14]See "Time to Privatize Social Security," by Martin Feldstein, *Wall Street Journal*, March 8, 1996.

Many other nations have already shifted their versions of our Social Security system from unfunded pay-as-you-go systems to funded privatized systems. Although the approach in these countries differs in detail, the common thread is requiring that employer and employee contributions be invested in mutual funds or similar private assets.

It has been argued that a privatized system could not be achieved immediately. There would be a transition period during which the Social Security Administration would have to continue to pay benefits to existing retirees while new funds are accumulated and invested through the individual accounts.

Report of the Advisory Council on Social Security   In January 1997, a special Advisory Council on Social Security appointed in 1994 to examine the long-term financing of Social Security issued its report. The Council concluded that the program faces "serious problems in the long run," requiring attention in the near term. Although there was agreement about the problems facing the system, the Council could not agree on a single proposal to address the system's financial problems.

Instead the report offered three proposals, none of which was supported by a majority of the Council. Although some strategies are common to all three proposals (i.e., accelerating the scheduled increase in the retirement age, decreasing benefit levels, and bringing state and local employees into the program), the most significant differences among the proposals relate to privatization. One proposal—the *Maintenance of Benefits Proposal*—recommended "a study of the possibility of investing up to 40 percent of Trust Fund assets in common stocks, corporate bonds, and other investments." A second proposal—the *Personal Security Accounts Proposal*—would allow 5 percent of the current 12.4 percent payroll tax to be redirected to individual Private Security Accounts, which would not be taxed. The third proposal—called the *Individual Account Proposal*—would establish an individual account system to provide benefits in addition to the traditional

Social Security benefit. Individuals would be permitted to direct the investment, choosing from among fund options provided by the federal government. Benefits would be payable in the form of an annuity at retirement. All Council members agreed that the current pay-as-you-go system should be changed and recommended that there be partial advance funding for Social Security.

The extent to which any of the proposals for change will be implemented and whether they will solve the financial problems of the Social Security system remains to be seen. The difficulties in financing the Social Security system will remain a haunting problem for our society.

Workers Compensation

Workers compensation is a social insurance program that provides covered workers with protection against work-related disability and death. Workers compensation provides benefits for the cost of medical care and income to workers and their dependents when a worker is disabled or killed as a result of a work-related injury or occupational disease. The workers compensation system is based on statutes that exist in all states, which require covered employers to provide benefits specified by the law to covered workers and their dependents.

Historical Background

The workers compensation laws were enacted in the early 1900s in response to a growing dissatisfaction with the system then in use for compensating injured employees and their dependents. The system, known as *employers liability law*, was based on the concept of negligence. Under employers liability law, a worker who was injured on the job could collect for the injury only if he or she could prove that the injury resulted from the employer's negligence. To establish fault, the employee had to prove that the employer had violated one of five employer obligations that had

---

Tidbits, Vignettes, and Conundrums 11.1

Social Security Retirement Age

When Congress created our Social Security System in 1935, it set the normal retirement age at 65, the same age that had been adopted for the German system a half-century earlier in 1884. German Chancellor Otto Von Bismarck set the age for the German program at age 65 after he was assured by actuaries that few, if any, workers would live beyond this age. It has been estimated that a corresponding age today would be 105.

---

developed under common law: (1) to provide the employee with a safe place to work; (2) to provide safe tools and equipment; (3) to provide sane and sober fellow employees; (4) to set up safety rules and enforce them; and (5) to warn of any dangers in the work that the worker could not be expected to know about.

Although these common-law obligations established a basis for recovery of damages, the employer could interpose three common-law defenses that were often sufficient to defeat the worker's claim. The first was *contributory negligence.* Under this doctrine, if the employee's own negligence contributed to the accident in the slightest degree, he or she lost all right to collect damages.

The second defense was the *fellow servant rule,* which held that the employer was not liable when the worker was injured by a fellow employee. Finally, the *assumption-of-risk doctrine* held that an employee was presumed to accept the normal risks associated with the job. If a worker continued employment while knowing, or when he or she might have been expected to discover, that the premises, tools, or fellow employees were unsafe, he or she was deemed to have assumed the risks connected with the unsafe conditions.

Although the severity of the common-law defenses was eventually softened, the modifications did not solve the fundamental problems inherent in a system based on the principle of negli-

---

Tidbits, Vignettes, and Conundrums 11.2

Milton Friedman on Privatization Transition Costs

One of America's most respected economists, Nobel recipient Milton Friedman, calls the argument about transition costs "balderdash." According to Friedman, the current obligations for OASDI benefits are simply a part of the federal government's debt. When the benefits that are due exceed the proceeds from payroll taxes, as it now appears that they will in the not-very-distant future, the difference will have to be financed by raising taxes, borrow-

ing, creating money, or reducing other government spending. The assurance that workers will receive benefits when they retire doesn't depend on the particular tax used to finance the benefits or on any "trust fund." It depends solely on the expectation that future Congresses will honor promises made by earlier Congresses.

Source: Milton Friedman, "Social Security Chimeras," *New York Times* (January 11, 1999).

gence.[15] To establish negligence, litigation was necessary, and in most cases, the worker did not have the resources to bring suit. Even if the worker won the suit, a substantial portion of the judgment went to the attorney who had accepted the case on a contingency basis. It was not unusual for the size of the attorney's fee to represent 50 percent of the amount of the judgment. Finally, there were some cases in which workers were injured where there was no employer negligence. Although there was no one the injured worker could sue, the financial loss in such instances was no less severe than when the employer was at fault. The unsatisfactory status of the worker under common law, and the social and economic consequences of industrial injuries, finally led to a new way of distributing the financial costs of industrial accidents.

Rationale of Workers Compensation Laws

The workers compensation principle is based on the notion that industrial accidents are inevitable in an industrialized society. Since the entire society gains from industrialization, it should bear the burden of these costs. Workers compensation laws are designed to make the cost of industrial accidents a part of the cost of production by imposing absolute liability on the employer for employee injuries regardless of negligence. The costs are thus built into the cost of the product and are passed on to the consumer. The basic purpose of the laws is to avoid litigation, lessen the expense to the claimant, and provide for a speedy and efficient means of compensating injured workers.

Workers compensation laws were enacted by the states shortly after the turn of the century and

now exist in all 50 states. All but two laws are compulsory and require every employer subject to the law to accept the act and pay the compensation specified. Coverage is elective in New Jersey and Texas. In these states either the employer or employee can choose to be exempt from the law.

Principles of Workers Compensation

Although the laws of the various states differ somewhat in detail, the basic principles they embody are the same. There are five general principles on which all the laws are based.

Negligence Is Not a Factor in Determining Liability

As a basic principle of law, liability for injury to another is generally based on the concept of negligence or fault. Workers compensation laws represent an exception to this principle and impose liability on the employer for injury to an employee that arises *out of and in the course of employment* regardless of fault. If the worker is injured, the employer is obligated to pay benefits according to a schedule in the law regardless of whose negligence caused the injury.[16]

Indemnity Is Partial but Final

The second principle of workers compensation involves the amount of the benefit. The indemnity to the worker is partial, meaning that the benefits are usually less than the employee might receive if he or she were permitted to sue (and if the employer were found to have been negligent). On the other hand, the worker is entitled to the benefits as a matter of right, without having to sue. In addition, the benefit is final. In return

---

[15]The doctrine of contributory negligence was replaced by the doctrine of *comparative negligence,* under which the worker was allowed recovery in inverse relationship to his or her own negligence. The fellow servant doctrine was modified to the less severe *vice-principal rule,* which provided that supervisors did not fall under the fellow servant doctrine.

[16]The law dealing with liability for injuries arising out of negligence is called *tort law.* The law of torts is discussed in Chapter 20. Workers compensation laws represent an exception to the law of torts, since they impose liability on the employer for injuries to employees without regard to the question of fault.

for the entitlement to benefits regardless of the employer's fault, workers compensation is an *exclusive remedy,* which means that the worker gives up the right to sue the employer for work-related injuries covered by the law.[17]

Periodic Payments

The third principle concerns the basis of payment of benefits, which is arranged to ensure a greater degree of security for the recipients. Usually, the indemnity is paid periodically instead of in a lump sum, although the periodic payments may sometimes be commuted to a lump sum. The requirement of periodic rather than lump-sum payments is designed to protect the recipient against financial ineptness and the possibility of squandering a lump sum.

Cost of the Program Is Made a Cost of Production

Unlike many other social insurance coverages, the employees are not required to contribute to the financing of workers compensation coverage. The employer must pay the premium for the insurance coverage, or pay the benefits required by law, without any contribution by workers. The employer can predict the cost of accidents under a workers compensation program and build this into the price of the product, thereby passing the cost of industrial accidents on to the consumer.

Insurance Is Required

All states require the employers that are subject to the workers compensation law to insure their obligations either through commercial insurance companies or a state fund or by qualification as a self-insurer. In 5 states the insurance must be purchased from a monopolistic state insurance fund. In 20 states the private insurance industry operates side by side with the state workers compensation insurance funds.[18] Under the workers compensation insurance policy, the insurer promises to pay all sums for which the insured (i.e., the employer) is obligated under the law.

Penalties for failure to insure are severe. Forty-four states make failure to insure punishable by fines (ranging from $25 to $50,000 depending on the state), imprisonment, or both. Other laws provide that the employer may be enjoined from doing business in the state. In addition, about four-fifths of the states allow common lawsuits by the employee against a noninsuring employer. States that allow common lawsuits against noninsuring employers give the employee the option of a common lawsuit or the benefits under the workers compensation law. If the employee elects the common lawsuit option, the employer is denied use of the three common-law employer defenses.

An Overview of State Workers Compensation Laws

Although it is difficult to generalize about state workers compensation laws, there are general similarities among the laws. The following discussion is intended to provide an overview of the laws and to identify the major areas in which the laws differ.

---

[17]The employers liability law still applies to employments that are not covered under workers compensation. For example, in some states an injured farm worker or domestic servant has a remedy against the employer only under employers liability laws, which means that the negligence of the employer must be the cause of the injury and the employer would usually have the right to interpose the common-law defenses.

[18]The 5 states that maintain monopolistic workers compensation programs are North Dakota, Ohio, Washington, West Virginia, and Wyoming. Prior to July 1, 1999, Nevada also had a monopolistic state fund, but it now operates as a competitive fund. The 20 states in which the workers compensation fund operated by the state competes with private insurers are Arizona, California, Colorado, Idaho, Kentucky, Louisiana, Maine, Maryland, Minnesota, Missouri, Montana, Nevada, New Mexico, New York, Oklahoma, Oregon, Pennsylvania, Rhode Island, Texas, and Utah.

Persons Covered Under State Laws

None of the state workers compensation laws cover all employees in the state. The classes most often excluded are agricultural and domestic employees. Only 20 states cover agricultural workers on the same basis as other categories, and only 7 provide full coverage on domestic employees. About three-fourths of the states exclude *casual employees*—those whose work is occasional, incidental, or irregular. In addition, about a fourth of the states have numerical limitations, providing that if the employer has fewer than a specified number of employees (ranging from two to five), the employees need not be covered under the act. The remainder of the states and the federal laws require the employer of one or more people to be covered under the law. The laws usually permit the employer of persons omitted from the law to bring these workers under the law voluntarily. This applies to excluded classes of employment and employers with fewer than the number of employees specified in the law.

Injuries Covered

The workers compensation laws cover work-related injuries and generally require that the injury arise *out of and in the course of employment.* Questions may arise whether the injured employee was "in the course of employment" when the injury was sustained while coming to or from the job or while participating in social events connected with employment. The greater problem arises when it is clear that the injury occurred in the course of employment, but there is a question whether it was caused by the employment. Generally, injuries sustained while at work are considered to arise out of the work, but there are exceptions. Injuries may be noncompensable if they are deliberately self-inflicted or result from intoxication. In addition, there may be difficulties in such cases as heart attacks, mental or nervous disorders, or even suicide. Often, the only way these questions can be settled is by litigation, and litigation involving these issues has been almost end-

less. The courts have usually taken a liberal attitude and more often than not favor the injured worker or his or her dependents.

Occupational Disease

In addition to the traumatic type of injury, all laws provide compensation for *occupational disease.* All states provide coverage for all occupational diseases, either under a separate occupational disease law or by defining injury broadly enough under the workers compensation law to include disease. Some states have specific conditions for particular diseases, such as silicosis, asbestosis, and AIDS.

Workers Compensation Benefits

There are usually seven classes of benefits payable to the injured worker or his or her dependents under the workers compensation laws:

1. Medical expenses
2. Total temporary disability
3. Partial temporary disability
4. Total permanent disability
5. Partial permanent disability
6. Survivors' death benefits
7. Rehabilitation benefits

Medical Expense Benefits   *Medical expense benefits* account for about 40 percent of total benefit payments under workers compensation. Medical expenses incurred through employment-connected injuries are covered without limit. In an effort to control costs, many states have established medical fee schedules that limit payments to providers of medical care, and a number of states have placed limits on the employee's choice of physician.

Total Temporary Disability   There are four classes of disability income benefits under the workers compensation laws. The most frequent type of disability is *total temporary disability*, which exists when the worker is unable to work because of an injury but will recover and eventually return to work. All states provide for a waiting period before disability benefits are payable. This waiting period is a deductible, eliminating coverage for short periods of disability, thereby reducing administrative costs. The normal waiting period is one week, although some states have waiting periods as short as three days. Normally, the waiting period does not apply if the disability lasts beyond some specified number of weeks, usually four.

The amount of the benefit is set by statute and varies with the worker's wage and in some cases with the number of dependents. The most frequently used percentage of the injured worker's wage is $66\frac{2}{3}$ percent, subject to a dollar maximum and minimum also imposed by the law. In 1999, the dollar maxima ranged from a low of $271 per week to a high of $873 per week. Some states provide for a sliding scale of benefits based on the number of dependents. More than 90 percent of the states provide benefits for the entire period of disability. In the remaining jurisdictions there is a time limit (ranging from 104 to 500 weeks) or a dollar limit on the benefits.

Partial Temporary Disability Many states provide disability benefits for *partial temporary disability*, to cover those cases in which the worker cannot pursue his or her own occupation but can engage in some work for remuneration. In these cases, compensation is based on a percentage of the difference between the wages received before the injury and those received afterward. This benefit is also subject to a maximum and minimum and is usually payable for the same period as total temporary disability.

Total Permanent Disability A worker is *totally and permanently disabled* when he or she is unable to obtain any gainful employment because of the injury and is expected to remain so. In practice,

total permanent disability benefits are payable to a worker who remains disabled after exhausting total temporary disability benefits. The benefit for total permanent disability is usually computed on the same basis as the total temporary disability benefit and is subject to the same minima and maxima, but the benefits are payable for life or, in some states, for a specified number of additional weeks.

In addition to the inability to obtain gainful employment, most laws specify that the loss of both hands, arms, feet, legs, or eyes, or any combination of two of these constitutes total and permanent disability.

Partial Permanent Disability An injury resulting from an industrial accident may be deemed a partial disability on one of two bases. In one instance, the loss of a member such as an arm or a leg is considered a *partial permanent disability*. In addition, the disability may consist of a disability to the body generally (e.g., an injured spine). In the case of a disability not involving the loss of a limb, a percentage disability is usually determined, and a benefit equal to some multiple of the weekly disability benefit as specified by law is payable for the various percentages so determined. The compensation for the loss of a limb such as an arm or leg is determined by a schedule (these are therefore called *scheduled injuries*). The compensation for scheduled injuries is usually some multiple of the weekly disability benefit, which may be commuted and paid as a lump sum (for example, 230 weeks for an arm or 125 weeks for an eye). There are variations among the states in the amount of compensation for the various extremities and also in the stated value of one member as opposed to another. For example, some states place a greater value on an arm than on a leg, while other states value a leg more highly.

In most states, the compensation for scheduled injuries is payable in addition to any benefits otherwise given the injured worker under the total temporary disability benefit. However, some states limit the total temporary disability benefit when payment is made for a scheduled injury, and a few states deduct the amount paid under total temporary disability from the allowance for the scheduled injury.

Death Benefit Benefits are also payable when a worker is killed, and all laws allow two types of death benefits. Under the first, payment is made for the reasonable expenses of burial, not to exceed some maximum amount, ranging from $800 to about $7500.

The second death benefit is a *survivors' benefit* payable to dependents. The survivors' benefit is usually paid as a weekly sum, determined by the usual formula. Although the definition of dependent varies from state to state, most laws provide that a dependent may be a spouse, a child of the deceased worker, or a dependent parent.

Under about three-fifths of the laws, the survivors' benefit is payable to a surviving spouse for life or until remarriage, without limit. Eleven states provide for a maximum number of weeks (250 to 1040), and six others set an aggregate dollar maximum. In about half of the states, survivors' benefits are based on the number of dependents.

Rehabilitation Benefits Virtually all of the state laws contain specific *rehabilitation benefit provisions,* but even where state law does not enumerate such benefits, they are provided. Under these provisions, the injured worker may be entitled to additional compensation during a period of vocational training, transportation and other necessary expenses, artificial limbs and mechanical appliances, and other benefits. The funds for payment of the rehabilitation benefits may or may not come from the employer or its insurance company. In some cases, state funds are used. In others, funds come from insurers in death cases in which no surviving dependents receive benefits. Finally, the Federal Vocational Rehabilitation Act provides for federal funds to aid states in this program.

Second-Injury Funds

Under most workers compensation laws, the loss of both arms, feet, legs, eyes, or any two thereof constitutes permanent total disability. As a result, situations may arise in which a partial injury leaves a worker totally disabled; a worker who has lost an arm or a leg in an industrial accident and who has returned to work will be totally disabled by another such accident. To assist in meeting the problem of injuries to workers with preexisting industrial disabilities, *second-injury funds* have been established in all states except Alabama, Maine, and Wyoming. When a worker suffers a second injury that causes total permanent disability, and the injury is of a type that would constitute only partial permanent disability except for the previous injury, the employer is liable only for the partial disability benefits. The second-injury fund pays the difference between the partial and the total permanent disability. Second-injury funds are supported by required contributions from insurance companies operating in the state, either as a percentage tax or through payments into a fund in death cases where there are no dependents.

Unemployment Insurance

In addition to the perils of death and disability, the individual faces loss of income from another source: unemployment. Commercial insurance companies cannot deal with the peril of unemployment; the government has therefore undertaken a system of unemployment compensation to protect members of the society against loss from this ever-present threat.[19]

---

[19]A few private insurers offer private unemployment insurance in connection with consumer installment debt. The insurance covers the payments on an installment debt when the insured debtor becomes involuntarily unemployed. The amounts of insurance are small, and the coverage is generally overpriced.

The unemployment insurance program of the United States is subject to control by both the federal and state governments. This division of control resulted from the reluctance of the states to enact unemployment insurance programs and the manner in which the federal government encouraged the states to do so.

Although reformers had long argued for a system of unemployment insurance, by the mid–1930s, only two states (Wisconsin and New York) had established such programs. Most states were reluctant to enact such programs because they feared that their industries would suffer a competitive disadvantage with other states whose firms were not burdened by the cost of such programs. Eventually, the federal government used its power to tax to force states to establish unemployment insurance programs.

The Social Security Act of 1935 imposed a payroll tax of 1 percent on the total wages of all employers who had eight or more employees in each of 20 weeks during the year and who were not exempted because of occupational classification.[20] The law then provided that employers would be permitted to offset 90 percent of the tax through credit for taxes paid to a state unemployment insurance program that met federal standards. This meant that any state that did not enact a qualified unemployment insurance law would experience a financial drain that could be avoided by creating an unemployment insurance system. It is not surprising that all the states elected to create programs meeting the conditions required by the federal law and thereby qualify for the tax offset.

Over time, participation has been expanded to include employers of one or more employees in 20 separate weeks or firms that have a quarterly payroll of $1500 or more. In addition, coverage has been extended to nonprofit institutions, state hospitals and educational institutions, municipalities and school districts, and certain agricultural and domestic workers. The tax rate has been increased several times and was 6.2 percent in 2000. The wage base has been reduced from total wages and now applies to the first $7000 of each worker's wages.[21] Because each state has enacted separate legislation and operates a separate program, the programs differ considerably in almost every respect. However, it will be useful to discuss their general nature.

Eligibility for Benefits

The eligibility requirements vary from state to state, but all call for previous employment in a covered occupation. A few states cover occupational classifications excluded under the federal standards, but in general the occupations omitted under the federal law are also left out under the state laws.

In most states, the worker must also have earned a certain minimum income during the preceding year, referred to as the base period. Some states require that the worker must have been paid a stated dollar minimum during the base period, and a few demand a specified number of weeks of employment with a minimum amount of earnings each week. Most states require the employee to have earned some multiple of the weekly benefit amount that he or she will receive (e.g., 30 times).

---

[20]The occupations exempted from the act included agricultural employees, domestic employees, crews of vessels on navigable waters of the United States, immediate members of the employer's family, federal government or federal agency employees, state and local government or agency employees, and employees of nonprofit organizations of a religious, charitable, scientific, literary, or educational nature.

[21]The actual tax is 6 percent and the federal retention is 10 percent of the tax, or 0.6 percent. There is also 0.2 percent temporary tax that will be levied by the federal government until all outstanding advances to the Federal Extended Unemployment Compensation Account are repaid, making the federal retention 0.8 percent. The total tax and the federal retention will drop from 6.2 percent and 0.8 percent to 6.0 percent and 0.6 percent, respectively, when the Federal Extended Unemployment Compensation Account advances are repaid.

Continued attachment to the labor force is also required. This means that the unemployment must be involuntary and the worker must be willing and able to work. This is the principal reason that benefits are payable through the state employment offices. The worker desiring to draw benefits must present himself or herself at the employment office to collect the money and must be willing to accept suitable work if it is offered.[22] Following the philosophy that only those who are involuntarily unemployed are entitled to benefits, most state laws deny or limit benefits to workers who quit without sufficient reason or who are discharged for misconduct.[23]

Amount and Duration of Benefits

There is no uniformity among the states in the amount of benefits to which the qualified worker is entitled, and the benefits payable in some states are far higher than those in others. In all states the amount of the benefits to which the worker is entitled is related to previous earnings. In most states, the benefit is 1/26 of the worker's wages during the quarter of highest earnings in his or her base year. If the worker was fully employed during the quarter, the 1/26 benefit provides a weekly benefit equal to about 50 percent of his or her normal full-time earnings. The benefit is subject to a weekly maximum and minimum. Most states automatically adjust the benefit maximum

based on changes in the state's average weekly wage in covered employment. A few states provide for a sliding maximum based on the number of dependents the unemployed worker has. In addition to imposing limits on the amount, all states limit the period for which benefits are payable. In 45 states, this is 26 weeks, while in 5 states and the District of Columbia it is longer. The maximum in any state is 39 weeks.[24]

Most states provide for a one-week waiting period before benefits begin, but some states use a shorter waiting period, and in 10 states there is no waiting period.

In all states, benefits may be extended during periods of high unemployment by 50 percent for up to 13 weeks under the federal–state extended unemployment compensation program. Extended benefits are triggered when the unemployment rate in a state averages 5 percent or more over a 13-week period and is at least 20 percent higher than the rate for the same period in the two preceding years.

Financing

The federal law permits the states to impose tax rates higher than the 6.2 percent specified by the federal statute and also to increase the tax base. A number of states (39 in 1999) have increased the tax base above the federal $7000, and 35 have also elected to levy taxes at a higher rate.

All states have enacted "experience-rating" provisions that link the taxes paid by an employer to the benefits that have been paid to its former workers who were involuntarily terminated. The intent of the experience-rating plans, which vary widely, is to promote employment stability by rewarding employers exhibiting a low turnover rate with a lower premium requirement. The rate paid

---

[22]For example, students not available for work while attending school and women who quit their jobs because of pregnancy or to get married are not eligible for benefits. However, since 1978, states have been prohibited from automatically disqualifying women from unemployment benefits solely on the basis of pregnancy.

[23]In such circumstances benefits may be completely or only partially forfeited. For example, under the Iowa law a worker discharged for misconduct forfeits from four to nine weeks of benefits. A worker who voluntarily quits a job forfeits all benefits for which he or she had accumulated credit in that particular job, but the benefits given up are those accumulated only during the job that was quit.

[24]In Alaska, California, Connecticut, Hawaii, and Oregon, benefits are extended under exclusively state-funded programs when unemployment in the state reaches a specified level.

by the employer under an experience-rated plan is based on the ratio of past premiums paid to past benefits paid. The lower the benefits in relation to tax deposits made by the employer, the lower its current tax rate.[25]

Unemployment Compensation Laws Appraised

State unemployment insurance programs serve several functions. They are designed to provide income to the worker who is temporarily idle—the "between-jobs" worker. Although they provide only a modest level of benefits for a limited period of time, they represent an important part of the individual's floor of protection against fundamental risks. In addition, unemployment insurance exerts a countercyclical influence on the economy. During periods of high employment, payroll taxes drain purchasing power from the economy, dampening inflationary pressures. During periods of high unemployment, benefit payments return purchasing power to consumers and can have a stimulating effect. Finally, state experience-rating programs may have an effect on employment stability, although this influence is probably modest.

Although the program was devised during a period of mass unemployment, it is not designed to cope with large-scale unemployment over an extended period. Structural and technological unemployment must be met through other income redistribution techniques and retraining of workers.

Compulsory Temporary Disability Insurance Laws

Workers who are incapacitated because of an injury resulting from an industrial accident are entitled to disability income benefits under the workers compensation laws. In addition, persons in covered employment who are able to work, and are available, and who are involuntarily unemployed, are entitled to unemployment compensation benefits. The OASDHI program, as we have seen, provides disability income benefits for covered employees who become totally and permanently disabled. In spite of the broad coverage of these three programs, there exists an income risk that is not generally protected under the social insurance programs: loss of income from temporary nonoccupational disability. While many private employers have established plans covering their employees against loss of income due to nonoccupational injuries, only six jurisdictions require such coverage by law: California, Hawaii, New Jersey, New York, Rhode Island, and Puerto Rico. The basic emphasis of these laws differs from both workers compensation and unemployment insurance. Workers compensation provides protection against job-connected disabilities; unemployment compensation pays benefits to the healthy person who is out of work. The temporary disability laws of these six jurisdictions provide benefits for loss of income from nonoccupational disabilities.

---

[25]Only the state portion of the tax is subject to experience rating. The federal 0.8 percent remains unchanged.

Important Concepts to Remember

Social Security	quarter of coverage	survivors' benefits
social insurance	FICA tax	disability benefits
OASDHI	fully insured	children's benefit
OASDI	currently insured	mother's (father's) benefit
Medicare	retirement benefits	parents' benefit

widow's (widower's) benefit
lump-sum benefit
averaged indexed monthly earnings
   (AIME)
primary insurance amount
disqualifying income
pay-as-you-go system
floor of protection
common law

employers' common-law obligations
employers' common-law defenses
contributory negligence
fellow servant rule
assumption-of-risk doctrine
casual employee
out of and in the course of employment
medical expense benefits

total temporary disability
partial temporary disability
total permanent disability
partial permanent disability
rehabilitation benefits
second-injury fund
occupational disease
absolute liability

Questions for Review

1. Identify and briefly describe the four classes of benefits available to those covered under OASDHI.

2. Explain how benefit levels are automatically adjusted under OASDHI. How are the increases in benefits financed?

3. Outline the requirements for *fully insured* status under OASDHI.

4. What benefits does a *fully insured* worker have that a *currently insured* worker does not? What benefits does a worker who is only currently insured have?

5. Under what circumstances can a person who is entitled to Social Security benefits become ineligible for benefits?

6. Explain the nature of the common-law obligations and the common-law defenses of employers liability. Are these obligations and defenses ever used today? Under what circumstances?

7. Identify and explain the five general principles on which workers compensation laws are based.

8. Identify and briefly describe the classes of benefits that are provided to injured workers under the workers compensation laws.

9. Individual states were initially reluctant to enact unemployment insurance laws, fearing that such laws would place industries in their states at a competitive disadvantage. Describe the strategy the federal government used to encourage the individual states to enact unemployment insurance laws.

10. Unemployment comes in many forms and is caused by many factors. With what particular forms of unemployment are the state unemployment compensation programs designed to deal?

Questions for Discussion

1. Social Security provides protection against financial loss to dependents resulting from premature death of the wage earner, and also provides wage earners with retirement benefits. Do you think that the enactment or expansion of the Social Security Act has encouraged or discouraged life insurance sales? Why or why not?

2. Many observers have voiced concern about the soundness of the Social Security system, pointing to the growing number of recipients and the increasing benefit levels. To what extent do you believe that the OASDHI system is still in trouble? What would you recommend in the way of corrective action?

3. The Old Age, Survivors', Disability, and Health Insurance program has been called "the greatest chain letter in history." To what aspect of the Social Security system does this probably refer? Do you agree or disagree with the observation and why?

4. The Social Security trust funds are invested in U.S. Treasury securities. Although there is little question regarding the safety of these instruments, many observers have expressed alarm over this arrangement. Do you believe that the current arrangement, in which the trust funds are invested in Treasury bonds is a good thing, a bad thing, or a matter of no consequence? Why?

5. Which, if any, of the three proposals contained in the report of the Advisory Council on Social Security released in 1997 do you personally prefer? Why?

Suggestions for Additional Reading

Black, Kenneth, Jr., and Harold D. Skipper, Jr. *Life Insurance*, 13th ed. Englewood Cliffs, NJ: Prentice Hall, 2000. Chapter 22.

Chamber of Commerce of the United States. *Analysis of Workers Compensation Laws*. Washington, DC: U.S. Chamber of Commerce, annual.

Hardy, Dorcas R., and C. Colburn Hardy. *Social Insecurity: The Crisis in America's Social Security System and How to Plan Now for Your Own Survival*. New York: Villard Books, 1991.

Rejda, G. E. *Social Insurance and Economic Security*, 6th ed. Old Tappan, NJ: Prentice Hall, 1998.

Robertson, A. Haeworth. "Is the Current Social Security Program Financially Feasible in the Long Run?" *Benefits Quarterly*, vol. 1, no. 3 (Third Quarter 1985).

State Workers Compensation Laws. Washington, DC: U.S. Department of Labor, revised annually.

Thomas, William W., III, ed. *Social Security Manual*. Cincinnati, OH: National Underwriter Co., 1999.

Unemployment Insurance Reporter. A loose-leaf reporting service. New York: Commerce Clearing House.

Workmen's Compensation Law Reporter. New York: Commerce Clearing House, Biweekly.

Websites to Explore

National Council on Compensation Insurance: http://www.ncci.com

Social Security Administration: http://www.ssa.gov/

CHAPTER 12

Introduction to Life Insurance

A man's dying is more the survivors' affair than his own.
—Thomas Mann

CHAPTER OBJECTIVES

When you have finished this chapter, you should be able to

- Distinguish between the two broad types of life insurance contracts

- Explain how the cash value arises in some life insurance contracts

- Distinguish between participating and nonparticipating life insurance contracts

- Explain the importance of renewability and convertibility features in term life insurance policies

- Describe the distinguishing characteristics of universal life insurance, adjustable life insurance, and variable life insurance

- Identify and describe the four major marketing classes of life insurance

- Describe the distinguishing features of group life insurance and explain the basis for its cost advantages

Some Unique Characteristics of Life Insurance

Life insurance is a risk-pooling plan, an economic device through which the risk of premature death is transferred from the individual to the group. However, the contingency insured against has characteristics that make it unique; as a result, the contract insuring against this contingency is different in certain respects from other types of insurance. The event insured against is an eventual certainty. No one lives forever. The insurer's chance of loss under a life insurance contract is greater the second year of the contract than it was the first year, and so on, until the insured eventually dies. Yet life insurance does not violate the requirements of an insurable risk, for it is not the possibility of death itself that is insured, but rather untimely death. The risk in life insurance is not whether the individual is going to die, but when, and the risk increases from year to year.

There is no possibility of partial loss in life insurance as there is in the case of property and liability insurance. Therefore, all policies are cash payment policies. In the event that a loss occurs, the company will pay the face amount of the policy.

Life Insurance Is Not a Contract of Indemnity

The principle of indemnity applies on a modified basis in the case of life insurance. In most lines of insurance, an attempt is made to put the individual back in exactly the same financial position after a loss as before the loss. For obvious reasons, this is not possible in life insurance. Insurance cannot compensate for the loss of a loved one. It can only help to replace the funds that are cut off by death.

As noted in Chapter 9, the requirement of insurable interest is applied somewhat differently in life insurance than in property and liability insurance. When the individual taking out the policy is also the insured, there is no legal problem concerning insurable interest. The courts have held that every individual has an unlimited insurable interest in his or her own life and that a person may assign that insurable interest to anyone. In other words, there is no legal limit to the amount of insurance one may take out on one's own life and no legal limitations as to whom one may name as beneficiary.[1]

Actually, the question of insurable interest seldom arises in life insurance, because the person whose life is insured purchases most life insurance policies. In addition, the consent of the individual insured is required in most cases even when there is an insurable interest. The exception to this requirement exists in certain jurisdictions where a husband or wife is permitted to insure a spouse without the other's consent.

Types of Life Insurance Contracts

Based on their characteristics, it is possible to identify five distinct types of life insurance contracts: term insurance, whole life, endowment, universal life, and variable life policies. Term insurance, whole life, and endowment contracts were the traditional forms of life insurance and have existed for many years. Universal life and variable life are relatively recent innovations, and date from the 1970s. Ignoring the subtle differences among some of these types of policies for the moment, we can divide life insurance products into two classes: those that provide pure life insurance protection, called *term insurance,* and those that include a savings or investment element, which we will call *cash value policies.* Based on this classification system, life insurance products are divided as follows:

---

[1]While there is no legal limit, insurance companies often impose limits for underwriting reasons. Not only is the amount of insurance a company is willing to write on a life limited, but companies are also reluctant to issue a policy with a beneficiary where there is no apparent insurable interest.

Term Insurance (Pure Protection)	Cash Value Insurance (Insurance and Savings)
Term Insurance	Whole Life Insurance
	Endowment Insurance
	Universal Life Insurance
	Variable Life Insurance

Although there are important differences among the policies that we have classified together as cash value policies, these contracts are more similar than they are different. For the moment, let us focus on the difference between term insurance, which provides pure insurance protection, and cash value life insurance, which combines insurance with an investment element. Because whole life is the prototype cash value contract, it can serve as a representative in our discussion for cash value policies generally.

Rationale for Different Forms

The simplest form of life insurance is yearly renewable term. This type provides protection for one year only, but it permits the insured to renew the policy for successive periods of one year, at a higher premium rate each year, without having to furnish evidence of insurability at the time of each renewal. This is life insurance protection in its purest form.

The easiest way to understand the operation of any mechanism is to try it. Mortality data tell us that at age 21, 1.07 out of every 1000 females will die. To simplify the mathematics, let us assume that there are 100,000 females in the group. On the basis of past experience, we may expect 107 of them to die, and if we wish to pay a death benefit of $1000 to the beneficiary of each woman who dies, we will need $107,000. Ignoring, for the present, the cost of operating the program and any interest that we might earn on the premiums we collect, and assuming that the mortality table is an accurate statement of the number who will die, it will be necessary to collect $1.07 from each individual in the group to provide the needed

$107,000.[2] During the year, 107 members of the group will die and $107,000 will be paid to their beneficiaries. The next year we would find that the chance of loss has increased, for all the members of the group are now older and past experience indicates that a greater number will die per 1000. At age 25, it will be necessary to collect $1.16 from each member. At age 30, the cost will be $1.35.

At age 40, the cost per member will have almost doubled from the cost at age 21, and it will be necessary to collect $2.42. By the time the members of the group reach age 50, we will have to collect $4.96 from each. At age 60, we will need $9.47, and at age 70, we will need $22.11 from each member. It does not take a great deal of insight to recognize that before long the plan is going to bog down, if it has not already done so before the members reach age 70. At age 70, when the probability of death is greater than ever before, the members of the group may find that they cannot afford the premium that has become necessary. At age 80, we will need $65.99 from each member, and at age 90, $190.75. The increasing mortality as the group grows older makes yearly renewable term impractical as a means of providing insurance protection at advanced ages. Yet many insurance buyers want coverage that continues throughout their lifetimes. Insurers have found a practical solution.

The Level Premium Concept

It has been found that a practical method of providing life insurance for the entire lifetime of the insured is to use a level premium, under which

---

[2]The $1.07 indicated in our simplified calculation reflects mortality only. In actual practice, life insurance rates include two additional factors: interest and loading. Life insurers specifically recognize the investment income that will be earned on premiums by assuming that premiums will be paid at the beginning of the year and that deaths will occur at the end of the year. The discounted value of future mortality costs is called the net premium. A loading for expenses is added to the net premium to derive the gross premium, which is the amount the buyer pays.

the premium is higher than necessary to fund the cost of death claims during the early years of the policy, and the excess premiums are used to meet the increasing death claims, as the insured group grows older. Ordinary whole life insurance embodies this principle.

The level premium for an ordinary life policy of $1000 purchased by a female at age 21 and the one for yearly renewable term insurance beginning at age 21 are illustrated in Figure 12.1. The line that constitutes the level premium is the exact mathematical equivalent of the yearly renewable term premium curve. This means that the insurance company will obtain the same amount of premium income and interest from a large group of insureds under either plan, assuming that neither group discontinues its payments.

The level premium plan introduces features that have no counterpart in term insurance. From a glance at Figure 12.1 it is clear that under the level premium plan, the insured pays more than the cost of pure life insurance protection during the early years the policy is in force. This overpayment is indicated by the difference between the term and the level premium lines up to the point at which the lines cross. This overpayment, when accumulated at compound interest, will be sufficient to offset the deficiency in the later years of the contract. The excess payments during the early years of the contract create a fund that is held by the insurance company for the benefit and credit of the policyholders. The fund is invested, usually in long-term investments, and the earnings are added to the accumulating fund to help meet the future obligations to the policyholders. The insurer establishes a reserve or liability on its financial statement to reflect these future obligations.

Referring again to Figure 12.1, it appears that the reserve should increase for a time and then diminish. It also appears that the area of redundant premiums in the early years of the contract will never be enough to equal the deficit in the later years. In the case of a single individual, this would be true, but many insureds are involved, and the law of averages permits a continuously in-

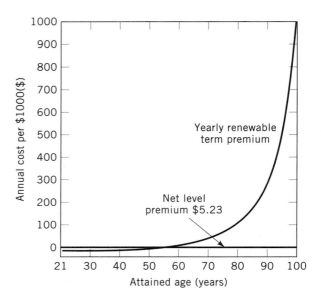

Figure 12.1 Comparison of Net Premiums per $1000 Yearly Renewable Term and Whole Life

creasing reserve for each policy in force. Some insureds will die during the early years of the contracts, and the excess premiums that they have paid are forfeited to the group. The excess premiums forfeited by those who die, together with the excess premiums paid by the survivors will not only offset the deficiency in later years but, with the aid of compound interest, will also continue to build the reserves on the survivors' policies until they equal the face of the contract at age 100. Death is bound to occur at some time, and in a whole life policy, the insurance company knows that a death claim must ultimately be paid.[3] While aggregate reserves for the entire group of insureds increase and then decrease, individual policy reserves continue to climb, mainly because the aggregate reserves are divided among a smaller number of survivors each year. Figure 12.2 shows

[3]The mortality table indicates that all policyholders will have died by age 100. If the insured has not died by this time, the insurance company will declare him dead and pay the face of the policy.

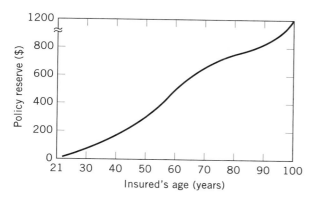

Figure 12.2 Increase in Reserve on Whole Life Policy

the growth in the reserve on an ordinary life policy purchased at age 20.

The level premium plan introduces the features of the redundant premium during the early years of the contract and the creation of the reserve fund. The insured has a contractual right to receive a part of this reserve in the event the policy is terminated, under a policy provision called the *nonforfeiture value* (discussed in Chapter 13). The contractual right to receive a part of the excess premiums that are paid under the level premium plan, therefore, represents an investment element in the contract for the insured. When a policyholder dies, the death benefit could be viewed as being composed of two parts—the portion of the reserve to which the insured would have been eligible and an amount of pure insurance. Under this view, the face amount of the policy is seen as a combination of a decreasing amount of insurance (the net amount at risk) and the increasing investment element (the growing reserve). The decreasing insurance and the increasing investment element always equal the face of the policy.

It should be stressed that the policy reserve is not, strictly speaking, the property of the insured. It is the insured's only if and when the policy is surrendered. If this occurs, the contract no longer exists, and the insurance company is re-

lieved of all obligations on the policy. As long as the contract is in full force, the reserve belongs to the insurance company and must be used to help pay the death claim if the insured should die.

The preceding analysis suggests that there are two distinct advantages in the use of level premium insurance. First, by paying an amount in excess of the cost of pure life insurance during the early years of the contract, the insured avoids a rising premium in the later years; this will make it financially possible to maintain the insurance until the policyholder's death, even though it occurs at an advanced age. Second, if the insured survives, he or she has accumulated a savings fund that can be used for income in old age (or any other purpose the insured decides).

Tax Treatment of Life Insurance

Life insurance policies are granted favorable tax treatment in two ways. First, amounts payable to a beneficiary at the death of an insured are generally not included in taxable income.[4] In addition, income earned on the investment element of life insurance policies is not taxed currently to the policyholder. The investment gain on a life insurance policy is taxed only when the contract is terminated prior to the death of the insured and the cash value is withdrawn. Then, the cash value is taxed only to the extent that the cash value exceeds the policyholder's investment in the contract (i.e., the sum of all premiums paid on the contract). Since the total amount of premiums paid includes the cost of life insurance protection, this represents an understatement of

[4]An exception exists in the case of "transfer for value." An example of a policy transferred for value would be if A purchases from B an existing policy for $10,000 on B's life, paying B $3000 for the policy. If B dies, A will be taxed on the $7000 gain. The taxation of policies transferred for value does not apply if the transferee is the person insured, a partner of the insured, or a corporation of which the insured is a director or stockholder.

the taxable gain. Both features of this tax treatment are obviously beneficial to the insured or beneficiaries.

To qualify for favorable tax treatment as life insurance, a contract must meet the definition of life insurance in the *Internal Revenue Code* (IRC). This definition applies two tests for determining if a contract is a "life insurance contract." A contract that meets either of the two tests is considered life insurance as long as the test is met at all times for the life of the contract. Both tests are designed to limit the types of contracts that qualify as "life insurance" to those contracts that involve only a modest investment and yield a modest investment return. The first test measures the premium under the contract against the premium required to fund death benefits until age 95. The second test requires that the amount of death protection in a policy exceed the policy's cash value by a specified margin. If the contract fails to meet one or the other of these two tests at any time, it does not qualify as life insurance. The cash surrender value is treated as a deposit fund, and income earned on the fund is currently taxable. In addition, all income previously deferred will be included in the insured's income in the year the contract fails to qualify as a life insurance contract.

Current Life Insurance Products

Now that we have an idea about why term insurance differs from cash value life insurance, we can take a closer look at some of those differences as they are reflected in the insurance products from which consumers can choose. We will begin this examination by returning once again to term insurance.

Term Insurance

We already know that term insurance provides temporary protection. It is called term because the coverage is for a limited term. The period for which the coverage will be provided may be 1 year, 5 years, 10 years, or 20 years. It may be "term to expectancy," which is term insurance for the period the insured is expected to live, according to the mortality tables.

In its purest form, a term policy is purchased for a specified period of time and the face is payable only if the insured dies during this period. Nothing is paid if the insured survives the term period. It is customary, however, for term policies to include provisions relating to renewability and convertibility.

Renewable Term

Renewable term policies include a contractual provision guaranteeing the insured the right to renew the policy for a limited number of additional periods, each usually of the same length as the original term period. For example, if the insured purchases a 10-year term policy at age 25 and survives this period, he or she has the option of renewing the policy for an additional 10 years without having to prove insurability. The level premium for this 10-year period will be higher than that for the first 10 years, because of the insured's more advanced age. The insured may renew the policy at age 45 and perhaps also at age 55. However, all insurance companies, because of the element of adverse selection, impose an age limit beyond which renewal is not permitted.

Some term policies grant the insured a lower renewal premium if he or she "reenters" the pool of insured lives by undergoing a somewhat abbreviated underwriting process, including a new physical exam. If the insured does not requalify, he or she may keep the policy, but at a higher premium. Often, this premium is a multiple of the prior premium, subject to a guaranteed maximum that is stated in the policy.

Convertible Term

The conversion provision grants the insured the option of exchanging the term policy for some type of permanent life insurance without evidence of insurability.[5] The conversion is usually effected at the policyholder's attained age, but it can also be made retroactive to his or her original age. For example, if the insured decides to convert the term policy purchased at age 25 to whole life at age 32, and to convert at the attained age, the premium on the whole life policy will be the same as if it had been purchased at age 32. However, the policy could also be converted at the original age of 25, and the premium rates on the converted policy will be those the insured would have paid if the whole life policy had originally been purchased at age 25. However, the insured will be required to pay a lump sum of money to the insurer equal to the larger of (1) the difference in the reserves under the policies being exchanged or (2) the difference between the premiums paid on the term policy and those that would have been paid had the permanent policy been purchased at age 25, plus interest at 5 or 6 percent.

Advantages and Disadvantages of Term Insurance

The advantages and disadvantages of term insurance stem from its dual character as pure protection and temporary protection. Because the premium for term insurance covers protection only, term insurance provides the greatest amount of protection for a given dollar outlay. Because it is temporary protection, it may be better suited to meet temporary insurance needs than would be permanent insurance.

The disadvantages of term insurance also stem from its nature as pure protection and temporary

[5]To minimize the element of adverse selection, most companies impose a time limit within which the conversion must take place. In the 10-year term policy, the insured could be required to convert within 7 or 8 years after the date of issue of the original contract. If the policy is renewable, however, the only limitation is that conversion must take place before the limiting age for renewal or that it be converted within a certain period before the expiration of the last term for which it can be renewed.

protection. Term insurance is misused when it is used to meet permanent needs. In addition, because insurers are subject to a greater element of adverse selection in term policies than in policies that include an investment element, the cost of term insurance may be somewhat greater than the cost of death protection in permanent insurance.

Cash Value Insurance

There are four types of cash value life insurance; whole life, universal life, variable life, and endowment life insurance.

Whole Life Insurance

In our discussion of the difference between term insurance and cash value insurance, we used the whole life policy as the representative of cash value type contracts. This seems entirely appropriate, since the whole life policy is the standard approach to permanent insurance, and other cash value policies may be described in terms of the way(s) in which they differ from whole life.

Straight Whole Life The term "straight" whole life refers to a contract in which the premiums are payable for the entire lifetime of the insured (i.e., until age 100). It is also called continuous premium whole life. The principal advantage of straight whole life is that it provides permanent protection for permanent needs and can be continued for the entire lifetime of the insured. In addition, because it includes a cash value, it serves the dual function of protection and saving. The savings element in the policy can be borrowed for emergencies, or it can be used to pay future premiums under the policy.

Straight whole life has disadvantages when it is used to fill a need for which it was not designed. When it is used to meet a temporary need, the amount of coverage that may be purchased may be less than if the need were met with term insurance. On the other hand, there are permanent life insurance needs, and permanent insurance should be used to meet such needs. Insurance to provide liquidity for estate tax purposes, for example, is a permanent need that cannot be met by temporary life insurance such as term insurance.

Limited-Pay Whole Life   Limited-payment whole life is a variation of the whole life policy, differing only in the manner in which the premium is paid. As in the case of a straight whole life policy, protection under the limited-pay whole life policy extends to age 100, but the premium payments are made for some shorter period of time. During the period that premiums are paid, they are sufficiently high to prepay the policy in advance. Thus, under a 20-payment life policy, during the payment period, one pays premiums that are high enough to permit one to stop payment at the end of 20 years and still enjoy protection equal to the face amount of the policy for the remainder of one's life.

Single-Premium Whole Life   As its name suggests, a *single-premium whole life* (SPWL) policy is one for which there is a single premium. SPWL insurance is usually subject to a minimum premium of $5000 or more. This premium creates an immediate cash value in the policy, which, together with future investment income will be sufficient to cover the cost of the policy's benefits. Single-premium life insurance is written on both a traditional whole-life and variable basis.

Unlike traditional forms of life insurance, single-premium life does not usually have a front-end "load." Instead, the policy is subject to a surrender charge, usually in the range of 5 to 10 percent, which applies if the policy is cashed in during a specified period of time, generally 7 to 10 years. The surrender charge diminishes and eventually disappears after 7 to 10 years.

In the *Technical and Miscellaneous Revenue Act of 1988* (TAMRA), Congress imposed new restrictions on life insurance contracts—such as SPWL—that contained what it considered to be an excessive investment feature. To identify such

contracts, the *IRC* now includes a test—called the "7-pay test"—that measures the investment element in a life insurance contract. The 7-pay test compares the premiums paid for the policy during the first seven years with seven annual net level premiums for a 7-pay policy. The net level premium for a 7-pay policy is an arbitrary standard that measures whether the premiums paid into the policy are excessive relative to the death protection. If the policy fails the test, it is a *modified endowment contract* (MEC).

Modified endowment contracts are subject to two important provisions. First, funds withdrawn from MECs are subject to a "last-in, first-out" treatment. This assumes that the investment income is withdrawn from the policy before the insured's basis. In addition, MECs are subject to a 10 percent penalty on any taxable gains withdrawn before age $59\frac{1}{2}$. This is essentially the same penalty that applies to early withdrawals from qualified pension plans, individual retirement accounts, and annuities.

Universal Life

Universal life was introduced in 1979 by Hutton Life, a subsidiary of the stockbrokerage firm, E. F. Hutton. The essential feature of universal life, which distinguishes it from traditional whole life, is that, subject to specified limitations, the premiums, cash values, and level of protection can be adjusted up or down during the term of the contract to meet the owner's needs. A second distinguishing feature is the fact that the interest credited to the policy's cash value is geared to current interest rates, but is subject to a minimum such as 4 percent.

In effect, the premiums under a universal life policy are credited to a fund (which, following traditional insurance terminology, is called the cash value). This fund is credited with the policy's share of investment earnings, after a deduction for expenses. The cost of the death protection under the policy, which may be increased or decreased, subject to the insurer's underwriting standards is deducted from the fund. Universal policyholders receive annual statements indicating the level of life insurance protection under their policy, the cash value, the current interest being earned, and a statement of the amount of the premium paid that has been used for protection, investment, and expenses.

Some insurers set the minimum amount of coverage for their universal life products at $100,000; other companies offer contracts with an initial face amount as low as $25,000. As in the case of other forms of permanent insurance, the policyholder may borrow against the cash value, but in the case of universal life, he or she may also make withdrawals from the cash value without terminating the contract.

Variable Life Insurance

Variable life insurance is a whole life contract in which the insured has the right to direct how the policy's cash value will be invested and the insured bears the investment risk in the form of fluctuations in the cash value and in the death benefit. Variable life is patterned after the variable annuity, which has been available to groups since 1952 and to individuals for well over a decade. Like the variable annuity, variable life is designed as a solution to the problem of the decline in the purchasing power of the dollar that accompanies inflation.

Under a variable life policy, the amount of the premium is fixed, but the face amount of the policy varies up and down, subject to a minimum, which is the original amount of insurance. The cash value of the policy is not guaranteed and fluctuates with the performance of the portfolio in which the insurer has invested the premiums. This fluctuating cash value provides the funds to pay for the varying amount of death protection. Typically, the insurer will offer policyholders a choice of investments, including stock funds, bond funds, or money market funds.

Variable Universal Life The latest innovation, variable universal life insurance, was introduced in 1985. It combines the flexible premium features of universal life with the investment component of variable life. The policyholder decides how the fund will be invested, and the fund's performance is directly related to the performance of the underlying investments.

Endowment Life Insurance

Under endowment life policies, which, like term insurance, are issued for a period such as 10 years or 20 years, the insurer promises to pay the face of the policy if the insured dies during the policy period, but also promises to pay the face of the policy if the insured survives until the end of the period. ("You win if you live and you win if you die.") Because they require premiums far in excess of the amount required to fund the death benefit, they do not qualify as life insurance under the current provisions of the U.S. *IRC* and are rarely sold in the United States. They remain an important part of the life insurance market in other countries.

Participating and Nonparticipating Life Insurance

A participating life insurance policy is one for which the policyholder "participates" in the divisible surplus of the company through the payment of annual dividends. Originally, only mutual life insurers issued such policies, but today many stock life insurers also offer them. Under a participating policy, a substantial margin of safety is built into the premium, sufficient to reflect an intentional overcharge, but justified on the assumption that if the extra premium is not needed, it will be returned to the policyholder as a dividend.

Because of the long-term nature of life insurance contracts, substantial shifts in the premium factors can occur: mortality rates may change; the expenses of operating the company may increase; and investment income can change, going down as well as up. The participating concept permits the insurer to establish a more generous margin

---

Tidbits, Vignettes, and Conundrums 12.1

Endowments and the Tontine

Endowment life insurance was formerly a popular approach to saving, especially for education. Endowment life insurance policies combined a pure endowment with life insurance protection, thereby guaranteeing the completion of the targeted saving whether an individual lived or died. A *pure endowment* is a contract that promises to pay the face amount of the policy only if the insured survives the endowment period. Pure endowment policies trace their roots to the tontine principle, a concept invented by the Neapolitan banker, Lorenzo Tonti and introduced in France in 1653. Under the tontine system, a fund was created by the contributions of members or subscribers.

The fund was invested and at the end of each year the interest was divided among the survivors. As subscribers died, the dividends were divided among the decreasing number of participants. In a number of early tontines sponsored by governments, the principal remained with the government after the death of the last participant. In later variations, the principal was paid to the last survivor. In a sense, the tontine was a seventeenth-century version of our modern state-run lotteries. Insurance companies in the United States aggressively marketed tontine policies until about the time of the Armstrong investigation of 1905.

---

for changes in the form of an intentional overcharge, which will be returned to the policyholder if not needed. The safety margin on nonparticipating policies is narrower, because the cost of the insurance to the policyholder cannot be adjusted at a later time. The gross premium charged on nonparticipating policies must reflect, at least for competitive reasons, the actual cost of providing the insurance. Any profit realized in the operation will be used to provide dividends to stockholders as well as surplus funds that may be used as a buffer for future adverse experience.

Specialized Life Contracts

Many life insurance policies have been designed to fit special situations. Other policies include features designed to make them appealing to consumers. These forms are simply combinations or modifications of the five basic types of life insurance, and the manner in which they may be combined is limited only by the imagination of the policy writers.

Increasing and Decreasing Term Insurance

Term life insurance is written on a level basis and for a decreasing or increasing amount. Decreasing term insurance is often combined with whole life to create package policies that cover the family income need during child-raising years. Because the period decreases as children age, decreasing term insurance can fund a monthly amount for a diminishing period. This combination policy is called a *family income policy*.

Another popular decreasing term policy is the *mortgage protection policy* (also called a *mortgage redemption policy*), which is designed to provide coverage in an amount sufficient to pay off the mortgage at any given time. Although some insurers refer to virtually any decreasing term policy as their "mortgage redemption policy," other insurers offer contracts with different time periods and amortization rates that facilitate a close match between the decreasing level of coverage and the amount of the unpaid mortgage.

Increasing term insurance is used to support cost-of-living adjustment riders to life insurance policies. An increasing amount of insurance is written to coincide with the increases in the cost of living reflected by the consumer price index (or other standard on which the increases are based).

Increasing term is also written with a base policy to create contracts such as the *return-of-premium policy*. The return-of-premium policy agrees to pay the face of the policy at the death of the insured, plus all the premiums that have been paid, if the insured dies within a certain period of time (usually 20 years). This agreement is supported by an additional amount of insurance (for which the insured pays an additional premium) equal to the premiums that have been paid on the policy. If the insured does not die within the 20-year period, the term portion of the policy expires without value.

Insurance for Multiple Lives

Some life insurance contracts are written to cover multiple lives. One example of a multiple-life policy is the *family protection policy*, which provides insurance on all members of a family in predetermined amounts. The unit on the wage-earning spouse might be $10,000 on an ordinary life basis, with $1000 term insurance on the spouse (extending to the time the wage earner is 65) and $1000 term coverage on each child—including future children—to a designated age such as 21 years.

Other multiple life policies agree to pay only at the death of the first to die (called *joint life*) or at the death of the second to die (called *survivorship life insurance*). For example, when the mortgage protection policy discussed above is written on two lives and agrees to pay at the death of the first, it is called a *joint mortgage protection policy*. A *survivorship whole life* or the *second-to-die* policy insures two lives with the promise to pay only at the

second death. Survivorship whole life was developed in response to a feature in the federal estate tax law under which the tax burden at the death of the second spouse is often greater than at the death of the first spouse.[6]

Policies with Special Premium Modes

Another group of specialized contracts are those that have modified premium arrangements. The *modified whole life* policy is typical. Under a modified whole life policy, the premium for the first three or five years is slightly more than that on the same amount of term insurance. After the end of the three- or five-year period, the premium increases to a level that is slightly more than the whole life premium at the age at which the policy was taken out, but also slightly less than the premium on permanent insurance at the attained age of the insured. Modified whole life is essentially equivalent to automatically convertible term. As in the case of term, during the first three to five years, there is rarely a cash value.

Another contract closely related to modified whole life is graded-premium whole life. *Graded-premium whole life* is a contract in which the initial premium is quite low (say, $2 per $1000 at age 21) but increases yearly until it levels off sometime between the tenth and twentieth years. Cash values are not generally available until year 10, and even by year 20 the cash values are quite low.

Interest-Sensitive Whole Life

In response to the competition from universal life, some companies introduced interest-sensitive whole-life policies, in which the dividends under participating policies are geared to current money rates. The sale of interest-sensitive policies generally requires a new approach for crediting interest in the company's dividend formula. Under the traditional dividend allocation method (called the *portfolio average method*), excess invest-

---

[6]The federal estate tax is discussed in Chapter 14.

ment earnings included in dividends are allocated to all policies, old and new, at a single rate, regardless of the pattern of premium payments over the years. The new approaches that have been adopted are collectively called the *investment generation method* (IGM). Under IGM, dividends are allocated on a basis that recognizes the year (or generation of policies) during which money was invested by the policyholder.

Current Assumption Whole Life

Current assumption whole life (CAWL) insurance is the nonparticipating version of interest sensitive participating whole life policies. CAWL uses new-money investment income and current mortality charges in determining premiums and cash values. CAWL policies include a *redetermination provision* under which the insurer can, after an initial guarantee period, increase or decrease the premiums based on current interest and mortality. If the current assumption produces a lower premium the insured can pay the lower premium or continue to pay the old higher premium and thereby increase the cash value. Subject to evidence of insurability, the insured can use the difference between the old and new premiums to increase the death benefit. If the new premium is higher than the previous premium, the insured can pay the new premium, reduce the face amount of the policy, or use a part of the cash value to cover the difference.

General Classifications of Life Insurance

There are four basic classes of life insurance, distinguished by the manner in which they are marketed:

1. Ordinary life insurance
2. Industrial life insurance
3. Group life insurance
4. Credit life insurance

Our discussion thus far has been concerned with ordinary life insurance. It would not be complete without at least a brief description of the other three types.

Ordinary Life Insurance

Ordinary life insurance constitutes the oldest and largest of the classes. In ordinary life, individual policies are marketed with a face amount of $1000 or more. The premiums are paid annually, semiannually, quarterly, or monthly. The main characteristics of ordinary life are that it is sold on an individual basis and policy amounts are $1000 or more. It currently accounts for 59 percent of all life insurance in force in the United States.

Industrial Life Insurance

Industrial life insurance is characterized by individual policies with face amounts of less than $1000, with premiums payable as frequently as weekly and collected by an agent at the home of the insured. In most instances, industrial life insurance is sold in premium units (which vary from $0.25 to $1.00 a week). Generally, it is decided how much weekly premium the insured can pay, and the amount of insurance will depend on the amount of coverage this premium will purchase under the plan selected at the attained age of the insured. As a general rule, the insurance is provided without medical examination. Although industrial life insurance once represented an important segment of the market, it now represents less than 1 percent of all legal reserve life insurance in force as compared with more than 10 percent five decades ago.

Although industrial life insurance has virtually disappeared over the past five decades, a variation of this product called Monthly Debit Ordinary (MDO) life insurance has emerged as its successor. MDO life insurance—also known as *home service life insurance*—is a form of cash value life insurance with relatively low face amounts and high premiums. Like industrial life insurance, MDO life insurance is sold by agents who go door-to-door to sell the coverage and collect premiums. Because the volume of MDO life insurance is included in insurance company reports as ordinary life, there are no dependable data on the size of this market. A number of insurers specialize in this field, and others write MDO in addition to other forms of ordinary life insurance.

Group Life Insurance

Group life insurance is a plan whereby coverage can be provided for a number of persons under one contract, called a master policy, usually without evidence of individual insurability. It is generally issued to an employer for the benefit of employees, but may also be used for other closely knit groups. The individual members of the group receive certificates as evidence of their insurance, but the contract is between the employer and the insurance company. Group life insurance programs sponsored by an employer may be contributory or noncontributory. Under a contributory plan, which is the more common approach, employer and employees share the cost of the insurance. Under a noncontributory plan, the employer pays the entire cost.

In most states, laws patterned after an NAIC Model Group Life Insurance Law define the groups to which group life insurance may be issued. The model law permits group coverage for current and retired employees of a single employer or multiple employer groups, the members of a labor union, debtors of a common creditor, members of credit unions, and members of associations formed for purposes other than to obtain insurance.

The basic feature of group life insurance was originally the substitution of group underwriting for individual underwriting. This meant that there were no physical examination or other individual underwriting methods applicable to individual employees. Under the first group life insurance laws, the definition of *groups* for insurance purposes was restrictive, requiring a minimum number of members, usually 50 or 100

lives.[7] Over time, the minimum number of individuals in a group required by statute have shrunk, and with the decrease in the number, the nature of group underwriting has changed. As the minimum number of members required for group coverage fell, insurers introduced elements of individual underwriting for smaller groups. Although group underwriting is still used for large groups, state laws now allow insurers to require evidence of individual insurability on groups. Whether an insurer will require evidence of individual insurability for group coverage depends on the size and nature of the group.

The cost of group life insurance is comparatively low for several reasons. The first is that the basic plan under which most group life insurance is provided is yearly renewable term insurance, which provides the lowest-cost form of protection per premium dollar. In addition, when true group underwriting is applied, the expenses of medical examinations and other methods of determining insurability are largely eliminated. Third, group life involves mass selling and mass administration, with the result that expenses are lower under group policies than under the marketing of individual policies. Finally, when group life insurance is part of an employee's compensation, there are tax advantages that further reduce the cost. Under current federal tax laws, an employer may deduct as a business expense premiums on group term life insurance up to $50,000 per employee, and amounts paid by the employer for such insurance are not taxable as income to the employee.

In addition to the lower cost, coverage under group life insurance contracts is very liberal. There are no exclusions, and the insurance pays for death from any cause, including suicide, without restrictions as to time. In addition, most policies include a conversion provision, under which the insured employee may, within 31 days after

[7]The first NAIC model group law, adopted in 1917, set the minimum for groups at 50. Many states reduced this to 25, and the number has gradually dropped to 10. Group underwriting is discussed in Chapter 17.

termination of employment, convert all or a portion of the insurance to any form of individual policy currently offered by the insurance company, with the exception of term insurance. Conversion would be at the attained age of the employee and could not be refused by the insurance company because of the worker's uninsurability.

Group life insurance has become an important branch of life insurance today, accounting for 39.6 percent of all such protection in force in 1998. For many persons who would not be insurable under ordinary life insurance, it provides the only means for obtaining coverage. For others, the low-cost group life insurance is an excellent supplement to the individual life insurance program.

Credit Life Insurance

Credit life insurance is sold through lending institutions to short-term borrowers contemplating consumer purchases and through retail merchants selling on a charge account basis to installment buyers. It also includes mortgage protection life insurance of 10 years' duration or less that is issued through lenders.[8] The insurance protects both the lenders and the debtors against financial loss should the debtor die before completing the required payments. The life of the borrower is insured for an amount related to the outstanding balance of a specific loan, and the policy generally provides for the payment of the scheduled balance in the event of the debtor's death. The insurance is term insurance, generally decreasing in amount as the loan is repaid.

The major sellers of credit life insurance (and the lenders who are usually the beneficiaries of

this coverage) include commercial banks, sales finance companies, credit unions, personal finance companies, and retailers selling goods and services on a charge account or installment basis. Some insurers specialize in writing credit life, while for other insurers, it represents only a small part of their total business. The coverage is sold on both an individual and group basis. In the former, borrowers receive individual policies. In the latter, a master policy is issued to the lending institution, and the individual borrowers receive certificates outlining their coverage. Approximately 85 percent of the credit life insurance in force is written on a group basis.

Total Life Insurance in Force in the United States

Total life insurance in force in 1998 exceeded $14 trillion, well over twice the amount held a decade earlier. The bulk of this amount—over 97.5 percent—was issued by legal reserve life insurance companies operating under state insurance laws specifying the minimum basis for the reserves that the company must maintain on its policies.[9] The remainder was issued by other private insurers and government insurers discussed in the paragraphs that follow. Table 12.1, which lists the insurance in force with legal reserve life insurance companies from 1900 through 1998, indicates the distribution of the insurance by class, and also depicts its growth and changing distribution by class over time.

Other Types of Life Insurance

In addition to the life insurance issued by legal reserve life insurance companies, a small amount (about 2.5 percent of life insurance in force) is written by other types of insurers.

---

[8]Credit life insurance is frequently sold in conjunction with a companion coverage, credit accident and health insurance. This insures against the disability of the borrower through accident or illness and provides benefits by meeting required payments for a specific loan during the debtor's disability. Benefits are commonly subject to some dollar maximum per payment and some maximum number of payments.

[9]Insurers that do not qualify as legal reserve life insurers include fraternals and assessment societies.

Table 12.1   Life Insurance in Force in the United States, 1900–1999 (000,000 omitted)

Year	Ordinary Number	Ordinary Amount	Group Number	Group Amount	Industrial Number	Industrial Amount	Credit Number[a]	Credit Amount	Total Number	Total Amount
1900	3	$6,124			11	$1,449	—	—	14	$7,573
1910	6	11,783	—		23	3,125	—	—	29	14,908
1920	16	32,011	2	$1,570	48	6,948	b	$4	66	40,540
1930	32	78,576	6	9,801	86	17,963	b	73	124	106,413
1940	37	79,346	9	14,938	85	20,866	3	380	134	115,530
1950	64	149,116	19	47,793	108	33,415	11	3,844	202	234,168
1960	95	341,881	44	175,903	100	39,563	43	29,101	282	586,448
1970	120	734,730	80	551,357	77	38,644	78	77,392	355	1,402,123
1975	134	1,083,421	96	904,695	70	39,423	80	112,032	380	2,139,571
1980	148	1,760,474	118	1,579,355	58	35,994	78	165,215	402	3,541,038
1985	142	3,247,289	130	2,561,595	44	28,250	70	215,973	386	6,053,107
1990	141	5,366,982	141	3,753,506	36	24,071	71	248,038	389	9,392,597
1995	151	7,547,537	145	4,777,912	30	19,977	66	231,251	392	12,576,677
1998	158	8,505,894	147	5,735,273	27	17,365	64	212,917	396	14,471,449

Note: "Credit" is limited to life insurance on loans of 10 years' or less duration. "Ordinary" and "Group" include credit life insurance on loans of more than 10 years' duration.

[a] Includes group credit certificates.

[b] Fewer than 500,000.

Sources: Spectator Year Book and American Council of Life Insurance. Totals for "In the United States" represent all life insurance (net of reinsurance) on residents of the United States, whether issued by U.S. or foreign companies. Beginning with 1959, the data include Alaska and Hawaii.

In three states—New York, Massachusetts, and Connecticut—the law authorizes mutual savings banks to issue life insurance policies under prescribed conditions to residents of the state and to persons regularly employed there. The amount of savings bank life insurance in force in these states is a small percentage of the total insurance in force: about 3 percent in Massachusetts, 2.5 percent in New York, and less than 2 percent in Connecticut.[10]

Another source of life insurance is fraternal organizations that provide life insurance to their members. Most fraternals originally used the assessment principle, but the majority currently operate on a legal reserve basis. The total amount of insurance in force with fraternals at the end of 1999 was less than 2 percent of all effective life insurance.

The U.S. Veterans Administration has sold life insurance to veterans since World War I. No veteran can own more than $10,000 in government life insurance under any one or a combination of these plans. The total amount of government life insurance in force under these programs was about $26.2 billion at the end of 1999. Only one of the programs—designed for veterans separated from the service with a service-connected disability—is still open to new issues, so it may be assumed that the amount of insurance of this type will decline in the future.[11]

[10]In Massachusetts, individuals may purchase up to $500,000 in savings bank life insurance. In New York, the maximum is $50,000 for individual coverage and $250,000 for group coverage. The maximum insurance allowable in Connecticut is $100,000 for individual coverage and $200,000 for group coverage.

[11]Servicemen's Group Life Insurance (SGLI) and Veterans Group Life Insurance (VGLI), which is sold by private insurers, are included in the private insurance industry totals in Table 12.1.

Finally, the Wisconsin State Life Insurance Fund issues policies with a $1000 minimum and a $10,000 maximum to persons in the state at the time of issuance. Although the program has been in effect since 1911, the total amount of insurance in force under the program is less than 1 percent of all life insurance in force in the state.

Annuities

Annuities have been called *upside-down life insurance*, and in a sense they are a reverse application of the law of large numbers as it is used in life insurance. An *annuity* is a contract that provides periodic payments for a specified period of time or, more commonly, for the duration of a person's life or the lives of more than one person.[12] The person whose life governs the duration of the payments is called the *annuitant*.

Nature and Functions of Annuities

The basic function of a life annuity is to liquidate a principal sum. The annuity may involve the liquidation of a sum derived from a person's savings (including the annuity itself or the cash value of life insurance policies) or the liquidation of life insurance death benefits in the form of a life income to the beneficiary of the policy. Regardless of how the principal fund was annuitized, the annuity is designed to protect against the risk of outliving the income from that fund.

To illustrate the annuity principle, let us assume that Mr. X reaches age 65, retires, and has exactly $100,000 to provide for his needs during the balance of his lifetime. How much of this $100,000 can he afford to spend each year so that the principal will be used up when he dies, but not before? Because X is uncertain as to how long he will live, he cannot answer the question with certainty. If he assumes that he will live another 16 years, he can withdraw $6250 annually plus, say, $3650 in interest, which will provide him with $9,900 annually. But what if he lives 20 or 25 years? If he assumes that he will live 25 years, he can only withdraw about $4000 plus interest annually, or about $7800, which is 20 percent less.

If X uses his $100,000 principal as a single premium to purchase a life annuity, he will be guaranteed an income for life, with a payout rate that will maximize his withdrawals without premature exhaustion of his capital. His income from this contract will be guaranteed at a rate of $9900 (and could be as much as $12,000 or $13,000), but more important, it will be guaranteed for the rest of his life, regardless of how long he lives.

Under the annuity principle, the law of averages operates to permit a lifetime-guaranteed income to each annuitant. Some people who reach age 65 will die before they reach 66. Others will live to be 100. Those who live longer than average will offset those who live for a shorter period than average, and those who die early will forfeit money to those who die later. Every payment the annuitant receives is part interest and part principal. In addition, each payment is part survivorship benefit, in that it is composed in part of the funds of group members who have died.

Insurance companies have found that annuitants live longer than most people. This is simply a result of adverse selection. People who feel that they have short life expectancies do not normally purchase annuities, while the individual whose parents and grandparents all lived to be 115 years old will probably look on an annuity as a good investment. The annuity principle favors the long-lived, and in general, these are the people who purchase these policies. For this reason, insurance companies use different mortality tables for computing the cost of annuities than they use for life insurance. The older the annuitant, the lower

[12]If the payments are to be continued for a specified period but only for as long as the annuitant lives, the contract is known as a temporary life annuity. Because the temporary life annuity is used infrequently, our discussion of annuities will concentrate on life annuities.

the cost for a given amount of monthly income.[13] Obviously, there is no requirement that the annuitant be in good health.

In addition to their function in liquidating an accumulated principal, annuities may also serve as investment instruments through which the principal may be accumulated. When the commencement date for annuity payments is set at some time in the future, the annuity principal may be accumulated by the periodic installment payments by the annuity purchaser. As in the case of life insurance, the investment income on the growing fund accumulates on a tax-deferred basis and is not taxed until it is paid out to the annuitant.

If the annuitant dies during the accumulation period—that is, before the contract is annuitized—a death benefit is payable to a beneficiary or to the insured's estate. Annuities therefore represent a part of the individual's protection against premature death. The most common approach is to provide for a return of gross premiums without interest, or the cash value (whichever is larger).

Classification of Annuities

Annuities may be classified in various ways. Traditionally, annuities have been classified according to the following distinctions:

- Individual versus group annuity
- Immediate versus deferred annuity
- Single-premium versus installment annuity
- Single life versus joint life annuity
- Pure life annuity versus annuity certain
- Fixed-dollar versus variable annuity

[13]Since on average women live longer than men, life annuities are more expensive for women. The amount of monthly income produced by a given amount for a female at age 65 is approximately the amount produced for a male who is 60 years old.

Individual versus Group Annuities

Annuities, like life insurance, are sold on both an individual and a group basis. Group annuities often serve as a funding mechanism for the qualified retirement programs discussed in Chapter 17. Although the discussion that follows focuses primarily on individual contracts, the basic principles are essentially the same in group annuities.

Immediate versus Deferred Annuities

Annuities may be grouped according to when payments to the annuitant commence. With the immediate annuity, annuity payments begin the month after the annuity is purchased. Under a deferred annuity, there is a spread of several years between the date of purchase and the beginning of the annuity payments. A deferred annuity is purchased at some time before retirement and the purchase price is augmented by investment income during the interval between the time of purchase and the time the benefits commence.

Single Premium versus Installment Annuities

Annuities may also be classified according to the method of premium payment. They may be purchased with a single premium (the annuity to begin immediately or at some future date), or they may be purchased on an installment basis over a period of years. Installment annuities will, of course, always be deferred annuities.

Single Life versus Joint Life Annuities

The annuity may be paid only for the duration of a single life or for the duration of two or more lives. When the annuity involves two lives, the amount payable after the death of the first annuitant may be the same as during the lifetime of both annuitants, it may be lower, or payments may cease. Under the *joint and survivor annuity*, the insurer promises to make payments until both annuitants have died. A variation of this form provides for a reduction in the income payments at the death of the first annuitant, with lower annuity payments (usually one-half or two-thirds of the original income payments) being continued until the death of the second annuitant. Under the *joint life annuity*, payments cease at the death of the first annuitant; the other annuitant then receives no further benefits under the program. This form is useful when there is a secondary source of income that is sufficient to support one, but not both, of the annuitants.

Pure Life Annuities versus Annuity Certain

Annuities may be classified according to the nature of the insurer's obligation. Under a pure life annuity, payments are made only for the balance of the annuitant's lifetime, regardless of how long or short this period might be. The annuity is considered fully liquidated at the annuitant's death, with nothing payable to his or her estate. Even though the pure life annuity provides the maximum income per dollar of principal sum, some people object to placing a substantial sum into a contract that promises no return if death should occur shortly after the annuity payments begin. As a result, insurers have found it necessary to add some sort of refund feature to annuities to make them more salable.

Life annuities may include one of two guarantee features; a period certain or refund feature. Under a life annuity with period certain, payments are made for the lifetime of the annuitant, but at least for some minimum number of years. Guarantee periods are available for 5, 10, 15, and 20 years. Under a life annuity with refund, if the entire purchase price has not been paid by the time the annuitant dies, the difference between the purchase price and the payments that have been made is refunded to a beneficiary, either as a lump sum or by continu-

ing installment payments until the purchase price has been recovered.

Fixed and Variable Annuities

Finally, the annuity may be a *fixed-dollar annuity* or a *variable annuity*. Under a fixed-dollar annuity, premiums paid by the annuitant are converted into a lifetime payout, and the annuitant is guaranteed a fixed number of dollars monthly or annually for the rest of his or her lifetime. While the number of dollars payable is guaranteed, those dollars may have reduced purchasing power if inflation occurs. Under a variable annuity, the premiums are invested in common stocks or other investments and maintained in *separate accounts* by insurers (i.e., accounts separated from an insurer's other assets and for which state laws allow greater discretion with respect to investment). Premiums paid into a variable annuity are converted into *accumulation units* as they are received. The number of accumulation units credited to the purchaser depends on the current value of the accumulation units, which is determined in much the same way as the value of mutual fund shares—by dividing the current value of all securities in the portfolio by the total number of accumulation units outstanding. Variable annuities may be variable during the accumulation period and fixed during the payout period or variable during both the accumulation period and the payout period.

The underlying philosophy of the variable annuity is that while the value of the dollar will vary over time, the value of a diversified portfolio of common stocks will change in the same direction as the price level. Over time, the value of the accumulation unit rises and falls with the market price of the securities held by the insurer. By contributing a fixed amount each month regardless of the fluctuations in the value of the securities, the annuity purchasers make use of the principle of dollar averaging. Many companies selling variable annuities offer *self-directed annuities*, in which the insurer gives the purchaser a choice among several stock, bond, and money portfolios. The purchaser can allocate premiums among the stock and bond options and can transfer the funds from account to account as conditions change.[14]

Variable annuities are regulated by both the SEC and the state insurance departments. Agents who sell variable annuities must be licensed by state insurance departments for the sale of life insurance products and must be registered with the National Association of Securities Dealers (NASD). By 2000, more than 15 million persons had variable annuities. Persons insured are about equally divided between group and individual plans, with about 51 percent of those insured covered under group plans.

Equity-Indexed Annuities Equity-indexed annuities first appeared in early 1996 and quickly captured a significant share of the annuity market. An equity-indexed annuity is a fixed annuity that earns interest or provides benefits that are linked to the performance of an equity index, such as the S&P 500. Generally, the crediting rate is a function of the relative change in the index, the participation rate (i.e., the percentage of the index growth that is passed on to policyholders), and any caps imposed on the crediting rate. These annuities also typically have minimum interest guarantees and comply with the minimum nonforfeiture law. Because of the complexity of equity-indexed annuities, the NAIC produced a buyers guide in 1998 and encourages insurers to make it available to consumers considering an annuity.

---

[14]The variable annuity was developed by the Teachers Insurance and Annuity Association of America (TIAA), a nonprofit organization founded in 1918 by the Carnegie Foundation to provide college professors with retirement programs. In 1952, TIAA created a companion organization, called the College Retirement Equity Fund (CREF). The fund issued its first variable annuity in 1952, and now serves over 3 million participants.

Annuity Rate of Return and Expense Ratio

The return that will be earned over the life of a fixed dollar annuity depends on the interest rate, the surrender charge, and administrative expenses. There is a guaranteed interest rate both during the accumulation period and during the payout period. The actual rate payable—called the "current interest rate"—may be higher than the guaranteed rate, depending on the insurer's investment income. A current rate is guaranteed for an initial period of years, after which it may be changed, subject to the guaranteed minimum. The guarantee period may range from one year up to ten, and some insurers offer the buyer a choice as to the period for which the current rate will be guaranteed. Usually, the longer the period for which the rate will be guaranteed, the lower the rate.

Although some insurers charge a front-end sales fee of 4 or 5 percent of the premium on individual annuities, most insurers have eliminated front-end commission charges on annuities and use a surrender fee for early withdrawals. The surrender fee usually begins at a high level (8 to 10 percent), and then diminishes until it disappears after a specified period (ranging from 7 to 15 years). A few insurers charge an annual management fee, particularly on small policies.

Tax Treatment of Annuities

As in the case of life insurance, investment income earned on annuities during the accumulation period is not taxable until distributed to the policyholder. Distributions are taxed to the extent that payments exceed the investment in the contract. In addition, a 10 percent premature penalty is imposed on "early withdrawals" from annuities, which is any distribution prior to the time the annuitant reaches age $59\frac{1}{2}$. The penalty on premature distributions does not apply if the contract holder becomes disabled or if the distribution is over the life of the annuitant.

The taxation of distributions requires apportioning annuity payments between recovery of capital and income. This is done by a formula that excludes from taxable income the portion of each payment that the price of the annuity bears to the expected return under the contract. The expected return is the annual amount to be paid to the annuitant multiplied by the annuitant's life expectancy, using IRS annuity tables. Separate tables are used for single life annuities and for joint-and-survivor annuities. The exclusion ratio formula is

$$\text{Payment} \times \frac{\text{Investment in contract}}{\text{Expected return}} = \frac{\text{Nontaxable}}{\text{return of capital}}$$

Assume that Brown has purchased an annuity for $60,000 and that the annuity will pay $500 a month for life. He is 66 years old and has a life expectancy of 15 years, which means that he "expects" to receive $90,000 ($6000 per year for 15 years). Applying the *exclusion ratio formula* to the $6000 benefit Brown receives in the first year:

$$\$6000 \times \frac{\$60,000}{\$500 \times 12 \times 15 \text{ years}} = \$4000$$

The $4000 is a nontaxable return of capital and $2000 is taxable income. Once the annuitant has recovered the investment in the annuity, the exclusion ratio does not apply and subsequent payments are fully taxable. If the annuitant dies before recovering the total basis, the unrecovered basis may be deducted from the decedent's final tax return.

If the contract holder dies after annuity payments have begun but before the entire interest has been distributed, the remaining portion of the annuity must be distributed at least as rapidly as the original method of distribution and will be taxable to the beneficiary. If the annuitant dies before the annuity starting date, unless the beneficiary of the annuity is a spouse, the annuity proceeds must be distributed within five years from the date of death or be annuitized within one year. If the beneficiary is a spouse, the annuity contract may be continued (and the tax on the earnings deferred) until distribution of the benefits to or the death of the spouse.

Important Concepts to Remember

term insurance	group life insurance	endowment life insurance
nonforfeiture value	variable life insurance	adjustable life policy
ordinary life insurance	straight whole life	yearly renewable term
cash value life insurance	limited-pay life insurance	participating life insurance
renewable term insurance	credit life insurance	fraternal insurer
industrial life insurance	pure endowment	level premium plan
whole life insurance	universal life insurance	policy dividend
convertible term insurance	savings bank life	

Questions for Review

1. Distinguish between term insurance policies and cash value policies.

2. Explain what is meant by the statement that term insurance is "pure protection."

3. Under a whole life policy, the overpayment by the insured during the early years of the contract offsets underpayments in later years. This being the case, the reserve should reach a peak and then gradually decline. How do you explain the fact that it does not?

4. Under a whole life policy, the amount payable in the event of the insured's death can be viewed as consisting of two parts. Explain this concept.

5. Describe the ways in which life insurance policies receive favorable tax treatment.

6. John Jones buys *a renewable, convertible, nonparticipating term* insurance policy. Explain the precise meaning of each of the italicized words.

7. Describe the distinguishing characteristics of universal life insurance and variable life insurance.

8. What is the difference between a participating and a nonparticipating life insurance contract? How do their premiums reflect this difference?

9. Life insurance may be classified according to the manner in which it is marketed. Identify the four classes of insurance based on this classification and explain the distinguishing characteristics of each.

10. Explain what is meant by the observation that annuities are "upside-down life insurance" and describe the various ways in which annuities are classified.

Questions for Discussion

1. Insurance people are always calling things by names that don't apply. What they call health insurance should be called "sickness insurance" and what they call life insurance should be called "death insurance." Do you agree or disagree with the author of this statement?

2. The *Internal Revenue Code* provides certain tax advantages to life insurance. Some observers argue that this gives life insurance an unfair advantage over other savings vehicles, such as mutual funds. Do you agree or disagree? Why?

3. The variable annuity has been described as an ingenious solution to the problem that inflation poses for persons attempting to accumulate funds for retirement. In what way, if any, does the variable annuity suggest possible solutions for the problems facing the Social Security System?

4. Dividends paid to policyholders on participating policies are treated by the IRS as a return of premium and are not subject to income tax. Dividends to shareholders in a stock company, however, are taxable income to the recipients. Do you believe this difference in treatment is justified? Why or why not?

5. Discuss the potential for adverse selection when insureds exercise the renewability or convertibility option in a term life insurance policy. Which is more likely to be affected by adverse selection?

Suggestions for Additional Reading

Black, Kenneth, Jr., and Harold D. Skipper, Jr. *Life Insurance,* 13th ed. Englewood Cliffs, NJ: Prentice-Hall, 2000. Chapters 4, 5, 6.

Crawford, Muriel L. *Life and Health Insurance Law,* 7th ed. Homewood, IL: Richard D. Irwin, 1994.

Graves, Edward E., (ed.). *McGill's Life Insurance.* Bryn Mawr, PA: American College, 1994. Chapters 2, 3, 4, 33.

Hallman, G. Victor, and Karen L. Hamilton. *Personal Insurance: Life, Health & Retirement.* Malvern, PA: American Institute for CPCU, 1994. Chapter 4.

Websites to Explore

American College: http://www.amercoll.edu/

American Council of Life Insurance: http://www.acli.com/

American Society of CLU & ChFC: http://www.agents-online.com/ASCLU/web/index.html

Association for Advanced Life Underwriting: http://www.agents-online.com/AALU/

Insurance News Network: http://www.insure.com/

Life Office Management Association (LOMA): http://www.loma.org/

Life-Line: http://www.life-line.org/

LIMRA: http://www.limra.com/aboutlim.htm

Newsedge News Page: http://www.newspage.com/browse/46622/

National Underwriter Company: http://www.nuco.com/

CHAPTER 13

The Life Insurance Contract

Youngsters read it, grown men understand it, and old people applaud it.
—Miguel de Cervantes
Don Quixote

CHAPTER OBJECTIVES

When you have finished this chapter, you should be able to

- Describe the common provisions of life insurance contracts

- Explain the purpose and importance of the incontestable clause in life insurance contracts

- Identify and explain the distinction among the various types of beneficiaries that may be designated in a life insurance contract

- Identify and describe the settlement options and explain the circumstances in which each of the settlement options might be used

- Describe the nonforfeiture options in life insurance contracts and explain the source of these values

- Identify and describe the dividend options in life insurance policies and explain the source of dividends

- Identify and describe the major optional provisions of life insurance contracts and discuss their value to the policyholder

In this chapter, we turn to the life insurance policy itself. Like other insurance contracts, the policy embodies the agreement between the insurer and the insured. The focus of our discussion will be on the terms of that agreement. Before turning to the contract provisions, we will digress briefly and examine some considerations related to the inception of the policy.

Inception of the Life Insurance Contract

Coverage under the life insurance policy is effective as soon as the contract comes into existence. The fundamental question, then, is When does the policy come into existence? The answer hinges on a detail relatively small in the eyes of many insureds—whether the first premium accompanies the application for insurance. If the application is sent to the insurance company without the premium, the company draws the contract and offers it to the applicant. It is not a contract until it has been accepted by the insured, which the latter does by taking the policy and paying the first premium. If the insured should die during the period between making the application and receiving the policy and paying the first premium, no benefits will be paid, for the policy has not yet come into existence. For the most part, this is not the usual procedure.

Normally, the premium accompanies the application for insurance. The company acknowledges receipt of the premium with a conditional binding receipt. The typical binding receipt makes the policy effective as of the date of application, provided the applicant is found to be insurable according to the underwriting rules of the company. A situation might arise in which the underwriter is forced to determine whether a deceased person would have qualified for insurance if he or she had not died. If the applicant would have qualified, then the company is bound to pay the death benefit, since the policy went into effect conditionally at the time of the application.[1]

General Provisions of Life Insurance Contracts

Unlike many other insurance contracts, there is no standard policy form that must be used in life insurance. However, while there is no uniform contract, the states have enacted legislation that makes certain provisions mandatory in life insurance policies. The most commonly required provisions include the following:

- The policy shall constitute the entire contract.
- There must be a grace period of 30 days or one month.
- The policy shall be contestable only during the first two years.
- Misstatement of age shall be cause for an adjustment in the amount of insurance.
- Reinstatement must be permitted.
- Participating policies shall pay dividends on an annual basis.
- Nonforfeiture values must be listed for at least 20 years.
- The nonforfeiture values to which the insured is entitled must be listed after the payment of three premiums.
- Loan values must be listed.
- Installment or annuity tables shall show the amount of benefits to which the beneficiary is entitled if the policy is payable in installments or as an annuity.

---

[1]Although the conditional binding receipt is the normal procedure, some companies use a binding receipt that is not conditional. Here, coverage is effective immediately under *interim term insurance,* which continues until the contract is issued.

Although certain provisions are required by law, in many cases their exact wording is not spelled out. However, the commissioner of insurance must approve the final wording adopted by the insurance company. In addition, even in the case of those provisions not required by law, competition generally forces them to be substantially similar. So, while there is no "standard" life insurance policy, the provisions discussed in the chapter are typical of those in most life insurance policies.

Entire Contract Clause

When the application is incorporated as a part of the policy contract, the representations of the insured become contract provisions and can be used as evidence to contest the contract's validity. To prevent the use of other evidence, most states require the inclusion of a clause in life insurance policies stating that the policy and the application attached to it constitute the entire contract between the parties and that in the absence of fraud, all statements in the application will be considered representations and not warranties. In declaring the statements of the insured to be representations and not warranties, the clause requires the insurer to prove the materiality of any misrepresentations by the insured. This provision is clearly beneficial to the insured.

Ownership Clause

A life insurance policy is a piece of property. The owner of the policy may be the individual on whose life the policy is written, it may be the beneficiary, or it may be someone else. In most cases, the insured is also the owner of the policy. The person designated as the owner has vested privileges of ownership, including the right to assign or transfer the policy, receive the cash values and dividends, or borrow against it. At the death of the insured, the beneficiary becomes the owner of the policy.

Beneficiary Clause

The beneficiary is the person named in the life insurance contract to receive all or a portion of the proceeds at maturity of the policy. There are several classifications of beneficiaries, but for our purpose the most important distinctions are between a "primary" or "contingent" beneficiary and a revocable or irrevocable one.

A primary beneficiary is the person first entitled to the proceeds of the policy at the death of the insured. A contingent beneficiary is entitled to the policy benefits if the primary or direct beneficiary dies before the insured.

The distinction between a revocable or irrevocable beneficiary relates to the insured's right to change a beneficiary once designated. When the beneficiary designation is revocable, the insured reserves the right to change the designation at any time. The insured is the complete owner of the policy, and the revocable beneficiary cannot interfere in any manner with the insured's exercise of these rights. The insured may borrow on the policy, surrender the contract for cash value, assign the policy, or anything else that he or she wishes, without legal interference by the beneficiary. The only time the beneficiary acquires a legal interest in the contract is at the death of the insured. But even here the right of the beneficiary to the proceeds is subject to the conditions of any settlement options selected by the insured.

If an irrevocable beneficiary is named, the insured loses complete ownership of the policy, which then becomes the joint property of beneficiary and insured. The insured cannot change the designation of the beneficiary without the latter's consent. In addition, the acquisition of a policy loan or an assignment of the contract will require the permission of the beneficiary. If the irrevocable beneficiary dies before the insured, most policies provide that the interest of the beneficiary ends and all rights in the contract revert to the insured. As a consequence, the irrevocable beneficiary does not become the complete owner of the policy; this person's interest is conditionally vested along with that of the insured.

To make certain that his or her intentions will be accomplished, the insured should designate the beneficiary or beneficiaries with care. For example, a man may wish his present wife to be the primary beneficiary and his children by this wife to be the class-contingent beneficiaries. Proper identification could be accomplished in this case by the designation of "my wife, Elizabeth Hallquist Jones, and the children of our marriage." The wife would be the primary beneficiary and the children contingent beneficiaries. The children then would receive, and share equally, the proceeds if the wife should predecease the insured.[2]

Problems: have extra kids after beneficiary named or ex-wife named, then divorce

Incontestable Clause

One unusual provision that is required in life policies is the incontestable clause. The usual policy provision reads as follows: "This policy shall be incontestable after it has been in force during the lifetime of the insured for two years from the date of issue." This means that the validity of the contract cannot be questioned for any reason whatsoever after it has been in force during the lifetime of the insured for two years. The reason for this restriction is based on the long-term nature of the life insurance contract. The intent is to relieve the insured or a beneficiary of disproving fraud at a time when all evidence of the original transaction has disappeared and original witnesses have died. The effect of the clause is not that of justifying a contract involving fraud. The courts justify the clause on the grounds that they are not condoning fraud, but that after an insurance company has been given a reasonable opportunity to investigate the validity of the contract, it should then relinquish its right on the grounds that the

social advantages will outweigh the undesirable consequences.[3]

The clause is applicable for two years during the lifetime of the insured. If this were not the case, if the beneficiary knew that the insured had made material misrepresentations in the application, he or she could wait until the end of the two-year period before submitting the claim, and thus would be protected against voidance of the contract because of the insured's fraudulent acts.[4]

Misstatement of Age Clause

The incontestability clause does not apply to a misstatement of age by the insured. Since the amount of insurance a given premium will purchase varies with the age of the insured, there is a marked tendency on the part of applicants for insurance to understate their age.[5] The misstate-

---

[2]There are many reasons for the use of care in the designation of the beneficiary. For example, if the insured designates "my children" as a class beneficiary, which children does he intend to include? Would adopted or illegitimate children be included? And what about children of a former wife? These difficulties may be avoided with a little care. Otherwise, a disgruntled former wife or an illegitimate child may cause difficulty.

[3]There are some instances in which strict enforcement of the incontestable clause would be a violation of public policy. For example, courts will permit insurers to deny liability after the contestable period when an insurable interest did not exist at the inception of the contract. Liability could also be denied if it is discovered that a healthier person impersonated the applicant in the medical examination, particularly should this person have been the beneficiary under the policy.

[4]In years past, the incontestable clause did not contain the language "for two years during the lifetime of the insured." In a celebrated case, *Monahan v. Metropolitan Life Insurance Company* (283 Ill. 136, 119 N.E. 68), an insured had died during the contestable period and the company denied liability, alleging breach of warranty. The beneficiary, however, waited until the two-year period had expired and then sued the company. The Supreme Court of Illinois held that the policy was incontestable and ordered the insurance company to make payment.

[5]For rating purposes, life insurers assume that the individual's age changes at the midpoint between birthdays. (Health insurers, in contrast, usually use the applicant's age at his or her last birthday until the next birthday is reached.) Insurers will often agree to backdate a life insurance policy to allow the insured to purchase the coverage at a lower age if the insured pays the premium for the backdated period of coverage. Most state insurance laws limit the period for which a policy may be backdated to not more than six months.

ment of age clause provides that in the event that the insured has misstated his or her age, the face of the policy will be adjusted to the amount of insurance that the premium paid would have purchased at the correct age. In other words, the amount of the policy is adjusted; the contract is not voided.

For example, the premium on a certain policy is $20 per $1000 at age 40. The premium on the same policy is only $15 per $1000 at age 31. The insured in question was a particularly youthful-looking individual and convinced the agent and the insurance company that she was 31 years old, when in reality she was 40. She purchased a $100,000 policy, paying the annual premium of $1500. Upon her death, the insurance company discovered that she was actually 40 years old when the policy was issued. In this event, the company would pay 15/20 of the face amount, or $75,000. This is the amount of insurance the individual could have purchased for the premium that she paid if she had given her correct age.

Grace Period

A premium due date is designated in the policy, and the premium should be paid on or before that date. Premiums may be payable annually, semiannually, quarterly, or monthly. If the insured does not pay the premium on the due date, technically the contract will lapse. The time of lapsing, however, is subject to a modification by a grace period that is almost universally required by statute. This provision states that a grace period of 31 days shall be allowed for payment of a premium in default, during which the policy will continue in full force. If the insured dies during the grace period, the premium in default is deducted from the policy's death benefit. If the insured pays the premium before the end of the grace period, the policy continues in effect as if payment had been on time. The purpose of this clause is not to encourage procrastination in the payment of premiums (although it does), but rather to keep the policy

from lapsing when the owner of the policy inadvertently neglects to pay the premium.

Reinstatement

Practically all permanent life insurance contracts permit reinstatement of a lapsed policy. The provisions of a typical contract read as follows:

> This policy may be reinstated within five years after the date of premium default if it has not been surrendered for its cash value. Reinstatement is subject to (a) receipt of evidence of insurability of the insured satisfactory to the Company; (b) payment of all overdue premiums with interest from the due date of each at the rate of 6% per annum; and (c) payments or reinstatement of any indebtedness existing on the date of premium default with interest from that date.

Reinstatement is not an unconditional right of the insured. It can be accomplished only if the risk has not changed for the insurance company and only if, by payment of the back premiums with interest, the reinstated policy would have the same reserve as it would have had if the policy had not been lapsed. The conditions necessary are quite specific. First, reinstatement is possible only if at the time of lapsing the insured did not withdraw the cash value of the policy. Withdrawal of the surrender value in cash terminates the contract forever. Second, reinstatement must be effected within a specific time period, normally five years after the lapse. Third, the insured must provide proper evidence of insurability. Not only must his or her health be satisfactory, but other factors such as financial income and morals must not have deteriorated substantially. Fourth, reinstatement can be effected only if the insured pays the overdue premium plus interest and pays or reinstates any indebtedness that may have existed. These conditions may appear burdensome, and some may appear unnecessary. However, they are required if the contract is to be maintained in its original form, and are important if the insurance company is to avoid what would otherwise be a substantial element of adverse selection.[6]

Suicide Clause

Almost universally, suicide during a stated period after inception of the contract is excluded. A typical suicide exclusion reads as follows: "If within two years from the date of issue the insured shall die by suicide, whether sane or insane, the amount payable by the Company shall be the premiums paid." Some companies, however, limit the suicide exclusion period to one year. The reason for the exclusion is, of course, to protect the insurer against a person who might purchase the insurance with the deliberate purpose of committing suicide.[7] The assumption of the two years is that during this length of time, if the insured has not committed suicide, the reason for doing so will probably have disappeared.[8]

Aviation Exclusions

At one time, virtually all life insurance policies excluded death resulting from aviation. Today, most

[6]The question may arise concerning the application of the incontestability clause to the reinstated policy. There is some difference of opinion in the courts. However, the majority opinion is that a reinstated contract is contestable for the same period as prescribed in the original contract, but only with respect to the information supplied for the reinstatement. Representations in the original application for the policy may not be contested.

[7]The courts have evolved the doctrine that the love of life in and of itself is sufficient grounds for a presumption against suicide. The burden of proof of suicide is on the company, and the insurer must prove conclusively that the death was a suicide or pay the face of the policy.

[8]Some states have statutes that impose restrictions on the right of the insurer to avoid liability if the insured commits suicide. In Missouri, for example, the law does not permit any exclusion at all. The insurer can deny liability only if it can prove that the insured contemplated suicide at the time the policy was purchased. Needless to say, this intent is difficult, if not impossible, to prove, so insurers in Missouri do not even attempt to do so. This may be an advantage of residing in Missouri.

policies cover loss from aviation accidents, although an additional premium may be required for pilots. The single area in which aviation exclusions are still found are with respect to military aircraft, and even here the exclusion can usually be eliminated for an additional premium.

passenger on plane Ø covered

War Clause

created to avoid adverse selection

As a general rule, life insurance policies do not contain a war-risk exclusion. During time of war, or when war appears imminent, insurance companies may insert clauses in their policies that provide for a return of premium plus interest rather than payment of the policy amount if death occurs under excluded circumstances. Some exclusions deny coverage for any death while serving in the military, while other versions apply only if death results directly from war.

The purpose of the war clause is not so much to avoid payment to beneficiaries of insureds who are killed in the war as to prevent adverse selection. If the clause were not put into policies sold during wartime, those who faced a higher chance of loss would obtain larger amounts of insurance than they might otherwise purchase. The result would be selection against the company.

Settlement Options

Although the vast majority of death benefits are paid in a lump sum, the contract provides other options for payment of the policy proceeds. In addition to the lump-sum settlement, there are optional modes of settlement that may be used to pay out the proceeds of the policy. Normally, the owner (who in most cases is also the insured) elects the option under which the proceeds of the policy are to be paid. If no election is in force when the policy becomes payable, the beneficiary is entitled to select the option desired. Unless the insured (owner) has made provision that denies the right, the beneficiary may also change to some other mode of settlement.

amt paid out ≠ to amt paid in, they will refund

Tidbits, Vignettes, and Conundrums 13.1

What? No Double Indemnity?

When General George Armstrong Custer died at the Battle of the Little Big Horn on June 24, 1876, he was covered by a $5000 whole life insurance policy that had been issued by New York Life Insurance Company two years earlier on June 4, 1874. Custer was age 34 at the time of issue and his wife was named as the beneficiary. The premium for the policy was $25.56 per thousand, or $127.80 annually, including a 5% surcharge for war risk. The records at New York Life reveal that the death payment under the policy was $4750, indicating that there was probably a loan against the policy at the time of Custer's death.

Source: http://garryowen.com/ins.htm.

Interest Option

Under the interest option, the proceeds of the policy may be left with the insurance company, to be paid out at a later time, and only the interest on the principal amount is paid to the beneficiary. A minimum rate of interest is guaranteed in the policy, but under participating options, many insurance companies pay excess interest above the guaranteed rate if the company earns additional interest.[9] Normally, the interest option is selected when there are proceeds from other policies available for income and the principal of the policy is not needed until some later time.

Installments for a Fixed Period

The insured may specify (or the beneficiary may elect) to have the proceeds of the policy paid out over some specified period of time (e.g., monthly for 5 or 10 years). The insurance company simply computes the amount it can pay out each month over the designated period so that the entire principal and interest will be distributed by the end of the period. The rate of interest credited to the unpaid balance is specified in the policy, but as in the case of the interest option introduced earlier, excess interest may be payable under participating policies. A typical schedule of installments for a fixed period is reproduced in Table 13.1. The longer the period of time for which the company promises to pay the installments, the smaller each installment will be. According to Table 13.1, a $100,000 policy would provide $1812 per month if paid over a 5-year period and only $983 if paid out over a 10-year period. The fixed period selected may be any number of years, usually up to 30. This option is most valuable where the chief consideration is to provide income during some definite period, such as the child-raising years.

Table 13.1 Installments for a Fixed Period

Minimum Monthly Installments for Each $1000 of Net Proceeds

Period (Years)	Monthly Payment	Period (Years)	Monthly Payment	Period (Years)	Monthly Payment
1	$84.65	11	9.09	21	5.56
2	43.05	12	8.46	22	5.39
3	29.19	13	7.94	23	5.24
4	22.27	14	7.49	24	5.07
5	18.12	15	7.10	25	4.93
6	15.35	16	6.76	26	4.84
7	13.38	17	6.47	27	4.73
8	11.90	18	6.20	28	4.63
9	10.75	19	5.97	29	4.53
10	9.83	20	5.75	30	4.45

[9]For example, while most policies issued today guarantee interest of 3 percent, $3\frac{1}{2}$ percent, or 4 percent, many companies are actually paying 6 to $6\frac{1}{2}$ percent. In addition, some interest-sensitive policies pay higher rates.

Installments of a Fixed Amount

The owner of the policy (or the beneficiary) may elect to have the proceeds of the policy paid out in payments of some fixed amount ($500, $1000, $1500, and so on) per month for as long as the principal plus interest on the unpaid portion of the principal will last. Since the amount of each installment is the controlling factor under this option, the length of time for which the payments will last will vary with the amount of the policy. In a sense, the installment of fixed amount option is similar to the installment for a fixed period. Under one option, the amount to be paid determines the length of time the benefits will last, and under the other, the length of time for which the benefits are to be paid determines the amount of the benefits.

Life Income Options

In addition to the options listed, the policy gives the insured's beneficiary the right to have the proceeds paid out in the form of an annuity. In such cases, the proceeds of the policy are used to make a single premium purchase of an annuity. Most policies offer several options for either a single life or for two or more lives. Table 13.2 illustrates a typical life income option for single lives. The amount payable under the life income options depends on the age and sex of the beneficiary, plus the plan selected.

Straight Life Income Under a straight life income option, the policy proceeds are paid to the beneficiary based on his or her life expectancy. The beneficiary is entitled to receive a specified amount for as long as he or she lives, but nothing more. If the beneficiary dies during the first year of the pay period, the company has fulfilled its obligations, and no further payments are made. Beneficiaries who live longer than the average are offset by those who live only a short time.

To illustrate the operation of Table 13.2, assume that the policy proceeds are $100,000 and that the beneficiary is a 65-year-old female. Since the life expectancy of women is greater than is that of men, a given number of proceeds dollars will provide a higher monthly income to a male than to a female. If our 65-year-old female beneficiary selects a life income without a period certain, she will receive $564 a month for life, but payments will cease at her death, regardless of the amount that has been paid.

Life Income with Period Certain Under this option, the beneficiary is paid a life income for as long as he or she lives, but a minimum number of payments is guaranteed. If the beneficiary dies before the number of payments guaranteed has been made, the payments are continued to a contingent beneficiary. Normally, the period certain, as the time for which payments are guaranteed is known, is 5, 10, 15, or 20 years.

If the 65-year-old female in our example selects a life income with 10 years certain, the policy will pay $550 a month for as long as she lives, but at least for 10 years. The slight decrease in the amount payable under the 10-year certain option as compared with the payment without a period certain results from the fact that there is no mortality gain to survivors during the first 10 years. If a 20-year period certain is selected, the amount of the monthly benefit is reduced even more. Under the 20-year certain option, the monthly benefit amount will be only $505.

Life Income with Refund Under the life income with refund option, the beneficiary is paid a life income for as long as he or she lives, and if the entire policy proceeds have not been paid out by the time the beneficiary dies, the unpaid balance will be paid to a contingent beneficiary. The remaining proceeds may be paid on an installment basis or in a lump sum. Under a *life income with installment refund option,* installments are continued until the contingent beneficiary has received the difference between the original policy proceeds and the amount received by the direct beneficiary. Under the *cash refund option,* installments do not continue to the contingent beneficiary, but are paid in a lump sum. If the female beneficiary in our exam-

Table 13.2   Single Life–Life Income Payments

Minimum Monthly Life Income Payments per $1000 Proceeds

Male Adjusted Age	Chosen Period (years)				Female Adjusted Age	Chosen Period (years)			
	Zero	*10*	*20*	*Refund*		*Zero*	*10*	*20*	*Refund*
55	$4.99	$4.91	$4.66	$4.73	55	$4.54	$4.51	$4.38	$4.40
56	5.09	5.00	4.72	4.81	56	4.62	4.58	4.44	4.47
57	5.20	5.10	4.78	4.90	57	4.71	4.66	4.51	4.54
58	5.32	5.20	4.85	4.99	58	4.80	4.75	4.57	4.62
59	5.44	5.31	4.91	5.08	59	4.90	4.84	4.64	4.70
60	5.57	5.42	4.97	5.18	60	5.00	4.93	4.70	4.78
61	5.71	5.54	5.04	5.29	61	5.11	5.03	4.77	4.87
62	5.86	5.67	5.10	5.40	62	5.23	5.14	4.84	4.96
63	6.02	5.80	5.16	5.51	63	5.36	5.25	4.91	5.06
64	6.20	5.94	5.22	5.63	64	5.49	5.37	4.98	5.17
65	6.38	6.08	5.28	5.76	65	5.64	5.50	5.05	5.28
66	6.54	6.23	5.33	5.90	66	5.79	5.63	5.12	5.39
67	6.70	6.38	5.38	6.04	67	5.94	5.77	5.19	5.52
68	6.87	6.54	5.43	6.19	68	6.09	5.91	5.25	5.65
69	7.05	6.71	5.48	6.35	69	6.25	6.07	5.32	5.79
70	7.21	6.87	5.52	6.52	70	6.42	6.23	5.37	5.94
71	7.40	7.05	5.55	6.69	71	6.59	6.40	5.43	6.09
72	7.58	7.21	5.59	6.88	72	6.78	6.58	5.48	6.26
73	7.77	7.40	5.62	7.07	73	6.96	6.76	5.52	6.44
74	7.95	7.57	5.64	7.28	74	7.16	6.95	5.57	6.63
75	8.14	7.75	5.66	7.49	75	7.35	7.14	5.60	6.83
76	8.32	7.92	5.68	7.72	76	7.56	7.34	5.63	7.04
77	8.49	8.09	5.70	7.96	77	7.77	7.54	5.66	7.26
78	8.84	8.26	5.71	8.21	78	7.97	7.74	5.68	7.51
79	9.18	8.42	5.72	8.47	79	8.18	7.94	5.70	7.76
80	9.51	8.57	5.73	8.74	80	8.37	8.13	5.71	8.03
81	9.84	8.71	5.74	9.04	81	8.57	8.32	5.72	8.32
82	10.18	8.85	5.74	9.34	82	8.93	8.50	5.73	8.61
83	10.49	8.97	5.75	9.65	83	9.28	8.67	5.74	8.93
84	10.82	9.09	5.75	9.98	84	9.62	8.83	5.74	9.27
85 and over	11.13	9.20	5.75	10.34	85 and over	9.96	8.97	5.75	9.62

ple selects a life income with installment refund, the insurer will pay her $528 a month for life, and at least until the full $100,000 has been paid out.

Joint and Survivor Income

The joint and survivor income option is designed to provide income to two payees. The payments continue after the first of the two payees has died and stops only with the death of the second. A variation of this plan provides that the amount of the benefit will be decreased when the first of the two payees dies. The benefit to the surviving payee will then be either two-thirds or one-half (or some other fraction) of the original income amount. The benefit is computed on the basis of

Table 13.3 Joint and Survivor Life Income Option

Minimum Monthly Joint and Survivor Life Income with Payments Certain for 10 Years per $1000 of Proceeds

Male Adjusted Age	Female Adjusted Age						
	55	60	65	70	75	80	85 and Over
55	$4.16	$4.34	$4.51	$4.65	$4.76	$4.84	$4.88
60	4.26	4.51	4.75	4.98	5.16	5.29	5.37
65	4.35	4.65	4.98	5.31	5.61	5.84	5.98
70	4.41	4.76	5.17	5.62	6.07	6.44	6.68
75	4.46	4.84	5.32	5.88	6.48	7.03	7.42
80	4.48	4.89	5.41	6.05	6.79	7.52	8.07
85 and Over	4.50	4.92	5.46	6.15	6.99	7.85	8.53

two lives, its amount depending on the age of both beneficiaries. Table 13.3 indicates the payment that will be made under a joint and survivor life income option, with a 10-year period certain.

Assuming the same $100,000 in policy proceeds, with male and female beneficiaries both age 65, payment would be made in the amount of $498 a month. Payments would continue until the second payee had died—that is, jointly and to the survivor. If both payees die before the end of the 10-year period, payments will continue to a contingent beneficiary. Under other contracts, provisions might be made for a reduction in the benefit at the death of the first beneficiary.

Taxation of Policy Proceeds under Various Settlement Options

As a general rule, benefits payable to a beneficiary under a life insurance policy are not subject to the federal income tax, except insofar as the benefits are composed in part of interest on the policy proceeds. When a life insurer pays death benefits to a beneficiary in a series of installments (under one of the installment options or a life income option), a part of each payment is considered a nontaxable death benefit and a part is treated as taxable interest income.

If the face of the policy is $100,000 and the beneficiary selects a monthly income for ten years (under the installments for a fixed-period op-

tion), the guaranteed monthly installments indicated in Table 13.1 will be $983, or $11,796 annually. One-tenth of the face amount, or $10,000 annually, is the tax-exempt death benefit. Taxable income includes the $1,796 annually that is guaranteed plus any excess interest paid.

When proceeds are payable under one of the life income options, the taxable interest is determined by computing the portion of each installment that represents payment of principal. Total expected payments are calculated based on the beneficiary's life expectancy as indicated by "gender-neutral" mortality tables prescribed by the IRS. The portion of those payments representing principal is excluded, and the remainder is taxed as interest income.

Nonforfeiture Values

Under the Standard Nonforfeiture Law, today, at any time after the policy has begun to develop a cash value, the insured may discontinue premium payments and obtain the return of a part of the overpayment. Normally, policies do not begin to accumulate a cash value until after the end of the second policy year, and although there is a relationship between the policy reserve and the cash value, the cash value of the policy rarely equals the full amount of the policy reserve until the policy has been in force for 10 to 15 years.

When terminating a policy that has developed a cash value, the insured is entitled to take that cash value in one of three ways:

1. The insured may take the cash listed in the table of nonforfeiture values.

2. The insured may take a paid-up policy in some reduced amount. The amount of the reduced policy will be the amount the cash value would purchase as a net single premium.

3. The policy may be continued in force as term insurance for as long as the cash value will permit. The cash value is used to make a net single premium purchase of a term policy in the face amount of the policy with the nonforfeiture value. If the insured does not request another option, the insurer normally provides extended term insurance.

Table 13.4 is a typical table of nonforfeiture options. It lists the guaranteed values at the end of each policy year. The law requires that these values be listed for at least the first 20 years of the policy, but they are also commonly given for advanced ages of the insured.

Table 13.4 Nonforfeiture Table (dollar values are per $1,000 of face amount)

End of Policy Year	Cash or Loan Value	Paid-Up Insurance	Extended term Insurance	
			Years	Days
1	$ 0.00	$ 0	0	0
2	10.78	50	3	165
3	22.01	98	6	118
4	33.71	144	8	256
5	45.88	187	10	268
6	58.52	229	12	162
7	71.65	268	14	37
8	85.28	305	15	284
9	99.42	341	17	44
10	114.11	374	18	72
11	129.33	406	19	13
12	145.15	437	19	250
13	161.56	466	20	70
14	178.60	493	20	213
15	196.29	519	20	321
16	214.66	544	21	31
17	233.70	568	21	77
18	253.41	590	21	96
19	273.80	611	21	92
20	294.86	631	21	70
Age 60	383.28	718	19	302
Age 65	475.45	788	18	36
Age 70	567.41	844	16	48

Paid-Up — continues until death (handwritten annotation)

Paid-up additions and dividend accumulations increase the cash values, indebtedness decreases them.

Cash Option

To illustrate the operation of the surrender provision, let us assume that Mr. X purchases a whole life policy with a face value of $100,000 at age 35. He surrenders the policy after 10 years and chooses to withdraw the cash surrender value. The insurance company would send him a check for $11,411.[10] If he should decide to drop the policy and take the surrender value in cash at age 65, the guaranteed amount would be $47,545.[11] If the insured surrenders the policy for its cash value, the entire contract is terminated and the company has no further obligations. At the time that the policy is surrendered, the excess of cash surrender value over net premiums paid is taxable as income.

The Standard Nonforfeiture Law permits the insurer to delay or postpone payment of the cash value for a period of six months after surrender of the policy. This is known as a delay clause and is now mandatory in all policies. Its purpose is to prevent substantial investment losses in case many insureds cash in their contracts in a relatively short period, as might occur during a major economic recession. Insurers pay little attention to the clause and perhaps would use it only under the most unusual circumstances.

Paid-up Reduced Amount

The second surrender option is paid-up whole life or endowment insurance. Here, in lieu of obtaining the cash surrender value in cash, with complete termination of any insurance, the insured will receive a reduced amount of paid-up insurance that will be payable under the same

---

[10]Remember that the values in the table are for each $1000 of insurance, so if the insured has a $100,000 policy, the cash value and paid-up policy amount will be multiplied by 100.

[11]These figures are the guaranteed surrender values. If the policy is participating, that is, if dividends are paid on the contract, and if the dividends are left with the insurance company, the actual cash surrender value could be substantially greater than those shown in the table.

conditions as the original policy. Referring back to Table 13.4, if the insured lapses the $100,000 ordinary life policy at the end of 10 years, the cash value could be used as a net single premium at his or her attained age to purchase a paid-up whole life contract with a face value of $37,400. At age 65, the reduced paid-up insurance would be $78,800. The paid-up contract will have a cash and loan value on the same general terms as those of the original policy. If the original policy is a limited-payment contract, the paid-up insurance of reduced amount will be whole life.

This option perhaps has its greatest appeal to older insureds who no longer have a substantial need for life insurance protection. It allows the insured to discontinue premium payments and still have a substantial amount of life insurance in force.

Extended Term Insurance

The third surrender option is paid-up term insurance, commonly referred to as extended term insurance. The amount of the term insurance will be the same as the face value of the original contract. The variable will be the length of the term period rather than the amount of the insurance. The length of the period will be that which the cash value used as a net single premium will purchase at the insured's attained age. For example, Table 13.4 shows that if the insured lapses the policy at the end of the tenth year and chooses the extended term option, he or she would have a paid-up term policy with a face value of $100,000 for a period of 18 years and 72 days. If the insured dies during this term, the insurer will pay the $100,000 to the beneficiary. But if the policyholder outlives the term, the insurer's commitment will be terminated.

The extended term option normally subjects the insurer to an element of adverse selection. Many insureds in poor health, who must discontinue premium payments, are inclined to select the extended term option. As a result, the death rates under extended term insurance tend to be greater than normal. For this reason, insurance companies are permitted to calculate net premiums for extended term on mortality factors higher than those shown in the mortality table.

Policy Loan Provisions

One of the important secondary benefits of life insurance cash values is the policy loan provision. The insured may, at any time, obtain a loan from the insurance company, usually equal to the full amount of the cash surrender value, using the policy as collateral for the loan. The loan provision is subject to a delay clause, under which the insurer may delay making the loan for up to six months. As in the case of the cash-surrender delay clause, the option of delay is rarely exercised. The loan will bear interest at a rate stated in the policy (5 or 6 percent in older policies but up to 8 percent in newer contracts) or the loan may be subject to a variable rate. Although some insurers charge interest in advance, the more common practice is to charge interest at the end of the year. If the interest is not paid when due, it is added to the policy loan. If the insured dies while the indebtedness exists, the loan plus interest will be deducted from the policy proceeds.

Automatic Premium Loan

Most policies today contain an automatic premium loan provision. A typical provision reads as follows:

> A premium loan shall be automatically granted to pay a premium in default. A premium for any other frequency permitted by this policy shall be loaned whenever the loan value, less any indebtedness, is sufficient for such premium but is insufficient for a loan of the premium in default. A revocation or reinstatement of this provision shall be made by written notice filed at the Home Office.

If this provision is included in the contract and the insured does not pay the premium on the due date, the company automatically will pay the premium and charge it as a loan against the cash value of the policy. The loan will bear interest at the rate applicable to policy loans as stipulated in the contract. The effect of the provision is to extend the original face amount of the insurance, decreased by the amount of the loan plus interest, for as long as the remaining cash value is sufficient to permit the payment of premiums. The policy does not lapse and the insured will not be subject to the conditions imposed in the reinstatement clause. Another advantage is that any special coverages such as double indemnity and disability coverages will remain in force, which would not be the case under the extended term or paid-up insurance nonforfeiture options. In addition, if the policy is participating, dividends will continue to be paid, which would not be true under the extended term option.

After the policy has been in effect for a period of time, it is possible for the increase in cash value each year to exceed the premium payment. In these cases, the policy is capable of sustaining itself, since a loan against the cash value to pay the premium permits an increase in the cash value that is sufficient to pay the next year's premium.

There are also disadvantages in the automatic premium loan provision. Most important, if the premium payments are not resumed by the insured and the cash value of the policy is low, the contract may eventually terminate. It is even possible that the period in which the policy will remain in force under automatic premium loan will be shorter than under the extended term option, and the amount of insurance coverage will be considerably less.

Most companies now offer this provision, but various companies handle the option differently. Some specify that the insured must notify the company if he or she wants the provision to apply, while others make the provision automatic and the insured must specify if it is not wanted.

Dividend Provisions

The dividend provision, which will appear only in participating policies, outlines several options available to the insured regarding the payment of policy dividends. The dividend may be taken in cash, applied toward the payment of the policy's current premium, applied to the purchase of paid-up additions to the policy, or left on deposit with the insurance company to accumulate at interest. The first two options are so simple they require little explanation. The insurer sends the insured a check for the annual dividend or indicates the dividend on the premium due notice and the insured remits the net premium payable.

If the insured chooses to use the dividend to purchase paid-up additions to the policy, the dividend will be used as a net single premium at his or her attained age to purchase whatever amount it could purchase at that age. The paid-up additions, like the basic policy, are participating, and they may be surrendered for their cash value at any time.

The insured may also choose to leave the dividends on deposit with the insurance company. Interest at some guaranteed rate will be paid on the deposit and the insured will also share in the company's excess interest earnings.[12] If the insured should die, the accumulated deposits will be paid in addition to the face of the basic contract. If the policy is surrendered, the deposits will be added to the surrender value.

Some insurers offer still another dividend option—generally referred to as the fifth dividend option—under which dividends may be used as a single premium to purchase one-year term insurance at net rates. This is an attractive alternative to the insured, permitting an increase in protection at favorable rates.

If the dividends are left with the insurer either as deposits or to purchase paid-up additions, it is possible for the insured to convert the basic contract into a fully paid-up policy at an earlier date than that called for by the terms of the original contract. A policy is considered to be fully paid-up when the reserve of the basic contract plus the value of the dividend additions or deposits equals the net single premium for the policy at the insured's attained age. The insurer will inform the policyholder when this point is reached. The insured will then surrender the paid-up additions or the deposits, and from this time on will have no premium payment obligation on the policy.

In some companies, the dividend payable on a particular policy may reflect the existence of a policy loan. Under a system called *direct recognition* the dividend is reduced to recognize the difference between the interest on the policy loan and the investment income that would otherwise be earned on the funds by the insurer. Direct recognition usually applies only to policies with a fixed rate on policy loans. For policies with a variable loan rate, dividends generally continue as if no borrowing took place. Failure to reflect the existence of outstanding loans in the dividend scale would result in a subsidy from nonborrowers to borrowers.

The policyholder normally makes an election as to the disposition of the dividends when purchasing the policy. However, a new election may be made at any time with just one possible qualification: if the insured does not elect to use the dividends to purchase paid-up additions to the face of the policy or one-year term insurance at the inception of the contract, the insurer may require evidence of insurability if this option is selected at some later date.

Important Optional Provisions

In addition to the provisions just outlined, many of which are required by law, there are a number of optional endorsements to life insurance contracts.

---

[12]This interest will be taxable as income to the insured. The dividends themselves are obviously not taxable, for they are not income, but merely the return of an overcharge.

Disability Waiver of Premium Provision

Under disability waiver of premium provision, the insurer agrees to waive all premiums coming due after the insured has become totally and permanently disabled as a result of sickness or bodily injury. When premiums are waived, the contract continues in effect as if the premiums were actually paid. This means that the cash value will increase and the dividends will be paid to the insured just as if payment of the premiums was continuing. The provision is so important and so desirable, while at the same time so inexpensive, that many companies include it automatically in their policies. If it is not an automatic provision, the insured should certainly elect to have it included.

The disability waiver of premium provisions currently in use require that the disability commence before some specified age, usually age 55 or 60, but as high as 65 in some contracts.[13] In addition, the disability must have lasted for six months. Once the disability has lasted for the required six months, premiums will be waived from the commencement of the disability, including the first six months.

Disability is usually defined as the inability of the insured to engage in his or her own occupation during the first two years of incapacity. Thereafter, disability is defined in terms of an occupation for which he or she is reasonably fitted by education, training, or experience. Most disability waiver of premium provisions also agree that the total and irrecoverable loss of the sight of both eyes, or the use of both hands, or of both feet, or of one hand and one foot, will be considered total disability, even if the insured can engage in an occupation.

---

[13]The time at which the disability must begin should not be confused with the duration of the benefits. If the disability commences before the limiting age, then it could continue for the lifetime of the insured. However, if it should commence after the limiting age, the company would have no liability under the contract.

Accidental Death Benefit

Another coverage, commonly known as double indemnity, can be added to a life insurance contract for an additional premium. Here, if the death of the insured is caused by accident, an additional sum equal to the face of the policy, called an accidental death benefit, will be paid.[14] The benefit is payable only if three conditions are satisfied. First, death must result, directly and independently of all other causes, from accidental bodily injury. This means that the accidental bodily injury must be the proximate cause of the death and that no other factor, such as sickness, was a cause. Second, the death must occur within 90 days after the injury. This limitation is included to minimize the influence of other factors that could contribute to the death. Third, the accidental bodily injury and the death must occur before some limiting age, usually age 70.

The exclusions to which the accidental death benefit is subject are (1) death by suicide, whether sane or insane, (2) death resulting from or contributed to by bodily or mental infirmity or disease, (3) death caused by any act of war, and (4) death arising while riding in or descending from aircraft if the insured is participating in training or in any duties aboard the aircraft, or if the aircraft is being operated by or for the armed forces.

There is little to commend and much to criticize in the accidental death benefit. There is no economic justification for its existence, since the termination of the insured's income through death is the same whether death is caused by an automobile accident or lung cancer. In addition, its existence will tend to create an illusion of having more insurance coverage than will be the case for most causes of death. In this respect, it is a contributing factor in many of the inadequate insurance programs people are counting on today.

---

[14]Some companies offer triple and quadruple indemnity.

Guaranteed Insurability Option

Many companies now permit an insured to purchase additional amounts of insurance at stated intervals without providing evidence of insurability. The option under which this is possible is known as guaranteed insurability, "additional purchase option," or some similar designation, and is applicable only to the permanent types of contracts such as whole life and endowment. The insured has the option of purchasing additional insurance, regardless of his or her insurability, at three-year intervals and up to a specified age, the most common maximum being age 40. In most cases, the amount of the additional insurance is limited to the face amount of the basic policy or an amount stated in the policy for the additional purchase option, whichever is the smaller. Although the maximum amount of each option was originally $10,000, a number of companies now offer up to $25,000 per option date. The option requires an extra premium that is based on the company's estimate of the extra mortality that will be experienced on policies issued without evidence of insurability. The premium is payable to the last option date and, for the insured, is the cost of insuring his or her insurability.

For purposes of illustration, assume that the insured purchases a $25,000 ordinary life policy at age 21 and that the guaranteed insurability option is a part of the policy. The insurer agrees to issue an additional policy on the life of this insured, without evidence of insurability, at each option date. The customary option dates are at ages 25, 28, 31, 34, 37, and 40. So if our insured desires, he or she can add $25,000 insurance at each of these six dates, despite having become uninsurable. This could result in the addition of $150,000 coverage to the original policy for $25,000.

The option is not standardized, and there is some variation in the provisions used by different insurance companies. One of the most important variations involves the waiver of premium provision. Under the most liberal version, a waiver of premium benefit is included in the new contract if it exists in the original contract. In this case, premiums will be waived on the additional insurance if they are being waived on the basic contract on the purchase option date. A new contestable period applies to additional purchase options.

Some versions of the guaranteed insurability option provide for an acceleration of the next option date in the event of the insured's marriage or birth of a child. Some companies will also provide automatic term insurance equal to the next exercisable option, beginning on the date of marriage or of the birth of the child. The term insurance ends on the day preceding the expiration of the privilege to purchase the additional insurance.

Cost-of-Living Riders

As a result of chronic inflation in our economy, cost-of-living riders have become increasingly popular additions to permanent life insurance policies. Under the basic model of a cost-of-living rider, the insurer offers the insured additional coverage (for which the insured pays an added premium) when the Consumer Price Index increases. The principal advantage of the cost-of-living rider is that the additional insurance is offered without evidence of insurability by the insured. However, to continue eligibility to additional insurance without evidence of insurability, the insured must accept each additional offering of coverage. If the insured rejects any of the increases, the insurer may require evidence of insurability for the next increase.

Common Disaster Clause

The widespread use of the automobile and the airplane has given rise to circumstances in which the insured and the beneficiary are both killed in the same accident. To develop a rule for the disposition of insurance proceeds in such cases, most states have adopted the *Uniform Simultaneous Death Act.* The act states that where the insured and the beneficiary have died and there is not sufficient evidence that one survived the other, life insurance proceeds shall be distributed as if the insured survived the beneficiary. In other words, the benefits are paid to the contingent beneficiary or to the insured's estate. However, this does not totally solve the problem, since in some instances it is known that the beneficiary did survive the insured, if only for a short time. In such cases, the policy proceeds are payable to the beneficiary and upon the subsequent death of the beneficiary, to the beneficiary's estate. This may be contrary to the insured's intent. The situation is addressed more effectively by a policy provision called *the common disaster clause.* Under the common disaster clause (sometimes called the time clause), settlement of the policy proceeds is withheld for a designated number of days (usually 30) after the death of the insured, and for the purpose of making settlement, any beneficiary surviving the insured but dying within that specified period is considered to have predeceased the insured.

Spendthrift Clause

It is sometimes the practice to include a provision in the policy called the spendthrift clause, which denies the beneficiary the right to commute, alienate, or assign his or her interest in the policy proceeds. The provision is used only in conjunction with an installment settlement option. In addition to providing some protection against the beneficiary's extravagance that might result in the dissipation of the policy proceeds, the clause also provides some protection against claims made by creditors of the beneficiary. A typical spendthrift clause reads as follows:

> Unless otherwise provided in this settlement option agreement, no beneficiary may commute, anticipate, encumber, alienate, withdraw, or assign any portion of his share of

the proceeds. To the extent permitted by law, no payments to a beneficiary will be subject to his debts, contracts, or engagements, nor may they be levied upon or attached.

It should be noted that the provision protects the policy proceeds only while they are being held by the insurer. Once the proceeds have been paid out to the beneficiary, creditors are free to attempt to obtain them.

Rights of Creditors to Life Insurance Proceeds

While on the subject of creditor claims, we should note that all states grant at least some exemption to life insurance proceeds from the claims of the deceased insured's creditors. While it has sometimes been maintained that this represents discrimination against creditors, it seems justifiable, since the insured also has obligations to dependents that are even more fundamental than are those to creditors. In some states, the exemption applies only if the benefits are payable to certain beneficiaries, such as a spouse or children. The laws differ in scope, and the broadest laws exempt the proceeds of life insurance policies not only from the claims of the insured's creditors but also from the claims of the beneficiary's creditors. The exemption may be limited to a specific dollar amount.

Universal Life Policy Provisions

Universal life policies include many of the standard policy provisions noted earlier in the chapter. These include, for example, the misstatement of age provision, suicide provision, incontestability provision, reinstatement provision, and settlement options. The special nature of the universal life policy also requires certain specialized provisions that do not appear in traditional life insurance policies. For the most part, these provisions are unique to universal life policies, although some also appear in adjustable life and variable life policies. The most important universal life provisions are the following.

Universal Life Premium and Cost of Insurance Provision

Universal life policies contain several provisions relating to premiums. First, universal life policies include a cost of insurance table that specifies the maximum rate per $1000 of insurance chargeable under the policy for the life insurance protection. The rates actually charged are usually below the specified maximum by a considerable margin.

Because premiums under universal life are variable at the option of the insured, most policies also make a distinction between "scheduled" or "planned" premiums and unscheduled additional premiums. The policy indicates when additional premiums may be paid and the procedure for changing the level of planned premiums.

Finally, universal life policies may include a cumulative premium limit table, setting a maximum to the premiums payable under the policy. The maximum premium payable in any given year is limited to the cumulative premium limit specified for the year less the sum of premiums paid in prior years. The purpose of this is to ensure that the policy continues to meet the Internal Revenue Code definition of life insurance, and is therefore eligible for the special tax advantages of life insurance.

Changes in the Amount of Insurance

Universal life insurance policies will also have a provision governing changes in the amount of insurance. For increases in coverage, the provision generally requires proof of insurability and states when the increased coverage is effective (usually the day following receipt of the request by the company). The insured is normally required to

submit a supplemental application, which will become a part of the policy.

Decreases in the amount of insurance, like increases, are usually effective the day following receipt of the request. However, most policies stipulate a minimum level of coverage that must be continued under the policy. The following amounts used by one insurer are typical:

Insured's Age on Policy Date	Minimum Level of Coverage
0 through 54	$25,000
55 through 59	20,000
60 through 64	15,000
65 and older	10,000

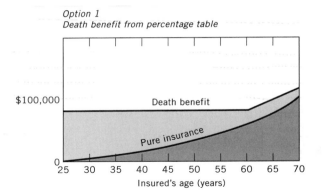

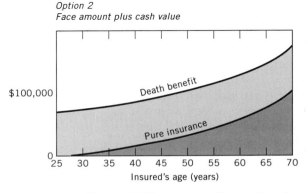

Figure 13.1 Universal Life Insurance Death Benefit Options

Death Benefit Provision

Some provisions in universal life policies are designed to maintain the policy's status as "life insurance" and avoid disqualification under the Internal Revenue Code. Because interest earnings in excess of the guaranteed minimum increase the cash value of the policy, a part of the cash value must be withdrawn periodically or the amount of protection must be increased as the cash value increases. Otherwise, the excess accumulation in the cash value of the policy will result in disqualification. In this respect, universal life policies use two approaches. Under one approach, the policy includes a provision maintaining the required corridor between the cash value and the face amount of protection. Under the second approach, increases in the cash value in excess of the guaranteed minimum are payable as a death benefit. In some cases, policies provide death benefit options, and the insured may select one of the two approaches at the time the policy is taken out. The payment then varies with the death benefit option that is in effect at the time of the insured's death. The insured may change from one option to the other upon request. Figure 13.1 illustrates the difference in the two approaches and the manner in which the amount of life insurance varies with the option selected.

Important Concepts to Remember

entire contract clause	misstatement of age clause	additional purchase option
ownership clause	grace period	installments for fixed amount
primary beneficiary	reinstatement provision	straight life income option
contingent beneficiary	suicide exclusion	life income with period certain
direct beneficiary	settlement options	life income with installment refund
revocable beneficiary	interest option	joint and survivor income
incontestable clause	installments for fixed period	nonforfeiture values
delay clause	dividend options	guaranteed insurability option
cash surrender value	fifth dividend option	common disaster clause
paid-up reduced amount option	disability waiver of premium provision	spendthrift clause
extended term option		cost-of-living rider
policy loan provision	accidental death benefit	
automatic premium loan	double indemnity	

Questions for Review

1. Some life insurance contract provisions are designed for the protection of the insured and some for the protection of the insurance company. Indicate whether each of the following provisions is designed for the benefit of the insured, the company, or both: (a) the entire contract provision; (b) the incontestability provision; (c) the suicide provision; (d) the misstatement of age provision.

2. Explain the difference among the insured, the owner, and the beneficiary of a life insurance policy. Give a specific example in which each party might be a different person.

3. Briefly distinguish between a direct beneficiary and a contingent beneficiary; between a revocable and an irrevocable beneficiary.

4. Explain in detail the obligation of the insurer under a straight life income option, life income with ten years certain, and life income with installment fund.

5. Settlement options of life insurance policies include lump sum, the interest option, installments for a fixed period, installments of a fixed amount, and life income options. Explain each.

6. Joe Smith purchased a $10,000 whole life policy with an accidental death (double indemnity) provision on December 1, 1998. He committed suicide on December 15, 2000. Discuss the liability of the insurance company.

7. To what extent does the accidental benefit or "double indemnity" provision of a life insurance policy violate the rules of good risk management?

8. What are the four standard dividend options available under a participating life insurance policy? What is the so-called "fifth dividend option"?

9. Describe the nonforfeiture options. Under what circumstances would you advise the choice of each in preference to the other two?

10. The settlement option providing a life income with cash or installment refund seems too good to be true. How can the insurance company agree to pay for as long as the beneficiary-annuitant lives and also agree to pay out at least the face amount of the policy?

Questions for Discussion

1. The incontestability clause seems to permit fraud to go unpunished. Do you think that this exception is justified? On what grounds?

2. John Jones dies leaving $100,000 in life insurance policy proceeds to his widow. Widow Jones elects to have the $100,000 paid out under the life income option. At the end of the first year, after having received $7176 in income, widow Jones is struck by a car and killed. Selection of a straight life income option was a foolish mistake on her part. Discuss.

3. The exposure of insurers to adverse selection is not restricted to the underwriting process. To what extent, if any, is the insurer subject to any form of adverse selection under policy settlement options?

4. On January 1, 1998, Sam Smith gave his application for life insurance to his agent, including his first premium payment. On the application, he neglected to notify the company of a mild heart attack he had suffered eight years earlier. On February 15, he received notification from the company that his application had been accepted. He failed to pay the premium due on January 1, 2000, and on January 30, 2000, he died of a massive coronary. Discuss in detail the liability of the insurance company, with reference to specific clauses that apply in this instance.

5. It is often said that policyholders should not have to pay interest on policy loans since they are "borrowing their own money." Explain specifically the fallacy of this argument. Assuming that policyholders did not pay interest on any policy loans, what would happen?

Suggestions for Additional Reading

Black, Kenneth, Jr., and Harold D. Skipper, Jr. *Life Insurance,* 13th ed. Englewood Cliffs, NJ: Prentice Hall, 2000. Chapters 9, 10.

Crawford, Muriel L., and William T. Beadles. *Law and the Life Insurance Contract,* 6th ed. Homewood, IL: Richard D. Irwin, 1989.

Graves, Edward E. (ed.). *McGill's Life Insurance.* Bryn Mawr, PA: American College, 1994. Chapters 10, 25.

Hallman, G. Victor, and Karen L. Hamilton. *Personal Insurance: Life, Health & Retirement.* Malvern, PA: American Institute for CPCU, 1994. Chapter 4.

Websites to Explore

American College: http://www.amercoll.edu/

American Council of Life Insurance: http://www.acli.com/

American Society of CLU & ChFC: http://www.agents-online.com/ASCLU/web/index.html

Association for Advanced Life Underwriting: http://www.agents-online.com/AALU/

Insurance News Network: http://www.insure.com/

Life Office Management Association (LOMA): http://www.loma.org/

Life-Line: http://www.life-line.org/

LIMRA: http://www.limra.com/aboutlim.htm

National Underwriter Company: http://www.nuco.com/

Newsedge News Page: http://www.newspage.com/browse/46622/

S.S. Huebner Foundation for Insurance Education: http://rider.wharton.upenn.edu/~sshuebne/

CHAPTER 14

Buying Life Insurance and Estate Planning

The measure of choosing well is whether a man likes what he has chosen.
—Charles Lamb

CHAPTER OBJECTIVES

When you have finished this chapter, you should be able to

- Identify the three major decisions that must be made in buying life insurance and the sequence in which the decisions should be made

- Identify the ways in which a consumer can determine the financial strength of a life insurer

- Discuss the relative merits of term insurance and cash value insurance for meeting financial security needs

- Briefly summarize the advantages and disadvantages of life insurance as an investment

- Explain how differences in cost among traditional life insurance policies can be compared

- Explain how differences in cost among universal and variable life insurance policies can be compared

In this chapter, we turn to the subject of buying life insurance. The purchase of life insurance differs in many ways from the other purchases that the average consumer makes day in and day out. In many ways, it also differs from the purchase of other forms of insurance, since it sometimes combines protection with savings. In addition, the long-term nature of most life insurance contracts makes the purchase a long-term commitment. The fact that one out of every five life insurance policies purchased today is dropped within the first two years of its purchase is a clear indication of the consumer regret sometimes associated with the purchase of life insurance.

In addition to life insurance buying, we will briefly examine the process of estate planning, the process by which one minimizes the shrinkage of an estate as it passes from one generation to the next.

Decisions in Buying Life Insurance

There are three fundamental decisions that must be made in the purchase of life insurance:

1. How much should I buy?
2. What kind should I buy?
3. From which company should I buy it?

In Chapter 10, we examined one approach to answering the first question. Here we are concerned with the remaining two questions. As explained in the discussion that follows, the first and most important question to be addressed in the purchase of life insurance is the amount. Only after this question has been answered should the type of policy to be purchased be addressed.

Buy Term and Invest the Difference?

"Buy term and invest the difference" are the six most controversial words in the area of life insurance buying. They summarize the philosophy of those who argue that the individual would be better off by purchasing term insurance and investing, separately, the difference in premiums between term and permanent insurance. The long-raging controversy between the proponents of permanent insurance as an investment and the advocates of insurance for the sake of pure protection will probably never be settled. For a significant portion of the population, however, the argument is an irrelevant one.

The first question to be addressed in buying life insurance is "how much should I buy?" This is the risk management question that considers what should be done about the risk of premature

death. Often, the answer to this first question will provide an answer to the second question, the type of insurance that should be purchased. If the amount of insurance needed is substantial, term insurance may be the only alternative. When the money available for life insurance is limited (and it usually is), the savings feature of permanent insurance forces the individual into a compromise in setting up protection for the family during the critical years. The arguments about term versus other forms of life insurance are meaningless for at least a portion of the population, because with limited resources available to spend on life insurance, there may be very little "difference" left after providing adequate protection.

In the cold realism of mathematics, we noted that the insurable value of a person whose earnings will average $60,000 over his or her lifetime has a life value of $600,000 or more. If the individual chooses to purchase cash value coverage for this amount, the premiums would be more than $6000 a year. Even based on the needs approach, we saw that significant amounts of insurance may be required. The buyer opting for permanent life insurance must make a choice between savings and protection. This is not intended as a criticism of cash value life insurance. It is a criticism of the misuse of cash value life insurance and the violations of good risk management practice that it entails. With a limited number of dollars available for the purchase of life insurance, cash value life insurance carries an opportunity cost in the death protection that must be forgone. As a result, many individuals leave their families inadequately protected. They commit the error of permitting the question of the type of policy to purchase to determine the answer to the question of how much to purchase instead of vice versa.[1]

---

[1] Wouldn't it be absurd if an insurance company approached the owner of a $1 million building with the proposal that the owner purchase $100,000 in coverage on the building and use the premium "saved" for an investment program? Yet this is essentially what occurs when individuals are persuaded to purchase high-premium cash value life insurance in an amount less than the required level of protection.

Sometimes, life insurance sellers attempt to pose the choice between term and permanent insurance in terms of "protection" rather than an investment decision by pointing out that term insurance cannot be continued beyond age 65 or 70. "Term insurance is only temporary protection," they criticize, as if there were something inherently good about insurance that is not temporary. When one recalls that the income-earning period and the economic life value of an individual are also temporary, it is "permanent" that takes on the undesirable connotation. By age 65, a person's economic value has declined to zero in most cases; in addition, by this time the economic responsibility to dependents is also normally fulfilled. One has little need for income-earning protection at this age; yet it is during the 35-year period following this age that the cost of life insurance becomes prohibitive. Insuring an asset that no longer has value hardly seems like a wise choice.[2]

In deciding on the form of life insurance to be purchased, we leave the area of risk management and enter the field of finance. The question of term insurance versus permanent cash value insurance is a separate issue, unrelated to the problems of risk management. Once the individual has decided to transfer the risk of the loss of $200,000 or $300,000 in income-earning ability to an insurance company, the rules and principles of risk management are no longer helpful. The choice of the type of insurance contract that should be used is an investment question and should be evaluated by the same standards that are used in ranking investments of other types. As a matter of fact, the question is not really one of term versus permanent insurance at all, but rather a choice between permanent insurance and alternative forms of investment. The only logical reason for the purchase of cash value insurance is that it is superior to the other investments available to the insured for his or her purpose.

Life Insurance as an Investment

The long-raging controversy between the proponents of permanent insurance as an investment and the advocates of insurance for the sake of pure protection will probably never be settled. There is a considerable amount of literature—much of it generated by vendors of competing investments—that condemns life insurance as an investment. The issue, however, is much more complex than this literature suggests, and anyone who states that "life insurance is a poor investment" is oversimplifying the issue. In fact, the assertion that any investment is "good" or "poor" rests on a variety of unstated assumptions that may or may not hold true for a particular set of circumstances. There are some situations in which life insurance may compare favorably with other investment alternatives, and the student should at least be aware of these situations.

The first feature that is often cited in support of life insurance as an investment is the compulsion it entails. Many people do not have the self-discipline and determination required to follow through with their plans for the regular accumulation of a savings fund. Once a policy is taken out, an individual usually will pay the premiums rather than deprive the family of the protection the policy gives, and paying the premiums means making regular contributions to the savings element of the contract. Frankly, this argument is not particularly compelling.

A more persuasive advantage of life insurance as an investment is the fact that it enjoys certain tax advantages that some other forms of investment do not enjoy. First, increments in the cash

---

[2]Another criticism of term insurance, which hardly deserves comment, is "You have to die to collect," undoubtedly the most absurd criticism that can be made. The implication is that if you do not collect under an insurance policy, you have somehow lost in the transaction. One might just as well say that your house has to burn down in the case of fire insurance or that you have to run over someone to collect under your automobile liability insurance. The best approach to use on someone who makes such a comment is to refer the person to any insurance textbook that explains the operation of the insurance principle. Perhaps he or she will learn that the insured receives something under an insurance policy even without collecting.

value are not taxable until actually received by the insured. At the time that the policy is surrendered, the excess of the cash surrender value over the premiums paid is taxable as ordinary income. Furthermore, in computing the gain, the insured is permitted to deduct the total amount of premiums paid, which includes the cost of death protection. To earn a net return on investments that do not share the tax advantage enjoyed by life insurance, the gross rate of return on the alternative investment must be higher than that available under the life contract.

The major criticism usually leveled at traditional life insurance as an investment is the relatively low rate of return—usually between 6 and 8 percent (but sometimes, depending on the company, much lower). For many forms of life insurance, the front-end load (commission) makes the return during the early years negative, and in the long run less attractive than alternative investments. The actual rate of return that will be earned on the investment element, then, depends on the time for which the policy is maintained. If it is to be considered as an investment, life insurance should be considered only as a long-term investment.[3]

Besides the expense factor, another legitimate criticism of traditional life insurance as an investment is that inflation may seriously erode the value of the dollars contributed, but this is a legitimate criticism of all fixed-dollar instruments. If the future economy is marked by inflation and a rising price level, then traditional cash value life insurance (or any other fixed-dollar investment) will be less attractive than those investments that ride the inflationary trend. Universal life, variable life, and the newer interest-sensitive policies make it possible to realize significantly higher returns than those guaranteed in traditional cash value whole life insurance.

The most appealing feature of life insurance as an investment is its complementary functions of providing protection against premature death at the same time it provides an accumulation that may be used if the individual does not die prematurely. If the individual has no need for protection against premature death, it is unlikely that life insurance will match other investment alternatives. At the risk of oversimplification, the premium for cash value life insurance covers three things: a part goes to pay the death benefits for those members of the group who die, a part goes to pay insurer operating expenses (including agents' commissions), and a part contributes to the accumulating savings element. The individual who has no need for death protection but purchases life insurance as an investment incurs costs for death benefits and commissions that are avoided with other investments. To the extent that life insurance is an attractive investment, its appeal is based primarily on its role in simultaneously meeting the diametrically opposed risks of premature death and superannuation.

For many individuals, traditional cash value life insurance may be an attractive and dependable investment. On the other hand, there are many individuals who are not content with the fixed-dollar nature of traditional life insurance, preferring equity investments with their potentially greater return. The choice, however, is a matter of finance rather than of insurance.

Choosing the Company

In choosing from among the approximately 2000 life insurance companies doing business in the United States, the insurance buyer may consider many factors—some more important than others. Among the weightier considerations are the company's financial strength and integrity, its policy

---

[3]Low-load and no-load life insurance products are available from a limited number of insurers. The term *low-load* refers to a contract in which the commission for the first and subsequent years is lower than the traditional commission rates. A *no-load* policy is one on which no commission is payable. Initially, low-commission products were offered only by insurers that do not have a conventional distribution system (such as TIAA/CREF and mail-order insurers). Increasingly, however, both low-load and no-load life insurance has become available through specialty agents or brokers who charge a fee for placement.

forms and their suitability to the insured's needs, and the cost.

Financial Strength and Integrity

Since the life insurance policy represents a long-term promise on the part of the seller, the financial strength of the insurer and its ability eventually to meet its promise rank as the first consideration. In Chapter 5, we discussed the insurer ratings that are published by A. M. Best and other financial rating services. These rating agencies are far from infallible, as evidenced by their failure to anticipate the approaching difficulties of several large life insurers that were taken over by regulators in the 1990s. Still, given the complexities in insurance company accounting, the insurer-rating services are a valuable source of information. It makes sense to compare the ratings from several rating agencies. The higher the ratings and the more the rating services agree, the less is the likelihood that the company will encounter financial problems.

Types of Policies Available

Most major companies offer a wide range of policy forms, including those discussed in the preceding chapters plus many others. However, a given company may not write a particular form of coverage in which the buyer is interested.

The availability of participating and nonparticipating contracts may also be an important consideration. Mutual companies offer only participating policies, while some stock companies offer both kinds, and other stock insurers issue only nonparticipating forms. Under participating agreements, there is an opportunity cost to be considered in the excess payment that may be returned as a dividend. On the other hand, with nonparticipating policies, the insurer gets only one chance in pricing, and there is no provision for returning gains that may be realized from improved mortality experience or favorable investments. While some people favor participating policies and others favor the nonparticipating

kind, the preference of the buyer in this respect will be a determining factor in choice of company.

Cost Consideration

Although most life insurance companies invest in approximately the same securities and start with similar mortality tables, there are significant differences in the premiums different companies charge for the same type of policy. This wide range of premiums makes the selection of a company and a policy a complicated process. The fact that the premium for a whole life policy with Company A is $10 per $1000 and the premium for a whole life policy with Company B is $12 per $1000 does not necessarily mean that Company A is offering the best "deal" and that Company B is overcharging its customers. The differences in premiums do not mean differences in cost. In the case of cash value policies, the premium paid by the insured does not represent a true cost, since a part of the payment goes toward the accumulation of the cash value. The cash value of Company B's policy may increase more rapidly than that of Company A. In addition, the settlement options or other internal policy provisions may be more liberal.[4] Unfortunately, it is also true that the provisions of Company A's policy may be more liberal or its cash value may increase more rapidly.

One of the most common fallacies about differences in premiums among life insurance companies is that these variations can always be traced to actuarial differences in the benefits of the contracts, and that in the field of life insurance, you get exactly what you pay for. While some differences in premiums among companies may be traced to differing rates at which the saving elements of the contracts accumulate, to differences in dividends, and to differences in the liberality of policy provisions, the differences may also be due

---

[4]The first point to recognize in comparing cost among companies is that the policy provisions of the contracts are probably not identical. Disregarding cash values and dividends for the moment, there are other differences of great importance, and a price comparison of two contracts is valid only if the two contracts are identical in other respects.

to varying levels of expense and insurer profit. Commissions and other acquisition costs differ significantly among companies, resulting in wide differentials in the actual costs to the insured. New companies in particular, which are attempting to grow rapidly, often pay substantially higher commissions to their agents, and these commissions must be passed on to the consumer as higher premiums. For this reason, many authorities suggest avoiding new life insurance companies. Others recommend dealing only with companies licensed to do business in New York State, because New York imposes a statutory maximum on commission levels and requires companies operating in the state to observe this maximum in other states in which they operate as well. It is a simple principle of mathematics that higher costs incurred by the company will mean higher costs to the consumer.

Comparing Differences in Cost

The simplest cost comparison in life insurance is between two nonparticipating term policies. Since neither policy provides dividends or cash value accumulations, a simple and straightforward comparison is possible. Once dividends or cash values are introduced, the process of comparison becomes more complicated. Differences in premiums may reflect differing rates at which the cash values accumulate, or may be reduced by dividends. With an increasing number of variables to be considered, and a complex pricing structure based on the variables, it is easy for the insurance buyer to be misled.

Traditional System of Net Cost Comparisons

One method of selling life insurance widespread in the past uses an illustrative projected net cost. Such proposals are not only misleading, but the manner in which they are usually presented is fundamentally invalid as well. The basic technique is to make a summation of the total premiums paid over some period of time (usually 20

years), subtract projected dividends, then subtract the cash value, and call the answer the net cost of the policy. The fallacy in this technique is that it completely ignores the time value of money. An accurate appraisal of a proposed contract must include consideration of the opportunity costs involved.

To illustrate, let us consider two term contracts without cash values, one a nonparticipating contract and the other a participating contract. Company A charges $4 per $1000. The premium for a $50,000 policy will be $200 a year, and at the end of a 20-year period, the net cost will be $4000. Company B, on the other hand, charges $300 for the $50,000 policy and returns the overcharge at the end of the year as a dividend. Assuming that the Company B can earn 5 percent on the $100 overcharge, it can return a dividend of $105, making the "net cost" to the policyholder $195 for the year and the net cost over the 20-year period $3900. Thus, the overcharge on participating policies can permit a "net cost" comparison, which, ignoring the interest on the insured's overpayments, makes the cost appear lower. When dividends are left to accumulate, the opportunity cost becomes even greater. Although our example has used a nonparticipating policy and a participating policy for the purpose of simplification, it should be clear that the same distortion can result when comparing policies with different savings components.[5]

Interest-Adjusted Method

In 1976, the National Association of Insurance Commissioners (NAIC) adopted a "Life Insurance Solicitation Model Regulation" and recom-

---

[5]Comparisons between participating and nonparticipating policies involve additional difficulties. Some allowance must be made for dividends under the participating policies, and since dividends usually increase under a policy as time goes by, they must be considered over the long run. At the same time, it should be recognized that future dividends cannot be guaranteed and are mere estimates based on past experience or future projections.

mended it to the states for enactment. One part of this regulation requires that insurers provide buyers with an alternate cost-comparison method known as the interest-adjusted method. As its name implies, the interest-adjusted method considers the time value of money by applying an interest adjustment to the yearly premiums and dividends. The regulation requires insurers to provide buyers with a *surrender cost index* and a *net payment cost index*, which are two slightly different versions of the interest-adjusted measure of cost. The regulation also requires the insurer to provide the buyer with an equivalent annual dividend for the policy under consideration. Most insurers voluntarily comply with this regulation, even in states where it has not been adopted.

Surrender Cost Index   The manner in which the interest-adjusted method differs from the traditional cost method can best be explained through an example. Assume that the policy under consideration is a $10,000 whole life policy with a $240 annual premium. Projected dividends amount to $1300, and the cash value at the end of the twentieth year is $3420. The traditional cost calculation uses simple arithmetic:

Total premiums paid over 20-year period	$4800.00
Less: Dividends received during the 20 years	1300.00
Net premiums over the 20-year period	3500.00
Subtract year 20 cash value	3420.00
Net insurance cost	80.00
Net cost per year ($80/20 years)	4.00
Net cost per $1000	0.40

From this calculation, it appears that the insured's cost per $1000 of coverage over the 20-year period has been a mere 40 cents per $1000. As we have seen, this is misleading in that it ignores the time value of money.

Calculating the interest-adjusted cost index for the same policy calls for a more involved computation:

Twenty years' premiums accumulated at 5% interest	$8333
Less: Twenty years' dividends accumulated at 5%	2256
Net premiums over the 20-year period	6077
Subtract year 20 cash surrender value	3420
Insurance cost	2657
Amount to which $1 deposited annually will accumulate in 20 years at 5%	34.719
For interest-adjusted surrender cost index, divide $2657 by $34.719	76.52
Interest-adjusted surrender cost index per $1000 per year at the end of year 20	7.65

By accumulating both the premiums paid by the insured and the dividends at interest, the interest-adjusted method considers the opportunity cost by reflecting the amount the premiums paid could generate at a conservative rate over the years used in the comparison. Although we have used a 20-year period, the computation is also often made for 10 years. Subtracting the cash value from the accumulated premiums minus dividends indicates the insured's actual cost if the policy is terminated at the end of the 20 years, considering the time value of money. Dividing the cost by $34.719 indicates the number of dollars per year it would be necessary to invest and allow to accumulate at 5 percent to equal the $2657 cost of insurance.

Net Payment Cost Index   The net payment cost index is a variation of the interest-adjusted method that attempts to overcome some of the criticisms that have been leveled at the surrender cost index. It differs from the surrender cost index only in the fact that the cash value is not deducted at the end of the 10 or 20 years used in the computation. In our example policy, the net payment cost index is computed by dividing the net premiums over the 20-year period ($6077) by the value of $1 annually at 5 percent ($34.719). The net payment cost index for the policy is $175.03, or $17.50 per $1000 per year.

Significance of the Indexes   It should be clear that both the surrender cost index and the net payment cost index are meaningless in themselves; they merely provide a basis for comparing one policy with another. It is the difference in the index between two policies that is important. Small differences that may be indicated between two companies by either index are probably not significant. The cost index is determined by the interest rate used, and a slightly different rate could result in a different cost advantage between two policies, particularly when the difference is small.

When the indexes were introduced, some companies manipulated their cash value tables for the tenth and twentieth years—the years for which the index is usually computed. This may make the policy appear more attractive at those points in time, while it is far less attractive at all other times. NAIC model legislation now requires a notation in the disclosure document when an unusual pattern of premiums or benefits makes the comparison of the cost index with other policies unreliable. It also requires notation when the dividend illustration for a particular policy is not made in accordance with the contribution principles.

Despite these shortcomings, the interest-adjusted indexes represent a significant improvement over the traditional net cost approach to comparing policies. Published information sources are available that list interest-adjusted cost data for all of the larger and better-known companies.[6] For the consumer who is willing to spend the time and effort to compare costs, the interest-adjusted indexes represent an important source of information.

Other Cost-Comparison Techniques

The interest-adjusted method represents one of two basic approaches designed to deal with the fact that the life insurance premium consists of a payment for protection and a contribution to savings. Under the interest-adjusted method, an assumption is made concerning the rate of yield on the savings, and the cost of protection is calculated. A second approach is to make an assumption concerning the cost of the protection, and then calculate the yield on the savings element. Several models have been devised under which the rate of return on the investment element of a life insurance policy is calculated by assuming that the cost of the protection is the same as the cost of an amount of term insurance equal to the difference between the face amount of the policy and an increasing investment fund.[7] The obvious advantage of this approach is that it provides a basis for comparisons not only between two cash value life insurance policies, but also between cash value life insurance and alternative investments.

Shopping for Universal and Variable Life

While universal life and variable universal life have widened the range of consumer choices, they have also compounded the difficulty in shopping for life insurance. In fact, there is a strong possibility that the increased flexibility of universal life and variable life will require consideration of so many variables that the decision process will become unmanageable. Before leaving the sub-

[6]For example, see the current editions of *Best's Flitcraft Compend* (Oldwick, NJ: A. M. Best Company) or Price Gains, *Interest Adjusted Index: Life Insurance Payment and Cost Comparisons* (Cincinnati: National Underwriter Company).

[7]For example, see Michael L. Murray, "Analyzing the Investment Value of Cash Value Life Insurance," *Journal of Risk and Insurance*, vol. 43, no. 1 (March 1976), pp. 121–128.

ject of buying life insurance, it seems appropriate that we at least touch on the subject of purchasing universal and variable life.

Factors to Consider in Universal and Variable Life Costs

The same three factors that are used in ratemaking in life insurance—interest, mortality, and loading—are the factors that must be considered in evaluating a universal life policy. Unfortunately, it may be very difficult to bring these elements into focus, since they are uncertain at the time the policy is purchased and are often interrelated. The expense charges, for example, will determine the portion of each premium that will be available for addition to the cash value. This, in turn, will determine the rate at which the cash value will increase.

Interest Although the minimum interest rate guaranteed in the policy is of some passing interest, it will not provide much in the way of information that can be helpful in evaluating the product. More important by far is the actual interest credited to the policy. (Interest earned and interest credited to policies may not be the same.) In most cases, the interest rate actually credited to universal life policies is determined by the insurer from time to time, subject to the minimum specified rate. Prospective customers should ask the agents for recent fund performance reports. Such reports, while useful in comparing different policies, should not be taken as an indication of future performance.

Mortality The charge for the life insurance protection under most universal life policies is usually competitive with that of other universal life insurers and with traditional insurers. Nevertheless, the prospective buyer should determine the level of these charges, as indicated by past and current practice of the insurer. While universal life policies indicate guaranteed mortality charges, these guar-

anteed rates are generally far more than the actual charges currently being made and are not of much use in evaluating the contract. Again, information on the insurers' current practice is of much greater significance than the guaranteed rates.

Loading The differences among insurers with respect to expense charges and the complexities such charges introduce into the analysis are almost overwhelming. One company may charge a fixed fee of, say, $30 to $50 a month for the first year of the policy with only modest charges thereafter (a front-end load). Some companies make no charge when the policy is sold, but charge a withdrawal fee when cash is withdrawn (a rear-end load). Another might charge 5 percent of each premium paid plus a charge for withdrawals. Sometimes the additional charge for withdrawals remains fixed, and sometimes it decreases over time. Some companies charge a monthly or an annual contract maintenance fee, others charge an investment adviser's fee, and some retain a part of the investment income generated. With the wide range of approaches to the expense charges for a universal life policy, comparing differences among policies is exceedingly difficult.

Marketing Reforms in Life Insurance

In the mid-1990s, many segments of the life insurance industry were subject to extensive criticism for their market conduct. Headlines referred to practices such as churning, or improper replacements, vanishing premiums that did not vanish, and misrepresentations during the sales process. Many insurers were subject to class action lawsuits and regulatory actions. In response, the NAIC developed new model regulations to address life insurance marketing practices. Two areas of concern were illustrations used in marketing and the replacement of older policies with the newer interest-sensitive contracts.

Although deceptive illustrations have probably existed from the earliest days of life insurance, they intensified in the 1980s, when microcomputer software became available that permitted insurance agents to make policy projections using "illustrative" rates of return. A typical example was the so-called *vanishing premium policy*, a concept that was widely marketed in the 1980s. In theory, dividends would be allowed to accumulate until the accumulated dividends plus anticipated future dividends were sufficient to pay all future premiums under the policy, at which point the premium would "vanish." The policy illustrations that were used in the sale of these policies projected interest rates of 10, 12 and 15 percent into the future, giving prospective buyers delusions of astronomical returns on their investments. In fact, in some instances, the agents represented the contracts as investments, retirement accounts, or even as pension plans. Once interest rates fell, premiums that "vanished" reappeared for many insurance buyers.[8]

The NAIC Life Insurance Illustrations Model Regulation

In 1995, in response to alleged abusive practices in life insurance policy illustrations, the NAIC adopted a new Model Life Insurance Illustrations Regulation. Although the Regulation applies only in those states where it has been adopted, most major life insurers have elected to abide by the Model.[9]

The purposes of the Model are first, to ensure that life insurance policy illustrations do not mislead consumers, and second, to make illustrations more understandable. It provides formats, prescribes standards to be followed when illustrations are used, and specifies disclosures that are required in connection with illustrations. It prohibits using future policy values that are higher than possible under the actual recent history of the insurer. In addition, the Model forbids the use of the term "vanish" or "vanishing premium" or similar terms that imply a policy will become paid up dependent on nonguaranteed elements. The Model prohibits representing a policy as anything other than a life insurance policy.

Under the Model Regulation, insurers must inform the Commissioner whether a policy form will be sold with or without illustrations. If a policy form is identified as one that will be marketed without an illustration, no illustration may be used in its sale. If a policy is identified as one that will be marketed with an illustration, the illustration *must* be delivered to the prospect and the prospect and agent must sign the illustration indicating they have discussed it. The prospect's signature confirms that he or she understands the nonguaranteed elements and that the final results could be different than projected.

The regulations require that an officer of the insurance company and a designated *illustration actuary* certify that the proposal system used by the company is based on a *disciplined current scale*. The disciplined current scale means a projection that is reasonably based on actual recent historical experience of the company, as certified by the illustration actuary designated by the insurer. The Actuarial Standards Board defines the standard for a disciplined current scale.

The illustration must show three scenarios: the *current scenario* as described above, the *guaranteed worst-case scenario*, which shows what to expect if investment income declines to the minimum level and expenses increase to the maximum level guaranteed in the contract, and the *midpoint scenario*, which shows the policy's performance with investment income and operating expenses at a

---

[8]The disappointing return on vanishing premium policies generated thousands of lawsuits against the insurers who sold them. Many of the lawsuits were class actions, which purported to represent all the policyholders in the country or all the people in a particular state. Companies that were sued in these actions include Prudential, Metropolitan Life, New York Life, Crown Life, The Equitable, and other giants in the industry.

[9]The Model Regulation applies to all group and individual life insurance policies except variable life, credit life, and life insurance with death benefits not exceeding $10,000. Although the Model applies only to sales of nonvariable life insurance, the NAIC is drafting Model Regulations applying to variable life insurance products and to annuities.

point halfway between their current level and their guaranteed level.

The format for the policy illustration includes three sections;

1. *Narrative summary.* The narrative summary is a detailed summary of the policy and riders and an explanation of terms.

2. *Numeric summary.* This summarizes the projected values for certain mandated years using average guaranteed and current interest rates and charges called "midpoint assumptions."

3. *Policy detail.* This is a ledger of the guaranteed and projected values for all years. Concept selling or any yellow-pad representation of values does *not* qualify as a basic illustration under the Regulation.

The insurer must provide an annual report on the status of the policy to the policyholder.

NAIC Model Replacement Regulation

In 1998, the NAIC adopted another model regulation related to the marketing of life insurance, the Life Insurance and Annuities Replacement Model Regulation. This regulation established a new regulatory scheme for replacements and "financed purchases" of life insurance and annuities. (A financed purchase occurs when policy values from an existing policy, such as the cash value, are borrowed or surrendered to provide funds to purchase another policy.) Where a sale involves a potential replacement, the agent must provide a notice that identifies some disadvantages of replacements and recommends the insured make a comparison between his or her current policy and the proposed policy. Insurance companies that are replacing an existing policy must provide the insured with a 30-day "free look" period, during which the policyholder can cancel that new policy and receive a full refund. The agent and the insurer planning to replace a policy must provide written notification to the insurance company whose policy is being replaced and, if re-

quested, provide a copy of the policy illustration or policy summary for the proposed policy. The replacing company must provide credit for prior periods of coverage toward satisfying the suicide clause, and, where the replacing insurer is the same as the original insurer, must provide credit toward meeting the incontestability period. The model does not apply to sales of credit life insurance or to group life or annuities where there is no direct solicitation of individuals.

Insurance Marketplace Standards Association (IMSA)

In addition to the regulatory changes, the industry itself responded to the increasing negative publicity by creating the Insurance Marketplace Standards Association (IMSA). Participating life insurers adopt IMSA's *Principles of Ethical Market Conduct* for life insurance and annuity products sold in the individual market:

- To conduct business according to high standards of honesty and fairness and to render that service to its customers, which, in the same circumstances, it would apply to or demand for itself.

- To provide competent and customer-focused sales and service.

- To engage in active and fair competition.

- To provide advertising and sales materials that are clear as to purpose and honest and fair as to content.

- To provide fair and expeditious handling of customer complaints and disputes.

- To maintain a system of supervision and review that is reasonably designed to achieve compliance with these *Principles of Ethical Market Conduct.*

An insurer that wishes to become a member of IMSA must submit to a thorough self-assessment of its marketing practices, followed by a review by an independent assessor. If the application meets the requirements of IMSA, the insurer will be given a three-year membership and be permitted to use the IMSA logo for marketing purposes.

Estate Planning

Estate planning is the process through which one arranges one's affairs so as to yield most effective accumulation, management, and disposition of capital and income. It involves decisions regarding how an individual's financial affairs will be managed following his or her death and who will do the managing. A major goal of estate planning is to reduce the shrinkage of an estate as it passes from one generation to the next. Estates shrink as they pass to heirs for several reasons. First, there is the shrinkage that results from the debts of the decedent, which must be paid before the estate passes to heirs. In addition, there is the cost of probate—the legal process of transferring the estate—which generally amounts to between 4 percent and 5 percent of the estate. Finally, and frequently the most burdensome, there is the cost of the federal estate tax and state inheritance taxes.

The greatest shrinkage of the estate has historically come from the federal estate tax, a tax that is imposed on the transfer of assets at the time of death. Virtually from the time it was enacted in 1916, there has been pressure for repeal of the federal estate tax. Congress actually passed legislation repealing the estate tax in 2000, but President Clinton vetoed it. Then, in 2001, Congress passed and President Bush signed into law the Economic Growth and Tax Relief Reconciliation Act of 2001 (EGTRRA-2001), which, among other things, enacted significant changes in the federal estate tax.

EGTRRA 2001 Estate Tax Changes

To understand the changes enacted in 2001, it is useful to know something about what it was that the legislation changed. The basic features of the estate tax in effect in 2001 were adopted by the Tax Reform Act of 1976, which unified the previ-

Table 14.1 Phase-Out and Ultimate Repeal of the Federal Estate Tax

Year Of Death	Estate Tax Exemption	Maximum Rates	
		Estate Tax	Gift Tax
2001	$675,000	55%	55%
2002	$1,000,000	50%	50%
2003	$1,000,000	49%	49%
2004	$1,500,000	48%	48%
2005	$1,500,000	47%	47%
2006	$2,000,000	46%	46%
2007	$2,000,000	45%	45%
2008	$2,000,000	45%	45%
2009	$3,500,000	45%	45%
2010	Tax repealed	0%	35%
2011	$675,000	55%	55%

ously-separate federal gift and estate taxes. Under the unified estate-gift tax, gifts during one's lifetime that exceed $10,000 per year (indexed for inflation) are combined with the taxable estate and are subject to a single tax rate. The indicated tax is subject to a *unified credit* that reduces the actual tax payable. The unified credit was $220,550 in 2001, which exempted $675,000 from the estate tax.[10] Estates in excess of the exempt amount are taxed at rates from 37 percent to 55 percent (applicable to estates in excess of $3 million). A 5 percent surtax applies to estates from $10 million to $21 million.

EGTRRA-2001 phases out, repeals, and then resurrects the federal estate tax. The "repeal" process began in 2002, with a reduction in the

---

[10]The unified credit's equivalent exemption was set at $600,000 in 1997 with scheduled increases to $1 million in 2006. The scheduled increases were to $625,000 for decedents dying and gifts made in 1998; $650,000 in 1999; $675,000 in 2000 and 2001; $700,000 in 2002 and 2003; $850,000 in 2004; $950,000 in 2005; and $1 million in 2006. An additional estate tax credit was added in the TRA-97, making a family-business owner's total exemption from the estate tax to $1.3 million. This family-business credit was scheduled to decrease as the unified credit increased, so the combined unified credit and family business credit would remain at $1.3 million.

maximum tax rate from 55% to 50 percent, elimination of the 5 percent surtax on estates over $10 million, and an increase in the exemption equivalent credit from $675,000 in 2001 to $1 million in 2002. Thereafter, as indicated in Table 10.5, the maximum tax rate will continue to decrease and the unified credit will increase until 2010, when the estate tax is repealed. Then, in 2011, unless a future Congress acts to make the repeal permanent, a sunset provision in EGTRRA-2001 brings everything back to where it was in 2001. The maximum tax rate returns to 55 percent, the 5 percent surcharge tax is restored, and the estate tax credit returns to $675,000.[11]

EGTRRA-2001 does not repeal the federal gift tax. Beginning in 2002, gift tax rates are reduced according to the schedule in Table 10.5. The unified credit exemption amount for gift tax purposes will be increased to, *and remain at*, $1 million. Once the estate tax is fully phased out, beginning in 2010, the top gift tax rate will be equal to the top individual tax rate (i.e., 35% under EGTRA-2001).

Estate Planning Strategies

The bizarre scenario created by EGTRRA-2001 obviously creates uncertainties for estate planners. However, during the period over which the estate tax is phased out, the traditional estate planning strategies will remain relevant, *albeit* on a modified basis.

The taxable estate is determined by deduction of certain allowable exemptions from the gross es-

tate. The gross estate includes the fair market value of all real and personal property owned by the individual at the time of death, including the individual's interest in any property that is owned jointly with another.[12] In addition to other assets, the gross estate also includes the proceeds of life insurance policies on the individual's life, if the deceased possessed any *incidents of ownership* in the policies. By *incidents of ownership* is meant such ownership rights as the right to change beneficiaries, to borrow against the cash value of the policies, or to collect the cash values. Inclusion of life insurance proceeds in an estate can be avoided if proceeds are payable to a named beneficiary such as a spouse, child, or friend and if the insured avoids incidents of ownership in the policy at death (and at any time within three years before death).[13]

Deductions

The gross estate is subject to certain deductions in determining the portion that is *taxable*. These include credit for death taxes paid to the states as well as foreign death taxes.[14] The most important deduction from the gross estate is the marital deduction. An individual can give his or her spouse gifts in any amount without gift tax liability, and

---

[11]Under current law (effective until 2010), heirs who receive property from a decedent get a step-up in basis (the deductible cost in computing taxable gain when an asset is sold) to the fair market value of the property at the date of the decedent's death (or six months after death in some cases). Thus, any appreciation that occurs from the time the decedent acquired the property until his or her death is permanently shielded from the capital gains tax. Under EGTRRA-2001, the increase to a date-of-death basis is limited to $1.3 million in value, plus a bequest to a surviving spouse of $3 million (making the total property to a spouse eligible for the step-up basis $4.3 million).

[12]Property that is held in joint ownership with the right of survivorship passes outside the will, but is still taxable under the estate tax to the extent of the deceased's original contribution to the purchase price or other interest in the property.

[13]When incidents of ownership already exist, they may be transferred to another party, such as a spouse or child. If the transfer occurs within three years of the individual's death, the insurance proceeds may be brought back into the estate as a gift that was made *in contemplation of death*.

[14] Every state imposes an estate or inheritance tax on taxable estates. About two-thirds of the states have a "sop tax" or "sponge tax" law, so-called because it is limited to the allowable credit for state death taxes in the federal estate tax (that is, the amount that will sop up or sponge up funds that would otherwise be payable as federal estate taxes). During the phase-out of the federal estate tax, the state death tax credit will be reduced from the 2001 level by 25% in 2002, by 50% in 2003, by 75% in 2004. In 2005 the state death tax is completely repealed and replaced by a deduction for death taxes actually paid to any state or to the District of Columbia.

property passing from one spouse to the other is not subject to the federal estate tax. However, the estate tax marital deduction applies only to the part of the estate that actually passes from the deceased to a surviving spouse.

Although the unlimited marital deduction will protect an individual's entire estate from the federal estate tax, at the subsequent death of the surviving spouse, the spouse's estate (including amounts he or she received from the first partner to die) will be subject to the federal estate tax. This means that in some cases, the marital deduction merely defers the taxation of the property, since property passed to a surviving spouse becomes a part of that spouse's estate and will be taxed without the benefit of the marital deductions when he or she dies.

A first strategy for reducing the estate tax is through the use of the marital deduction. This usually requires use of a will, the legal document by which an individual directs the disposition of the estate. Someone who dies without having left a will is said to have died "*intestate.*" In such cases, the property owned at the time of death is distributed in accordance with the fixed provisions of the laws in the state in which the person lived. In many states, if an individual dies without a will and is survived by a spouse and children, the spouse receives one-third and the remaining two-thirds is divided equally among the children.[15] This distribution deprives the estate of the full benefit of the marital deduction, since the marital deduction applies only to that part of the estate actually left to a surviving spouse. The desired estate distribution, leaving an appropriate share to the spouse, can be achieved under the terms of a will.

A second strategy for the individual with a substantial estate is to arrange for the distribution of that estate in a way that maximizes the effect of

the unified estate-gift tax credit. Consider, for example, the case of Bill Smith, who has an estate of $2 million. If he leaves his entire estate to his wife Mary, it will pass without estate tax liability, but the tax is merely deferred. At Mary's death, there will be no marital deduction and the entire $2 million estate will be taxable, subject to the unified tax credit. Instead of passing his entire estate to the Mary, Bill might pass a part of the estate to other heirs (such as children) in order to use part or all of the unified tax credit. If Bill dies in 2002, $1 million of his estate could pass to children or other heirs without tax liability. The remaining $1 million may pass to Mary without tax liability and Mary will have the benefit of the unified estate-gift tax credit at the time she dies. By passing a part of his estate to heirs other than Mary, Bill Smith can maximize the effect of the unified credit.

A third strategy for reducing estate taxes is to reduce the value of the estate to be transferred by making gifts prior to death. Although lifetime gifts are combined with the taxable estate for the purpose of the unified tax, the annual gift tax exclusion permits the transfer of assets during one's lifetime without tax consequences.

Trusts

A common tool for implementing estate-planning strategies and for the administration of an estate is a trust. A trust is an arrangement under which the holder (called the trustee) undertakes the management of another's property (called the *corpus* of the trust), for the benefit of designated persons. The person establishing the trust is called the *grantor, trustor,* or simply the creator of the trust. Those who receive income from the trust are known as *beneficiaries,* and persons to whom the corpus of a trust will pass at the death of the beneficiary or beneficiaries are called *remaindermen.*

The most widely used trusts are the *testamentary trust,* which is a part of the will and, as the

---

[15] The *Uniform Probate Code* was revised in 1990, introducing significant changes in the provisions related to intestacy. By 1998, the 1990 version of the *Code* had been adopted, at least in part, by slightly less than half the states. Other states continue to follow the intestacy provisions of the previous version of the *Code.*

name implies, takes effect after death, and the living or *inter vivos trust,* which is established during the lifetime of the creator and which may be revocable or irrevocable.

Testamentary Trust

A testamentary trust does not reduce estate taxes upon the death of the testator, nor does it lighten estate settlement costs. The potential trust property remains in the estate of the testator until distribution after the will has been probated. It is handled and taxed like all other property. However, it can reduce taxes and administration costs when the trust beneficiary dies.

In our previous example, Bill Smith wants to leave property to his children to maximize use of the unified credit, but at the same time he wants to ensure that Mary will have an adequate income. To achieve these goals, he establishes a testamentary trust with Mary as the beneficiary and his children as remaindermen. For estate tax purposes, the property in trust is not subject to the marital deduction, but instead uses all or part of the unified credit. Although Mary will enjoy the income from the trust, the property will not be included in her estate at the time of death. This permits full use of the tax credit by the trust grantor, while at the same time providing an adequate level of income to the surviving spouse.[16]

Living Trusts

Living trusts or *inter vivos trusts* may be revocable or irrevocable. A *revocable inter vivos trust* is one in which the creator reserves the right to terminate the trust and acquire the property. A living trust can reduce estate administration costs if the trust

remains in force after his or her death, since the property will pass outside the will. The beneficiaries will not have to wait until the will is probated to receive their allotted income and principal. The revocable trust does not, however, reduce the estate tax liability.

An *irrevocable inter vivos trust* is one in which the creator relinquishes the right to terminate the trust and acquire the property. An absolute and irrevocable trust takes the property out of the grantor's estate, thereby eliminating certain administrative costs. In addition, estate taxes may be reduced to the extent that the trust is established through gifts subject to exclusion from the federal gift tax (e. g., the annual $10,000 exemption per donee or the spouse gift exemption).

Irrevocable Life Insurance Trust One type of living trust that deserves special note is the *Irrevocable Life Insurance Trust* (ILIT), which is used to avoid the incidents of ownership in a life insurance contract. Under an ILIT, the trustee purchases life insurance on the person to be insured, normally with the trust named as the beneficiary. At the insured's death, the life insurance proceeds are paid to the trust, and then distributed from the trust to the trust beneficiaries. The premiums are paid from funds transferred to the trust as gifts. The $10,000 annual gift tax exemption will apply if beneficiaries are given the right to withdraw amounts gifted to the trust on a yearly, non-cumulative basis. The trustee notifies each trust beneficiary when a gift is received by the trust on his or her behalf and, unless the beneficiary elects to receive the gift now, the trustee will use the contribution to pay the premium on the life insurance policy. Obviously, a key feature of the ILIT is the willingness of the beneficiaries to not withdraw the gift, which they must have the right to do if it is to qualify as a gift.[17]

---

[16]However, generation skipping transfers (GST), in which property is transferred to a person more than one generation below the transferor are subject to a special GST tax. Generation-skipping transfers are taxed at the maximum estate tax rate of 55 percent, subject to a $1 million tax credit, indexed for inflation. Like the estate tax, the generation-skipping transfer tax is phased out over the period from 2002 to 2010.

[17]The right to withdraw gifts to a trust is called "Crummey powers," after the individual involved in the case in which the principle was established. *Crummey v. Commissioner,* 397 F,2,d 82 (9th Cir. 1968).

Important Concepts to Remember

Buy term and invest the difference
net cost comparison
estate planning
interest-adjusted method
surrender cost index
net payment cost index
policy illustrations

vanishing premium policy
Insurance Marketplace Standards
  Association (IMSA)
gross estate
unified credit
incidents of ownership
marital deduction

intestate
testamentary trust
inter vivos trust
living trusts
irrevocable inter vivos trust
irrevocable life insurance trust
  (ILIT)

Questions for Review

1. List the three important considerations in selecting a life insurance company. How important is each relative to the other two?

2. Briefly outline the factors you would consider in deciding the answer to each of the three basic decisions involved in the process of buying life insurance.

3. Explain how the traditional net cost system of life insurance cost comparison can be misleading to the consumer.

4. List and explain the most commonly offered objections to term insurance. How valid is each of these objections?

5. Briefly describe the tax advantage enjoyed by cash value life insurance as an investment. Does it have any disadvantages? Explain.

6. Why is it more difficult to evaluate a universal life product than a traditional whole life product?

7. Identify the three factors used in life insurance ratemaking and explain how they are recognized in universal life insurance policies.

8. When selling universal life and other interest sensitive life insurance policies, insurance agents frequently use a policy illustration, which projects accumulated premiums and investment income. Identify the difficulties in making these projections. What should an individual look for when evaluating a policy illustration?

9. Identify the factors that are important in choosing a company.

10. "In life insurance, differences in premiums do not mean differences in cost." Explain this statement.

Questions for Discussion

1. Income may be divided into two components: consumption and savings. Into which of these components do you feel expenditures on insurance should be put?

2. What underlying assumptions are embodied in the advice, "Buy term and invest the difference?" What do you think of this advice?

3. When deciding on the type of insurance to buy, "the question is not really one of term versus permanent insurance at all, but rather a choice between permanent insurance and alternative forms of investment." In comparing permanent insurance with alternative forms of investment, what do you consider to be the most attractive features of insurance?

4. Some companies specialize in selling life insurance to college students. In many instances, the student is permitted to pay the first annual premium (and sometimes the second and third annual premiums) with a note. What do you think of this practice?

5. The guaranteed insurability option is a valuable form of protection, permitting an individual to insure his or her insurability up to some multiple of the face amount of the policy to which the option is attached. What do you think of the idea of marketing the guaranteed insurability option by itself, without any form of current protection? Would it be marketable? Why or why not?

Suggestions for Additional Reading

Belth, Joseph M. *Life Insurance: A Consumer's Handbook*, 2nd ed. Bloomington, IN: Indiana University Press, 1985.

Best's Flitcraft Compend. Oldwick, NJ: A. M. Best, annual.

Black, Kenneth, Jr., and Harold D. Skipper, Jr. *Life Insurance*, 13th ed. Englewood Cliffs, NJ: Prentice Hall, 2000. Chapters 11, 12, 13.

Crowe, Robert M., and Charles E. Hughes (eds.). *Fundamentals of Financial Planning*, 2nd ed. Bryn Mawr, PA: American College, 1993.

Gains, Price. *Interest Adjusted Index: Life Insurance Payment and Cost Comparisons.* Cincinnati, OH: National Underwriter Company, annual.

Hallman, G. Victor, and Karen L. Hamilton. *Personal Insurance: Life, Health, and Retirement.* Malvern, PA: American Institute for CPCU, 1994. Chapters 1, 2.

Websites to Explore

American College: http://www.amercoll.edu/

American Council of Life Insurance: http://www.acli.com/

American Society of CLU & ChFC: http://www.agents-online.com/ASCLU/web/index.html

Association for Advanced Life Underwriting: http://www.agents-online.com/AALU/

Consumer Insurance Guide: http://www.insure.com/life

Insurance News Network: http://www.insure.com/

Life Office Management Association (LOMA): http://www.loma.org/

Life-Line: http://www.life-line.org/

LIMRA: http://www.limra.com/aboutlim.htm

Money Magazine: http://www.pathfinder.com/money/depts/insurance/

Newsedge News Page: http://www.newspage.com/browse/46622/

S.S. Huebner Foundation for Insurance Education: http://rider.wharton.upenn.edu/~sshuebne/

CHAPTER 15

Health Insurance: Disability Income Insurance

He jests at scars that never felt a wound.
—William Shakespeare
Romeo and Juliet

CHAPTER OBJECTIVES

When you have finished this chapter, you should be able to

- Compare the severity of the risk of disability and the risk of premature death

- Describe the nature of disability income insurance, including the types of contracts

- Identify and contrast the alternative definitions of total disability

- Identify ways in which benefits are provided for partial disabilities

- Explain how the maximum benefit period and the waiting period affect the cost of a disability income insurance policy

- List and explain the common continuance provisions of individual health insurance contracts and identify the uniform provisions

- Explain the way in which disability income needs can be estimated and how disability income insurance can be integrated with social insurance benefits

Two separate types of insurance are included in the term health insurance: disability income insurance, which provides periodic payments when the insured is unable to work because of sickness or injury; and medical expense insurance, which pays the costs of medical care that result from sickness or injury. In this chapter, we will deal with the first of these two forms of health insurance, disability income. Coverage for the expenses relating to health care will be discussed in the next chapter.

Disability Income Insurance

Disability income insurance is the oldest of the health insurance coverages and has been marketed for over a century. The coverage provides periodic payments to the person insured when he or she is unable to work because of injury or illness. Coverage may be provided for disabilities resulting from accidents only or for disabilities resulting from accidents or sickness. Coverage for disability resulting from sickness only is rarely written. Benefit eligibility presumes a loss of income, but in practice this is usually defined as the inability to pursue an occupation.

Types of Insurers and Methods of Marketing

Disability income insurance is sold by property and liability insurers, life insurance companies, and specialty insurers that operate only in the health insurance field. With the advent of all-line groups, many company fleets transferred the bulk of their health insurance operations from their property and liability affiliates to the life insurers in the group.

Disability income insurance is marketed in two principal ways: through groups and to individuals. Approximately four-fifths of the disability income insurance in the United States is sold on a group basis. Group underwriting in the disability income field employs much the same principle as does group life insurance. A minimum-sized group is required and the group must have been formed for some purpose other than purchasing the group insurance. The coverage available under group plans is usually broader than under individual policies, and the cost is almost always less. The lower cost of group disability insurance arises from the same features found in group life insurance: group coverage enjoys relative freedom from adverse selection, the employer usually performs certain administrative functions, and the agent receives a lower commission rate. Although individual disability income policies are more expensive than group coverage, they are an important source of protection for the self-employed and persons who do not have access to group coverage.

Need for Disability Income Insurance

Some authorities argue that loss-of-income protection should come even before life insurance. When a wage earner is disabled, his or her earnings stop just as surely as if death had occurred. The "living death" of disability can be economically more severe than actual death. If the breadwinner of the family dies, the family's income stops; if he or she is disabled, not only does the income stop, but expenses remain the same and usually increase. Because a disabled person—by definition—is one whose ability to work is impaired, he or she must depend on sources other than employment for income. When other persons were also supported by the lost income, the problem is compounded.[1]

---

[1]In addition to a policy to cover living expenses, some self-employed persons carry "overhead" insurance, which is designed to pay business expenses, such as rent and clerical costs, while they are disabled. Disability policies can also be obtained with provision for a lump-sum settlement, rather than periodic payments, to be used in purchasing a disabled partner's interest in a business.

Protection Available from Other Sources

In Chapter 10 we noted the protection that is available under social insurance programs for the disability risk. For disability that arises out of and in the course of employment, most injured workers are entitled to benefits under state workers compensation laws. In addition, workers who are totally and permanently disabled and who meet the special eligibility requirements for disability under the federal Old-Age, Survivors', and Disability Insurance program qualify for disability benefits under that program. Finally, workers in California, Hawaii, New Jersey, New York, Rhode Island, and Puerto Rico are covered under the compulsory temporary disability program of those states.

Besides these government-sponsored or -supervised programs, the most common source of recovery is through group or individual disability income policies. In some instances, employers self-insure a program of disability benefits for their employees, providing either cash benefits or paid sick leave. In others, the paid sick leave plans are integrated with disability income insurance purchased from commercial insurers.

Extent of Coverage for Disability

Because there is some overlapping, it is difficult to measure precisely the extent of disability income coverage applicable to the labor force. Excluding the coverage under workers compensation laws and the OASDI program, approximately two-thirds of the U.S. labor force had some sort of disability income coverage by 1999. About 57 percent of nongovernment workers and self-employed persons were covered under short-term disability plans, including sick leave programs.[2] Of this total, about two-thirds were insured with commercial insurers.[3] At the same time, slightly less than 30 percent of the nongovernment labor force had long-term disability protection, all of which was provided through commercial insurers. Because some workers participate in both short- and long-term programs, total coverage is less than would be suggested by combining these two categories.

Disability Income Contracts

Because there is no such thing as a standard disability income policy, the discussion of this kind of coverage must focus on the differences in the provisions likely to be included in such contracts. Individual disability income policies must include certain mandatory provisions discussed later in the chapter, but there are wide variations in both individual and group contracts. The following provisions and options are common to both individual and group policies.

Length of Time for Which Benefits Are Payable

Disability income policies offer benefits for varying periods. In this respect, a distinction is made between short-term disability and long-term disability. Short-term disability insurance provides coverage for disabilities up to two years, whereas long-term disability protects the individual for a longer time, often until age 65 for illness and for life in the case of accident. Short-term disability policies are written with benefit periods of 13, 26, 52, or 104 weeks. Since most disabilities are short term, the insurer's risk decreases as the contract lengthens. A 26-week plan does not cost twice as much as one for 13 weeks. Most disabilities will not exceed 13 weeks, so the insurer does not have to pay out twice as much in benefits under a 26-week plan. The longer the contract, other things being equal, the lower the cost of the additional

[2]When persons covered under the state compulsory temporary disability plans and railroad workers are excluded, the total covered for short-term disability is less than 50 percent of the nongovernment labor force.

[3]Health Insurance Institute, *Source Book of Health Insurance Data* (New York: The Institute, 1999).

protection. Most short-term disability coverage—about 82 percent—is employer-provided group coverage, usually covering blue-collar workers.

Long-term disability policies, also called LTD policies, provide benefits for 5 years, 10 years, until age 65, or even for the lifetime of the insured. About 76 percent of the long-term disability coverage is sold through groups and covers both blue-collar and white-collar workers. LTD for blue-collar workers is usually limited to five years, while coverage for white-collar workers can be provided to age 65 or lifetime. For individual long-term disability, coverage to age 65 or 70 is becoming the standard. Although lifetime benefits are still available from some insurers, increasingly, lifetime benefit periods are being replaced with "to age 70" plans.

Perils Covered

The disability income policy may provide coverage for loss of income caused by accident, or it may cover loss of income that results from either accident or sickness. Coverage for sickness is rarely written alone. When a disability income policy is written to cover both sickness and accidents, the intervals for which benefits are payable may be different, depending on the cause of the disability. Thus, one policy will pay benefits for two years if the disability is brought on by illness and for five years if it results from accident. Long-term contracts often pay to age 65 for sickness and for life if the disability results from accident.

Occupational-Nonoccupational Disability

Another important distinction in the disability insurance field is between policies that cover both occupational and nonoccupational disabilities and those that cover nonoccupational disabilities only. Some disability income policies exclude losses arising out of the occupation of the insured for which the insured is entitled to receive workers compensation benefits. These contracts are called nonoccupational disability insurance. Other contracts provide for a reduction in benefits equal to the amount received under workers compensation, while still others pay the full policy benefit regardless of the occupational or nonoccupational character of the injury.

Waiting Periods

The waiting period or elimination period in disability income policies acts like a deductible, forcing the insured to bear a part of the loss. It eliminates coverage for brief periods of disability and helps to control the morale hazard. In short-term disability policies, waiting periods of 3, 7, 15, 30, and 60 days are available. Short-term disability policy waiting periods may differ for accident and sickness losses. One widely used short-term disability plan is the "1–8–26" formula. This coverage provides benefits from the first day if the disability results from an accident, and from the eighth day if it is caused by illness. The "26" indicates the number of weeks for which benefits are payable.

In the case of individual long-term disability, plans with 14-day and 30-day elimination periods are virtually extinct and the 60-day elimination period is disappearing. Lowering the cost of the plan by extending the elimination period has become an increasingly necessary strategy in recent years as the rates for disability income coverage have increased. While some insurers still offer elimination periods as short as 30 days, the high cost of elimination periods less than 90 days has made them unattractive for the average consumer.

Limitations on Amount of Coverage

Ideally, the disability income policy should restore the income of the incapacitated worker as closely as possible to what was earned before the disability. However, insurance companies typically limit the amount of coverage under short-term policies to about 60 percent of the worker's weekly wage. Under long-term contracts, coverage is sometimes written for as much as 75 or 80 percent of the worker's monthly wage. Such limits are considered necessary to prevent moral hazard. If a policy could be purchased that would pay as much as or more than the worker's regular income, there would be little incentive for a worker to return to the job as quickly as possible.[4] Insurer underwriting tables indicate the amount of monthly disability income coverage that can be purchased on specific earning levels. The maximum issue limits for most insurers are now $4,000 to $5,000 per month, although some insurers offer coverage as high as $15,000 to $20,000 per month. In the case of application for high levels of coverage, the required underwriting information may include documentation of past income, including tax forms.

Definitions of Disability Income Policies

The definitions are of utmost importance in disability income policies, for the broadness of the coverage is based on the definitions of "disability," "injury," and "sickness."

Definition of Disability

The traditional approach to disability income insurance has been to define disability as the insured's inability to engage in a designated occupation due to accident or sickness. Most definitions fall into one of four categories:

1. The inability of the insured to engage in his or her own occupation

2. The inability of the insured to engage in his or her own occupation and not working in any gainful [or reasonable] employment

3. The inability of the insured to engage in any reasonable occupation for which he or she is or might easily become qualified

4. The inability of the insured to engage in any occupation

The most liberal definition defines disability as the inability of the insured to engage in his or her own occupation. The narrowest definition is the inability to engage in any occupation. Short-term disability coverage almost universally uses the *any* occupation definition.

Although the first definition (referred to as *own occupation*) provides the broadest coverage, unfavorable loss experience with this definition has caused many insurers to shift to the second definition (referred to as *modified own occupation*). Under this definition, if the insured cannot perform the duties of his or her own occupation, benefits will be payable unless the insured enters another occupation. The modified own occupation definition is becoming increasingly prevalent and, for most insurers, represents the current standard.

Some policies use a split definition that defines disability as the inability of the insured to engage in his or her occupation for some initial period (e.g., two years), and the inability to engage in any occupation for which he or she is suited or might become qualified after that period. For example, if a dentist should lose his or her right arm in an accident, he or she will be totally disabled in the occupation of dentistry, and the benefits would be paid. After a period of two years, if the dentist is able to pursue an occupation as a faculty member in a dental college or a sales representative for a dental supply firm, benefits would cease.

In addition to those discussed already, there are several more restrictive definitions. When the disability results from sickness, some policies make it a requirement that the insured be confined indoors to collect full benefits for sickness. The most restrictive contracts provide benefits only if the policyholder is hospitalized. Typically, these policies pay $50, $100, or some higher limit a day, regardless of expenses incurred and in addition to any other coverage the insured may have, for each day in the hospital. These contracts are frequently sold through the mail. It should be

---

[4]Insurers question the amount of an applicant's insurance in force with other insurers and, if the total exceeds the percentages cited, decline to insure the excess. If the applicant does not truthfully disclose the total amount of coverage, the insurer may attempt to avoid its contract on the grounds of fraud.

recognized that they represent an extremely limited form of coverage and hardly qualify as disability income protection.

Loss of Income Coverage Approach

The newest approach to the definition of disability abandons the effort to define the disability in terms of the cause of the loss (e.g., the inability to engage in a defined occupation) and focuses instead on the result—which is the loss of income. Today, many insurers are offering a *loss of earnings (income replacement)* coverage that pays benefits when the insured suffers a *loss of income due to illness or injury,* and the loss continues for the elimination period.

Because the level of income insured reflects the after-tax income underwriting limits of the insurer, the monthly limit is payable in the event of total disability, which occurs when the insured's income ceases. Coverage also applies for partial disabilities, measured by the reduction in income suffered by the insured. For partial disabilities, a percentage of the monthly benefit is payable, based on the percentage reduction in the insured's income. This approach, which focuses on the income loss, rather than on inability to perform functions of a specific occupation, is the only form of disability insurance that will pay a claim on a progressive disease such as multiple sclerosis or muscular dystrophy, before the insured is totally disabled.

Definition of Injury

The most common definition of injury today is "accidental bodily injury," which requires that the result (bodily injury) be accidental or unintended. Older policies sometimes used the definition of "bodily injury by accidental means," which required not only that the result must have been accidental, but that the cause of the injury also must have been accidental. Most states now prohibit the use of insuring agreements based on the "accidental means" requirement.

Definition of Sickness

The definition of sickness is often used to exclude preexisting conditions in individual disability contracts.[5] For example, the definition of sickness in one contract specifies that

> The company will pay the total disability benefit for total disability resulting from sickness first manifesting itself while the policy is in force.

Thus, coverage would be provided for a preexisting condition that did not manifest itself until after the inception of the policy. Some earlier contracts used a definition that covered "sickness contracted or commencing while the policy is in force." In that case, there would be no coverage for a sickness or disease that the insured had at the inception of the policy, even if the condition were unknown to the insured. Since ailments can go undetected for many years, this is a severe limitation. Courts do not look favorably on those definitions. In most states, insurers may exclude only those preexisting conditions that manifested themselves during the five years prior to the inception of coverage.

Group disability income plans tend to have either no exclusions or less restrictive exclusions for preexisting conditions. A typical exclusion might eliminate coverage for a disability starting within one year of inception if the sickness was diagnosed or treated in the year prior to being covered.

Exclusions in Disability Income Contracts

While the coverage of the policy is generally defined and limited by the insuring agreement and the policy definitions, disability income policies also have exclusions. The number of exclusions is

---

[5]Preexisting conditions are not normally excluded under group contracts.

usually limited. Common exclusions include war, self-inflicted injuries, and normal pregnancies.[6] In some individual policies, preexisting conditions are eliminated by an exclusion rather than by the definition of sickness. The trend is toward a reduction in the number of exclusions, but each policy should be examined individually.

In group contracts, the number of exclusions is even smaller. Nonoccupational contracts may bar work-connected injuries by an exclusion or in the insuring agreement. Pregnancy is generally not excluded in group plans. Federal and state laws require that disability plans offered by most employers treat disability from pregnancy or childbirth the same as any other disability.

Payments for Other than Total Disability

Although disability coverage is usually payable only when the insured is totally disabled, some contracts provide for payment of a reduced benefit when the insured resumes work on a partial basis after a period of total disability. There are two approaches to the payment of such benefits: a partial disability benefit and a residual disability benefit.

Partial Disability Benefit

Partial disability is usually defined as the inability to perform some specified percentage of the duties of the insured's usual occupation. A common definition of partial disability is "the inability of the insured to perform some, but not all of the important duties of his or her occupation," or "the inability to engage in his or her regular occupation for longer than one-half the time normally spent in performing the usual duties of the

regular occupation." If the individual cannot perform the duties of the job, it is presumed that his or her income will decrease, but partial disability does not base its benefits on the reduction in income. It is based on the inability to perform the specified percentage of the functions that constitute the person's normal job. The customary payment under a partial disability benefit is a monthly indemnity equal to one-half the monthly benefit for total disability. Usually, the partial disability benefit is payable for the period of partial disability, but not exceeding a specified term, such as five or six months, but sometimes up to a full year. The provision is usually payable only for a partial disability that immediately follows a period of total disability for which benefits were payable. In fact, one of the motivations for offering partial disability coverage was as an encouragement for the insured to resume employment as quickly as possible, even on a part-time basis.

Residual Disability Benefit

Increasingly, a somewhat different provision called *residual disability* is used to provide benefits for partial disabilities. Like the coverage for partial disability noted in our discussion of the loss of income approach to disability coverage, a residual disability benefits provision provides coverage for partial disabilities but focuses on the amount of income lost rather than on the physical inability to work. Residual disability coverage is particularly appropriate for self-employed persons, who may suffer a loss of income after returning to work, even though they are now capable of performing all of the functions of their occupation (due to a loss of clients, for example).

The payment for residual disability is a percentage of the total disability benefit based on the percentage reduction in the insured's income. If the insured's income is reduced by 40 percent, 40 percent of the total disability monthly amount is payable. Some policies include a provision entitled *significant loss of earnings*, which provides that if the income loss reaches a stipulated percentage

---

[6]While disability from a normal pregnancy may be excluded (depending on the state) in an individual policy, disability from complications of pregnancy would generally be covered.

of prior earnings (75 or 80 percent), the disability will be deemed total. Although some policies require a prior total disability, it is increasingly common for residual disability benefits to cover income lost because of accident or sickness even in the absence of prior disability.

Insureds must usually have a 20 percent income loss to be eligible for the residual disability income benefit. To determine the amount of income loss under the residual disability provision, a benchmark against which loss of earnings will be measured is needed. This benchmark is the amount of income earned while the insured was healthy. Usually, the insured has a choice of earning periods prior to disability to be used in determining the income base. The first choice is usually a monthly average for the 12-month or 6-month period immediately preceding the disability. Usually, the insured's highest earnings will have been during this period. If earnings were higher during an earlier period, the insured can use the highest average monthly earnings for any 24 consecutive months in the 60 months prior to disability.

Rehabilitation Provision

In addition to the partial disability and residual disability benefits, some long-term disability contracts include a rehabilitation provision, which provides for continuation of disability benefits or other financial assistance while a totally disabled person is retraining or attempting to acquire skills to return to the work force.

Presumptive Disability

Some contracts include a provision entitled presumptive disability, which provides that loss of the use of two bodily members or the loss of sight will be considered as total disability, regardless of whether the insured can do any work for remuneration. This means that an insured who suffered a stroke, for example, and lost the use of an arm and leg, would be entitled to full benefits under the policy, even though the crippling of these members did not affect the person's income-earning ability.

Optional Benefit Provisions

Some insurers offer additional benefits that liberalize the coverage of their disability income contracts. The following are among the more common optional benefit provisions.

Guaranteed Insurability Option

Some insurers offer a guaranteed insurability option similar to the one available in life insurance contracts. The disability income version of the guaranteed insurability option permits an individual whose income increases after the policy is purchased to increase the amount of coverage at specified dates after the inception of the policy.

Cost-of-Living Adjustment Benefit

The cost-of-living adjustment benefit is designed to offset the decline in purchasing power of disability benefits that result from inflation. Under the terms of this provision, disability benefits are increased by the lesser of the increase in the Consumer Price Index or a percentage specified in the policy. The percentage specified is usually 5 to 10 percent, and the increase applies after disability benefits have been paid for a year.

Waiver of Premium

Nearly all disability income policies include provisions that waive premiums if the insured becomes totally disabled and the disability lasts for some specified minimum period. The provision may waive premiums only while the insured is receiving benefits or for as long as the insured remains disabled. Premiums may also be waived during a residual disability.

Social Insurance Substitute Benefit

Although Social Security and workers compensation provide benefits for disability, both forms of social insurance provide benefits only under specified circumstances, and it is difficult to predict whether benefits will be payable in the event of disability. First, there is the 5-month waiting period under Social Security, during which no benefits are payable. In addition, there is no coverage under Social Security for disabilities when it is clear that the disability will last less than 12 months. Finally, the demanding definition of "disability" under Social Security requires that the individual must be unable to engage in *any kind* of substantial work.[7] Like Social Security, workers compensation provides coverage for some disabilities (namely, those that arise out of injuries in the workplace), but not others. If the worker counts on social insurance benefits and they are not paid, income during a period of disability may be inadequate. If the social insurance benefits are ignored, the amount of coverage purchased may be excessive in other cases. The Social Insurance Substitute (SIS) benefit offered by some commercial insurers permits the insured to coordinate the individual's disability insurance with the social insurance programs.

The SIS benefit is designed to serve as a contingency ("just in case") coverage. It pays additional monthly benefits for a disability when Social Security or workers compensation benefits are not payable. In a sense, the coverage is excess over any benefits provided by the social insurance programs. If social insurance benefits are not payable, the SIS benefit provides coverage. If social insurance benefits are forthcoming from OASDI or workers compensation, the SIS benefit terminates or is reduced by the amount of the social insurance benefits. Because it does not pay when social insurance benefits are paid, the premiums for SIS coverage are less expensive than coverage that does not include a social insurance offset.

Although the SIS benefit addresses the problem of disabilities in which social insurance benefits are payable and eliminates duplicate coverage and costs, it does not deal specifically with the 5-month waiting period under Social Security. Neither does it address disabilities that it is known will last less than 12 months and that are therefore not covered under Social Security. These exposures may be addressed by another specialized form of disability coverage, a short-term additional monthly indemnity benefit.

Short-Term Additional Monthly Indemnity

A short-term additional monthly indemnity benefit is an optional endorsement that provides an additional amount of monthly indemnity during the first few months of total disability. Usually, this additional monthly benefit is payable for a maximum of five or six months. This makes it ideally suited to dovetail with the Social Security waiting period. Ideally, this benefit would be written in an amount approximately equal to the individual's expected family Social Security disability benefit. The coverage can be written to cover both sickness and accident, and it can also be written on a Social Insurance Substitute basis, which means that it will pay only if Social Security benefits are not payable. This benefit, combined with the long-term disability coverage, will provide reasonably adequate protection against the loss connected with a short-term disability not covered by Social Security.

Programming and Buying Disability Income Insurance

For the individual, disability income insurance is an essential coverage. For some fortunate individuals, the coverage will be provided by the employer as a part of an employee benefit package.

---

[7]According to the Social Security Administration, slightly fewer than half of those who apply for disability benefits under OASDI are approved for benefits. *Social Security Bulletin—Annual Statistical Supplement—1997.*

Usually, such programs are integrated with the available social insurance coverages, and little or no decision will be required by the individual. When coverage is not provided by the employer, however, the individual will be responsible for decisions relating to the design of the disability income program and for purchasing the coverages designed to implement those decisions.

Determining Disability Income Coverage Needs

Measuring needs for disability income insurance follows the same general principles discussed earlier in connection with life insurance. It involves predicting future income needs, measuring the extent these needs will be met by existing sources of recovery, and then designing an insurance that will fill the gap between the future needs and existing sources of protection.

Income Needs in the Event of Disability

As in the case of life insurance, the disability income program should be viewed as a potential flow of income, capable of replacing the income lost as a result of the inability to work. In determining the amount of insurance necessary, the same needs discussed in connection with life insurance are appropriate. Because it is impossible to determine in advance the length of a disability, protection should be provided for the worst eventuality, a disability that is permanent in nature.

As explained in Chapter 9, the disability income need is fundamentally different from the life insurance need, where the absence of dependents may eliminate the need for insurance. A single person without dependents who is disabled still needs income to replace his or her wages. Because the single person does not have the cushion of a possible second family income, a greater percentage of the future income needs may have to be insured. In addition, since there are no family members to serve as care providers, the need for

disability income is not diminished by the individual's marital status. The specific amount of income that would be needed in the event of disability is determined in essentially the same way as income needs are determined for life-insurance programming—by constructing a budget for the various expenditures that will be required.

Since insurers do not offer lifetime disability coverage for illness, a disability protection program should make provision for income when the disability income policies stop making payments at age 65. The need for income after age 65 will exist whether or not the person is disabled. Sufficient income should be provided in the disability protection program to allow the individual to complete the accumulation for retirement in the same manner as would have been the case in the absence of the disability.[8]

Evaluating Existing Sources of Protection

Once income needs have been determined, the existing sources of protection available to meet those needs should be inventoried. Sources of funds during a period of disability include, first, any sick leave or short-term benefits available in connection with the job. Many employers provide their employees with a salary continuation plan or sick leave. A standard model is to grant 2.5 days of sick leave a month, which the employee may accumulate up to 30 days a year. Some plans are more generous and some are less. Although some corporate pension plans provide disability benefits, unless the individual has a significant accumulation in his or her plan, or unless the disability benefits are separately insured, this is not likely to be of much help.

The next important source of protection is the coverage available under social insurance programs, such as Social Security and workers com-

---

[8]Alternately, the insured may purchase cash value life insurance with a disability waiver of premium provision. The accumulation of cash values will then serve to provide funds to supplement Social Security benefits when the disability income benefits terminate at age 65.

pensation. Some "advisers" suggest that one disregard these benefits in determining the amount of disability income benefits to purchase. A better approach is to integrate these forms of protection into an overall program using the Social Insurance Substitute Benefit and the Short-Term Additional Monthly Indemnity Benefit to make private disability insurance dovetail with social insurance coverages.

Taxation of Disability Income

The tax treatment of disability income benefits has an important effect on the amount of income that needs to be replaced. Benefits received from individually owned disability income policies are not subject to federal income tax. Since the individual will not have to pay taxes on the benefits, something less than 100 percent of the predisability income needs to be replaced. The amount of income that needs to be replaced is also affected by the reduction in expenses associated with employment (such as work clothing and transportation expenses), however this reduction will probably be small. Premiums paid by individuals for disability income insurance are not deductible for federal income tax purposes.

The tax treatment of disability income benefits provided through employment is somewhat more complicated. Sick pay and other disability income payments that have been paid for by the employee are treated essentially the same as wages and are taxable to the employee. If the employee was required to contribute to the cost of the disability income plan as a condition for being covered, however, the portion of the benefits paid for by the employee is received tax free.

Cost of Disability Income Insurance

The cost of disability income insurance varies widely, depending on whether the coverage is purchased through a group or individually. Even among individual contracts, there can be wide variations in cost. The premium depends on the occupation, age, and sex of the insured, the length of time for which benefits are payable, the extent of the coverage, the amount of the weekly or monthly benefit, and the length of the waiting period.

Because most disabilities are short term in duration, coverage for longer periods of disability costs proportionately less than coverage for short periods. If the employer provides only short-term disability coverage (or does not provide any coverage at all), the major focus should be on the purchase of long-term disability coverage with the longest waiting period affordable. Because most disabilities are short term in duration, the waiting period under disability policies will also have a significant influence on cost. The longer the waiting period, the lower, other things being equal, will be the premium. The principles of risk management suggest that the appropriate trade-off is to accept the highest waiting period one can afford and purchase coverage for the longest duration available. Often, a higher waiting period will make it possible to purchase the longest duration coverage available, which pays benefits for lifetime in the event of accident and until age 65 for sickness. For example, the cost of a $1000 monthly benefit under a policy that pays until age 65 for accident or illness, and subject to a 30-day waiting period, is about $800 annually. With a 90-day waiting period, the cost is about $400. This means that for the same dollar outlay, the buyer can obtain $1000 per month with the 30-day waiting period and $2000 per month with a 90-day waiting period.

For the lower-income family, a short waiting period may be a necessity. However, the individual should consider other disability income protection he or she may have as sick leave. If the length of the waiting period can be increased, the resulting premium reduction may well permit a substantial increase in the amount of benefits or the length of time for which benefits are payable. Families in the middle-income group ($25,000–$35,000) should consider a waiting period of at least two weeks.

Families in higher-income brackets should be able to carry themselves for three to six months, or even a year.

Limited Health Insurance Policies

Before leaving the subject of disability income policies, a few comments on the related field of limited health insurance policies is in order. These contracts do not fit conveniently into either disability income insurance or medical expense insurance, but represent a separate class of health insurance contracts. They provide coverage for only certain types of accidents or for only certain types of disease. They are referred to as limited policies and often bear the admonition on the face of the policy, "This is a limited policy. Read the provisions carefully."

Accidental Death and Dismemberment

Accidental death and dismemberment (AD&D) insurance is sometimes sold in conjunction with life insurance, but is generally considered a form of health insurance. When AD&D coverage is written as a standalone coverage, it provides a principal amount when the insured dies as a result of an accident ($100,000, $200,000 or more). Coverage is provided for a lesser amount, according to a schedule, for the loss of a limb (dismemberment) or for the loss of sight. The principal sum is usually payable for the loss of any two limbs or the loss of sight in both eyes. The loss of a single limb or the sight of one eye usually provides a lesser amount, typically 50 percent of the principal sum. Because the loss of a limb or sight is likely to have an effect on the individual's income earning ability, the coverage for loss of a member is an extremely limited form of disability income. AD&D is sometimes sold as an endorsement to

disability income coverage, in which case the benefit is expressed as some multiple of the policy's weekly disability benefit (e.g., 200 weeks). There is a scaled-down benefit for the loss of one eye, arm, leg, hand, or foot.

Travel Accident

Travel accident policies are a good example of limited health insurance contracts. These policies cover if the insured is killed or suffers serious injury while a passenger on a public transportation facility. Some also provide payment in the event of death from an auto accident.

Dread Disease Policy

[handwritten: originally just polio, but now vaccine]

The *dread disease policy* is an example of a limited sickness policy. This contract provides protection against the expenses connected with diseases such as polio, cancer, meningitis, and certain others. Policies of this type are generally a poor buy. More important, they represent a logical inconsistency and a violation of the principles of risk management. If the individual cannot afford the loss associated with any of the dread diseases covered under such policies, he or she also cannot afford the loss associated with other catastrophic illness not so covered. Because dread disease policies have received a good deal of negative press, some insurers have renamed them with the new title *critical disease policies*. Remember, a proper approach to risk management emphasizes the effect of the loss rather than its cause.

[handwritten: pays for days in hospital amt]

Individual Health Insurance Policy Provisions

There has never been a "standard" health insurance policy. While group contracts differ one from another in various ways, the greatest varia-

---

Tidbits, Vignettes, and Conundrums 15.1

Career-Ending Injuries and College Athletes

Are there athletes on the teams at your school that seem destined for the pros? College athletes with professional potential face a special disability exposure—the possibility of a career-ending injury arising out of collegiate competition. Many athletes with the potential for a promising professional career purchase career-ending injury insurance. Peyton Manning, the Tennessee quarterback in 1995 and 1996, purchased a $5 million policy from Lloyd's of London his senior year. (The maximum Lloyd's was willing to sell Manning in his junior year

was $1 million.) In addition to the coverage available through Lloyd's, the NCAA sponsors a disability insurance program for exceptional student athletes in men's football, men's and women's basketball, baseball, and men's hockey. The program offers coverage for career-ending injuries (with preapproved financing if necessary) to student athletes with remaining eligibility at NCAA institutions who are projected to be high picks in the professional drafts.

---

tions are among the individual contracts. Thus far in our discussion, we have dealt with provisions that are used in group and individual contracts. The following provisions appear in individual contracts only.

Individual Health Insurance Continuance Provisions

The right to continue a health insurance contract may be crucial for the insured, particularly if he or she has become uninsurable. Since individual health insurance policies provide coverage for a specified term, the absence of a cancellation provision does not guarantee continuing protection, for even when it cannot cancel, the insurer may retain the right to refuse to renew the policy. Individual health insurance policies (including both disability and medical coverage contracts) have a variety of provisions stating the respective rights of the company and the insured to continue or discontinue the policy. There are three types of contracts that cannot be canceled during the term and in which a guarantee to renew is provided. In addition, there are three forms in which the con-

tract may be canceled or where there is no guarantee of renewability. The six main types of policies, classified according to their continuance provisions, are as follows:

1. *Noncancelable.* Noncancelable policies provide the most liberal continuation provision. The noncancelable policy is a continuous term contract guaranteeing the insured the right to renew for a stated number of years or to a stated age (normally 60 or 65), with the premium at renewal guaranteed. In trade jargon, these policies are called *noncan.* Although noncancelable LTD policies were once common, poor claims experience caused most disability income insurers to abandon this type of renewable provision. It is not the inability to terminate coverage that has been a problem for insurers, but the inability to adjust the rates on a particular block of business. In place of noncancelable provision, insurers have adopted a guaranteed renewable provision.

2. *Guaranteed renewable.* Under a guaranteed renewable policy, the insured is protected

against cancellation and is guaranteed the right to renew the policy, but with a provision permitting the company to adjust the premium for an entire class of insureds. While the premium rate for renewal is not guaranteed under the guaranteed renewable contract as it is under the noncancelable policy, the company may not increase the rate for a single individual, but only for an entire class.

3. *Conditionally renewable.* Conditionally renewable policies are continuous-term policies under which the insurer may terminate the contract by not renewing it under certain conditions stated in the contract. This form provides some guarantee of continuance, but *usually* less than either the noncancelable or the guaranteed renewable. There are exceptions, however, depending on what is conditioned. Some companies offer contracts that may be conditionally renewed beyond age 65 if the insured is still working full time. The premiums are based on the current rate for the insured's age at the time of renewal.

4. *Renewable at the company's option.* Some continuous-term policies are renewable only at the option of the company. This in effect means that the insured has no guarantee whatsoever of continuation.

5. *No provision.* Policies that have no provision for continuation are simply single-term policies. They provide coverage for the stated period only.

6. *Cancelable.* A contract that may be terminated by the insurer during its term is called a cancelable policy. The provision for cancellation usually requires the insurer to give the insured a specified number of days of notice. Under such a policy, not only does the insured lack a guarantee with respect to continuation at the expiration of the policy, but coverage may be terminated during the policy period as well.

For obvious reasons, the noncancelable policy is more expensive than the guaranteed renewable policy, and the guaranteed renewable policy is more expensive than a conditionally renewable one. While it has been pointed out that only a very small percentage of the policies not written on a noncancelable basis are refused renewal, the loss of health insurance at the time it is most needed might be a serious financial blow.

Uniform Provisions

In an attempt to induce some uniformity in conditions and operating procedures in health insurance contracts, the various states have enacted laws requiring that certain uniform provisions recommended by the National Association of Insurance Commissioners (NAIC) be included in all individual health insurance policies. These laws provide that policies submitted to the state insurance departments must be drafted according to the standards imposed by the uniform provisions put forward by the NAIC and must meet certain other requirements. (Some requirements of the laws have to do with style, arrangement, and size of type.)

There are 23 uniform provisions: 12 of these are required and must be included in every contract. The other 11 are optional and may be included or omitted. An insurance company may reword any of the provisions, if the new wording is not less favorable in any respect to the policyholder or the beneficiary.

Mandatory Provisions for Individual Policies

There are 12 required provisions under the uniform policy provisions law, which must be included in all individual health insurance contracts, including both disability and medical expense policies. Many of the required provisions are similar to the general provisions of life insurance contracts we examined in Chapter 12. The following is a brief summary of the mandatory provisions for individual health insurance policies.

Provision 1: Entire Contract. The policy, including endorsements and attached papers, constitutes the entire contract. No changes can be made unless approved by the insurer and attached to the contract.

Provision 2: Time Limit on Certain Defenses. After three years from the date of issue, the contract is incontestable except for fraudulent misstatements in the application. (Some insurers have reduced the time to two years.)

Provision 3: Grace Period. A grace period of not less than 7 days must be provided in weekly premium contracts and 31 days on all other contracts.

Provision 4: Reinstatement. Lapsed policies can be reinstated by the insurer by acceptance of an overdue premium. If the insurer requires a new application, the reinstatement is not effective until approved by the insurer or until 45 days have passed and the applicant has not been notified that reinstatement has been refused.

Provision 5: Notice of Claim. The insured must furnish the insurer with a notice of claim within 20 days after the occurrence or commencement of a loss, or as soon as reasonably possible. Notice to an agent is considered sufficient.

Provision 6: Claim Forms. If the insurer insists that claims be submitted on company forms, forms must be furnished to the insured within 15 days of the receipt of notice. If the forms are not furnished, the insurer must accept any reasonable written proof of loss submitted by the insured.

Provision 7: Proofs of Loss. The insured must furnish a written proof of loss within 90 days after the end of a period for which the insurer is liable for payments unless it is not possible for the insured to do so. Except in cases of legal incapacity, the proof of loss must be filed within one year from the date otherwise required.

Provision 8: Time of Payment of Claims. Benefits are payable by the insurer immediately upon receipt of the proof of loss. Income benefits are to be paid at specified intervals not less frequent than monthly.

Provision 9: Payment of Claims. Death benefits are payable to the named beneficiary or, if no beneficiary has been named, to the insured's estate. All other indemnities will be payable to the insured.

Provision 10: Physical Examinations and Autopsy. The insurer may, at its own expense, have the insured physically examined at reasonable intervals during a claim period and have an autopsy performed when death benefits are payable, provided it is not prohibited by law.

Provision 11: Legal Action. No legal action may be brought to recover on the contract in the 60 days immediately following the proof of loss. A suit may not be brought under the policy unless it is instituted within three years from the date the proof of loss is required to be filed.

Provision 12: Change of Beneficiary. Unless the policyholder has specifically relinquished the right to change the beneficiary, the beneficiary may be changed or the policy assigned as the insured wishes.

Optional Uniform Provisions

Any or all of the following 11 optional provisions may be included in individual health insurance policies.

Optional Provision 1: Change of Occupation. If the insured changes to a more hazardous occupation, benefits are reduced to the amount that the premium paid would have been purchased at the more hazardous classification. If the insured changes to a less risky occupation, the premium rate is reduced accordingly, and any overpayment will be refunded upon request.

Optional Provision 2: Misstatement of Age. If the insured's age has been misstated, benefits under the policy are adjusted to the amount that the premium paid will purchase at the correct age.

Optional Provision 3: Other Insurance in This Insurer. If the insured already has coverage with the insurer that, with the additional policy, provides benefits in excess of some maximum allowed by the company, only the maximum is payable and the excess premiums will be returned to the policyholder or his or her estate.

Optional Provision 4: Insurance with Other Insurer. If the policyholder has duplicate coverage for medical expenses with other companies and does not notify the insurer of the other policy, the insurer's liability is limited to its proportionate share of the expenses incurred. The premiums for the unused part of the coverage are refunded to the insured.

Optional Provision 5: Insurance with Other Insurer. This is the same as optional provision 4, except that it relates to income benefits rather than medical expenses. It is seldom used since the relation of earnings to insurance provision discussed next provides more effective protection against overinsurance.

Optional Provision 6: Relation of Earnings to Insurance. This provision is generally known as the average earnings clause, and is used only in noncancelable and guaranteed renewable contracts. If, at the time of disability, the insured's total disability income exceeds earned income

or average earned income for the preceding two years (whichever is greater), the income benefits under the policy will be reduced proportionately. In no case, however, will the benefits under all policies be reduced to less than $200 per month. Premiums for the excess coverage are returned to the insured.

Optional Provision 7: Unpaid Premium. This clause states that the company may deduct from a claim any unpaid premium that is due.

Optional Provision 8: Cancellation. The cancellation clause gives the insurer the right to cancel at any time with at least five days' notice. Excess or unearned premiums must be refunded. Of course, cancellation does not affect any claim originating before cancellation.

Optional Provision 9: Conformity with State Statutes. Although this is an optional provision, some states require that it be included. It amends the policy, if necessary, so that it will conform to minimum state requirements.

Optional Provision 10: Illegal Occupation. The insurer is not liable for loss for which a contributing cause was the insured's commission of a felony or being engaged in an illegal occupation.

Optional Provision 11: Intoxicants and Narcotics. This provision relieves the insurer of liability for losses while the insured is under the influence of liquor or narcotics.

Important Concepts to Remember

short-term disability coverage
long-term disability coverage
occupational disability
nonoccupational disability
waiting period
disability
accidental bodily injury
sickness
rehabilitation provision

partial disability
residual disability
presumptive disability provision
accidental death and dismemberment
social insurance substitute provision
noncancelable
guaranteed renewable
conditionally renewable

renewable at insurer's option
uniform provisions
change of occupation
misstatement of age
average earnings clause
relation of earnings to insurance clause

Questions for Review

1. Identify the ways in which disability income insurance is marketed. Which approach accounts for the greatest percentage of disability income insurance sold?

2. What sources of protection other than disability income insurance may the individual have to protect against loss of earnings? Why is disability income insurance a necessary supplement to these forms of protection?

3. List the four definitions of "disability" that may be found in disability income contracts. Which is the most beneficial to the insured? Which is the narrowest form of coverage?

4. In your own words, explain the basic difference between the two broad approaches to defining disability in disability income policies. Explain which would be preferable from the insured's point of view and why.

5. Briefly distinguish between long-term and short-term disability income contracts.

6. Briefly distinguish between occupational and nonoccupational disability income contracts.

7. Identify and briefly describe three optional benefits that may be included in disability income policies.

8. List and explain the alternative continuance provisions of individual health insurance policies.

9. What provisions may an insurer incorporate in an individual health insurance policy to guard against overinsurance and morale hazard?

10. Compare and contrast the uniform health insurance optional provisions that deal with a change in occupations by the insured and misstatement of age.

Questions for Discussion

1. Joe Smith is considering the purchase of a disability income policy and is trying to decide between two policies sold by two different companies. Although both will pay until age 65 for disability arising out of sickness, and for lifetime for disability resulting from accident, the cost of one policy is almost twice that of the other. What provisions in the two contracts would you advise Smith to compare?

2. In his best seller, *Wealth Without Risk*, Charles J. Givens, the self-styled expert on "low-risk ways to achieve and hold onto wealth," offers the following advice as his "strategy #32": "Buy disability insurance only if you are in poor health or accident prone." What is your reaction to this "strategy?"

3. Which type of hazard (physical, moral, or morale) do you believe would pose the greatest problem for an insurer writing disability income insurance?

4. You have been retained by an insurer to design a disability income policy covering both accident and sickness, but with appropriate provisions to protect against the special hazards associated with writing sickness coverage. What provisions or conditions would you incorporate into the policy?

5. One of the major problems facing a person who is permanently disabled is the possibility of erosion of purchasing power when price level changes occur during the period of disability. To what extent could the concept of variable annuity or variable life insurance be used in the field of disability income?

Suggestions for Additional Reading

Beam, Burton T., Jr., and John J. McFadden. *Employee Benefits,* 4th ed. Brookfield, WI: Dearborn Financial Publishing, 1996. Chapter 8.

Black, Kenneth, Jr., and Harold D. Skipper, Jr. *Life Insurance,* 13th ed. Englewood Cliffs, NJ: Prentice Hall, 2000. Chapters 7, 18.

Graves, Edward E. (ed.). *McGill's Life Insurance.* Bryn Mawr, PA: American College, 1994. Chapter 7.

Health Insurance Association of America. *Group Life and Health Insurance Parts A and B,* 5th ed. Washington, DC: Health Insurance Association of America, 1994.

————. *Group Life and Health Insurance Part C,* 4th ed. Washington, DC: Health Insurance Association of America, 1994.

Rosenbloom, Jerry S. (ed.). *The Handbook of Employee Benefits: Design, Funding and Administration,* 3rd ed. Homewood, IL: Richard D. Irwin, 1991.

Websites to Explore

Association of Health Insurance Advisors: http://www.ahia.net/

Health Insurance Association of America: http://www.hiaa.org

Insurance News Network: http://www.insure.com/

Money Magazine: http://www.pathfinder.com/money/depts/insurance/

National Underwriter Company: http://www.nuco.com/

Quicken InsureMarket: http://www.insuremarket.com/

CHAPTER 16

Health Insurance: Coverage for Medical Expenses

Physicians of the utmost fame
Were called at once; but when they came
They answered, as they took their fees,
"There is no cure for this disease."
—Hilaire Belloc

CHAPTER OBJECTIVES

When you have finished this chapter, you should be able to

- Identify and describe the major problems associated with the current health care system

- Identify the past efforts that have been made to address the problems associated with the financing of health care in the United States

- Distinguish between the traditional fee-for-service approach to health insurance and the capitation system of managed care providers

- Identify common cost-containment activities that have been adopted by health insurers

- Identify and describe the traditional forms of medical expense insurance, distinguishing between basic policies and major medical insurance

- Describe the nature of medical savings accounts and explain the way in which they are used

- Describe the benefits provided by the traditional Medicare program

- Explain how Medicare supplement policies dovetail with traditional Medicare coverage

- Describe the alternatives to the traditional Medicare coverages that were added to Medicare by the Medicare+Choice coverage options

- Describe the features of long-term care insurance

- Identify the three broad approaches that have been proposed as methods of providing universal health care in this country

Medical expense insurance provides for the payment of the costs of medical care that result from sickness and injury. It helps to meet the expenses of physicians, hospital, nursing, and related services, as well as medications and supplies. Benefits may be in the form of reimbursement of actual expenses (up to a limit), cash payments, or the direct provision of services. Like disability income and life insurance, medical expense coverage is sold on both an individual and a group basis.

Although insurance is an important tool for financing health care expenditures, most health care costs are paid from sources other than private health insurance. State and federal governments cover a staggering 46.4 percent of health care expenses in the United States. Out-of-pocket expenditures from private resources cover about 21.8 percent of total expenditures for health care. Finally, private insurance, written by various types of insurers, provides financing for the remaining 31.9 percent of health care expenditures.[1]

Background on the Current Health Insurance Market

Before turning to a discussion of health insurance, it will be helpful to examine the system of health care delivery in this country and the ways in which the delivery of health care is financed. Both will be useful in understanding some of the coverage features one encounters in the health insurance market.

Historical Development of Health Insurance in the U.S.

Health insurance is a phenomenon of the twentieth century. Although accident insurance was first offered in 1863, coverage for expenses associated with sickness did not become popular until after World War I. Interestingly, it was not traditional insurance companies that popularized medical expense coverage, but hospitals. Early in the 1920s, a number of innovative hospitals began to offer hospitalization on a prepaid basis to individuals.

Blue Cross and Blue Shield

In 1929, a group of schoolteachers arranged for Baylor University to provide hospital benefits on a prepaid basis. This plan is considered the forerunner of Blue Cross plans, which were organized by a group of hospitals to permit and encourage prepayment of hospital expenses. They offered subscribers contracts that promised a semiprivate room in a participating hospital when the insured was hospitalized. In 1939, the first Blue Shield plan was organized by physicians in California to offer prepaid surgical expense coverage.[2]

Commercial Insurance Companies

In the 1930s, commercial insurance companies began to market hospital and surgical expense insurance. Unlike the blues, commercial insurers provided coverage on a reimbursement basis, providing payment up to a specified dollar maximum per day while the insured was confined to a hospital, or a specific limit of coverage for various surgical procedures. In 1949, commercial insurers introduced a form of catastrophe medical expense coverage called major medical insurance. When written with basic hospital insurance and surgical expense insurance, this major medical insurance became the stan-

---

[1]Health Care Financing Administration, *HFCA Annual Report for Fiscal Year 1997;* see http://www.hcfa.gov/stats/nheoact/nhe.htm.

[2]The laws under which Blue Cross and Blue Shield plans were organized originally exempted the plans from the state insurance premium tax and from other provisions of insurance laws. A number of states have eliminated the exemption from the premium tax in recent years. Prior to the Tax Reform Act of 1986 (TRA–86), Blue Cross and Blue Shield plans were exempt from federal taxes, but TRA–86 repealed this exemption for years after 1986. In recent years, a number of Blue Cross/Blue Shield plans have converted to mutual insurance companies.

dard against which other health insurance plans were measured.

Fee for Service

The health insurance provided by Blue Cross and Blue Shield organizations and insurance companies is now referred to as *fee-for-service* coverage. Under this approach, the insured had complete autonomy in the choice of doctors, hospitals, and other health care providers. Insureds were free to choose any specialist without getting prior approval and insurers did not attempt to decide whether the health care services were necessary. Insurers attempted to control costs through deductibles and share-loss provisions called *coinsurance*, under which the patient was required to bear a part of the cost.

Medicare

In 1965, Congress amended the Social Security system by establishing the Medicare program to provide medical expense insurance to persons over age 65. The same legislation created Medicaid, a state-federal medical assistance program for low-income persons. During the years immediately following Medicare in 1965, the cost of health care (and of private health insurance) increased dramatically. Attention turned to the problems inherent in the fee-for-service system. Many experts argued that this system provided an incentive to overutilize health care. When the insurer (or government) paid the costs, insureds and providers had no incentive to reduce costs. In fact, it was argued, the provider stood to gain when more services were provided. Insurers, employers, and public policy makers began to look for ways to change the way in which health care is financed in order to give providers an incentive to control medical expenses.

Managed Care Organizations

The solution was the concept of managed care, which represented a change not only in the fi-

nancing of health care, but in its delivery as well. New types of "insurers" emerged that not only offered risk financing, but the delivery of health care as well. The prototype for this type of organization was the *health maintenance organization,* which offered a more direct relationship between the provision of health care and its financing.

Health Maintenance Organizations The distinguishing characteristic of a health maintenance organization (HMO) is that the HMO not only provides for the financing of health care—as do commercial insurers and the blues—it also delivers that care. HMOs often operate their own hospitals and clinics and employ or maintain contracts with physicians and other health care professionals that deliver health care services. The insurance element in the operation of HMOs derives from the manner in which they charge for their services, which is called *capitation.* Under the capitation approach, subscribers pay an annual fee and in return receive comprehensive health care. The HMO may be sponsored by a group of physicians, a hospital or medical school, an employer, labor union, consumer group, insurance company, or Blue Cross and Blue Shield plans.

Although HMOs have been around for at least as long as the Blue Cross and Blue Shield plans, it was not until the 1970s that public and government attention was focused on them, bringing them their current popularity.[3] In 1971, the federal government adopted a policy of encouraging and promoting HMOs as an alternative to

---

[3]Although the roots of the HMO idea can be traced back to the 1800s, their modern history dates from 1938, when industrialist Henry Kaiser adopted the idea of prepaid group medical practice and capitation for his employees working on the Grand Coulee Dam. The idea spread to Kaiser shipyards and other Kaiser industries during World War II, and the result was the Kaiser Permanente Medical Care Program, the largest HMO in the country. Other early HMOs include the New York Health Insurance Plan (HIP), the United Mine Workers' Plans, the Ross-Loos Medical Group in Los Angeles, the Metro Health Plan of Detroit, and the San Joaquin Plan.

the fee-for-service approach to health care financing.[4] Two years later, Congress passed the Health Maintenance Organization Act of 1973, which provided funding for new HMOs and the expansion of existing ones. The law also required employers with 25 or more workers who are subject to the Fair Labor Standards Act to offer, as a part of their health benefit programs, the option of membership in a federally qualified HMO if one is available.

During the period since 1973, HMOs have grown at a phenomenal rate. HMOs increased from about 25 in the early 1970s to more than 800 by the year 2000. Although the original organizations were independent plans, commercial insurers and the Blue Cross and Blue Shield organizations have embraced the idea. By 2000, insurance companies were administering over 200 HMO projects. Blue Cross and Blue Shield organizations have been equally active, with 89 HMOs in operation by 2000.

HMOs include a variety of arrangements but consist mainly of three types: the *staff model*, the *group model*, and the *independent practice association* or IPA type. Under the staff model HMO, physician services are provided through a group of multispecialty physicians who are salaried employees of the HMO. Under the group model, physicians' services are provided by a group of physicians who are independent of the HMO, but who contract with the HMO to provide service. The physicians primarily serve members of the HMO, but may serve other patients as well. The physicians' group is compensated on a capitation basis. Finally, the individual practice association (IPA) type of HMO involves physicians who practice in their own offices but agree to provide medical services to the HMO. IPA physicians are reimbursed on a fee basis within agreed ranges by the association and the association provides compre-

hensive health care to its enrolled population on a capitation basis.[5]

Whatever the arrangement with the physicians, from the subscriber's point of view, the fee-for-service system is replaced by a system of capitation. In return for a fixed monthly fee, the individual receives virtually all the medical care required during the year. There may be a nominal charge, on the order of $5, paid by the participant when visiting the physician, but this charge is the same regardless of the service rendered. The subscriber is required to choose a primary-care physician (also known as the *gatekeeper*), who is responsible for determining what care is received and when the individual is referred to specialists. If the primary care physician decides the patient requires the services of a specialist, the patient is referred to a specialist in the HMO network. If the network does not include a specialist of the type required, referral is made to a specialist outside the network. Emergency care services are provided outside the network when there is a sudden onset of an illness or injury, which, if not immediately treated, could jeopardize the subscriber's life or health.

Preferred Provider Organizations Given the successes of HMOs in controlling costs, commercial insurers began to look for ways to copy their success. Noting that many individuals objected to the limitations placed on their ability to select the physicians and hospitals, insurers sought other ways they could reduce costs by contracting with providers, while still allowing insureds the option to choose their provider. This led to the development of *preferred provider organizations* (PPOs). A preferred provider organization is a network of health care providers (doctors and hospitals) with whom an insurance company (or an employer) contracts to provide medical serv-

---

[4]In that year, Elliott L. Richardson, secretary of HEW, described the administration's health-care strategy; the HMO was central to the core of that strategy. Elliott L. Richardson, *A White Paper: Toward a Comprehensive Health Policy for the 1970s* (Washington, DC: Department of Health, Education and Welfare, May 1971).

[5]In addition to the three main types of HMOs, there are two additional models: the *network model* and the *direct contract model*. The network model is similar to the group practice model, except that the HMO enters into contracts with several multispecialty groups of physicians. Under the direct contract model, also called an "open-ended HMO," physicians who are not affiliated with the HMO may provide services.

ices. The provider typically offers to discount those services and to set up special utilization review programs to control medical expenses. In return, the insurer promises to increase patient volume by encouraging insureds to seek care from preferred providers. The insurer does this by providing higher rates of reimbursement when the care is received from the network. The insured is still permitted to seek care from other providers, but will suffer a penalty in the form of increased deductibles and coinsurance.

This arrangement preserves the employee's option to choose a provider outside the network, should he or she desire. Where the insured stays in the network, the discounted fees to providers should provide some cost savings, although the potential for savings is lower than with an HMO. In 2000, there were over 1000 preferred provider organizations operating countrywide.

Point-of-Service Plans Eventually some HMOs adopted procedures that made them more like PPOs, adopting what are known as *point-of-service plans* (POS). In one respect, a POS plan operates like a PPO, since the employee retains the right to use any provider, but will have to pay a higher proportion of the costs when he or she uses a provider outside the network. On the other hand, a POS plan is like an HMO, since care received through the network is managed by a primary care physician, or "gatekeeper." In fact, the first POS plans were created when HMOs allowed their subscribers to use non-network providers. The penalties for using a non-network provider are usually greater than the penalties under a PPO. It is hoped that the use of the gatekeeper approach in POS plans will provide greater cost control than that provided by a PPO arrangement.

Dominance of Managed Care Collectively, HMOs, PPOs, and POS plans are referred to as *managed care plans.* Although there are important differences among these plans, there are greater similarities. All managed care plans involve an arrangement between insurers and a selected network of providers and they offer policyholders significant financial incentives to use the providers in the network. The term *managed care* is also used to refer to the variety of case management procedures that are now used by virtually all health insurers as cost control measures. Even where indemnity plans are offered, they now contain cost-containment features that encourage efficient provision of care.

The dramatic growth in popularity of HMOs, PPOs, and POS plans can be seen by examining the trends in enrollment in recent years. Thirty years ago, 90 percent of individual employees were covered under traditional fee-for-service plans offered by commercial insurers and Blue Cross and Blue Shield plans. By 2000, that had fallen to less than 20 percent. Approximately 32 percent of employees are enrolled in PPOs, 33 percent are enrolled in HMOs, and 17 percent are enrolled in POS plans. Fee-for-service plans now cover about 18 percent of insured individuals.

ERISA

A final event of significance in the evolution of our current health care financing system occurred in 1974 with the passage of the Employee Retirement Income Security Act (ERISA). Although the primary focus of ERISA was employee retirement plans, it also included a broad preemption of state regulation for employee welfare benefit plans, specifically providing that states may not regulate self-funded health insurance arrangements as insurance. As a result, group health insurance in the U.S. has evolved into two separate but unequal parts—one subject to regulation by the state insurance departments and the other almost free of regulation. Employers that self-fund the costs of employee health care are exempt from most state laws regulating health insurance.

Current Deficiencies in the System

Rapidly rising costs, inadequate health care services for some segments of the population, and the failure of past measures to solve the problems of health care have contributed to a growing dissatisfaction with the health care financing system. Although they are manifest in many ways, the U.S. health care system faces two main problems: access to health care and cost.

Access to Health Care

A part of the dissatisfaction with the present system results from the uneven distribution of health care. It is estimated that 44 million Americans have no health insurance coverage. Individuals may be uninsured for a number of reasons. About three-fourths of the uninsured are employees and their dependents. About half of these workers have insurance available at their place of employment but elect not to purchase it. Many of the uninsured are low-income workers. Some of the uninsureds are unemployed and about one-third have incomes at or below the poverty level but do not qualify for Medicaid. Others are between jobs or have taken early retirement and are not yet eligible for Medicare.

The problem of access is not limited to the economically disadvantaged. It also exists for persons who, because of personal hazards, are unable to obtain health insurance in the standard market. Plans of small employers may no longer exclude coverage for some employees, but persons who must purchase insurance individually sometimes find that they cannot obtain it. It is estimated, however, that only 3 percent of uninsured lack insurance because they are unable to obtain it from a provider.

High Cost of Health Care

Ensuring access to health care for the poor is only part of the problem. For insured and uninsured persons alike, the most distressing problem is cost—not only the absolute level of health-care costs, but their escalation from year to year. National expenditures for health care, as a percentage of GNP, have increased from 4.4 percent of GNP in 1950 to over 13 percent by 2000. For con-

sumers, the increases in the cost of health care have come in two ways. The first is the annual increase in premiums, which at times in the past has been 15 to nearly 20 percent a year. A second increase in costs has come in the form of increased deductibles and cost-sharing features adopted by employers. Although these measures reduce the employer's cost, the reduction is achieved by shifting the cost to employees. The increasing cost of health care is due to many causes. These include an aging population, improved technology, excess capacity, and defensive medicine.[6] In addition, the use of insurance tends to worsen some problems.

The Aging Population One factor that contributes to increasing health care costs is our aging population. People are living longer, and in doing so incur increased costs for health care. Older persons tend to experience more frequent and more costly need for medical services. The Medicare system made access available to the elderly, but in doing so has acted as a cost driver.

Improved Medical Technology By far the greatest cause of escalating health care costs is the high cost of medical technology and the advances in medical knowledge. Medicine is constantly learning new procedures, but seldom does the new medical miracle save money over the old method of treatment. Human organ transplants such as heart, liver, and kidney transplants have become more common, and their enormous cost intensifies the problems of financing health care.

Excessive Capacity Although advances in medical technology create justifiable increases in cost, they can also be a source of waste and inefficiency. When new technology comes onto the market, it tends to spread rapidly throughout the

---

[6]The Health Care Financing Administration (HCFA) estimates that population growth accounts for about 10 percent of health care cost increases between 1980 and 1993, technology-driven increases in utilization account for 26 percent, general inflation accounts for 44 percent, and other health-care inflation accounts for 21 percent.

medical community. Once an expensive machine is purchased, the incentive to use it to recoup the investment, combined with the desire to improve medical care, work naturally to increase health-care costs.

Defensive Medicine The increasingly litigious atmosphere in the country, evidenced by an epidemic of malpractice suits, encourages physicians to practice "defensive medicine," an inclination that compounds the impact of technology on costs. Advances in technology create increasingly expensive testing equipment with vastly expanded diagnostic powers; the threat of malpractice suits strengthens the physician's inclination to use the equipment to perform more and higher-cost diagnostic testing. Patients rarely object to more testing, especially if it is covered by insurance, because it might do them some good, even if it is not cost effective for society as a whole.[7]

Insurance as a Complicating Factor

Despite the varied causes of the problems in the health care financing system, the insurance mechanism has become a focal point in the debate. Based on what we know about how insurance operates, this was probably inevitable. The health care financing problem is brought into focus and perhaps worsened by the ways in which insurance operates to spread risk.

Insurance-Encouraged Utilization Medical expense insurance has a natural tendency to increase utilization of health care services, because it alters the cost barriers for consumers. Individuals who have full coverage essentially face a price of zero at the time health care service is delivered. Where deductibles and coinsurance exist, they

pay some price, but not the full cost of the service. There is a tendency for people to use more health care when someone else is paying the cost. Although the problem is less pronounced in managed care plans than in fee-for-service plans, it is pervasive.

Segmentation and Adverse Selection Another problem with a free, competitive health insurance market is the tendency toward risk segmentation—the classification of insureds into groups that reflect their hazards. The reason this is a problem is the highly skewed distribution of health expenditures. The most expensive 1 percent of our population accounts for 30 percent of all health spending. The most expensive 50 percent of the population produces 97 percent of total national health spending, meaning that the least expensive 50 percent account for only 3 percent of spending.[8]

In a private insurance market, competitors have incentives to identify and compete for insureds with lower-than-average expected losses, which they do by offering these insureds lower premiums. This inevitably results in segmentation of the market. In every insured group, there are some individuals whose predictable losses are less than the average of the group. These better-than-average insureds are those who are most likely to be attracted to a competing insurer whose rates better reflect their hazard. When the better-than-average insureds are removed from a group, the average loss of the remaining population increases. While risk segmentation of the insurance market provides benefits for low-risk populations, higher-risk populations may find it prohibitively expensive or impossible to obtain insurance for themselves and/or their families.

The distribution of health-care costs across the population also suggests a significant potential for adverse selection. Some people have an incentive to not buy insurance because they have lower than average expected loss costs. The problem

---

[7]ERISA establishes penalties for fiduciaries that fail in their obligations and exempts such fiduciaries from tort liability. One of the major issues in the health-care debate during the late 1990s was the exemption of health maintenance organizations from tort liability.

[8]M. Berk and A. Monheit, "The Concentration of Health Expenditures: An Update," *Health Affairs* (Winter 1992).

with this is that today's healthy person may be to-morrow's sick person. Those who do not feel that they need health insurance change their minds after the onset of a serious illness and would then like to join the mechanism that spreads the high cost of health care.

Insurance Market Reform Options

Historically, insurers could refuse to issue cover-age to groups or individuals based on their past health care use or general indicators of their health status. Insurers could also refuse to renew policies based upon previous years' claims experi-ences, and could deny coverage for preexisting ill-nesses or conditions. In response to the problems encountered by insurance buyers, there have been continuing attempts to reform the market in ways that will make insurance available to those who have difficulty in obtaining it. These efforts generally take the form of restrictions on the abil-ity of insurers to select from among prospective buyers. These reforms, which tend to be grouped together in reform proposals, are *guaranteed issue, renewability, portability, limits on preexisting condition exclusions,* and *mandated benefits.*

Guaranteed issue is a requirement that insurers sell health insurance to any eligible party that agrees to pay the applicable premiums and to ful-fill the other plan requirements. It can be thought of as a "take all comers" rule. Guaranteed issue does not regulate the premium charged to a given individual or group. This means that for some buyers, the guaranteed issue coverage could be prohibitive in cost.

Guaranteed renewability ensures that those cur-rently insured cannot have their coverage discon-tinued by their insurer in a subsequent year as long as the insurer continues to do business in that particular market. As with the guaranteed-is-sue, guaranteed renewability alone does not limit the premium that can be charged a covered group or individual.

Preexisting condition exclusions disallow coverage related to any previous conditions. Without such

restrictions, there would be no incentive to pur-chase insurance until the onset of an illness or in-jury. Recognizing that a complete elimination of preexisting conditions exclusions would create chaos, reform proposals generally limit the time for which preexisting conditions can be excluded, usually for 6 to 12 months.

Portability refers to the ability to change insur-ers without encountering a gap in coverage. Re-forms relating to portability take the form of lim-its on preexisting condition exclusions. Under the proposed reforms, individuals maintaining continuous coverage are exempt from all preex-isting condition exclusions applying to new poli-cies. The objective of such a rule is to decrease the problem of "job-lock," the limit on worker mobility that results from the potential loss of in-surance coverage if the worker changes jobs.

Mandated benefits laws are an attempt to guar-antee that particular health services are covered in every insurance product sold in a state. The ra-tionale for mandating particular benefits is to avoid segmentation of persons who are subject to the illness or medical needs that are mandated and thereby spread the cost of treatment. Man-dated benefits include such diverse benefits as in-patient alcohol and drug abuse programs, infer-tility treatment, coverage for mental health, and the services of chiropractors and podiatrists. Man-dated benefits provisions, by forcing coverage of particular services, have the potential for spread-ing risk. Mandated benefits may also increase the incentives for insurers to select risks, worsening the degree of risk segmentation, as insurers at-tempt to write those who are least likely to have need for the mandated benefits.

Previous Attacks on the Access Problem

The problems in health care delivery and financ-ing have existed for many years. In view of the critical importance of medical expense insurance, it is not surprising that both the state and federal governments have enacted legislation that addresses access and cost problems of health insurance.

State Efforts to Improve Access

Most states have attempted to address the problem of availability of health insurance by creating subsidized state health insurance pools for the uninsurable.[9] Individuals who are not eligible for Medicare or Medicaid and who cannot buy private health insurance obtain coverage from the pools, usually at a subsidized rate. Although the plans differ in detail, the pools provide comprehensive medical coverage that includes in-hospital services, skilled nursing facility care, and prescription drugs. Although the pools are subsidized, even with the subsidy, premiums range from 125 to 200 percent of the state's average premiums. Costs in excess of the premiums are covered by a subsidy. The source of the subsidy varies by state, and includes state general revenues, a tax on hospital revenues, and assessments on health insurers. Most states fund their plans with an assessment on health insurers.

In addition, during the 1990s, many states passed "small-group reform" laws, which require insurers to offer plans to small groups on a guaranteed issue basis. The insurer may not exclude individual employees and may exclude preexisting conditions only for a limited period. Having met the preexisting conditions requirement in one plan, coverage must be "portable," that is, a new insurer may not impose a new preexisting conditions requirement. Rating rules limit the rate the insurer may charge and also limit annual rate increases. Insurers are allowed to nonrenew only for certain specified reasons.

---

[9]By 1999, the following 27 states had created such pools: Alaska, California, Colorado, Connecticut, Florida, Georgia, Illinois, Indiana, Iowa, Kansas, Louisiana, Maine, Minnesota, Mississippi, Missouri, Montana, Nebraska, New Mexico, North Dakota, Oregon, South Carolina, Tennessee, Texas, Utah, Washington, Wisconsin, and Wyoming.

Federal Legislation to Increase Access

Federal legislation has been enacted to ensure, to some extent, access to health care.

COBRA

The Consolidated Omnibus Budget Reconciliation Act of 1986 (COBRA) requires that employees and certain beneficiaries be allowed to continue their group health insurance coverage following a qualifying loss of coverage. The law applies to the employers with group plans covering 20 or more persons and permits continuation when coverage would otherwise end as a result of termination of employment, divorce, legal separation, eligibility for Medicare, or the cessation of dependent-child status. The employer must provide the coverage for up to 18 months for terminated employees and up to 36 months for spouses of deceased, divorced, or legally separated employees and for dependent children whose eligibility ceases. Generally, the COBRA participant pays a premium based on the existing group rate.

The Health Insurance Portability and Accountability Act of 1996 (HIPAA)   The second federal attempt to address access was the Health Insurance Portability and Accountability Act of 1996, also known as Kassebaum–Kennedy, which became effective on July 1, 1997. Although most states had already enacted small group and individual insurance reforms similar to those contained in HIPAA, HIPAA was significant because, for the first time, minimum federal standards were enacted for all plans nationally, including self-insured plans. HIPAA imposed reforms on the large group market (employers with more than 50 employees), the small group market (employers with 2 to 50 employees), and the individual market.

Reforms in the group market (both large and small) include guaranteed renewability, limitations on preexisting conditions, and portability. Preexisting conditions (defined as a medical condition diagnosed or treated within the previous six months) may not be excluded for more than 12 months. Credit toward satisfying the preexisting condition exclusion must be granted for prior coverage (with no gap greater than 63 days).

In the small group market (2 to 50 employees), insurers must provide all products on a guaranteed-issue basis and may not single out an individual in the group to be charged higher premiums or excluded from coverage. Insurers may use underwriting requirements such as minimum employee enrollment or minimum employer contribution levels.

In the individual market, policies must be guaranteed renewable. Also, certain *eligible individuals* must be given access to coverage in the individual market. An eligible individual is a person who has at least 18 months of prior health insurance coverage, with the most recent coverage being employer-provided, and no break in coverage greater than 63 days. HIPAA permits states to use one of two approaches in meeting this access requirement; the *federal fallback approach* (so-called because it applies if the state does nothing) and an *approved alternative mechanism*. Under the federal fallback approach, all insurers who operate in the individual market must offer eligible individuals a choice between at least two health plans. Most states (37 plus the District of Columbia) opted to use an approved alternative mechanism. The most common choice is a qualified high-risk pool (chosen by 22 states), which many states already had in place. Thirteen states implemented the federal fallback standards.

Significantly, the federal fallback standards did not contain rating reforms. Although insurers are required to provide individual insurance to eligible individuals, there is no limit on the premium they can charge. Not surprisingly, a GAO report issued in early 1998 questioned the effectiveness of the reforms in the federal fallback states, noting that many consumers who lost group coverage experienced difficulty obtaining individual market coverage or paid significantly higher rates for the coverage, reportedly up to 600 percent of the standard rate.

Efforts to Reduce Costs

Efforts to reduce cost have come mainly in the form of managed care initiatives that were pioneered by HMOs, but that have been adopted by other insurers.

Covering Alternative Sites of Care

Originally, hospital insurance policies covered only care administered in a hospital. Today, most policies recognize that there may be less costly alternative, but still appropriate, sites for delivering care. Policies are likely to cover outpatient surgery and ambulatory care. Birthing facilities are often covered as a less expensive alternative to in-hospital maternity care. Policies are also likely to cover care delivered in skilled nursing facilities, home health care, and hospice care (i.e., services to terminally ill patients, with emphasis on pain relief and other support).

Addressing Utilization

A number of policy provisions adopted by insurers are designed to encourage the cost-effective delivery of care. *Second surgical opinion* programs will pay for the cost of a second opinion prior to surgery, with the belief that this might reduce the incidence of unnecessary surgeries. *Preadmission certification* programs require the insured to receive approval of the insurer prior to being admitted to the hospital for certain conditions. The object is to prevent unnecessary admissions for ailments that can be treated on an outpatient basis. Under a *concurrent review* program, the insurer reviews the care while the insured is in the hospital to determine whether continued hospitalization is necessary. It authorizes an appropriate length of confinement and may authorize more inpatient days if the patient's condition requires it. Many companies have *case management programs* under which cases that have very high medical expenses are reviewed individually, with an attempt to design a plan of care that will reduce overall costs. This plan may result in the insurer covering expenses that are otherwise excluded but that will result in the elimination of other unnecessary costs.

Medical Savings Accounts

Medical savings accounts (MSAs) are a reform initiative that has been proposed as a way of reducing health care costs by giving consumers a stake in the level of expenditures.[10] The basic idea of the MSA is to allow individuals to make tax-sheltered contributions to a fund that is used to cover medical expenses. This fund is used with a high deductible health insurance policy and covers the expenses that fall within the policy deductible. It is hoped that MSAs will serve as an incentive to consumers to control medical care expenses.

As a pilot experiment, HIPAA authorized up to 750,000 MSAs for employees of small businesses and self-employed persons who purchase high-deductible health insurance. For individual-only coverage, the deductible for the high-deductible plan was between $1500 to $2250 and for family coverage was $3000 to $4500. These amounts are adjusted for inflation after 1998. The MSA pilot program was scheduled to end in the year 2000 but has been extended through 2002.

Generally, MSA contributions made by an employer are excluded from the employee's income. MSA contributions by individual taxpayers are deductible from income up to 65 percent of the annual deductible for individual coverage and 75 percent of the annual deductible for family coverage. Distributions from an MSA to pay for qualified medical expenses are not taxed to the MSA holder. Distributions for any other purpose are taxable as income and are also subject to a penalty tax of 15 percent. Distributions received after an MSA-holder becomes disabled, dies, or

---

[10]The idea of Medical Savings Accounts has been around at least since 1965. See Thomas L. Wenck, "Financing Senior Citizen Health Care: An Alternative Approach," *Journal of Risk and Insurance*, vol. XXXII, no. 2, pp. 165–175.

reaches Medicare eligibility are taxable income, but are not subject to the 15 percent penalty tax.

The Health Insurance Market

The ability to segment the insurance market has created a multitiered system of coverage. Coverage is found in both the public and private sector, although public sector coverage is limited to particular categories of individuals.

The Public Sector

Persons whose health-care financing is provided by government includes those covered by Medicare, Medicaid, and the new Children's Health Insurance Programs (CHIP).

Medicare

The Medicare program covers most persons over age 65 and disabled persons who meet specific eligibility requirements. Approximately 60 percent of Medicare-covered persons purchase private insurance to supplement the protection under Medicare. The Medicare program is discussed in greater detail later in the chapter.

Medicaid

Title XIX of the Social Security Act, popularly known as Medicaid, is a federal-state program of medical assistance for needy persons that was enacted simultaneously with the Medicare program. It provides medical assistance to low-income persons and to some individuals who have enough income for basic living expenses but cannot afford to pay for their medical care. States administer the program and make the payments, which are then partially reimbursed by the federal government. The federal proportion of the cost is based on a formula tied to state per-capita income and varies from about 50 percent to 80 percent in 2000, with the poorest states receiving the greatest proportion.[11]

The federal government establishes regulations and minimum standards related to eligibility, benefit coverage, and provider participation and reimbursement. States have options for expanding their programs beyond the minimum standards, subject to federal criteria. The benefit package is fairly similar from state to state and is generally quite comprehensive. Coverage is provided for services traditionally included in a commercial group-health-insurance package, as well as some services, such as long-term care, that are not. States are permitted to incorporate reasonable utilization management provisions in their Medicaid programs. Some states have implemented fairly restrictive limits on the amount, duration, and scope of care without conflicting with the federal requirements.[12]

Child Health Assistance Program

The Balanced Budget Act of 1997 (BBA–97) introduced a new Child Health Assistance Program (Title XXI of the Social Security Act), from fiscal year 1998 through fiscal year 2007. The law committed new federal spending of $24 billion over 5 years for children's health, with a total commitment to expend more than $48 billion for the initiative over the next 10 years. The funding will allow states to provide health insurance coverage to poor uninsured children who do not qualify for Medicaid. States can provide the coverage by expanding coverage under Medicaid or by providing insurance under a *State Children's Health Insurance Program* or by a combination of the two approaches. The federal funds can be used to purchase coverage under group health or individual insurance plans.

Federal CHAMPUS Program

All active and retired military personnel and their dependents are eligible for medical treatment in any Department of Defense installation medical facility. In addition, the Department of Defense operates an insurance program called *Civilian Health and Medical Program of the Uniformed Services* (CHAMPUS) for those persons who cannot obtain required medical treatment at a military medical facility. In 2000 the CHAMPUS program covered approximately 3.7 million persons.

The Private Sector

Slightly fewer than 10 million persons, less than 5 percent of the total population, obtain their health insurance coverage under individually purchased health insurance policies. The overwhelming majority of persons covered by private health insurance obtain their coverage under group plans, usually sponsored by an employer, that cover the worker and his or her dependents.

There are two reasons for the overwhelming dominance of the group approach. The first is that most people obtain their health insurance as an employee benefit. The economies of the group approach make group coverage cheaper than individually written coverage. The potential for cost savings inherent in the operation of the group

---

[11]The eligibility requirements for Medicaid are extensive and complex. Students who are interested in a more detailed description of eligibility requirements are referred to the Health Care Financing Administration (HCFA) website (http://www.hcfa.gov).

[12]The state of Oregon, in a revolutionary but controversial experiment, obtained a waiver that allows the state to cover a list of services, based on a ranking of the assessed value of each service. Various medical treatments are ranked according to their effectiveness and cost, and those that ranked low (e.g., life-saving measures for very-low-weight premature babies) will not be covered. State budget constraints determine which services will be covered, based on their ranking. Critics argue that this results in health-care rationing to Medicaid recipients. Proponents counter that it is necessary to extend the benefits of Medicaid to all of Oregon's needy population at a cost the state can afford.

mechanism was discussed in Chapter 12. The second major reason that medical expense insurance is typically provided through an employment relationship is taxes. Contributions by an employer for employee health insurance premiums are deductible as a business expense by the employer, but are not taxable as income to the employee. The employee is not taxed on benefits received under such a program if they are reimbursement of medical expenses actually incurred.

ERISA Plans

The largest group of workers covered by group plans consists of those covered by ERISA-exempted plans—that is, self-insured plans that are exempt from state regulation. It is estimated that more than two-thirds of large employers are self-insured, with programs covering over 62 million persons. Employers favor the ERISA preemption of state insurance laws because it allows them to avoid state premium taxes (usually 2 percent to 3 percent of premiums) and the costs associated with state-mandated benefits.

Originally, the ERISA exemption from state regulation applied to self-insured plans of a limited number of large employers. Over time, smaller and smaller employers have shifted to self-insurance, often as a part of a *multiemployer welfare arrangement* (MEWA). After a number of MEWA failures due to the absence of regulatory oversight, the 1982 amendments to ERISA authorized states to regulate self-funded MEWAs.[13] The U.S. Department of Labor and the states now have concurrent jurisdiction for regulation of MEWAs.

---

[13]In 1994, Secretary of Labor Robert Reich cited a General Accounting Office report showing that fraudulent MEWAs had left at least 398,000 health plan participants with more than $123 million in unpaid claims between January 1988 and June 1991. Reich went on further to say that "We have every reason to believe that problem has gotten worse since then." *Labor Secretary Reich Files Lawsuits to Raise Pressure on Fraudulent MEWAs,* Health L. Rep. (BNA). April 7, 1994.

Capitating Health Care Providers

Capitating health care providers include health maintenance organizations (HMOs) and provider-sponsored organizations (PSOs). HMOs insure an estimated 60.4 million persons, including about 8.7 million persons enrolled in HMOs operated by commercial insurance companies and 9 million enrolled in Blue Cross/Blue Shield HMOs. Because PSOs are relatively new, they presently insure a small number of persons, but that number is growing.

Commercial Insurance Companies

Private commercial insurance companies selling medical expense protection include property and liability insurers, life insurers, and monoline health insurers. These insurance companies cover about 78.4 million persons. This includes 38 million persons covered under fully insured group plans and 7.2 million persons covered under individual policies. The remainder are persons in programs that are fully or partially self-insured by employers and administered by insurance companies.

Blue Cross and Blue Shield Plans

Blue Cross and Blue Shield organizations insure an estimated 67.1 million persons, a part of whom represent participants in employer self-funded plans that are administered by the Blue Cross and Blue Shield organizations.

Distribution of Insurance Buyers

Approximately 190.8 million persons, or slightly more than 70 percent of the population, are insured by the private sector. Government programs (Medicare and CHAMPUS) cover 47.5 million. Because there is some overlapping between private and government programs, the total insured population is about 227.4 million, or roughly 84 percent of the total population. About 44.3 million persons, or 16.3 percent of the population, are uninsured. Many uninsured persons receive reimbursement for medical expenses under the Medicaid program. Table 16.1 summarizes the distribution of the U.S. population according to the source of health insurance protection.

Because there is some overlapping among the categories, it is difficult to be precise in measuring the percentages of the population in each category. Self-insured plans, for example, are partially insured by commercial insurers. In addition, about 60 percent of those persons covered by Medicare also purchase private insurance.

Table 16.1 Distribution of Health-Insured Population

	Persons Insured (millions)	Percentage of Population
Insured Coverage	130.2	47.90%
Self-Insured Plans	60.7	22.34%
Total Private Sector	190.9	70.24%
Medicare	38.8	14.28%
Champus	8.7	3.22%
Total Government	47.5	17.50%
Total Insured Population	227.5	83.73%
Uninsured	44,281	16.30%
Medicaid	37,500	13.80%
Total Population	271,743	100.00%

The Insurance Product

Medical expense policies are not standardized. There are, however, certain benefits that are common to all policies. For these common benefits, the major difference among plans is in the percentage of the costs that are paid.

Traditional Forms of Medical Expense Insurance

Traditional medical expense insurance available from private insurers is divided into four major classes; hospital expense coverage, surgical expense coverage, physicians expense coverage, and major medical coverage. Today, these four classes of coverage are generally merged into a single package of health-care benefits.

Base Plan Coverage

Hospitalization, surgical expense coverage, and physician's expense coverage are generally written together and are referred to as a base plan or sometimes as basic coverage. The coverage is pro-

vided in two ways: expense reimbursement contracts, marketed by insurance companies; and service contracts, originally offered by Blue Cross and Blue Shield organizations. Either type may be written to cover the individual or an entire family.

Hospitalization Insurance Blue Cross service plans provide a semiprivate room in a participating hospital for a stated number of days, rather than a cash benefit. The number of days varies, but generally ranges from 70 to 365 days. If the subscriber desires a private room, he or she may reimburse the hospital for the difference between the cost of the private room and the charges paid by Blue Cross. The Blue Cross plan pays the hospital a fee for each day the subscriber is in the hospital, based on a prenegotiated contract rate. Not all hospitals are members of Blue Cross, and when a subscriber is admitted to a nonmember hospital, the insured is reimbursed for the Blue Cross organization's cost of a semiprivate room in a member hospital.

Hospital expense policies offered by commercial insurers reimburse some or all of the cost of room and board when the insured is confined to a hospital. Like Blue Cross plans, coverage applies for a stated number of days. Early contracts paid a maximum daily benefit (e.g., $100, $200, or $300), with charges in excess of the daily benefit paid by the insured. Although this approach is still used, many policies have dropped the dollar limit and instead pay benefits based on "reasonable and customary" charges. Under this arrangement, the policy pays a benefit based on the prevailing charges for hospitals in the region. These plans operate very much like service benefit policies.[14]

In addition to the room benefit, policies of both Blue Cross and commercial insurance companies cover incidental hospital expenses such as the use of the operating room, X-rays, drugs, anesthesia, and laboratory charges. These services and facilities are generally referred to as "hospital miscellaneous expenses" or "incidental hospital expenses."

Surgical Expense and Physicians' Expense Insurance Two types of basic coverages pay for physicians' fees. *Surgical expense insurance* provides coverage for surgeons' fees, and *physicians' expense insurance* covers nonsurgical doctors' fees. Blue Shield plans cover surgical and physicians' services in much the same way that Blue Cross plans provide hospital benefits. Blue Shield organizations agree to pay the physician's usual, customary, and reasonable charges. Surgical expense contracts sold by insurance companies originally reimbursed the policyholder according to a schedule that assigned a dollar value to different types of operations but most commercial insurers have switched to the "reasonable and customary" basis of coverage. Physicians' expense insurance (formerly called "regular medical expense insurance") covers a physician's fees for nonsurgical

care in a hospital, home, or doctor's office, usually with a limit per visit (e.g., $25 to $50) and a maximum number of calls per sickness or injury.

Major Medical Policy

A distinguishing characteristic of the major medical policy is the high limit per loss and the relative absence of exclusions. Major medical policies are commonly written with a limit as high as $500,000 or $1 million. The policy maximum may apply to each accident or illness, or it may apply as a lifetime maximum. Some policies, especially group contracts, are written without a maximum limit on the amount payable. Some major medical policies include internal limitations, restricting the amount payable for specific types of expense (e.g., mental illness).[15] In general, however, major medical policies go beyond the usual health insurance contracts, providing payment for blood transfusions, prescriptions and drugs, casts, splints, braces and crutches, and durable medical equipment such as artificial limbs or eyes, and even the rental of wheelchairs.

A second characteristic of the major medical policy is its deductible, which may be $100, $200, $250, $300, $500, or even higher. The application of the deductible differs from contract to contract. Most policies make the deductible applicable to a time period, such as a calendar year. Under this form, the deductible applies only once per member of the family during the stated period. Other policies apply the deductible on a disability basis, requiring that the deductible be paid only once for any disability. Many policies have both individual and maximum family deductibles.

---

[14]A third type of hospitalization coverage is the cash payment policy, which is also referred to—somewhat illogically—as a hospital indemnity policy. These contracts agree to pay a specified amount per day, regardless of expenses incurred, when the insured is hospitalized, up to a maximum number of days stated.

[15]The Mental Health Parity Act of 1996 (MHPA) bars health plans from imposing lower limits for mental illness than for other disorders. The requirements do not apply to group health plans of employers with not more than 50 employees or if their application would result in an increase in the plan's cost of at least 1 percent. The MHPA includes a sunset provision under which the MHPA requirements do not apply to benefits for services furnished on or after September 30, 2001.

Finally, the major medical policy also requires the insured to share a part of the loss in excess of the deductible. For example, the insurance company may pay 80 percent of the loss in excess of the deductible, with the insured paying the other 20 percent. The insurer may pay a lower percentage for certain classes of expenses (e.g., mental illness). There is usually a cap on out-of-pocket costs borne by the insured—commonly $2000 or $3000—beyond which the insurance pays 100 percent of covered expenses up to the policy limit.

Historically, major medical contracts were either *supplemental major medical policies* or *comprehensive major medical policies*. A supplemental major medical policy is written with a base plan and is subject to a corridor deductible, which represents out-of-pocket expenses the insured must incur before the major medical plan applies. With the transition to managed care, medical expense insurance increasingly resembles the comprehensive major medical policy, which combines the best features of a base plan and the major medical contract into a single policy. Although some supplemental major medical policies still exist in the marketplace, the comprehensive major medical policy has become the standard approach that most insurers now follow.

Originally, comprehensive major medical plans applied the deductible and coinsurance provision to all covered medical expenses, including hospital and surgical expense. Current versions have eliminated the deductible for hospital charges, and sometimes for surgical charges as well. They provided for payment of these expenses without a coinsurance provision up to some specified maximum, with coinsurance applicable above this limit. The initial level of deductible- and coinsurance-free coverage—usually from $2500 to $5000 or $6000—reflects the base plan origins of these policies. A sample comprehensive major medical plan is depicted in Figure 16.1

To illustrate the elements in the comprehensive major medical depicted in Figure 16.1 and the operation of major medical policies generally, assume that the insured under this program incurs expenses as follows:

	Expenses	Insured Pays	Insurer Pays
Hospital & surgical expenses	$25,000	$2,000	$23,000
Rehabilitation therapy	3,000	500	2,500
Total medical expenses	28,000	2,500	25,500

The first $5000 in hospital and surgical expense coverage is covered without a deductible and without coinsurance. Expenses in excess of this initial $5000 are subject to 80 percent coinsurance, up to a $2000 out-of-pocket maximum. Expenses other than hospital and surgical expense are subject to the $500 deductible and the 80 percent coinsurance provision. Because the insured's share of the hospital and surgical expense above $5000 satisfies the out-of-pocket maximum on coinsured losses, coverage for the rehabilitation therapy in the example is subject only to the $500 deductible.

HMO Contracts

In HMO contracts, hospital room and board and in-hospital physicians' medical and surgical services are provided on a fully prepaid basis with no limit on the number of days covered. In addition to these basic benefits, managed care plans often include additional benefits such as preventive care and checkups, well-baby care, and similar health care services.

Subscribers are encouraged to have regular medical checkups and see their physician as often as necessary. Outpatient services, such as visits to a doctor's office for diagnostic services, treatment, and preventive care (i.e., routine physical examinations), may be subject to a nominal copayment charge (e.g., $10 or $15), with no limit on the number of visits. The copayment charge is usually the same, regardless of the service rendered. Some HMOs provide prescription benefits as a part of the capitation fee. Prescriptions are usually subject to a $10 or $15 copayment applicable to each 100-day supply of a drug. There is no lifetime maximum dollar limits under the coverage of an HMO.

Virtually all care is provided within the network. The major exceptions are when the primary care physician refers the patient to a specialist outside

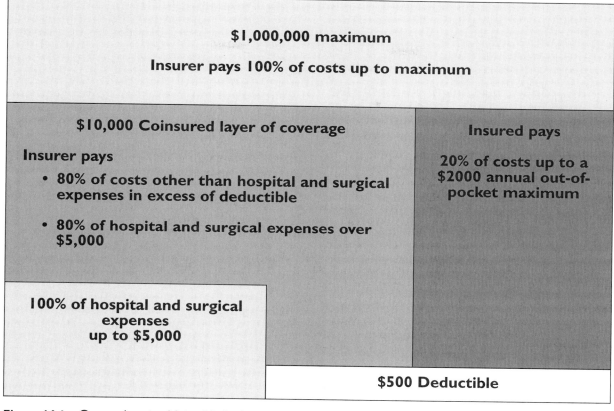

Figure 16.1   Comprehensive Major Medical

the network or when the subscriber requires emergency services.

Exclusions Under Health Insurance Policies

All health insurance policies are subject to exclusions. Exclusions in individual policies tend to be more extensive than those in group policies and some group contracts contain more exclusions than others. The following exclusions are typical of those that may be in either individual or group contracts, depending on the insurer.

- Expenses payable under workers compensation or any occupational disease law

- Personal comfort items (e.g., television, telephone, air conditioners)
- Elective cosmetic surgery
- Routine medical care (e.g., annual physical exams, birth control, well-baby care)
- Hearing aids and eyeglasses
- Dental work
- Experimental procedures
- Expenses resulting from self-inflicted injuries
- Expenses resulting from war or any act of war
- Expenses incurred while on active duty with the armed forces
- Services received in any government hospital not making a charge for such services

- Expenses arising out of mental or nervous disorders (Some policies cover mental and nervous disorders subject to a lower maximum or only for a percentage of the costs covered.)

Most policies contain limitations on coverage for preexisting conditions. These tend to be less restrictive in group policies, which are subject to the requirements of state small group reform laws and HIPAA.

Maternity benefits may or may not be included in individual contracts. If they are included, they usually have a specified maximum payment. It is also customary to include maternity benefits in individual contracts only after the dependent has been covered under the policy for 9 or 10 months. Under group contracts, maternity benefits are usually covered on the same basis as any other condition.[16] The Newborn and Mothers Health Protection Act of 1996 (NMHPA) requires all health plans that provide maternity coverage to allow new mothers and their infants to stay in the hospital at least 48 hours after a normal birth and 96 hours after a Caesarian birth.

Other exclusions not listed here may be found in the policies issued by a particular insurer. Similarly, some of the exclusions listed here may not be present. It is increasingly common for policies to cover preventive health care, such as annual physical exams. Each policy must be examined individually to determine the extent of the coverage.

Coordination of Benefit

With the increase in the two-income family, situations often arise in which a married couple will both be covered under medical expense policies provided by their employers. When an employer-provided policy includes coverage on depend-ents, one or both partners may be covered under two policies: the policy provided by their own employer and the policy provided by their spouse's employer.

Insurers developed the *coordination of benefits provision* to eliminate double payment when two policies exist and to establish a coverage priority for payment of losses. Under a standard coordination of benefits provision, if a wife is covered by her employer and as a dependent under her husband's policy, her policy applies before the husband's policy. The husband's policy pays nothing if the wife's policy covers the total cost of the expenses. Children are covered under the policy of the parent whose birthday is earliest in the year.

Other Medical Expense Coverages

Besides the various forms of medical expense coverage we have discussed, there are several other health contracts with which you should be familiar. In general, these contracts meet specialized needs, or are limited contracts providing coverage for particular types of medical expenses.

Dental Expense Insurance

Dental expense insurance is a specialized form of health expense coverage, designed to pay for normal dental care as well as damage caused by accidents. Most of the coverage is written on a group basis. It is offered by insurance companies, the Blue Cross and Blue Shield organizations, and dental service corporations, similar in nature to the blues. The blues and dental service corporations typically provide benefits on a service basis.

Dental expense coverage is written on a scheduled or nonscheduled basis. Scheduled plans provide a listing of various dental services, with a specific amount available for each. Unscheduled plans generally pay on a "reasonable and customary" basis, subject to deductibles and coinsurance. Coinsurance rates tend to vary with the type of service provided. Because of the proven benefits of preventive care in dental treatment, the insurer may encourage preventive care by reimbursing it at a

---

[16]The Pregnancy Discrimination Act of 1975 amended the Civil Rights Act of 1964 to prohibit employment discrimination with respect to pregnancy, childbirth, or related medical conditions. All employer-sponsored health and disability insurance plans must provide equal benefits for pregnancy-related conditions and other medical conditions.

higher percentage (e.g., 90 percent) than basic services such as extractions (80 percent). Orthodontia services are often subject to a separate limit and a lower reimbursement percentage (e.g., 50 percent).

Prescription Drug Insurance

Prescription drug insurance is a limited form of health insurance designed to cover the cost of drugs and medicines prescribed by a physician. The coverage is written on a group basis, often as an adjunct to other types of health care coverage. Coverage is written on a reimbursement basis, under which payment is made for the usual and customary charges for covered drugs and prescriptions. Often, there is a coinsurance or deductible arrangement, under which the insured is required to bear a part of the cost. The typical deductible is from $2 to $5 for generic drugs and from $5 to $20 for name-brand drugs. Under an alternate approach, the coverage is subject to an annual deductible, such as $25 or $50. Coverage may be subject to an annual maximum.

An alternative to reimbursement coverage is coverage for prescription drugs from a service plan, which operates in a manner similar to the Blue Cross/Blue Shield organizations. Under this approach, the insurer makes payment directly to participating pharmacists or, sometimes, to a third-party administrator. When drugs or prescriptions are obtained from a nonparticipating pharmacy, payment is limited to the amount that would have been payable to a participating pharmacy. Coverage under both reimbursement plans and service plans typically excludes contraceptive drugs, dietary supplements, beauty aids, and cosmetics.

Health Insurance for the Elderly

Because they often need more extensive care than other members of society, and because their resources are often limited, senior citizens face special problems in the area of health care costs.

Three broad types of coverage exist for insuring the health care needs of the elderly: Medicare, Medicare supplement (or Medigap) policies, and long-term care insurance. In addition to these forms of social and private insurance, the federal Medicaid program also provides financing for the health care needs of senior citizens.

The Medicare Program

From its creation in 1965 until 1999, the Medicare program consisted of two programs: Medicare: Part A, *Hospital Insurance*, which provides coverage for the cost of hospital care, nursing home care, hospice care, and home visits; and Part B, *Supplementary Medical Insurance*, an optional coverage for which the insured pays a monthly premium ($45.50 in 1999), which covers doctors' fees and certain other costs. In 1997, Congress added several new options to the program, collectively called *Medicare Part C* or *Medicare+Choice*. We will begin our discussion with the traditional Medicare Parts A and B.[17]

Part A—Hospital Insurance

The basic benefits under the hospital insurance coverage fall into four broad categories: (1) hospital care, (2) care in a nursing home or extended care facility, (3) home health services, and (4) care in a hospice.

Part A hospital insurance provides coverage for the cost of hospital care in excess of a deductible ($776 in 2000) during the patient's first 60 days in the hospital. From day 61 to day 90, the insured pays a specified charge per day ($194 in 2000), and Medicare pays the remainder of the costs. In addition to the 90 days for each spell of illness, the insured has a 60-day "lifetime reserve," which may be used after the 90-day limit is exhausted in a spell of illness. The insured pays a greater part of the costs during the reserve days

[17]The Health Care Financing Administration (HCFA), which administers Medicare, maintains an excellent website at http://www.hcfa.gov/.

($388 per day in 2000). A spell of illness starts on the first day the insured receives covered services as a bed patient in a hospital or extended care facility and ends when he or she has been out of the hospital or skilled nursing home for 60 consecutive days.

Medicare Part A also provides benefits for up to 100 days per benefit period in a skilled nursing facility. Medicare covers all costs for the first 20 days of care, after which the insured pays a daily charge ($97.00 in 2000) for the remaining 80 days. Benefits are provided only when the insured is confined to a hospital for at least 3 days and enters the facility within 14 days after discharge from the hospital. There is no coverage for custodial care.

Home benefits under Medicare Part A are provided to beneficiaries who require home health care—such as part-time nursing and physical, occupational, or speech therapy—or part-time services of a home health aide after being confined to a hospital for at least 3 days. A doctor must prescribe the home health care within 14 days after the discharge from a hospital or extended care facility. Benefits are provided for up to 21 days of consecutive care per illness.

Finally, Medicare Part A covers hospice care for individuals with a life expectancy of six months or less. Benefits are provided for up to two 90-day periods, plus one 30-day period, plus one extension period of unlimited length.

Payments to hospitals under Medicare are determined under the prospective payment system (PPS), based on diagnostic related groups (DRGs).[18] Under this system, the hospital is paid a flat amount based on the patient's diagnosis, rather than an amount that varies with the number of days the patient is hospitalized. The flat amount is based on the "average" resource use for the patient's diagnostic related group.

[18]Medicare DRGs are derived by taking all possible diagnoses identified in the International Classification of Diseases system, classifying them into major diagnostic categories (MDCs) based on organ systems, and further breaking them into distinct diagnostic related groupings (DRGs).

Part B—Supplementary Medical Insurance

Supplementary Medical Insurance (SMI) covers the cost of physicians' and surgeons' services, no matter where rendered, including those in a hospital, clinic, doctor's office, or even in the home. Home health services are covered up to 100 visits during the calendar year (even if the insured has not been hospitalized), as are all outpatient services of a participating hospital, including diagnostic tests and treatments. Coverage also applies for diagnostic tests, surgical dressings, splints, and rental or purchase of medical equipment.

The coverage under the SMI is much like a major medical contract. Benefits begin after a deductible ($100 in 2000), and nothing is paid until this initial expense has been met by the insured. Medical insurance pays 80 percent of the covered expenses in excess of the deductible, provided that the charges are "reasonable" (based on customary and prevailing charges). Besides the deductible and coinsurance, the individual may have additional out-of-pocket costs if the physician or medical supplier does not *accept assignment* of the Medicare claim and charges more than Medicare's approved amount. Charges above the Medicare-approved amount (called the *excess charge*) are subject to a maximum of 15 percent above the Medicare-approved charge. This means that when the physician refuses to accept assignment, the beneficiary must pay 20 percent of the approved amount plus the amount of any excess charges, which are limited to 15 percent above the approved amount.

Medicare-approved payments to physicians are determined according to the *Resource Based Relative Value Schedule* (RBRVS), which measures the time, training, and skill required to perform a given service, adjusted for overhead costs and geographic differences.

Employer Group Medicare Coverage

Employers with more than 20 employees must permit persons who are eligible for Medicare but who are still employed to enroll (with their spouses) in the employer's health insurance plan.

This rule applies only to workers between ages 65 and 69. Employers must also offer health care coverage to employees' spouses who are between 65 and 69 even if the employee is under age 65. If the employee chooses coverage under the employer's plan, Medicare coverage becomes excess. If the employee elects not to participate in the employer's plan, Medicare is primary coverage. In that case, the employer may not offer coverage to supplement Medicare benefits.

Medicare Supplement Policies

Commercial insurers and Blue Cross and Blue Shield organizations have developed special policies called *Medicare supplement policies* or *Medigap* policies to fill the gaps in coverages arising from Medicare's deductibles and coinsurance provisions. Most states have adopted an NAIC model act for regulating the sale of Medicare supplement policies, which includes provisions relating both to sales practices and to policy benefits. State laws require delivery of a *Medicare Supplement Buyer's Guide* to purchasers of Medicare supplement policies. Buyers are also granted a 30-day "free look," during which the policy can be canceled and returned for a full refund.

In 1990, Congress enacted legislation to encourage the states to regulate Medicare policies even more rigidly. This legislation required the NAIC to set standards for coverage provided by Medicare supplement policies and for the sale of those policies. Responding to this federal mandate, the NAIC set standards for ten levels of coverage under Medicare supplement policies, designated Plans A through J. As required by the federal law, all ten policies include a core of basic benefits, which covers certain coinsurance and deductible features of Medicare. This core includes five coverages:

1. Reimbursement for insured's share of hospital charges (coinsurance) under hospital insurance (Part A coverage) for days 61 through 90 ($192 per day in 2000) and days 91 through 150 ($384 per day in 2000)

2. Coverage for all charges for an additional 365 days in hospital

3. Reimbursement for hospital insurance blood deductible (3 pints)

4. Reimbursement for medical insurance (Part B) blood deductible (3 pints)

5. Reimbursement for insured's 20 percent share of expenses covered under medical insurance (Part B)

Other coverages are added to the basic core coverage in different combinations, as indicated in Table 16.2. In all states except Minnesota, Massachusetts, and Wisconsin, all insurers must offer Plan A and may offer any of the other plans, subject to state laws.

Medigap insurers must accept all applicants for coverage within the first 6 months after they enroll in Medicare after age 65, regardless of their health. No one can be rejected because of illness, injury, or a preexisting condition. The benefits under Medicare supplement policies that are designed to cover cost-sharing features of Medicare must change automatically when Medicare deductible and coinsurance percentages change. Insurers are permitted to change the premiums to reflect the changes in coverage.

The law also limits the use of preexisting condition provisions and requires that all Medicare supplement policies be guaranteed renewable. Insurance agents are required to obtain, in writing, a statement from the buyer about his or her eligibility for Medicare and whether he or she has other Medicare supplement insurance. Finally, the law mandates a minimum loss ratio of 65 percent for individual Medicare policies and requires the states to establish a counseling program to help senior citizens in selecting a policy.

Medigap Premiums

Although the benefits are identical for all Medigap plans of the same type, the premiums may

Table 16.2 Medicare Supplement Policies

Benefits Included	Plan									
	A	B	C	D	E	F	G	H	I	J
Basic Medicare supplement benefits	yes	yes	yes	yes	yes	yes	yes	yes	yes	yes
Hospital deductible ($776 in 2000)		yes	yes	yes	yes	yes	yes	yes	yes	yes
Skilled nursing facility coinsurance, days 21–100 ($97 in 2000)		yes	yes	yes	yes	yes	yes	yes	yes	yes
Emergency care while traveling overseas			yes	yes	yes	yes	yes	yes	yes	yes
Doctors' services deductible ($100 in 2000)		yes				yes				yes
Excess doctors' charges						100%	80%		100%	100%
Health care services provided at home				yes			yes		yes	yes
Prescription drugs—$250 deductible, 50% coinsurance								$1250	$1250	$3000
Preventive medical care					yes					yes

vary from one company to another and from area to area. Insurance companies use three different methods to calculate premiums: issue age, attained age, and no-age rating. Under the issue age method, the premium varies with the insured's age at which the contract was purchased, but does not increase as the insured becomes older. Under the attained age method, the premium is based on the insured's current age and increases as the insured ages. Under no-age rating, everyone pays the same premium regardless of age.[19]

Medicare+Choice

In 1997, as part of the Balanced Budget Act of 1997 (BBA-97), Congress added a new option for Medicare beneficiaries: Medicare+Choice (also called Medicare Part C). The goal of the Medicare+Choice initiative—which some have characterized as the *privatization of Medicare*—is to contain costs in Medicare by injecting private competition into the system and encouraging more beneficiaries to enroll in managed care plans.[20] Medicare beneficiaries may continue to participate in the traditional fee-for-service program, or they may elect one of three new alternatives to the traditional program. These new options are:

- Coordinated care plans
- Private fee-for-service Medicare
- Medical savings accounts (MSAs)

Except in the case of medical savings accounts, Medicare+Choice plans must provide the same services and benefits (other than hospice care) as are covered under Parts A and B of original Medicare. In addition, Medicare+Choice Plans (other than MSA plans) are required to pass on to beneficiaries in the form of additional benefits

[19]State Medicaid offices offer two programs that are designed specifically to help certain low-income Medicare beneficiaries meet the cost of Medicare. One is called the *Qualified Medicare Beneficiary (QMB) program* and the other is called the *Specified Low-Income Medicare Beneficiary (SLMB) program.*

[20]At the time Medicare+Choice was enacted, more than 5.5 million Medicare beneficiaries (or about 14 percent of the Medicare population) were already enrolled in managed care plans under special arrangements between HCFA and the managed care plans. The majority of the beneficiaries in managed-care plans were concentrated in six states: Arizona, California, Florida, Hawaii, New York, and Oregon.

any "savings" they achieve because their costs are less than the Medicare payment. To participate in Medicare+Choice, the Medicare beneficiary must be eligible for coverage under Part A and must pay the Part B monthly premium.

Coordinated Care Plans

Medicare+Choice *coordinated care plans* include HMOs (with or without POS options), PPOs, and plans offered by provider-sponsored organizations (PSOs). When Medicare beneficiaries enroll in a particular plan, HCFA contributes a Medicare+Choice capitation payment directly to the plan. Initially, beneficiaries who enroll in a Medicare+Choice plan will be allowed to change to another plan monthly. Beginning in 2003, beneficiaries may disenroll from a Medicare+Choice plan and choose another plan or return to Medicare fee-for-service only one time during the first 3 months of the calendar year.

Private Fee-for-Service

In addition to "original" fee-for-service, BBA–97 allows Medicare beneficiaries to enroll in a private indemnity insurance plan offering unrestricted use of participating physicians. The plans will pay providers a specified amount for each service, and physicians will be limited to charging their patients up to 15 percent above the plan's payment. Medicare will make monthly payments to these plans to cover traditional Medicare benefits and the beneficiaries will pay the difference between the full cost of coverage and the Medicare payment. There will be no limit on the premiums that insurers can charge beneficiaries.[21]

Medical Savings Accounts

Under a demonstration project, up to 390,000 Medicare beneficiaries will be able to establish a *Medicare medical savings account* (MSA) to pay for qualified medical expenses.[22] Beneficiaries who choose this option will purchase a high-deductible (up to $6000 in 1999) catastrophic health insurance policy to accompany their medical savings account. Payments from HCFA to beneficiaries will be used to pay the premium for the high-deductible/catastrophic plan, with any remainder deposited into the beneficiary's MSA. The catastrophic plan will provide coverage for at least the services that are available under Medicare Parts A and B, after the deductible has been met. Withdrawals from an MSA to pay medical expenses are not taxable. However, withdrawals for non-medical purposes will be subject to income tax, and in some cases, a 50 percent penalty. The 50 percent penalty applies to withdrawals that reduce the MSA fund below 60 percent of the annual deductible for the high-deductible policy. Withdrawals from accumulations that exceed 60 percent of the annual deductible of the high-deductible policy are taxable income, but are not subject to the penalty. Thus, over time, Medicare dollars could be used for any consumer purchase.

Medicare+Choice Medicare Supplement Insurance

The BBA–97 added a new guaranteed-issue requirement for Medicare supplement plans, which allows persons returning to regular Medicare from a Medicare+Choice plan to purchase Medigap coverage without new preexisting-conditions

---

[21]The BBA–97 also allows doctors to opt out of Medicare and to enter into private contracts with beneficiaries to provide Medicare-covered services for a fee in excess of 115 percent of the Medicare-approved rate. Neither the beneficiary nor the physician will be able to obtain Medicare reimbursement for the services and the doctor is barred from participating in the Medicare program for 2 years.

[22]Enrollments in Medicare+Choice MSAs will not be allowed after the number of persons enrolled reaches 390,000 or after January 1, 2003. The secretary of HHS is required to report to Congress no later than March 1, 2002 on whether the time limit for enrollment in MSAs should be extended or removed and whether the numerical limit should be ended.

exclusions. The BBA–97 also added two additional benefits to the 10 standard packages by specifying that a high-deductible feature is added to Plans F and J.

The Future of Medicare

Whether the changes in the Medicare program enacted by the BBA–97 will have a positive effect on the program's costs remains to be seen. Authorities speculate that at least initially, most beneficiaries will elect to stay in the traditional fee-for-service Medicare plan. Over time, however, the other options, which may offer more benefits at a lower cost, might attract an increasing number of beneficiaries. Some critics suggest that the Medicare+Choice option will create a multitiered Medicare system, in which wealthy beneficiaries will opt for fee-for-service, healthy individuals will shift into managed care plans, and sicker and more expensive beneficiaries will stay in the traditional fee-for-service program.

Although the Congressional Budget Office predicts that the BBA–97 changes will ensure the solvency of Medicare through 2007, the longer-range problem remains. Future Medicare cost increases will reflect more beneficiaries, increases in the cost of medical services, and increases in the utilization and intensity of medical services. Beginning in 2010, the demographic shift that will occur with the retirement of baby-boomers will worsen the imbalance between expenditures and revenues. After that time, a larger proportion of our population will be eligible for Medicare, and a correspondingly smaller percentage will be paying the taxes that support the Health Insurance (HI) trust fund.

Long-Term Care Insurance

With the increase in life expectancy and improved medical care, Americans age 65 and older are increasing more rapidly than the remainder of the population. For a variety of social and economic reasons, an increasing number of our aged are spending their final days in nursing homes and extended care facilities, with annual costs of $30,000 to $80,000 per year. In 1999, about seven million people over age 65 required long-term care and it is estimated that this number will increase to nine million by the year 2005 and to 12 million by 2020. According to a study by the U.S. Department of Health and Human Services, people age 65 have a 40 percent lifetime risk of entering a nursing home. Of those who enter nursing homes, one in ten will stay five years or longer.

Although Medicare covers short-term skilled nursing home care following hospitalization, it does not cover custodial care. Medicare supplement policies issued by private insurers supplement Medicare, but generally do not provide for extended care. The need therefore exists for a form of insurance that will assist in meeting the costs of long-term care for the aged. Individual and group LTC policies have been introduced by insurers into the marketplace to meet this need.

Regulatory Standards

At the state level, most states have adopted the NAIC model law that sets minimum standards for LTC policies. The NAIC model law requires that long-term care policies be guaranteed renewable, and must be incontestable on the basis of misrepresentations after two years. Coverage for Alzheimer's disease must be included. Insurers must offer an inflation-protection option, either by automatic annual increases in benefit levels or through the right to purchase increased benefits without evidence of insurability. Finally, the model law specifies a minimum loss ratio for LTC policies of 60 percent.[23]

At the federal level, HIPAA establishes standards for *tax-qualified long-term care insurance* (TQ-LTCI). Policies that meet these standards are granted favorable tax treatment under the Inter-

---

[23]By the end of 1995, 43 states had adopted some version of the NAIC model Long-Term Care Coverage Act. Seven additional states adopted standards that differ significantly from the NAIC model law.

nal Revenue Code. TQ-LTCI must be guaranteed renewable and may not, in general, cover services that are reimbursed by Medicare. In addition, the policy must not provide a cash surrender value or other money that can be paid, assigned, pledged, or borrowed. Dividends may be used only to reduce future premiums or increase future benefits.

Coverage of LTC Policies

There are two broad approaches to the benefit structure of LTC policies. Under the earliest approach—which still predominates—coverage is provided for a specified limit per day, with benefits payable for from 1 to 5 or 6 years and, in the case of some insurers, for life. The maximum daily limit available in 2000 varied by company, but daily limits up to $300 were available from some insurers. Some policies pay the full daily benefit selected, regardless of the actual charges for the services provided and others reimburse only for actual charges incurred up to the daily limit. Waiting periods generally range from 20 to 100 days.

The second type of benefit is called a *pool of money policy*. Rather than specify a period of time, benefits for LTC services are paid from a single lifetime maximum number of dollars. A $100-per-day benefit payable for 5 years represents $182,500 (365 × 5 × $100). Under a pool of money policy, a $182,500 policy limit is available to pay for whatever long-term care expenses are incurred and benefits are payable for as long as the maximum amount lasts, regardless of the time period.

Although there is a tendency to think of long-term-care insurance in the traditional terms of *accident and sickness*, the need for long-term care is different from the need for other types of medical care. Many people who require long-term care are not "sick" in the traditional sense. They are old and frail, and while they may not require traditional types of medical services, they do need assistance with the activities of daily living. Generally, long-term care insurance pays benefits based on the insured's inability to perform certain per-

sonal functions or *activities of daily living*, such as bathing, dressing, or eating, or when care is required because of cognitive impairment (i.e., Alzheimer's disease). The standard for TQ-LTCI established by HIPAA, for example, provides that coverage is triggered when the insured cannot perform, without substantial assistance, at least two activities of daily living for at least 90 days. The activities of daily living specified by HIPAA are (1) eating; (2) toileting; (3) transferring; (4) bathing; (5) dressing; and (6) continence. HIPAA also requires coverage for Alzheimer's by mandating coverage for a person "who requires substantial supervision to be protected from threats to health and safety due to severe cognitive impairment."

Home Care and Other Benefits LTC policies are not required to include home care benefits, but under the NAIC model law if a home care benefit is provided, it may not be subject to a step-down requirement (a requirement that the insured was previously confined in a hospital or skilled nursing facility). In addition to licensed nursing homes, some policies provide coverage for *assisted living facilities,* in which a lesser level of care is provided to residents. Some policies limit home care benefits or benefits for assisted living facilities to 50 or 60 percent of the daily limit for nursing-home care but most policies pay the same amount for these services as for nursing-home care. Finally, some policies now include a *respite care benefit,* which provides payment for a substitute caregiver when the primary caregiver (usually a relative) takes a vacation or break from the care-giving task.

Cost of LTC Insurance

The cost of LTC insurance varies widely among companies. The Health Insurance Association of America reports the following *average* premiums for LTC coverage in 1999. At age 50, the cost of LTC coverage is about $380 annually. At age 65, the premium increases to about $1000 annually, and by age 79, it is about $4000. Some insurers offer a two-policy discount (usually 10 or 15 percent) when two spouses purchase coverage. The discount may be applied to the cheaper of the two policies or to both policies.

Tax Treatment of TQ-LTCI

For employer-provided plans, premiums for TQ-LTCI are deductible by the employer and are not included in the taxable income of the employee. For individuals who itemize, premiums paid on qualified TQ-LTCI are deductible as medical expenses for itemized-deduction purposes. The annual amount of premiums deductible as medical expenses is limited, depending on the insured's age. The annual dollar limits are indexed to reflect increases in health care costs.[24]

Benefits payable under TQ-LTCI are treated as amounts received for sickness and personal injuries, which are generally excludable from income. If recoveries under TQ-LTCI exceed the cost incurred for care and a statutory per diem limit, the excess is taxable as income. The per diem limit, which is adjusted for inflation, was $175 per day in 2000.

Success of LTC Insurance in the Market

Sales of long-term care insurance have been less than spectacular. According to the industry's own estimates, less than 7 percent of those in the target market (age 55 and older) have purchased the coverage. One reason for this poor performance may be that there are other more appealing options for financing long-term care. Persons of modest means may qualify for Medicaid. Persons who do not qualify for Medicaid may be able to arrange their finances so they *do* qualify through *Medicaid planning,* a euphemism for the strategy of becoming artificially impoverished by disposing of assets. Another alternative is a *reverse mortgage,* in which the individual borrows the equity in

his or her home if necessary to finance long-term care. Still another approach is to tap the proceeds of existing life insurance.

Life Insurance Accelerated Benefits

Although cash values in life insurance policies can provide a source of cash in the event of a terminal illness or the need for long-term care, cash values may be limited or nonexistent. An alternative is an agreement by the insurer to advance the policy proceeds under an *accelerated benefits rider* (also known as a *living benefits rider*). These riders agree to pay a part of the policy death benefit to policyholders who choose this way of paying nursing home or other bills. The accelerated benefits rider defines the conditions under which the benefit is payable. These usually include a designated catastrophic illness, a terminal illness, or the need for custodial or nursing-home care that occurs after the insured has reached a specified age ranging from 65 to 85. Most policies specify a maximum limit for the benefit, expressed as a dollar amount, a monthly benefit, or a percentage of the death benefit. Initially, many companies charged for the coverage. A number of companies now offer living benefit riders on all new and existing policies as a no-additional-cost benefit.

For the terminally ill, the IRC treats accelerated benefits as an amount paid by reason of the death of the insured (i.e., nontaxable). Amounts paid to a chronically ill person for long-term care costs are subject to the same tax treatment as benefits under TQ-LTCI.

Viatication

Another alternative with respect to life insurance policy proceeds is *viatication,*[25] which refers to the

---

[24]In 2000, if the taxpayer is not more than 40 by the end of the tax year, the annual limit is $200; age 41 through 50, $375; 51 through 60, $750; 61 through 70, $2000; 71 or older, $2500.

[25]The term comes from the Latin word *viaticum,* meaning money or supplies provided as traveling expenses to an officer on an official journey in ancient Rome. The suggested meaning is that the proceeds from the sale of the life insurance policy provide "supplies" for the individual's final journey.

Tidbits, Vignettes, and Conundrums 16.1

The Granny Goes to Jail Law

Medicaid Planning refers to the disposal of assets to become eligible for Medicaid. Under current rules, the transfer of assets at less than fair market value during the 36 months prior to application for Medicaid can result in a period of Medicaid ineligibility. The number of months for which Medicaid benefits are denied is equal to the amount that was transferred divided by the average monthly cost of nursing home care in the region. For example, if the regional rate is $3000 per month and the individual transfers $30,000 in assets, he or she would lose Medicaid eligibility for 10 months. There is no limit to the length of the penalty period, but the look-back period is limited to 36 or 60 months.

In 1996, Congress enacted a law that criminalized the transfer of assets to become eligible for Medicaid. The law was widely criticized in the press as the "Granny Goes to Jail Law." It was repealed in 1997 and replaced with a provision that makes it a crime to counsel or assist an individual in making asset transfers. Instead of Granny going to jail, her lawyer or financial planner goes; the penalty for violation is a fine of up to $25,000 and five years in prison. The irony is that the new 1997 law makes it a crime to discuss with clients matters that, in themselves, are perfectly legal.

sale of a terminally ill person's life insurance policy to a business firm that specializes in such transactions. These firms are generally referred to as viatical settlement companies. In 1993, the NAIC adopted a model act on viatical settlements, placing viatical settlement companies under the jurisdiction of the state insurance department. The model act requires viatical settlement companies to file a plan of operation with the state insurance department. It also requires disclosure to prospects of the alternatives to viatication and the tax consequences of the transaction.

The IRC provides that any part of the death benefit under a life insurance policy on a terminally or chronically ill insured that is sold or assigned to a viatical settlement provider will be treated as an amount paid by reason of the insured's death (i.e., as nontaxable income).

Buying Health Insurance

Sometimes, the decisions relating to health insurance coverage of the individual and his or her family are simple: when the employer provides a noncontributory plan, there is no decision to make concerning that coverage. Usually the employee's only concern is whether the program provided is adequate for the family's needs or if a supplement is needed. Sometimes, when the option is provided, the individual may have to choose between a traditional form of health insurance and membership in a health maintenance organization. Such decisions are generally a matter of personal preference.

In those cases in which the employee must pay part or all of a group plan, or where the insurance must be purchased individually, there are several considerations, all of which serve to complicate the decision.

First-Dollar Coverages

During recent years, the first-dollar insurance coverages have been increasingly condemned as an improper application of the insurance principle. In the case of health insurance, this criticism may not apply. Because group insurance plans can achieve economies for participants through managed care and by participating in a PPO network, the cost of health care acquired through an insurance plan is generally less expensive than when the same services are purchased by the individual consumer on a fee-for-service basis. For insurance obtained as a part of a large group, administrative fees are extremely modest and can be more than offset by the reduction in loss costs.

Taxes and Health Care Costs

Decisions regarding the purchase of first-dollar coverages are complicated to a certain extent by the federal tax code. As already noted, employer-paid premiums for employee health insurance are deductible as a business expense by the employer and are not taxable to the employee as income. The employee is not taxed on benefits received under such a program as specified reimbursement of medical expenses actually incurred.

For the individual, medical insurance premiums receive no special tax treatment. They are considered simply another medical expense that, combined with other medical costs, are deductible to the extent that the total exceeds 7.5 percent of the individual's adjusted gross income.

The Tax Reform Act of 1986 introduced a new tax deduction for medical expenses of the self-employed, allowing self-employed persons to deduct 25 percent of the cost of health insurance premiums from their gross income. Subsequent legislation increased this 25 percent to 50 percent by 2000, with scheduled increases raising the deduction to 100 percent in year 2007 and later years. Premiums for LTC insurance are now included in these deductible premiums. The deduction is not available to a self-employed person who is eligible to participate in a subsidized health plan maintained by his or her spouse's employer.

The deduction is not subject to the 7.5 percent adjusted gross income limitation on medical expenses. For years prior to 2007, the nondeductible portion of health insurance cost may be combined with other medical expenses and is deductible only to the extent that it and other medical expenses exceed 7.5 percent of adjusted gross income.

The Future of Health Insurance

The Failure of Past Efforts

In spite of these efforts, health care costs continue to rise, and the uninsured population continues to grow. (The number of uninsured is estimated to have increased from 32.6 million in 1988 to 44 million in 1999.) In addition, although the rate of growth has slowed, the cost of health care continues to increase in the face of the efforts of the federal government, insurers, and managed care consultants. Although it can be argued that the situation would be worse without past efforts, the attempts that have been made to address the problems of the system have failed to correct its deficiencies. No single party is totally to blame, and none are totally free from blame.

Both the fee-for-service system and managed care contain built-in incentives to practice bad medicine. Under the fee-for-service system, the incentive is to provide unneeded services. Under the managed care approach, there is an incentive to deny needed services. Insurance companies and employers continue to support managed care as the most effective approach to cost control, but increasingly they are standing alone. Although it is indisputable that the growth of managed care has had a positive effect on medical inflation, cost controls have come at a price.

The Attack on Managed Care

By 1999, the health care financing problem had become even more complex, as consumer dissatisfaction with the cost-saving features of managed care programs turned the focus of reformers to the quality of the health care being delivered.

Managed care, which was once heralded as the solution that promised affordable health insurance to most Americans, became the target of a consumer backlash.

Managed care came into being out of a desperate need to cut health-care costs. It was conceived as one answer to the increasing level of health care costs in the country. Measured against this goal, managed care has been reasonably successful in controlling utilization and associated costs, but the cost controls have been accompanied by changes in the traditional relationship between patients and providers. Physicians and hospitals have become disenchanted with the discounting arrangements of preferred provider organizations and other network organizations. Health care providers have complained about the interference of "outsiders" in medical decisions, such as the appropriate hospital stay for a particular illness or procedure. Arbitrary decisions by the claims personnel of insurance companies and third-party administrators have become the new crusade for consumer activists. The crusade was fueled by congressional hearings and daytime talk shows, where HMO patients recited horror stories about HMOs denying care to patients, resulting in serious injury or death. Newspapers and magazines attacked health maintenance organizations over the allegations of bonus payments to physicians for not treating patients and for blocking people from even seeing their doctors.

Patients' Bill of Rights Legislation

Eventually, the debate culminated in legislative proposals to address patients' rights, which were introduced in 1998. Congress failed to reach agreement on a patients' rights bill, and new versions were introduced in 1999 and 2000. Democrats and Republicans introduced different versions of the legislation. Both bills include provisions to provide better access to physicians, coverage for services outside the network in case of emergencies, increased information for patients, and improved appeal processes for patients who have complaints. Both versions also prohibit

"gag clauses in contracts with participating physicians, which prohibit physicians in managed care organizations from discussing costly options with patients. The major difference in the legislation was the provision in the Democrats' *Patient's Bill of Rights* to repeal a provision in ERISA that exempts employee benefit plans from tort liability. The repeal would make HMOs and other managed care plans subject to tort liability for medical malpractice. Republicans, who oppose lifting the ban on suits against HMOs, argue that to do so would only encourage managed care providers to practice defensive medicine. In June 2000, Senate Republicans moved toward compromise, passing a Patients' Bill of Rights bill that allows health plans to be sued for failure to comply with an external review decision or for a wrongful determination where the decision maker acts in bad faith. The importance of this concession may become moot. In 1995, the U.S. Supreme Court ruled that ERISA was not designed to replace general health care regulation and an increasing number of courts are deciding that patients can sue their HMOs for malpractice over decisions about treatment that results in harm to those patients.

A second major difference between the Democrat and Republican proposals is with respect to the groups to which they would apply. The Democrats' plan would apply to all employer-sponsored plans, covering about 168 million persons. The Republican plan would apply only to the single-employer, self-insured plans that are exempt from state regulation under ERISA, on the premise that state regulation protects the patients of other HMOs from the excesses of HMOs.[26]

While Congress has been debating the issue of patients' rights, the states have and are enacting legislation incorporating quality care protections such as those embodied in the congressional legislation. However, these state laws do not apply to the ERISA-exempt self-funded plans that have come to dominate employer-sponsored health plans.

[26]Most of the patients' rights proposals parallel recommendations contained in the 1997 report of the President's Advisory Commission on Consumer Protection and Quality in the Health Care Industry.

Tidbits, Vignettes, and Conundrums 16.2

Physicians Who Are Willing to Lie to Help Patients Obtain Benefits

According to an article published in the October 25, 1999 issue of the *Archives of Internal Medicine,* many doctors are willing to lie to insurance companies to help patients get care, especially life-saving or emergency care. A team of researchers surveyed 169 randomly selected internists, who were each given six hypothetical cases in which patients with described illnesses or maladies would not be eligible for treatment under their insurance, but in which coverage would apply if the physician misrepresented the facts to the insurer. The hypothetical cases included a woman with chest pain whose insurance would authorize coronary bypass surgery only if the doctor stated that her condition was worsening, a dy-

ing cancer patient who would benefit from intravenous pain medication and nutrition, a depressed patient at risk for suicide who is willing to be admitted to a psychiatric hospital, and a patient who feels life would be better if she had plastic surgery on her nose. In their responses to the hypothetical cases, nearly 60 percent of the doctors stated that they would misrepresent the facts to the insurer to help the patient obtain bypass surgery, about half would lie to obtain intravenous pain medication for the dying patient, and a third would lie to obtain psychiatric help for the depressed patient. (Less than 3 percent would lie to the insurer for the nose job.) About a fourth of the doctors state that they would not lie in any of the cases.

The current focus by the federal government on patients' rights is ironic in light of the historical origins of the practices that are now considered to be violations of the traditional relationship between doctor and patient. It was the federal government, in its administration of the Medicare system, that invented utilization review and diagnostic-related groups. The growth of health maintenance organizations as an alternative to the fee-for-service system was significantly promoted by a federal agenda, embodied in the Health Maintenance Act of 1973.

Proposals for National Health Insurance

Some critics of our current system point out that the one thing the United States lacks that every other industrialized country has is some form of national health insurance. These critics argue that the solution to the health care crisis in this country is a national health insurance program, coupled with more emphasis on coordinated

planning of health services. Whether the United States is likely to have a national health insurance plan depends in part on how one defines national health insurance. Although many approaches have been suggested, most fall into three broad categories.

Single-Payer Plan

One approach to a national health insurance scheme is a government-run and -financed health insurance similar to Medicare, but applicable to the entire population. Under this approach, a universal system of comprehensive health insurance would be funded by taxes and administered by a federal agency. It would eliminate private health insurance and substitute a federal insurance system with benefits for hospital, dental, optometric, home, and nursing care. The federal agency would establish a national budget for health care and set the fees paid to providers. One clear advantage of this approach is that it would provide universal coverage. Proponents also argue that it would be more efficient than the current privately financed system. Critics, on the other hand, argue that this approach would involve the most dramatic change from the current system and would result in a massive restructuring of the way health care is delivered, giving excessive control to a government agency. They believe this would ultimately reduce the quality of care, since the current price-based system of allocating health care would be replaced by another form of rationing. Finally, they argue that this dramatic change is not necessary to solve problems that affect only a few and point to the moderating rate of increase in private plans as evidence that the current system can be fixed.

Employer-Mandated Health Insurance

A second group of proposals for reforming health care would build on the current employment-based system. In its basic form, employers would be required to provide health care to their employees or to pay a payroll tax that would help fund benefits provided by a government program. This is often referred to as the *play-or-pay approach*. Persons who did not receive insurance from their employer may be required to purchase insurance either individually or from the government program.

Individual Mandates

This approach places the burden for purchasing health insurance on the individual. All individuals would be required to purchase insurance for themselves and their dependents. They would be permitted to arrange this through their employment, through other group plans, or through individual insurance. Those that could not afford health insurance would be eligible for tax credits to subsidize the cost. Typically, this plan would also eliminate the current tax advantage of employer-provided plans, up to a certain level. The proposed change in the tax treatment of employer-provided health insurance is intended to increase employee awareness and concern about price and encourage price competition across plans.

The Future

There are many people in the United States who believe that a comprehensive national health insurance program for all Americans is an idea whose time has come. Regardless of whether some form of national health insurance is eventually adopted, however, one point is clear: a fundamental change in our health-care system is inevitable. The pressure of health-care costs, both for the individual and for society as a whole, will force us to take steps to deal with the problem.

The challenge in designing a health care system to meet the nation's future needs is to somehow reconcile two competing objectives. Ideally, we would have a system that provides quality health care to everyone who needs it, while at the same time containing costs at a level society can afford. Unfortunately, there is no simple solution to this problem, and the health-care debate will continue into the future.

Important Concepts to Remember

fee-for-service benefits
service benefit contract
reimbursement contract
usual, customary, and reasonable
   (UCR) contract
surgical-expense contract
benefit schedule
physician's expense insurance

major medical policy
coinsurance
corridor deductible
comprehensive major medical
health maintenance organization
   (HMO)
capitation
primary care physician

gate keeper
preferred provider organization
   (PPO)
point-of-service (POS) plan
cost containment
coordination of benefits provision
dental expense insurance
medical savings accounts

Medicaid	mandated benefits	employer-mandated health
first-dollar coverage	Consolidated Omnibus Budget	insurance
single-payer plan	Reconciliation Act (COBRA)	individual mandates
insurance-encouraged utilization	Health Insurance Portability and	physician hospital organization
defensive medicine	Accountability Act (HIPAA)	(PHO)
cost shifting	small-group reform	national health insurance

Questions for Review

1. Identify the major problems associated with health care listed in the chapter. What measures have been taken in the past to address these problems?

2. Compare and contrast the typical provisions and benefits of a commercial hospitalization policy with a Blue Cross contract, and a commercial surgical expense contract with a Blue Shield contract.

3. Explain what is meant by an ERISA-exempt health insurance plan. Why are these plans popular with employers?

4. Briefly describe the distinguishing characteristics of a comprehensive major medical policy.

5. Give reasons for the coinsurance feature and the deductible in the major medical policy. Are both really necessary?

6. Briefly describe the distinguishing characteristics of a health maintenance organization (HMO). How does an HMO differ from the other insurers operating in the health insurance field?

7. To what do you attribute the rapid increase in the number of HMOs throughout the country?

8. In what ways does the operation of the private insurance mechanism complicate the problem of health care access?

9. To what extent can the provisions of the tax code influence the decision to insure or retain the health care exposure? Your answer should include a discussion of the provisions of the code with respect to

   a. Employer-paid medical expense insurance

   b. Premiums paid by the individual for medical expense insurance

   c. Costs incurred directly by the individual for health care

10. Describe generally, the coverage provided by Part A and Part B of the traditional Medicare program and the options for Medicare beneficiaries under Medicare Part C (Medicare+ Choice).

Questions for Discussion

1. Movie audiences cheered when the heroine in the movie *As Good as It Gets* referred to her HMO with an expletive. Do you agree or disagree with the sentiment expressed by the audiences? Why?

2. Briefly explain the basic features of each of the three approaches that have been sug-

gested for a national health insurance plan. Which do you prefer, and why?

3. In a 1999 survey, a significant percentage of physicians stated that they would misrepresent a patient's symptoms to an insurer if the misstatement would result in payment for treatment that would otherwise be denied. In

your opinion, is this a positive or a negative phenomenon?

4. State mandates are intended to spread the cost of covering certain treatments such as infertility treatments. Do you agree or disagree with the exemption of ERISA plans from these mandates?

5. "Much of the increase in the cost of medical care can be attributed to unnecessary and undesirable overutilization of health services, often prompted by the existence of insurance." Do you agree or disagree? What policy provisions have been designed to control overutilization of health services?

Suggestions for Additional Reading

Beam, Burton T., Jr., and John J. McFadden. *Employee Benefits*, 4th ed. Brookfield, WI: Dearborn Financial Publishing, 1996.

Black, Kenneth, Jr., and Harold D. Skipper, Jr. *Life Insurance*, 13th ed., Englewood Cliffs, NJ: Prentice Hall, 2000. Chapters 19, 20.

Enthoven, Alain C. "Consumer Centered vs. Job Centered Health Insurance." *Harvard Business Review* (Jan.–Feb. 1979).

Gorham, William. *Medical Care Prices: A Report to the President.* Washington, DC: U.S. Department of Health, Education, and Welfare (Feb. 1967).

Health Insurance Association of America. *Group Life and Health Insurance Parts A and B,* 5th ed. Washington, DC: Health Insurance Association of America, 1994.

———. *Group Life and Health Insurance Part C,* 4th ed. Washington, DC: Health Insurance Association of America, 1994.

Richardson, Elliott L. *A White Paper: Toward a Comprehensive Health Policy for the 1970s.* Washington, DC: U.S. Department of Health, Education, and Welfare (May 1971).

Rosenbloom, Jerry S. (ed.). *The Handbook of Employee Benefits: Design, Funding and Administration,* 4th ed. Homewood, IL: Richard D. Irwin, 1996.

Websites to Explore

American Association of Health Plans: http://www.aahp.org

American Association of Managed Care Providers: http://www.aapso.com/

Association of Health Insurance Advisors: http://www.ahia.net/

Blue Cross/Blue Shield Association: http://www.bluecares.com/

Consumer Insurance Guide: http://www.insure.com/health

Health Care Financing Administration: http://www.hcfa.gov/

Health Insurance Association of America: http://www.hiaa.org

Insurance News Network: http://www.insure.com/

International Association of Health Funds: http://www.fhf.com/

Managed Care Magazine: http://www.managedcaremag.com/

Money Magazine: http://www.pathfinder.com/money/depts/insurance/

National Senior Citizens Law Center: http://www.nsclc.org/

Quicken InsureMarket: http://www.insuremarket.com/

CHAPTER 17

Employee Benefits and Business Uses of Life and Health Insurance

And they call these "fringes."
—Will Rogers

CHAPTER OBJECTIVES

When you have finished this chapter, you should be able to

- Identify the major classes of employee benefits that are provided by employers to their employees, and describe the tax treatment of these benefits

- Explain the way in which employer contributions to a qualified pension plan are treated under federal tax laws and the way in which this treatment benefits workers covered under such plans

- Identify and explain the difference between the defined contribution and defined benefit approaches in qualified retirement plans

- Explain the statutory requirements that must be met by qualified retirement programs

- Identify and explain the characteristics of the funding alternatives available to employers with respect to qualified retirement plans

- Explain the nature of the business-continuation exposure facing business owners and describe the measures that may be used to address this exposure

- Explain the nature of the key-person exposure facing a business organization and describe the measures that may be used to address this exposure

- Explain the purpose and operation of nonqualified deferred-compensation programs and describe the characteristics that distinguish them from qualified programs

Businesses use life and health insurance for two general purposes. First, many businesses provide life insurance, health insurance, and retirement benefits to employees as an employee benefit. In addition to their use in employee benefits, organizations may use life and health insurance arrangements to protect against risks they themselves face. These may involve loss to the business from death or disability of a key employee. Businesses may also use life insurance to arrange the continuation of the business following the death of the owner. We begin our discussion with the use of insurance as an employee benefit.

Employee Benefits Generally

There is no uniform definition of what constitutes employee benefits. The U.S. Chamber of Commerce defines employee benefits broadly, to include virtually any benefit provided to employees by an employer other than wages and salary for work performed. This definition includes the employer's share of the cost for mandated social insurance programs (i.e., Social Security, workers compensation, and unemployment compensation). It also includes such things as tuition assistance, childcare assistance programs, vacation benefits, holidays, paid rest periods, subsidized parking, and similar nonwage compensation. Finally, the broad definition includes group life and health insurance and qualified retirement plans, such as pensions. Using this definition, it is estimated that U.S. employers spend over 40 percent of payroll on employee benefits. Table 17.1 indicates the cost of employee benefits under the broad definition.

For our purposes, a more limited definition of employee benefits is of interest: those benefits offered voluntarily by the employer and confined to benefits that address the employees' personal risks of premature death, disability, superannuation, and health care. Even under this more limited definition, employee benefits represent a significant part of the compensation of many

Table 17.1   Cost of Employee Benefits

Mandated social insurance programs	8.8%
Retirement and savings	6.3%
Life insurance and death benefits	0.4%
Health care benefits	9.6%
Paid rest periods, breaks	3.7%
Paid vacations, holidays, sick leave	10.2%
Miscellaneous benefits	2.3%
Total	41.3%

Source: Chamber of Commerce of the United States, Employee Benefits, 1997.

employees. The nature and scope of the employee benefit package varies by the size of the employer. As indicated in Table 17.2, large employers tend to have more extensive benefit packages than do small employers.

Group Life and Health Insurance

Group life and group health insurance are widely used as part of the compensation package for workers. In part, the growth of group life and health has been encouraged by collective bargaining and the demands of unions. A more important factor has been the favorable tax treatment of these benefits. As already noted, wages are taxable income to the employee, while most employer-provided insurance benefits are not. In addition, most life and health insurance benefits are provided under group contracts, which tend to be less expensive than individual insurance. There are several reasons for this, including lower underwriting expenses and administrative costs, as well as reduced costs from adverse selection.

When group underwriting is used, the flow of insureds through the group maintains a stable average age as older employees retire, die, or leave the firm and younger workers take their place. The major problem of the insurance company is that of holding adverse selection to a minimum, and many of the features of group life and health insurance derive from this requirement. In group

Table 17.2 Percent of Full-Time Employees Offered Employee Benefits

Benefit	Small Establishments	Medium & Large Establishments
Short-term disability	29%	53%
Long-term disability	22%	42%
Health care benefits	64%	77%
Dental care	31%	57%
Life insurance	62%	87%
Retirement plans	46%	80%
Retirement deferrals with matching funds	24%	45%
Retirement deferrals without matching	4%	9%

Source: U.S. Bureau of Labor Statistics Annual Survey.

life insurance, for example, when the premium is paid entirely by the employer, 100 percent of the eligible employees must be included. When the plan is contributory, with the premium paid jointly by the employer and employees, a minimum of 75 percent of the eligible employees must participate. Also, the amount of insurance on each participant must be determined in a way that precludes individual selection. Usually, the amount of insurance is a flat amount for all employees, or is determined as a percentage or multiple of the individual's salary. These safeguards are required in group underwriting to prevent and minimize adverse selection.

Group Life Insurance as an Employee Benefit

Group life insurance is one of the most common employee benefits. Although the majority of this life insurance is term, some employers also provide other types of life insurance.

Group Term Life Insurance

The most common life insurance benefit offered to employees is group term life insurance. Under the *Internal Revenue Code* (IRC) Section 79, the employer-paid premium on $50,000 of group term life insurance is deductible by the employer

as a business expense, but is not taxable to the employee as income. The coverage must be provided on a nondiscriminatory basis. This requirement can be satisfied if the amount of insurance bears a uniform relationship to total compensation of the persons covered. A formula that provides life insurance equal to, say, two times the individual's annual salary, is nondiscriminatory, even though it produces a higher amount of life insurance for more highly compensated individuals.[1] Term life insurance in excess of $50,000 is taxable to the employee as income, based on an imputed cost contained in IRS regulations.

Other Employer-Sponsored Life Insurance

In addition to group term life insurance, some employers also sponsor various forms of permanent life insurance.

Group Ordinary Life Insurance Group ordinary life insurance is group insurance with an accumulating cash value. Usually, the employer pays and takes a tax deduction for that part of the premium that represents the cost of group term insurance. The employee pays the remainder of the premium, which represents the cash value element of the policy. If the employer pays the entire

[1]If a group term insurance plan discriminates in favor of key employees, the key employees are taxed on the value of the benefits, but the benefits remain tax exempt to other workers.

premium, the employee is taxed on the nonterm portion of the premium.

Group Universal Life Group universal life is similar in most respects to individual universal life, and differs primarily in the same ways that other forms of group life differ from individual contracts. Coverage is usually written without evidence of insurability, and is usually subject to lower administrative costs than individually written universal life. There is no tax advantage in employer funding, and employees generally pay the premiums.

Postretirement Life Insurance Benefits Some employers sponsor programs that provide life insurance to employees after retirement. Under one approach, workers themselves purchase paid-up units of single premium life insurance during their working years. Under a second approach, called *retired lives reserve,* the employer makes contributions to a trust fund during the employee's working years to fund the cost of term insurance after the worker retires.

Group Health Benefits

The prevalence of group health insurance as an employee benefit was noted in Chapter 16. Health care benefits are offered in many varieties, and many employers offer employees a choice from among several options. These different plans may vary significantly in terms of the proportion of costs the employee must bear, maximum limits of coverage, and types of expenses included. They are also likely to impose different limitations on the ability of the employee to choose who delivers the health care.

Most group health insurance coverage is contributory. That is, the employee is required to contribute to the cost of the coverage. For small businesses, 52 percent of employees contribute to the cost of single coverage, and 75 percent contribute to the cost of family coverage. In medium

and large firms, 69 percent of employees contribute to the cost of single coverage, and 80 percent contribute to the cost of family coverage.

Funding Issues

The options available to an employer for financing life and health benefits for employees range from a fully insured plan to a fully self-funded plan, with many variations in between. Employers elect to self-fund their employee benefits for the reasons discussed in Chapter 5, because there are economies in self-funding. Self-funding of life and disability insurance tends to be limited to the very largest employers. Self-funding of employee health benefits, in contrast, is widespread.

Historically, only very large employers self-insured their medical expense plans, because of the potential severity of loss. In the past two decades, it has become increasingly common for smaller employers to engage in some degree of self-funding, while capping their exposure through the use of stop-loss insurance. *Specific stop-loss insurance* caps the amount of claims for one individual. When the claims of one employee or dependent exceed the stop-loss limit, the insurer covers any excess. With *aggregate stop-loss insurance,* the employer agrees to pay all claims up to an agreed on limit for the year, and the insurer pays for all the claims beyond the limit. In a sense, the stop-loss limit acts as an annual deductible, and the policy caps the employer's loss exposure for the year. In a given program, stop-loss coverage may be triggered if an individual's covered expenses exceed $20,000, or if the group's covered expenses exceed 120 percent of expected aggregate costs. The lower the individual and aggregate thresholds, the more risk that is actually borne by the stop-loss insurer rather than by the self-insured employer or group. At some level, there is a question of whether the employer is actually buying health insurance and not merely protection from financial catastrophe. At some point, the employer is not really "self-insured" and the ERISA exemption from state laws may be inappropriate. The NAIC has developed a *Model Stop Loss Insurance Act*, to standardize the definitions of health insurance and self-insurance in reasonable ways.

As alternatives to self-funding in conjunction with stop-loss insurance, employee benefits may also be insured under a *retrospective rating plan* or under a *minimum premium plan* (MPP). A retrospective rating program is a cost-plus contract under which the final premium depends on the claims under the program, but subject to a maximum and a minimum. Under a minimum premium plan, the employer retains liability for small claims and pays these directly. The insurance company provides coverage only for large claims in excess of stated levels. Because most states levy premium taxes only on premiums actually received by the insurer, the MPP avoids premium taxes on a significant part of the benefit costs, those paid directly by the employer.

Third-Party Administrators

Most employers that self-fund their medical expense benefits use the services of a third-party administrator (TPA). The TPA makes benefit determinations, pays benefits, assists in plan design, and otherwise administers the plan. Where the employer arranges stop-loss insurance, it is common for the stop-loss insurer to serve as the administrator. If the plan is fully self-funded, the contract between the insurer and employer is often called an *administrative-services-only* (ASO) agreement, in recognition of the fact that no insurance is being provided. With the growth of managed care plans, one motivation for the use of TPAs is to gain access to their networks of providers.

Cafeteria Employee Benefit Plans

A *cafeteria plan* is an employee benefit plan that meets the design conditions outlined in Section 125 of the IRC, and in which employees have the right to choose from a range of benefits. Cafeteria plans have become popular because they permit employees to select the benefits that are most appropriate to their needs.

The normal approach in a cafeteria plan is for the employer to grant employees credits that may be used to "buy" benefits. Credits can be based on salary, years of service, or a combination of factors, but cannot discriminate in favor of key employees.[2] The employee then selects benefits most appropriate to his or her needs from the choices offered. The choices can include most nontaxable benefits, such as group term life insurance, health insurance, dependent care, or participation in a group legal service plan. The employer may also permit the employee to take some or all of the credit as cash compensation (but not as taxable benefits). Section 401(k) cash or deferred profit-sharing or stock-bonus plans can be included in the list of choices. Other deferred compensation plans (such as pensions) and long-term care insurance must be provided separately from the cafeteria plan.

In some cases, flexible benefits are funded by a salary reduction; employees can reduce their salaries by a certain amount and use the money tax free to pay for certain benefits. Such arrangements, while technically cafeteria plans, are called *flexible spending accounts*.

Pensions

Although private pension plans have existed in the United States since the late 1800s, their greatest growth has taken place since World War II. In 1940, about 4 million people—less than 20 percent of all employees in government and industry—were covered by private pensions. By 2000, over 100 million persons, including about one-

---

[2] Key employees are taxed on otherwise nontaxable benefits in any year for which the qualified benefits for key employees exceed 25 percent of such benefits for all employees under the plan.

half of all workers in private business and three-fourths of all government workers, were enrolled in retirement programs other than Social Security. Pension plans are established by employers, and sometimes jointly by unions and employers, to provide individual workers with a retirement income that will supplement Social Security retirement benefits. The plan may be set up for the employees of a particular firm, or it may be a "multi-employer" plan, serving workers from several unrelated firms.

Qualified Retirement Plans

A "qualified" retirement plan is one that conforms to the requirements of the *Internal Revenue Code (I.R.C.)*, which defines the conditions that must be met for favorable tax treatment. When these conditions are met, employer contributions to the plan are a tax-deductible expense for the employer when they are made, and the employee is not taxed on the employer's contributions or the investment income until benefits are actually received (usually at retirement).

Contributory and Noncontributory Plans

Retirement plans may be noncontributory, in which case the entire cost of the pensions is borne by the employer, or they may be contributory, with employees making contributions in addition to those of the employer. Employee contributions may be voluntary, or they may be required for participation. When employees contribute their own funds to a plan, the plan is sometimes called a *thrift* or *savings plan*. While employee contributions are not usually deductible by the employees, the investment income on such contributions is exempt from federal taxes until distributed, which makes savings plans a form of tax-favored deferred compensation.[3]

---

[3]Section 401(k) plans, Simple plans, and Section 403(b) plans, discussed later in the chapter, are exceptions to the rule that employee contributions are not deductible.

Federal Regulation of Private Retirement Plans

Any discussion of private pension plans in the United States today must begin with the *Employee Retirement Income Security Act of 1974* (ERISA), the most sweeping overhaul of private pensions in the history of the country. The act was passed in response to a growing concern over the soundness and equity of the pension system. Although few pension plans had actually failed, there were many instances in which workers lost the benefits they had been counting on for retirement. Funding provisions of many plans were unsound and the vesting requirements, under which an employee's right to the pension was established, were often severe.

The goal of ERISA was to increase the rate of national participation in pension plans, prevent loss of benefits by persons who terminate employment before retirement, establish minimum standards for funding and vesting, and provide for the overall control of pension plans. ERISA prescribes which employees must be included in a plan, establishes minimum vesting requirements, specifies the amounts that may be contributed, and sets minimum funding requirements. The act also requires extensive reporting and disclosure information about pension and welfare programs to the Secretary of Labor, to the Internal Revenue Service, and to those covered by the plan and their beneficiaries.

Pension plans are also subject to various provisions of the I.R.C., which defines the requirements for qualifications and establishes the maximum allowable contributions. The contribution limits have been changed over the years (generally upward). Most recently, the Economic Growth and Tax Relief Reconciliation Act of 2001 (EGTRRA-2001) significantly liberalized the contribution limits for most plans and scheduled increases over the next several years.

Finally, retirement plans are subject to laws relating to employment practices. The U.S. Supreme Court has ruled that a plan may not violate the equal employment provisions of the Civil Rights Act of 1964. In particular, a retirement plan cannot pay women lower retirement benefits and cannot require women to make higher contributions to pension plans because of their average longer life expectancy. In a 1978 case,[4] the court ruled that when pension benefits to men and women are equal, the employer cannot require higher contributions to the plan by women than by men. In another case, the Court ruled that when men and women make equal contributions to a plan (or when equal contributions are made by the employer on their behalf), women cannot receive a smaller monthly benefit than men, either directly from the plan or under an annuity purchased from an insurer by the employer.[5]

Qualification Requirements

To meet the *I.R.C.* requirements for qualification, a retirement plan must be designed for the exclusive benefit of employees and their beneficiaries, must be in writing and communicated to the employees, and must meet one of several vesting schedules. Contributions and benefit formulas cannot be designed to discriminate in favor of officers, stockholders, or highly compensated employees, and the plan must provide either for definite contributions by the employer or a definite benefit to the worker at the time of retirement. (Profit-sharing plans are an exception in which the contributions vary with the profits of the firm.) Life insurance benefits may be included in the plan only on an incidental basis.[6] Finally, top-heavy plans—plans that provide a disproportionate share of their benefits to owners or other highly paid executives—are subject to special requirements designed to guarantee that they provide minimum benefits or contributions for rank and file workers.[7]

Vesting Requirements

The term *vesting* refers to the right of a covered employee to retain a claim to the benefits accrued, even though his or her employment terminates before retirement. Under current law, qualified retirement plans are generally subject to the following vesting requirements.

1. No vesting for three years, with 100 percent vesting after three years (called *cliff vesting*).

2. After two years of service, 20 percent vesting, with 20 percent per year thereafter, so that 100 percent vesting exists after six years of service.

These vesting schedules are minimum requirements, and an employer may provide vesting at a more rapid rate. In a contributory plan, employees have a nonforfeitable right to their contributions, meaning that they are always 100 percent vested.

Types of Qualified Plans

The *I.R.C.* recognizes several types of qualified plans, including corporate plans, plans for self-employed persons and their employees and several "simplified" plans for small employers. In addition to the various plans offered by employers, federal tax law also provides tax-sheltered treatment to *individual retirement accounts* (IRAs), under which individuals may accumulate funds for retirement.

---

[4]*City of Los Angeles Department of Water and Power v. Manhart* (435 U.S. 702).

[5]*Norris v. Arizona Governing Committee for Tax Deferred Annuity and Deferred Compensation Plans.* This 1983 ruling on defined contribution plans was limited to future retirees. A later case (*TIAA v. SPIRT*, 1984) reached the same conclusion and required retroactive correction.

[6]Life insurance is considered incidental if the cost of the life insurance is less than 50 percent of the employer contribution or does not exceed 100 times the expected monthly retirement benefit.

[7]Generally, a plan is top-heavy if 60% or more of the account balances or accrued benefits are allocated to a group of participants known as the *key employees*. A key employee is defined as any plan participant employee who, during the preceding plan year was (i) an officer earning over $130,000, (ii) a five-percent owner, or (iii) a one-percent owner earning over $150,000.

IRAs are also used as funding vehicles for several types of simplified employer-sponsored qualified plans under which employers make contributions to an IRA plan on behalf of their employees. Finally, IRAs provide a basis for portable pensions. Regulations permit persons who terminate employment and receive a lump-sum distribution from a qualified plan to "roll over" the distribution into an IRA. This defers taxation until the proceeds are withdrawn from the IRA at a later date.

Defined Contribution Pension Plan *401 K*

A defined contribution plan (also called *money purchase plans*), works exactly as its name implies. The employer's contribution to the plan is set as a percentage of compensation, such as, for example, 5 percent or 10 percent of the employee's wages. The employee's retirement benefit is simply the amount that the contributions and investment earnings on those contributions will provide at retirement age.

The employer's maximum annual contribution on behalf of any employee is limited to 25 percent of the individual's earnings for the year, subject to a dollar maximum, which is indexed for inflation. The dollar maximum was $40,000 in 2002 and is indexed for inflation in increments of $1000. The compensation to which the contribution percentage applies is subject to a dollar maximum that is indexed for inflation in increments of $5000. In 2002, the dollar limit on income to which the contribution percentage could be applied was $200,000.[8] This means that a plan that provides an employer contribution equal to 10 percent of compensation would provide a $10,000 contribution for a person earning $100,000, but only $20,000 for a person earning $250,000.

Prior to EGTRRA-2001, Section 415 of the *IRC* imposed a limit on the amount of *annual additions*

to an individual's account during the year that was the same as the limit on employer deductions (i.e., the dollar maximum or 25% of compensation). Effective for years after 2001, EGTRRA-2001 increases the limit on annual additions to an individual's account to the current dollar maximum (i.e., $40,000 in 2002) or 100% of compensation.

Defined Benefit Pension Plan

Under a defined benefit pension plan, the employer promises to pay the employee a specific income at retirement. The benefit the employee will receive at retirement is specified in a benefit formula, and the employer's contribution is the amount that will be required, together with the investment earnings on the contributions, to provide the specified benefit and pay the expenses of the plan.[9] Benefit formulas for defined benefit plans are usually based on the employee's salary, the benefit accrual rate, and the employee's years of service. Under *final average salary plans*, the benefit depends on the salary earned in the later years of employment. For example, a plan may promise a monthly benefit equal to 1 percent of the average monthly salary during the last three years of employment for each year worked. An employee who worked for the employer for 40 years would receive a benefit equal to 40 percent of the final three-year average salary. Other plans are *career average salary plans*, and the benefit is a function of the salary earned in all years of employment

The maximum deductible contribution to a defined-benefit plan is expressed in terms of the maximum benefit that the contribution may provide. The maximum retirement benefit that may be provided by a defined-benefit plan is 100 percent of the employee's earnings in his 3 consecu-

---

[8]Prior to the changes enacted in EGTRRA-2001, the dollar maximum was $35,000 and was indexed in increments of $5000. The dollar limit on compensation to which the percentage limit applied was $170,000 and was indexed for inflation in increments of $10,000.

[9]Some plans use a *target benefit plan*, which is a cross between a defined benefit and a defined contribution plan. The annual contribution is the amount needed each year to accumulate (at an assumed rate of interest) a fund sufficient to pay a defined retirement benefit (the *target benefit*) at retirement age.

tive years of highest earnings, subject to an inflation-adjusted dollar maximum. In 2002, the maximum annual benefit permitted under a defined benefit plan was $160,000, with future adjustments for inflation in increments of $5000. This maximum benefit is the amount that may be paid to participants age 62 to 65. If benefits are paid earlier the maximum is reduced and if later it is increased.

Qualified Profit-Sharing Plans

A qualified profit-sharing plan is a form of defined contribution plan, since ultimate benefits depend on the amount contributed by the employer. A major distinction between a qualified profit-sharing plan and a defined contribution pension is that the contribution under a profit-sharing plan need not be fixed; employers may vary the contribution from year to year (theoretically, according to profits). Although a profit-sharing plan does not require annual contributions, the IRS does require that recurring and substantial contributions be made (generally interpreted to mean that a contribution should be made at least once every three years). In addition, while a profit-sharing plan need not contain a formula for determining the annual contributions, it must provide a formula for allocating the contributions that are made among employees on a nondiscriminatory basis. The most common approach is to allocate contributions according to the ratio of each employee's earnings to the earnings of the group.

Historically, the contributions limit for profit-sharing plans was 15 percent of employee compensation. Effective for tax years beginning 2002, the allowable deduction is increased to 25 percent of the participant's compensation.

Employee Stock Ownership Plan

An employee stock ownership plan (ESOP) is a qualified stock bonus plan closely related to the qualified profit-sharing plan. The principal difference is that under an ESOP instead of giving the employees a part of the profits of the firm, the employer gives them part of the firm itself, in the form of stock in the corporation. Although contributions to an ESOP may be made in cash or in stock, the accumulation in the employees' portfolio is based on the value of the employer's stock. Because an ESOP is basically a type of profit-sharing plan, it is subject to the same limits as those outlined above for profit-sharing plans.

Keogh Plans

Keogh plans are qualified retirement plans for self-employed persons and their employees. Self-employed persons are permitted to make tax-deductible contributions to a retirement plan, provided the plan includes coverage for all other eligible employees on a nondiscriminatory basis. A Keogh plan may be established as a defined benefit plan, a money purchase plan, or a profit-sharing plan, subject to essentially the same limitations, deductions, and benefits that apply to corporate pension or profit-sharing plans. A special definition of *earned income* is used to make contributions by a self-employed person correspond to those for a common-law employee. First, the self-employed business owner's net earnings must be reduced by the income tax deduction for one-half of the owner's self-employment (FICA) tax. In addition, the contribution percentage applies to the owner's net income *excluding* the contribution itself. For example, if a partnership establishes a 25 percent money purchase Keogh plan, and a partner earned $100,000, the deductible contribution on his or her behalf would be $20,000 (25 percent of earned income of $80,000), not $25,000.[10] With this adjustment, earned income for a self-

---

[10]For a common-law employee, the employer's contribution to a qualified retirement plan is added to earned income, creating a maximum for taxable income and nontaxable deferred income equal to 125 percent of earned income. This means that 80 percent of the total compensation is taxable and 20 percent is a nontaxable deferral. A self-employed person qualifies for the 2002 maximum contribution of $40,000 if he or she has $200,000 in earned income [25 percent of ($200,000—$40,000)].

employed person corresponds to a common-law employee's compensation. This special definition of earned income also applies to the contributions to self-employed persons under other non-corporate plans.

Section 401(k) Plans

Section 401(k) plans are a special type of profit sharing or stock bonus plan that permits employees to make contributions to the plan on a pre-tax basis. Employees elect to contribute a part of their income into the 401(k) plan and instruct their employer to reduce their wages and contribute the reduction to the plan. The *I.R.C.* provides that amounts an employee elects to defer under Section 401(k) are treated as contributions by the employer rather than by the employee. The effect is that the plan is a tax-deductible savings account for employees.

EGTRRA-2000 set the dollar limit on employee's elective deferrals to a 401(k) plan at $11,000 for 2002, with scheduled increases of $1000 annually through 2006, when the elective deferral limit will be $15,000. Thereafter, the limit will be indexed for inflation in $500 increments. In addition, for participants who are age 50 and older, EGTRRA-2001 authorizes additional *catch-up* deferrals. Beginning in 2002, the annual limit on catch up contributions is $1,000. This limit will increase in $1,000 increments until it reaches $5,000 in 2006, after which it will be indexed for inflation in increments of $500.

The employer may make matching contributions to a 401(k) plan and can also make contributions (other than matching contributions) without giving the employee the choice to take cash instead. The maximum employer contribution is 25 percent of employee compensation.[11]

Simplified Employee Pension (SEP) Plans

A *simplified employee pension* (SEP) permits employers to provide retirement benefits under a less complex arrangement than a qualified pension plan. Under a SEP, the employer contributes to a traditional IRA (individual retirement account or individual retirement annuity) that is owned and controlled by the employee. The employer makes contributions to the financial institution where the IRA is maintained. The maximum employer contribution to a SEP is 15 percent of employee compensation (up to the $200,000 limit, or $30,000). Employee contributions are not allowed and employer contributions are immediately vested.[12]

Section 403(b) Plans for Employees of Nonprofit Organizations

The employees of certain non-profit organizations (referred to in the *I.R.C* as Section 501(c)(3) organizations) are permitted to make before-tax contributions to tax-sheltered annuities under what are called 403(b) plans. As in 401(k) plans, the employee makes an agreement with the employer to reduce his or her salary by an amount equal to the contribution to the retirement plan. The contribution limits for 403(b) plans is the same as that for 401(k) plans, including the over-age 50 catch-up contribution limits.[13]

---

[11]Elective deferrals by participants are not considered part of the employer's contribution, which means that the 25 percent limit applies only to the employer's matching or nonelective contributions to the plan. The maximum annual addition to the plan is the lesser of the employer's 25 percent of employee compensation plus employee deferrals or the 2002 $40,000 dollar maximum indexed for inflation.

[12]Prior to 1997, SEPs could be established on a salary-reduction basis (much like a 401(k) plan) in which case the plan was referred to as an SARSEP. New SARSEPs have not been permitted since 1997 but the plans in existence before 1997 may continue to operate and can add new employees. The contribution limit to SARSEPs is the same as for a 401(k) plan and is scheduled to increase according to the same schedule, along with the catch-up deferrals for persons over age 50.

[13]Prior to EGTRRA-2001, a 403(b) plan participant's contributions for a year was limited by an *exclusion allowance*, which was 20% of the participant's compensation for the year, multiplied by the participant's years of service, less tax-excludable contributions in prior years to qualified plans maintained by the same employer. EGTRRA-2001 eliminated the exclusion allowance beginning in 2002.

SIMPLE Plans

The Small Business Job Protection Act of 1996 (SBJPA) introduced a new type of retirement plan known as a *Savings Incentive Match Plan for Employees* (SIMPLE). Eligibility is limited to employers with 100 or fewer employees that do not maintain any other type of employee retirement plan. The key feature of a SIMPLE plan is its exemption from many of the complicated rules applicable to other qualified plans, such as the top-heavy rules and some of the more complex nondiscrimination rules. Subject to certain exceptions, all employees with two years earnings of at least $5000 in each year and compensation of at least $5000 for the current year must be eligible to participate. The employer can choose to be less restrictive. Eligible employees make annual voluntary salary deferral contributions up to a statutory dollar maximum, regardless of their compensation level. The employer must either match employee contributions up to 3 percent of annual compensation or make nonelective contributions for all eligible employees of 2 percent of compensation. EGTRRA-2001 increased salary deferral maximum for SIMPLE plans from $6,500 in 2001 to $7,000 in 2002, with phased increases to $10,000 in 2005. After 2005, the limit adjusts for inflation in $500 increments. As in the case of 401(k) and 403(b) plans, individuals age 50 or older will be permitted to make additional catch-up contributions beginning in 2002. The catch-up contribution will be phased in gradually and will ultimately be $2,500 by 2006. After 2006, the $2,500 catch-up contribution will be indexed to inflation in $500 increments.

Nonrefundable Tax Credit for Employee Contributions

EGTRRA-2001 introduces an entirely new feature with respect to qualified retirement plans—a tax credit for certain low-income workers. The credit is available to joint filers with adjusted gross income below $50,000, heads of household with AGI below $47,500, and all other filers (excluding full-time students and any person who is claimed as a dependent by another taxpayer) with AGI below $25,000. The credit is a percentage of the first $2000 of the individual's annual contribution to a qualified retirement plan and varies inversely with the individual's income. For joint filers, the credit is 50% of the IRA contribution if the AGI is $30,000 or less, 20% if AGI is $30,000 to $32,500, and 10% if AGI is $32,500 to $50,000.[14] If the taxpayer does not have a tax liability prior to application of the credit, the credit is lost.

Roth Contributions to 401(k), 403(b) and SAR-SEP Plans

Beginning in 2006, Section 401(k) plans and Section 403(b) plans can include provision for after-tax employee contributions to the plan. These contributions will be referred to as *Roth contributions*, after the member of Congress who introduced the concept of after-tax IRA contributions. The contributions and investment income on the accumulation will be withdrawn tax-free after the employee has completed five years of service and reaches age 59½.

Minimum Contribution or Benefit for Top-Heavy Plans

Top-heavy plans are required to provide a minimum contribution on behalf of non-key employees. For defined-contribution plans, the minimum annual contribution is 3 percent of the employee's compensation. In defined-benefit plans, it is the amount required to provide a single life annuity beginning at the plan's normal retirement age, equal to 2 percent of the employee's average annual compensation during the 5 highest paid years with the employer, multiplied by the employee's years of service with the employer. However, the minimum benefit need not exceed 20 percent of average annual compensation.

[14]The corresponding AGI brackets for heads of households are $0 to $22,500, $22,500 to $24,375, and $24,375 to $37,500. For all other filers, the brackets are $0 to $15,000, $15,000 to $16,250, and $16,250–$25,000.

Tidbits, Vignettes, and Conundrums 17.1

Defined Benefit and Defined Contribution Plans

According to the U.S. Department of Labor, the percentage of workers covered by defined benefit plans has declined from about 86 percent in 1975 to 50 percent in 1995, while the number of workers covered by defined contribution plans has increased from 13 percent to 50 percent. There were two reasons for the shift to the defined contribution approach. The first was passage of ERISA, which required that employers insure defined benefit plans with the PBGC, thereby increasing their cost. The second was the creation of the 401(k) account, which was authorized by the Revenue Act of 1978 and which has become one of the most popular forms of pension funding.

Some observers believe that the shift from defined benefit to defined contribution plans has had an effect on the stock market. Under a defined benefit plan, employers need only contribute as much to the pension plan as needed to pay the benefits promised. When stock values increase by more than anticipated, defined benefit plans hold more assets than needed to pay promised benefits. In this case, the employer can reduce contributions or even reclaim excess contributions. In a defined contribution plan, when the stock market increases, the employees keep the gains. The increase in demand for stocks that accompanied the growth of defined contribution plans coupled with the maturing of the baby boom generation may have contributed to the steady increase in the stock market since 1982.

Source: Bruce R. Bartlett, *The Defined Contribution Plan Revolution* (June 1999), http://www.lexingtoninstitute.org/whtwrks2.htm.

Integration: Adjusting Benefits for Social Security

Although *I.R.C.* rules require that contribution rates and benefits be nondiscriminatory, employers are permitted to recognize their share of the FICA payments already being made on behalf of employees in determining the level of contributions or benefits. This process is referred to as "integration." In a defined contribution-type plan, the integration is usually accomplished by providing a higher contribution rate on salaries above the Social Security wage base. In defined benefit pension plans, integration may be accomplished by using a higher benefit accrual rate on higher salaries. Alternatively, the employer may apply the same accrual rate to all salary levels, but deduct some percentage (e.g., 50 percent) of Social Security benefits received from the benefit.

This latter arrangement is referred to as an "offset" plan.

Although the provisions for integration initially appear to discriminate against lower-paid workers, they are designed to compensate for the fact that Social Security benefits provide for replacement of a higher percentage of a lower-paid worker's preretirement income than they do for the higher-paid employees.

Characteristics of Qualified Retirement Plans

Although each of these programs is similar to the others in its use as a tax-sheltered retirement program, there are fundamental differences among them. Their differences have implications both for employers and employees.

The Nature of the Employer's Promise

In a defined benefit plan, the employer promises to provide a certain level of retirement benefits to the employee, starting at normal retirement age. The employer determines the required contributions to the pension fund by making assumptions about the number of employees that will reach retirement age, the time for which benefits will be paid, and the rate of investment income earned on the fund. The higher the assumed investment income, the lower the employer's required contribution. However, if investment income goes down and the accumulation is insufficient to fund the benefits, the employer must increase the contributions because the employer's obligation is to provide the promised benefits.

Under a defined contribution plan (which includes defined contribution pension plans, profit-sharing plans, ESOPs, Section 401(k) plans, and SEPs), the employer's only promise is to make contributions to the plan. Because the level of benefits depend on contributions and on investment income, the employee bears the investment risk in a defined contribution plan. Since the employee bears the investment risk in a defined contribution plan, he or she is likely to have some say in how the funds are invested. Employers often provide a number of investment options from which the employee may choose.

In addition to the difference regarding who bears the investment risk, defined benefit and defined contribution plans differ in their relative advantages to young and older employees. In a defined contribution plan, a higher proportion of the ultimate retirement benefits result from contributions in the early years of participation. This is because the contribution in early years will accumulate with investment income for a longer period than the contribution in later years. Hence, the accumulation at retirement will be larger, and the benefits it can purchase will be greater. On the other hand, the present value of the benefits promised to a young worker under a defined benefit plan tends to be small compared to the present value of the benefits promised to an older worker who is closer to retirement.

ERISA Pension Plan Termination Insurance

ERISA established the Pension Benefit Guarantee Corporation (PBGC) within the Department of Labor and requires employers with defined-benefit plans to insure the benefits of their plan with the PBGC. The premium varies with the nature of the plan. In 2002, the rate for multi-employer plans was $2.60 per participant. For single-employer plans, a variable rate applies; $19 per plan participant, with an additional charge of $9 per participant for each $1000 of underfunding. Benefits of an insured plan are guaranteed up to 100 percent of the average wages of the worker during his or her 5 highest-earning years, subject to an indexed dollar maximum. The dollar maximum was originally set at $750 per month. By 2001, the maximum coverage per employee had increased to $3,392.05 per month by 2001.

If a plan is terminated with insufficient assets, the employer must reimburse the PBGC for the deficiency. This *contingent employer liability* is limited to 30 percent of the net worth of the employer plus 75 percent of the remaining liability. The payments collected are paid to the plan beneficiaries along with the assets from the plan.

Forfeitures

Defined contribution and defined benefit plans may differ in how they deal with forfeitures by employees who terminate before being fully vested. In a defined contribution plan, forfeitures by employees who leave before being fully vested may be used to reduce future employer contributions, or they may be reallocated among remaining participants on a nondiscriminatory basis. In a defined benefit plan, gains from employee termination may be used only to reduce future employer contributions.

The Shift to Defined Contribution Plans

Since the mid-1970s, there has been a significant shift in the percentage of defined benefit and defined contribution plans. According to the U.S. Department of Labor, the percentage of workers covered by defined benefit plans has declined from about 86 percent in 1975 to 50 percent in 1995, while the number of workers covered by defined contribution plans has increased from 13 percent to 50 percent. There were two reasons for the shift to the defined contribution approach. The first was passage of the Employee Retirement and Income Security Act of 1974 (ERISA), which required that employers insure defined benefit plans with the PBGC, thereby increasing their cost. The second was the creation of the 401(k) account, which has become one of the most popular forms of pension funding.

Other Benefits

Although the basic purpose of a pension plan is to provide retirement benefits, some plans include other features such as death benefits and disability benefits.

Survivor Benefits

Current law requires that the pension benefit for any participant who has been married for at least a year must include a joint and survivor spousal benefit of at least 50 percent. In addition, a qualified plan must provide benefits to the surviving spouse of a vested participant who dies before retirement. Spousal consent is required for a participant to elect out of either the joint-and-survivor annuity or the preretirement survivor benefit. Other than this requirement, a death benefit prior to retirement of the employee is an optional feature in pensions, except in the case of a contributory plan, where the employee's contribution is payable as a death benefit. Some employers provide a preretirement death benefit to a participant's survivors, either out of plan accumulations or through life insurance.

Disability Benefits

Some pension plans provide benefits if the employee becomes totally and permanently disabled.

Under some plans, disability is simply treated as a form of early retirement, with a reduced retirement benefit payable. A more favorable approach provides for continued contributions to the plan on behalf of the disabled employee. The election to continue deductible contributions for a disabled employee cannot be made for a disabled employee who is an officer, owner, or highly compensated employee.

Distribution Requirements

In addition to the limits on contributions, the I.R.C. establishes rules regarding the time at which benefits *may* commence and the time at which they *must* commence.

Commencement of Benefits

Until 1997, the *I.R.C.* required that distributions from a tax-qualified retirement plan commence no later than April 1 of the calendar year following the calendar year in which an employee attained age 70½, even if the employee had not retired. The Small Business Job Protection Act of 1996 (SBJPA) amended the required beginning distribution date for most employees beginning in 1997. Under the new law, distributions may be deferred beyond age 70½ until actual retirement.[15] When distribution begins, it must be made over one of the following periods:

- The life of the participant or the lives of the participant and a designated beneficiary *or*

- A period not extending beyond the life expectancy of the participant and his or her beneficiary

---

[15]For employees who are 5-percent owners, the required beginning date remains April 1 of the calendar year following the calendar year in which the 5-percent owner attains age 70½. The SBJPA amendments do not apply to the required beginning date for distributions from an IRA, including an IRA established in conjunction with a Simplified Employee Pension (SEP) or a SIMPLE Plan.

Under the first option, the accumulation is annuitized, and the plan administrator makes payments for the entire lifetime of the participant (and beneficiary if the joint life option is selected). The annuity may be based on one or two lives, and the annuitant may elect a minimum guaranteed number of payments.

Under the second option, payments are made for a period *based* on the life expectancy of the retired worker, but cease when the funds are exhausted. If the entire accumulation is not paid out before the individual dies, the balance is paid to the designated beneficiary or to the decedent's estate. The accumulation is distributed based on a life expectancy, but is not guaranteed for life.

Premature Withdrawals

A 10 percent penalty applies to withdrawals that are made before the individual reaches age 59½. The penalty does not apply to withdrawals that are rolled over into another qualified plan or an IRA. The penalty also does not apply if (1) the distribution is made on account of the employee's death or disability; (2) the distribution is used to pay deductible medical expenses; (3) the distribution is received as an annuity over the lifetime of the employee or under a joint life annuity including a beneficiary; or (4) the individual is at least age 55 and meets the requirements of a plan that permits retirement at his or her age.

Distributions From SIMPLE IRAs A special rule applies to distributions from a SIMPLE IRA during the first two years of an individual's participation. Taxable distributions during this period are subject to a 25 percent penalty (rather than the 10 percent penalty applicable to other plans).

Taxation of Distributions

Distributions from a qualified pension are taxable to the recipient when received. In addition, if the participant dies, a distribution to his or her dependents is taxable as income and, in some cases, is also subject to estate taxes.

Installment Distributions

Retirement benefits have traditionally been paid to participants as lifetime annuities, which are taxable under special annuity rules of *I.R.C.* Section 72. Under a contributory plan, where the employee made nondeductible contributions, distributions are taxable only to the extent that they exceed the employee's investment in the contract. Every payment, beginning with the first, is considered part taxable income and part nontaxable. The nontaxable part consists of the portion of the payment that represents the employee's nondeductible contribution and is referred to as the *exclusion ratio*.[16]

Lump-Sum Distributions

An employee who receives a lump-sum distribution from a qualified plan can "rollover" the distribution into an IRA or another qualified retirement plan, in which case there is no tax on the distribution until it is eventually received from the IRA or other plan. As an alternative, within 60 days of receiving a lump-sum distribution, an employee may use the distribution to purchase a single-premium, nontransferable annuity, in which case the distribution will be taxed under the annuity rules. Otherwise, lump sum distributions are taxable in the year received.

Death Benefits

The distribution resulting from the death of a covered employee is usually taxed to the beneficiary in the same manner as it would have been to the deceased worker. If an employee dies before his or her entire interest is paid and a joint-and-survivor option is not in effect, or if payments are being made to a surviving spouse who dies before the entire interest is received, the balance generally must be distributed to beneficiaries within 5 years.

---

[16]Annuity payments beyond the individual's life expectancy will be fully taxable. Should the retired person die before reaching full life expectancy, his or her heirs may take a deduction on the deceased's final return for the amount of any unrecovered contributions.

Limitations on Loan Transactions

The accumulation of funds in qualified pension plans has been an appealing source of loans to the plan participants, but such loans are subject to restrictions imposed by the *I.R.C.* A loan from a qualified plan to an employee is treated as a distribution (and is therefore taxable) to the extent that it exceeds prescribed limits. Furthermore, a loan to a participant may not exceed the lesser of $50,000 or one-half of the participant's vested accrued benefit (but not less than $10,000). The loan must be repaid within 5 years, and the repayment must be on an amortized basis. An exception to the 5-year payback rules applies to a loan used to acquire the principal residence of the participant.[17]

Pension Funding

The term *funding* refers to the advance preparation that the employer makes for payment of the benefits under the plan. ERISA now requires full funding for currently incurred liabilities. An employer failing to meet the funding requirement is subject to an excise tax equal to 5 percent of the unfunded liability. If the deficiency is not corrected within a period allowed after notice by the IRS, a 100 percent tax is imposed.

Two principal types of funding agencies are used for pension plans: trustees and insurance companies. In either case, the employer's contributions are paid to the funding agency, where they accumulate with investment earnings until they are paid to the pension plan participants. The use of two or more agencies for the funding of a single pension plan is called split *funding*.

Trust Fund Plans

Under a *trust fund plan,* the employer usually retains a consulting actuary to determine the contributions necessary to fund the benefits specified in the plan. Contributions by the employer (and by employees in a contributory plan) are paid to a trustee, usually a bank or trust company. The trustee holds and invests the contributions and pays benefits according to the terms of the trust agreement and the pension plan provisions. Although a trustee holds the assets, trust fund plans are self-insured by the employer, who is ultimately responsible for the payment of benefits. The trustee makes no guarantee as to the adequacy of the employer's contributions to meet the obligations under the plan.

Insured Plans

For *insured plans,* the funding agency is an insurance company. There are two approaches to funding by an insurance company; allocated funding instruments and unallocated funding instruments.

Allocated Funding Approaches Allocated funding instruments include individual and group annuities. Individual annuity policies (and sometimes cash value life insurance) may be used by smaller employers as funding devices. When individual contracts are used to fund a pension plan, plan contributions are paid to an *individual policy pension trust,* a trustee who arranges for the purchase of the individual policies, serves as a custodian, and pays the premiums.

In a *group deferred annuity plan,* the employer's annual contributions are used to purchase a deferred annuity for each employee each year. Under the defined-contribution plan, the annual contribution is used to purchase a single-premium deferred annuity, payable to the employee at retirement. A defined-benefit plan might purchase an annuity equal to 2 percent of the employee's current income so that over a period of, say, 30 years, the cumulative value of such annuities would equal 60 percent of the employee's average earnings.

Unallocated Funding Instruments In the case of *unallocated funding instruments,* funds paid to the insurer are not allocated to individual plan

---

[17]Prior to EGTRAA-2001, loans from qualified plans to owner employee were not permitted, but EGTRRA-2001 makes owner-employees eligible to receive loans from qualified plans subject to the same limitations as other participants.

participants, but reside in an aggregated pool until they are required for the payment of benefits. Unallocated funding instruments used by insurers for pension funding include deposit administration plans, immediate participation guarantee plans, and separate accounts. Under a deposit administration plan, a withdrawal is made from the fund to purchase a single-premium immediate annuity to provide the retirement benefits due the employee. In an immediate participation plan, annuities are not purchased for retiring workers; instead, annuity payments are made directly out of the IPG fund.

A *separate account* is a fund held by an insurance company apart from its general assets, to be used for investment of pension assets in equities. The accounts are "separate" in the sense that the funds are not commingled with the insurer's other funds, but contributions from a particular pension plan are usually commingled with those of other plans. Separate accounts are authorized by legislation enacted by the states in the 1960s as an exception to statutory limits on the investment of life insurer assets in equities.

Individual Retirement Arrangements

Although individual retirement accounts (commonly known as IRAs) are not an employee benefit *per se*, they were originally conceived as a substitute for employer-provided pensions. The idea was to allow persons who are not covered by an employer-sponsored retirement plan to make tax-deductible contributions to an IRA, where the contributions and investment earnings would accumulate tax deferred until distributed at retirement. The provisions applicable to IRAs have been changed numerous times. In 1998, a new type of IRA called the Roth IRA was introduced that does not allow tax deductible contributions but has other advantages.

Traditional Individual Retirement Accounts

The traditional IRA was created by the Pension Reform Act of 1974, which authorized persons who are not covered by an employer-sponsored retirement plan to make tax-deductible contributions to an individual retirement account or an individual retirement annuity.

Eligibility

Under the current rules, a person who is not covered by an employer retirement plan can make deductible contributions to an IRA up to a specified dollar maximum or 100 percent of compensation. A person who is covered by an employer-sponsored plan may still be entitled to a deduction, depending on his or her income. The deduction begins to decrease when the taxpayer's adjusted gross income (AGI) rises above a certain level and is eliminated altogether when it reaches a higher level. In 2002, the AGI levels at which the IRA deduction is phased out were $34,000 to $44,000 for single persons and heads of households and $54,000 to $64,000 for joint filers. These limits will increase, respectively, to $40,000 to $50,000 and $60,000 to $70,000 in 2003. Thereafter, the phaseout limits will increase by $5000 annually so that the limit for single persons and heads of households will reach $50,000 to $60,000 in 2005 and the limit for married filing jointly will reach $80,000 to $100,000 in 2007.

Maximum Deduction

For many years, the dollar maximum contribution limit to a traditional IRA was $2000. Under EGTRRA-2001, the maximum annual contribution will increase to $3000 for 2002 through 2004, to $4000 for years 2005 through 2007, and to $5000 in 2008. After 2008, the $5,000 contribution limit will be indexed to inflation in $500 increments. New rules introduced by EGTRRA-2001 allow individuals age 50 or older by the end of the taxable year for which a contribution is made to make additional "catch-up" contributions of $500 per year in 2002 through 2005 and $1000 a year in 2006 and thereafter. Unlike catch-up contributions to 401(k) plans, 403(b) plans, 457 plans, SEP-IRAs and SIMPLE IRAs, the catch-up contribution for Traditional and Roth IRAs is not indexed for inflation but will remain at $1000 after 2006.

A spouse who is not employed outside the home can make tax-deductible IRA contributions up to the maximum limit a year even if his or her partner is covered by an employer's retirement plan. In other words, if only one spouse is a participant in an employer's plan, the limitation only applies to that spouse. The deduction for such spousal contributions phases out for married couples with incomes between $150,000 and $160,000.[18]

Taxpayers whose income exceeds the AGI phaseout levels can still make nondeductible contributions to a traditional IRA up to the dollar maximum. Although these contributions are not deductible, earnings on the contributions are not taxed until distributed.

Taxation of Traditional IRAs

Deductible contributions and investment income are taxable when distributed and premature distributions (i.e., distributions before age 59½) are subject to a 10-percent tax penalty. When the IRA is funded by both deductible and nondeductible contributions, withdrawals are considered to consist in part of deductible and in part of nondeductible contributions, with the nondeductible contributions exempt from tax on the distribution.

Penalty-free withdrawals (prior to age 59½) are permitted to cover tax-deductible medical expenses (i.e., medical expenses that exceed 7.5

percent of adjusted gross income) of the taxpayer, a spouse, or dependents. The withdrawal is subject to income tax, but if the taxpayer itemizes, the income can be partially offset by the itemized deduction of the medical expense. In addition, the 10 percent penalty does not apply to withdrawals by unemployed persons to pay health insurance premiums. Penalty-free (not income-tax-free) withdrawals are also permitted for qualified first-time homebuyers or for the first home purchase by a spouse, child, or grandchild (subject to a $10,000 lifetime limit). Finally, penalty-free withdrawals are allowed for qualified higher education expenses for individuals, their spouses, children, or grandchildren.

Generally, IRA accounts may be funded with any investments that are acceptable for other tax-qualified plans. The most common funding instruments are custodial accounts established by banks and retirement annuities. The *I.R.C.* forbids IRAs to invest in life insurance contracts.

The Roth IRA

Since 1998, an improved version of the nondeductible IRA called the "Roth IRA" has been available to taxpayers. The distinguishing feature of the Roth IRA is that contributions are made only on a non-deductible basis and the tax benefit is realized when the funds are withdrawn. All earnings on the contributions compound tax-free as long as they are not withdrawn for at least five years and there are no taxes due when the funds are withdrawn for retirement (i.e., after age 59½).

Annual contributions up to the lesser of 100% or the same dollar maximum applicable to traditional IRAs are permitted for single taxpayers with annual income of up to $95,000 or couples filing jointly with annual income up to $150,000.[19] The contribution amount is gradually reduced to zero

---

[18]Prior to the 1997 tax law changes, a nonworking spouse (or a working spouse not covered under an employer-sponsored plan) could not make a deductible contribution to an IRA if the other spouse participated in an employer-sponsored plan and the spouses had an income above a certain limit.

[19]Unlike the dollar limits for other retirement programs, the IRA contribution phase-out AGI limits are not indexed for inflation.

at income levels between $95,000 and $110,000 for single taxpayers, and $150,000 and $160,000 for couples. There is no requirement that withdrawals commence at 70½ and contributions to a Roth IRA may continue after age 70½ as long as the individual or spouse has earned income.

Taxpayers with adjusted gross incomes less than $100,000, whether single or joint filers, can roll over assets from traditional IRAs into a Roth IRA. Once rolled over, these assets continue to accumulate tax-deferred until withdrawn. Income taxes apply to the taxable amount that is rolled over, but there is no premature distribution penalty.

There is no penalty on early withdrawals of the after-tax contributions to a Roth IRA. Under the *Code* provisions applicable to Roth IRAs, the first money taken out of the account is considered to be the after-tax contributions, rather than earnings. Premature withdrawals of earnings (i.e., before age 59½) are taxable income, subject to a 10% penalty except in the event of death, disability, or a first time home purchase. The first-time homeowner withdrawal is subject to a 10,000 one-time limit.

Individuals can have a traditional IRA and a Roth IRA, but they cannot contribute more than the traditional IRA dollar maximum to both accounts combined. Individuals who are not eligible for deductible contributions to a traditional IRA or to make contributions to a Roth IRA may still make nondeductible contributions to a traditional IRA.

Some Specialized Uses of Life Insurance in Business

In addition to providing protection to employees under the fringe benefit programs and funding retirement benefits, life insurance serves several other functions in the business firm. They include funding business purchase agreements, protecting the firm against the loss of a key employee, and providing additional compensation to executives and other valuable employees.

Business Continuation Insurance

The death or disability of the owner of a business, a member of a partnership, or a stockholder of a close corporation may create serious problems for that business. The heirs of the deceased owner may not want to continue their ownership or the other owners may not want to share ownership and control with the heirs. The recommended solution to this problem is to make arrangements for the sale of the individual's interest in the business prior to death through a buy-and-sell agreement. Under a buy-sell agreement, each owner agrees that his or her share of the business is to be sold to the remaining owners at death, and each owner agrees to buy the shares of a deceased owner. The buy-and-sell agreement should contain a formula for setting the value of the business at the time of the sale, thus eliminating later difficulties regarding the value.

Unless the owners have sufficient cash or liquid assets to purchase each other's interest, the most satisfactory method of funding a buy-sell agreement is through life insurance on the lives of the owners. The partners, partnership, stockholders, or the corporation—whoever is to be the purchaser—would pay the premiums and receive the proceeds of the policy on the life of the party whose interest in the business is to be purchased.[20]

The operational aspects of the funding may vary, depending on the circumstances. Under the arrangement known as a *cross-purchase plan*, each partner or stockholder carries enough life insurance on the lives of the others to permit the purchase of a proportionate share of the deceased member's interest. For example, if Abner, Baker, and Cole each own one-third of a business valued at $300,000, Abner would buy $50,000 in life in-

---

[20]Although this discussion describes the need and solution in the event of death, the same problems apply to disability. Business continuation disability policies are available that pay a lump-sum benefit for use in purchasing a disabled owner's interest.

Tidbits, Vignettes, and Conundrums 17.2

Key Person Life Insurance and the Movies

Motion picture makers sometimes purchase cast insurance to protect against the financial loss that could result from the death of a cast member. In 1994, the producers of the movie

Wagons West collected $14.5 million when actor John Candy suffered heart failure and died when the shooting was about 80 percent completed.

---

surance on Baker and $50,000 on Cole, Baker would buy $50,000 on both Abner and Cole, and Cole would buy $50,000 on Abner and Baker. If one partner dies, the remaining two will receive sufficient proceeds from their policies to permit them to purchase the decedent's interest.

Under an alternate arrangement known as the *entity plan*, the firm itself purchases the policies and is the beneficiary. Under the entity plan, the partnership or corporation purchases the interest of the deceased owner, and the interest of the survivors is increased proportionately.[21] Premiums paid by the firm are not a deductible expense, but the policy proceeds are exempt from income taxation.

Key Person Insurance

One of the most valuable assets of any business is the skill of its employees. Since every employee contributes to the success of a business, the death of any one of them is a source of loss to the firm. The extent of this loss varies with the individual's part in the firm's success. Those employees who

make a critical contribution to this success are key employees, and sometimes the risk of their loss may be sufficient to warrant *key person insurance* protection. When the death of an individual associated with the business might cause a financial loss through imperiled credit, loss of leadership, lower profits, or reduced ability to secure new business, the firm has an insurable interest in that individual. The most difficult aspect of insuring key personnel is the determination of their value. The valuation may be based on an estimate of the probable loss of income that might result from the employee's death or an estimate of the additional expenses of obtaining a replacement. In the last analysis, the value will be an educated guess, based on a combination of factors.

Split-Dollar Plan

Split-dollar insurance is an arrangement by which an employer and employee share the cost of an insurance policy on the life of the employee. The parties usually enter into an agreement under which the employer agrees to pay that portion of each annual premium equal to the increase in the cash value resulting from such premium payment. The employee pays the balance of the premium. The employer is usually the owner of the policy and is also a beneficiary to the extent of the cash value. The employee designates the beneficiary to the extent of the balance of the death proceeds.

Split-dollar insurance is intended to give the employee an incentive to remain with the firm. It

---

[21]A stock retirement agreement is a contract between stockholders and the corporation in which the corporation agrees to purchase the stock in the corporation owned by an employee on the employee's death. A stockholders' buy-sell agreement is an agreement for the purchase and sale among stockholders, under which survivors agree to buy the stock of a deceased shareholder.

permits the employee to obtain additional life insurance with a minimum outlay of personal funds and, because it is permanent insurance, it can be continued beyond retirement age. One drawback to the basic split-dollar plan is that the amount payable to the insured's personal beneficiary decreases year by year as the cash value of the policy and the employer's interest increase. However, in the case of participating policies, this drawback can be partially offset through the use of dividends to purchase one-year term insurance (the fifth dividend option).

Deferred Compensation

Deferred compensation is an arrangement in which the employer agrees to make payments to an employee after retirement or future payments to the employee's spouse if the worker should die before retiring. The arrangement usually reflects the employer's desire to retain the services

and loyalty of key personnel. The employee incurs no federal income tax liability prior to retirement under an orthodox deferred compensation agreement, because the employer's mere promise to pay, not represented by notes or secured in any way, is not regarded as the receipt of income by a cash-basis taxpayer.

Employers often use cash value life insurance on the life of the employee to fund the deferred compensation agreement. If the employee lives to retirement age, the employer uses the policy cash surrender value to make payments to the retiree. The employer cannot deduct premiums paid for the insurance, and the cash value is taxable when received to the extent that it exceeds the premiums paid. If the employee dies before retirement, the death proceeds are not taxable when received by the employer. Amounts paid to the employee at retirement or to dependents if the employee dies—if reasonable in amount—are a deductible expense to the firm and taxable as income to the employee or dependents.

Important Concepts to Remember

employee benefits	501(c)(9) trusts	Pension Benefit Guarantee Corporation (PBGC)
group life insurance	split funding	
group health insurance	group deferred annuity	cafeteria plan
group term life insurance	top-heavy plan	allocated funding instrument
group ordinary life	trust fund plan	unallocated funding instrument
group universal life insurance	insured plan	cross-purchase plan
retired lives reserve	deposit administration plan	deferred compensation
stop-loss insurance	immediate participation guarantee plan	key-person life insurance
aggregate stop-loss insurance	separate account	entity plan
flexible spending account		split-dollar insurance

Questions for Review

1. Identify and briefly describe the employee benefits discussed in the chapter for which the tax code provides favorable tax treatment.

2. Explain the advantages granted to employees under the tax laws governing

a. Health insurance plans for which the employer pays the premium, and

b. Contributions made by an employer for life insurance on the lives of employees.

3. Identify and briefly explain the requirements for a pension plan to be "qualified" under ERISA. What are the advantages of qualification?

4. Identify and explain the differences in the funding agencies that an employer may use for funding a qualified pension plan.

5. What is the basic difference between *allocated funding instruments* and *unallocated funding instruments*? Identify the funding instruments that fall into each category.

6. The PBGC guarantees insured plan participants against loss of benefits that can result from funding deficiencies. How can funding deficiencies arise?

7. In what way does the employer assume a greater element of risk under an immediate participation guarantee pension plan than under a group deferred annuity?

8. Briefly describe the special requirements that apply to a top-heavy plan. Why were these requirements enacted?

9. Briefly outline the provisions of the tax code relating to deductibility of premiums and taxation of policy proceeds in key-person life insurance.

10. In what way(s) does the Pension Benefit Guarantee Corporation protect (a) employees and (b) employers?

Exam 3 Ch. 10-17

Questions for Discussion

1. Many of the decisions relating to pension plans were formerly regarded to be management prerogatives, but are now dictated by federal regulations. To what extent does ERISA violate the freedom of choice of business managers with respect to pension plans? Is this violation justified?

2. The text notes that the business continuation exposure involves the possibility of the death or the disability of owners. From the perspective of other owners, in what ways is the effect of the disability of an owner the same as and different from the risk of the death of an owner?

3. For what reasons might an organization decide to establish a nonqualified deferred compensation program? Has the number of nonqualified programs increased or decreased since enactment of ERISA? Why?

4. A self-employed chiropractor has three full-time employees and is considering establishing a qualified retirement plan. What are the options with respect to the type of plan that she should establish and the features that will be included in the plan?

5. Employee benefits are sometimes referred to as "fringe" benefits, suggesting that they represent a form of somewhat gratuitous compensation granted by an employer. This view considers pensions as a reward for long and faithful service. The opposing view is that employee benefits are a part of a total compensation package and that pension benefits are simply deferred compensation accepted by the employee in lieu of higher current wages. With which of these views are the provisions of ERISA consistent? To what extent are the provisions of ERISA fully consistent with this view?

Suggestions for Additional Reading

Allen, Everett T., Joseph J. Melone, Jerry S. Rosenbloom, and Jack L. Vanderhei. *Pension Planning: Pension, Profit-Sharing, and Other Deferred Compensation Plans*, 8th ed. Homewood, IL: Irwin/McGraw Hill, 1997.

American Council of Life Insurance. *Pension Facts*. Washington, DC: American Council of Life Insurance, published annually.

Beam, Burton T., Jr., and John J. McFadden. *Employee Benefits*. Dearborn Financial Publishing, 1998.

Black, Kenneth, Jr., and Harold D. Skipper, Jr. *Life Insurance*, 13th ed. Englewood Cliffs, NJ: Prentice Hall, 2000. Chapters 7, 19, 20.

Fundamentals of Employee Benefit Programs, 5th ed. Washington, DC: Employee Benefit Research Institute, 1997.

Hallman, G. Victor, and Karen L. Hamilton. *Personal Insurance: Life, Health, and Retirement*. Malvern, PA: American Institute for CPCU, 1994. Chapters 7, 8.

Rosenbloom, Jerry S. (ed.). *The Handbook of Employee Benefits: Design, Funding and Administration*, 4th ed. Homewood, IL: Richard D. Irwin, 1996.

Websites to Explore

American Society of Pension Actuaries: http://www.aspa.org/

Association of Private Pension and Welfare Plans: http://www.podi.com/appwp/retire.htm

Benefit Links: http://www.benefitslink.com/

Employee Benefit Research Institute: http://www.ebri.org

Employee Benefits Survey: http://www.bls.gov/ebshome.htm

Health Insurance Association of America: http://www.hiaa.org/

Insurance News Network: http://www.insure.com/

Integrated Benefits Institute: http://www.ibiweb.org

International Foundation of Employee Benefit Plans: http://www.ifebp.org/

Pension and Welfare Benefit Administration: http://www.dol.gov/dol/pwba/

Pension Benefit Guarantee Corporation: http://www.pbgc.gov/

TIAA-CREF: http://www.tiaa-cref.org/

U.S. Pension Law-Cornell University: http://www.law.cornell.edu/topics/pensions.html

SECTION THREE

PROPERTY AND LIABILITY INSURANCE

CHAPTER 18

The Homeowners Policy

A combination and a form indeed.
—William Shakespeare
Hamlet

CHAPTER OBJECTIVES

When you have finished this chapter, you should be able to

- Explain the general nature of the Homeowners program

- Identify and distinguish among the Homeowners forms and describe the individual for whom each form is designed

- Explain the difference between named-peril and open-peril coverage

- Identify the coverage parts of the Homeowners Policy

- Interpret loss-settlement provisions

- Recognize significant exclusions and limitations in the Homeowners Section I coverage

- List and describe the optional coverages available to broaden the Homeowners forms

The home is one of the most important, and probably the most expensive, investments that the average consumer will ever make. Understandably, protection against damage to the dwelling is a central part of every family's insurance program. Also, insurance protection on the individual's personal property is an important part of a personal insurance program. Finally, but by no means of lesser importance, is the liability coverage needed to protect against the financial consequences of legal liability. In this chapter, we turn to the Homeowners Policy, which is a package policy approach to insuring these exposures.

Historical Development

The Homeowners Policy is a product of the multiple-line transition, which resulted from the removal of the legal barriers that separated property insurance from casualty insurance. One of the significant effects of the multiple-line transition was the package policy, in which property and casualty coverages are combined in a single contract. The Homeowners policies, which combine fire insurance coverages with theft insurance and personal liability insurance, are the most widely sold and by far the best known of the package policies. The Homeowners program was introduced in 1958. Within a short time after their introduction, the Homeowners forms had become the standard approach to insuring residential property. The policy has been revised numerous times since its introduction. The following discussion is based on the year-2000 edition of the Homeowners program.

General Nature of the Homeowners Program

In most jurisdictions, there are six standard Homeowners forms:

HO 00 02, Homeowners 2 Broad Form (Narrow)

HO 00 03, Homeowners 3 Special Form (Broad)

HO 00 04, Homeowners 4 Contents Broad Form Apt Dwellers

HO 00 05, Homeowners 5 Comprehensive Form (Ext Broad & sold much

HO 00 06, Homeowners 6 Unit-Owners Form (condos)

HO 00 08, Homeowners 8 Modified Coverage Form (Houses w/ ++ Repl. Cost than market)

Four of these forms (2, 3, 5, and 8) are designed for individuals who own their homes, one (Form 4) is designed for tenants, and one (Form 6) is designed for condominium unit-owners.[1]

There are strict eligibility requirements under the program. Forms 2, 3, 5, and 8 may be written only for the owner-occupant of a one-to-

four family dwelling used exclusively for private residential purposes (although the rules permit incidental office or professional occupancy, such as a physician who may have an office in his or her home). Homeowners Form 4 may be written for a tenant who lives in a rented dwelling or an apartment or for a homeowner who owns a dwelling that does not meet the eligibility requirements for one of the other forms (i.e., because it contains more than four families). Form 6 may be written only for condominium unit-owners and members of cooperatives. (Members of cooperatives are eligible for either Form 4 or Form 6.) Owners of older dwellings that insurers are unwilling to insure under Forms 2, 3, or 5 may be insured under Form 8, which provides the most limited coverage of the six forms.

All the forms include two sections: Section I, which provides coverage on the insured's own property, and Section II, which provides liability and medical payments coverage. The coverage under Section II is identical under all the forms, and it is only with respect to Section I that the forms differ. The provisions of Section II will be discussed in Chapter 20. Here we are concerned only with the coverage under Section I.

older homes

Homeowners Section I Coverages

The Section I coverages of the Homeowners forms provide coverage on the insured's own property, and the forms differ from one another in the protection they provide. Differences exist both in terms of the items covered under some of the forms and in the perils insured.

Section I Coverages: An Overview

There are four items of coverage under Section I, designated A, B, C, and D. The basic philoso-

---

[1]Earlier versions of the Homeowners program included another form, the Homeowners Basic Form (HO 1). The Homeowners Basic Form is being phased out nationally and was still used in only six states in 1994. The Homeowners Comprehensive Form (HO 5) was eliminated in 1984 but was resurrected in the 2000 revision.

phy of the Homeowners program is to require certain minimum limits for each coverage with a mandatory relationship among the minimums for the various coverages.

Coverage A provides protection on the dwelling. Individual insurers' eligibility rules for each of the forms set minimum levels of coverage for the dwelling under Forms 2, 3, 5, and 8. Form 4 does not cover the dwelling and does not include Coverage A. Under Form 6, Coverage A provides $1000 on the condominium unit-owner's building items. This nominal amount may be increased if there is a need for greater coverage.

Coverage B provides a specific amount of insurance on other structures (such as a garage) on the premises, equal to 10 percent of the amount on the dwelling. The insurance on other structures may be increased above this standard 10 percent when there is a need.

Coverage C provides coverage on personal property or "contents." Under Forms 4 and 6 the minimum coverage on personal property is $6000. Under the other forms, it is 50 percent of the amount on the dwelling. The coverage on personal property may be increased when its value exceeds the standard 50 percent, or it may be reduced, but not below 40 percent of dwelling coverage.

Coverage D, designated *loss of use*, provides coverage for additional living expense and loss of rental income. The standard limit for the loss of use coverage is 20 percent of the amount on the dwelling under Forms 2, 3, and 5 and 10 percent of the amount on the dwelling under Form 8. The limit for Coverage D under Form 4 is 20 percent of personal property coverage, and under Form 6 it is 40 percent of the amount on personal property.

In addition to the four coverages designated A, B, C, and D, each form also includes several extensions, called Additional Coverages, that further broaden the coverage. The additional coverages are discussed later in the chapter.

Perils Insured

Although it is common to use the term "fire insurance" when referring to property insurance at fixed locations, coverage is seldom written to cover against loss by fire only. At the minimum, modern property insurance is written to include the perils of fire and lightning plus the perils of *Extended Coverage* and vandalism. The term *extended coverage* refers to a group of perils that are sold as a package and that became a more-or-less standard endorsement under monoline fire insurance policies. (The perils of extended coverage include windstorm and hail, explosion, riot or civil commotion, aircraft, vehicles, and smoke.) This minimum level of coverage is referred to as the *Basic* or *Standard* form, depending on the contract. Coverage may be broadened to include additional named perils, in which case the coverage is referred to as *Broad Form* coverage. Finally, coverage may also be written under a *Special Form*, which provides coverage on an *open-peril* basis. The Homeowners forms are based on these three standard levels of property coverage (*Basic, Broad,* and *Special*), but include the peril of theft, a coverage that was not generally included in traditional "fire insurance" perils. With the exception of Homeowners Form 8 (HO 8), which is designed for older homes that do not qualify for the "normal" Homeowners Policy, coverage under the Homeowners forms is on a Broad or Special basis.[2] That is, coverage is on a broad named-peril basis or on an open-peril basis. The broad named-peril coverage includes 16 perils, with wording that is essentially identical from form to form. HO 2 covers buildings and contents on a broad named-peril basis. HO 4 and 6 cover contents only for the same broad named perils. HO 3 covers contents for the same named perils as do Forms 2, 4, and 6 and covers buildings on an

---

[2]The Homeowners 8 Modified Coverage Form and the Homeowners 1 Basic Form, which is still used in a limited number of states, provide coverage for a smaller number of named perils.

open-peril basis. Finally, HO Form 5 covers both buildings and contents on an open-peril basis.

For the convenience of the reader, the coverage of the six Homeowners forms used nationally, the minimum amounts of coverage, and the perils insured are summarized in Table 18.1.

Coverage A: Dwelling

With a few exceptions noted in the following discussion, all the forms that provide coverage on the dwelling and other structures (that is, Forms 2, 3, 5, and 8) contain the same definitions with respect to this property. Coverage A specifies that "dwelling" includes structures attached to the dwelling and also covers material and supplies located on the premises or adjacent to the premises, which are intended for use in construction, alteration, or repair of the dwelling. The extension of coverage to cover construction materials is important because the Homeowners Policy can be used to cover a dwelling under construction. (The dwelling must be intended for occupancy by the insured.) The form specifically states that land is not covered.

Coverage B: Other Structures

The coverage on *other structures* applies only to structures separated from the dwelling by a clear space. It includes buildings, such as a detached garage, but also includes nonbuilding structures, such as fences, patios, or even swimming pools. The coverage on other structures excludes buildings that are rented to anyone other than a tenant of the residence unless used solely as a private garage. Other structures used to store business property are also excluded. Here, an exception applies for business property owned by an insured or a tenant of the building, provided such business property does not include gaseous or liquid fuel (other than fuel in a vehicle parked in the structure).

Replacement Cost Coverage

The coverage on the dwelling and other buildings under the Homeowners forms is on a replacement cost basis. It provides that if at the time of a loss the amount of insurance covering a building is at least 80 percent of the building's replacement cost, the loss will be paid on a replacement cost basis (without deduction for depreciation) rather than on an actual cash value basis. Replacement cost coverage applies only to buildings, and specifically does not include carpeting, domestic appliances, awnings, outdoor antennas, and outdoor equipment.[3]

If the amount of insurance is less than 80 percent of the replacement cost of the building, the company will pay the larger of the following two amounts:

- The actual cash value or
- The proportion of the replacement cost of the loss that the amount of insurance bears to 80 percent of the replacement cost value of the building

If the loss is more than $2500 or 5 percent of the amount of insurance, the building must actually be repaired or replaced before the insured can collect on a replacement cost basis.

To illustrate the operation of the replacement cost provision (and at the same time indicate the effects of the misconceptions about insurable value), consider a dwelling built 30 years ago at an original cost of $25,000. The owner has just purchased this dwelling for $60,000, and insures it for the purchase price of $60,000. Now assume that a loss occurs, causing damage to the roof in the amount of, say, $8000. In adjusting the loss, the adjuster determines that the current replacement cost of the building is $100,000. The roof on the building is determined to be 10 years old,

---

[3]Replacement cost coverage is available on personal property in many jurisdictions under a special Personal Property Replacement Cost Endorsement, which is discussed later in the chapter.

Table 18.1   Homeowners Forms

Coverage	Form HO 00 02	Form HO 00 03	Form HO 00 04	Form HO 00 06	Form HO 00 08
A. Dwelling	Covered	Covered	Not covered	$1,000	Covered
B. Other Structures	10% of A	1% of A	Not covered	Part of A	10% of A
C. Personal Property	50% of A	50% of A	$6000 minimum	$6000 minimum	50% of A
D. Loss of Use	20% of A	20% of A	20% of C	40% of C	10% of A
	Fire or lightning	Open-peril on building	Same perils as Form 2	Same perils as Form 2	Fire or lightning
	Windstorm or hail				Windstorm or hail
	Explosion	Same perils as Form 2 on contents			Explosion
	Riot or civil commotion				Riot or civil commotion
	Aircraft				Aircraft
	Vehicles				Vehicles
	Smoke				Smoke
	Vandalism				Vandalism
	Theft				Theft
	Falling objects				Volcanic eruption
	Weight of ice, snow, or sleet				
	Accidental discharge or overflow of water or steam				
	Sudden and accidental tearing apart, cracking, burning or bulging				
	Freezing of plumbing, heating, air-conditioning systems or appliances				
	Damage from artificially generated electricity				
	Volcanic eruption				

Handwritten annotations:

See p. 584 for details

$100,000

coverage on prop. (can go to 10% but it can↑)

open on A (coverage)

cost to live elsewhere while house being repaired

→ items in dwelling.

under const → unoccupied

unoccupied → still items in bldg.

vacant → no one lives there

open 15

with a life expectancy of 20 years. In settling the $8000 loss to the roof, the insurer will pay the greater of the actual cash value of the loss (50 percent of $8000, or $4000) or that proportion of the loss that the amount of insurance carried bears to 80 percent of the replacement cost. Since 80 percent of the replacement cost is $80,000 and only $60,000 in coverage has been purchased, the insurer will pay 60/80 percent of the $8000 loss, or $6000. The policyholder will be forced to bear $2000 of the loss personally. If the insured had purchased insurance equal to 80 percent of the replacement cost, payment for the same $8000 loss would have been made in full without a deduction for depreciation or a penalty for underinsurance.

There are two basic measures of insurable value in dwelling property: replacement cost and actual cash value. Replacement cost is simply the cost of rebuilding the structure with materials of like kind and quality at current prices. Actual cash value, on the other hand, means "replacement cost less depreciation."

Some insureds think of insurable value in terms of some other inappropriate measure such as loan value or market value. The mortgagee usually requires insurance equal to its interest in the property, reinforcing the mistaken notion that market value somehow coincides with insurable value. There is no reason that market value will be the same as either actual cash value or replacement cost; there is even good reason to assume that it will not. Market value is based on the supply and demand for a particular type of real estate. It includes the value of the land on which the building stands, yet the land value is not a part of the insurable worth.

Although the form requires that only 80 percent of the replacement cost be insured, this does not and should not preclude the insured from purchasing 100 percent replacement cost coverage. When the insured purchases coverage for 80 percent of the replacement cost of the building, losses are paid without a deduction for depreciation, but in the event of a total loss, the insured is underinsured to the extent of 20 percent of the value of the building.

Inflation Guard Endorsement The Inflation Guard Endorsement is an optional coverage that automatically increases the amount of insurance under the policy by some percentage of the original face amount each calendar quarter. The increase applies not only to the building but to other items of coverage as well. The insured may select a quarterly percentage increase (e.g., 1%, 2%, 3%, and so on), and the premium for the endorsement varies with the percentage increase selected. The endorsement protects against unintended underinsurance, which might result from increasing construction costs.

Guaranteed Replacement Cost The most attractive approach to coverage on the dwelling is an option offered by some insurers for *guaranteed replacement cost* coverage. The standard ISO endorsement for this coverage is called *Additional Limits of Liability for Coverage A, B, C, and D* (HO 04 11). The endorsement provides that the insured must notify the insurer of additions or improvements to the dwelling that increase its replacement cost by 5 percent or more within 30 days of the completion of the improvements. The insurer agrees to pay for the repair or replacement of the dwelling even if the cost to do so exceeds the limit for Coverage A shown in the declarations. In effect, the limit for Coverage A is increased retroactively to equal the current replacement cost of the building. Coverages B, C, and D limits are increased by the same percentage as the increase in the Coverage A limit. The premium is also adjusted to reflect the higher limits of coverage.

Under a second endorsement, *Specified Additional Amount of Insurance for Coverage A—Dwelling* (HO 04 20), the insured may choose 25 or 50 percent of the Coverage A limit as an additional amount of insurance on the dwelling, to be used for payment of dwelling losses that exceed the limit listed in the declarations.

Personal Property Coverage

The limit for personal property is 50 percent of the dwelling limit under Forms 2, 3, and 5. This limit may be increased when there is a need for greater coverage. The limit may be decreased if the insured does not own personal property equal to 50 percent of the value of the dwelling, but it cannot be decreased below 40 percent. Under Forms 4 and 6, the minimum coverage on personal property is $6000. The Personal Property coverage can, of course, be increased under any of the forms if the need exists.

The Personal Property insuring agreement of all forms is identical:

We cover personal property owned or used by any insured while anywhere in the world.

Note, first, that coverage is provided on both owned and borrowed property. For example, if an insured borrows property from a friend, and the property is damaged or lost as a result of an insured peril, the Homeowners Policy will cover the property as if it had been owned by the insured.

The reference to property owned or used *by any insured* grants coverage for the property of all persons that fall within the definition of *Insured.* The policy definition defines "Insured" to include the named insured ("You"), residents of the named insured's household who are relatives of the insured, and other persons under the age of 21 who are in the care of the named insured or a resident relative. The definition of insured also extends to full-time students who were residents of the household before moving out to attend school if they are under age 24 and related to the insured, or under 21 and in the care of the insured or a resident relative.

The entire personal property coverage applies "anywhere in the world," subject to one excep-

tion. Coverage on personal property located at a secondary residence is limited to 10 percent of the Coverage C limit, subject to a $1000 minimum. For example, if the insured has a summer cottage, coverage on personal property at the cottage is limited to 10 percent of the total Personal Property coverage.[4] With this exception, property located elsewhere than on the premises is covered up to the full limit specified for personal property.

If the insured requests at the time of loss, coverage also applies to property owned by others while on that part of the premises occupied by an insured or on the property of a guest or residence employee while in any residence occupied by an insured. The requirement that the insured request coverage on the property of others is intended to protect the insured in case the value of property of others that is damaged or destroyed, when combined with the insured's destroyed property, exceeds the limit of coverage.

Personal Property Replacement Cost

Coverage on personal property is on an *actual cash value* basis. The optional Personal Property Replacement Cost Endorsement provides replacement cost coverage on personal property and on certain building items that are excluded from the replacement cost coverage applicable to buildings. These building items are awnings, carpeting, household appliances, outdoor antennas, and outdoor equipment. Like the replacement cost on buildings, the personal property replacement cost provision agrees to pay losses without a deduction for depreciation. When the replacement cost of the loss is over $500, payment is made on a replacement cost basis only if the

---

[4]The 10 percent limit on property at a secondary residence does not apply to property at a newly acquired residence acquired as a principal residence for 30 days after the insured begins to move property to that location. Neither does it apply to property that has been moved while the principal residence is being repaired, renovated, or rebuilt and is not fit to live in or store property in.

Tidbits, Vignettes, and Conundrums 18.1

The Homeowners Policy and Nontraditional Families

The growth of nontraditional households has prompted the insurance industry to change some of its policy provision. The definition of insured in the Homeowners policy, for example, does not extend coverage to a resident of the named insured's household who is not a relative and is not a person under age 21 in the care of an insured. In the year-2000 revision of the Homeowners program, ISO introduced a new endorsement titled *Other Members of Your Household* (HO 04 58) that may be used to modify the definition of insured to include a person of any age or gender living with the named insured to share expenses or in a personal relationship.

A second area in which changing family patterns are recognized is with respect to the elderly. A new *Assisted Living Care Coverage* endorsement (HO 04 59) extends the definition of insured to provide limited third-party liability coverage for bodily injury and property damage to a relative of an insured who resides in an assisted living care facility. The endorsement also extends the coverage on personal property to cover personal property of such relatives. Finally, the endorsement provides additional living expense coverage in the event of loss or damage to the assisted living expense facility.

---

property is actually replaced. Certain designated classes of property (antiques, fine arts, memorabilia, souvenirs, collectors items, and similar property; property not kept in good or workable condition; and obsolete articles that are stored or not being used) are specifically excluded from the replacement cost coverage.

Property Excluded under Personal Property Coverage

The Personal Property insuring agreement provides coverage on a "blanket" basis. This means that all personal property owned or used by the insured is covered by a single amount of insurance. Blanket coverage is contrasted with specific or scheduled coverage, where items are listed and insured individually. Some types of property, such as jewelry, furs, guns, and other property with high values are commonly insured on a scheduled basis, usually for broader perils than the perils applicable to property covered on a blanket basis. The blanket coverage of the Homeowners forms excludes or limits coverage on certain classes of

property for which coverage is available on a scheduled basis or under other more specialized contracts. The following property is excluded:

1. Articles that are separately described and specifically insured under the Homeowners or any other insurance

2. Animals, birds, or fish

3. Motor vehicles, their accessories, equipment and parts, and electronic apparatus designed to be operated solely by the vehicle's electrical system, and tapes, discs, or other media for use with such equipment, while in or on the vehicle

4. Aircraft and their parts (except model or hobby aircraft)

5. Hovercraft and their parts

6. Property of roomers, boarders, and other tenants not related to the insured

7. Property in an apartment regularly rented or held for rental to others by the insured, except as provided under the Landlord's Furnishings additional coverage

8. Property rented or held for rental to others away from the premises

9. Business data, including such data stored in books of account, drawings, paper records, and electronic data processing (EDP) software media

10. Credit cards, electronic fund transfer cards, or access devices used for deposit, withdrawal, or transfer of funds (except as provided under Additional Coverages)

11. Water or steam

Most of these excluded classes are self-explanatory, but a few may require comment.

First, the exclusion of property separately described and specifically insured eliminates coverage on scheduled items and property insured under other policies from the blanket coverage on personal property.

The exclusion of motor vehicles and their equipment excludes not only automobiles, motorcycles, motorscooters, and the like, but also go-carts, minibikes, golf carts, and snowmobiles. An exception to the exclusion of motor vehicles provides coverage on vehicles such as riding lawn mowers or garden tractors, and motorized wheelchairs, as long as they are not subject to motor vehicle registration. Coverage is also available on owned golf carts by endorsment.

The Motor Vehicle exclusion extends to the vehicle's equipment and accessories only while in or on the vehicle. This means that the theft of a tire from the vehicle is excluded, while theft of the same tire while stored in the insured's garage would be covered. The exclusion of motor vehicle electronic apparatus includes tape players, CB radios, cellular telephones, fax machines, or any other electronic equipment only if it can be operated *solely* by the vehicle's electrical system. Electronic equipment that can be operated by the power system of the vehicle, but which can also be operated from other power sources, is not excluded, but is subject to a dollar limit discussed later in this chapter.

The exclusion of Hovercraft and their parts was added to the policy in the 2000 revision, to address an ambiguity over whether hovercraft were motor vehicles or watercraft.

Exclusions 6 and 7 are related. Property of roomers and boarders who are not members of the insured's family is excluded along with the property of other tenants. Furnishings owned by the insured in that part of the premises rented to roomers or boarders is covered. Furnishings in an apartment (a living unit with its own cooking and bathing facilities) are limited to the amount of coverage provided by the Landlord's Furnishings additional coverage.

Exclusion 8 eliminates coverage on property rented or held for rental to others away from the premises. Such property represents a business exposure beyond the scope of the Homeowners Policy.

The exclusion of business data stored in records and electronic data processing media eliminates coverage for the cost of reconstructing the information that is lost. The cost of blank or unexposed records and media is covered. Coverage is also provided for standard software such as word processing or spreadsheet programs available in the retail market.

The exclusion of water and steam is intended to make clear that water or steam delivered through public water mains is considered a utility and, therefore, not owned by the insured. Coverage will not apply, for example, for the loss of water or steam through a broken pipe on the premises that results in a massive increase in the insured's utility bill.

Personal Property Subject to Dollar Limits

In addition to excluding certain classes of property just described, the Homeowners forms impose dollar limits on other classes of property. Some of these limits may be increased for an additional premium. In other cases, the property may be scheduled with a higher limit of coverage of insured under another policy. The property subject to dollar limits is indicated in Table 18.2

The $200 limit on money applies not only to currency, but to coin collections, scrip, stored

Table 18.2   Dollar Limits on Specified Types of Personal Property

Item	Class of Property	Limit Dollar
1.	Money, bank notes, bullion, gold other than goldware, silver other than silverware, platinum other than platinumware, coins, medals, scrip, stored value and smart cards	$200
2.	Securities, accounts, deeds, evidences of debt, letters of credit, notes other than banknotes, manuscripts, personal records, passports, tickets and stamps, regardless of the medium (paper or computer software) on which the material exists	1500
3.	Watercraft, including their trailers, equipment and motors	1500
4.	Other trailers	1500
5.	Loss of jewelry, watches, furs, and precious and semiprecious stones by theft	1500
6.	Loss of firearms and related equipment by theft	2500
7.	Loss of silverware, silver-plated ware, goldware, gold-plated ware, platinumware, platinum-plated ware and pewterware by theft	2500
8.	Property on the residence premises used primarily for business purposes	2500
9.	Property away from the residence premises used for business purposes	500
10.	Electronic apparatus and accessories that may be powered by electrical system of a motor vehicle but that retains its capability of being operated by other sources, while in or on a motor vehicle	$1500
11.	Electronic apparatus and accessories used primarily for business that may be powered by electrical system of a motor vehicle but that retains its capability of being operated by other sources, while away from the premises	$1500

value cards, and smart cards. Stored value cards are instruments like prepaid phone cards with a magnetic strip or computer chip that are loaded with some amount of spendable credits. Smart cards can also be loaded with spendable credits, but serve other functions as well. The limitation on such cards reflects their increasing role as substitutes for cash. The $200 limit may be increased to $500 for an additional premium.

Note that the dollar limitations applicable to jewelry and furs, silverware, and firearms and related equipment (classes 6, 7, and 8) apply only to loss by theft. Property of these types valued at more than the specified limits may be scheduled for their full value.

Coverage on business property ("property used primarily for business purposes") is limited to $2500 while on premises. Coverage on business property away from the premises is limited to $500. The limit for business personal property on premises may be increased by endorsement up to $10,000 for an additional premium. When the on-premises business property limit is increased, the off-premises limit is increased to 20 percent of the on-premises limit.

Two separate provisions limit coverage on electronic apparatus (including accessories, antennas, tapes, discs, or other media) that is equipped to be operated by the power system of a vehicle, but that retains the capacity of being operated by another source. The first limit on such equipment is $1500 while it is in or on a motor vehicle. The second provision imposes a $1500 limit on the same types of equipment while it is away from the premises, but not in an auto, if the equipment is used primarily for business purposes. Although the distinction between the two limitations is perhaps confusing, the intent is to limit coverage on such property that is used for both personal and business purposes to $1500 while it is in a vehicle.

Electronic apparatus that is used for business is also limited to $1500 while it is away from the insured premises whether or not it is in a vehicle. This $1500 limit supersedes the $500 limit on business property away from the premises.

Loss of Use Coverage

The *Loss of Use Coverage*, designated Coverage D, provides protection against loss involving both the part of the premises occupied by the insured and any part rented to others. For the part of the premises occupied by the insured, the *Additional Living Expense* coverage pays for the necessary increase in living expenses incurred by the insured to continue as nearly as practicable the normal standard of living of the household when the premises are rendered uninhabitable by an insured peril. Payment is made only for the period required to repair or replace the damage or, if the insured permanently relocates, for the period required to settle the household elsewhere.

For damage to a part of the premises rented to others, coverage applies for the fair rental value. Again, coverage applies for the shortest period in which the property could be repaired or replaced. Under Form 4 and Form 6, Coverage D applies not only for loss arising out of damage to covered property (i.e., personal property) but also for loss to the building containing the covered property that makes the building uninhabitable.

Additional Coverages

The Homeowners forms include 12 supplementary extensions of coverage under Section I, called Additional Coverages. Although most of the additional coverages are common to all forms, a few of the additional coverages are included in some forms but not others.

1. Debris Removal

The Debris Removal additional coverage covers expenses incurred in removing the debris of insured property damaged by an insured peril. If the policy limit is exhausted by payment for damage to the property, the Debris Removal additional coverage provides up to 5 percent of the limit applicable to the property damaged as an additional amount of insurance to cover the removal of debris.

The debris removal additional coverage also covers up to $500 per tree with a $1000 aggregate for the removal of certain fallen trees from the premises. Coverage is provided for the removal of trees that have been "felled" by the perils of windstorm, hail, the weight of ice, snow, or sleet, and any tree belonging to a neighbor that is felled by any of the named perils applicable to Coverage C (the contents coverage) if, in falling, the tree damages a covered structure, blocks a driveway denying access to the premises, or blocks a ramp or fixture designed to assist a handicapped person entering or leaving the premises. As explained below, these are not perils for which damage to trees is covered and there is no indemnity for the loss of the tree itself. In other words, the extension applies only for the removal of trees that are not insured (i.e., a neighbor's tree) or that suffer damage that is not insured.

2. Reasonable Repairs

The policy requires the insured to take all reasonable steps to protect and preserve the property at and after a loss (under the Conditions section of Section I). Under the Reasonable Repairs additional coverage, the insurer agrees to pay the costs incurred by the insured in providing such protection. This extension is not additional coverage, but the cost of reasonable repairs is included in the amount of loss payable, up to the policy limit.

3. Trees, Shrubs, Plants, and Lawns

An extension is also provided to cover trees, shrubs, plants, and lawns. Under Forms 2, 3, 5, and 8, the extension is 5 percent of the amount on the dwelling. Under Forms 4 and 6, it is 10 percent of the amount of coverage on personal property. The coverage is subject to its own specific perils (fire, lightning, explosion, riot or civil commotion, aircraft, non-owned vehicles, vandalism and malicious mischief, and theft). A $500 limit applies per tree, shrub, or plant, except in Form 8, where the limit is $250.

4. Fire Department Service Charge

Many municipal fire departments will respond to calls outside the city limits, but a charge is usually made, which can amount to several hundred dollars. The Fire Department Service Charge coverage provides up to $500 to cover the insured's liability under a contract or agreement for fire department charges when the fire department is called because the property is threatened by an insured peril (normally fire).

5. Property Removed

Insured property may be damaged while attempting to preserve it from destruction by removing it from a building that is threatened by an insured peril. It would be grossly unjust to penalize the insured for attempting to prevent a loss to the property or to reduce the amount of loss if the property were somehow damaged in the process. For this reason, the Homeowners forms (and most other property insurance policies) provide coverage for damage to property that is being removed to protect it from one of the perils insured against. Coverage applies for loss by any cause during the process of removal and also for 30 days following the removal.

6. Credit Card, Electronic Funds Transfer Card or Access Device, Forgery, and Counterfeit Money

This additional coverage provides protection up to $500 for losses resulting from the unauthorized use of a credit card, electronic funds transfer

card, or other electronic access device, issued or registered to any insured.[5] It makes no difference whether the card was stolen, lost, or simply misplaced, as long as the loss results from its unauthorized use. Coverage is also provided for depositor's forgery, which protects against loss resulting from the forgery or alteration of any check drawn on or by the insured, up to the $500 limit. In addition, the insured is protected up to $500 against loss sustained through the acceptance of bogus paper currency. Finally, this coverage agrees to defend the insured and pay court costs arising in connection with any of the covered losses.

7. Loss Assessment Coverage

Loss Assessment coverage provides payment for assessments against the insured by a condominium association or a corporation or association of property owners. Separate Loss Assessment coverages apply to Section I and Section II of the policy. With respect to Section I, coverage applies up to $1000 per loss for assessments resulting from direct loss to property owned by all members collectively, when such damage is caused by a peril insured under the policy. Increased limits are available by endorsement.

8. Collapse

Prior to 1984, Collapse was included in many property insurance forms as an insured peril, a logical inconsistency, since Collapse is not a peril, but a result that is caused by some peril. Collapse is now defined as an additional coverage and is covered only if it results from specific causes. The collapse additional coverage is included in all Homeowners forms except Form 8 (and Form 1,

---

[5]Federal legislation effective since October 1970 provides a maximum limit of $50 for a credit card holder's liability in the event of the unauthorized use of the card. Even though the limit applies to each card, it has reduced the possible severity of credit card losses.

where still in use). Collapse is defined to mean the abrupt falling down or caving in of a building or part of the building with the result that it cannot be occupied. Coverage applies only if the collapse is caused by a specific group of perils. The specific perils that must cause collapse for coverage to exist are

1. The perils insured against in Coverage C
2. Decay that is hidden from view, unless the insured knew of such damage
3. Insect or vermin damage that is hidden from view, unless the insured knew of such damage
4. Weight of contents, equipment, animals, or people
5. Weight of rain on a roof
6. Defects in materials or methods used in construction, if the collapse occurs during the course of the construction

Coverage applies for damage to all insured property that results from a covered collapse.

9. Glass or Safety Glazing Material

The additional coverage covers breakage of glass that is part of the building, including glass in storm doors and windows, by any cause. There is no coverage for breakage if the building has been vacant for over 30 days, but a building under construction is not considered vacant. Loss for breakage is settled based on the replacement with safety glazing material when such replacement is required by law.

10. Landlord's Furnishings

The Landlord's Furnishings additional coverage is included in Forms 2 and 3. It provides $2500 to cover appliances, carpeting, and other household appliances in each apartment on the residence premises that is rented or held for rental to others. The perils for which landlord's furnishings

are covered are identical under Forms 2 and 3: the broad named perils applicable to contents, but excluding theft.

11. Ordinance or Law

In many cities, building codes specify that new buildings must meet certain construction requirements. Owners of buildings that do not conform to the code provisions (because they were constructed before these laws were passed) face a special exposure. Usually, the building code requires that if a structure is destroyed, it must be replaced with one that meets code provisions. This is normally more costly than replacing the existing building. The building codes also provide that if a noncomforming building is damaged beyond a specified percentage (e.g., 40 percent or 50 percent), it cannot be repaired. This creates a gap in coverage, since the 40 percent or 50 percent loss would be only a partial loss under the property policy, but would be a total loss to the insured.

Like most other property insurance forms, the Homeowners forms contain an Ordinance or Law exclusion (discussed later in the chapter), which excludes any increase in the amount of loss due to the enforcement of building laws. The Ordinance or Law Additional Coverage provides up to 10 percent of the Coverage A limit, as additional insurance, to pay for increased costs made necessary by the enforcement of an ordinance or law when the building is damaged by an insured peril. This 10 percent may be increased to 25, 50, 75, 100 percent or more of the Coverage A limit. In form HO 4, the Ordinance or Law additional coverage is 10 percent of the Building Additions and Alterations coverage.

12. Grave Markers

Grave markers, including mausoleums, on or away from the premises, are covered up to $5000. Coverage is provided for loss caused by the perils insured against under Coverage C. This extension was added to the policy in the 2000 revision.

Homeowners Deductibles

In most states, there is a $250 deductible under the Homeowners Policy that applies to loss by any of the perils under Section I, including Loss of Use coverage. However, the deductible does not apply to scheduled items or to the Credit Card, Forgery, and Counterfeit Money coverage. In many states, the deductible may be reduced to $100 for an additional premium. If the insured desires a higher deductible, options of $500, $1000, and $2500 are provided under the Insurance Service Office rules, with substantial rate credits.

Homeowners Form 3—Perils Insured

As is the case with most forms of property insurance, the scope of the coverage provided under the Homeowners forms is determined by the perils against which protection is provided. We turn now to an examination of the perils for which coverage is provided under the Homeowners forms. For the purpose of this review, we will examine a single form, Homeowners Form 3. Because this form includes both the broad named-peril coverage applicable under forms HO 2, HO 4, and HO 6, and the open-peril coverage applicable to the dwelling and other structures under Form 3 and 5, we are, in effect, also examining the perils of these forms.

Open-Peril Coverage—Dwellings and Other Structures

Coverage on the dwelling and other structures under Homeowners Form 3 is on an "open-peril" basis, with coverage provided against all physical loss except by those causes that are specifically excluded. In addition, the Loss of Use coverage also applies on an open-peril basis. The open-peril in-suring agreement of Form 3 is simple and straightforward:

1. We insure against risk of direct physical loss to property described in Coverages A and B.
2. We do not insure, however, for loss: . . . .

A list of excluded losses for which coverage is not provided then follows. Any loss that does not fall within one of the exclusions is covered. The number of exclusions required in an open-peril form is usually extensive, since all uninsurable perils must be excluded. The exclusions that immediately follow the open-peril Dwelling and Other Structures insuring agreement include the general Section I exclusions (designated exclusion a), losses involving collapse, except as covered under the Collapse Additional Coverage (designated exclusion b), and a group of seven exclusions (designated c(1) through c(6) that are more or less standard exclusions in all open-peril contracts.

General Section I Exclusions

The General Section I exclusions are divided into two groups designated A.1 through A.9 and B.1 through B.3.

A.1 Ordinance or Law With the exception of the 10 percent extension for Ordinance or Laws provided under the Additional Coverage previously discussed (and any increase in this extension added by endorsement), the form excludes loss caused by the enforcement of any ordinance or law regulating construction, repair, or demolition of any building.

A.2 Earth Movement The Earth Movement exclusion eliminates coverage for loss caused by earth movement except direct loss by fire, explosion, theft, or breakage of glass. Earth movement is defined in the policy to include earthquake, including land shock waves or tremors before, during, or after a volcanic eruption; landslide; mine subsidence; mudflow; and other types of earth movement such as earth sinking, rising, or shifting. Coverage for earthquake and other types of earth movement is available by endorsement for an additional premium.

A.3 Water Damage The Water Damage exclusion eliminates coverage for certain types of enumerated water, including flood in all its forms, water or water-borne material that backs up through sewers or drains or overflows from a sump, and water or water-borne material below the surface of the ground that seeps through basement walls, foundation floors, and similar structural components. An exception to the exclusion provides coverage for loss by fire, explosion, or theft that is caused by any of the excluded forms of water. In most jurisdictions the exclusion of water and water-borne material that backs up through sewers or drains can be deleted by endorsement for the payment of an additional premium. The *Water Back Up and Sump Discharge or Overflow* endorsement provides coverage up to $5000 for loss resulting from such backup.

A.4 Power Failure The Power Failure exclusion denies coverage for losses resulting directly from interruption of power or other utility service, if the interruption takes place away from the residence premises. The exclusion contemplates a special form of consequential loss damage that may result from power interruption. The best example as it applies to the dwelling risk is food in a deep freezer. If lightning strikes the dwelling, and burns out the motor on the freezer, food in the freezer may spoil as a result. The damage to the food in the freezer results from the "interruption of power." The net effect of the Power Interruption exclusion is to provide coverage for such consequential losses when equipment on the premises is damaged by an insured peril and to deny coverage for such losses when the damage takes place away from the premises.

A.5 Neglect The policy excludes loss resulting directly or indirectly from neglect of the insured to use reasonable means at or after a loss to save the property. The insured cannot collect for damage that he or she has a reasonable chance to prevent. Note, however, that neglect of the insured before a loss does not affect coverage. The exclusion merely relieves the insurer from liability for that part of the loss attributable to the insured's neglect *at or after* a loss (i.e., when a loss occurs).

A.6 War As do most forms of property insurance, the Homeowners forms exclude loss caused by war in all its forms, including undeclared war, insurrections, rebellion, or revolution. Any discharge of a nuclear weapon—even though accidental—is excluded under this provision.

Tidbits, Vignettes, and Conundrums 18.2

Water's Not the Problem

The reference to "water-borne material that backs up through sewers or drains" was added to the water damage exclusion in 2000 in response to court decisions that held the earlier wording to be ambiguous. In a Florida case, for example, the insured made claim for payment of damage caused by raw sewage that backed up through the sewer. Because only damage caused by water was excluded, the court ruled that coverage applied. *Florida Farm Bureau Insurance Company v. Birge et ux.* 1994 Fla App. Lexis 12600.

A.7 Nuclear Hazard The Nuclear Hazard exclusion refers to loss defined in the Section I conditions and provides that losses from such hazard are not covered. The nuclear hazard includes nuclear reactions, radiation, or radioactive contamination. The one exception is direct loss by fire, which is covered even if it results from the nuclear hazard.

A.8 Intentional Loss The Homeowners Policy excludes coverage for intentional loss "by or at the direction of an insured" and "with the intent to cause a loss." While this exclusion aims at eliminating payment to persons who commit arson losses, it goes beyond this. It also eliminates payment to other persons insured, who were not involved in the intentional act. These could include an innocent spouse or even a person with an interest in the dwelling who has been added as an additional insured under the policy.[6]

A.9 Government Action Loss resulting from government actions—such as the destruction, seizure, or confiscation of property by order of any government authority—is excluded. This could include property illegally held or used for illegal purposes. Sometimes, government authorities will seize or confiscate not only illegal substances, but the structure in which such property is located. The exclusion does not apply to acts of destruction taken to prevent the spread of fire.

B.1-B.3 Concurrent Causation Exclusions Exclusions B.1 through B.3, usually referred to as the "concurrent causation" exclusions, were added to the policy (and to most other broad form and special form property contracts) in the 1980s in response to a series of adverse court decisions.[7]

Exclusion B.1 applies to loss caused by weather conditions that contribute to an otherwise excluded peril. For example, landslide caused by excessive rain or rain combined with wind is excluded. Loss caused directly by the weather condition such as windstorm damage would be covered.

Exclusion B.2 applies to loss caused by acts or decisions, including failure to act or decide, of any person, group, organization, or governmental body. Loss resulting from failure of a governmental body to maintain flood control structures or failure to enforce zoning or building codes would be excluded.

Exclusion B.3 relates to loss caused by faulty, inadequate, or defective activities such as planning, design, maintenance, or faulty materials. Loss resulting solely from inadequate design of a building would not be covered, but the ensuing loss such as by fire arising from faulty installation or repair would be covered.

Dwelling and Other Structures Exclusions

The remaining exclusions applicable to Coverage A and B fall into two broad classes. First, four exclusions (designated C1 through C4) relate to

---

[6]In 1998, the NAIC adopted a model law which, when adopted by a state, nullifies the intentional loss exclusion of the homeowners policy with respect to damage suffered by a victim of domestic abuse and caused by a co-insured. The model law prohibits insurance companies from denying, canceling, or nonrenewing coverage based on abuse status and requires insurers to pay claims filed by innocent co-insureds.

[7]These exclusions were added to the policy in 1984 in response to a doctrine adopted by some courts called *concurrent causation*, which held that when a loss results from two causes—one of which is excluded and the other not excluded—the loss is covered. This stretched the coverage of broad form and special form contracts beyond the intent of its drafters, providing coverage for flood and earthquake losses on the grounds that although these causes of loss were excluded, they were concurrently caused by perils that were not excluded (zoning laws that allowed structures to be built in flood or earthquake areas or negligence of a contractor in not making the structures earthquake resistant). The concurrent causation exclusions merely bring the scope of the coverage back to its original intent.

perils that are covered as named perils in the other Homeowners forms. These exclusions relate to freezing of plumbing, and damage to fences, pavements, patios, and certain other property by freezing, thawing, or the pressure of water or ice, theft in or to a dwelling under construction, and vandalism and any ensuing loss if the building has been vacant for more than 60 days. We will discuss these exclusions when we examine the named-peril coverage applicable to personal property.

The second class of exclusions (C5 and C6) are a series of open-peril exclusions that appear in virtually all open-peril contracts. They exclude losses that are considered to be uninsurable, either because they are inevitable or because it is difficult to fix the time at which the damage takes place. The first of these exclusions (C5), excludes loss caused by mold, fungus, or wet rot. An exception applies to loss caused by mold, fungus, or wet rot that is hidden in walls, ceilings, or floors that results from accidental discharge, leakage, or overflow of water from the plumbing system or domestic appliances.

The remaining open-peril exclusions are grouped together as exclusion (C6), and include the following:

a. Wear and tear, marring, or deterioration

b. Mechanical breakdown, latent defect, inherent vice or a quality in property that causes it to damage or destroy itself

c. Smog, rust or other corrosion, or dry rot

d. Smoke from agricultural smudging or industrial operations

e. Discharge, release, or dispersal of contaminants or pollutants, unless caused by one of the named perils for which personal property is insured

f. Settling, cracking, shrinking, bulging, or expansions of pavements, patios, foundations, walls, floors, or ceilings

g. Birds, vermin, rodents, or insects

h. Animals owned or kept by an insured

Any ensuing loss to property insured under Coverages A and B that is not excluded by another provision of the policy is covered. For example, if a mechanical breakdown resulted in a fire, the resulting fire would be covered.

Coverage C—Personal Property Perils Insured

Homeowners Form 3 covers damage to personal property against loss by 16 named perils. Because the coverage on personal property under Forms 2, 4, and 6 covers loss by the same 16 perils, the following discussion of the perils covered under this form will also serve to illustrate the coverage under these other forms. A complete analysis of these perils requires a close examination of the form itself, but the following explanation provides an indication of the scope of their coverage.

I. Fire and Lightning

The basic peril against which coverage is provided in virtually all property insurance forms is fire. Surprisingly, the term "fire" is nowhere defined in the policy. Although the term is not defined, court decisions over many years have established that the fire contemplated in insurance policies is of a specific type. Fire, according to the courts, is "combustion proceeding at a rate rapid enough to generate flame, glow, or incandescence."[8] In other words, there must be light. Mere smoke, scorching, or charring is not sufficient to constitute a fire.

Not all fires are covered under the fire peril. The courts distinguish between a *friendly* fire and a hostile or *unfriendly* fire. A friendly fire is one that is within the confines for which it was intended; the friendly fire was intentionally kindled and burns where it is supposed to. A hostile fire, on the other hand, has escaped its intended con-

---

[8] *Western Woolen Co. v. Northern Assurance Co.*, 139 Fed. 637 (1905).

fines. Only hostile or unfriendly fires are covered under the named fire peril.

In addition to the destruction by the actual fire itself, the "direct loss by fire" peril provides coverage for any damage that results from the smoke from a hostile fire, or is caused by water or attempts by firefighters to extinguish a hostile fire.

2. Windstorm and Hail

The wind and hail insuring agreement excludes damage caused by rain, snow, sleet, sand, or dust to the interior of the building unless the exterior walls or roof are first damaged by direct action of the wind or hail. Thus, if an insured leaves a window open and the wind blows rain into the house, damaging the contents, there is no coverage. However, if the window were first broken by the wind, damage to the contents would be covered.

In addition to the exclusion relating to damage to the interior of the structure, there is an exclusion of damage by wind or hail to watercraft, their trailers, or equipment, unless such items are inside a fully enclosed building.

3. Explosion

Explosions are covered whether they originate within or outside the building. There are no exceptions or exclusions.

4. Riot or Civil Commotion

Damage caused by rioters and persons engaged in civil commotion is covered, subject to few exceptions. Even "pillage and looting" are covered, if they occur during and at the place of the riot. The only area in which an issue has arisen is in the distinction between a riot (which is covered) and an insurrection (which is excluded as a form of war). The courts have differentiated between the two: an insurrection is distinguished by its intent—to overthrow duly constituted authority. A riot, in contrast, is a "tumultuous disturbance of the peace"—something that happens in response

to police brutality, civil unrest, or sometimes after a loss at the NCAA basketball tournament.

5. Aircraft

The aircraft peril provides coverage against damage to insured property caused by aircraft, including self-propelled missiles or spacecraft. This includes damage resulting from direct physical contact of the insured property with aircraft, but could also include damage resulting from objects falling from aircraft or even "sonic boom."

6. Vehicles

Coverage applies for damage to insured property caused by vehicles, including vehicles owned or operated by an insured.[9]

7. Smoke

Although the fire peril includes coverage for damage caused by smoke from a hostile fire, the smoke peril broadens this to include coverage for sudden and accidental smoke damage from other sources, including the emission or puffback of smoke, soot, fumes, or vapors from a furnace or boiler. Smoke from agricultural smudging and industrial operations are excluded.

8. Vandalism and Malicious Mischief

Vandalism and malicious mischief refers to the willful and malicious damage to or destruction of property. Loss by vandalism is not covered if the building has been vacant for over 60 days.[10] The

---

[9]Form 8 (and Form 1 where it is still used) excludes all damage caused by vehicles owned or operated by a resident of the premises. Form 2 excludes damage to fences, driveways, or walks by owned vehicles.

[10]Insurance contracts frequently reduce or exclude coverage when the insured property is "vacant" and some contracts restrict coverage in case of "unoccupancy." A building is vacant when it has neither occupants nor contents. It is unoccupied when it has contents, but no occupants.

policy also provides that a dwelling under construction is not considered "vacant."

9. Theft

Except for Forms 5 and 8, the theft coverage of the Homeowners forms is identical.[11] The theft peril provides coverage for theft, including attempted theft or loss of property from a known location when it is likely that the property has been stolen. The phrase "loss of property from a known location when it is likely that the property has been stolen" is intended to reduce the insured's burden of establishing that the loss actually resulted from theft where there is no conclusive proof. The policy requires the insured to give immediate notice to the police if an article is stolen.

There are two sets of exclusions applicable to the theft peril: a set of general theft exclusions and a set that applies only to property that is away from the insured premises.

General Theft Exclusions There are three general theft exclusions.

1. Theft committed by any insured
2. Theft in or from a dwelling under construction or of materials or supplies for use in the construction until the dwelling is completed and occupied
3. Theft from any part of a residence rented by an insured to anyone except another insured

With respect to the first, theft from one family member by another is not covered. In addition, while the definition of the dwelling includes lumber, materials, and appliances on the premises and intended for use in construction, the second general theft exclusion eliminates insurance against the stealing of such items. The exclusion with respect to theft from any part of the

---

[11]Theft coverage under Forms 5 and 8 is discussed later in the chapter.

dwelling that is rented relates not only to portions of the house that may be let to roomers and boarders, but also to the occasional rental of that portion of the dwelling customarily occupied by the insured. Such a situation might arise, for example, if the insured were leaving town for an extended period and decides to rent out the residence.

Off-Premises Theft Exclusions Three exclusions apply to property while away from the premises.

First, theft of property from any residence owned, rented to, or occupied by any insured is not covered for loss by theft except while an insured is actually residing at the location. For example, if the policyholder owns a summer cottage, its contents are covered for other perils (subject to the 10 percent limitation on contents at a secondary residence), but the theft coverage does not apply except while the individual is actually residing at the cottage. An exception to this exclusion provides that coverage will apply to the property of a student residing away from home if the student has been at the residence at any time during the 45 days immediately preceding the loss. While there would be no coverage for loss by theft on property left at a dormitory, sorority, or fraternity over an entire summer, coverage would apply on other occasions such as spring break, Christmas, or Thanksgiving, when students leave the campus.

The second off-premises exclusion excludes theft of watercraft or their furnishings, equipment, and outboard motors, and the third exclusion eliminates coverage for campers or trailers stolen while away from the premises.

10. Falling Objects

This peril covers damage caused by falling objects such as tree limbs, but is not limited to this. Contents of a building are not covered for loss by falling objects unless the exterior of the building first sustains damage. Also, damage to the falling object itself is excluded. The exclusion of "damage to the falling object itself" eliminates coverage for damage to contents items that are damaged by being dropped or otherwise falling. Thus, if a heavy mirror fell from the wall, damaging the interior of the building and itself, there is no coverage under the Falling Objects peril.

11. Weight of Ice, Snow, or Sleet

Damage caused by the weight of ice, snow, and sleet is covered, but the damage must actually result from the *weight*. Melting snow that leaks into the dwelling causing damage would not be covered. Damage to awnings, fences, patios, pavement, swimming pools, foundations, retaining walls, bulkheads, piers, wharves, or docks is also excluded.

12. Accidental Discharge or Overflow of Water or Steam

Coverage is provided for the accidental discharge, leakage, or overflow of water from a plumbing, heating, or air-conditioning or automatic sprinkler system from within a domestic appliance. This includes not only burst or leaking pipes, but overflow of plumbing fixtures such as bathtubs, or appliances such as automatic dishwashers. Coverage includes the cost of tearing out and replacing part of the building to make repairs, but the loss to the system or appliance itself is excluded.

13. Sudden and Accidental Tearing Apart, Cracking, Burning, or Bulging of Heating or Air-Conditioning Systems

This insuring agreement provides coverage against loss caused by "Sudden and accidental tearing apart, cracking, burning or bulging of a steam or hot water heating system, an air-conditioning system or of a household appliance." Damage to steam or hot water heating systems of the type specified can occur if the water level for such systems becomes too low and damage of this type was the original rationale for this coverage.

Damage of the types specified, from any cause, is covered.

14. Freezing of Plumbing, Heating, and Other Systems and Appliances

Loss resulting from freezing of plumbing, heating, or air-conditioning or automatic sprinkler systems or domestic appliances is covered, provided the insured has used reasonable means to maintain heat in the building or if the water has been shut off and the system has been drained. (If the building is protected by a sprinkler system, draining is not an allowable option.) Unlike the water leakage peril, coverage applies for damage to a system or appliance damaged by freezing.

15. Sudden and Accidental Damage from Artificially Generated Electrical Current

Sudden and accidental injury to wiring and appliances from artificially generated currents is covered as an insured peril. The major exclusion with respect to artificially generated electricity is damage to tubes, transistors, electronic components, or circuitry, which are excluded. Although damage to television sets, stereos, and the like that is caused by artificial electricity is excluded, the same damage, if caused by lightning (natural electricity), is covered.

16. Volcanic Eruption

The volcanic eruption peril covers "aboveground" effects of volcanic eruption, such as damage caused by lava and debris from an earthquake. As noted earlier, the general exclusions exclude damage by shock waves and ground tremors caused by volcanic eruption.

Optional Perils

There are three endorsements available to extend the coverage of the policy to include additional perils, the Sinkhole Collapse Endorsement, the

Earthquake Endorsement, and a Refrigerated Property Coverage Endorsement.

1. Sinkhole Collapse

All Homeowners forms except Forms 4 and 6 may be endorsed to provide coverage against sinkhole collapse. The sinkhole collapse peril covers damage to insured property caused by underground erosion of limestone or similar rock caused by water. The cost of filling the sinkhole is not covered.

2. Earthquake

The Earthquake Endorsement modifies the basic Earth Movement exclusion of the policy, reimbursing for loss to insured property resulting from earthquake or volcanic eruption, excluding only loss by flood or tidal wave generated by these catastrophes. The coverage does not apply to damage to land. In most jurisdictions, the earthquake deductible is 5 percent of the value of each item insured. In some areas, where the earthquake hazard is severe, a 10 percent deductible is used.

3. Refrigerated Property Coverage

The Refrigerated Property Coverage Endorsement (HO 04 98) covers damage to property stored in freezers or refrigerators against loss caused by the interruption of electrical service to the refrigeration unit or by the mechanical failure of the unit. The coverage is subject to a $500 limit and is subject to a $100 deductible.

Features of Other Homeowners Forms

Homeowners 4 Contents Broad Form

The Homeowners 4 Contents Broad Form (HO 00 04), which is designed for tenants, provides protection against the same named perils as does the contents coverage of Homeowners Form 3. It does not cover the building, but includes an additional coverage for Building Additions and Alterations. The Building Additions and Alterations

---

Tidbits, Vignettes, and Conundrums 18.3

Waiting for the Big One

Based on research conducted since the 1989 Loma Prieta earthquake, U.S. Geological Survey (USGS) and other scientists conclude that there is a 70 percent probability of at least one magnitude 6.7 or greater quake, capable of causing widespread damage, striking the San Francisco Bay region before 2030. It is estimated that if a 7.0 magnitude quake hit the Los Angeles area, it would cost as much as $120 billion in insured damages and up to $220 billion in total losses.

Earthquakes in the United States are by no means confined to California. In the winter of 1811–12, the central Mississippi Valley was struck by three of the most powerful earthquakes in U.S. history, centered at the New Madrid fault in Missouri. The San Francisco, California, earthquake of 1906 (magnitude 7.8) was felt 350 miles away in Nevada, whereas the New Madrid earthquake of December 1811 (magnitude 8.0) rang church bells in Boston, Massachusetts, 1,000 miles away and changed the course of the Missouri River. Scientists estimate that the probability of a magnitude 6 to 7 earthquake occurring in this Mississippi Valley within the next 50 years is higher than 90 percent.

Source: http://quake.wr.usgs.gov/

coverage applies to building additions, alterations, fixtures, improvements, or installations made by the insured in a rented apartment or dwelling. This coverage, also sometimes called *tenant's improvements and betterments*, covers the insured's "use value" in such improvements. A tenant who installs extensive renovations in rented property does so in the expectation that he or she will have the use of the property for a period of time. If the property is destroyed, the tenant loses the use of the additions or improvements. The Building Additions and Alterations additional coverage provides compensation for this loss. The coverage on Building Additions and Alterations is limited to 10 percent of the coverage on contents.

Coverage on personal property insured under HO 4 may be extended to an open-peril basis by the *Special Personal Property Coverage—Form HO 00 04 Only Endorsement*. The open-peril coverage of this endorsement parallels the coverage on personal property under Form HO 00 05, discussed next.

Homeowners Comprehensive Form 5

Coverage on the Dwelling under Form 5 is identical with the dwelling coverage of Form 3. In addition, HO 5 provides open-peril coverage on contents. HO 5 includes several exclusions applicable to personal property that are common to most contracts providing open-peril coverage on personal property. These include breakage of fragile or brittle articles (other than jewelry, watches, bronzes, cameras, and photographic lenses) unless such breakage is caused by specifically named perils[12] and losses resulting from dampness or extremes of temperature. Loss to watches, jewelry,

and furs as a result of refinishing or renovation is also excluded.

The theft coverage of Form 5 is subject to only one exclusion, theft in or to a building under construction until completed and occupied. The other exclusions of the named-peril forms—theft by an insured and theft from a secondary residence—are not excluded and are therefore covered. Furthermore, in a revised statement of the limit on jewelry, furs, silverware, and firearms, Form 5 makes it clear that coverage applies not only to loss by theft, but to misplacing and losing such property as well.

Condominium Unit-Owners Form 6

Homeowners Form 6 is designed to cover the special exposures of a condominium unit-owner. To understand these special exposures, it may be helpful first to review the nature of a condominium. Basically, a condominium is a multiple-occupancy building in which individuals own units of living space—a cube of air formed by the four walls, ceiling, and floor. The common areas of the building are jointly owned by all unit-owners as tenants-in-common. These common areas include the basic structure, the grounds, halls, stairways, and other facilities. Because the condominium arrangement involves two kinds of ownership—individual and joint—the responsibility for insurance is also divided. The individual unit-owners grant the right to purchase insurance on the common elements of ownership to a condominium association. Although the condominium association purchases insurance on the common elements of ownership, the unit-owner is generally responsible for the insurance additions to his or her own unit. The exact definition of the unit-owner's responsibility varies with state law, and sometimes with the bylaws of the association. In some instances, the unit-owner is responsible for all real property within the confines of the perimeter of the condominium unit. This could include interior partitions, appliances, and even plumbing fixtures and the interior décor, such as wallpaper, paneling, and carpeting. In addition to the need for coverage on unit-owner's ad-

---

[12]The specific perils for which loss by breakage is covered are fire, lightning, perils of extended coverage, vehicles, vandalism and malicious mischief, collapse of a building, earthquake, water not otherwise excluded, theft or attempted theft, or sudden and accidental tearing apart, cracking, burning, or bulging of a steam or hot water heating system, air-conditioning system, or appliance for heating water.

ditions, the condominium unit-owner needs coverage on his or her own personal property. HO 6 is designed to meet both needs.

Coverage of Form 6

The coverage under the Homeowners 6 Unit-Owner's form generally parallels the coverage of Form 4, providing protection against loss by the broad named perils discussed in detail above. Coverage A of Homeowners Form 6 (which, like Coverage A of other forms is designated "Dwelling Coverage") covers building alterations and additions, plus certain other items of real property identified in the Dwelling insuring agreement. The standard limit for Coverage A, which must usually be increased, is $1000. The definition of insured property under the Dwelling coverage includes alterations, appliances, fixtures, and improvements within the residence premises, other items of real property that pertain exclusively to the insured's premises (such as balconies or patios and could even include trees or shrubs), property that is the insured's responsibility under the condominium association agreement, and other structures owned solely by the insured (such as a garage or tool shed).

Although the Condominium Unit-Owner's form provides basic coverage for the owner of a condominium, it may be modified by endorsement to provide broader coverage and coverage tailored to the specific needs of the unit-owner.

Open-Peril Coverage

The named-peril coverage on real property may be extended by endorsement to an open-peril basis, providing essentially the same coverage on unit-owner's additions as is provided on the building under Homeowners Form 3. In addition, coverage on personal property insured under HO 6 may be extended to an open-peril basis by the *Unit-Owners Coverage C Special Coverage*. The open-peril coverage of this endorsement parallels the coverage on personal property under Form HO 00 05.

Rental Unit Coverage

Many condominium units, especially those in recreational areas, are rented to others, at least for parts of the year. A *Rental Unit Coverage* endorsement may be added to the policy to cover personal property in the residence premises regularly rented or held for rental to others. (The Basic Form covers personal property only if "occasionally" rented to others.)

Assessment Coverage

As in the other Homeowners forms, the Section I Loss Assessment Additional Coverage covers assessments by the condominium association for damage to common property by the perils insured under the policy. An increased limit for loss assessment coverage is available by endorsement. A provision in the Loss Assessment Endorsement for HO 6 sets a $1000 limit on payment for assessments that arise from a deductible in the association's property insurance policy.

Homeowners Form 8

The Homeowners forms were conceived as a program for superior exposures in the dwelling field; as a result, there are some dwellings that are not eligible for the program. One major class of buyers who could not obtain coverage under the original Homeowners forms were owners of certain types of older dwellings that were built many years ago, when the home-building industry was more labor intensive. These dwellings often involve obsolete types of construction or are too large in relation to the insured's needs. Usually, the replacement cost of such structures far exceeds their market value. These older obsolete dwellings may have a replacement cost of $500,000 or more, while the market value is $100,000 or $200,000. Owners of such property often do not see any sense in insuring their dwellings for two or three times fair market value. At the same time, insurers are reluctant to provide replacement cost coverage for the full replacement cost of such buildings. To meet this dilemma, the Insurance Services Office introduced a new Homeowners form in 1978, the Homeowners Modified Coverage Form 8. Form 8 is a named-peril form and provides the most limited coverage of any of the Homeowners contracts. Coverage applies only for *Basic*-level perils: the perils of fire and lightning, windstorm and hail, explosion, riot and civil commotion, aircraft, vehicles, smoke, vandalism and malicious mischief, theft, and volcanic eruption. Theft coverage applies only on premises, and is limited to $1000 per occurrence. Finally, the policy does not include the standard replacement cost provision, but substitutes a unique "functional replacement cost" approach to building losses. For partial losses, the contract agrees to pay for *functionally equivalent repairs*, meaning current construction materials and methods that are functionally equivalent to but less costly than obsolete, antique, or custom construction materials and methods. This means that hand-plastered walls will be replaced with plasterboard, and marble will be replaced by Formica. If the building is not repaired, payment is limited to the lowest of (1) the limit of insurance, (2) the market value of the property (excluding the land), or (3) the actual cash value of the loss.

Although the coverage of Form 8 is more limited than is that of the other Homeowners forms, the introduction of this form has made package buying available to many personal insurance buyers that previously were forced to purchase individual coverages.

Homeowners Policy Conditions

There is a set of conditions applicable to Section I of the policy, a separate set for Section II, and a set of General Conditions applicable to the entire contract.

Section I Conditions

Most of the 17 Section I conditions relate to the amount payable at the time of loss or otherwise deal with the loss settlement process.

1. Insurable Interest and Limit of Liability

The insurer will not be liable for more than the insured's interest in the property, or for more than the limit of liability under the policy.

2. Your Duties After a Loss

The insured is required to give notice to the company in the event of loss, protect the property from further damage, prepare an inventory of the damaged property indicating the items damaged or destroyed and the amount of loss, and submit a signed statement within 60 days of the company's request. The insured is also required to notify the police in the event of a theft loss and notify the credit card company in the event of a loss under the credit card coverage. Compliance with the conditions relating to loss settlement is a requisite to payment by the insurer.

3. Loss Settlement

Loss to personal property or to structures that are not buildings is on an actual cash value basis, but not exceeding the cost to repair or replace the property. With respect to buildings, the condition sets forth the replacement cost provision previously discussed.

4. Loss to a Pair or Set

In the situation in which a single item in a pair or set is lost or destroyed, the insurer may repair or replace the lost part, restoring the pair or set to its value before the loss, or it may elect to pay the difference between the actual cash value of the property before the loss and after the loss. The provision prevents the insured from collecting for a total loss when a part of a pair or set is lost.

5. Appraisal

The Appraisal provision establishes a framework for the settlement of losses when the company and the insured cannot agree on the amount of loss. In such cases, each party selects a competent and impartial appraiser and together the two appraisers select an umpire. If the appraisers cannot agree on an umpire, the court with jurisdiction will appoint one. The appraisers then evaluate the loss, each setting their value on the loss. Their differences are submitted to the umpire, and an agreement in writing of any two of the three persons is binding on both parties. Each appraiser's fee is paid by the party represented, and the umpire's fee is paid by both parties. The appraisal provision is not used when the insurer and insured disagree over whether a loss is actually covered under the policy. Such disputes can be settled through the courts.

6. Other Insurance and Service Agreement

The insurer agrees to pay that proportion of the loss that the limit of liability under the policy bears to the total insurance covering the loss. The policy provides coverage in excess of any amounts payable under a home warranty or other type of service agreement.

7. Suit Against Us

Before a suit can be brought against the insurer, the insured must have complied with all the provisions of the policy, and the suit must be brought within one year of the loss or damage.

8. Our Option

The insurer—at its option—may pay for the loss in cash, or it may repair or replace the damaged property. In most situations, the insurer exercises the cash option, but the right to repair or replace operates as a safeguard against unreasonable cash claims.

9. Loss Payment

The Loss Payment clause requires the insurer to pay a loss within 30 days after an agreement on the amount of loss has been reached with the insured.

10. Abandonment of Property

Although the insurer has a right to take salvage upon payment for a total loss, this provision stipulates that the insurer need not accept salvage and that property cannot be abandoned by the insured.

11. Mortgage Clause

A mortgagee occupies an unusual position in the Homeowners Policy (and many other property insurance contracts). Although not involved in the formation of the contract, a mortgagee listed in the policy becomes a party to the contract with rights distinct from those of the insured.[13] The Mortgage Clause grants those rights and imposes certain conditional obligations on the mortgagee. The mortgagee is entitled to receive payment for loss or damage to the extent of its interest in the property, regardless of any default of the insured with respect to the insurance. This means that the mortgagee's protection under the policy is unaffected by any violations of the policy

---

[13]The mortgagee could, if it so desired, take out a separate policy covering its interest in the mortgaged property. However, this would result in a duplication of coverage, since the owner-mortgagor would insure the property to the extent of his or her insurable interest, which includes not only the owner's equity but also the obligation to the mortgagee for the unpaid loan balance. The normal practice is for the owner to purchase a policy naming the mortgagee as an insured under the standard mortgage clause.

provisions or breach of the contract by the insured. The mortgagee's interest would still be covered even if the insured committed arson. The mortgagee is also entitled to receive separate written notice of cancellation and to sue under the policy in its own name.

The mortgagee must notify the insurer of any change in occupancy or increase in hazard of which the mortgagee is aware. In event of loss, the mortgagee must render proof of loss to the insurer if the owner fails to do so, and abide by the policy provisions with respect to appraisal, time of payment, and bringing suit. The mortgagee must also pay premiums due if the insured fails to do so. Finally, the mortgagee must also surrender to the insurer any claim it has against the mortgagor to the extent that it receives payment in those cases where the company has ruled that no coverage exists for the owner. Note that these are conditional obligations. They must be met only if the mortgagee wishes to enjoy the coverage of the policy; they are not conditions the mortgagee can be required to keep.

12. No Benefit to Bailee

Because the Personal Property coverage of the Homeowners forms applies both on premises and off premises, situations may arise in which insured property is in the custody of a bailee, such as a laundry, dry cleaner, or storage firm. The No Benefit to Bailee provision denies coverage for any person or organization having custody for a fee (i.e., a bailee for hire).

13. Nuclear Hazard Clause

Nuclear hazard is defined to include nuclear reaction, radiation, and radioactive contamination. Loss caused by these perils will not be considered fire, explosion, or smoke. The policy does not apply under Section I to Nuclear Hazard.

14. Recovered Property

If property for which a loss payment has been made to the insured is recovered by either party, the insured may elect to have the property returned or may relinquish ownership to the insurer. If the insured elects to have the property returned, the loss payment will be adjusted based on the amount that was paid for the recovered property.

15. Volcanic Eruption Period

All volcanic eruptions within a 72-hour period will be considered as a single volcanic eruption. This prevents the application of multiple deductibles when a series of eruptions occur within a short period.

16. Concealment or Fraud

No insured is entitled to payment under the policy if, whether before or after a loss, an insured has intentionally concealed or misrepresented any material fact, engaged in fraudulent conduct, or made false statements relating to the insurance.

17. Loss Payable Clause

If a loss payee is listed for insured personal property, the definition of insured is changed to include the loss payee. In case of cancellation or nonrenewal, the loss payee will be notified in writing.

General Conditions Applicable to Sections I and II

In addition to those conditions that apply separately to the Section I or Section II coverages, the Homeowners forms include a third set of conditions, applicable to the entire policy. These eight conditions deal with such items as cancellation, subrogation, and the death of the insured—areas that are of importance to both the property coverage and the liability section coverages.

1. Policy Period

Coverage applies only to the losses that occur during the policy period. The inception time of the Homeowners Policy is 12:01 A.M.

2. Liberalization Clause

If the insurer adopts a new form or endorsement during the term of the policy that would broaden the policy without additional premium, such change is automatically made a part of the policy.

3. Waiver or Change of Policy Provisions

Any waiver or change in the policy provisions must be in writing by the insurer.

4. Cancellation

The insured may cancel at any time by returning the policy or notifying the insurer in writing of the date the cancellation is to take effect. Cancellation by the insurer must be in writing and is permitted only under specified conditions. If the insured has not paid the premium, the insurer may cancel with 10 days' written notice. When the policy has been in effect for less than 60 days, the insurer may cancel for any reason, with 10 days' written notice to the insured. For policies that have been in effect for more than 60 days and for all renewal policies, the insurer can cancel only if there has been a material misrepresentation or if the risk has changed substantially. In either case, 30 days' written notice is required. Continuous policies written for more than one year can be canceled for any reason on the anniversary date with 30 days' written notice. If the policy is canceled, a pro rata return premium is payable to the insured for the period from the date of cancellation to the expiration date.

5. Nonrenewal

If the insurer decides not to renew the policy, it must notify the insured in writing 30 days prior to the expiration date of the policy.

6. Assignment

Assignment is not valid without the written consent of the insurer.

7. Subrogation

The Subrogation clause requires the insured to assign his or her right of recovery against a third party to the insurer, to the extent of the payment made under the policy. Under the Homeowners forms, the subrogation provision also grants the insured permission to waive right of recovery against a third party before a loss, as long as the waiver is in writing. Landlords sometimes waive rights of recovery against tenants in the lease, to the extent that a loss is covered by insurance. This protects the tenant from subrogation by the insurer and is specifically permitted under the terms of the subrogation provision.

8. Death

Some provision must be made for the possibility that the insured might die. Coverage is provided for the legal representative of a deceased named insured (or spouse) with respect to insured property. In addition, resident relatives continue as insureds under the policy. Finally, any person having custody of insured property pending appointment of a legal representative is also an insured.

Important Concepts to Remember

package policy
Homeowners Form 2 (Broad)
Homeowners Form 3 (Special)
Homeowners Form 4 (Tenant's)
Homeowners Form 5 (Comprehensive)
Homeowners Form 6 (Condominium Unit-Owner's)
Homeowners Form 8 (Modified Coverage)
Dwelling Coverage
Other Structures Coverage
Personal Property Coverage
Loss of Use Coverage
additional living expense
rental value
replacement cost

Collapse Additional Coverage
Inflation Guard endorsement
Debris Removal Additional Coverage
Property Removed Additional Coverage
Subrogation provision
Loss Assessment Additional Coverage
Landlord's Furnishings Additional Coverage
Building Additions and Alterations Additional Coverage
Ordinance or Law Additional Coverage
improvements and betterments
fire
friendly fire

hostile fire
Assignment clause
Appraisal provision
Mortgage clause
Pair and Set clause
Liberalization clause
Ordinance or Law exclusion
Earth Movement exclusion
Power Failure exclusion
Neglect exclusion
Earthquake Damage Assumption endorsement
Special Personal Property Coverage endorsement
sinkhole collapse

Questions for Review

1. Without going into great detail, explain the essential difference among the Homeowners Broad Form, the Homeowners Tenant's Form, and the Homeowners Special Form.

2. Identify and briefly describe the four coverages that are included under Section I of the Homeowners forms. Explain the relationship among the limits of these four coverages.

3. Explain the special exposures of a condominium unit-owner that led to the development of a separate Homeowners form for such individuals. Explain the manner in which these exposures are handled under the Condominium Unit-Owner's Form.

4. List the classes of personal property that are (a) excluded from the definition of covered property under the Homeowners forms, and (b) subject to dollar limitations.

5. Of what significance is the wording "owned or used by the insured . . ." in the definition of in-

sured personal property under the Homeowners forms?

6. Briefly explain the exclusion pertaining to motorized vehicles under Section I of the Homeowners Policy. What vehicles are excluded? Which are covered?

7. Is the term "fire" defined in the Homeowners forms? What is meant by "direct loss by fire?" Upon what do you base your answer?

8. What procedure is followed when the insured and the insurer disagree on the amount of a loss under the Homeowners Policy? What if they disagree as to whether the loss is covered?

9. The theft coverage under the Homeowners policies is subject to a number of exclusions and other limitations. Identify the exclusions applicable to the theft peril, and any other limitations imposed by the Homeowners forms

with respect to theft losses. For each of the exclusions or limitations identified, indicate the manner in which additional protection might be obtained.

10. List and briefly explain the general exclusions under Section I of the Homeowners forms. Which of these exclusions can be deleted or modified?

Questions for Discussion

1. Although replacement cost coverage on buildings has been available since the inception of the Homeowners program, replacement cost coverage on contents is a recent innovation. Do you feel that this is a logical extension of the replacement cost principle or does it violate the principle of indemnity to a greater extent than does the replacement cost coverage applicable to the dwelling?

2. Jones Jr. and his wife Mary store their household goods at his parents' home while they are looking for an apartment. A fire at the parents' home damages $3000 worth of their property. Assuming that the parents have a Homeowners Form 3, explain whether or not coverage would be provided under Jones', Sr. policy for the $3000 loss.

3. Your Homeowners policy is about to be renewed. It is written to cover your dwelling for its original construction cost. The policy is a Homeowners Form 3, and is standard in all respects: the coverages are all standard percentages and there are no endorsements or modifications to the policy. What changes to this basic contract should you consider?

4. Sue and Mary share a small apartment. Some of the property in the apartment belongs to Sue and some belongs to Mary, while some items are owned jointly. Mary purchases a Homeowners Tenant's Form, with herself as the named insured. What coverage is provided under this form for the personal property owned by Mary, by Sue, and by the two jointly?

5. A distant uncle dies, leaving you his $150,000 condominium unit in Aspen, Colorado. It is rented to skiers during the winter months, and is managed by a local realtor. You elect to spend your summers living in the unit yourself. Upon investigation you find that the uncle has been insured under a Homeowners Form 6, with $25,000 in coverage on the contents of the unit. All other features of the policy are standard. What modifications in this policy would you consider?

Suggestions for Additional Reading

Fire, Casualty and Surety Bulletins. Personal Lines Volume. Cincinnati: National Underwriter Company. (Loose-leaf manual service with monthly supplements.) See "Dwellings" section.

Hamilton, Karen L., and Donald S. Malecki. *Personal Insurance: Property and Liability.* Malvern, PA: American Institute for CPCU, 1994. Chapter 2.

Huebner, S. S., Kenneth Black, Jr., and Bernard L. Webb. *Property and Liability Insurance,* 4th ed. Englewood Cliffs, NJ: Prentice Hall, 1995. Chapter 30.

Launie, J. J., George E. Rejda, and Donald R. Oakes with Anita W. Johnson. *Personal Insurance.* Bryn Mawr, PA: Insurance Institute of America, 1991. Chapters 2–4.

Policy, Form and Manual Analysis Service, Property Coverages Volume. Indianapolis: Rough Notes Company. (Loose-leaf manual service with monthly supplements.) See "Homeowners Policy Program" section.

Taylor, Barbara. *How to Get Your Money's Worth in Home and Auto Insurance.* New York: Insurance Information Institute, 1991. Chapters 5, 6.

Vaughan, E. J. "What Is Insurable Value?" *American Agency Bulletin* (Sept. 1965).

Wood, Glenn L., Claude C. Lilly, III, Donald S. Malecki, Edward E. Graves, and Jerry S. Rosenbloom. *Personal Risk Management and Insurance*, 4th ed., vol. 1. Malvern, PA: American Institute for Property and Liability Underwriters, 1989. Chapter 4.

Websites to Explore

Best's Review—Property/Casualty Edition: http://www.ambest.com/review/lh/index.html

Consumers Guide to Homeowners Insurance: http://www.iiaa.iix.com/homeguid.htm

Independent Insurance Agents of America, Inc.: http://www.iiaa.org

Insurance News Network: http://www.insure.com/

National Association of Professional Insurance Agents: http://www.pianet.com/

Newsedge News Page: http://www.newspage.com/browse/46622/

Quicken InsureMarket: http://www.insuremarket.com/

Rough Notes Company: http://www.roughnotes.com/

CHAPTER 19

Other Personal Forms of Property Insurance

Like—but oh how different!
—William Wordsworth
"Yes, It Was the Mountain Echo"

CHAPTER OBJECTIVES

When you have finished this chapter, you should be able to

- Describe the purpose and uses of the monoline dwelling forms

- Explain how coverage under the Mobilehome program differs from coverage on dwellings under the Homeowners program

- Identify the coverage limits on residential property available under the Federal Flood Insurance program

- Explain the reasons that an individual might choose to purchase scheduled coverage under an inland marine floater

- Identify the classes of property that may be insured under the scheduled coverage endorsement to the Homeowners

- Explain the coverage features of watercraft policies

Although the Homeowners Policy does a good job of protecting the assets of persons eligible for coverage under the program, there are some properties that are not eligible for a Homeowners Policy. In addition, while the Homeowners Policy protects many types of personal property owned by individuals, some property is excluded, and the coverage on other classes is limited. Finally, while the Homeowners Policy protects against a wide range of perils, it does not cover flood, and protection against this peril must be obtained separately. For these reasons, individuals frequently need additional forms of coverage for specialized exposures.

In this chapter, we conclude our discussion of property insurance for the individual and the family with a brief look at several additional forms of protection. The specific coverages that remain to be considered include the monoline fire Dwelling policies, the Mobilehome Policy, the Federal Flood Insurance program, and inland marine coverages designed for personal exposures.

Finally, we will examine the process of purchasing property insurance and provide some additional guidelines in this area, applying the principles originally encountered in Chapters 2 and 4.

Monoline Fire Dwelling Program

Although the Homeowners forms represent the most attractive approach to insuring residences and their contents, there are many dwellings that are not eligible for coverage under these forms. Such properties must be insured under monoline fire forms, which have less demanding eligibility requirements. The monoline fire forms used to insure residential property are referred to as "Dwelling forms." As monoline forms, the Dwelling policies have traditionally differed from the Homeowners policies in that they do not provide personal liability insurance or personal theft coverage. (Theft coverage and personal liability coverage are now available under the Dwelling policies by endorsement.) Although the coverage of the Dwelling policies is still somewhat narrower than that of the Homeowners policies in certain respects, the Dwelling policies provide an alternative for those property owners whose buildings are not eligible for one of the Homeowners forms.[1]

Monoline Dwelling Forms

There are three forms in the Dwelling '89 program, designated the Dwelling Property 1 Basic Form (DP 00 01), Dwelling Property 2 Broad Form (DP 00 02), and Dwelling Property 3 Special Form (DP 00 03). In general, each of the Dwelling forms parallels one of the Homeowners forms. DP 1 is the equivalent of HO 8, and DP 2 and DP 3 are roughly equivalent of HO 2 and HO 3.

There are five insuring agreements used in the Dwelling '89 policies:

Coverage A, Dwelling

Coverage B, Other Structures

Coverage C, Personal Property

Coverage D, Rental Value

Coverage E, Additional Living Expense

All forms include Coverages A, B, C, and D, and the terminology affecting these coverages is identical under all three forms. Coverage E (Additional Living Expense) is included only in the Broad and Special Forms, but is available by endorsement to the Basic Form. Any of the three forms may be used to provide coverage on the dwelling only, personal property only, or both the dwelling and personal property.

As its title indicates, the "Basic" Form provides the most limited coverage available on dwellings and their contents. The form makes provision for three levels of coverage. The first level consists of coverage for loss by fire, lightning, and "internal explosion." For an additional premium, coverage may be extended to include *extended coverage* (windstorm and hail, explosion, riot or civil commotion, aircraft, vehicles, smoke, and volcanic eruption).[2] For yet an additional premium, coverage is extended to include Vandalism and Malicious Mischief. The Broad Form includes the perils of the Basic Form, plus most of the broad-form

---

[1]Residential property may be ineligible for coverage under the Homeowners program for a variety of reasons but the main class of ineligible dwellings consists of rental property. The Dwelling forms may be used to insure most dwelling property, including dwellings in the course of construction, whether or not owner occupied.

[2]Although volcanic eruption was not an insured peril under the separate *Extended Coverage Endorsement*, it is included in the extended coverage perils of the Dwelling Basic Form.

perils of Homeowners HO 00 02. The Dwelling Special Form—like the Homeowners Special Form—insures the dwelling and other structures on an open-peril basis and insures personal property for the same perils as the Broad Form.

Differences Between Dwelling Forms and Homeowners Forms

Our previous analysis of the Homeowners program and the forms that are contained in that program permit a somewhat briefer discussion of the Dwelling forms. The three Dwelling forms differ from their Homeowners counterparts in the following five ways.

1. The Dwelling forms do not include the peril of theft of personal property. Coverage for loss by theft is available by endorsement.

2. The Dwelling forms do not include personal liability coverage (as provided under Section II of the Homeowners). Personal liability coverage is available as an option for an additional premium.

3. Coverage on property away from the insured premises is limited to 10 percent of the on-premises limit under all three forms.

4. In addition to the classes of personal property excluded under the Homeowners forms, the Dwelling Basic Coverage Form excludes boats other than rowboats and canoes.

5. The Dwelling forms do not provide coverage on money or valuable papers.

Endorsements to the Dwelling Program Forms

A variety of endorsements are available to modify the Dwelling '89 forms. They include an Auto-matic Increase in Insurance Endorsement, Sinkhole Collapse Endorsement, Dwelling Under Construction Endorsement, Condominium Unit-Owners Coverage Endorsement, and a Loss Assessment Endorsement. These provide coverage that parallels the similarly titled coverages of the Homeowners forms. In addition, a Modified Loss Settlement Endorsement is used only with the Dwelling Property 1 Basic Form. The endorsement modifies the loss-settlement provisions of the Basic Form to coincide with those of the Homeowners 8 Modified Coverage Form discussed in Chapter 18.

Mobilehome Program

It has been estimated that one-half of the new homes being sold today are mobilehomes. In view of the increasing popularity of this type of dwelling, it is not surprising that a special program has been developed to meet the special insurance needs of mobilehome owners.

IS0 Mobilehome Program

Coverage on mobilehomes is available under the Insurance Service Office (ISO) Mobilehome Supplement to the Homeowners program. Under this program, coverage for mobilehomes is provided by endorsement to a Homeowners Policy. The program rules allow the use of Homeowners 2 Broad Form or Homeowners 3 Special Form with a Mobilehome Endorsement that tailors the Homeowners forms to accommodate the needs of mobilehome owners. In addition, the Homeowners 4 Contents Broad Form may be used without endorsement for a tenant of a mobilehome. In addition to the ISO program, some specialty insurers offer mobilehome policies that are similar to the ISO program.

To be eligible for coverage under the Mobilehome Policy, the unit must be a trailer; that is, it must be a portable unit, designed and built to be towed on its own chassis, comprised of a frame and wheels, and must be designed for year-round living. The unit must be not less than 10 feet wide and 40 feet in length. These requirements eliminate from eligibility small trailers of a "camper type" that may be pulled by private passenger auto. Such trailers are insured under the auto policy.

Coverage on the Mobilehome

The Mobilehome Endorsement amends the definition of Dwelling in the Homeowners form to include utility tanks attached to the mobilehome and permanently installed floor coverings, appliances, dressers and cabinets, and other built-in or attached items of a similar nature. Replacement cost coverage applies to the mobilehome, subject to the requirement that it be insured for a minimum of 80 percent of replacement cost. The policy can be endorsed to provide coverage on an actual cash value basis.

There is a special loss settlement provision, addressing the difficulties that can arise in repairing a mobilehome when part of a series of panels used in the construction of the unit are damaged. In the event of damage to pieces or panels of the mobilehome, the insurer agrees to pay

The reasonable cost of repairing or replacing the damaged part to match the remainder as closely as possible, or

The reasonable cost of providing an acceptable decorative effect or utilization as circumstances may warrant.

This means if the repairs to the unit result in a mismatch (appearance damage), the insurer will pay for recovering (or perhaps painting) the unit.

Coverage on Personal Property

The basic limit of personal property under the Mobilehome program is 40 percent of the limit on the mobilehome (rather than the standard 50 percent under other Homeowners forms). The reason for the reduced limit of contents is the fact that a substantial number of normal contents items are "built in" in mobilehomes. The coverage on contents may be increased if the need exists.

Other Coverage Features

In addition to the special loss-settlement provision applicable to the mobilehome, there are several other unique coverage features designed to accommodate the special insurance needs of mobilehome owners.

A special Property Removal coverage provides payment for the expense of moving the mobilehome, when the movement is required to protect the property from an insured peril. Coverage is provided up to $500, with an option to purchase a higher limit up to $2500 (in increments of $250).

A *Transportation/Moving Endorsement* is available to cover the mobilehome for up to 30 days while it is being moved to a new location. Coverage applies for loss by collision, upset, stranding, or sinking while being moved to a new location.

When the mobilehome is financed by a dealer on a time payment basis or when there is a lienholder interest in the unit, special coverage protecting the interest of such parties may be provided under the *Lienholders Single Interest Endorsement.* This endorsement provides coverage for the interest of the vendor or lienholder against loss caused by collision, conversion, embezzlement, or secretion of the mobilehome by the insured.

Flood Insurance

The Housing and Urban Development (HUD) Act of 1968 established a federal flood insurance program. The Federal Insurance Administration, a part of the Federal Emergency Management Agency, administers the program.[3] It is conducted

[3]FEMA maintains a useful Web site at http://www.fema.gov/.

as a partnership between the federal government and the private insurance industry, under what is known as the "Write-Your-Own" program. Flood insurance policies are issued both by the government and by the private insurers participating in the program. The private insurers collect premiums and settle losses, retaining a percentage of the premium to cover operating expenses. The National Flood Insurance Program (NFIP) reimburses insurers for losses not covered by their retained premiums and investment income. Profits in excess of the service fee must be paid to the federal government. Residents in eligible communities purchase flood insurance through licensed agents and brokers in their state who are paid a commission.

Eligibility

Cities, counties, and other governmental units qualify for the program by submitting a request to the Federal Insurance Administration, indicating the need for the insurance and a desire to participate in the program. The community must agree to adopt certain land-use regulations and flood-control measures, including zoning laws that prohibit new construction in areas where the chance of loss by flood is 1 percent or more each year. Once the community has agreed to adopt the specified controls, it becomes eligible for the Emergency program,[4] under which limited amounts of coverage are available at subsidized rates. Rates under the Emergency program are identical for all eligible cities and towns.

When the community actually implements the controls and actuarial studies have been completed, it becomes eligible for the Regular program. Under the Regular program, a second layer of coverage is available, but on an actuarial-rate basis. The actuarial rate may be more or less than the subsidized rate. The amounts of subsidized and nonsubsidized coverage available under the Emergency program and the Regular program, and the subsidized rates for the Emergency program are indicated in Table 19.1.

Property owners in any special flood hazard area—a specifically designated area with a 1 percent or greater probability of flood—must purchase insurance as a condition to receiving any form of financing from financial institutions under the supervision of or insured by a federal instrumentality.[5] Furthermore, owners of property in any special flood hazard area are ineligible for federal disaster funds following a flood unless the individual has purchased flood insurance.

Virtually all residential, industrial, commercial, agricultural, and public buildings are now eligible for coverage. By 1999, there were more than 18,000 communities in the program with about 2.6 million property owners insured. Insurance in force exceeds $183.2 billion.

✳Flood Insurance Policy

There are two flood insurance forms: one provides coverage on dwellings and their contents; the second insures other types of eligible property. Here we are concerned only with the coverage for residential buildings and their contents.

The Residential Flood Insurance Policy provides protection under three items, designated coverages A, B, and C, insuring the dwelling, contents, and debris removal, respectively. Coverage may be purchased on the dwelling, its contents, or both. The Debris Removal coverage is included in the limit of liability applicable to the property

---

[4]Under the original 1968 act, a community did not become eligible for flood insurance until the U.S. Corps of Engineers completed a study for the purpose of determining actuarial rates. Slow progress in completing the studies led Congress to amend the act in 1969, creating the "Emergency Flood program," under which flood insurance is available prior to the completion of the ratemaking studies.

[5]This includes all lending institutions under the supervision of or insured by the Board of Governors of the Federal Reserve System, the Federal Deposit Insurance Corporation, the Comptroller of Currency, the Federal Home Loan Bank Board, and the National Credit Union Administration.

Table 19.1 Limits on Residential Property under Federal Flood Insurance Program

	Emergency Program	Basic Insurance Limits	Additional Insurance Limits	Total Insurance Availiable
Single-Family Residential	$35,000	$50,000	$200,000	$250,000
2–4 Family Dwelling		50,000	200,000	250,000
Other Residential	100,000*	135,000	115,000	250,000
Residential Contents	10,000	15,000	85,000	100,000

*Single-family residential in Alaska, Guam, Hawaii, and U.S. Virgin Islands is $50,000, and other residential is $150,000.
Source: *National Flood Insurance Manual*, 1995.

insured. Although no minimum amount of insurance is required, there is a minimum premium per policy of $50.

Insuring Agreement

The Residential Flood Policy provides coverage for "direct physical loss by or from flood" as defined in the contract. Flood is defined as "a general and temporary condition of partial or complete inundation of normally dry land areas, resulting from overflow of inland or tidal waters or the unusual and rapid accumulation or runoff of surface waters from any source." This means that the policy will not cover as "flood damage" accumulations of water from a broken or stopped-up sewer or a faulty sump pump in the insured's basement. Neither would accumulations of water on the insured property caused by the slope of the lot be covered in the absence of general flooding in the area. The policy defines "flood" to include mudslides that are caused or precipitated by accumulations of water on or under the ground.

Building Coverage

The definition of the dwelling generally follows that of the Homeowners forms. The building item includes a 10 percent extension to cover appurtenant structures on the premises, but only those that are fully enclosed and the 10 percent is not additional coverage. Coverage is on an actual cash

value basis, but replacement cost coverage is available for one- to four-family dwellings occupied by the owner for at least 80 percent of the year.

There is an extensive list of excluded property. In addition to land values, lawns, trees, shrubs, and plants, the policy excludes fences and outdoor swimming pools, waterfront structures (e.g., docks and wharves) and walks, driveways, or other paved surfaces outside the building. Underground structures (like wells) and equipment outside the foundation walls of the dwelling (such as an air-conditioning unit) are also excluded. Finally, flood policies also exclude certain property in basements, including finished walls, floors, ceiling or other similar construction or improvements and contents located in the basement area.

Contents Coverage

Coverage is provided on personal property owned by the insured and members of his or her family, or for which the insured may be liable. At the option of the policyholder, the contents coverage may be extended to cover the property of guests or servants on the premises. Personal property is covered against loss by flood only while inside a fully enclosed building on the premises and there is no off-premises coverage.

The policy contains an extensive list of Property Not Covered. In addition to money, securities, and valuable papers, the form excludes animals, birds, fish, aircraft and motor vehicles, trailers, watercraft (including their furnishings and equipment), and business property. There is a $500 aggregate limit on fine arts (such as statuary, paintings, antiques, and similar articles) and a separate $500 aggregate limit on jewelry; watches; articles of gold, silver, and platinum; and furs.

Removal

Property removed from the premises to protect it from the insured peril is covered pro rata at its new location for up to 30 days. The coverage during removal and for the 30 days afterward is limited to the peril of flood (and is not open-peril coverage as in the case of the Homeowners Policy). The removal coverage also covers reimbursing the insured for reasonable expenses of moving insured contents to a safe area and temporary storage for up to 45 days when the property is in imminent danger of flood. The reimbursement is limited to the amount of the minimum deductibles ($500 on the building and $500 for contents). No deductible applies to removal expense reimbursement.

Debris Removal

The coverage for debris removal applies only to removal of debris *of* or *on* the property insured. This is an important limitation. The property owner may incur considerable expense in clearing away debris following a flood, but the cost is covered only to the extent of removing the debris of the covered property itself or removing other debris from the covered property. Reimbursement for debris removal is a part of, and not in addition to, the coverage provided on the dwelling or the contents.

Deductible

The Residential Flood Policy is subject to a $500 deductible that applies separately to building and contents. An insured suffering loss to both would be subject to an aggregate deductible of up to $1000. Higher optional deductibles are available, ranging from $1000 up to $5000, in increments of $1000.

Inception of Coverage and Cancellation Provision

During the first 30 days in which flood insurance is available in a community, policies are in force immediately upon issuance. Policies issued after the thirtieth day become effective only after a 30-day waiting period. The policy may be canceled by the insurer only for nonpayment of premium, and even in this case 20 days' written notice is required. The policy may be dropped by the insured at any time, but if the insured retains title to the property, the premium for the current term is considered fully earned, and there is no premium refund. If the insured disposes of the property, the return premium is calculated on a short-rate basis. Finally, if the community in which the insured property is located ceases participation in the NFIP during the term of the policy, the policy ends effective at the end of the policy year in which the cessation occurred and will not be renewed.

Personal Inland Marine Floaters

The term "floater" originally suggested a coverage that protected property while away from the insured's premises. This was to contrast the coverage with the coverage of the monoline fire policies, which provided only limited coverage on property away from the premises. With the introduction of the worldwide coverage of the Homeowners forms, the term "floater" has lost its original significance, since the coverage on personal property under the Homeowners forms also "floats"; that is, it provides coverage not only on

---

Tidbits, Vignettes, and Conundrums 19.1

Flood Insurance Premiums

Premiums for coverage under the National Flood Insurance Program vary considerably, depending on the location of the property. The highest premiums apply to property near the ocean, which is subject to the hurricane exposure. Coverage on a $100,000 dwelling in these areas can exceed $1,000 annually. Coverage on inland property located near a river, lake, or stream is about half the ocean-side rate, and coverage in low-risk areas is about 30 percent of the ocean-side rate.

---

the premises, but off the premises as well. Nevertheless, the term "floater" retains its original meaning of an inland marine form that provides coverage on property that by its nature is mobile. Today, "floater" coverage on personal property is provided under inland marine forms purchased either as a separate Personal Articles floater or by endorsement to the Homeowners.

Scheduled Personal Property Endorsement

The Homeowners "Scheduled Personal Property Endorsement" provides open-peril coverage on nine classes of property under the same terms as if separate contracts were purchased for each type of property.[6] Regardless of whether the coverage is purchased as a separate floater policy or by endorsement to the Homeowners, it is extremely broad and provides an attractive means of insuring valuable types of personal property. The following discussion is based on the coverage under the Homeowners Scheduled Personal Property Endorsement. Coverage under this form is virtually identical with the coverage on the same items under a separate Personal Articles floater.

Valuation Options

There are two versions of the Scheduled Personal Property Endorsement: one that provides coverage on a valued basis (HO 04 60) and one that provides coverage either on an *actual cash value* basis or on a replacement cost basis (HO 04 61). Prior to the year-2000 revision, there was a single version of the Scheduled Personal Property Endorsement, which covers all property on an *actual cash value* basis, except fine arts, which are insured on a *valued basis*. The Personal Property Replacement Cost endorsement discussed in the previous chapter provides that the replacement cost coverage it provides applies both to the blanket personal property coverage of Coverage C, and to scheduled items under the Scheduled Personal Property Endorsement (HO 04 61). Under HO 04 60, the *Scheduled Personal Property Endorsement (With Agreed Value Loss Settlement)* that was introduced as part of the year-2000 revision, coverage applies to all scheduled property on a valued basis.

Scope of Coverage

All property is covered on an open-peril basis anywhere in the world, with exclusions for different types of property that reflect the nature of the

---

[6]Jewelry, furs, cameras, musical instruments, silverware, golfers' equipment, fine arts (including antiques), stamp collections, and coin collections.

property. Coverage on jewelry, furs, silverware, and cameras, for example, is quite similar. The breadth of the coverage is indicated by the fact that there are only three exclusions. The first eliminates loss caused by wear and tear, gradual deterioration, insects, vermin, or inherent vice (a quality within a good that causes it to destroy itself); the second excludes loss by nuclear radiation or radioactive contamination; and the last excludes war.

Each item must be scheduled, with an amount of insurance applicable to each. Insurers often require an appraisal of each article before it is insured; however, the sales slip on a recently purchased item is sufficient to establish a value. The coverage is worldwide.

Additionally acquired property of an insured class is covered automatically, subject to a limitation of 25 percent of the amount of insurance scheduled or $10,000, whichever is less, and with the requirement that the acquisitions be reported within 30 days and an additional premium paid.

Coverage on cameras may include a blanket limit of coverage to cover miscellaneous photographic articles such as sunshades and filters. The coverage on personal jewelry is subject to a "pairs or sets" clause, which prevents collecting for a total loss if one item in a pair or set is lost or destroyed.

Coverage on golfing equipment includes clubs, golf clothing (but excluding watches and jewelry), and other clothing kept in a locker in a clubhouse or other building used for golfing. The description of eligible property is quite broad and could even include a motor-driven golf cart. The coverage is open-peril for most items and generally is written on a blanket basis. Coverage on golf balls is limited to loss by the perils of fire and burglary.

The coverage on stamp and coin collections is subject to additional provisions, reflecting the nature of the property. The property in both cases may be insured on a schedule or on a blanket basis. There is no automatic coverage of newly acquired property. In addition to the customary ex-

clusions, there are several unique to this contract. For example, damage resulting from fading, creasing, denting, scratching, tearing, thinning, or transfer of colors or from working on the property is excluded. The policy also does not cover mysterious disappearance of individual stamps unless the item has been specifically scheduled or mounted in a volume and the page to which the stamp is attached is also lost. Theft from an unattended automobile is also excluded except when a package is being shipped by registered mail. The policy also sets a limit of no more than $250 on any one stamp or any one pair, block, or series and $1000 on unscheduled numismatic property.

Coverage on musical instruments is similar to that on jewelry and furs, but includes an agreement that none of the instruments insured will be played for remuneration during the term of the policy unless permitted by endorsement and the payment of an additional premium. The purpose of this exclusion is to allow the insurer to differentiate pricing for amateur and professional musicians.

The fine arts and antiques coverage is written to cover objects of art such as paintings, statuary, rare manuscripts, and antiques.[7] These classes of property are usually insured on a *valued basis* rather than for their actual cash value. The insurance company agrees to the value of each item insured and this is the sum paid in the event of a loss. Appraisals are usually mandatory, and some insurance companies even retain art appraisers who advise them on the values. Each insured item is scheduled with an amount of insurance applicable. Newly acquired property is covered automatically but subject to a limit of 25 percent of the amount of insurance. However, reports of additional items must be made within 90 days and the proper pro rata additional premium paid.

---

[7]For an item of property to be eligible as an antique, it must have a real antique value; that is, the value must be something more than just sentimental. An arbitrary rule followed by most insurance companies requires that the object be at least 100 years old before it can be considered an antique.

Coverage on Computers

Computers are not scheduled under the Scheduled Personal Property Endorsement, but may be insured under a Special Computer Coverage Endorsement (HO 04 14). Although there is no specific exclusion of computers under the blanket personal property, the named peril coverage for sudden and accidental damage by artificially generated electrical current specifically excludes damage to tubes, transistors, electronic components, or circuitry, eliminating coverage for a major cause of loss to computers and their equipment. The Special Computer Coverage Endorsement provides open-peril coverage on the insured "computer equipment." The endorsement covers "computer equipment" defined to mean: "1. Computer hardware, software, operating systems or networks and 2. Other electronic parts, equipment or systems solely designed for use with or connected to equipment in 1. above."

Other Floater Policies

Other floater policies available to persons who desire broader coverage on some types of personal property include gun floaters and fishing tackle floaters, or sporting goods floaters, contact lens floaters, and a wedding present floater.

Coverage is available for owned golf carts by endorsement to the Homeowners policy. The *Owned Motorized Golf Cart—Physical Loss Coverage Endorsement* (HO 05 28) covers loss to an owned motorized golf cart, including permanently installed accessories and equipment, scheduled in the endorsement. Coverage is on an open-peril basis, with the option of including or not including collision. Coverage is subject to a $500 deductible. Physical damage coverage on other recreational motor vehicles is usually written under a recreational motor vehicle policy, which combines physical damage coverage with liability coverage.

Insurance on Watercraft

Although the Homeowners policies provide some coverage on watercraft and their equipment, this coverage is limited to $1000, and excludes coverage for loss by theft away from the premises. Because of this $1000 limit, and to a lesser degree because of the theft exclusion, many boat owners will need specific coverage on their boats. In addition, boat owners need coverage for liability arising out of the operation of watercraft. Although Section II of the Homeowners forms provides coverage for some liability arising out of watercraft, the coverage applies only to smaller watercraft. Liability coverage for other watercraft must be extended by endorsement to the Homeowners Policy or specifically insured under a separate contract.

Types of Policies

Policies used to insure boats are not standardized, but they fall into two general classes: y*acht policies*, which are used to insure larger vessels, and the *Boatowners Policy*. The distinction between the two has become somewhat blurred, but yacht policies are considered to be ocean marine coverages, while the Boatowners Policy was developed by combining liability coverage with an inland marine form, Outboard Motor and Boat Policy.[8] Here we will focus primarily on the Boatowners Policy.

The Boatowners Policy

The Boatowners Policy is a package contract, similar to an automobile policy, which provides cov-

---

[8]When watercraft liability is insured under the Homeowners Policy, the boat owner may obtain broader physical damage coverage on boats under an inland marine Outboard Motor and Boat Policy, which provides open-peril coverage on boats and their trailers.

erage for liability, physical damage, medical payments, and uninsured watercraft. The Boatowners Policy sold by most companies includes two sections, designated Physical Damage Coverages and Liability Coverages.

Section I Physical Damage Coverages

Physical damage coverage of the Boatowners Policy provides coverage for the actual cash value of the boat, the motor(s), and the boat trailer described in the declarations. When coverage includes a boat, coverage also applies to equipment and accessories manufactured for marine use. Coverage is on an open-peril basis, subject to the usual exclusions of wear and tear, gradual deterioration, inherent vice, and mechanical breakdown. Some policies also exclude loss when the boat is used to carry persons or property for a fee, while the boat is rented to others, or while watercraft (other than sailboats) are being operated in an official race or speed contest.

Section II Liability Coverages

The Section II coverages of the Boatowners Policy parallel the coverages of the Personal Auto Policy. They include watercraft liability, medical payments coverage, and uninsured boaters coverage. The liability coverage protects the named insured and permissive users against liability arising out of the operation of the boat. The medical payments coverage pays for medical expenses resulting from boating accidents when a person (including the named insured and family members) is injured "in, upon, getting into or out of the insured watercraft." The broadest policies include medical payments coverage for persons who are water-skiing. Finally, the uninsured watercraft coverage is a special form of accident insurance, which is available under the Boatowners Policy as an option. It provides payment up to a specified limit—usually $10,000—when the in-

sured or a family member suffers bodily injury that is caused by an uninsured boater.[9]

Navigation and Territorial Definitions Most policies limit usage of the insured watercraft to a specified territory. The broadest policies cover the watercraft while being operated on any inland body of water within the continental United States and Canada, and coastal waters of the same areas, up to a limit of from 10 to 25 miles. The most restrictive policies provide coverage only on a specified body of water and within a narrow parameter around that particular area. Between these extremes, there are policies that provide coverage only in inland lakes, only in certain states, and some that provide coverage options to extend coverage to areas such as the Bahamas.

Buying Property Insurance for the Individual

Before turning to a discussion of buying property insurance for the individual or family, a brief review of the factors that influence the cost of such insurance seems in order. Aside from the differences in prices among companies, there are differences in cost based on the characteristics of the individual exposure.

As the reader will recall, the "rate" is the cost per unit of insurance. The premium is determined by multiplying the amount of insurance to be purchased by the rate. In property insurance, the rate varies with the scope of the perils insured against and the loss potential carried by those perils. The loss potential (i.e., the likelihood that the loss will occur) is a function of the property itself and is measured in part by the characteristics of the property. Although the Homeowners Policy

[9]Uninsured Boaters coverage is patterned after the automobile insurance coverage, "uninsured motorists coverage," which is discussed in Chapter 23.

uses an "indivisible premium" approach, in which the premium is the cost for the package of coverages, this indivisible premium is influenced by the loss-producing characteristics of the exposure. Homeowners premiums vary, for example, with the type of the construction, the fire protection of the city, and the number of families housed in the structure. The premium for frame dwellings is higher than the premium for brick dwellings. Premiums also differ by location. Cities and towns are evaluated on certain critical factors such as the fire department and water supply and are placed in one of 10 classes, numbered 1 through 10, with class 1 towns being the lowest rated and class 10 the highest.[10] The premiums for dwellings in class 10 towns are significantly higher than those in a town with a lower rating. Location also influences the cost for other coverages in the package, and premiums are higher in areas susceptible to windstorms and tornadoes or in areas in which the incidence of crime is greater.

Choosing the Form

If the residence is eligible, coverage on the building and personal property should be purchased under a Homeowners Policy. In keeping with the principles of risk management, coverage should be obtained against the widest range of perils possible. Thus, Form 5 is preferred over Form 3 and Form 3 is preferable to Form 2. If the higher cost of Form 5 is a problem, the insured might consider a higher deductible. Table 19.2 indicates the premium credits available for increased deductibles under the Homeowners policies. The choice of a Form 5 with a $500 deductible in preference to a Form 3 with a $250 deductible follows the principles of risk management. By sacrificing coverage on the potential $250 difference in deductibles, the purchaser secures coverage against disastrous losses caused by perils not listed in Form 2 or 3 that would be covered under Form 5.

---

[10]These classes are established by the Insurance Services Office.

Table 19.2

Homeowners Deductible Premium Credits

Insurance on Dwelling	$500 Deductible	$1000 Deductible	$2500 Deductible
$10,000–59,999	9%	17%	25%
$60,000–99,999	7%	15%	25%
$100,000–250,000	5%	12%	25%

Source: Insurance Services Office, Inc.

Tailoring the Coverage Under the Homeowners Policy

The dwelling should be insured for its full replacement cost. Even though the replacement cost condition of the Homeowners forms requires that the amount of insurance on the dwelling be 80 percent of the full replacement cost value, it is good practice to insure for 100 percent of the replacement cost value. This cushion, plus the Inflation Guard Endorsement, should prevent possible underinsurance from inflation and increases in the cost of construction. An even better approach is a policy that provides the guaranteed replacement cost coverage.

The Homeowners forms provide coverage on the contents equal to 50 percent of the value of the dwelling. Yet there is no reason to think that the actual value of contents will be this amount, and the insurance buyer should estimate the value of his or her personal property so as to avoid underinsurance. Although coverage on personal property is on an actual cash value basis, replacement cost coverage on contents is highly recommended. The replacement cost of personal property can be estimated from a complete inventory of the family's personal property. An inventory of this type is of immeasurable value in loss settlement, and a copy should be maintained in a safety deposit box or elsewhere away from the premises.

The inventory of personal property compiled in estimating the value of contents should also note any valuable jewelry and furs or other items on which open-peril scheduled coverage is needed. Although the Homeowners forms provide adequate coverage on most personal property, it may be desirable to specifically insure certain items of personal property under a Scheduled Personal Property Endorsement or an inland marine form. Obvious examples would include property specifically excluded under the Homeowners Policy, such as various types of recreational motor vehicles or items on which coverage under the Homeowners Policy is limited. Perhaps not so obvious is the need for broader coverage on certain classes of property than that afforded under the named-peril coverage of the Homeowners or for valued coverage in the case of fine arts or antiques.

Finally, the insured should consider adding other perils or broadening those that are included under the form selected. Even when coverage on the dwelling is written on an open-peril basis under HO 3 or HO 5, two potentially catastrophic exposures remain uninsured; earthquake and flood. The earthquake peril should be added to the Homeowners form. It protects against a potentially catastrophic loss at an extremely reasonable (in most areas) premium.

Property owners in special flood hazard areas may have no choice in the purchase of federal flood insurance. If the real estate is financed through one of the specified types of lending institutions, flood insurance will be required as a condition of the loan. When the property is not in a flood hazard area, the purchase of the coverage is optional with the property owner. However, flood insurance, even in the minimal amount provided for the minimum $50 policy premium, seems like a sound way of protecting a substantial investment.

Important Concepts to Remember

monoline fire forms
Dwelling Property Basic Form
Dwelling Property Broad Form
Dwelling Property Special Form
Mobilehome endorsement
Collision endorsement
Lienholder's Single Interest endorsement

Scheduled Personal Property Endorsement
Personal Furs floater
Personal Jewelry floater
Silverware floater
Camera floater
Fine Arts and Antique floater
Stamp and Coin Collection floater

Musical Instrument floater
Golfer's floater
Personal Property floater

Questions for Review

1. Under what circumstances might dwelling property be insured under one of the monoline dwelling forms rather than under one of the Homeowners forms?

2. Briefly describe the difference in coverage on the insured's own property under Section I of the Homeowners forms and the coverage on that property under the equivalent monoline dwelling forms.

3. In what fundamental respect is the coverage on personal property owned by the insured under the Mobilehome Policy different from the coverage under the Homeowners policies?

4. Describe the general nature of the Lienholder's Single Interest Conversion Endorsement. Why would a mobilehome owner elect this coverage?

5. Explain the manner in which eligibility for coverage under the Federal Flood Insurance program is determined. What limits of coverage are currently available to residential applicants under the Federal Flood Insurance program?

6. Briefly describe the provisions of the Flood Insurance Policy relating to inception of coverage and cancellation.

7. For what reasons might an individual decide to insure property under the Homeowners Scheduled Personal Property Endorsement? What classes of property are typically insured under this form?

8. List and briefly describe the coverages that may be included in the Boatowners Policy.

9. What factors, other than the value of the property insured, determine the cost of coverage under the monoline dwelling policies and the Homeowners forms?

10. In what way does the coverage on antiques differ from coverage on other items insured under the Homeowners Scheduled Personal Property Endorsement?

Questions for Discussion

1. Most people elect the standard percentage of coverage on contents when purchasing a Homeowners policy, yet there is no reason to suppose that the value of contents for a given family will be equal to 50 percent of that of the dwelling. Unfortunately, few people have any idea what the true value of their contents is. How do you believe one should go about determining the amount of contents coverage to be purchased? What additional benefits might be derived from the technique you recommend?

2. The cancellation provisions of the Federal Flood Insurance Policy are different from those of any contracts previously encountered in the text. In what ways do these provisions seem necessary for the protection of (1) the insured, and (2) the insurer?

3. Do you believe that persons owning property in the city in which you live should purchase the Earthquake Assumption Endorsement to their Homeowners Policy? Why or why not?

4. What are the advantages of open-peril coverage compared to name peril coverage?

5. The open-peril coverage of inland marine policies is generally subject to exclusions of damage caused by wear and tear, gradual deterioration, insects, vermin, and inherent vice. For what reason are these causes of loss excluded? Are these causes of loss uninsurable or, in your opinion, are they excluded for some other reason?

Suggestions for Additional Reading

Fire, Casualty and Surety Bulletins. Personal Lines Volume. Cincinnati, OH: National Underwriter Company. (Loose-leaf manual service with monthly supplements.) See "Dwellings" section.

Hamilton, Karen L., and Donald S. Malecki. *Personal Insurance: Property and Liability.* Malvern, PA: American Institute for CPCU, 1994. Chapter 6.

Launie, J. J., George E. Rejda, and Donald R. Oakes with Anita W. Johnson. *Personal Insurance.* Bryn Mawr, PA: Insurance Institute of America, 1991. Chapter 5.

Policy, Form and Manual Analysis Service. Property Coverages Volume. Indianapolis, IN: Rough Notes Company. (Loose-leaf manual service with monthly supplements.) See "Homeowners Policy Program" section.

Taylor, Barbara J. *How to Get Your Money's Worth in Home and Auto Insurance.* New York: McGraw-Hill, 1990.

Websites to Explore

Best's Review—Property/Casualty Edition: http://www.ambest.com/review/lh/index.html

FEMA National Flood Insurance Program: http://www.fema.gov/nfip/

Independent Insurance Agents of America, Inc.: http://www.iiaa.org

Insurance News Network: http://www.insure.com/

National Association of Professional Insurance Agents: http://www.pianet.com/

Rough Notes Company: http://www.roughnotes.com/

CHAPTER 20

Negligence and Legal Liability

That man may err was never yet denied.
—John Dryden
The Hind and the Panther

CHAPTER OBJECTIVES

When you have finished this chapter, you should be able to

- Distinguish between criminal acts and torts and define negligence, giving the requirements to support a claim of negligence

- Explain what is meant by vicarious liability

- Explain the obligations of property owners to those on their property

- Identify and describe the types of damages that may be awarded to an injured party and explain how each is determined

- Explain the defenses to negligence

- Apply the law of negligence to specific fact situations

- Explain the problems in the tort system and identify the proposals for change

A risk confronting almost every person or business is that of behavior that could result in an injury to another person or damage to property of others. The basis of the risk is the liability imposed by law upon one responsible for injury or damage to other people or their property. It is a risk that can, and in many instances has, attained catastrophic proportions, and one that can materialize at any time. There is no way of estimating the amount of legal liability in advance. It may be a few thousand dollars, a half-million, or more. It is a risk that has no maximum predictable limit.[1] Before we study the role of insurance in protecting the individual from the legal liability hazard, we will examine

[1]For many risks, the maximum predictable loss can be calculated precisely. For example, owning a car entails the possibility of the loss of the value of the auto itself, a loss with a maximum limit equal to the value of the car. But with respect to the legal liability arising from driving it, the loss will depend on the severity of the accident and the amount the jury is willing to award the injured parties.

the hazard itself, with emphasis on the doctrines of negligence that give rise to the liability exposure.

Criminal and Tortious Behavior

Basically, a person can commit two classes of wrongs: public and private. A public wrong is a violation of one of the laws that govern the relationships of the individual with the rest of society; it is called a crime and is the subject of criminal law. Crimes include a wide range of acts: treason, murder, rape, arson, larceny, trespass, disorderly conduct, assault, vagrancy, and so on. Criminal acts are prosecuted by the state as the moving party (plaintiff) against any citizen for violation of a duty prescribed by statute or common law. They are punishable by fine, imprisonment, or death.

A private wrong, on the other hand, is an infringement of the rights of another individual. A private wrong is called a tort, and the person who commits such a wrong is called a tort feasor. Commission of a tort may give the person whose rights were violated a right of action for damages against the tort feasor. Such an action is called a civil action. Torts may be subdivided into intentional and unintentional. Intentional torts include such infringements on the rights of others as assault and battery, libel, slander, false arrest or imprisonment, trespass, or invasion of privacy. Persons who suffer injury as a result of these intentional torts have the right to sue for damages.[2] Unintentional torts are those that result from negligence or carelessness. In these cases the injured party may also be entitled to damages in a civil action even though the tort feasor had no malicious intent, as in an intentional tort.

Liability insurance is rarely concerned with the legal penalties resulting from criminal behavior or intentional torts. It is considered against public policy to protect an individual from the consequences of an intentional injury he or she inflicts. Although insurance is available to protect against loss resulting from some intentional torts, most liability policies exclude injury or damage caused deliberately or at the direction of the insured. In liability insurance, we are concerned primarily with unintentional torts or losses arising from negligence.

Negligence and Legal Liability

We have already determined that there are many causes of legal liability.[3] The most important, and the most significant for insurance, is that of negligence. While many of the doctrines relating to the law of negligence are found in statutes, its primary development has been through common law. The basic principle of common law is that most people have an obligation to behave as a reasonable and prudent individual would. Failure to behave in this manner constitutes negligence, and if this negligence leads to an injury to another, or to damage of another's property, the negligent party may be held liable for the damage. Legal liability is imposed by the courts when it has been established that all the following occurred:

- There was negligence.
- There was actual damage or loss.
- The negligence was the proximate cause of the damage.

There Must Be Negligence

The basic concept of our law holds that unless a party is at fault—unless he or she has unreasonably and unlawfully invaded the rights of another—he or she is not liable. The basic question

---

[2]It is possible for an act to be both a crime and a tort. If Brown assaults White, he commits a crime and he may go to jail, but in addition he has committed a tort and he may be liable for civil damages if White decides to sue.

[3]Liability may also arise from contracts. Civil law is composed of two branches: the law of contracts and the law of torts. Here we are concerned primarily with the area of torts.

Tidbits, Vignettes, and Conundrums 20.1

An Eye for an Eye

The concept of tort liability grew out of the ancient and deep-rooted *lex talionis*—the law of retaliation. Originally, absolute liability was the rule, and it was harshly applied. The concept was one of measured retaliation—thus the rule "an eye for an eye." If a stone fell from a building and killed an occupant, the builder was put to death. Later, someone realized that it made more sense to pay damages that would support the building owner's dependents than to kill him too and the idea of compensation developed. Gradually, the courts shifted away from the concept of absolute liability, under which liability was imposed regardless of fault, to the doctrine of negligence, under which a person cannot be held responsible unless proven negligent or at fault.

in all cases concerning legal liability must be, "Has there been negligence?" Negligence is defined as the failure of a person to exercise the proper degree of care required by the circumstances.

Who May Be Held Liable?

To be held legally negligent, it must be established that the individual had a duty to act and that he or she failed to act or acted incorrectly. The duty to act is the first of the prerequisites.

At the beginning of this discussion, we stated that "Most people have an obligation to behave as a reasonable and prudent individual would." The question arises, "What persons do not have this obligation?" There are certain classes of individuals and certain institutions who are excepted from the obligation.

Infants To be duty bound to behave in a reasonable and prudent manner, one must be capable of determining what is reasonable. In terms of the law, the person must have reached the "age of reason." In some states this has been set by law at 7 years of age; in other jurisdictions the court determines what constitutes the age at which the individual can distinguish between right and wrong. While children below this age are immune from legal liability, a minor who has attained the age of reason may be held legally liable for his or her own negligent acts.[4] Although minors can be held legally liable, the degree of care demanded of a child is often different from that required of an adult.

Mentally Incompetent For obvious reasons, certain mentally incompetent persons are not expected to exercise the care required of the sane. In the eyes of the law, a mentally incompetent person is approximately the same as an "infant." However, if it can be shown that the deficient person could have been expected to exercise some degree of care, the courts will hold the individual to that degree of caution.

Government Bodies At common law, sovereign powers can be sued only with their permission. Any government unit that shares in the sovereignty is immune from liability unless it is engaging in proprietary functions. When performing strictly government functions, it is normally im-

[4]In addition to confusion over the liability of children themselves, the liability of parents for the acts of their children is often misunderstood. Fundamentally, parents are not liable for their children's acts. This point will be discussed in greater detail later in the chapter.

mune from liability. This government immunity is based on the old common law maxim that "the king can do no wrong." The doctrine has been modified significantly, both by statute and by court decision. One of the most important qualifications is the Federal Tort Claims Act, which provides that the United States shall be liable for money damages to the same extent as a private individual. Government immunity also has been modified at the state level in many jurisdictions by similar statutes. Finally, in a growing number of instances, the courts have attempted to find exceptions to the doctrine of government immunity, and some have rejected it entirely.[5]

It should be noted that even in those areas where the doctrine has not been abrogated, the immunity does not extend to the employees of the government unit who are acting in their capacity as employees. If Brown is struck by a city vehicle and the damage is the result of the negligence of the vehicle's driver, the city itself may not be held liable, but the driver does not enjoy the same immunity.

Charitable Institutions Formerly there was a distinct difference between the liability exposure of a charitable institution and that of a profit-making one, but this distinction has gradually disappeared. Although courts were once reluctant to hold charitable institutions liable, the recent trend has been to treat them in the same manner as profit-making institutions.

What Constitutes Negligence?

As we noted previously, negligence is defined as the failure of a person to exercise the proper degree of care required by the circumstances. As a rule, the duty to exercise care is owed to anyone who might suffer injuries as a result of a person's breach of duty, even if the negligent party could not have foreseen a risk of harm to someone because of the behavior.

One problem is to determine what constitutes correct action in any given situation. To make this determination, the courts apply what is known as the "prudent person rule," which seeks to ascertain what would have been a reasonable course of action under the circumstances. The mere fact that some other course of action might have avoided the accident does not make the individual liable. The negligent person is entitled to have his or her actions judged by this "prudent person standard" rather than hindsight. The judge and jury are not permitted to look back at the situation in light of what happened and judge liability on whether some other course of action would have prevented the accident. The action must be judged by what a reasonable and prudent individual, confronted with the same situation, might normally and properly have done.

Since the standard is rather vague and the variety of circumstances and conditions precludes hard and fast rules, in the final analysis whether the duty has been breached will be for a court of law to decide.[6] Normally, the burden of proof of negligence is on the injured party. However, there are certain doctrines that impose liability by statute or shift the burden of proof from the injured party to the defendant.

Negligence Per Se In some circumstances, what constitutes the standard of care to be met by an individual is set arbitrarily by statute. For example, speed limits in most states set the rate of

---

[5]States in which government immunity has been substantially affected by statute include Alaska, Hawaii, Illinois, Iowa, Kansas, New York, Oregon, Rhode Island, Utah, Vermont, and Washington. The doctrine has been judicially invalidated in the states of Arizona, California, Colorado, Idaho, Indiana, New Jersey, New Mexico, Pennsylvania, and Wisconsin. In some states, the immunity is waived if insurance is in effect; these include Georgia, Maine, Mississippi, Missouri, Montana, North Carolina, North Dakota, Ohio, and Tennessee.

[6]Not all situations arising from negligence, particularly those in which insurance is involved, become subjects of court litigation. Adjusters can determine the existence or nonexistence of legal liability in the vast majority of cases without court action. Only those in which the facts or issues are debatable reach court, and these constitute a relatively small percentage of the total.

speed for driving an automobile. These speed limits represent a rule that no reasonable person should violate. If the law is violated, it is referred to as negligence *per se* (negligence of itself), and the injured party is relieved of the obligation to prove that the speed was unreasonable.

Absolute Liability Under certain circumstances, liability may be imposed simply because "accidents happen," and it is imposed regardless of whether anyone was at fault. In such cases we have the application of the rule of strict or absolute liability. The injured party will be awarded damages even though there was nothing legally wrong in what the other person was doing or the manner in which it was done.

One of the most important examples of absolute liability is employment-connected injuries. All the states have enacted workers compensation laws, which impose absolute liability on employers for injuries to employees who are covered under the laws. These laws represent an exception to the rule that there can be no liability without fault, and the injured worker is entitled to indemnity regardless of the negligence or lack of it on the part of the employer.

The second example of the rule of strict liability is with respect to extra-hazardous activities. The principle is that one who maintains a dangerous condition on his or her premises, or who engages in an activity that involves a high risk to the person or property of others in spite of all reasonable care, will be strictly liable for the harm it causes. Customary examples are keeping wild animals,[7] blasting, explosives manufacture, oil well

drilling, crop spraying by airplane, and containment of water.

Res Ipsa Loquitur A significant doctrine in the operation of the law of negligence is that of *res ipsa loquitur*. This means that "the thing speaks for itself" and is concerned with circumstances and types of accidents that afford reasonable evidence, in the absence of some specific explanation, that negligence existed. The accident is of a type that normally does not occur without someone's negligence and the doctrine recognizes the persuasive force of a particular kind of circumstantial evidence. The characteristics of the event constitute an inference or prima facie evidence of negligence. In the operation of the doctrine, the law reverses the burden of proof. When the instrumentality causing the damage was under the exclusive control of the defendant, and the accident is the type that would not usually happen in the absence of negligence, the law holds that the very fact the accident happened is proof that the defendant was negligent. For example, if Mr. Brown walks down the sidewalk and a 2000-pound safe being lowered by a rope falls on him, he is not required to prove that the person or persons lowering the safe failed to exercise due care. The fact that the safe fell on him (or that he is now 18 inches tall) is evidence of this. The burden of proof is shifted, and the defendants must prove that care was exercised.

For the doctrine to be applicable, certain conditions are required. First, the event must be of a type that normally does not occur in the absence of negligence. Second, the instrumentality causing the injuries must be shown to have been under the defendant's exclusive control. Finally, the injured party must in no manner have contributed to his or her own injuries. The injured party must be completely free from fault.

There Must Be Actual Damage or Loss

The mere fact that carelessness existed is not, in itself, sufficient cause for legal liability. The party seeking recovery must have actually suffered injury or damage. In most cases it is not difficult to

---

[7]Pets represent a separate case. Up until a few years ago, most states still operated under the English common law doctrine that permitted a dog "one free bite." According to the doctrine of *scienter* (knowledge), the owner of the animal is liable for the injuries caused by the animal only if the animal is known to be vicious. Hence the one "free bite." How could the owner know that the dog bites people until it has bitten one? Recently, however, this doctrine has been changed in most jurisdictions. The prevailing current rule holds that anyone who keeps a pet that he or she knows or should know to be dangerous can be held strictly liable for any injuries caused by the animal. This doctrine of the owner's liability is known as the doctrine of *vicious propensity*.

prove that injury or damage has occurred, but establishing the amount of damages can be extremely difficult.

The tort may result in two forms of injury to another: bodily injury and property damage. In the case of property damage, the extent of the loss is relatively simple to determine. Generally, it is measured by the actual monetary loss the injured party suffers. For example, if another driver negligently collides with your auto and "totals" it, it is relatively simple to place a value on the car. Market or depreciated value is the normal measure. An additional loss could involve the loss of use of your car. If you needed an auto in your business and had to rent one, the rental expenses would be included in the damages. The loss of use of property could amount to a large sum if, for example, a large building were destroyed. In some cases, punitive damages (discussed shortly) may also be awarded for property damage.

In the case of bodily injury, fixing damages can be considerably more complicated. Bodily injuries may lead to claims for medical expenses, lost income (present and future), disfigurement, pain and suffering, mental anguish, and loss of consortium.[8] Three classes of damages may be awarded.

1. *Special Damages.* Special damages are designed to compensate for measurable losses, such as medical expenses and loss of income caused by the injury.

2. *General Damages.* General damages compensate the injured party for <u>intangible losses</u>, such as <u>pain and suffering</u>, disfig-

urement, mental anguish, and loss of consortium. Determination of the amount that should be awarded for these damages is clearly subjective.

3. *Punitive Damages.* Punitive damages are amounts assessed against the negligent party as a <u>form of punishment when</u> the <u>injury resulted from gross negligence or willful intent.</u> They are intended not only as punishment, but also to deter others from similar behavior in the future.

The great difficulty in determining the award for each of these types of losses should be fairly obvious. First, although the medical and hospital expenses incurred by an injured party are subject to fairly accurate measurement, an injury that will require expenditures for many years into the future can pose valuation problems at the time damages are determined. The same is true with respect to loss of future earnings. If the injury will prevent the victim from ever working again, the problem becomes one of determining the present value of his or her probable future earnings.

In determining the amounts that should be awarded as general damages, we enter the world of fantasy. What, for example, is the "price" for the pain and suffering and mental anguish over the loss of an arm or leg? The best answer is, "The amount that an attorney can convince a jury it is worth."

Finally, with respect to punitive damages, there is no necessary relationship between the extent of the injured party's loss and the amount awarded. Punitive damages tend to vary with the conduct of the negligent third party rather than with the extent of the injured party's loss and, in a sense, represent a windfall to the injured party.

> can collect twice

Collateral Source Rule It should be noted that <u>damages for bodily injury could be assessed against the negligent party</u> even when the injured person recovers the amount of his or her loss from other sources. A basic principle of common law, the collateral source rule, holds that the damages assessed against a tort feasor should not

---

[8]Loss of consortium originally referred to the loss of a wife's companionship. Under a common law rule still retained in most states, a husband has the right to the services and consortium of his wife. A husband has an ancillary cause of action against a negligent party who is responsible for the loss of his wife's services and consortium, as well as for reasonable expenses incurred for her recovery. Originally, loss of consortium applied only to the husband's right to sue for loss of the wife's services, and a wife had no corresponding right vis-à-vis her husband's services, but most jurisdictions now permit damages for loss of consortium by either husband or wife.

[handwritten margin note: car accident: → lend car to someone & they wreck it → owner's ins. pays 1st, driver's pays 2nd.]

be reduced by the existence of other sources of recovery available to the injured party, such as insurance or a salary continuation plan provided by an employer. If X is injured by Y and X has full insurance to compensate for the injury, he or she can still sue Y for the amount of medical expenses and lost income he or she would have incurred had there been no insurance.

Negligence Must Be the Proximate Cause of the Damage

The negligence must have been the proximate cause of the damage if the injured is to collect. This means that there must have been an unbroken chain of events beginning with the negligence and leading to the injury or damage. The negligence must have been the cause without which the accident would not have happened.

The negligent person is usually held to be responsible not only for the direct consequences of his or her action, but for the consequences that follow naturally and directly from the negligent conduct. Even if an intervening force arises, the negligent party may still be held responsible for the damage if the intervening force was foreseeable. For example, suppose that Brown decides to burn his leaves but takes no precautions to confine the fire. The wind begins to blow (an intervening cause), and the flying embers set Brown's neighbor's house on fire. The negligence began the direct chain of events, and in spite of the intervening cause, Brown could be held liable. The wind is an intervening cause, but one that Brown should have foreseen and for which he should have provided.[9]

---

[9]In addition to an intervening cause, the chain of casualty can be interrupted by a "superseding" cause. A superseding cause is one that is more immediate to the event and "replaces" a prior event as the proximate cause. The doctrine of last clear chance discussed later in the chapter is an example of a superseding cause.

Vicarious Liability

There are circumstances in which one person may become legally liable for the negligent behavior of another person. This type of liability is known as "imputed" or *vicarious* liability and is based on the common law principle of *respondeat superior:* "let the master answer." For example, principals are liable for the negligent acts of their agents. Employers are liable for the negligence of their employees when they are acting within their capacity as employees. In some instances, vicarious liability is imposed by statute. For example, in many states a car's owner is held liable for the negligent acts of anyone driving it with his or her permission. Note that this is not liability without negligence; there is negligence, but the negligence of one person makes another person liable.

To illustrate the principle of vicarious liability, suppose that an employee who uses her car in the business of her employer has no auto liability insurance. Through her negligent driving, a pedestrian is injured seriously. The injured party has a right of action against both the employee and the employer, and any judgment would be binding on both. The purpose of the doctrine of respondeat superior is to increase the number of defendants to include parties who will be better able to pay for the injury. Note that vicarious liability does not relieve the agent of liability. It merely makes it possible to impute his or her negligence to additional persons. If the employee is not financially responsible, the vicarious liability rule will obligate the employer to pay the damages.

Under English common law, a husband was liable for the torts of his wife. This is no longer recognized, and today the wife is liable for her own torts. As a rule, parents are not liable for torts committed by their children. Here, again, the child is liable for his or her own carelessness. While this is true as a basic principle, there are some circumstances in which the parents may be held liable for the acts of their children. First, the parent may be held liable if it can be shown that the parent was negligent in supervising the child. For example, if a parent was aware that the child's hobby was vandalism and did not at least tell the child to stop, the courts would probably consider this to be negligence on the part of the parent. In the same manner, in allowing a child to possess a dangerous weapon, the parent may be deemed negligent and be held liable for any injuries caused by the child with the dangerous weapon.[10] In addition, the parents may be held liable under the doctrine of respondeat superior if the child is acting as an agent of the parent. Several states have enacted statutes that hold that the child is considered to be acting as an agent of the parent when driving the family car. Finally, many states have passed special laws that impose liability upon the parents for willful and malicious destruction of property by their children. For example, the legal code in Nebraska reads as follows:

> The parents shall be jointly and severally liable for the willful and intentional destruction of real and personal property occasioned by their minor or unemancipated children residing with them, or placed by them under the care of other persons.[11]

The statutes may impose liability without limit, as in Nebraska, or the vicarious liability of the parent may be subject to a maximum, as in Kansas, where the limit is $300.

Joint-and-Several Liability

Instances sometimes occur in which the negligence of two or more parties contributes to the injury or damage. In such cases, the question of who is to be held liable is of critical importance. One of the important doctrines in this area is the concept of joint-and-several liability. A liability is said to be joint and several when the plaintiff obtains a judgment that may be enforced against multiple tort feasors collectively or individually. In effect, this doctrine permits an injured party to recover the entire amount of compensation due for injuries from any tort feasor who is able to pay, regardless of the degree of that party's negligence. If A and B are both negligent and C is injured, the doctrine of joint-and-several liability permits C to collect the entire amount of damages from either A or B, even if A were 98 percent at fault and B were 2 percent at fault. The doctrine has been attacked by critics who argue that it is merely a manifestation of the "deep pocket" theory of recovery. Over two-thirds of the states have passed laws since 1986 to abolish or modify the doctrine of joint-and-several liability[12] replacing it with several liability or a system for apportionment of damages based on the degree of fault.

Obligations of Property Owners to Others

The owner of real property or its occupant has an obligation to persons who come onto it. The degree of care that must be exercised depends on the status of the person coming onto the land and on the specific circumstances. Common law generally recognizes four classes of persons with differing degrees of care due them: trespassers, licensees, invitees, and children.[13]

Trespassers A trespasser is a person who comes onto the property without right and without consent of the owner or occupier. As a rule, the land

---

[10]An automobile is not considered a "dangerous weapon" in this context. The subject of legal liability arising out of the ownership and use of autos will be discussed in Chapter 22.

[11]Section 43–801, *Revised Statutes of Nebraska*, Reissue of 1960. Unemancipated means that the child is not freed; an emancipated child is one who has left home and is self-supporting.

[12]Alaska, Arizona, California, Colorado, Connecticut, Florida, Georgia, Hawaii, Idaho, Illinois, Indiana, Iowa, Kentucky, Louisiana, Michigan, Minnesota, Mississippi, Missouri, Montana, Nebraska, Nevada, New Hampshire, New Jersey, New Mexico, New York, North Dakota, Ohio, Oregon, South Dakota, Texas, Utah, Vermont, Washington, Wisconsin, and Wyoming.

[13]The courts in some jurisdictions have modified the once firmly established distinction among trespassers, licensees, and invitees. For example, courts in California and Hawaii have abolished the distinction. See William L. Prosser, *Handbook of the Law of Torts* (St. Paul, MN: West, 1971), pp. 398ff.

Tidbits, Vignettes, and Conundrums 20.2

Parental Liability

In the aftermath of the 1999 shootings in Littleton, Colorado, the parents of one of the students shot to death filed a $250 million lawsuit against the parents of the two shooters for failure to supervise their children. The family is represented by Geoffrey Fieger, an attorney who won a $25 million jury verdict against the *Jenny Jones* TV show over the murder of a guest on the show by another guest.

---

occupant has no duty to exercise care to protect trespassers upon his or her land from injury. Trespassing children (discussed shortly) and "discovered trespassers" are exceptions. Once a trespasser has been discovered, the occupier must exercise ordinary care for the trespasser's safety. Otherwise, the only obligation is to avoid doing the intruder intentional injury.[14]

Licensees A licensee is a person who comes onto the property with the knowledge or toleration of the owner but for no purpose of, or benefit to, the latter. This classification includes door-to-door salespeople, business visitors who have strayed from the part of the premises they were invited or authorized to enter, and perhaps visiting friends and relatives.[15] As with trespassers, the property owner must avoid intentional harm to a licensee. In addition, the owner must warn the licensee of, or make safe, conditions or activities posing risk or harm that would not be obvious to a reasonable person coming onto the land.

If the land occupant knows that persons continuously or habitually trespass on his or her land, then the occupant has a higher degree of responsibility to such persons than to ordinary trespassers. This is based on the principle that if the owner knows that persons are in the habit of trespassing and does nothing to stop it, the toleration gives implied consent to the presence of the trespassers, changing their status to licensees. Perhaps the best evidence of this implied consent is a beaten path. The land occupier might overcome the implied consent by posting "no trespassing" signs.

Invitees An invitee is a person who has been invited in or onto the property for some purpose of the owner. If the person coming onto the premises of the land occupier is a business visitor—an invitee—rather than a licensee, the degree of care required of the land occupier is significantly increased. Invitees, as a classification, include customers and any person on premises open for admission to the general public, free or paid—such as theaters, churches, railroad stations, and the like. It also includes letter carriers, delivery people, workers, garbage collectors, and similar persons, who come onto the land to further the use to which the land occupier is putting the prem-

---

[14]The fact that the person was a trespasser is not a defense for injuries caused intentionally; intentional injury to another is permitted only in self-defense. The rule is that one is privileged to use force likely to cause death or serious bodily harm only if there is reason to believe the behavior of the other party would cause one's death or serious bodily harm. In addition, if someone intrudes on your land, you have the privilege to use force not likely to cause death or serious bodily harm if you have demanded that the intruder leave or desist and the demand has been ignored.

[15]The situation with respect to social guests varies in different jurisdictions. The majority of the courts hold that a social guest is a licensee, although some courts have held that a social guest is an invitee.

ises. With respect to invitees, the person occupying the land has a duty to inspect and discover the presence of natural and artificial conditions or activities carrying any risk of harm, and should exercise due care to warn invitees of such dangers or make them safe. Any condition that could cause harm to an invitee is a possible source of legal liability.

Children   The law imposes a greater responsibility in the degree of care that must be exercised with regard to children. It is an accepted fact that children do not always act prudently. This being the case, the law requires the property owner to protect children from themselves, regardless of their status as trespassers, licensees, or guests. Under the doctrine of an attractive nuisance, a high degree of care is imposed on the land occupier for certain conditions on the land—attractive nuisances—that might attract and injure a child of tender years. The doctrine is based on the principle that there is a greater social interest in the safety of children than in the land occupier's right to do as he or she pleases with the land. For the doctrine to be applicable, the child must be so immature as to be unable to recognize the danger involved. Or it must be something the land occupant would realize could involve an unreasonable risk of harm to such children.[16]

Many types of artificial conditions have been held to be attractive nuisances. However, there does not appear to be any consistent criterion that the courts have utilized. Unattended vehicles, explosives, guns, window wells in basements, trees, construction machinery, and fences have all been held to qualify. In fact, almost anything in or about premises has at one time or another been considered as qualifying. We might note that it is difficult to eliminate the possibility of legal liabil-

ity from an attractive nuisance even by dying, because gravestones have even qualified under the doctrine.

Defenses to Negligence

Thus far in our discussion of negligence, we have been concerned with the existence of a duty owed to others and a breach of that duty. But an individual's negligent behavior does not necessarily mean that a person has a legal liability. For many torts predicated on negligence alone, the presumed negligent parties may have certain defenses that could free them from legal liability in spite of the negligent behavior.

Assumption of Risk

An excellent defense to tort actions is that of assumption of risk by the injured party. If one recognizes and understands the danger involved in an activity and voluntarily chooses to encounter it, this assumption of the risk will bar any recovery for injury caused by negligence. Perhaps the most common application of this doctrine is attendance at certain types of sporting events such as baseball and hockey. Courts have held that in seeking admission, a spectator must be taken to have chosen to undergo the well-known risk of having his or her face smashed by a baseball or a hockey puck. Another common example is the guest passenger in an automobile. If the car is driven in a grossly negligent manner and the guest fails to protest the dangerous driving, he or she may be considered to have assumed the risk of injury.

Negligence on the Part of the Injured Party

Negligence on the part of the injured party may also serve as a bar to recovery or, in some jurisdictions, reduce the amount to which the injured party is entitled as damages. Two doctrines have

---

[16]The courts regard the doctrine either as an exception to the general rules of negligence, or as an application of the rules of negligence to a special class of persons, that is, children. The doctrine, however, is rarely applicable to a child over age 12.

developed: contributory negligence and comparative negligence.

Contributory Negligence As an outgrowth of the idea that every person has an obligation to look out for his or her own safety and cannot blame someone else for damage where personal negligence is to blame, the common law principle of contributory negligence developed.[17] To collect, the injured party must come into court with clean hands. Under the doctrine of contributory negligence, any negligence on the part of the injured party, even though slight, will normally defeat the claim. Note that the degree of negligence is of no consequence; any contributory negligence on the part of the injured party, no matter how slight, will defeat the claim.

Contributory negligence is an important and effective defense, but it is an extremely harsh doctrine to apply in modern society. It seems unfortunate that some courts continue to follow the common law maxim of refusal to apportion blame. For example, one could seriously question the virtue of a legal doctrine under which a person who is 90 percent to blame for an accident should be free of liability just because the injured party was 10 percent responsible.[18] In spite of its harshness, the doctrine is still applied in several states.

Comparative Negligence Because of the harshness of the contributory negligence doctrine, the majority of the states have adopted a somewhat more lenient doctrine, that of comparative negligence. Here contributory negligence on the part of the injured party will not necessarily defeat the claim, but will be used in some manner to mitigate the damages payable by the other party. Comparative negligence rules divide into two broad types. One is the so-called "pure" rule, sometimes called the "Mississippi" rule because it was first adopted by that state in 1910. Under this rule, any defendant who is only partly at fault must still pay in proportion to his or her blame.[19] Most other states follow the Wisconsin rule, first asserted in 1933, under which the defendant who was least at fault is not required to pay at all.[20] By 1994, all but seven states had adopted one or the other of these rules.

To illustrate the difference between the two approaches, and to provide a contrast with the common law principle of contributory negligence, assume that Brown and White are injured in an accident, each suffering losses in the amount of $10,000. Assume also that Brown is 40 percent and White 60 percent at fault. Recovery under each of the systems would be as indicated by the table below.

The comparative negligence principle has much to commend it. It has the effect of tempering the harshness of the contributory negligence doctrine, particularly in situations in which only a slight degree of contributory negligence will de-

---

[17]Contributory negligence is a defense only to tort actions based on negligence. It is not a defense to intentional torts such as assault and battery or to any tort predicated on strict liability.

[18]Because of the obvious and unjust harshness of the doctrine, some courts are inclined perhaps to ignore very slight degrees of contributory negligence.

[19]States following the "pure" comparative negligence rule are Alaska, California, Florida, Illinois, Louisiana, Michigan, Mississippi, Missouri, New Mexico, New York, Rhode Island, and Washington.

[20]States that follow the Wisconsin rule may be divided into two classes: those that permit recovery when the injured party's negligence is "less than that of the other person" (the 49 percent rule) and those that permit recovery when the injured party's negligence is "not greater than the other person" (the 50 percent rule). States that follow the "less than" rule are Arkansas, Colorado, Georgia, Idaho, Kansas, Maine, North Dakota, Utah, West Virginia, and Wyoming. In addition, Arizona, Nebraska, South Dakota, and Tennessee have a special version of the "less than" rule and use the terms "slight" and "gross" negligence. States following the "not greater than" rule are Connecticut, Hawaii, Indiana, Iowa, Massachusetts, Minnesota, Montana, Nevada, New Hampshire, New Jersey, Ohio, Oklahoma, Oregon, Pennsylvania, Texas, Vermont, and Wisconsin.

	Recovery Under Common Law Rule (7 states)	Recovery Under Wisconsin Rule (31 states)	Recovery Under Mississippi Rule (12 states)
Brown, 40 percent at fault, $10,000 loss	0	$6000	$6000
White, 60 percent at fault, $10,000 loss	0	0	$4000

feat an injured party's claim. It seems unfair to disallow a claim in cases in which the negligence of the injured party is slight, but it also seems illogical to allow one to recover complete damages in such instances. If the jury can separate degrees of negligence, the comparative negligence principle will produce logical and fair results.

Last Clear Chance The doctrine of last clear chance is an additional modification of the doctrine of contributory negligence. Under this tenet, as utilized in practically all legal jurisdictions, it is recognized that the contributory negligence of an injured party will not bar his or her recovery if the other party immediately prior to the accident had a "last clear chance" to prevent it but failed to seize that chance. Its logic is obvious. If one can avoid an accident and does nothing to prevent its occurrence, one should be legally liable for damages, regardless of the contributory negligence of the injured party.

Survival of Tort Actions

Under common law, tort actions do not survive the death of the person committing the injury or the person injured. This obviously prevents any recovery by the deceased individual's estate or personal representative. The responsible person could be held criminally but not civilly responsible. It is clear, therefore, that this rule had the unusual characteristic of making it more profitable to kill a person than to maim him or her. In almost every jurisdiction, this rule has been changed to some extent. Some statutes declare

merely that cause of action for damage to property survives the death of either the plaintiff or the defendant. But most go further and allow the survival of causes of action for personal injuries as well.

Every jurisdiction now has some sort of statute of wrongful death. The most common creates a new cause of action for the benefit of particular surviving relatives—usually the spouse, children, or parents—which permits the recovery of the damage sustained by such persons. The new cause of action, however, does not eliminate any defenses available to the responsible party. Thus, the decedent's contributory negligence, assumption of risk, or a release executed by him or her before death for the full recovery of a judgment by the deceased are all held to bar wrongful death actions in most states.

Legal Liability and Bankruptcy

The risk of legal liability is one fraught with potential catastrophic losses. Naturally, the question must arise as to whether the guilty party, confronted with a large judgment, has any alternative but to pay, even if it takes the balance of his or her lifetime to make complete settlement. Bankruptcy is, of course, an alternative, and perhaps is the only possible course of action. The negligent party will lose most of what he or she has accumulated up to this point in life, but will be released from the balance of the judgment. The discharge of the judgment may appear to be desirable to the guilty party, but the stigma of bankruptcy will be lifelong and will hamper practically all his or her future business and personal activities.

A judgment for liability arising from a willful or malicious tort, on the other hand, cannot be discharged by bankruptcy. The guilty party will be obligated to pay the judgment if it takes the rest of his or her life. That bankruptcy will not discharge a judgment arising from a willful or malicious act is a fact that should be appreciated, particularly by young people who are inclined to drive in a manner that could amount to willful and malicious behavior.

Possible Changes in the Tort System

In the 1980s, a debate over the tort system, which had begun with dissatisfaction over the cost of auto insurance, moved from the auto field into the field of general liability. Initially, agitation for reform came from the medical profession, whose members complained that the costs of insuring against medical malpractice losses had become unbearable. Later, manufacturers complained that liability suits involving defective products had also reached an unbearable level. Eventually, the high cost of insuring against liability losses produced what many called a liability insurance crisis, affecting classes as diverse as day care centers, recreational facilities, medical practitioners, architects, product manufacturers, governmental bodies, and the officers of major corporations. Dissatisfaction with the system reached a peak in the late 1980s, when many buyers faced astronomical increases for liability insurance, which the insurance industry blamed on a tort system out of control. Pressure for reform came from a coalition of insurance buyers and the insurance industry. Opposition to reform has come principally from the American Trial Lawyers Association and other groups representing the plaintiff's bar.

The changes in the tort system that are collectively considered to be tort reform include

1. Alternative dispute resolution mechanisms, such as binding arbitration for small claims to reduce the cost of litigation

2. Elimination of the doctrine of joint-and-several liability

3. Establishing a sliding fee schedule for plaintiffs' attorneys in place of the contingency system

4. Limitations or "caps" on awards for non-economic damages (pain and suffering)

5. Elimination of the collateral source rule (subtracting from the award for economic damages any reimbursement from other sources, such as personal health insurance)

6. Periodic payment of awards (also called structured settlements) in place of lump-sum awards

7. Elimination of punitive damages or making punitive damages payable to the state rather than to the injured party

In response to the pressure, most states have enacted some elements of tort reform. In general, however, the impact of reform on liability insurance costs has been modest. The failure of the reform measures that have been adopted thus far to reduce insurance costs is blamed on two factors.

First, the reforms were virtually all at the state level, which means that their impact would be localized. Those who advocate serious tort reform have always been skeptical that state-by-state reform would solve the problem. In the case of products liability, for example, they point out that we are a national market, and that only a national system of product liability tort reform will eliminate the problems that underlie the crisis.

Furthermore, because insurers had not maintained loss data in a form that indicates the proportion of liability losses attributable to pain and suffering, punitive damages, or contingency fees, they have had difficulty in judging the amount by which the reforms were likely to reduce future losses. As a result, many states enacted legislation requiring insurers to accumulate loss data according to categories that will permit measurement of such factors in the future.

Although the impact of tort reform on insurance prices has not met consumer expectations, there is evidence that even the regional changes in the tort system had a positive effect on insurer losses and on premiums. The limitations on joint-and-several liability, pain and suffering, and punitive damages significantly reduced insurers' losses, and the reductions were passed on to buyers in the form of premiums that were lower than otherwise would have been the case.[21]

Although we have surveyed only the more fundamental aspects of legal liability, the tremendous exposure that the individual faces in this area should be evident.[22] The catastrophic proportions that the liability loss can assume suggest that the appropriate risk management technique for this exposure is transfer. This is accomplished for the most part by transfer of the risk to an insurance company through the purchase of liability insurance, the subject of Chapter 21.

[21]See Glenn Blackmon and Richard Zeckhauser, "State Tort Reform Legislation: Assessing Our Control of Risks." *Tort Law and the Public Interest* (New York: The American Assembly, W. W. Norton, 1991).

[22]The tort system is an evolving body of legal doctrines. It has undergone significant change in the past and is likely to change in the future. Changes in the tort system as it relates to automobiles are discussed in Chapter 23.

[Handwritten notes in margin:]
CO - INS —
100,000 house
80% Co-Ins
60,000 Policy
20,000 Loss
$$\frac{60,000}{80,000} \times 20000 = 15000 \text{ Ins pays}$$
5000 you pay
INS. carried / Ins req'd

Important Concepts to Remember

tort	sovereign immunity	consortium
intentional torts	negligence *per se*	proximate cause
unintentional torts	absolute liability	special damages
negligence	*res ipsa loquitur*	general damages
lex talionis	*scienter*	punitive damages
law of retaliation	vicious propensity	collateral source rule
vicarious liability	licensees	contributory negligence
joint-and-several liability	invitees	comparative negligence
respondeat superior	attractive nuisance	last clear chance
trespassers	assumption of risk	

Questions for Review

1. What conditions must exist before an individual may be held legally liable in a tort action?

2. Distinguish among invitee, licensee, and trespasser, and describe a property owner's responsibilities to each.

3. Give an example of each of the following legal doctrines: *res ipsa loquitur*, negligence *per se*, last clear chance.

4. Explain fully what is meant by the term vicarious liability, giving examples of several situations in which vicarious liability is likely to exist.

5. Identify the defenses that may be used against a tort action.

6. To what extent may parents be held liable for the acts of their minor children? Be complete and specific.

7. Distinguish between the concepts of contributory negligence and comparative negligence. Which doctrine is used in your state? Which do you feel is the more reasonable, and why?

8. What factors are considered in determining the amount of damages to which a person who suffers bodily injury is entitled in a tort action?

9. What is meant by the term absolute liability? Give three examples of absolute liability.

10. To what extent are the risk management techniques of avoidance, reduction, and retention suitable and adequate techniques for dealing with the liability risk?

Questions for Discussion

1. At one time, it was felt that liability insurance would undermine the tort system, which has as its central theorem the concept that the individual responsible for injuring another should be made to pay for that injury. Do you think that the existence of liability insurance causes one to be less careful than he or she might be otherwise?

2. Schwartz had been troubled by burglars, so he installed a trap in his building with a shotgun rigged to fire when an intruder opened the door. Sam Burglar broke into the building and lost both legs when the shotgun discharged. Sam thereupon brought suit against Schwartz for damages. What defenses might Schwartz offer? Do you believe that a court would permit recovery under such circumstances?

3. Bodily injury awards have increased at a significant rate during the past two decades. To what do you attribute this increase? Were previous awards inadequate, or are the current ones excessive?

4. The text lists several proposed changes in the tort system that are collectively considered to be tort reform. Which, if any, of the proposed changes do you believe would be most beneficial? Why, in your opinion, has there not been greater progress toward tort reform?

5. The subject of punitive damages is one of the more fiercely debated facets of the tort system. What is your personal opinion on assessment of punitive damages against a negligent party? Do you favor or oppose the concept of punitive damages? Does your opinion differ depending on whether punitive damages are payable on behalf of the negligent party by an insurance company?

Suggestions for Additional Reading

Anderson, R. A. *The Insurer's Tort Law*. Ocean City, NJ: Insurance Press, 1964.

Huebner, S. S., Kenneth Black, Jr., and Bernard L. Webb. *Property and Liability Insurance*, 4th ed. Englewood Cliffs, NJ: Prentice Hall, 1995. Chapter 25.

Kulp, C. A., and John W. Hall. *Casualty Insurance*, 4th ed. New York: Ronald Press, 1968. Chapter 4.

Lorimer, James J., et al. *The Legal Environment of Insurance*, 3rd ed., vol. 2. Malvern, PA: American Institute for Property and Liability Underwriters, 1987.

Prosser, William L., et al. *Handbook on the Law of Torts*, 5th ed. St. Paul, MN: West Publishing, 1984.

Websites to Explore

American Tort Reform Association: http://www.aaabiz.com/ATRA/default.html

American Trial Lawyers Association: http://www.atlanet.org/

Arbitration Forum: http://www.arb-forum.com/

Best's Review—Property/Casualty Edition: http://www.ambest.com/review/Ih/index.html

Independent Insurance Agents of America, Inc.: http://www.iiaa.org

Insurance News Network: http://www.insure.com/

National Association of Professional Insurance Agents: http://www.pianet.com/

CHAPTER 21

General Liability Insurance for the Individual

He that scatters thorns, let him not go barefoot.
—Benjamin Franklin
Poor Richard, 1736

CHAPTER OBJECTIVES

When you have finished this chapter, you should be able to

- Explain the distinction between a denial of payment by an insurer because there is no liability and denial because there is no coverage

- Identify the coverage features under Section II of the Homeowners forms

- Describe the insuring agreements of liability insurance contracts generally and explain the insurer's obligation to defend the insured

- Explain the insuring agreement of the Section II Personal Liability coverage

- Explain the insuring agreement of the Section II Medical Payments coverage

- Recognize significant exclusions under the Homeowners Section II

- Describe the personal umbrella liability contracts, including qualification requirements and typical exclusions

Liability Insurance in General

In Chapter 20, we examined the principles of negligence that give rise to the legal liability exposure. We noted that the risk of legal liability is a pervasive aspect of the life of every individual and that it is a risk of catastrophic potential. In this chapter, we turn to liability insurance, the form of coverage designed to protect against the financial consequences of negligence, legal liability.

Liability insurance undertakes to assume the obligations imposed on the negligent party in the event of legal liability. A liability insurance policy agrees to pay the sums that the insured becomes legally obligated to pay, up to the limit of the policy, when such liability arises out of acts of an insured that are within the defined coverage. Liability insurance is commonly called *third-party coverage*, because it undertakes to compensate someone who is not a party to the contract, the injured person to whom the insured is liable. It is important to recognize that this "third party" is not an insured under the policy and has no direct claim against the insurer. Contractually, the insurer has no *legal* obligation to the injured third party unless and until the insured's liability has been established in a court of law.

Besides the promise to pay sums that the insured becomes legally obligated to pay, most liability policies also include a promise by the insurer to defend the insured in suits involving the type of liability covered under the policy. Thus, automobile liability policies will provide defense for suits alleging negligence in the operation of an automobile, while a premises liability policy will pay defense costs related to insured premises. The basic principle is that the insurer must pay defense costs if it would be obligated to pay damages if the insured should be held liable.

As a practical matter, few liability claims reach trial. Insurers realize that the best interests of all concerned will be served if a settlement can be reached without litigation, and the insurer normally seeks an out-of-court settlement with the injured party. Most liability policies reserve this right to the insurer.

An area frequently misunderstood by the public is the distinction between the liability of the insured and coverage under the liability policy. When presented with a claim, an insurer may attempt to negotiate a settlement, or it may refuse to consider payment. An insurer may refuse payment under a liability policy for one of two reasons. One is that the loss is not covered under the policy. Here, the insured must assume his or her own defense and, if held liable, must pay the claim. An entirely different situation exists when the company denies payment because it does not feel that the insured is legally liable for the damage or injury. In this instance, the insurer is obligated to defend the insured, and if the insured is eventually found to be liable, the insurer will pay for the loss up to the policy limits.

Types of Liability Insurance

By custom and practice, liability insurance has divided into three branches of coverage:

1. Automobile liability
2. Employers liability and workers compensation
3. General liability

Usually, these three types of liability insurance are provided under separate contracts. Most general liability policies exclude liability arising out of automobiles and liability for injuries to employees. Liability arising out of the operation of automobiles is insured under a separate automobile liability policy, and coverage for injury to employees is available under the Workers Compensation and Employers Liability Policy. The discussion in this chapter is concerned primarily with the field of general liability.[1] General liability insurance can

---

[1]As will be noted in the discussion that follows, Comprehensive Personal Liability coverage is an exception to the general principle since it includes coverage for injuries to domestic employees.

be subdivided further into coverages (1) designed to protect business firms and other institutions and (2) designed to protect the individual. We will confine our discussion to coverage for the individual.

Comprehensive Personal Liability Coverage

The general liability coverage designed to protect the individual is called Comprehensive Personal Liability (CPL) insurance. The coverage is "comprehensive" in the sense that it insures against all types of liability hazards falling within a broad insuring agreement, except those that are specifically excluded. In general, the coverage is intended to protect against the nonbusiness, nonautomobile exposures of the individual or family unit. Protection exists for legal liability arising out of the premises and also for liability arising out of the personal activities of the insured or family members, both on and away from the premises. In addition, the coverage includes employers liability coverage for injury to domestic employees in those jurisdictions where such workers are not subject to the workers compensation laws. In other states, the policy can be endorsed to provide workers compensation coverage for domestic employees.

Comprehensive Personal Liability coverage may be purchased as a monoline contract, it may be added to monoline dwelling forms by endorsement, and it is automatically included as Section II of the Homeowners Policy. Because the most widely used means of obtaining the coverage is under the Homeowners forms, we will use Section II of the Homeowners as the basis for our discussion.

There are two coverages under Section II of the Homeowners, designated Coverage E, Personal Liability, and Coverage F, Medical Payments to Others. In addition, there are four supplementary insuring agreements, called Additional Coverages.

Personal Liability Coverage

The Personal Liability coverage is the major coverage of the Comprehensive Personal Liability coverage. Its insuring agreement is simple and straightforward:

> If a claim is made or a suit is brought against any insured for damages because of bodily injury or property damage to which this coverage applies, we will:
>
> a. pay up to our limit of liability for the damages for which the insured is legally liable; and
> b. provide a defense at our expense by counsel of our choice. We may make any investigation and settle any claim or suit that we decide is appropriate. Our obligation to defend any claim or suit ends when the amount we pay for damages resulting from the occurrence equals our limit of liability.

This is a fairly typical liability insuring agreement. In addition to the promise to pay sums that the insured becomes legally obligated to pay, the agreement also promises defense, and reserves to the company the right to make an out-of-court settlement.

Persons Insured

One of the most important parts of any liability policy is the definition of "persons insured," because the insurer promises to pay damages or defend under the liability coverage "if a claim is made or suit is brought against any insured." Like most liability policies, coverage is provided for certain individuals other than the person listed in the declarations of the policy. In Chapter 18, we noted that the definition of Insured under the Homeowners Policy includes the named insured and resident relative, other persons under age 21 in the care of the insured, and certain students enrolled in school full-time who were residents of the household before leaving to attend school.

(Insured students include persons under age 24 related to the insured and students under age 21 who were in the care of an insured.) These persons are also insureds under Section II of the policy. In addition, for Section II coverages only, the Homeowners Policy contains the following definition:

> Under Section II, "insured" also means:
> c. with respect to animals or watercraft to which this policy applies, any person or organization legally responsible for these animals or watercraft which are owned by you or any person included in 5.a. or 5.b. above. "Insured" does not mean a person or organization using or having custody of these animals or watercraft in the course of any "business" or without consent of the owner.
> d. with respect to a "motor vehicle" to which this policy applies,
>   1. Persons while engaged in your employ or that of any person included in 5.a. or 5.b. above; or
>   2. Other persons using the vehicle on an "insured location" with your consent.

Under both Section I and II, when the word an immediately precedes the word "insured." the words an "insured" together mean one or more "insureds".

The inclusion of persons legally responsible for animals or watercraft to which the insurance applies extends coverage for persons to whom the insured may have loaned such animals or watercraft or who have custody for other reasons. If a neighbor takes care of the insured's dog while the insured is on vacation, the neighbor would be covered under the policy in the event of any suit arising out of the dog's actions. However, the exclusion of anyone having custody of an animal or watercraft in the course of business denies coverage to organizations such as kennels or marinas.

The exclusion of persons having custody without permission is self-explanatory.

Finally, the definition of persons insured includes certain persons while operating a vehicle to which the insurance applies. As we will see shortly, this is limited to unlicensed motor vehicles, such as those used for the maintenance of the premises, and recreational vehicles. The intent is to provide coverage, for example, to a gardener operating a riding lawn mower. Coverage applies for "any other person using the vehicle on an insured location with your (the named insured's) permission."

Liability Exclusions

There are two sets of exclusions applicable to the liability coverage. One set of twelve exclusions (designated 1 through 4 and 5.a through 5.h) applies to both liability and medical payments, and a second set of six exclusions (designated 6.a through 6.f) applies to liability coverage only.

1. Motor Vehicle Liability Liability arising out of motor vehicles owned or operated by any insured is excluded in a complex and somewhat wordy series of provisions. These include the exclusion itself (which denies coverage for "motor vehicle liability"), the definition of "motor vehicle," and a definition of "motor vehicle liability." There have been attempts in the past (mostly unsuccessful) to find coverage under the Homeowners Policy for automobile liability losses through claims against an insured other than the operator of the auto. These attempts were usually based on the argument that a parent was negligent, not in the operation of an auto, but in supervising a minor or by negligently entrusting someone with the auto. In an effort to address these arguments, in addition to excluding liability arising out of the ownership, maintenance, occupancy, operation, use, and loading and unloading of a motor vehicle, the policy also excludes liability arising out of entrustment, failure to supervise or negligent supervision, or vicarious liability for the actions of a child or minor involving a motor vehicle. The

---

Tidbits, Vignettes, and Conundrums 21.1

Nice Doggie

According to the Western Insurance Information Service (a nonprofit consumer organization), in 1998 alone there were more than 4.7 million dog-bite injuries, which accounted for one of every three claims under the liability section of Homeowners' policies. Dog-bite claims exceed $1 billion annually, and insurers are reportedly nonrenewing policies under which they have had to pay claims for dog bites. About 70 percent of the insurers surveyed responded that they will not renew policyholders whose dogs have been the source of claims. *Newsweek*, March 6, 2000.

---

exclusions of watercraft, aircraft, and hovercraft include similarly worded provisions.

The Motor Vehicle exclusion distinguishes between motor vehicles that are registered for use on public roads or property (or which should be so registered) and other vehicles. These are completely excluded. Other vehicles, which are not registered and are not required to be registered, may be excluded or covered, depending on the vehicle. Unregistered vehicles are excluded if they are operated in (or practicing for) any prearranged or organized race, speed contest, or other competition. Unregistered vehicles rented to others, used to carry persons or cargo for a charge, or used for business purposes are also excluded.

Unregistered motor vehicles for which coverage exists include a motor vehicle in dead storage on an insured location, motor vehicles used solely to service an insured's premises, and motor vehicles designed to assist the handicapped if actually being used for this purpose or parked at the time of the occurrence.

Recreational motor vehicles such as snowmobiles, all-terrain vehicles, go-carts, and other land motor vehicles designed for recreational use off public roads are divided, for coverage purposes, as owned and nonowned. Nonowned recreational motor vehicles are insured on and off premises. Owned recreational motor vehicles are covered only when on an insured location.

A motorized golf cart owned by an insured is covered while at a golfing facility and parked or stored there, or being used by an insured to play golf or for other recreational activities allowed by the facility. The golf cart must be designed to carry no more than four persons and cannot have been modified after manufacture to exceed 25 miles per hour. Coverage also applies while the cart is being used for travel to and from an area where motor vehicles or golf carts are parked or while crossing public roads at designated points to access other parts of the golf course. Finally, owned golf carts are covered while in a private residential community (e.g., "Sun City") where the insured's residence is located. If it is legal for golf carts to travel on the public roads of the private community, coverage applies to such usage.

2. **Watercraft Liability** Watercraft Exclusion 1.g excludes liability (including negligent entrustment, negligent supervision, and vicarious liability) arising out of the following types of boats:

- Inboard or inboard-outboard motorboats with more than 50 horsepower owned by or rented to an insured

- Sailing vessels (with or without auxiliary power) over 26 feet in length owned by or rented to an insured

- Any boats powered by an outboard motor or motors in excess of 25 horsepower if such motor or motors were owned by the insured at the inception of the policy and not listed or reported to the insurer

Note that the exclusion with respect to outboard motors, unlike that with respect to inboards or sailing vessels, does not apply to rented motors. Coverage applies to boats below these limits, and the exclusion with respect to larger units may be removed by endorsement for an additional premium. The policy also provides that none of the exclusions relating to watercraft apply while the watercraft is stored.

3. Aircraft Liability   Next, legal liability arising from the ownership, maintenance, or use of aircraft (including negligent entrustment, negligent supervision, and vicarious liability) is excluded by exclusion 1.h. If the insured owns or rents a private airplane, he or she must purchase aircraft insurance specifically designed for this purpose. The policy defines an aircraft as "any contrivance used or designed for flight, except model or hobby aircraft not used or designed to carry people or cargo." In addition to airplanes, the exclusion eliminates coverage for ultralights and hang gliders.

4. Hovercraft Liability   The Hovercraft Liability exclusion was introduced in the year-2000 revision to address the ambiguity regarding the nature of these vehicles. Although the policy excluded aircraft, motor vehicles, and watercraft, it was argued that hovercraft were technically none of these. The wording of the hovercraft liability exclusion parallels the wording of the motor vehicle exclusion.

5.a. Intentional Injury   It is considered contrary to public policy to protect an individual from the consequences of intentional injury to another. For this reason, the policy excludes coverage for bodily injury or property damage that either is expected or is intended from the standpoint of the insured.

5.b. Business Activities   The Personal Liability coverage of the Homeowners Policy is designed to provide coverage for legal liability arising from the dwelling premises and personal activities of the insured. It is not designed to provide coverage for business or professional activities. Exclusion 5.b makes this clear; it excludes liability "arising out of or in connection with a "business" conducted from an insured location or engaged in by an insured." The exclusion applies not only to a business owned by the insured, but a business by which the insured is employed as well. The scope of the exclusion is defined, in part, by the policy definition of "business." "Business" means a trade, profession, or occupation engaged in on a full-time, part-time, or occasional basis. It also means any other activity engaged in for money or other compensation. Four types of activity are excepted from the definition of business (and are therefore covered). These include volunteer activity for which no money is received (other than payment for expenses), providing day care services without compensation (other than the mutual exchange of services), and providing home day care services to a relative of the insured. The final exception is any activity (other than the first three) for which no insured received more than $2000 in compensation in the 12 months before the inception of the policy.

In addition to the qualifications in the definition of "business," there are two exceptions to the business exclusion itself. The first relates to rental activities.

The definition of "business" is sufficiently broad to include rental activities of an insured. The rental activities exceptions to the business exclusion provide coverage for (1) the occasional rental of an insured's residence, (2) rental of part of the insured premises for use as a residence only (but with no more than two roomers or boarders per family), or (3) rental of part of the residence as an office, school, studio, or private garage.

The first exception is self-explanatory. The insured is permitted to rent the insured residence to others on a short-term or temporary basis (e.g., while the insured is on a temporary assignment in another city). The second exception permits rental of a single-family unit in the residence (provided there are no more than two roomers or boarders per single-family unit). Finally, a part of the insured residence may be rented to others for use as an office, school, studio, or private garage. Other rental activities may be covered by endorsement to the Homeowners Policy or under a separate business general liability policy.

Coverage for Business Activities Coverage is available by endorsement to the Homeowners Policy for some types of business activities, including businesses conducted from the residence premises. There are four separate endorsements, designed for different business exposures.

Employees who want liability coverage for their activities as employees (as opposed to business owners) may obtain coverage under the *Business Pursuits Endorsement.* This endorsement is available to clerical office employees, salespersons, collectors, messengers, and teachers. Although the liability insurance purchased by one's employer usually extends coverage to employees, an employee might desire coverage for exposures not covered by the employer's policy or where the employer's coverage is considered inadequate. The endorsement excludes coverage for acts of the insured in connection with a business owned by the insured and injury to fellow employees.

The Homeowners program rules allow coverage on dwellings with certain "incidental" business occupancies (an office, studio, or school). When a Homeowners Policy is written for one of these permissible "incidental occupancies, the business exclusion is modified to provide on-premises liability coverage relating to the incidental occupancy by attaching the *Permitted Incidental Occupancies (Residence Premises)* endorsement (HO 04 42).

The *Home Day Care Coverage* endorsement modifies the business activity exclusion to provide cov-erage for liability arising out of a home day care business operated in the dwelling or another building on the premises.[2]

Finally, coverage may be added to the Homeowners Policy for certain other home businesses under a new *Home Business Coverage Endorsement* (nicknamed the HOBIZ™) introduced by ISO in 1997. This endorsement provides coverage for business property, loss of business income, and general liability coverage appropriate for the home business activity. The business must be owned by the named insured (or by the named insured and a resident relative) or the named insured and a partner who is a resident of the household. Three types of businesses are eligible: offices, service businesses, and sales. Businesses engaged in the manufacture, sale, or distribution of food products or personal care products (e.g., cosmetics) and businesses eligible for coverage under either the Permitted Incidental Occupancy or the Home Day Care Coverage endorsements are ineligible. The business may have no more than three employees and must have receipts of less than $250,000 annually.

When a business exposure exists that cannot be insured under one of these four endorsements, it must be insured under a business liability policy.

5.c. Professional Liability Exclusion 5.c excludes professional liability, such as the liability that might be incurred by a physician, accountant, lawyer, or other professional. The intent of this exclusion is the same as the business pursuits exclusion discussed earlier. The excluded professional exposures must be insured under separate professional liability policies.[3]

5.d. Uninsured Premises A specific exclusion (1.e) eliminates liability arising out of any premises owned or rented to any insured that is not an

---

[2]A mandatory endorsement (HO 04 96, *No Section II—Liability Coverage for Home Day Care Business; Limited Section I—Property Coverage for Home Day Care Business*) is attached to the policy when the Home Day Care Coverage endorsement is not used.
[3]Professional liability insurance is discussed in Chapter 24.

"insured location." The definition of insured location includes all premises declared by the insured at inception, plus premises that are acquired by the insured during the policy period. Insured location also includes a location in which an insured is temporarily residing, such as a hotel or motel room. As long as the insured has disclosed the ownership and location of all owned premises and has paid the appropriate premium, coverage is afforded for liability arising out of the declared premises. A residence owned by the insured at the inception of the policy and not declared would be an uninsured location.

5.e. War The next exclusion (5.e) eliminates coverage for bodily injury or property damage arising out of war, civil war, insurrection, rebellion, revolution, and similar forms of conflict.

5.f. Communicable Disease The communicable disease exclusion (5.f) eliminates coverage for liability arising out of the transmission of a communicable disease by an insured. Prior to the addition of this exclusion, courts had held that such losses are "bodily injury" within the meaning of the policy coverage and that the bodily injury was not expected or intended by the insured.

5.g. Sexual Molestation or Abuse Exclusion 1.k was added to the Homeowners Policy in the 1990 revision. It excludes bodily injury arising out of sexual molestation, corporal punishment, or physical or mental abuse. Prior to the 1990 revision, the sexual molestation and abuse exclusion was used only in an endorsement that provided liability coverage for the operation of a child care business in the home.

5.h. Controlled Substance Exclusion 5.h was added in the 1990 revision of the Homeowners Policy. It excludes liability arising

> out of the use, sale, manufacture, delivery, transfer or possession by any person of a Controlled Substance(s) as defined by the Federal Food and Drug Law at 21 U.S.C.A.

Sections 811 and 812. Controlled Substances include but are not limited to cocaine, LSD, marijuana and all narcotic drugs. However, this exclusion does not apply to the legitimate use of prescription drugs by a person following the orders of a licensed physician.

The severity of this exclusion for some people and some life-styles does not require explanation.

6.a.(2) Assessments and Contractual Liability
In addition to the liability that arises out of negligence, liability may be incurred through contractual agreements. For example, a common clause in many leases shifts the liability in connection with premises from the landlord to the tenant or from the tenant to the landlord. Such agreements are called "hold-harmless agreements" because one party agrees to hold the other harmless from liability arising out of the premises. Brown, a tenant, may agree to hold Smith, the landlord, harmless from liability arising out of the premises. Jones is injured as a result of a defect in the premises and brings suit against Smith as the owner. Smith is held liable and is ordered to pay a judgment of $25,000. Under the terms of the hold-harmless agreement, Brown will be required to reimburse Smith. The Homeowners forms provide coverage for this exposure through an exception to an exclusion.

Under exclusion 6.a.(1), loss assessments charged against the insured as a member of an association, corporation, or community of property owners are excluded, except to the extent that such loss is covered under the Section II Additional Coverage for Loss Assessment (discussed later in this chapter). Such assessments are a type of contractual liability (since the association would not have the authority to level such assessments in the absence of an agreement by the insured).

Exclusion 6.a.(2) excludes other liability assumed under contract. Then, in two important exceptions to the exclusion, it provides a broad form of contractual liability to the insured. The exclusion of liability assumed under contract does not apply to (1) written contracts that relate directly to the ownership, maintenance, and use of an insured location or (2) contracts where the liability of others is assumed by the insured prior to an occurrence. The first exception provides coverage for the types of assumption discussed in our Smith-Brown example. The second exception provides coverage for other contractual assumptions, as long as the agreement is executed prior to the damage for which liability is assumed and as long as one of the other exclusions of the policy does not apply.

6.b. Property Owned by an Insured Section II of the Homeowners Policy, like most liability insurance contracts, excludes property damage to property owned by the insured. This exclusion prevents family members from suing one another for damage to their property.

6.c. Property Rented to, or in the Care of the Insured Damage to property occupied or used by the insured or rented to or in the care, custody, or control of the insured is excluded. Property of others in the insured's custody may be insured under Section I of the Homeowners Policy (or another form of first-party coverage). This exclusion has one important qualification. An exception to the exclusion makes it inapplicable to property damage caused by fire, smoke, or explosion. This exception provides what is known as *Fire Legal Liability Insurance,* a special form of protection designed to protect renters or lessees from claims arising out of fire damage to the rented or leased premises. The fact that the Care, Custody, and Control exclusion does not apply to damage caused by fire, smoke, or explosion could be important to an insured who has rented a dwelling or apartment. Coverage would apply both to the building and to furnishings.[4]

6.d. Workers Compensation and Other Statutory Benefits Exclusion 6.d eliminates payment for bodily injury to persons who are eligible for benefits under a workers compensation, nonoccupational disability, or occupational disease law.[5] The exclusion applies whether the benefits are required by law or the employer has voluntarily purchased workers compensation insurance. Note, however, that only liability under workers compensation is excluded, not injuries to employees. Although workers compensation benefits are excluded, coverage exists for suits by residence employees in jurisdictions where such employees are not covered by the workers compensation law. Residence employees are those employees whose duties relate to the maintenance of the premises, butlers, maids, gardeners, cleaning persons, babysitters, and domestic employees. Coverage is provided automatically for two full-time residence employees in the basic premium. An additional premium applies for each employee in excess of two employees.

6.e. Nuclear Exclusion The nuclear exclusion was inserted in virtually all liability policies very early in the development of nuclear energy as an alternate source of power. Coverage for liability arising out of nuclear reactors or other sources of potential nuclear damage is provided under Nuclear Energy Liability policies.

6.f. Injuries to Insured Persons The injury-to-insured persons exclusion (6.f) eliminates coverage for bodily injury to the named insured, resident relatives, other persons under the age of 21 in the care of the insured, and those students who qual-

---

[4]The tenant who negligently sets fire to the apartment or dwelling might be sued by the landlord. On the other hand, the landlord may not sue, but collect instead from his or her fire insurance company. What do you suppose the fire insurer will do?

[5]In most states, domestic servants in a private home are not subject to the workers compensation law, but the employer may voluntarily bring them under the law by purchasing the appropriate insurance. In California, New Hampshire, New Jersey, and New York, workers compensation insurance is required for all residence employees, and the coverage may be added to the Homeowners Policy under a Workers Compensation Endorsement. In other states, coverage for domestic employees is usually provided under a separate Workers Compensation Policy.

ify as insureds under the policy. Coverage for suits by one insured against another insured would encourage such suits in situations in which they would not otherwise occur.

Medical Payments to Others

The Medical Payments coverage provides payment for medical expenses incurred by persons who are injured while on the premises with the permission of any insured or who are injured away from the premises if the injury results from an activity of the insured or a member of the insured's family. Coverage for medical payments applies regardless of the insured's liability. The basic limit under the Homeowners Policy for this coverage is $1000 per person, which may be increased. The insuring agreement provides that medical payments will be paid under a variety of circumstances:

> We will pay the necessary medical expenses that are incurred or medically ascertained within three years from the date of an accident causing "bodily injury." Medical expenses means reasonable charges for medical, surgical, X-ray, dental, ambulance, hospital, professional nursing, prosthetic devices, and funeral services. This coverage does not apply to you or regular residents of your household except "residence employees." As to others, this coverage applies only:
> a. to a person on the "insured location" with the permission of an "insured"; or
> b. to a person off the "insured location," if the "bodily injury":
>   1. arises out of a condition on the "insured location" or the ways immediately adjoining;
>   2. is caused by the activities of an "insured";
>   3. is caused by a "residence employee" in the course of the "residence employee's" employment by an "insured"; or

4. is caused by an animal owned by or in the care of an "insured."

Medical Payments coverage applies regardless of fault. Furthermore, anyone injured within the scope of the coverage may claim directly under the policy. They do not have to have the consent of the named insured to enter a claim. The insuring agreement specifically provides that coverage does not apply to the insured or residents of the insured's household, *other than residence employees*. Residence employees are covered under medical payments for bodily injuries incurred on the premises or off premises if the injury arises out of or in the course of their employment by the insured.

The scope of covered medical expenses is inclusive, including even funeral expenses. The only requirements are that the expenses be "necessary" and that they be incurred or medically ascertained within three years of the accident.

Medical Payments Exclusions

The Liability exclusions relating to intentional injuries, business pursuits, professional acts, uninsured premises, aircraft, motor vehicles, watercraft, and war also apply to the Medical Payments coverage. In addition, four other exclusions apply to the Medical Payments coverage.

7.a. Residence Employees Away from the Premises Medical Payments coverage does not apply to injuries sustained by domestic servants or residence employees when they are away from the insured premises and the injury does not arise out of or in the course of their employment by the insured.

7.b. Workers Compensation and Other Statutory Benefits Just as the Liability section of the policy excluded liability imposed under any workers compensation law, medical benefits payable or required to be paid under any workers compensation, nonoccupational disability, or occupational disease law are excluded. This exclusion applies to any person eligible to receive such benefits, including, for example, workers who come on the premises and who are covered under a Workers Compensation Policy purchased by their employer.

7.c. Nuclear Exclusion   The nuclear exclusion under Medical Payments excludes coverage for bodily injury resulting from any nuclear reaction, radiation, or radioactive contamination.

7.d. Persons Residing on Premises   The final Medical Payments exclusion excludes coverage for any person other than a residence employee regularly residing at the insured location. The purpose of this exclusion is to eliminate Medical Payments coverage for roomers or boarders and the tenants of an apartment on the premises. However, coverage would exist under the liability section if such persons were injured and brought suit.

Additional Coverages

The Additional Coverages of Section II represent supporting promises by the insurer that provide payment for certain additional expenses that may be incurred by the insured in the event of injury or damage to the person or property of others. There are four Additional Coverages under Section II of the Homeowners Policy: Claim Expenses, First Aid Expenses, Damage to Property of Others, and Loss Assessment.

Claim Expense

The insurer promises to pay, in addition to the limit of liability, all expenses incurred in the defense of any suit under the policy, interest on judgments, plus certain other legal costs. These include expenses incurred by the insured in cooperating with the insurer in defending a suit, including loss of earnings up to $50 a day.

First Aid Expenses

The First Aid Expenses coverage promises to pay expenses incurred by the insured for first aid related to any bodily injury covered under the policy. First aid expenses, like defense costs, are payable in addition to the policy limit.

Damage to Property of Others Coverage

Damage to Property of Others coverage, like Medical Payments, is not a "liability" coverage. It provides some insurance for damage to the property of others that is caused by an insured but for which he or she would not be legally liable. It is intended to permit some payment for damage for which the insured feels a moral obligation, even though there is no legal one. It pays, up to $1000, for damage to the property of others that is caused by an insured, regardless of the insured's legal liability. The $1000 limit cannot be increased.

The insuring agreement of this coverage states

Damage to Property of Others: We will pay up to $1000 per "occurrence" for property damage to property of others caused by an "insured."

Note that the harm must be caused by an insured and that the property must have actually been damaged. If the insured borrows a neighbor's golf clubs and loses one, the loss would not be covered.

Damage to Property of Others Exclusions There are four exclusions relating to this coverage:

First, the Damage to Property of Others coverage does not apply to any loss if there is coverage for that loss under Section I of the policy as "property used by an insured." If the insured borrows personal property, it is insured property just as if it were owned by the insured. If such property is damaged by one of the perils insured against under Section I, the insured may collect for the damage under that section of the policy. However, subject to the coverage limit, payment can be made under Section II for any part of the loss (including the deductible) that is not covered under Section I.

The Damage to Property of Others coverage also does not apply to damage or destruction that is caused intentionally by any insured age 13 or older. The Intentional Damage exclusion under the *Liability Coverage* does not specify any age limit, thus eliminating all intentional damage. Under the Damage to Property of Others coverage, there is coverage up to a limit ($1000) for deliberate damage by insureds under the age of 13.

Damage to property owned by or rented to any insured or a resident of the insured's household or any tenant of the insured is also excluded. This is less restrictive than the exclusion of Damage to Property in Care, Custody, or Control of the Insured in the Liability coverage. The Damage to Property of Others exclusion does not mention property in the care, custody, or control of the insured, which means that coverage would exist for damage to borrowed property up to $1000.

The fourth exclusion relating to this insuring agreement has three parts. It excludes completely any damage from business pursuits of the insured. It also excludes damage resulting from acts or omissions in connection with uninsured owned or rented premises. Finally, it excludes all damage resulting from the ownership, maintenance, or use of aircraft, hovercraft, motor vehicles, or watercraft. An exception to this last exclusion provides that the exclusion does not apply to nonowned motor vehicles that are not subject to motor vehicle registration.

Loss Illustrations Several illustrations will clarify the intent of this coverage of damage to property of others. First, let us assume that the insured borrows a neighbor's lawnmower. While mowing the lawn, he inadvertently runs over a large rock and damages the machine extensively. Even if the insured were held liable for the damage, liability coverage will not apply because of the Care, Custody, or Control exclusion. Because the property

was damaged by an insured, the Damage to Property of Others coverage will be applicable up to $1000.[6]

As a second example, assume that the insured and her 2-year-old son are visiting friends. While the adults are talking, the child finds a bottle of laundry bleach, brings it into the living room, and before anyone can react, slams the bottle down on a glass-topped coffee table. The table is broken and the bleach damages a part of the rug. The facts imply that there is no legal liability on the part of the child or his parents, but still the parents might feel a moral obligation to pay for the property damage. Unless an insured is legally liable, the liability coverage of the policy does not apply. However, since the loss was caused by an insured (the son), payment would be made up to $1000 under the Damage to Property of Others coverage. The coverage will therefore pay for damage where the insured feels a moral obligation, even though legal liability does not exist.

Finally, suppose that the insured's 10-year-old son heaves a brick through the neighbor's plate glass picture window. This loss would not be paid under the liability coverage because it was an intentional act by the insured.[7] However, the cover-

---

[6]Not all losses involving property of others in the care, custody, or control of the insured are covered. If the borrowed lawnmower had been placed in the insured's garage overnight and had been stolen, the loss would not be paid, because there was no damage "caused by an insured." Similarly, if lightning struck the garage and burned it to the ground, destroying the lawnmower, this loss would not be paid for the same reason. Both the stolen lawnmower and the one destroyed in the fire would be covered under Section I of the insured's Homeowners Policy.

[7]In those states having special statutes making the parents liable for willful, malicious, and destructive acts to property by their minor and unemancipated children, perhaps this loss would be paid under the Liability section because of the parent's vicarious liability. In *Arenson v. National Automobile and Casualty Insurance Co.,* 286 PC. 2nd, 816 (1976), the court held that coverage applied where the parent was held liable for the son's intentional damage, in spite of the exclusion of damage caused intentionally by the insured. The court based its decision on the fact that the insured who was held liable (the parent) had not caused the damage intentionally.

age for Damage to Property of Others would pay up to $1000, since only intentional acts of insureds who have reached the age of 13 are excluded.

In summary, the coverage provides a limited amount of protection (up to $500) for damage to the property of others that the insured may have in his or her care, custody, and control. In addition, it serves as some coverage in those cases where there is no legal liability, but in which the insured feels a moral obligation. Finally, it provides limited restitution for intentional damage caused by the insured's minor children, provided that they are under age 13.

Loss Assessment Coverage

The Section II Loss Assessment coverage, like the Section I coverage, applies to assessments against the insured by a condominium association or other cooperative body of property owners. Coverage applies for assessments arising out of bodily injury or property damage that are not excluded under the terms of the Homeowners liability coverage. Coverage is limited to $1000, but an increased limit of coverage is available by endorsement. Coverage is included for the liability of the insured as an elected, uncompensated officer, director, or trustee of the corporation or association of property owners. However, the coverage excludes assessments charged against the insured or the group by any government body.

Homeowners Section II Conditions

Section II of the Homeowners Policy is subject to its own set of conditions as well as to the general conditions applicable to both Section I and Section II.

Limit of Liability

The limit of liability shown in the declarations for Coverage E is the maximum payable, regardless of the number of insureds involved, claims made, or persons injured. The maximum payable for all medical expenses of one person as the result of one accident will not be more than the limit listed for Coverage F in the declarations.

Severability of Insurance

The insurance applies separately to each insured. Historically, this has been interpreted to mean that it is possible for one insured to bring suit against another under the policy. Under the Comprehensive Personal Liability (CPL) form, however, suits by the named insured and residents of the household are specifically excluded.

Duties After Loss

In the event of loss, the insured must cooperate with the insurer in several ways. In addition to giving notice of loss to the insurer with information concerning the loss (e.g., name of the claimants and witnesses if possible), the insured is required to forward promptly to the insurer every notice, demand, summons, or other process relating to the loss and, at the company's request, cooperate in making settlement, attending trials, and so on. In addition, the insured may not admit liability or voluntarily make payment or assume any obligations at the time of a bodily injury, other than first aid.

Duties of Insured Persons—Coverage F—Medical Payments to Others

A person seeking payment under the Medical Payments coverage must give written proof of loss, authorize the insurer to obtain medical records, and submit to a physical examination by a doctor of the insurer's choice.

Payment of Claim—Coverage F

Payment of a claim under the Medical Payments coverage is not to be taken as an admission by the insurer of liability on the part of an insured.

Suits Against Us

No legal action may be brought against the insurer unless the insured has complied with the terms of the policy. The insurer cannot be sued by a claimant until the liability of the insured has been established, either by judgment or by agreement with the insurer.

Bankruptcy of Insured

Bankruptcy or insolvency of a covered person does not relieve the insurer of its obligation under the policy. If the insured is sued and declares bankruptcy, thereby discharging his or her portion of a judgment, the insurer is still obligated to pay the part of the judgment that is covered by insurance.

Other Insurance—Coverage E

The Liability coverage is excess over any other valid and collectible insurance, except for umbrella liability policies or other excess policies that are written specifically to cover on an excess basis.

Homeowners Section II Endorsements

There are a variety of endorsements available to tailor the Section II coverages to the needs of an insured. Some of these have already been noted. Others include endorsements that add coverage for excluded watercraft and recreational motor vehicles, or for excluded business activities. Most of these endorsements are dictated by specific needs of the individual or family. One endorsement, however—the Personal Injury Endorsement—is an essential addition to the policy for all insureds.

Personal Injury Liability Endorsement

The insuring agreement of the Liability Coverage provides protection against losses resulting from "bodily injury," which is defined as "bodily harm, sickness or disease, including required care, loss of services, and death resulting therefrom." This means that there is no coverage for losses from tort actions such as libel, slander, defamation of character, false arrest, or invasion of the right of privacy, none of which involves bodily harm. Coverage for such suits is provided under a separate form of coverage referred to as *Personal Injury Liability*, which is available by endorsement to the Homeowners Policy. Coverage is provided for three groups of hazards:

1. False arrest, detention, imprisonment, or malicious prosecution
2. Libel, slander, defamation, or violation of the right of privacy
3. Wrongful entry or eviction, or other invasion of the right of private occupancy

The coverage is subject to several exclusions, none of which should cause problems for the average insured. Exclusions apply with respect to (1) liability assumed under contract, (2) violation of law by or with the knowledge of the insured, (3) injury to employees of the insured, (4) business pursuits of the insured, or (5) any civic or public activities performed by an insured.

Cost of Personal Liability Insurance

The cost of Comprehensive Personal Liability (CPL) coverage is far less than one might imagine. Although the premium for the Liability section of the Homeowners Policy is included in the basic premium for the policy, the cost per year of a separate CPL policy with the basic $100,000 limit for liability and $1000 for medical payments is about $25. Increasing the limits of liability increases the cost of the policy only slightly. A $300,000 limit raises the cost to about $33, and a $500,000 limit increases the cost only to about $37. Higher limits of coverage are also available from most companies, but when limits in excess of $300,000 or $500,000 are desired, an Umbrella Liability Policy is generally used. In view of the catastrophic potential of the liability exposure and the low cost of increased limits, the sophisticated insurance buyer should elect the higher limits.

Umbrella Liability Policy *excess liability policy*

Many persons, particularly professional and well-to-do members of our society, are subject to liability claims of catastrophic proportions. These claims may stem from personal activities or professional or business pursuits and can exceed by hundreds of thousands of dollars the limits of the basic liability forms. The affluent are subject to high jury awards since they are always looked upon as fair game for large settlements.

To provide catastrophe liability protection for such individuals, insurance companies have developed a personal catastrophe liability contract, or as it is more commonly called, the Umbrella Liability Policy. While there is no standard form for the Umbrella Liability Policy, in general it may be described as a broad form of liability insurance, covering both general liability and automobile liability, which is purchased in addition to the separate basic liability contracts.

To qualify for an Umbrella Liability Policy, the insured is required to purchase certain underlying liability insurance. For example, the insurer may require automobile liability insurance with limits of $100,000/$300,000/$50,000 and CPL coverage in the amount of $300,000. If other special exposures exist, coverage will be required for these also in the basic program. For example, if the applicant owns watercraft of the type excluded under the basic CPL, such craft must be insured. The umbrella policy is then written as excess coverage over the limits of the basic policies. The limit of liability under the umbrella may range from $1 million to $5 million.

The Umbrella Liability Policy performs two separate functions, the net effect of which is to superimpose a blanket or umbrella of protection on the individual's other liability coverages. The first function is that of providing "excess coverage" in those instances where a liability loss covered under the basic policies exceeds the limit of those policies. For example, if the insured is the object of a liability claim for $500,000 that is covered by either the Homeowners Policy or automobile insurance, the basic liability policies involved would respond for the first $300,000, and the umbrella would pay the remaining $200,000.

The second function of the umbrella is to establish broader coverage than that provided under the basic contracts. Although there is no standard umbrella contract and it is, therefore, difficult to generalize, most such policies are written with broad insuring agreements and are subject to fewer exclusions than the basic policies, so that many losses normally excluded under the basic contracts are covered under the umbrella.[8] For example, the automobile liability coverage applies worldwide, with no restrictions regarding the type or use of the automobile.[9] In addition, the coverage is usually written to include personal injury hazards and blanket contractual liability.

When a liability claim is covered under the umbrella but not by one of the underlying contracts, the umbrella will respond, subject to a self-insured retention or deductible. The size of this deductible varies considerably among companies. On most personal umbrellas, it was originally $5000 or $10,000, but several companies now market policies with a retention as low as $250. It should be noted that this deductible applies only where the loss is not covered by the basic contracts. If the loss is covered under the basic contracts, the umbrella responds from the first dollar once these policies are exhausted.

Exclusions Under the Umbrella Liability Policy

While the coverage under the Umbrella Liability Policy is far broader than that of the individual contracts, it is not all risk. There are exclusions,

---

[8]In 1997, ISO filed the industry's first standardized personal umbrella policy. The new policy form is designed to complement ISO's homeowners, personal liability, and personal auto insurance products.

[9]As the reader will become aware of in Chapter 23, the automobile policy limits coverage to the United States and Canada and imposes restrictions on the type and use of automobiles that are covered.

Tidbits, Vignettes, and Conundrums 21.2

President Clinton's Umbrella Liability Policy

The breadth of umbrella liability policies is (perhaps) illustrated by the fact that two personal umbrella policies paid $1.5 million of the legal bills incurred by former President Clinton in the Paula Jones case. Umbrella liability policies were issued to the Clintons by State Farm Insurance Company and Pacific Indemnity Insurance Company (a subsidiary of Chubb Group Insurance). The payment of the defense costs provoked a debate over whether the president received preferential treatment because of his status or for some other reason.

Source: Washington Post. See http://www.washingtonpost.com/wp-srv/politics/special/pjones/stories/pj091097.htm and http://www.spectator.org/archives/96-06-york.html.

and some of them rather important. There is an exclusion of owned or leased aircraft, watercraft of the type excluded under the basic Homeowners Policy, business pursuits, and professional services—unless coverage for these exposures has been provided in the underlying insurance program. If such coverage is afforded by the underlying program, these exposures are covered by the umbrella. In addition, workers compensation obligations are generally excluded; however, as in the case of the underlying CPL or Homeowners Policy, employers liability coverage is provided. Any act committed by, or at, the direction of the insured with the intent to cause personal injury or property damage is also excluded. With the exception of aircraft or watercraft, there is no exclusion of property rented to or in the care, custody, and control of the insured; however, damage to rented or borrowed aircraft and watercraft is excluded. Finally, damage to property owned by the insured is excluded.

Cost of the Umbrella

In spite of the high limits and the extreme broadness of the insuring agreement, the cost of the Umbrella Liability Policy is not excessive. Although the premium will vary somewhat with the occupation of the insured and certain other variables such as the number of automobiles in the family, usually the annual cost is less than $100.

Important Concepts to Remember

third-party coverage
general liability insurance
business pursuits
Business Pursuits endorsement
insured location
motor vehicles
negligent entrustment
Comprehensive Personal Liability

contractual liability
fire legal liability insurance
care, custody, and control exclusion
Medical Payments to Others
   coverage
personal injury
single limit of liability
communicable disease exclusion

intrafamily suits
Damage to Property of Others
claim expense
first aid expense
Loss Assessment coverage
Personal Injury Liability
professional liability
Umbrella Liability Policy

Questions for Review

1. Why is liability insurance sometimes called "third-party" coverage?

2. Briefly explain the definition of the term "premises" as used in the Homeowners Policy with respect to Section II (liability) coverages.

3. Who is included within the definition of "persons insured" under Section II of the Homeowners Policy?

4. Briefly describe the coverage provided under the Medical Payments coverage of the Homeowners Policy Section II. To whom does the coverage apply? To whom does it not apply?

5. Jones is playing golf and runs over her partner's foot with a rented golf cart. Will the Personal Liability coverage or the Medical Payments coverage respond for the injury?

6. What coverage exists under Section II of the Homeowners Policy for those situations in which the insured feels a moral obligation but where no legal obligation exists?

7. Jones owns a vicious German shepherd. He (the dog) bites a mail carrier about three blocks away from Jones's premises. Discuss fully the coverage under Section II of the Homeowners Policy for this occurrence.

8. Briefly describe the Fire Legal Liability coverage found in Section II of the Homeowners Policy. To whom does it apply? What factors create the need for this coverage?

9. Explain the nature of the personal Umbrella Liability Policy. In your explanation, be sure to point out the relationship of the umbrella to the underlying coverage and the application of the deductible.

10. Briefly describe the coverage provided under the Personal Injury Liability endorsement to the Homeowners Policy.

Questions for Discussion

1. For each of the following losses, indicate whether or not coverage would exist under Coverage E, the liability coverage, of Section II of the Homeowners Policy:

   a. A young lady of the insured's acquaintance brings suit against him because of scurrilous remarks that he made about her virtue.

   b. A cleaning lady slips on the wet bathroom floor in the insured's home and brings suit to collect for her injuries.

   c. The insured throws a party at which one of the guests has too much to drink and injures a pedestrian while driving home. The injured party brings suit against the insured because the driver became intoxicated at the insured's party.

   d. The insured borrows a motorboat powered by an 85-horsepower outboard motor and runs over a water skier, who then brings suit.

   e. The insured's wife borrows a friend's mink stole and negligently burns a hole in it with a lighted cigar. The friend demands payment.

2. For each of the following losses, indicate whether or not coverage would exist under Coverage F, the medical payments coverage, of Section II of the Homeowners Policy:

   a. The insured's 65-year-old mother-in-law, who is living in his house, falls down the basement stairs and is injured.

   b. The insured's dog playfully nips a mail carrier, whose wounds require 14 stitches.

c. The insured's cleaning lady mistakes a bottle of cleaning fluid for gin and has to have her stomach pumped.

d. The insured's babysitter slips on a loose throw rug while carrying the insured's child, and both are injured.

3. For each of the following losses, indicate whether coverage would exist under the supplementary coverage for Damage to the Property of Others:

a. The insured borrows a neighbor's lawnmower, and while it is left outside overnight, it is stolen.

b. The insured's 9-year-old son pours sugar in his teacher's gas tank, resulting in extensive damage to the auto's engine.

c. The insured accidentally spills a glass of bourbon on his neighbor's dress, which is ruined as a result of the chemical reaction.

d. The insured backs his car over a neighbor's child's wagon, and although it is hardly worth a lawsuit, the insured would like to pay for the damage.

4. A friend, explaining his position with respect to liability insurance, states, "I don't feel that I really need high limits of liability, because I don't make that much money. If I were a doctor or a lawyer, I would carry higher limits of liability coverage, but since I am not, the $100,000 minimum included in my Homeowners Policy is enough." Do you agree or disagree? Why?

5. The Homeowners Section II liability coverage provides protection for liability arising out of bodily injury or property damage. Describe the coverage that is added by the Personal Injury Liability endorsement. How important, in your opinion, is this optional coverage?

Suggestions for Additional Reading

Fire, Casualty and Surety Bulletins. Personal Lines Volume. Cincinnati, OH: National Underwriter Company. (Loose-leaf manual service with monthly supplements.) See "Dwelling" section.

Hamilton, Karen L., and Donald S. Malecki. *Personal Insurance: Property and Liability.* Malvern, PA: American Institute for CPCU, 1994. Chapter 3.

Launie, J. J., George E. Rejda, and Donald R. Oakes with Anita W. Johnson. *Personal Insurance.* Bryn Mawr, PA: Insurance Institute of America, 1991. Chapter 5.

Policy, Form, and Manual Analysis Service. Personal Lines Volume. Indianapolis, IN: Rough Notes Company. (Loose-leaf manual service with monthly supplements.) See "Dwellings" section.

Wood, Glenn L., Claude C. Lilly, III, Donald S. Malecki, Edward E. Graves, and Jerry S. Rosenbloom. *Personal Risk Management and Insurance*, 4th ed., vol. 2. Malvern, PA: American Institute for Property and Liability Underwriters, 1989. Chapter 4.

Websites to Explore

Best's Review—Property/Casualty Edition: http://www.ambest.com/review/lh/index.html

Independent Insurance Agents of America, Inc.: http://www.iiaa.org

Insurance News Network: http://www.insure.com/

National Association of Professional Insurance Agents: http://www.pianet.com/

Rough Notes Company: http://www.roughnotes.com/

CHAPTER 22

The Automobile and Its Legal Environment

It's the Model T Ford made the trouble.
—Meredith Willson,
The Music Man

CHAPTER OBJECTIVES

When you have finished this chapter, you should be able to

- Explain the special provisions of tort law applicable to automobiles

- Explain the principles of vicarious liability and the special provisions applicable to guests

- Explain the legal requirements imposed by the states regarding automobile liability insurance

- Explain the no-fault concept and the basic philosophy on which this concept is based, and evaluate the arguments for and against no-fault laws

- Explain the differences among the approaches to reform of the automobile reparations system that have been adopted by the states

- Discuss the various systems for providing insurance to high-risk drivers

- Discuss the automobile insurance classification system and how rates are affected by various underwriting factors

The automobile is the most widely owned major asset in the United States. It is also one of the chief sources of economic loss. The ownership or operation of an automobile exposes the individual to many sources of loss: a person may be killed or injured while operating a car, or being struck by one, with resulting medical expenses and loss of income; one may also be held legally liable for injuries to others or for damage to the property of others; the car itself may be damaged, destroyed, or stolen.

In this chapter, we begin our study of automobile insurance with an examination of the legal principles governing the operation of the automobile, including a brief discussion of the no-fault laws that have been adopted by many states. In the next chapter, we will look at the automobile insurance policy itself.

Before turning to the legal environment, it may be helpful to review briefly the general nature of the automobile coverages available to protect against loss arising out of the automobile.

A Brief Overview of Automobile Coverages

For the purpose of our discussion that follows, it will be helpful if the reader will keep in mind the distinctions among the following four automobile insurance coverages: Automobile Liability Insurance, Medical Payments coverage, Physical Damage coverage, and Uninsured Motorists coverage.

Automobile Liability Insurance

Automobile Liability Insurance protects the insured against loss arising from legal liability when his or her automobile injures someone or damages another's property. This coverage is usually written today with a single limit similar to that of the Homeowners Policy, but it is also written subject to "split limits," usually expressed as $10,000/$20,000/$5000, or more simply as $10/$20/$5. The first two figures refer to the bodily injury liability limit, and the third refers to the property damage limit. Thus, $10/$20/$5 means that coverage is provided up to $10,000 for injury to one person and up to $20,000 for all persons injured in a single accident, and that property damage up to $5000 is payable for a single accident.

Medical Payments Coverage

Automobile Medical Payments coverage reimburses the insured and members of the insured's family for medical expenses that result from automobile accidents. The protection also applies to other occupants of the insured's automobile. Like the medical payments of the Homeowners Policy, automobile Medical Payments coverage is distinct from the liability coverage; it applies as a special form of accident insurance. Unlike the Homeowners, the coverage applies specifically to the insured and members of his or her family. It is written with a maximum limit per person per accident, which usually ranges from $500 to $5000.

Physical Damage Coverage

Automobile Physical Damage coverage insures against loss of the policyholder's own automobile and in this sense resembles Section I of the Homeowners. The coverage is written under two insuring agreements, Other Than Collision (formerly called Comprehensive) and Collision. Collision, as the name implies, indemnifies for collision losses; Other Than Collision is a form of open-peril coverage that provides protection against most other insurable perils. Physical Damage coverage applies to the insured auto regardless of fault. If the other driver is at fault, the insured who carries collision coverage has the option of proceeding against the other driver or collecting under his or her own collision and permitting the insurance company to subrogate. If the other driver is held liable, his or her property damage liability coverage will pay the loss.

Uninsured Motorists Coverage

Uninsured Motorists coverage is an imaginative form of auto insurance, under which the insurer agrees to pay the insured, up to specified limits, the amount the insured could have collected from a negligent driver who caused injury, when that driver is uninsured or is guilty of hit and run. Uninsured motorists coverage usually has the same limits as the bodily injury coverage in the liability section of the policy.

Understanding the following discussion will be much easier with a firm grasp of the distinctions among these four coverages.

Legal Liability and the Automobile

The liability of the owner or operator of an automobile is largely governed by the principles of negligence discussed in Chapter 20. However, special laws affecting automobile liability have been enacted to modify some of the basic principles of negligence. Several of these statutes relate to the responsibility of others when the driver is negligent. In addition, some laws deal with the liability of the operator toward passengers.

Vicarious Liability and the Automobile

As you will recall from Chapter 20, vicarious liability describes a situation in which one party becomes liable for the negligence of another. When one thinks of being held liable for the operation of a motor vehicle, one normally has in mind a situation in which he or she is the driver. However, because of vicarious liability laws and doctrines, it is possible for an individual to be held liable in situations where someone else is the operator. First, if the driver of the automobile is acting as an agent for another person, the principal may be held liable for the acts of the agent. In addition to this imputed or vicarious liability, the owner of an auto that is being operated by someone else may be held liable because of his or her own negligence, either in furnishing the auto to someone known to be an incompetent driver or in lending a car known to be unsafe. In addition to these situations based on common law principles, vicarious liability laws have been enacted by various states that greatly enlarge the exposure of imputed liability in connection with the automobile.

Under the family purpose doctrine, applicable in 18 states and the District of Columbia,[1] the owner of an automobile is held liable for the negligent acts of the members of his or her immediate family or household in their operation of the car. The family purpose doctrine is basically a part of the principal-agent relationship, in that any member of the family is considered to be an agent of the parent-owner when using the family car, even for the driver's own convenience or amusement. Somewhat related to the family purpose doctrine, about half the states[2] impose liability on the parents of a minor or on any person who signs a minor's application for a drivers license for any damage arising out of the operation of any automobile by that minor. Note that in this situation it is not only driving of the family car, but of any car, that gives rise to the vicarious lia-

---

[1]Arizona, Colorado, Connecticut, Georgia, Kentucky, Michigan, Minnesota, Nebraska, Nevada, New Jersey, New Mexico, North Carolina, North Dakota, Oregon, South Carolina, Tennessee, Washington, West Virginia, and the District of Columbia.

[2]Alaska, Arizona, Arkansas, California, Colorado, Delaware, Florida, Hawaii, Idaho, Indiana, Kentucky, Maryland, Mississippi, Montana, Nevada, New Mexico, North Dakota, Ohio, Oklahoma, Rhode Island, South Carolina, Tennessee, Texas, Utah, and Wisconsin.

bility. Other states[3] have enacted statutes that go farther and make any person furnishing an auto to a minor responsible for the negligent acts of that minor in the operation of the automobile. The most sweeping vicarious liability laws are the permissive use statutes, enforced in 12 states and the District of Columbia, which impose liability on the owner of an automobile for any liability arising out of someone's operating it with the owner's permission, regardless of the operator's age.[4]

One point bears mention again. The vicarious liability laws and doctrines do not relieve the driver of responsibility; they merely make the other party (owner or parent) jointly liable.

Guest Hazard Statutes

The second statutory modification of the principles of legal liability affecting the automobile defines the liability of a driver or owner toward passengers in the car. At one time, most states had so-called guest laws, which restricted the right of a passenger in an automobile to sue the owner or the driver.[5] The original reason for such laws was the allegation of insurers that suits by passengers presented an opportunity to defraud insurance companies. Without such laws, it was alleged, the guest in an automobile who is injured might easily induce the driver to admit liability in return for a portion of the settlement the driver's insurance company might make with the injured guest.

Under a standard guest law, the injured guest can collect from the negligent driver only if the driver was operating the auto in a grossly negligent manner or, in some jurisdictions, if the driver was intoxicated. Gross negligence is a "complete and total disregard for the safety of oneself or others." Even in the case of gross negligence, the guest may be denied recovery if he or she assumes the risk involved in it. Some laws provide that the failure of the guest to protest against the grossly negligent manner in which the auto is being operated constitutes acceptance of the risk.

Although there is room for disagreement, many observers believe that the guest statutes are ill-conceived laws. They were the result of a rash of state legislation in the 1920s and 1930s, the fruit of vigorous lobbying by the insurance industry. While a few collusive suits may have been prevented over the years, tens of thousands of "guests" have been denied access to the courts for recovery of compensation for their injuries. No American state has adopted a new guest law for many years; in many states the laws have been repealed or declared unconstitutional.[6] In those states where they still exist, the courts are now tending to construe them more narrowly.

Automobile Liability Insurance and the Law

As late as 1971, only Massachusetts, North Carolina, and New York had compulsory automobile liability insurance laws. However, with the enactment of the no-fault laws discussed later in this chapter, many legislatures also made automobile liability insurance compulsory. By 2000, 44 states and the District of Columbia had laws requiring the owners of automobiles registered in the state

---

[3]Delaware, Idaho, Kansas, Maine, Pennsylvania, and Utah.

[4]California, Connecticut, Florida, Idaho, Iowa, Massachusetts, Michigan, Minnesota, New York, North Carolina, Rhode Island, Tennessee, and the District of Columbia.

[5]States that have enacted guest laws include Alabama, Arkansas, California, Colorado, Delaware, Florida, Idaho, Illinois, Indiana, Iowa, Kansas, Michigan, Montana, Nebraska, Nevada, New Mexico, North Dakota, Ohio, Oregon, South Carolina, South Dakota, Texas, Utah, Vermont, Virginia, Washington, and Wyoming. In addition, the doctrine is applied by the courts in Georgia, although there is no statutory provision.

[6]States in which guest laws have been repealed or declared unconstitutional include Arkansas, California, Colorado, Connecticut, Florida, Idaho, Iowa, Kansas, Michigan, Montana, New Mexico, North Dakota, Ohio, Oregon, South Dakota, Vermont, Virginia, Washington, and Wyoming.

to have liability insurance or, sometimes, an approved substitute form of security.[7]

Before the widespread enactment of compulsory auto insurance laws, most states attempted to solve the problem of the financial responsibility of drivers through what are known as financial responsibility laws. These laws require a driver to show proof of insurance (or some other approved form of security) when he or she is involved in an accident. Because they require proof of "financial responsibility" only after an accident, these laws are sometimes called "free-bite laws." Most states that have enacted compulsory auto insurance laws retained their financial responsibility law, and drivers are subject to the requirements of both.[8]

In most states, the financial responsibility laws take the form of a "security-type" law. It provides that any driver involved in an auto accident that causes bodily injury or damage to the property of others (the latter must exceed a specified minimum, usually $100 or $200) must demonstrate the ability to pay any judgment resulting from the accident or lose his or her license. If a driver's license is suspended, then security for future accidents must be posted before it will be restored. The financial responsibility laws apply to all parties in an accident, even those who do not appear to have been at fault.

The requirements of the law will be met if an insurer files a certificate (called an "SR–21") indicating that, at the time of the accident, the driver had liability insurance with limits that meet the state's requirements. The limits of liability required by the various states and Canadian provinces in 1999 are indicated in Table 22.1. If the driver cannot provide evidence of insurance, the requirements of the law can be met by depositing security (money) with the specified authority in an amount determined by the authority.

A person who does not have liability insurance and cannot make any other arrangements for settlement of the loss will lose his or her driving privileges.[9] Driving privileges remain suspended until any judgment arising out of the accident is satisfied and until proof of financial responsibility for future accidents is demonstrated. Judgments are deemed satisfied, regardless of the amounts awarded, when the payment equals the required liability limits. The requirement that any judgment be satisfied may also be met by filing with the authority (1) signed forms releasing the driver from all liability for claims resulting from the accident, (2) a certified copy of a final judgment of nonliability, or (3) a written agreement with all claimants providing for payment in installments of an agreed amount for claims resulting from the accident. Financial responsibility for future accidents normally is proven by the purchase of automobile liability insurance in the limits prescribed by the state. The insurance company then submits a certificate, an SR–22, showing that the insurance is in force. Financial responsibility may also be demonstrated by posting a surety bond or, as a final resort, by the deposit of a stated amount of cash or securities (for instance, $25,000 or $50,000) with the proper authorities. The length of time for which proof is required varies from state to state, but the usual time is three years.

In many states, a person's drivers license may also be revoked or suspended if a person is convicted of certain traffic violations. After the period of suspension, the restoration of the license requires proof of financial responsibility. This can be accomplished as was just discussed. Offenses leading to suspension vary among the states. Practically all states suspend licenses for driving while intoxicated, reckless driving, conviction of a

---

[7]The states without compulsory auto insurance laws are New Hampshire, Rhode Island, Tennessee, Virginia, Washington, and Wisconsin.

[8]All states except Kansas, Maryland, Massachusetts, and Minnesota have some form of financial responsibility law (and these four states have compulsory insurance laws).

[9]The financial responsibility law of a particular state applies to nonresidents who have accidents in the state. The suspension of the license and registration of a nonresident normally affects driving privileges only in that state. But some states have reciprocal provisions, and if the nonresident's home state has reciprocity, his or her license and registration will be suspended in the home state as well.

felony in which a motor vehicle was used, operating a car without the owner's permission, or for a series of lesser offenses.

Insurance for High-Risk Drivers

For most American motorists, purchasing automobile insurance is fairly routine. Although the cost of the insurance may be irritating, there are many insurers that are willing to take the insured's premium dollars. There are some people, however, who find that insurers are generally unwilling to assume their risk and who have difficulty in obtaining automobile insurance. This is particularly true of youthful male drivers and some people who must demonstrate financial responsibility under state laws. It is also true of people whose poor driving records mark them as more hazardous risks than the average of the classification to which they would otherwise belong.

Automobile insurance companies, like most other businesses, want to make a profit, or at least cover all expenses of their business operations. They cannot do this if they accept a large number of applicants whose probability of loss is greater than the average. Yet if these high-risk drivers were to remain uninsured, their presence on the road would represent a financial risk not only to themselves but also to others who might be involved in the same accident.

The insurance industry has been concerned that if it does not provide coverage for high-risk drivers, a government plan might be instituted to do so. If the state undertook to insure high-risk drivers, it might decide to insure standard drivers as well, and private automobile insurance might disappear altogether. For these and other reasons, the insurance industry has established mechanisms to provide the necessary coverages for drivers who are unable to buy insurance through normal market channels. The most successful and widely used method of providing auto insurance to high-risk drivers is the Automobile Insurance Plan, now in operation in 42 states and the District of Columbia. Essentially, these are ap-

plicant-sharing plans under which each automobile insurance company doing business in the state accepts a share of the state's high-risk drivers. These systems were originally used in all states, but since 1972, 8 states have introduced other methods for providing such insurance.

Automobile Insurance Plans

An Automobile Insurance Plan is a risk-sharing pool in which all auto insurers operating in a particular state share in writing those drivers who do not meet normal underwriting standards.[10] It serves two functions. The first is to make auto liability insurance (and often other forms of auto insurance as well) available to those who cannot obtain it through normal channels. The second is to establish a procedure for the equitable distribution of these insureds among all the auto liability insurers in the state.[11]

With respect to the first function, the applicant must certify on a prescribed form that he or she has attempted, within 60 days before the application, to obtain liability insurance, but without success. In 38 states, coverage is provided to any applicant who presents a valid drivers license. In the remaining states, certain applicants, like habitual traffic violators, are ineligible. If the applicant is eligible, a company will be assigned to underwrite the insurance. The designated insurer will be obligated to provide coverage with limits equal to the financial responsibility requirements of the state law. In most states, the insurer will provide limits higher than the minimum required by state law. In addition, although the plans were originally designed to provide only liability insurance,

---

[10]These plans were originally called Assigned Risk Plans, but the name was changed to eliminate the stigma of being insured through a mechanism with "risk" in its title.

[11]Automobile Assigned Risk Plans were organized by insurers as voluntary risk-sharing mechanisms, but were later made compulsory. A U.S. Supreme Court decision in 1951 upheld the constitutionality of compulsory assigned-risk plans in *California State Automobile Association Inter-Insurance Bureau, Appellant, v. John R. Maloney, Insurance Commissioner*, 340 U.S. 105; 71 Sup. Ct. 601; 95 Law Ed. 788.

Table 22.1 State Financial Responsibility Limits, 2000

United States: States	Liability Limits[a]	United States: States	Liability Limits[a]
Alabama	$20/40/10 or 50,000	Missouri	25/50/10
Alaska	50/100/25 or 125	Montana	25/50/10
Arizona	15/30/10	Nebraska	25/50/25
Arkansas	25/50/15	Nevada	15/30/10
California	15/30/5	New Hampshire	25/50/25
Colorado	25/50/15	New Jersey	15/30/5
Connecticut	20/40/10	New Mexico	25/50/10
Delaware	15/30/10	New York	25/50/10*
District of Columbia	25/50/10	North Carolina	25/50/15
Florida	10/20/10 or 30	North Dakota	25/50/25
Georgia	15/30/10	Ohio	12.5/25/7.5
Hawaii	25/unlimited/10	Oklahoma	10/20/10
Idaho	25/50/15	Oregon	25/50/10
Illinois	20/40/15	Pennsylvania	15/30/5
Indiana	25/50/10	Rhode Island	25/50/25
Iowa	20/40/15	South Carolina	15/30/5
Kansas	25/50/10	South Dakota	25/50/25
Kentucky	25/50/10 or 60	Tennessee	25/50/10
Louisiana	10/20/10	Texas	20/40/15
Maine	20/40/10	Utah	25/50/15
Maryland	20/40/10	Vermont	25/50/10
Massachusetts	20/40/5	Virginia	25/50/20
Michigan	20/40/10	Washington	25/50/10
Minnesota	30/60/10	West Virginia	20/40/10
Mississippi	10/20/5	Wisconsin	25/50/10
		Wyoming	25/50/20

Canada: Provinces	Liability Limits	Canada: Provinces	Liability Limits
Alberta	$200,000	Nova Scotia	$200,000
British Columbia	200,000	Ontario	200,000
Manitoba	200,000	Prince Edward Island	200,000
New Brunswick	200,000	Quebec	50,000
New Foundland	200,000	Saskatchewan	200,000
Northwest Territories	200,000	Yukon	200,000

[a]The first two figures refer to bodily injury liability limits and the third figure to property damage. For example, $25/50/10 means coverage up to $50,000 for all persons injured in an accident, subject to a limit of $25,000 for one individual and $10,000 coverage for property damage.
*50/100 for wrongful death.

all the plans provide medical payments (or no-fault benefits) and most states offer Physical Damage coverage on the insured's own car.

An applicant cannot be assigned to a company for longer than three years, and the insurer may cancel an assigned risk under certain circumstances. The right to cancel is usually permitted only for nonpayment of premium, loss of the drivers license, or a number of major offenses while operating a motor vehicle.

The second function of the plan is to distribute the risks equitably among all automobile insurers operating in the state. This is accomplished by assigning to a particular insurer the percentage of

---

Tidbits, Vignettes, and Conundrums 22.1

Road Rage

According to a study by the National Highway Traffic Safety Administration (NHTSA), in 1996 the behavior known as *road rage* was involved in nearly two-thirds of motor vehicle deaths (nearly 28,000 deaths out of a total of 41,907). Another study (by the AAA Foundation for Traffic Safety) reported that during the period from 1990 through 1996, there were over 10,000 incidents in which drivers exhibiting road-rage behavior intentionally injured or killed another motorist or pedestrian.

---

the assigned-risk premiums that its total liability premiums bear to the total liability premiums of all automobile insurers operating in the state. Thus, if a particular company has 1/20 of all liability premiums written in the state, it would be assigned 1/20 of the risks. While this is only one of the methods of distribution available, it appears to be working reasonably well.

Alternate Approaches

Although the Automobile Insurance Plans exist in 42 states, 8 states use alternate systems for insuring high-risk drivers. In Maryland the insurance is available through a state-operated fund. The remaining seven states use one of two loss-sharing plans.

Reinsurance Pools In Massachusetts, New Hampshire, North Carolina, and South Carolina, all auto insurers participate in statewide automobile reinsurance pools, generally called the *facility*. Under this reinsurance system, every company accepts all applicants—good and bad. If the company considers a particular driver a high risk, it may place that driver in the statewide reinsurance pool. When this is done, all premiums paid and losses incurred by that driver are absorbed by the pool, but the policy is serviced by the originating company. The chief advantages to this system are that the stigma of purchasing insurance through an "assigned-risk plan" is eliminated and the con-

sumer may deal with the company of his or her choice.

Joint Underwriting Associations Three states—Florida, Hawaii, and Missouri—use a joint underwriting association approach to the problem of providing insurance for high-risk drivers.[12] Under this system, each agent or broker has access to a company that has been designated as a servicing company for high-risk drivers. A limited number of companies provide statewide service and claim-handling facilities for the high-risk drivers, but all automobile insurers in the state share in the losses. Like the reinsurance facility plans outlined, the joint underwriting association operates on the principle of sharing losses rather than sharing applicants.

Experience Under the Plans

As might be expected, the automobile insurance plans and the alternate loss-sharing arrangements have consistently experienced heavy dollar losses, currently more than $1 billion a year. These financial losses are passed on to other drivers in higher auto insurance rates. In a sense, the various plans all represent a continuing subsidy to problem drivers by other insureds.

---

[12]New Jersey established a type of joint underwriting association known as the New Jersey Automobile Full Underwriting Association in 1984, but replaced it with an Automobile Insurance Plan in 1990.

Distress Risk Companies

Although Automobile Insurance Plans provide a mechanism for insuring high-risk drivers, there are some drivers who are uninsurable even by the Automobile Insurance Plans and the alternative facilities in the other states. To purchase insurance coverage to meet the requirements of the state financial responsibility law, these persons must turn to what is commonly known as a distress risk company. Usually, these insurers specialize in insuring high-risk drivers. They have special ratings in which the premiums can attain almost incredible proportions and special policy forms that may be very limited. The distress risk companies perform a service, at least to the extent that they are making automobile liability insurance possible at some price.

The Automobile Insurance Problem and Changes in the Tort System

It is not at all unusual to hear complaints about automobile insurance today. Almost everyone connected with the automobile insurance business has what they consider to be a legitimate grievance. Insurance companies complain that they are losing money because of inadequate rates. The buyers complain that the rates are already too high. Young drivers (and to some extent older ones) complain that they frequently have difficulty in obtaining coverage. Finally, many who have suffered losses maintain that the settlements do not measure up to the economic loss. With all this dissatisfaction, it is not surprising that proposals for change have found widespread support.

Criticisms of the Traditional System

Dissatisfaction with auto insurance generally has fueled a debate that has been going on now since the mid-1960s. The debate has culminated in the passage of automobile no-fault laws or other legislation reforming automobile accident reparation in about half the states. While a part of the criticism has been aimed at insurance, some of the critics contend that the problem today is not so much with insurance as such, but rather with our method of compensating the injured. These critics maintain that our tort system is wasteful, expensive, unfair, and excessively time consuming, and they recommend that we abolish it for automobile accidents.

The effectiveness and rationale of the negligence approach have been questioned since the Columbia Report of 1932,[13] which pointed to many shortcomings of the tort system. One major criticism of that report, and also of today's critics, is that many persons who are injured remain uncompensated or are inadequately compensated. The accident victim may be unable to obtain reimbursement because he or she was contributorily negligent, because the guilty party is insolvent, or because the guilty party is unknown, as in the case of a hit-and-run driver. Additionally, the amount of compensation that is awarded may depend more on the skill of the victim's attorney than on the facts. Other criticisms of our traditional system attack the high cost of operating the insurance mechanism, the contingency fee system, and the congestion of the courts that results in long delays before the injured are finally compensated. Furthermore, the critics maintain that the traditional system is inequitable and that insurers overpay small claims to avoid litigation, but resist large claims in which the victim is seriously injured. Finally, the critics contend, the system is too expensive, paying more for the operation of insurance companies and the work of attorneys than it delivers to those who are injured.

For these reasons, the tort system has been under attack, and many proposals have been made

---

[13]Columbia Council for Research in the Social Sciences, *Report by the Committee to Study Compensation for Automobile Accidents* (New York: Columbia University, 1932).

to substitute a no-fault compensation system. Such proposals are not new, but they have generated increased interest since the middle of the 1960s, and, as noted, many states have actually adopted no-fault laws.

No-Fault Concept

The easiest way to understand the no-fault idea is to contrast it with the traditional tort system. Under the tort system, if you are involved in an accident and the accident is your fault, you may be held liable for injury to others or damage to their property. If you are found liable, you will be required to compensate the injured party through payment of damages. If you have liability insurance, your insurance company will pay for the other party's injuries. If the other party is found to have been negligent, his or her company will pay for your damages. If you are injured through your own negligence, you must bear the loss yourself, either out of existing resources or under some form of first-party insurance where the insurance company makes direct payment to you.

Under a no-fault system, there is no attempt to fix blame or to place the burden of the loss on the party causing it; each party collects for any injuries sustained from his or her own insurance company. Under a pure no-fault system, the right to sue the driver who caused an accident would be entirely abolished, and both the innocent victim and the driver at fault would recover their losses directly from their own insurance. Compulsory first-party coverage would compensate all accident victims regardless of fault. Although some no-fault proposals have included abolition of tort actions for damage to automobiles, the principal focus has been on bodily injuries.

Differences Among Proposals

Although the basic no-fault concept is simple enough, several modifications of the idea have developed, and there are significant differences

among the various proposals. We can distinguish among three different approaches.

1. **Pure No-Fault Proposals.** Under a pure no-fault plan, the tort system would be abolished for bodily injuries arising from auto accidents. (Some proposals would also abolish tort actions for damage to automobiles.) Anyone suffering loss would seek recovery for medical expenses, loss of income, or other expenses from his or her own insurer. Recovery for general damages (pain and suffering) would be eliminated.

2. **Modified No-Fault Proposals.** Modified no-fault proposals would provide limited immunity from tort action to the extent that the injured party was indemnified under a first-party coverage. Tort action would be retained for losses above the amount recovered under first-party coverage. In some modified no-fault plans, payment for pain and suffering would be limited or eliminated.

3. **Expanded First-Party Coverage.** Here there is no exemption from tort liability. Instead, the injured party collects benefits under a first-party coverage, retaining the right to sue for losses more than the amount paid by the first-party coverage. Most important, the responsibility of the negligent driver is retained by permitting subrogation by the insurer paying the first-party benefits.

Unfortunately, the "no-fault" label is sometimes applied to all three classifications. It is clearly a misnomer to refer to the expanded first-coverage approach as no-fault. Plans in this category, which do not change the tort system, cannot be called no-fault plans any more than fire insurance, health insurance, or even life insurance are no-fault plans. Before a plan qualifies as "no-fault," the requirement that motorists carry first-party coverage to protect themselves against medical expenses and loss of income must be accompanied by some restriction or outright elimination of the right to sue, together with the elimination of subrogation rights by the insurer making payment.

Existing State Laws

By 2000, 25 states and the District of Columbia had enacted laws that modify the automobile reparation system. None of the laws that have been passed thus far is of the pure no-fault variety. All the laws that have been enacted are either modified no-fault laws, under which the right to sue is not totally abolished but is subject to some restriction, or are laws that simply require some form of expanded first-party coverage.

Massachusetts became the first state with a compulsory no-fault automobile law when its legislature enacted the Personal Injury Protection (PIP) plan as an amendment to the state's compulsory automobile insurance law in August 1970.[14] The law, a modified no-fault plan, became effective January 1, 1971. Although it did not go nearly as far as many plans that had been proposed or that have been enacted since, it did contain many elements that were included in early proposals, and set a pattern that other states followed. The first-party coverage of the Massachusetts PIP plan provides coverage up to $2000 for medical expenses, lost wages, and loss of services. Reimbursement is limited to the "net loss" of wages, with a deduction to allow for the tax-free nature of the benefits. Loss of services includes coverage for reasonable expenses to replace services the injured person would have performed without pay (housekeeping, for example). The plan provides immunity from tort action up to the $2000 limit. One feature of the Massachusetts law later copied by other states was the provision for suits for general damages (pain and suffer-

ing) when the accident results in loss of a body member, disfigurement, or death, and when medical expenses exceed a specific dollar amount called a "threshold." The Massachusetts law originally set its threshold at $500; it has since been raised to $2000.

By 2000, a total of 16 states plus Puerto Rico and the District of Columbia had passed compulsory no-fault laws. Three states (Connecticut, Georgia, and Nevada) later repealed their laws and 2 states (Pennsylvania and New Jersey) changed their laws to optional no-fault laws. The Pennsylvania law, which had been in effect since 1975, was repealed in 1984, and then replaced by a "freedom of choice" no-fault law in 1990.[15] In addition to the 11 compulsory no-fault laws that remain, there are 3 optional no-fault laws, under which drivers who elect no-fault coverage are granted a partial tort exemption. In addition, 10 other states have laws that are frequently called "no-fault" but that in reality are expanded first-party coverage systems. In 3 states the first-party coverage is compulsory; in the remaining states it is optional. Table 22.2 lists the no-fault laws and other automobile reparation statutes in effect in mid-2000 on a state-by-state basis.

As can be seen, there is considerable diversity in the laws. In 6 states, the first-party coverage is optional and there is no restriction on tort suits. Three states require the first-party coverage, but still without restrictions or exemptions for tort suits. All these plans provide for subrogation by the insurer paying the first-party benefits.

There are also vast differences among the modified no-fault laws, not only in benefit levels, but also in the tort exemption. Benefits range from $8000 to unlimited medical expenses and wage-loss benefits. Most of the existing laws follow

---

[14]Although Massachusetts enacted the first state law, Puerto Rico had a government-administered and tax-supported no-fault system in 1969. The Social Protection Plan of Puerto Rico provides unlimited medical expenses and modest loss of income benefits. Private insurers do not participate in the plan.

[15]The 1990 Pennsylvania law requires motorists to select between a full-tort alternative, under which they are allowed to seek compensation through the courts for both economic and noneconomic loss, and a limited-tort alternative under which they may sue for noneconomic loss only in the event of serious injury.

the Massachusetts pattern and permit accident victims to sue for general damages when medical costs exceed a certain threshold level. In 5 states the threshold is $2500 or less. Florida and New York do not use a dollar threshold, but permit recovery for pain and suffering when disability exceeds 90 days or when there is "significant permanent injury." These thresholds, above which tort action is permitted for general damages, represent legislative compromises with the no-fault principle. In addition to suits when medical expenses exceed the threshold, all states permit suits for serious injuries such as those resulting in death, disability, dismemberment, or disfigurement. Michigan, which does not provide for suits above a threshold, does permit recovery for pain and suffering in cases of serious impairment of bodily function or permanent disfigurement.

In most states, the no-fault statutes apply only to private passenger automobiles, excluding both trucks and motorcycles. Only one state applies the no-fault principle to property damage. In Michigan, vehicle owners are responsible for damage to their own automobiles, with suits between drivers for recovery of collision damage forbidden. Damage to property other than automobiles in Michigan remains under the tort system.

Cost Experience in No-Fault States

There is an understandable interest in the cost experience of those states with no-fault plans, but it is difficult to compare costs over time because of other changes in the insurance environment. Premium reductions were mandated in many states when the no-fault laws were first passed, but like premiums elsewhere, rates have increased. Opponents of no-fault point to the rate increases and argue that while the plans were sold on the promise that they would cut premiums, the reverse has happened. No-fault advocates argue that costs have increased because the laws that have been enacted are weak and compromise the no-fault principle. Other advocates of no-fault maintain that premium costs are a relatively insignificant

consideration, and that the real issue is which plan—tort or no-fault—provides the greater benefits for the largest number of policyholders.

Prospect of Further No-Fault Legislation

At the state level, only two states have enacted new auto reparation laws in the past two decades. The District of Columbia enacted an optional no-fault law in 1983, and Washington passed an optional first-party coverage law in 1995. As already noted, the states of Connecticut, Georgia, and Nevada have repealed their no-fault laws and New Jersey and Pennsylvania have changed from compulsory to optional no-fault laws. Still, interest in the automobile no-fault idea endures. In 1988 a no-fault initiative appeared on the California ballot as an alternative to Proposition 103. California voters chose Proposition 103. In 1996, California voters again considered and rejected a no-fault initiative.

At the federal level, several no-fault bills were introduced in Congress during the period 1970 to 1978, but by the mid-1990s, the idea of a federal no-fault plan seemed to have been forgotten. Then, in 1997, legislation was introduced in Congress based on the no-fault approach known as *freedom-of-choice no-fault*.[16] The *Auto Choice Reform Act of 1997* (S. 625, HR 2021) would create a "choice" auto insurance system under which states would have the option of adopting or rejecting the system. Consumers in states that adopted the program would be allowed to choose one of two options, which generally parallel the existing tort system and a no-fault system. Under the no-fault *Personal Protection Insurance* (PPI) option, consumers would opt out of coverage for

---

[16]Freedom-of-choice no-fault was proposed by Jeffrey O'Connel, one of the authors of the Keeton-O'Connel *Basic Protection* plan in 1965, and Robert H. Joost in a 1986 article in the *Virginia Law Review.*

Table 22.2 Automobile No-Fault and Automobile Reparation Reform Laws, 2000

State	Effective Date	Type of Law	Maximum Benefits	Tort Exemption	Suits for Pain and Suffering	Dollar Threshold
Arkansas	1974	Optional First-Party	$20,920	No	No limitation	
Colorado	1974	Compulsory First-Party	125,829	Yes	Serious injury[b]	$2500
Delaware	1972	Compulsory First-Party	15,000[a]	No	No limitation	
D.C.	1983	Optional No-Fault	128,000	Choice	Serious injury	
Florida	1972	Compulsory No-Fault	10,000	Yes	Serious injury	
Hawaii	1974	Compulsory No-Fault	15,000	Yes	Serious injury	Variable[c]
Kansas	1974	Compulsory No-Fault	15,180	Yes	Serious injury	$2000
Kentucky	1975	Choice No-Fault	10,000	Yes	Serious injury	$1000
Maryland	1973	Compulsory First-Party	2,500	No	No limitation	
Massachusetts	1971	Compulsory No-Fault	8,000	Yes	Serious injury	$2000
Michigan	1973	Compulsory No-Fault	Unlimited	Yes	Serious injury	
Minnesota	1975	Compulsory No-Fault	40,000	Yes	Serious injury	$4000
New Jersey	1990	Optional No-Fault	260,580	Choice	Serious injury	
New York	1974	Compulsory No-Fault	50,000	Yes	Serious injury[d]	
North Dakota	1976	Compulsory No-Fault	30,000	Yes	Serious injury	$2500
Oregon	1972	Compulsory First-Party	46,425	No	No limitation	
Pennsylvania	1991	Optional No-Fault	177,500[e]	Choice	Serious injury	
South Carolina	1974	Optional First-Party	1,000	No	No limitation	
South Dakota	1972	Optional First-Party	15,120	No	No limitation	
Texas	1973	Optional First-Party	2,500	No	No limitation	
Utah	1974	Compulsory No-Fault	27,800	Yes	Serious injury	$3000
Virginia	1972	Optional First-Party	7,200	No	No limitation	
Washington	1994	Optional First-Party	77,000	No	No limitation	

[a]$30,000 per occurrence.
[b]State laws differ, but serious injury usually includes death, dismemberment, disfigurement, or permanent disability.
[c]Variable annually.
[d]90 days disability during 180 days following injury.
[e]Optional $1,100,000 medical.

pain and suffering. These drivers would recover economic damages from their own insurers up to the limits of their policy and could sue negligent drivers for any amount that exceeds their policy limits, but such suits would be permitted for economic damages only. PIP insureds could not sue or be sued for noneconomic damages unless the injury was intentional or was a result of alcohol or drug abuse. For those consumers who do not want to give up their right to collect for noneconomic damages, the *tort maintenance* option would allow them the right to retain this right by purchasing a new form of coverage called *tort maintenance coverage* (TMC). TMC is a form of *inverse liability coverage* that operates in much the same way as uninsured motorist coverage. TMC drivers would recover both economic damages and noneconomic damages from their own insurance companies up to the limits of their policies, based on who was at fault. TMC drivers not at fault in an accident would be permitted to sue negligent drivers for any damages that exceed the limits of their TMC coverage. Both TMC and PPI drivers would retain their rights to sue (and to be sued) for noneconomic damages if injuries are inflicted intentionally or as a result of drug or alcohol abuse. Also, both PPI drivers and TMC drivers could claim economic and noneconomic damages from an unlawfully uninsured motorist based on fault.

Cost of Automobile Insurance

Some of the dissatisfaction over automobile insurance relates to the manner that insurers use to spread the cost of accidents over the insured population. Many of the traditional rating factors are being challenged, and it seems appropriate that we examine those rating factors.

One of the most distressing aspects of automobile insurance, as far as youthful drivers are concerned, is the difficulty in obtaining adequate coverage and the cost of that coverage when it can be obtained. Because youthful drivers have a greater proportion of accidents, their premium rates are considerably higher than those of adults. Many factors enter into the determination of the premium for a specific individual. Understanding these factors can be helpful in purchasing insurance.

Insurance Services Office Automobile Rating Systems

The rating system used in most states for automobile insurance was adopted by the Insurance Services Office in 1965. Although individual companies use systems that differ in detail from this standard system, the factors considered under the various systems generally follow the pattern of the Insurance Services Office (ISO) system.

Most automobile rating systems begin with three basic factors:

1. Age and sex of the driver
2. Use of the automobile
3. The driver's record

In addition to these factors, the rates vary with the territory in which the automobile is principally garaged, the limits of coverage desired, and, for Physical Damage coverages, the value of the automobile and the deductible selected.

The starting point in the ISO system is a base premium for each coverage, which varies with the territory, the policy limits, and, for Physical Damage coverages, the value of the automobile. This is the premium charged for an automobile with no youthful drivers and which is used for pleasure only. All other drivers and uses are expressed as a percentage of this base premium. Each driver is assigned a rating factor that expresses the percentage of the base premium that individual is to be charged. Thus, a rating factor of 1.55 means that the driver would pay 155 percent of the base premium, and a 3.30 rating factor would require a premium equal to 330 percent of the base. The rating factor for each individual is based on a number of variables, including the driver's age, marital status, and past driving record; the use of the automobile; and the type of automobile.

Driver Classifications

There are ten general driver classifications under the Insurance Services Office rating plan; five for adult operators and five for youthful operators. The lowest-rated classes are drivers in the older age groups—from age 65 to 74 and age 75 and older. Female operators age 30 to 49 are the next lowest-rated class, followed by all other adult drivers. Youthful drivers are divided first by sex and then according to whether they are a principal or occasional driver of the vehicle.[17] Youthful male operators who are married are assigned to a separate category. Married youthful female operators are rated at the all-other-adult category.

Use Classification

In addition to the age of the principal operator, rating factors also vary with use. There are five

---

[17]The question may arise as to which classification applies when there is more than one occasional or incidental operator in the family. The basic rule is that the highest-rated operator class applies. If there is more than one automobile in the family, the highest-rated operator is assigned to the automobile with the highest basic premium, unless the driver is actually the owner or driver of another automobile.

Tidbits, Vignettes, and Conundrums 22.2

The More the Merrier

According to a study published in the March 22, 2000 edition of the *Journal of the American Medical Association (JAMA),* the likelihood of automobile accidents involving teen-age drivers increases in direct proportion to the number of teen-agers in the vehicle. The study, which was based on data for the years 1992 through 1997, found that 16-year-old drivers accompanied by one passenger were 39 percent more likely to get killed than those driving alone. With two passengers, the likelihood of driver fatality increased to 86 percent, and with three or more passengers the mortality rate increased to 182 percent. For 17-year-old drivers the rates were higher: 48 percent, 158 percent, and 207 percent, respectively.

---

use categories for those classes with no youthful operators:

1. *Pleasure Use:* The automobile is not used in business and is not customarily driven to work or school more than 3 miles each way. (Persons who participate in car pools and drive fewer than 15 miles each way are classed for pleasure, provided the car is not used more than two days a week or two weeks in each five-week period.)

2. *Drive to Work Fewer than 15 Miles:* The auto is not used in business but is driven to work or school more than 3 miles and fewer than 15 miles.

3. *Drive to Work More than 15 Miles:* The car is not used in business but is driven to work or school more than 15 miles each way.

4. *Business Use:* The car is customarily used in business.

5. *Farm Use:* The car is principally garaged on a farm or ranch and is not used in any other business and is not driven to school or any other work.

For youthful drivers, there are only two use categories. Pleasure and Farm Use are combined into a single class, as are the Drive-to-Work classes and the Business Use category.

The rating and use classifications and their corresponding rating factors are indicated in Table 22.3.

Youthful Operator Discounts

The automobile rating system contains two features that work to the benefit of some underage drivers. The first of these is the driver-training credit. If the youthful driver has completed an approved driver-training course, the rating factor is reduced by 5 to 35 points, depending upon the basic classification factor.

A second feature of considerable interest to youthful drivers is the good student discount, which applies to full-time students, 16 years of age or older, upon certification that the student, for the preceding semester or comparable period:

1. Ranked in the upper 20 percent of his or her class, or

2. Had a B average or higher, or

3. Had a three-point average or higher, or

4. Was on the dean's list, honor roll, or similar list.

As does the discount for driver training, the good student discount varies with the individual's basic rating factor. The discount results in a re-

Table 22.3   Driver and Use Rating Factors

Adult Driver	Age	Pleasure Use	Less than 15 Miles	15 Miles or More	Business Use	Farm Use
Principal Operator	75 or over	1.00	1.05	1.15	1.20	.85
Principal Operator	65 to 74	.85	.90	1.00	1.05	.70
Principal Operator	50 to 64	.80	.85	.95	1.00	.65
Only Operator Female	30 to 49	1.00	1.05	1.15	1.20	.85
Other Nonyouthful Drivers		1.00	1.05	1.15	1.20	.85

Youthful Drivers Without Discounts	Age	Pleasure or Farm Use	Drive to Work or School or Business Use
UnMarried Female	Under 21	2.10	2.25
Not Owner/Principal Operator	21–24	1.30	1.45
Unmarried Female,	Under 21	2.60	2.75
Owner/Principal Operator	21–24	1.60	1.75
Unmarried Male,	Under 21	2.50	2.65
Not Owner/Principal Operator	21–24	1.35	1.50
Unmarried Male, Owner or	Under 21	3.30	3.45
Principal Operator	21–24	1.75	1.90
Married Male Operator	Under 21	1.55	1.70
	21–24	1.25	1.40

Source: Insurance Services Office, Inc.

duction in the rating factor by 10 to 65 points, depending upon the basic classification factor. This credit is in addition to the driver-training credit. Table 22.4 indicates the rating factors for youthful drivers with and without driver training and the good student discount. These factors are for the Pleasure Use category and would be surcharged by the appropriate factor for Drive-to-Work and Business Use. Also, the rating factors listed in the table apply if the driver has not had any chargeable accidents in the past three years. If there are chargeable accidents and the insurer uses the safe-driver rating plan, additional surcharges will apply.

Safe-Driver Rating Plan

The safe-driver rating plan or a variation of the plan is used by most automobile insurers. The plan is based on the assumption that the past driving record is a valid indicator of the individual's future experience. The experience period is the three years immediately preceding the date of the

application for the insurance or the inception of the renewal policy. Points are assigned for traffic violations and certain accidents. Three points are assigned for a conviction for drunken driving, driving under the influence of drugs, failure to stop and report when involved in an accident, and homicide or assault arising out of the operation of a motor vehicle or for driving with a suspended or revoked license. Two points are assigned for an accumulation of points under a special state system of motor vehicle points or from a series of convictions requiring evidence of financial responsibility under a state financial responsibility law. One point is assigned for any other conviction or any other motor vehicle law violation for which one's operator's license is suspended or revoked, and for which the filing of financial responsibility is required as of the effective date of the policy. One point also is assigned for each accident causing bodily injury or death, or $500 or more in property damage. One point is also assigned if there were two or more accidents during the experience period, each of

Table 22.4   Youthful Driver Discounts

Youthful Driver Class	Age	Without Good Student Discount		With Good Student Discount	
		No Driver Training	With Driver Training	No Driver Training	With Driver Training
Unmarried Male,	Under 21	3.30	3.00	3.00	2.65
owner or principal operator	21–24	1.75	1.75	1.50	1.50
Unmarried Male,	Under 21	2.50	2.25	2.25	2.00
not owner or principal operator	21–24	1.35	1.35	1.15	1.15
Unmarried Female,	Under 21	2.60	2.35	2.35	2.10
owner or principal operator	21–24	1.60	1.60	1.35	1.35
Unmarried Female,	Under 21	2.10	1.90	1.90	1.70
Not owner or principal operator	21–24	1.30	1.30	1.10	1.10
Married Male	Under 21	1.55	1.40	1.40	1.25
	21–24	1.25	1.25	1.05	1.05

Source: Insurance Services Office, Inc., 1998

which resulted in damage to property in an amount of $500 or less. (No points are assigned if the insured's auto was legally parked at the time of the accident, if the damage was caused by a hit-and-run driver, or if the other driver was at fault for the accident.) Finally, one point is assigned to any principal operator who has been licensed less than two years.

If the insured has 1 point under the plan, his or her rating factor is increased by 40 points. For the second point, there is an additional surcharge of 50 points. The third point calls for a further 60-point surcharge, and the fourth point 70 more points. Thus, a driver with 4 points would incur a total surcharge of 220 percentage points.

Number and Type of Automobiles

When a person insures two or more automobiles with the same company, a special multicar discount applies. The rating factor applicable to each automobile is reduced by 0.20 points. In addition, any points developed under the safe-driver plan are applied to both automobiles, with the penalty developed divided in half and charged equally to each car.

The type and value of the automobile insured are obviously factors in the determination of collision and comprehensive premiums, but in some in-

stances they affect all coverages. For 1971 and later-model automobiles, the revised system imposes a 0.15-factor-point surcharge on sports cars and intermediate-performance cars and a 0.30-point surcharge on high-performance automobiles.

The Rating System and Equity

The various factors that are considered in determination of the final premium under the revised rating system can yield wide differences in premiums for different drivers, with some insureds paying considerably more for their insurance than others. For example, rating factors may range from 0.65 (for a driver over age 65, living on a farm, with no points and driving a standard performance automobile with the multicar discount) to 5.50 (for a 17-year-old male operator with his own high-performance car who has accumulated 4 points and is not entitled to the driver's education or good student discounts). Although the system is complex, it results in a more equitable allocation of insurance costs among drivers. Most people agree that the system is fair, since it has been established quite conclusively that the operator who cannot drive a car without accidents or traffic violations, as demonstrated in the past, will be no different in the future.

The Shifting View of Auto Insurance

The increasing cost of automobile insurance and the difficulty that some drivers have in obtaining coverage have raised automobile insurance to the status of a major social problem in this country. At least a part of this problem stems from the seldom-mentioned shift in the way that society views automobile insurance.

Originally, auto liability insurance—like personal liability insurance—was designed to protect the person insured against financial loss arising out of torts. When legislatures acted to make liability insurance compulsory, the motivation was not a paternalistic attempt to make sure that drivers were protected against lawsuits. It was an attempt to provide injured persons with a defendant who is worth suing. Imperceptibly, the function of auto liability insurance changed. While it still provides protection for insureds against liability losses, compulsory auto liability insurance is also viewed as a form of protection for accident victims. With this shift in objectives,

there has been an understandable shift in the attitude of consumers toward auto insurance.

Under the compulsory auto insurance system, some people are forced to purchase a product they don't want and don't need. They purchase insurance not for their own protection, but for the benefit of those they might injure. Economically disadvantaged people in particular have developed an animosity toward automobile insurance. It is a product from which they derive little benefit. After all, a person who doesn't have anything can afford to lose it. In the absence of a legal requirement, people who have little to lose in a lawsuit would "take their chances," going bare and driving without insurance.

Ironically, compulsory auto insurance doesn't really solve the problem. The compulsory levels of protection are inadequate to protect many people who might be injured, especially persons with higher incomes. Despite the compulsory laws, many people must purchase coverage to protect against losses they might suffer that are in excess of the auto limits carried by drivers with minimum limits.

Important Concepts to Remember

automobile liability insurance
Medical Payments coverage
Physical Damage coverage
Uninsured Motorists coverage
family purpose doctrine
permissive use statutes
guest laws
compulsory automobile liability insurance laws

financial responsibility laws
SR-21
SR-22
Automobile Insurance Plan
Assigned Risk Plans
facility
joint underwriting associations
distress risk company
no-fault

modified no-fault
expanded first-party coverage
threshold level
safe-driver rating plan
base premium

Questions for Review

1. What are the three major classes of loss associated with the ownership or operation of an automobile? What types of insurance coverage protect against each? What automobile coverages protect against each?

2. Briefly describe the general provisions of a financial responsibility law. Why are these laws often called "free-bite laws?"

3. Briefly distinguish between an SR-21 and an SR-22 that must be filed with the state depart-

ment of motor vehicles under a financial responsibility law.

4. What is the purpose and general nature of an Automobile Insurance Plan?

5. Outline the various ways in which one may be held vicariously liable in the operation of an automobile.

6. Describe the distinguishing characteristics of the four approaches currently used to provide automobile liability insurance to drivers who are unacceptable to insurers in the normal course of business.

7. Briefly describe the criticisms of the tort system that led to the enactment of automobile no-fault laws.

8. In what way is the automobile no-fault concept similar to workers compensation? In what way is it different?

9. List and briefly explain the differences among the three major approaches that automobile accident reparation reform legislation may take.

10. Briefly explain the factors that are considered in determining the premium for automobile liability insurance. What additional factors are considered in the rating of comprehensive and collision coverages? What factors apply in the case of youthful drivers that are not considered in the case of other drivers?

Questions for Discussion

1. How do you personally feel that we should cope with the problem of bad drivers who have difficulty in obtaining insurance through normal market channels?

2. Some states still have guest hazard statutes. Do you think that these laws are a logical extension of the assumption of risk doctrine, or should they be repealed?

3. What, in your opinion, is the strongest argument in favor of a no-fault system for compensating the victims of automobile accidents? What is the strongest argument against such a system?

4. Many people in the property and liability insurance industry complain about the "auto-

mobile problem." Actually, the "automobile problem" consists of a series of interrelated problems. What factors have combined to produce a problem in the automobile insurance area?

5. The insurance mechanism is based on the principle of loss sharing, with those who do not suffer losses paying to meet the costs of those who do. In view of this principle, would it make more sense to group all ages together for rating purposes, with older drivers subsidizing the cost of the losses incurred by younger drivers? Explain why insurance companies divide drivers into different classifications with preferential rates for some groups.

Suggestions for Additional Reading

Fire, Casualty and Surety Bulletins. Personal Lines Volume. Cincinnati, OH: National Underwriter Company. (Loose-leaf manual service with monthly supplements.) See "Auto" section.

Hamilton, Karen L., and Donald S. Malecki. *Personal Insurance: Property and Liability.* Malvern, PA: American Institute for CPCU, 1994. Chapter 5.

Huebner, S. S., Kenneth Black, Jr., and Bernard L. Webb. *Property and Liability Insurance,* 4th ed. Englewood Cliffs, NJ: Prentice Hall, 1995. Chapter 32.

Launie, J. J., George E. Rejda, and Donald R. Oakes with Anita W. Johnson. *Personal Insurance.* Bryn Mawr, PA: Insurance Institute of America, 1991. Chapter 9.

Mooney, Sean. *Auto Insurance: Critical Choices for the 1990s.* New York: Insurance Information Institute, 1989.

O'Connell, Jeffrey, and Robert H. Joost. "Giving Motorists a Choice Between Fault and No-Fault." *Virginia Law Review,* vol. 72 (1986).

Policy, Form and Manual Analysis Service. Personal Lines Volume. Indianapolis, IN: Rough Notes Company. (Loose-leaf manual service with monthly supplements.) See "Personal Auto" section.

Websites to Explore

Best's Review—Property/Casualty Edition: http://www.ambest.com/review/lh/index.html

Free Advice Web Site: http://freeadvice.com/law/595us.htm

Highway Loss Data Institute: http://www.hwysafety.org

Insurance Information Institute: http://www.iii.org/

Insurance Institute for Highway Safety: http://www.hwysafety.org

Insurance News Network: http://www.insure.com/

National Highway Traffic Safety Administration: http://www.nhtsa.org

National Safety Council: http://www.nsc.org

Quicken InsureMarket: http://www.insuremarket.com/

Rough Notes Company: http://www.roughnotes.com

CHAPTER 23

The Personal Auto Policy

Accidents will occur in the best regulated families.
—Charles Dickens
David Copperfield

CHAPTER OBJECTIVES

When you have finished this chapter, you should be able to

- Determine if an automobile is eligible for coverage under the Personal Auto Policy (PAP)

- Identify and explain the four coverage sections of the PAP

- Describe the coverage features of the PAP Liability coverage, including the persons and automobiles for which coverage is provided

- Describe the scope of coverage under the Medical Payments coverage of the PAP, including the persons to whom the coverage is applicable

- Describe the scope of coverage under the Uninsured Motorist coverage of the PAP, including the persons to whom the coverage is applicable

- Describe the scope of coverage under the Damage to Your Auto coverage of the PAP

- Identify and explain the Duties After Loss and general provisions of the PAP

In this chapter, we continue our study of automobile insurance, turning now to an examination of one of the contracts under which auto insurance is provided, the Insurance Services Office (ISO) Personal Auto Policy (PAP). The PAP is only one of several auto forms currently in use. Some insurers have developed their own contracts, which differ in detail from the ISO form. Still, the PAP is the most widely sold of the various auto policies and serves as a standard against which other policy forms may be compared.

General Nature of the Personal Auto Policy

The Personal Automobile Policy was introduced in 1977. It is written in the simplified terminology that has become common in the insurance field, but at the time of its introduction, it was considered a remarkable departure from the existing contracts. The policy has been revised several times, and the following discussion is based on the 1998 edition of the policy.[1]

The automobile insurance policy is one of the most complicated of all insurance contracts. The complicated nature of the contract results from the need to provide a contract that will provide coverage against different types of losses under diverse circumstances. The ownership or operation of an auto involves three types of loss:

1. Legal liability
2. Injury to the insured or members of the insured's family
3. Damage to or loss of the auto itself

The Personal Auto Policy is a package policy, providing protection for all three of these types of loss. It may be used to provide liability coverage, medical payments coverage, uninsured motorist coverage, and physical damage insurance. It may be endorsed to provide no-fault benefits in those states where such laws exist.

Besides covering different types of loss, the policy must provide protection in various situations. Most people in our society operate autos, and often the operator does not own the vehicle being driven. Jones may borrow Brown's car, and, as we have seen, Brown may be held liable with Jones if the latter is negligent. It is therefore necessary to devise a contract that will protect the owner when someone else is operating his or her auto. In addition, it is desirable that the contract protect the insured when he or she is driving someone else's car. Both requirements add to the complexity of the contract. In addition, the broadness of coverage in a policy designed to meet these various situations makes insurers limit its availability to specific classes. Before turning to an analysis of the policy itself, we will briefly examine the eligibility rules of the PAP.

Eligibility

The PAP is available only to certain classes of eligible persons and to cover specified types of vehicles. First, the auto must be owned by an individual or by a husband and wife who are residents of the same household.[2] For the purposes of eligibility and coverage, a vehicle that is leased under a written agreement for at least six months is treated as if it were owned.

Furthermore, the auto must be of a specific type. The first class of eligible vehicles consists of private passenger automobiles, defined as "a four-wheel motor vehicle, other than a truck type." The vehicle may not be used as a public or livery conveyance, and it may not be rented to others.

A pickup or van may also be eligible for coverage under the PAP if it is owned by an individual

---

[1]The Personal Auto Policy is a direct descendant of the Family Automobile Policy, the standard bureau auto policy that preceded it, and which is still used by a few companies. The Family Automobile Policy, as its name implies, was developed to provide auto insurance for the entire family.

[2]Autos owned jointly by resident relatives who are not husband and wife (e.g., father and son) may also be insured, but the coverage is limited by a special endorsement.

(or by a husband and wife who reside in the same household), depending on its size and use. The pickup or van must have a gross vehicle weight of less than 10,000 pounds and may not be used for the delivery or transportation of goods and materials (except incidental delivery or transport by someone in the business of installing, maintaining, or repairing furnishings or equipment or use for farming or ranching).[3]

Policy Format

The PAP is divided into six parts, designated as follows:

1. Part A, Liability Coverage
2. Part B, Medical Payments Coverage
3. Part C, Uninsured Motorist Coverage
4. Part D, Coverage for Damage to Your Auto
5. Part E, Duties After an Accident or Loss
6. Part F, General Provisions

Parts A through D are the four separate coverages that may be included in the policy. Each part has its own insuring agreement and exclusions. The parts are made effective by an indication in the declarations that the appropriate premium has been paid and that the coverage applies. Parts E and F apply to all sections of the policy. A specimen of the PAP should be referred to in the following discussion.

Liability Coverage

The liability part of the PAP, designated Part A, contains the liability insuring agreement, supple-

mentary payments, liability exclusions, and special conditions applicable to the liability coverage.

Liability Insuring Agreement

The liability insuring agreement obligates the insurer to pay, up to the policy limit, damages for which any "insured" becomes legally responsible because of an accident. Coverage for bodily injury and property damage is provided with split limits, with separate per-person and per-accident bodily injury limits and a separate limit for property damage. The minimum limits available vary with the financial responsibility law of the state. In most states the minimum bodily injury limits are $25,000/50,000, and the minimum property damage limit is generally $10,000 or $20,000. The bodily injury limits may be increased to $50,000/100,000, $100,000/200,000 or $100,000/300,000, $250,000/500,000 or higher. The property damage limit can be increased to $25,000, $50,000, $100,000, and higher. As in the case of most liability contracts, the insurer also agrees to defend the insured, but reserves the right to make any settlement it considers appropriate. The insuring agreement makes it clear that the insurer's obligation to defend ends when the policy limits are exhausted.

Persons Insured Under Liability Coverage

Since the policy agrees to pay sums an "Insured" becomes obligated to pay, the definition of *Insured* is a critical determinant of coverage. The PAP defines an "Insured" as follows:

"Insured" as used in this Part means:

1. You or any "family member" for the ownership, maintenance or use of any auto or trailer.
2. Any person using "your covered auto."
3. For "your covered auto," any person or organization but only with respect to legal responsibility for acts or omis-

---

[3]The PAP may also be used with a special endorsement to provide coverage on motorcycles, motor homes, golf carts and similar-type vehicles, and snowmobiles. The changes in the policy provisions when the PAP is used to insure motorcycles and other miscellaneous vehicles are so pronounced that it is almost a different contract than the standard PAP.

sions of a person for whom coverage is afforded under this Part.

4. For any auto or "trailer," other than "your covered auto," any person or organization but only with respect to legal responsibility for acts or omissions of you or any family member for whom coverage is afforded under this part. This provision (B.4.) applies only if the person or organization does not own or hire the auto or "trailer."

Although the provision is written in simplified terminology it considers a variety of situations and is therefore necessarily complex.

Initially, coverage is provided for "you" or any family member for the use of any auto or trailer. Reference to the policy definitions reveals that "you" means the named insured listed in the declarations, and his or her spouse if a resident of the same household. "You" also includes a spouse who ceases to be a resident of the household. Coverage is provided for 90 days after a spouse leaves the household, or until he or she obtains a separate policy, or the policy period ends, whichever comes first. The definitions section also indicates that the term "family member" means a person related to the named insured by blood, marriage, or adoption, including a ward or foster child, who is a resident of the named insured's household.

For the named insured and resident relatives, coverage applies to *any* auto, which means both the auto designated as the covered auto[4] and borrowed or rented autos. There is no restriction on the type of auto that may be borrowed or rented and it could include, for example, a bus or truck. Although the definition of *Insured* states that coverage applies to the named insured and resident relatives for *any* auto, this broad statement is subject to qualification by other provisions of the policy. Certain types of autos are eliminated from coverage by the exclusions that will be discussed shortly. In addition, while the definition of *Insured* does not refer to a requirement of permission, one of the exclusions (discussed shortly) eliminates coverage for anyone operating a vehicle without a reasonable belief that he or she is entitled to do so.

Persons other than the named insured and family members are covered while using the "covered auto" subject to the requirement that the use be with the reasonable belief that the person has a right to do so.

Parts 3 and 4 of the definition of insured extends coverage to persons or organizations held vicariously liable for the acts of an insured. Part 3 of the definition extends coverage to anyone vicariously liable for the operation of the owned auto. This would include, for example, the employer of any person operating a covered auto as an insured. Part 4 of the definition extends coverage to anyone held vicariously liable for the operation of a non-owned auto by the named insured or a family member. Note that for non-owned autos under Part 4 of the definition, there is no coverage for the owner of the non-owned auto, even if he or she is held vicariously liable for the acts of the named insured or the resident relative operating the vehicle.

To illustrate the coverage for vicarious liability with respect to owned and non-owned autos, consider the following example. Smith, an insured under a PAP, uses her car in her occupation. In the event of a loss in which her employer is joined in the suit, Smith's policy will provide coverage for both Smith and her employer. If Smith borrows a friend's car to use in her occupation, Part 4 of the definition provides coverage for the vicarious liability of Smith's employer. However, Smith's policy will not extend coverage to the friend if he is sued as the owner of the car. The owner of a non-owned auto must look to his own policy for protection.

Because the PAP provides coverage for the named insured and family members while operating borrowed autos, and also provides coverage

---

[4]The term *covered auto* is defined in the policy and has a precise meaning. For the present, we may consider the covered auto to be the auto described in the policy.

for other persons while operating the covered auto, situations will exist in which two policies will apply to the same loss. For example, if White borrows Brown's auto, Brown's policy will provide coverage for both Brown and White in the event of a loss. Brown is covered as "you" (the named insured), and White has coverage as a permissive user. In addition, White has coverage under his own policy as a "you" (named insured) while using a borrowed auto with permission. When two or more policies apply in the same loss, the policy on the auto being driven is primary and the policy of the permissive user is excess.

The "Covered Auto"

As is true of the definition of *insured*, the definition of insured autos is an important determinant of coverage. Because of its importance, the definition of *covered auto* is reproduced here in its entirety:

> J. "Your covered auto" means:
> 1. Any vehicle shown in the Declarations.
> 2. A "newly acquired auto."
> 3. Any "trailer" you own.
> 4. Any auto or "trailer" you do not own while used as a temporary substitute for any other vehicle described in this definition which is out of normal use because of its:
>   a. breakdown
>   b. repair
>   c. servicing
>   d. loss; or
>   e. destruction
>
> This provision (J.4.) does not apply to Coverage for Damage to Your Auto

A vehicle listed in the declarations is, of course, a covered auto. Certain newly acquired autos are also covered autos, as explained in greater detail in the paragraphs that follow. A trailer owned by the insured is also covered. There is no requirement that the trailer be listed, as long as it meets

the policy definition of "trailer." Finally, any non-owned auto is covered while used as a temporary substitute for a covered auto while the covered auto is withdrawn from use because of breakdown, repair, servicing, loss, or destruction.

The inclusion of a "newly acquired auto" in the definition of "your covered auto" provides coverage for autos acquired during the policy period, but on a qualified basis. First, the auto must be one that meets the eligibility requirements of the PAP (that is, it must be a private passenger auto or a pickup or van that does not exceed the gross vehicle weight limitation and is not used for delivery or transportation of goods except as allowed by the eligibility requirements).

For liability, medical payments, and uninsured motorist coverages, replacement autos are automatically covered for the remainder of the policy period, without notice to the insurer. For additional vehicles, the insurer must be notified and coverage must be requested within 14 days of the date of acquisition for these coverages. Note that if a loss occurs during the 14-day grace period and before notice is given to the company, coverage applies.

Liability Exclusions

There are 13 exclusions applicable to the liability coverage. Nine of these exclusions (designated *A*) eliminate coverage for certain persons. The other four (*B*) exclude specified vehicles.

Exclusion A.1 eliminates coverage for any insured who intentionally causes bodily injury or property damage. It would be contrary to public policy to provide protection against the financial consequences of injuries or damage caused intentionally.

Exclusion A.2 excludes coverage for damage to property owned or being transported by an insured. Damage to owned property or property being transported should be covered under a property insurance form, such as the Homeowners Policy, or a floater policy.

Exclusion A.3 is the PAP version of the care, custody, and control exclusion found in most liability contracts. It excludes coverage for any insured for damage to property rented to, used by, or in the care of that insured, excluding damage to property in a bailment status even when it is not being transported. However, an exception to the exclusion states that it does not apply to damage to a residence or private garage.

Exclusion A.4 eliminates coverage for injuries to employees in the course of their employment, except domestic employees in those states where workers compensation laws do not apply to domestic employees. This provision eliminates coverage for the driver's employer (who is otherwise covered for vicarious liability) if the liability involves injury to an employee of that employer.

Exclusion A.5 excludes coverage for liability while the auto "is being used as a public or livery conveyance" (i.e., as a taxi or a public delivery vehicle). An exception to the exclusion makes it clear that it does not apply to shared-expense car pools.[5]

Exclusion A.6 eliminates coverage for any person employed in the automobile business. However, the exclusion does not apply to the owned auto while being operated by the named insured or a family member (or by a partner, agent, or employee of the named insured or family member). There is no coverage for persons in the auto business (other than the named insured and family members) while operating the owned auto. If Abner takes his auto to a garage for a tune-up, there is no coverage under Abner's policy for Mike, the mechanic, while test-driving the car. Also, if the named insured or family member operates a non-owned auto while employed in the auto business, there is no coverage. If Mike the mechanic has a PAP, neither will his policy cover him while operating Abner's car. The excluded

exposures may be covered under a special business auto policy called the *garage policy*.

Exclusion A.7 is a "business pursuits" exclusion. It eliminates coverage for business use of commercial vehicles, but does so through a curious combination of exclusions, exceptions, and cross-references. Initially, the exclusion eliminates coverage for *any* insured using an auto in any business except farming or ranching (or in the auto business, which, as noted, is subject to Exclusion A.6). The provision then excepts private passenger autos, pickups and vans, and trailers used with these types of autos from the exclusion. This grants coverage for both owned and non-owned autos of these types used in business. What remains excluded are trucks (other than pickups and vans) while used in business.

Exclusion A.8 eliminates coverage for any person using a vehicle without a reasonable belief that he or she is entitled to do so. To illustrate, assume that Brown Jr. has his parents' car at school. White, another resident of the dorm, takes the car without permission and is involved in a spectacular accident. Many people are injured and the lawsuits promise to be astronomical. White appears to be in serious trouble. Although the policy covering Brown's car protects anyone operating it with "a reasonable belief" that he or she is entitled to do so, there is no basis for such belief and therefore no coverage. If White's parents have a PAP, the same exclusion will eliminate coverage under that policy.[6] The exclusion does not apply (and coverage is therefore provided) to a family member while using a covered auto owned by the insured.

The last exclusion in group A—Exclusion A.9—eliminates coverage for any insured who is

---

[5]A *livery conveyance* is a vehicle used indiscriminately in conveying the public, without limitation to certain persons or particular occasions or without being governed by special terms. A *public conveyance* holds itself out as a common carrier.

[6]Some students may say, "That may all be true, but the only thing necessary is for Brown to say that he had given permission; if he is willing to do this, both policies will apply." As you will recall from the discussion of vicarious liability as it relates to the auto, the owner of an auto may be held liable for its operation by anyone who is operating it with the owner's permission. Since by admitting that White had his permission Brown would leave himself open for a substantial amount of liability, he may be reluctant to do so.

also insured under a nuclear energy liability policy or who would be an insured under such a policy except for the exhaustion of its limits.

Exclusion B.1 eliminates coverage for liability arising out of motorcycles, other self-propelled vehicles with fewer than four wheels, and vehicles designed mainly for use off public roads (such as an all-terrain vehicle). The exclusion is subject to three exceptions. First, it does not apply if the vehicle is being used by an insured in a medical emergency. Second, it does not apply to trailers. Finally, the exclusion does not apply to any non-owned golf cart (i.e., a rented or borrowed golf cart).

Exclusion B.2 eliminates coverage on vehicles that are owned by or furnished for the regular use of the named insured, other than the Covered Auto. Automobiles owned by the insured at the inception of the policy and not declared are, of course, excluded. Less obvious to some insureds is the exclusion of autos furnished for regular use. A person who is furnished a company car by his or her employer must look to the employer's policy for coverage. Normally, the employer will have coverage to protect the employee. However, an individual who wants to arrange coverage on an auto that is furnished for his or her regular use may do so under the *Extended Liability Endorsement* to the PAP, which provides coverage for autos furnished for regular use.

Exclusion B.3 is related to Exclusion B.2 but differs in one important respect. This exclusion eliminates coverage for liability arising out of autos owned by or furnished for the regular use of family members. An exception to the exclusion states that it does not apply to the named insured or spouse. The intent is to exclude resident relatives for autos they own or that are furnished for their regular use. However, if the named insured or spouse should use an auto that is owned by or furnished for the regular use of a family member, coverage applies for the named insured or spouse. In the absence of this important exception to the exclusion, the coverage of the policy would never apply to an auto owned by another family member. This would be a serious gap in

coverage for the parent with high limits of coverage who occasionally operated a son's or daughter's auto with low limits.

Exclusion B.4 excludes coverage for any vehicle located inside a facility designed for racing for the purpose of competing in or practicing or preparing for any prearranged or organized racing or speed contest. (Although the insured's souped-up stock car is covered while being used on streets and highways, it is not covered while being raced at the fair grounds.)

Other Liability Coverage Provisions

In addition to the liability insuring agreement and exclusions, Part A contains the following additional provisions applicable to the liability coverage.

Supplementary Payments

In addition to the promise to pay sums that the insured is legally obligated to pay and the cost of defending suits, the insurer promises to pay certain other costs under the Supplementary Payments section:

1. First, the policy promises to pay the cost of bail bonds required of the insured because of an accident, provided the accident results in bodily injury or property damage covered under the policy. The limit of payment for such bonds is $250.

2. Premiums on appeal bonds and bonds to release attachments in suits covered under the policy are covered in full.

3. Interest on a judgment after the judgment has been entered is covered.

4. Loss of earnings up to $200 a day while attending hearings or trials at the company's request is covered.

5. Other reasonable expenses incurred at the request of the insurer are covered.

Amounts payable under the supplementary payments provision are payable in addition to the liability limit.

Out of State Coverage

The Out of State coverage provision makes two important qualifications in the liability insuring agreement when the insured is involved in an accident in another state. First, if the state in which the accident occurs requires higher limits under its financial responsibility law than those of the policy, the policy automatically adjusts to provide the higher required limits. In addition, if the state has a compulsory insurance law (such as a no-fault law) that applies to nonresidents, the policy changes automatically to include the minimum amounts of coverage required.

Limits of Liability

The Limit of Liability provision states that the policy limit (per person and per accident for bodily injury and per accident for property damage) is the most the insurer will pay, regardless of the number of insureds, claims made, vehicles insured under the policy, or vehicles involved in an accident. This provision also states that duplicate payments will not be made for the same elements of loss under liability coverage and under medical payments coverage, uninsured motorist coverage, or underinsured motorist coverage provided by the policy.

Medical Payments Coverage

Medical Payments coverage is a special form of accident insurance that covers medical expenses incurred by insured persons in automobile accidents. The basic limit of liability for medical payments coverage is $1000 per person, with no maximum per accident. For a small additional premium (a few dollars a year), this limit can be increased to $5000 or $10,000 per person, again with no aggregate per accident.

Medical Payments Insurance Agreement

The Medical Payments coverage insuring agreement is simple and straightforward:

We will pay reasonable expenses incurred for necessary medical and funeral services because of "bodily injury":

1. Caused by accident.
2. Sustained by an "insured."

We will pay only those expenses incurred within 3 years from the date of the accident.

The definition of *bodily injury* means "bodily harm, sickness or disease, including death that results." In the case of fatalities, funeral expenses are paid, again up to the limit for the coverage.

As in the liability insuring agreement, the definition of *Insured* is an important determinant of coverage. Coverage applies to two classes of persons.

First, coverage applies to the named insured and to any family member who suffers bodily injury caused by accident while occupying a covered auto. The term *occupying* is defined to include "in, upon, getting in, on, out, or off." This broad definition of occupying means that the occasional injuries caused by slamming car doors on hands and fingers are covered under the Medical Payments coverage.

Coverage also applies to the named insured and family members if, while a pedestrian, they are struck by any motor vehicle designed for use on public roads or by a trailer of any type. Under this "struck by" facet of the coverage, the injured party might be injured while a pedestrian. Although the insuring agreement makes specific reference to "pedestrian," an Insurance Services Office clarification states that there was no intent, by use of the term "pedestrian," to limit coverage to insureds when struck by a vehicle while walking. In other words, for example, an insured struck by a motor vehicle while riding a bicycle is entitled to Medical Payments coverage under the "pedestrian" provision.

Persons other than the named insured and family members are also covered for medical payments, but only while occupying the insured's covered auto. Persons injured while occupying a non-owned auto may have coverage for medical payments under the coverage on the non-owned auto or under their own policies.

Medical Payments Exclusions

Like the Liability coverage, the Medical Payments coverage is subject to its own set of exclusions. Several of the exclusions are almost identical with those of the liability section, and it is therefore unnecessary to repeat their discussion here. The exclusions under the liability section that also apply to the Medical Payments coverage are those that relate to

- Vehicles with fewer than four wheels (1)
- Autos used as a public or livery conveyance (2)
- Autos (other than a covered auto) owned by or furnished for the regular use of the named insured (5)
- Autos (other than a covered auto) owned by or furnished for the regular use of family members (6)
- Autos operated without a reasonable belief that the user is entitled to do so (7)
- Trucks being used in business (8)

Exclusion 3 denies coverage for injuries sustained while occupying a vehicle that is located for use as a residence or premises. Because the definition of *covered auto* includes a trailer owned

by the insured, this exclusion is required to prevent the policy from becoming a general accident policy when the insured owns or occupies a house trailer.

Exclusion 4 applies to individuals injured in the course of their employment and eliminates coverage if benefits are either available or required under a workers compensation law.

Exclusion 7, which involves vehicles used without permission, contains the same exception as the similarly worded liability exclusion, stating that it does not apply to a family member while using a covered auto belonging to the insured.

The next two exclusions under the medical payments coverage—Exclusions 9 and 10—eliminate coverage for injuries caused by the discharge of nuclear weapons, war, civil war, insurrection, rebellion, or revolution, and injuries caused by nuclear reaction, radiation, or radioactive contamination.

Exclusion 11 excludes injuries sustained while occupying a vehicle located at a facility designed for racing for the purpose of competing in or practicing or preparing for an organized racing or speed contest.

Limitations Applicable to Medical Payment Recoveries

The Medical Payments section of the PAP is subject to several provisions that limit the insured's recovery. First, the Limit of Liability provision states that duplicate payments will not be made for the same loss under Medical Payments coverage and the uninsured or underinsured motorist coverage (discussed shortly).

Recovery under medical payments is further limited by the Other Insurance clause. This clause provides that Medical Payments coverage of the policy is excess with respect to any non-owned auto, and that when other auto medical payments coverage exists, payment is made on a pro rata basis, based on the medical payment limits.

Finally, the Medical Payments coverage is subject to a subrogation clause that requires the insured to assign to the insurer any right of recovery against a third party to the extent that he or she receives payment from the insurer.

Uninsured Motorist Coverage

In spite of the financial responsibility laws and the dictates of common sense, some people still drive without auto liability insurance. Uninsured Motorist coverage, designated Part C in the PAP, is designed to protect the insured and his or her family for injuries sustained as a result of being struck by an uninsured or hit-and-run driver or a driver whose insurance company has become insolvent.[7]

Uninsured Motorist Insuring Agreement

Uninsured Motorist coverage promises to pay the amount that an injured insured could have collected from the insurer of an uninsured driver if such driver had carried auto liability insurance. The coverage is written with split limits of liability (per person and per accident). The standard limit for the coverage is the minimum limit required under the state's financial responsibility

---

[7]In most states, Uninsured Motorist coverage applies to bodily injury only, but in California, Delaware, Georgia, Indiana, New Jersey, New Mexico, North Carolina, Rhode Island, South Carolina, Tennessee, Texas, Virginia, Washington, West Virginia, and the District of Columbia, it also includes property damage. In these states, the property damage part of the coverage is subject to a deductible ranging from $100 to $300. In other states property damage caused by uninsured motorists is covered by the Collision coverage of the Damage-to-Your-Auto part.

law, but higher limits are available. Increased limits may be purchased up to the limit carried under the liability section (Part A) of the policy.

Coverage applies when an insured is injured by an "uninsured motor vehicle." *Uninsured motor vehicle* is defined to include (1) a motor vehicle that is not covered for bodily injury liability insurance or for which the bodily injury limits are less than the limits required by the state law, (2) a hit-and-run vehicle, and (3) a vehicle that was insured at the time of the accident, but the insurer becomes insolvent. Vehicles owned by or furnished for the regular use of the named insured or family members and vehicles owned or operated by qualified self-insurers or government bodies do not qualify as uninsured motor vehicles. Also, farm-type tractors or equipment designed for use off public roads while not on public roads and vehicles operated on rails or crawler treads are also excluded.

Persons Insured

Three classes of persons are insured under the Uninsured Motorist coverage: (1) the named insured and any family member, (2) any other person occupying the insured's covered auto, and (3) any person for damages that person is entitled to recover because of injury to a person described in (1) or (2). The named insured and family members are covered even when they are not occupying an auto and could recover if injured by an uninsured motorist as a pedestrian or, say, on a bicycle. Other persons are covered only if injured while occupying the insured's covered auto.

Uninsured Motorist Exclusions

Seven exclusions apply to the Uninsured Motorist coverage. Two of these are grouped as Exclusion A, three are grouped as Exclusion B, and the remaining two are designated Exclusions C and D.

Exclusion A.1 excludes injuries sustained while occupying an owned vehicle that is not insured for Uninsured Motorist coverage under the policy. Exclusion A.2 excludes bodily injury sustained by any family member while occupying or if struck by a vehicle owned by the insured and covered on a primary basis under another policy. This provision is designed to eliminate pyramiding of Uninsured Motorist coverage limits.

Exclusion B.1 excludes coverage under Uninsured Motorist coverage if the injured person settles with the negligent party without the insurer's consent. This is to preserve the insurer's right to recovery against the negligent uninsured motorist, which would be impaired by such settlement.

Exclusion B.2 is the standard exclusion of an auto being used as a public or livery conveyance, and B.3 is the exclusion of vehicles used without a reasonable belief that the person is entitled to do so. The exclusion requiring reasonable belief that the person is entitled to use a vehicle, like the same exclusions under liability coverage and medical payments coverage, does not apply to a family member using a covered auto.

Exclusion C stipulates that the coverage shall not apply directly or indirectly to benefit any insurer or self-insurer under any workers compensation, disability benefits, or similar law. Such insurers do not gain right to subrogation through Uninsured Motorist coverage when an injury is sustained in the course of employment and the insurer pays workers compensation benefits to the injured insured.

Exclusion D excludes coverage for punitive or exemplary damages under the Uninsured Motorist coverage. It was added to the policy in response to court decisions in some states that ruled that punitive damages were covered because they were not specifically excluded.

Limitations on Payment

Amounts otherwise payable under uninsured motorist coverage are reduced by amounts paid by or on behalf of the uninsured motorist. Payment under Uninsured Motorist coverage is also reduced

by amounts payable under a workers compensation law, disability benefits law, or any similar law. Finally, payments under Uninsured Motorist coverage are reduced by amounts the individual is entitled to receive under the Liability section of the policy.

The Other Insurance provision of the Uninsured Motorist coverage makes coverage excess over the coverage on any non-owned automobile. In addition, recovery under all policies is limited to the highest applicable limit for any one vehicle under any insurance providing either primary or excess coverage.

Basis for Settlement

The policy states that the question of whether the injured person is entitled to collect from the uninsured motorist, and if so, the amount to which he or she is entitled, is to be decided by agreement between the covered person and the insurer. If the parties are unable to agree on either point, either party may request arbitration of the matter. If both parties agree to the arbitration, each party selects an arbitrator, and the two arbitrators select a third. The three arbitrators then decide on the amount of damages. If the arbitrators cannot agree on a third arbitrator within 30 days, the court of jurisdiction appoints one. Each party pays the cost of his or her arbitrator, and they share the cost of the umpire.

Underinsured Motorist Coverage

Those insureds who purchase Uninsured Motorist coverage are eligible for an additional coverage, Underinsured Motorist coverage. Underinsured Motorist coverage, which is added to the PAP by endorsement, covers bodily injuries sustained by an insured when the negligent driver has insurance, but the limits are less than the limits of the Underinsured Motorist coverage. As is true in Uninsured Motorist coverage, the injured party's insurer agrees to pay the amount that the insurer of the other driver would have paid, if he or she had been adequately insured.

It should be understood that the Underinsured Motorist coverage does not in any sense duplicate or overlap with Uninsured Motorist coverage. Uninsured Motorist coverage applies only when the other driver does not carry insurance, is a hit-and-run driver, or is insured by an insurer that becomes insolvent. In the case of Underinsured Motorist coverage, the other driver has insurance, but the limits of coverage are less than the amount to which the injured party would be entitled based on his or her injuries. As in the case of Uninsured Motorist coverage, determination of the amount to which the injured party is entitled is decided by agreement between the insurer and the injured party or by arbitration.[8]

The Underinsured Motorist coverage must be written for the same limit as the Uninsured Motorist coverage and is available only when the insured has purchased increased limits for Uninsured Motorist coverage.

Physical Damage Coverage

The physical damage coverage of the PAP, Part D, is designated Coverage for Damage to Your Auto. Like the liability, medical payments, and uninsured motorist parts, the physical damage coverage includes its own insuring agreement, exclusions, and special conditions.

Physical Damage Insuring Agreement

There is a single physical damage insuring agreement, which provides coverage on an open-perils basis. However, the insuring agreement provides that loss by collision is covered only if the declarations section so indicates:

[8]In some states, Uninsured Motorist coverage and Underinsured Motorist coverage are merged into a single coverage.

We will pay for direct and accidental loss to "your covered auto" or any "non-owned auto," including their equipment, minus any applicable deductible shown in the Declarations. If loss to more than one "your covered auto" or "non-owned auto" results from the same collision, only the highest applicable deductible will apply. We will pay for loss to "your covered auto" caused by:

1. Other than "collision" only if the Declarations indicate that Other Than Collision Coverage is provided for that auto.
2. "Collision" only if the Declarations indicate that "Collision" coverage is provided for that auto.

If there is a loss to a "non-owned auto," we will provide the broadest coverage applicable to any "your covered auto" shown in the Declarations.

Earlier forms of auto physical damage coverage, such as the Family Auto Policy, divided physical damage coverage into two separate insuring agreements: comprehensive and collision. Although the PAP refers to loss by collision, the term *comprehensive* is not used. The open-perils coverage excluding collision will undoubtedly continue to be referred to as *comprehensive* as well as by its newer designation, *other than collision*.

Loss Other Than by Collision

The coverage for loss *other than by collision* is essentially an open-perils type of property coverage. Coverage applies to all losses except those that are specifically excluded. The policy specifically designates several perils as "not considered collision":

breakage of glass, loss caused by missiles, falling objects, fire, theft or larceny, explosion, earthquake, windstorm, hail, water, flood, malicious mischief or vandalism, riot or civil commotion, or contact with a bird or animal.

Because these losses are not considered collision losses, they are covered as *comprehensive* losses. Because the collision deductible is normally higher than for other losses, this is beneficial to the insured.

The policy also provides that the insured may, at his or her option, consider breakage of glass to be loss due to collision. This will be advantageous in two situations. First, if the insured carries collision, but does not carry comprehensive insurance, coverage would exist for glass broken in a collision. In addition, if glass is broken in a collision, the insured benefits by having the glass breakage subject to a single deductible with other damage to the vehicle, rather than subject to a separate comprehensive deductible.

Collision Coverage

Collision is defined as "the upset of your covered auto or its impact with another vehicle or object." Coverage for loss by collision applies to the covered auto regardless of fault and will respond when the insured cannot recover from another party because his or her personal negligence was the cause of the damage. But collision coverage can also be valuable in those cases where the insured is not at fault.

In those cases where the driver of the other auto is to blame, we would expect his or her Liability coverage to respond for damages to the owned auto. However, the other party may not have insurance. The innocent driver with Collision coverage can collect the amount of the loss (less any deductible) and then leave the job of collecting from the negligent driver to the insurance company. The PAP includes a subrogation provision under which the insured is required to assign to the insurer the right of claim against a negligent third party to the extent that he or she collects under the policy.

Newly Acquired Vehicles

For physical damage coverages, newly acquired autos—replacement vehicles and additional vehicles—are automatically covered for 14 days, for whatever physical damage coverage (Collision Coverage and/or Other Than Collision Coverage) is already provided by the policy for at least one insured auto. During this 14-day period, the newly acquired auto has the broadest physical damage coverage that is provided by the policy. If the policy covers two automobiles, one with physical damage coverage and one without, any newly acquired vehicle is automatically covered for physical damage for 14 days.[9] The same feature will apply when one vehicle has Collision coverage and the other does not or when two vehicles are insured with different deductibles. If the policy does not include physical damage coverage on any of the covered autos, newly acquired autos are automatically covered for 4 days. This automatic coverage is subject to a $500 deductible. If the insured does not request coverage within the grace period provided, coverage for a newly acquired auto begins at the time coverage is requested.

Physical Damage to Non-Owned Autos

We have already noted that the physical damage coverage of the PAP applies not only to the insured's covered auto, but to a non-owned auto as well. This means that when the individual has purchased physical damage coverage on his or her own auto, such coverage is extended to non-owned autos being used by or in the custody of the insured or a family member. If there is a loss to a non-owned auto, the insurer will provide the broadest coverage that is applicable to any covered auto shown in the declarations. If, for example, a policy insures one owned auto for collision

[9]It should be noted that the coverage on newly acquired pickups and vans applies only if the vehicle meets the eligibility requirements for the PAP.

and comprehensive and another owned auto for comprehensive only, a non-owned auto will be covered for both comprehensive and collision if a loss occurs.

The definition of "non-owned auto" under the physical damage section is an important determinant of coverage. A *non-owned auto* is defined as follows:

"Non-owned auto" means

1. Any private passenger auto, pickup, van or "trailer" not owned by or furnished or available for the regular use of you or any "family member" while in the custody of or being operated by you or any "family member"; or
2. Any auto or "trailer" you do not own while used as a temporary substitute for "your covered auto" which is out of normal use because of its

   a. breakdown   d. loss; or
   b. repair   e. destruction
   c. servicing

Note that the term *non-owned auto* includes two parts. The first refers to a private passenger auto, pickup, van, or trailer not owned by, or furnished, or available for the regular use of the named insured or any family member, while in the custody of or being operated by the named insured or any family member. The second part includes any non-owned auto or trailer used as a temporary substitute for a covered auto that is out of normal use because of its breakdown, repair, servicing, loss, or destruction.

There is a subtle distinction in the provisions of part 1 and part 2 of the definition of a non-owned auto. Under part 1 (when the non-owned auto is not used as a temporary substitute), it may not be owned by or furnished for the regular use of the named insured or a resident relative. Under part 2, which applies when the non-owned auto is being used as a temporary substitute, any auto not owned by the named insured qualifies.

Thus, under part 2, a non-owned auto could include one furnished for the regular use of the named insured or a vehicle owned by or furnished for the regular use of a resident relative.

The physical damage coverage on non-owned autos is excess over other coverage applicable to the non-owned auto. If Brian borrows Joan's car and demolishes it, Joan's policy will apply if she carries collision coverage. If Joan does not carry collision on her car, Brian's collision coverage will apply. The same is true with respect to a borrowed or rented trailer, since the definition of non-owned auto includes "trailer." The Limit of Liability provision sets a $500 limit on payment for damage to non-owned trailers.

One situation in which coverage for damage to non-owned autos can be important is the rental of an automobile. National car rental companies (such as Hertz and Avis) provide the renter with auto insurance covering liability, medical payments, and uninsured motorist coverage (plus no-fault benefits in those states with such laws), but do not provide the renter with physical damage coverage. Collision damage waiver (CDW) is offered at a cost of $10 or more per day. For those persons who carry comprehensive and collision on their own cars, the extension of physical damage coverage to non-owned autos under the PAP provides coverage on rented cars, subject to the policy deductible.[10]

Physical Damage Exclusions

In view of the fact that the physical damage coverage is on an "open-perils" basis, the number of exclusions in this section of the policy is surprisingly

---

[10]The National Association of Insurance Commissioners has developed a *Collision Damage Waivers Act*, which provides for the regulation of rental companies when issuing CDWs. The act provides definitions and establishes standards to which rental companies must adhere and makes certain practices unfair or deceptive practices under the statutory provisions on fraud.

small. There are 14 exclusions: 5 of these (Exclusions 1, 2, 3, 7, and 13) exclude loss to both owned and non-owned vehicles and their equipment under specified circumstances, 3 apply only to non-owned autos (Exclusions 9, 12, and 14), and 6 eliminate certain types of property from coverage (Exclusions 4, 5, 6, 8, 10, and 11). We will begin our examination of the exclusions with the 5 exclusions that deal with specific loss situations.

Exclusion 1 is the now-familiar exclusion of loss while the auto is being used as a public or livery conveyance.

Exclusion 2 eliminates coverage for damage due and confined to wear and tear, freezing, mechanical or electrical breakdown or failure, and road damage to tires. Losses of this nature are inevitable or at least controllable by the insured. However, the exclusion does not apply if the damage results from total theft of the insured auto.

Exclusion 3 eliminates coverage for damage caused by radioactive contamination or by the discharge of a nuclear weapon and war in all its forms.

Exclusion 7 excludes the total loss of an auto by destruction or confiscation by government or civil authorities. The exclusion was added in response to the increasingly frequent confiscation of vehicles by law enforcement agencies and decisions holding that such confiscation was a covered loss under the policy, because it was not excluded. The exclusion does not apply to the interests of a loss payee under the policy.

Exclusion 13 excludes any owned or non-owned auto while located inside a facility designed for racing, for the purpose of competing in or practicing for a prearranged or organized racing or speed contest.

Three exclusions (9, 12, and 14) apply to non-owned autos. Exclusion 9 excludes coverage for damage to a non-owned vehicle being used without a reasonable belief that the user is entitled to do so. It is similar in wording and intent to the permissive use exclusion discussed in connection with the liability coverage.

Exclusion 12 eliminates coverage for damage to non-owned autos being used by any insured

while employed in the automobile business. Coverage for this exposure is provided under the garage coverage form.

Exclusion 14 excludes coverage for loss to a rental vehicle, if the rental company is precluded from recovering for the loss because of the provisions in the rental agreement or in the applicable state law.

Exclusions 4, 5, 6, 8, 10, and 11 exclude damage to or loss of specific types of equipment.[11] Exclusion 4 excludes sound systems such as radios and stereos, tape decks, and compact disc players that are not either permanently installed in the vehicle or designed for operations solely by the auto's electrical system and removable from a permanent housing unit in the vehicle. Such equipment is covered if it is actually in or on the covered auto when the loss occurs.[12]

Exclusion 5 excludes coverage for electronic equipment capable of sending or receiving data signals, such as CB radios, telephones, video and audio cassette recorders, and computers. Accessories for such equipment are also excluded. The exclusion does not apply to equipment that is part of an auto's operating system or to telephones which are permanently installed and powered by the covered auto's electrical system.

Exclusion 6 eliminates coverage on tapes, records, disks or other media designed for use with the equipment excluded by Exclusions 4 and 5.

Exclusion 8 deletes coverage on camper bodies, trailers, or motor homes not listed in the declarations and facilities or equipment used with such vehicles. The exclusion does not apply to non-owned trailers or camper bodies (including facilities and equipment). (Under the Limit of Li-

---

[11]Coverage for loss to equipment described in Exclusions 4, 5, 6, 8, and 11 can be purchased on a stated-amount basis by endorsement for an additional premium.

[12]In addition to the exclusions related to sound equipment, under the physical damage limit of liability, there is a $1000 sublimit for sound-reproducing equipment and accessories that are permanently installed in a covered auto in a location not used by the auto manufacturer for such equipment. Such equipment might include, for example, a CD player or a set of humongous speakers installed in the trunk.

ability provision of the physical damage section, there is a $500 limit for loss to non-owned trailers, but there is no dollar limit on camper bodies.) In addition, the exclusion does not apply to newly acquired trailers or camper bodies. The insurer must be notified of the acquisition within 14 days.

Exclusion 10 excludes loss to equipment designed or used for the detection or location of radar (i.e., "fuzz-busters") or laser devices.

Exclusion 11 eliminates coverage on custom furnishings or equipment in or on any pickup or van. The exclusion cites carpeting and insulation, furniture or bars, facilities for cooking and sleeping, height-extending roofs, or custom murals, paints, or other decals or graphics. An exception to the exclusion extends coverage to caps, covers, and bedliners, which are covered while in or upon a pickup.

Other Physical Damage Provisions

In addition to the insuring agreement and exclusions, the physical damage section includes a number of other important provisions:

Limit of Liability—Payment of Loss

Loss payment under the physical damage coverage is limited to the lesser of (1) the actual cash value of the stolen or damaged property or (2) the amount required to repair or replace the property with other property of like kind and quality. An adjustment will be made for depreciation and physical condition in determining the actual cash value in the event of a total loss. If the repair or replacement results in betterment to the insured, the insurer will not pay for the betterment.

The Payment of Loss provision gives the insurer the option of repairing the damage, replacing the auto, or paying for the loss in cash. In the event of theft, the insurer has the right to return the stolen auto. If the stolen auto has been damaged, the company must, of course, pay for the repair of the damage.

Transportation Expense

Coverage is provided for temporary transportation expenses (the cost of renting a car or using public transportation) incurred by the insured in the event of loss to the covered auto or a non-owned auto. Coverage applies for loss by collision only if collision coverage has been purchased, and for loss other than collision if comprehensive coverage has been purchased. The limit for this coverage is $20 per day with a maximum of $600.[13] The coverage applies to expenses

[13]The limit of coverage may be increased by endorsement for an additional premium.

Tidbits, Vignettes, and Conundrums 23.1

Diminished Value

In some states, when a vehicle is involved in a collision requiring repairs in excess of a stated amount, say $3000, a notation of the damage and repair is made on the auto title. This can affect the trade-in or sale value at a later time. This loss (or potential loss) in the value of the vehicle is referred to as *diminished value,* a concept that has sparked considerable debate between consumers and insurers. In 1999, ISO filed a new endorsement in excluding diminished value in 47 states. The filing was approved in 29 states. Insurers are free to use or not use the diminished value endorsement and it remains to be seen to what extent it will find acceptance.

incurred by the insured for loss to an insured owned auto. For a non-owned auto, Transportation Expenses coverage applies for the loss of use expense for which the insured is legally liable. Except for losses caused by theft, coverage applies to expenses beginning 24 hours after the auto has been withdrawn from use. Coverage for transportation expenses resulting from theft begins 48 hours after the theft, and ends when the auto is returned to use or the insurer pays for the loss.

Towing and Labor Costs Coverage

Towing and Labor Costs coverage can be added to the PAP by endorsement. Limit of Liability options of $25, $50, and $75 are available. When purchased, Towing and Labor Costs coverage applies to both "your covered auto" and a "non-owned auto."

Policy Conditions

The two final parts of the contract, designated Part E and Part F, contain the general policy provisions, some of which have already been noted in passing.

Part E—Duties after an Accident or Loss

Part E of the PAP lists the duties of the insured and other persons seeking coverage under the policy in the event of loss. An introductory statement requires that the insurer be notified promptly of how, when, and where the accident or loss happened. In addition, a person seeking coverage under any of the provisions of the policy must cooperate with the insurer in the investigation, settlement, or defense of any claim. If required by the insurer, a person seeking coverage under the policy must agree to submit to examination under oath. Finally, the insured must submit a proof of loss when required.

A person seeking coverage under the uninsured motorist coverage must also promptly notify the police if a hit-and-run driver is involved.

With respect to the Physical Damage coverages (Damage to Your Auto), the insured must take

---

Tidbits, Vignettes, and Conundrums 23.2

After-Market Auto Parts

In November 1999, a Marion, Illinois, jury awarded a $1.2 billion judgment against State Farm, the nation's largest insurer, for their use of nonoriginal manufacturer equipment (OEM) parts (also sometimes called *after-market parts* or *competitive parts*). Competitive parts, or non-OEM parts, are replacement parts built by a manufacturer other than the original automaker. Competitive parts were initially developed to address the problem of skyrocketing costs to replace car parts, which were previously available only from the manufacturer of the auto. It is estimated that policyholders have saved $800 million a year since insurers began using non-OEM parts in the 1970s. Insurers argue that the use of competitive parts is a proven tool to encourage competition that provides consumers better products and lower prices. The Certified Automotive Parts Association (CAPA), a nonprofit organization with membership including collision repairers, distributors, and the insurance industry, was established in 1987 to certify quality after-market parts. For CAPA's view on the State Farm verdict, see http://www.capacertified.org.

reasonable steps after the loss to protect the auto and its equipment from further loss. The insurer will pay any expenses incurred by the insured in providing such protection. The insured must also notify the police if the covered auto is stolen. Finally, the insured must permit the insurer to inspect and appraise the damaged property before it is disposed of or repaired.

Part F—General Provisions

There are nine general provisions in the PAP, some of which are similar or identical in wording to their similarly titled provisions in the Homeowners General Conditions and Section II conditions already discussed: Bankruptcy, Changes, Fraud, Legal Action Against Us, Our Right to Recover Payment, and Transfer of Your Interest in This Policy. Three of the PAP General Conditions require comment.

Policy Period and Territory

The policy applies only to accidents and losses that occur during the policy period (shown in the declarations) and within the policy territory. The policy territory is the United States, its territories or possessions, or Canada. Coverage also applies for accidents or losses while the covered auto is being transported between ports of the United States, its territories or possessions, or Canada. Note that there is no coverage under the policy in Mexico. If the insured drives into Mexico, he or she must obtain coverage from an insurance company licensed to write auto insurance in Mexico.[14]

[14]Failure to purchase Mexican insurance can lead to serious complications in the event of loss. In Mexico, jurisdiction for criminal and civil law rests in a single court. It is customary to impound the vehicle and hold the driver in jail until an investigation is completed and a court hearing is held. If the driver has insurance with a Mexican-licensed insurer, the arresting officer has the authority to waive the incarceration and impounding of the auto.

Termination

The termination provision outlines the conditions under which either the insured or the company may cancel the policy and the rights of both parties with respect to nonrenewal. First, the named insured may cancel the policy at any time, either by returning the policy to the company or by giving written notice of the date of cancellation.

The insurer's right to cancel depends on the period for which the policy has been in force. If the policy has been in force for less than 60 days, the company may cancel by giving 10 days' written notice. However, once the policy has been in force for 60 days, the insurer can cancel only for nonpayment of premium, if the named insured or any resident relative has his or her drivers license suspended or revoked, or if the policy was obtained through material misrepresentation. Cancellation for nonpayment requires 10 days written notice. Cancellation for revocation or suspension of license requires 20 days written notice. Renewal policies or extensions of direct billed policies are considered to have been in force for more than 60 days.

Although the insurer's right to cancel is limited after the policy has been in force for 60 days, the company may refuse to renew a policy, in which case it must give the insured at least 20 days' written notice of its intent not to renew. Nonrenewal may take place only on the anniversary of the original effective date.

If laws in the state where the policy is sold impose greater restrictions on the insurer's right to cancel or to refuse renewal, the state law applies.

Two or More Auto Policies

This special "other insurance" clause provides that when an insured has two or more policies with the same company applicable to the same accident, the maximum payable under all policies will not exceed the highest applicable limit of liability under any one policy. For example, if Jones has two autos insured with the same company and has an accident while using a non-owned auto, the maximum payable under the two policies will be the highest limit under those policies.

Named Non-Owner Policy

A special form of coverage, called Named Non-Ownership coverage, may be written for a person who does not own an auto, but who desires his or her own coverage in the event that a borrowed auto is inadequately insured. Coverage is normally provided under the PAP, with a special endorsement called the Non-Owner Endorsement. Coverage applies for the named insured only; for liability arising out of the use of any auto not owned by the named insured or spouse or by any member of the named insured's household. Coverage does not extend to any other person—even to a resident spouse. The coverage is excess over any other coverage applicable to the borrowed auto, and does not apply to the owner of the auto. However, as in the PAP, other persons or organizations held vicariously liable for the operation of the borrowed auto by the named insured or spouse are covered.

Although the endorsement is designed to provide coverage on non-owned autos, it also provides automatic coverage for 30 days on a private passenger auto or a pickup, panel truck, or van not used in business other than farming, which is acquired by the insured during the policy period.

Buying Auto Insurance

Purchasing auto insurance should follow the principles of risk management and insurance buying we originally encountered in Chapter 5 and the priority ranking for *essential*, *important*, and *optional* insurance coverages. We will begin our discussion with the essential auto coverage, the liability coverage.

Liability Coverage

In purchasing auto insurance, one logically begins with liability coverage. The question is not whether to buy liability coverage, but rather how much to buy. While it is difficult to say how much is enough, it is clear that the minimum limits of coverage required by the financial responsibility laws fall short of adequate protection. Fortunately, the cost of increased limits of liability coverage is far less proportionately than the basic limits. Table 23.1 indicates the increased limit factors for the liability coverage of the PAP. For example, the $20,000/40,000 basic limit can be increased to $100,000/300,000 for an additional 41 percent in premium and the $15,000 property damage limit can be increased to $100,000 for an additional 10 percent. Although there is no scientific way to determine exactly what level of protection is adequate today, it makes good sense to purchase as much as you can reasonably afford (or the amount required as underlying coverage when a personal umbrella is purchased). The relatively small premium required for the higher limits of protection is a small price to pay for the security it provides.

Medical Payments Coverage

Automobile Medical Payments coverage represents something of a dilemma in the application

Table 23.1 Premium Factors for Increased Liability Limits: Personal Auto Policy

Bodily Injury Liability Limit	Rate Factor	Property Damage Liability Limits	Rate Factor
$20,000/40,000	1.00	$15,000	1.00
25,000/50,000	1.07	25,000	1.02
50,000/100,000	1.27	50,000	1.05
100,000/300,000	1.41	100,000	1.10
250,000/500,000	1.53	250,000	1.17
500,000/1,000,000	1.57	500,000	1.19

Source: Insurance Services Office, Inc. 1998.

of risk management principles. It can be argued that it violates the principles of risk management by focusing on the cause of a loss rather than on the effect. Clearly, protection against catastrophic medical expenses is important, but such protection is needed for medical expenses from any source, not just those caused by auto accidents. If an individual has purchased proper health insurance coverage to protect against catastrophic medical expenses, the auto Medical Payments coverage represents a duplication.

There is, however, an argument in favor of the coverage. Automobile Medical Payments coverage protects not only the insured and family members, but guests in the auto as well. Responsible motorists feel a sense of obligation to their passengers, and Medical Payments coverage serves as a mechanism for meeting this obligation. In some jurisdictions a guest statute may prevent a passenger from collecting medical expenses sustained as a result of the driver's negligence. Even where there is no guest statute, medical expense coverage may eliminate the need to make a federal case out of the accident. Adequate Medical Payments coverage may even serve as a loss-prevention device, reducing the possibility of a liability suit when a guest is injured. One of the main reasons for carrying auto medical expense coverage, then, is to provide for the payment of medical expenses incurred by guests or passengers.

Like the cost of increased liability limit, the cost of higher medical payments is relatively low. For example, in a midwestern city in 2000, the cost of medical payments coverage was as follows:

If $1000, medical payment limit costs $11, then $2000 medical payment limit costs $17, and $5000 medical payment limit costs $30.

In view of the fact that the cost of the coverage is low, it is probably a good idea to purchase Medical Payments coverage. But the coverage is not an essential one and certainly should not be purchased at the expense of adequate liability coverage.

Uninsured Motorist Coverage

Uninsured motorist coverage (and underinsured motorist coverage) represents a somewhat different dilemma from the Medical Payments coverage. Because it provides coverage based on the cause of loss rather than the effect, it falls short of the ideal from a risk management perspective. On the other hand, it covers a potentially catastrophic loss and is the only way in which some losses related to auto accidents can be covered. Although complete life insurance, disability coverage, and major medical insurance would cover a part of the loss caused by an uninsured driver, it would not cover disfigurement, physical impairment, or general damages (such as pain and suffering) for which a negligent uninsured driver might be liable. Most informed authorities treat Uninsured Motorist coverage as an essential form of protection and recommend that the highest limits possible be purchased.

Physical Damage Coverage

The decision to purchase or not to purchase auto physical damage insurance is influenced by a variety of factors. If the car is financed, the lender may insist on insurance to protect its financial interest. In this case, the only decision the buyer must make is with respect to the deductibles. In the case of an older car, insurers may be unwilling to provide the coverage. While some car owners have little choice in the matter, there are many owners who must make a decision on the physical damage coverage.

In those cases where the loss of the auto would be a serious loss beyond the individual's margin for contingencies, the risk management concept dictates that coverage should be purchased against as wide a range of perils as possible, which means that both comprehensive and collision would be purchased. Although the advice may seem wearisome at this point, the judicious use of deductibles can generate substantial economies.

Table 23.2 Personal Auto Policy Physical Damage Deductible Credits

Deductible	Comprehensive Percentage of $100 Deductible Premium	Collision Percentage of $200 Deductible Premium
None	118%	—
$50	109%	—
100	100%	105%
200	88%	100%
250	83%	98%
500	66%	89%
1000	49%	74%

Source: Insurance Services Office, Inc. 1998.

Table 23.2 indicates the premium credits available for differing levels of deductibles for both comprehensive and collision coverage. Because the credits are a percentage of the premium, larger deductibles will be most attractive to persons with high-priced autos or high rating classifications. In general, however, you should select as large a deductible as you can afford.

Cost Differences Among Companies

As a final note, it should perhaps be repeated that there are wide variations in price among automobile insurers. Although a comparison of costs should not be the sole criterion in selecting a company, the insurance buyer should at least investigate alternate sources and their costs. Although those companies with the lowest premiums are usually ultraselective, there are also wide differences in prices among insurers with similar underwriting philosophies, differences that result from different efficiencies and differences in expenses.

Important Concepts to Remember

Personal Auto Policy (PAP)
private passenger automobiles
insureds
your covered auto
split limit of liability

supplementary payments
physical damage coverage
comprehensive
collision
transportation expense

non-owned auto
Uninsured Motorist coverage
Underinsured Motorist coverage
named non-ownership coverage

Questions for Review

1. Briefly describe the four basic coverage sections of the Personal Auto Policy and explain the nature of the coverage under each section.

2. Who is included in the definition of *Insured* with respect to the owned automobile under the Personal Auto Policy? Who is included in

the definition of *Insured* with respect to non-owned automobiles?

3. What coverage is provided under the Personal Auto Policy for individuals or organizations held vicariously liable? Under what circumstances is there no coverage for a person who is held vicariously liable?

4. The definition of insured property under the homeowners policy includes property owned or "used by an insured." Briefly describe the coverage under the Personal Auto Policy that parallels this provision.

5. Briefly explain the coverage that is provided by the Out of State coverage provision of the PAP.

6. Ed Jones drives to work every day and carries two fellow employees, who pay him $10 per week for this service. He has been told that this voids his automobile liability insurance and comes to you for advice. What do you tell him?

7. Jones Jr. borrows a friend's pickup truck and is involved in a collision in which both the pickup and another car are demolished. Although Junior does not have an automobile himself, he lives with his parents who have a Personal Auto Policy, written to include liability and "Coverage for Damage to Your Auto." Describe the coverage that may be applicable to this situation, indicating the specific policy provisions that will determine whether coverage applies.

8. Smith is injured by an uninsured driver. He sues the driver and obtains a $100,000 judgment. Will the Uninsured Motorist coverage of his Personal Auto Policy pay this amount? Why or why not? Explain the manner in which amounts payable under the Uninsured Motorist coverage are determined.

9. Why might a person who does not own an automobile want to purchase automobile liability insurance? How can such a person obtain this protection?

10. Describe the coverage that is provided by the Personal Auto Policy on newly acquired autos.

Questions for Discussion

1. The agent delivering a Personal Auto Policy tells a client, "This policy will cover you when you are driving any car, and it will cover anyone when they are driving your car." How accurate is this statement?

2. Cassandra owns a late-model car that is insured under a Personal Auto Policy, with a $300,000 liability limit, $5000 medical payments, $100 deductible comprehensive, $200 deductible collision, and $300,000 Uninsured Motorist coverage. Which of the coverages would apply to each of the following losses? (If there is no coverage, indicate why not.)

a. Cassandra parks the car on a riverbank, but forgets to set the brake or put the car in park. It rolls into the river and the damage amounts to $800.

b. Cassandra is changing a tire when the car slips off the jack and breaks her leg.

c. Thieves break into the car and steal the car radio, a spare tire, and an overnight bag full of clothing.

d. Cassandra borrows a trailer from a neighbor (who has no insurance). While backing the car up to the trailer, Rosie misjudges the clearance and smashes into the trailer. Damage to the car amounts to $300, and the damage to the trailer is $250.

3. Robert and Francesca are not married, but live together. Robert owns an automobile, which they both use, and which is insured under a Personal Auto Policy. Are there any special dangers related to the automobile coverage of which they should be aware?

4. Robert carries full coverage on his automobile under a Personal Auto Policy, including Liability, Medical Payments, Physical Damage, and Uninsured Motorist coverage. He enjoys a financial windfall and decides to purchase a second car. He drives the new car home and parks it in the driveway, then goes into the house to call his insurance agent and report the purchase. Cassandra, who is driving Robert's old car, wheels into the driveway and is unable to stop, colliding with the new car and causing extensive damage to both vehicles. Robert is heartbroken because the agent's line was busy, and he had not yet completed his call. Attempt to console him.

5. In what sense does the purchase of automobile Medical Payments coverage violate the principles of risk management? Is the same criticism valid with respect to Uninsured Motorist coverage? Why or why not?

Suggestions for Additional Reading

Fire, Casualty and Surety Bulletins. Personal Lines Volume. Cincinnati, OH: National Underwriter Company. (Loose-leaf manual service with monthly supplements.) See "Personal Auto" section.

Hamilton, Karen L., and Donald S. Malecki. *Personal Insurance: Property and Liability.* Malvern, PA: American Institute for CPCU, 1994. Chapter 4.

Huebner, S. S., Kenneth Black, Jr., and Bernard L. Webb. *Property and Liability Insurance,* 4th ed. Englewood Cliffs, NJ: Prentice Hall, 1995. Chapter 32.

Policy, Form, and Manual Analysis Service. Casualty Coverages Volume. Indianapolis, IN: Rough Notes Company. (Loose-leaf manual service with monthly supplements.) See "Auto Liability" section.

Taylor, Barbara J. *How to Get Your Money's Worth in Home and Auto Insurance.* New York: McGraw-Hill, 1990.

Websites to Explore

Best's Review—Property/Casualty Edition: http://www.ambest.com/review/lh/index.html

Independent Insurance Agents of America, Inc.: http://www.iiaa.org

Insurance News Network: http://www.insure.com/

National Association of Professional Insurance Agents: http://www.pianet.com/

Nine Ways to Lower Your Auto Insurance Costs: http://www.iii.org/consumer/nineways.htm

Rough Notes Company: http://www.roughnotes.com/

CHAPTER 24

Commercial Property and Liability Coverages

By a small sample, we may judge the whole piece.
—Miguel de Cervantes
Don Quixote

CHAPTER OBJECTIVES

When you have finished this chapter, you should be able to

- Identify the seven broad classes of property and liability insurance for business firms

- Describe the general nature of coverage available to business firms with respect to fixed location property

- Distinguish between direct and consequential property losses

- Explain the principal features of boiler and machinery insurance and the feature that distinguishes it from other types of insurance

- Describe the general nature of the coverage available to business firms with respect to property that is not at a fixed location

- Describe the four coverages that may be written in ocean marine insurance

- Identify and briefly describe the six classes of inland marine insurance

- Identify and briefly explain the two standard coverages of the Workers Compensation and Employers Liability Policy

- Describe, in general, the coverage provided by the Commercial General Liability Coverage Form and the distinction between the claims-made and occurrence approach to this coverage

- Identify the three classes of automobiles that may be insured under the commercial automobile insurance forms

- Describe the coverages of a commercial Umbrella Liability Policy

Our discussion in Chapters 18 through 23 has focused on insurance coverages designed for the individual and the family unit. In the discussion of these coverages, many principles and provisions have been encountered that have counterparts in the coverages for businesses and other organizations. We turn now to a discussion of those coverages, generally referred to as *commercial line coverages*. Although a detailed discussion of the coverages available for business firms and other organizations is beyond the scope of this text, it seems appropriate that we at least describe these coverages. Commercial line coverages can be classified into the following seven classes:

1. Commercial Property Insurance
2. Boiler and Machinery Insurance
3. Marine Insurance
4. Crime Insurance
5. Commercial Liability Insurance
6. Commercial Automobile Insurance
7. Workers Compensation and Employers Liability Insurance

We begin our overview of commercial line insurance coverages with the field of commercial property insurance.

Commercial Property Insurance

Most businesses and organizations own property that is used in the conduct of their operations. Such property may include a building, machinery and equipment, and inventory. The possibility of damage to or destruction of these assets by a wide range of perils is a basic exposure for the organization. Although it is common to use the term "fire insurance" when referring to property insurance on buildings and contents, this is a misnomer, since coverage is rarely written to cover fire only. More generally, coverage is written to include the perils of *extended coverage*, vandalism, and other perils. Increasingly, coverage is provided on an open-peril basis. The term *fire insurance* is industry jargon for property insurance that was formerly written under a policy known as the Standard Fire Policy, a contract that has disappeared with the trend toward simplified policy language.

As you will recall, damage to property can be a source of two types of loss: direct loss, which consists of the loss of the asset itself, and indirect or consequential loss, which results from the loss of the use of the asset. Personal line contracts, such as the Homeowners forms, cover direct and indirect loss exposures in the same contract. In the commercial lines field, they are usually insured under separate coverage forms.

Commercial Property Direct Loss Coverages

Historically, fire insurance contracts covered insured property only on the insured's premises. Although some modern contracts provide limited coverage on property while away from the insured's premises, coverage applies primarily on premises. There are a variety of coverage forms, designed to cover specialized types of property, but most property is insured under a form known as the Building and Personal Property Coverage Form.

Building and Personal Property Coverage Form

The Building and Personal Property (BPP) Coverage Form is used to provide direct damage coverage on completed buildings and structures or business personal property, including personal property of others. Coverage may be written on buildings only, personal property only, or on both in the same contract. In addition, the form can be used to provide coverage on specific classes of property (such as stock, tenants' improvements and betterments, or machinery and equipment) by endorsements or by describing the property in the declarations. Coverage on both buildings and contents is available either on an actual cash value basis or for replacement cost.[1]

Perils The insured has several choices regarding the perils insured. Four *Causes of Loss* forms are available for use with the Building and Personal Property Coverage Form and other commercial property forms. They are titled the Basic Causes of Loss, Broad Causes of Loss, Special Causes of Loss, and Causes of Loss Earthquake Coverage Form. The first three forms more or less parallel the coverage of the similarly titled Homeowners forms and the fourth obviously provides earthquake coverage.

Coinsurance The Building and Personal Property Coverage Form—like many other commercial property forms—contains a coinsurance clause, a provision that requires the insured to maintain coverage at an agreed level or suffer a penalty. To understand the logic of the coinsurance concept, one must begin by recognizing that most fire losses are partial. Because fire insurance rates are based on the ratio of losses to the total values insured, the rate will be higher if owners insure a lower percentage of their property values than if they insure the property to some high percentage of its value. The coinsurance clause was

invented to support a concession in rates for policyholders who insure their property for a high percentage of its value. It is designed to enforce the insured's agreement to insure the property for a specified percentage of its value, which is made in return for a lower rate.

Under the provisions of the coinsurance clause, the insured agrees to maintain insurance equal to a specified percentage of the value of the property (e.g., 80 percent, 90 percent, 100 percent) in return for a reduced rate. In effect, the coinsurance rate is a quantity discount. If the insured fails to maintain insurance to value as agreed, he or she may suffer a penalty at the time of a loss. The simplified-language version of the coinsurance clause states that

> All property covered by this form must be insured for at least 80 percent of its total value at the time of "loss" or you will incur a penalty. The penalty is that we will pay only the proportion of any "loss" that the Limit of Insurance shown in the Declarations for the property bears to 80 percent of the total value of the property at the premises as of the time of "loss."

More simply, at the time of a loss, the company will make payment on the basis of the following formula:

$$\frac{\text{Amount of insurance carried}}{\text{Amount of insurance required}} \times \text{Amount of loss} = \text{Amount payable}$$

As long as the insured carries insurance equal to the required percentage, all losses covered by the policy will be paid in full up to the face amount of the policy. If the insured fails to maintain insurance to value as required, only a part of the loss will be collected.

To illustrate, let us assume that the insured has purchased coverage on a $100,000 building, subject to an 80 percent coinsurance clause. In keeping with the requirement of the clause, $80,000 in

---

[1]The Building and Personal Property Coverage Form and most other forms discussed in this chapter are part of the Insurance Services Office commercial portfolio program, introduced in 1986. This program introduced simplified policy language forms for most commercial insurance lines, including automobile insurance, property (fire) insurance, boiler and machinery, inland marine, crime insurance, and general liability insurance. All simplified portfolio commercial coverages follow the same general format, and the structure of the policy is essentially the same regardless of the type of coverage. The portfolio forms may be used to create monoline contracts, or they may be combined to create package policies; the same forms are used in either case.

coverage has been purchased. In the event of a $5000 loss, the company would pay:

$$\frac{\text{Amount of insurance carried (\$80,000)}}{\text{Amount of insurance required (\$80,000)}} \times \$5,000 = \$5,000$$

Now let us assume that construction costs rise, increasing the value of the building, but the insured continues to carry $80,000 in coverage. When the next $5000 loss occurs, it is found that the actual cash value of the building is $200,000. To comply with the 80 percent coinsurance clause, the insured should now be carrying $160,000 in coverage. In this case, the insured becomes a coinsurer and suffers a penalty equal to the coinsurance deficiency:

$$\frac{\text{Amount of insurance carried (\$80,000)}}{\text{Amount of insurance required (\$160,000)}} \times \$5,000 = \$2,500$$

Two important points are illustrated by the examples. First, the coinsurance requirement applies at the time of the loss, and the amount of coverage required for compliance is based on the value of the property at the time of loss—not the value of the property when the insurance is purchased. Second, the burden of maintaining the proper amount of insurance is on the insured. The insurance company does not check to see if the insured has kept his or her promise until a loss takes place.[2]

Agreed Value Optional Coverage The insurer may agree to suspend the coinsurance clause on a year-by-year basis, thereby guaranteeing that the insured will not suffer a coinsurance penalty as a result of an unintended insurance deficiency. After verifying the values insured, the insurer will activate the Agreed Value Optional coverage, which suspends the coinsurance provision for a one-year period.

Reporting Form Coverage

Reporting forms are designed to meet the needs of business firms whose stocks of merchandise fluctuate over time. A reporting form is written with a maximum limit sufficient to cover the highest values expected during the year, and the amount of insurance moves up and down with the values exposed to loss, subject to this maximum.[3] The insured makes periodic reports of current values on hand and is charged on the basis of these reports, paying only for the values exposed to loss, not the limit of liability.

The premium cannot be known until the year is over, so a provisional premium is paid at the inception of the policy and then adjusted at year's end to reflect the true cost of the protection provided. The insured must report 100 percent of the values of the property insured. Late reports or underreporting of values, intentional or otherwise, may result in a penalty at the time of a loss. In the event of a late report, the amount of insurance is limited to the values contained in the last previous filing. In addition, the full value reporting clause (also called the "honesty clause") provides that if the insured underreports, the company's liability is limited to that percentage of loss that the last stated values bear to the values that should have been reported. In effect, this represents a 100 percent coinsurance clause. If the insured reports value of $100,000, when the actual value of the property on hand was $200,000, recovery would be limited to 100/200, or 50 percent of the loss sustained.

---

[2]The policy deductible will apply to the loss payable after application of any coinsurance penalty.

[3]When the fluctuation in value is limited to an identifiable period, a Peak Season Endorsement may be used. Here the amount of insurance is increased pro rata for a specified period to cover the increased values, and a pro rata premium charge is made for the added coverage.

Builders Risk Coverage Form

Buildings under construction are usually insured under a contract known as the *Builders Risk Form.* Under this form, coverage is written when construction begins, with a provisional limit equal to anticipated value of the building when completed. The amount of insurance actually in force begins at zero and automatically increases as the building is completed. Because the insurer has an increasing amount of risk over the term of coverage, the premium is computed as 55 percent of the cost for the face amount of insurance. Coverage continues during the process of construction but terminates automatically when the structure is completed and occupied. Builders Risk coverage may be written to cover the interests of the building owner, the general contractor, and subcontractors, all of whom have an insurable interest in the building under construction.

Standard Property Policy

The Standard Property Policy is a self-contained property damage form that is used to insure buildings and personal property on a somewhat more restrictive basis than the BPP. It is used to insure property assigned to the insurer under FAIR plans or for other properties that do not meet high underwriting standards. The Standard Property Policy is similar to the BPP, but provides coverage only for the perils of the Causes of Loss Basic Form. The provisions regarding cancellation, increase in hazard, and vacancy are more restrictive than those of the BPP.

Plate Glass Insurance

Although the causes of loss forms applicable to building coverage cover glass constituting a part of the structure, such protection is subject to important exclusions. Business firms that want broader protection can purchase a Glass Coverage Form, which covers glass on an open-peril basis. Coverage applies for accidental glass breakage (except

by fire) and damage caused by acids or chemicals accidentally or maliciously applied. The only exclusions are fire, war, and nuclear damage.

Commercial Property Indirect Loss Coverages

The major consequential loss coverages are *business interruption insurance, extra expense insurance, contingent business interruption insurance, contingent extra expense insurance,* and *leasehold interest coverage.*

Business Interruption Insurance

Business interruption insurance indemnifies business firms for loss of income during the period required to restore property damaged by an insured peril to useful condition. It pays the expenses that continue and the profits that would have been earned during a period of interruption. The insured is required to resume operations as quickly as possible, and the insurance covers expenses incurred by the insured to resume operations. Although a valued form of coverage is available, most business interruption is written on an indemnity basis. Coverage may be written with a coinsurance provision or with a monthly limit. Under the coinsurance form, the insured agrees to insure a specified percentage (e.g., 50%, 60%, 70%, or 80%) of the firm's annual income. Under the monthly limit form, a fraction of amount of insurance (1/3, 1/4, or 1/6) of the face amount is payable for loss of income during any 30 days' period.

Extra Expense Insurance

Under some circumstances, it may be necessary for a business to continue operations after destruction of its facilities. Extra expense insurance is an alternative to business interruption insurance for those enterprises that can continue operations through the use of other facilities. It provides payment for expenses above normal costs when such expenses are incurred to continue operations after damage to the premises by an insured peril.

Contingent Business Interruption and Extra Expenses

Contingent business interruption insurance and contingent extra expense insurance protect a firm against interruption and extra expense losses resulting from damage caused by an insured peril to property that it does not own, operate, or control. It is used when the firm depends on a single supplier or a few suppliers for materials, or when it sells the bulk of its output to a single purchaser. It covers the loss sustained by the insured when its business is interrupted because of damage to property it does not own.

Leasehold Interest Insurance

Leasehold interest coverage protects against loss due to the termination of a favorable lease caused by fire or other insured peril. Consider, for example, a property leased for $1000 a month, subject to a lease that may be canceled in the event of fire or other damage to the premises. When prevailing conditions make it impossible to secure similar quarters at less than, say, $2500 a month, the existing contract would create a leasehold interest of $1500 a month for the remaining period of the lease.

Boiler and Machinery Insurance

Boiler and machinery insurance originated from the efforts of a group of engineers in Hartford, Connecticut, who offered an inspection service for steam boilers and, for a small additional charge, guaranteed their inspection by providing insurance against loss up to some limit selected by the client. The inspection service that originally served as the basis for this type of insurance remains an important part of the service provided by boiler and machinery insurers today. Boiler and machinery insurance is a highly specialized field, and insurers who offer this coverage employ trained engineers who provide the inspection service. The bulk of the boiler and machinery premium goes to pay the cost of inspections.

Although the inspection service is a critical part of the boiler and machinery product, indemnification for losses that do occur is equally important from the perspective of the insured. Hazards associated with boilers and machinery are usually excluded from other forms of property insurance, so boiler and machinery insurance is needed to fill this gap.

Boiler and machinery insurance insures against losses resulting from an accident to an insured object. Coverage is provided in a single insuring agreement both for damage to the insured's property and for liability arising out of damage to property of others in the care, custody, or control of the insured if caused by "a covered cause of loss." A "covered cause of loss" is an "accident" to an insured "object" shown in the declarations. One or more Object Definition forms are used to define the objects to be insured. Indirect loss coverages may be added by endorsement.

As in the case of fire coverages, business interruption and extra expense coverage may be added to the boiler and machinery portfolio form by endorsement.

Marine Insurance

The property forms used to insure business firms do not generally include off-premises coverage like that of the Homeowners or Dwelling forms; for this reason, special provision must be made for business property away from the premises. Historically, coverage on property away from the insured's premises developed as a separate line of insurance, known as marine insurance (sometimes called *transportation insurance*). Marine insurance is divided into two classes: ocean marine and inland marine.

Ocean Marine Insurance

As noted in Chapter 6, ocean marine insurance is considered to be the oldest of the modern fields of insurance. In spite of the technological advances in marine transportation, ocean disasters remain a hazard for those engaged in foreign trade. Ocean marine insurance provides coverage against four types of losses, corresponding to the four major classes of ocean marine insurance:

1. **Hull Insurance.** Hull insurance protects the owner of a vessel against loss to the ship itself. The coverage is written on a modified open-peril basis. A special provision in the hull policy called the "running-down clause" provides a form of property damage liability applicable to damage to other ships.

2. **Cargo Insurance.** Cargo insurance, which is written separately from the insurance on the ship, protects the owner of the cargo from financial losses that result from its destruction or loss.

3. **Freight Insurance.** Freight insurance is a special form of business interruption insurance. When a vessel is lost, this coverage indemnifies the ship owner for the loss of income that would have been earned upon completion of the voyage.

4. **Protection and Indemnity.** Protection and indemnity coverage is essentially liability insurance that protects the owner of the ship from the consequences of negligent acts of his or her agents.

Ocean Marine Policy

The traditional ocean marine insuring agreement is named peril, but with quasi-open-peril extensions. Coverage applies for perils of the sea (wind, waves, lighting, rocks, collision, and all damage arising from the elements), fire, assailing thieves, jettison and barratry, and all other like perils.[4] The reference to other *like* perils means that not all perils are covered, but only those that are similar in nature to those listed. Today, many ocean marine cargo policies are written on an open-peril basis.

Most ocean marine policies are valued policies, and the face amount of insurance is payable in the event of total loss. In addition, although the policy does not contain a 100 percent coinsurance clause, the legal custom of 100 percent insurance to value has been in existence for so long that it is considered a condition of the contract, and policies are interpreted as if they did contain a 100 percent coinsurance clause.

Originally, ocean marine policies covered insured cargo only while loaded on a vessel. However, because a shipment may originate at a point far from the place of ocean transportation, it became customary to endorse ocean marine policies to provide coverage during overland transportation under a provision known as the *warehouse-to-warehouse clause.*

Inland Marine Insurance

Inland marine insurance developed as an outgrowth of the ocean marine warehouse-to-warehouse clause. Eventually, marine insurers began to cover goods being transported over land and while otherwise away from the owner's premises. The distinguishing feature of inland marine insurance is that it covers property that is mobile in nature and that is subject to the perils of transportation. Because many inland marine contracts are written on an open-peril basis, there is sometimes a tendency to equate the term "inland marine" with "open peril." However, there are many

---

[4]Jettison is the voluntary act of destruction in which cargo is cast overboard to save the ship. Barratry refers to acts of the captain or crew in stealing the ship and its cargo, willfully sinking or deserting the ship, or imperiling the vessel by disobeying orders.

inline marine contracts that are written on a named-peril basis. For some exposures, there is both a named-peril form and an open-peril form. In addition, some inline marine forms are "manuscripted" or tailored to meet the specific needs of individual insureds.

Broadly speaking, inline marine forms may be divided into six broad categories, based on the similarity of the exposures that are insured by the contracts in each class. The six classes into which inline marine insurance is divided are

1. Transportation forms
2. Means of transportation forms
3. Business floater forms
4. Dealers forms
5. Bailee forms
6. Miscellaneous policies

We can illustrate the broad scope of exposures for which inline marine insurance provides protection and indicate the nature of the coverage by a very brief description of the major policies in each of these classes.

Transportation Coverages

Damage to property in transit may cause financial loss to two interests: the owner of the goods and the person or organization to whom the goods have been entrusted for transportation. Inline marine policies are available to cover both the interest of the owner and the liability of the carrier. Transportation forms may be written to cover property in transit by rail, truck, vessels, or aircraft. Coverage is available for goods being shipped on the owner's own vehicles or in the custody of a carrier for hire. There are also forms designed to cover property while it is being shipped by mail.

Liability Insurance for Common Carriers
Carriers that transport goods for others are classified as common carriers or contract carriers. A common carrier is one carrying goods for the public in a scheduled service between designated points;

it is distinguished from a contract carrier, which operates under contract with individual customers. The distinction is important, because the liability exposure of the common carrier is considerably broader than that of a contract carrier.

A contract carrier's legal liability is based on the principles of negligence. The legal liability of a common carrier for damage to goods that it carries is stricter, going far beyond liability resulting from negligence. The common carrier is responsible for all damage to the goods it carries except when the damage is caused by one of five specified causes: acts of God, acts of a public enemy, order of public authority, neglect of the shipper, and inherent vice. Acts of God are, of course, such things as floods, tornadoes, earthquakes, and the like. Damage by acts of a public enemy contemplates war. Damage caused by order of public authority might include several types of losses. For example, a government authority might order a dike cut to prevent flooding of a city down-river. If water from the cut dike damaged goods in the custody of a common carrier, the carrier would be excused from liability. Neglect of the shipper is concerned primarily with faulty packing of the goods by their shipper. Inherent vice is a quality in a good that causes it to destroy itself; for example, there will be a normal amount of spoilage of fresh fruit and vegetables shipped by carrier, and the carrier is not held liable for such loss.

Even in the case of these five exceptions, a common carrier may not be absolved absolutely from liability. It is still required to take all precautions possible to prevent loss if disaster threatens. For example, a flood is an act of God, but if a railroad could have moved the freight cars from the path of a flood and failed to do so, its negligence becomes a contributing factor and it could be held liable for the resulting damage.

The standard form for insuring a carrier's liability for damage to goods being transported is called the Motor Truck Cargo Policy—Truckers Form. Both common carriers and contract carriers use the policy. The Truckers Form is not a standardized contract, and is often tailor-made to the needs of the insured. However, the policies of most companies tend to be quite similar. The policy is a liability policy in the truest sense of the term: it pays only when the insured trucker is legally obligated to pay for the damages, and only to the extent of the trucker's liability. Further, coverage applies only when the damage is caused by an insured peril. Although an open-peril form is available, coverage is usually written on a named-peril basis. The named-peril form covers damage caused by fire and lightning and the perils of extended coverage (except strike, riot, and civil commotion, which are optional), plus the *perils of transportation*, which include flood, collision or overturn of vehicles; collapse of bridges; and the perils of the sea, lakes, rivers, or inland waters while on ferries. Coverage for loss by theft may be added, usually with a sizable deductible. Usually, only theft of an entire shipping package is covered, thus excluding loss by pilferage. Coverage applies to the cargo while loaded for shipment or in transit. If coverage is desired for cargo while it is off vehicles in terminals or other locations, it must be endorsed onto the policy.

Insurance for Owners of Goods in Transit Although the legal liability of a common carrier is extremely broad, the owner of goods being shipped may still need insurance on goods being shipped. First, there are those situations in which a common carrier is not liable for damage to goods in its custody: these include damage by acts of God or losses that are due to the negligence of the shipper. In addition, common carriers sometimes limit their liability through *released bills of lading*, under which the shipper agrees to a limitation of the carrier's liability.[5] Instances may also arise in which the carrier is liable for damage, but is not financially able to pay.

Coverage for the owner of goods being shipped by common carrier is available under the Annual Transit Policy, which may be written to cover all modes of transportation, including rail, air, and trucks. Coverage applies on a named-peril basis. For single shipments, a Trip Transit Policy is available.

A second approach to insurance for owners of goods in transit is a version of the Motor Truck Cargo Policy discussed above. In addition to the Truckers Form written to cover the liability of carriers, there is a Shippers Form of the Motor Truck Cargo Policy, which covers the interest of the owner who ships by common or contract carrier, and an Owners Form, which covers the owner's goods on the owner's own trucks.

Instrumentalities of Transportation and Communication

Means of Transportation forms include policies written to cover instrumentalities of transportation and communication, including mobile property such as railroad rolling stock, but also fixed objects such as bridges, tunnels, pipelines, power transmission lines, and radio and television transmitting equipment. Although some of this property is not mobile in nature, its inclusion in the field of inland marine insurance was justified on the grounds that it is subject to the perils of transportation. Coverage on bridges, tunnels, and other instrumentalities of transportation and communication is tailored to the specific needs of the insured and is often written under a manuscript policy designed for a particular exposure.

Business Floater Policies

Merchandise being shipped is not the only business property exposed to damage away from the business premises. There are many classes of property that are mobile in nature and, so, vulnerable to risk. Coverage on such property is provided under inland marine floater policies. In general, these floaters fall into one of three categories:

1. **Equipment Floaters.** These forms cover various types of personal property that is not held for sale or on consignment and

---

[5]Under a "released bill of lading," the carrier specifies the maximum amount for which it will be held liable. For example, a common carrier may use a bill of lading with the stipulation that its liability will be limited to a specific amount and grant the shipper the option of purchasing higher limits for an additional charge.

that is in the hands of the owner to be used for the purpose for which it was intended. The property insured is mobile in nature and is generally used away from the insured's premises. Common policies in this area include the Contractors Equipment floater, the Physicians and Surgeons Equipment floater, and the Salesmen's Sample floater.

2. **Processing and Storage Floaters.** These insure property in temporary storage and property undergoing processing outside the owner's premises. A good example is the Garment Contractors floater, which covers the stock of a manufacturer that has been sent off premises for processing.

3. **Consignment and Sales Floaters.** These policies protect goods being held for sale under consignment, being installed, or being sold under an installment plan. Examples include the Installment Sales floater, which covers goods sold on an installment basis; the Floor Plan Merchandise Form, which covers stock pledged as collateral under a "floor plan" arrangement; and the Installation floater, which covers machinery and equipment in transit for installation in a building and while being installed.

The coverage of business floater policies may be written on both an open-peril or named-peril basis. In several classes, the insured has a choice between open-peril and named-peril coverage. In addition, the coverage may be written on a scheduled or blanket basis.

Dealers Forms

Dealers forms represent something of an anomaly in inland marine insurance. Although inland marine forms usually cover property that is mobile and that is commonly away from the owner's premises, the dealers forms provide coverage on a dealer's stock of goods. Although coverage applies on and off premises, the major exposure is on premises. Dealers forms are available only for specific classes of dealers. They include jewelers, furriers, musical instrument dealers, camera dealers, equipment dealers, fine arts dealers, and stamp and coin collection dealers.

Bailee Forms

A bailment consists of the delivery of property of one person, the "bailor," to another, the "bailee," for some specific purpose. The property may be in the care of the bailee to be worked on, as in the case of an automobile being repaired, or in storage, or for some other purpose. If property in the hands of a bailee is damaged or destroyed, the bailee may be liable to the owner. A bailee may extend or limit its liability by contract or advertisement. The bailee may assume complete responsibility for damage to property of customers, regardless of negligence or a bailee may, by contract, limit its liability. For example, a furrier may specify that its total liability for a single fur coat in storage will be $200. Although bailees are permitted to limit their liability, the courts have frowned on attempts by bailees to completely relieve themselves of liability. The decided trend of modern decisions is against the validity of exculpatory clauses or provisions of parking lots, garages, checkrooms, and warehouses, where business firms undertake to protect themselves against liability by posting signs or printing limitations on the receipts delivered to the bailor-owner at the time of bailment.

The liability associated with bailed property has traditionally been insured under property insurance forms, most frequently under inland marine contracts.[6] Under some bailee forms, payment is made regardless of the liability of the

---

[6]The bailor may, of course, insure his or her property under all conditions, including the period while it is in the custody of the bailee, but the general principle is that coverage purchased by the bailor shall not benefit the bailee. If the bailor collects from his or her insurance company, the insurer may then subrogate against the bailee.

bailee, as long as the cause of the loss is a peril under the policy. This approach results from the expectation of customers that their property will be returned to them in good condition, regardless of the liability of the bailee. A merchant who refused to reimburse a customer for the loss of property because of not being liable under the specific set of circumstances might soon find himself or herself without customers.

The basic policy for bailees is the *Bailees Customer Policy*, which is completed by the attachment of a form designed for the particular class of business. Coverage may be provided under these forms for laundries, dyers, dry cleaners, processors, and service-type firms such as appliance repair stores, radio and television repair stores, and other similar establishments. Coverage applies for damage to or loss of customers' goods regardless of the bailee's liability. The normal perils insured against include fire, lightning, windstorm, riot, earthquake, sprinkler leakage, burglary, robbery, and confusion of goods caused by any of the perils insured against.[7] In addition, the usual perils of transportation are covered, and coverage applies to the property while in transit or at the insured's premises. Standard exclusions are loss due to shortage, misdelivery, or mysterious disappearance, loss resulting from delay, and losses from infidelity, nuclear energy, and war.

More specialized bailee forms include a Furriers Customer Policy, which covers customers' coats in storage; a Cold Storage Locker Bailee floater, which covers customers' property in public freezers; and a special form for hotels and motels, the Innkeepers Liability Policy. These forms have provisions that tailor the protection to the unique exposures of the particular type of business. In some instances, the coverage applies regardless of the bailee's liability. In others, it applies only when the insured is actually liable. In some cases, such as the Garagekeepers coverage, the insured may elect coverage on either basis.

Miscellaneous Inland Marine Forms

The miscellaneous class of inland marine commercial policies includes unrelated and unusual types of inland marine coverages such as Accounts Receivable and Valuable Papers coverages and Electronic Data Processing policies. Accounts receivable insurance and valuable papers insurance are the most common of these coverages.

Accounts Receivable Insurance Accounts receivable insurance protects against the inability to collect amounts owed to the insured because of destruction of records by fire or other insured perils. The coverage is written on an open-peril basis, on either a reporting or nonreporting form.[8] The coverage is on an indemnity basis and compensates the insured for any amounts that are uncollectible because of the destruction of the accounting records (with allowance for bad debts). In addition, payment is made for expenses incurred to reconstruct the records, for collection expenses above normal costs, and for the interest charges on loans taken out by the insured to offset the collections.

Valuable Papers Insurance Valuable papers insurance may be written on various types of important records, including maps, film, tape, wire or recording media, drawings, abstracts, deeds, mortgages, and manuscripts. Coverage is on an open-peril basis. Valuable papers may be insured on either a scheduled or blanket basis. The blanket coverage specifically excludes papers that cannot be reproduced, so valuable papers that cannot be replaced must be insured on a scheduled basis. Scheduled items are insured on a valued basis, and the amount scheduled for each item is

[7]Confusion of goods refers to the inability to identify the ownership of the goods even though they are not destroyed, but the confusion must result from an insured peril.

[8]It is important to distinguish accounts receivable insurance from *credit insurance*. As discussed above, accounts receivable coverage provides indemnification for losses that result from destruction of accounts receivable records by an insured peril. In credit insurance, the peril insured against is insolvency or default of a debtor to whom credit has been extended. Credit insurance is a highly specialized field, and the coverage is written only by a limited number of insurers.

payable in the event of loss. In the case of blanket coverage, payment is made for the actual cash value of the records.

Crime Insurance

The broad field of crime insurance includes all instances in which the cause of the loss is the wrongful taking of property belonging to the insured. Historical factors led to two distinct classes of dishonesty insurance: fidelity bonds, which cover employee dishonesty, and crime insurance, designed to cover dishonest acts of persons who are not employees of the insured. Each by itself provides incomplete protection against the perils of dishonesty.

Employee Crime Insurance—Fidelity Bonds

Fidelity bonds protect against loss resulting from employees' dishonesty and cover loss of money, securities, or other property resulting from acts (fraud, forgery, embezzlement, and theft) by the person bonded, up to the face amount of the bond, which is called the *penalty*. The penalty under a bond is never cumulative, and a series of thefts by one person is considered a single loss.

Employee crime coverage is written on a *loss sustained form* and a *discovery form*. The loss sustained form applies to criminal acts committed during the policy period and discovered within the policy period or in a one-year period after termination called the *extended period to discover loss* provision. The loss sustained form includes a provision entitled Loss Sustained During Prior Insurance, which states that any loss that would have been covered under prior insurance is covered under the current insurance, provided there has been no lapse in coverage from the old policy to the new one. The provision applies whether the current insurer or another insurer wrote the prior bond. The loss must be discovered and reported to the insurer during the policy period or

the discovery period. When the limits of the two policies are different, the lower limit applies if the previous insurance was written with a different insurer. If the current insurer wrote the previous policy, the higher limits apply.

The discovery form covers loss committed at any time, provided that the loss is discovered during the policy period. The *extended period to discover loss* provision in the discovery form grants coverage for loss discovered up to 60 days after the end of the policy period. The 60-day extension of the discovery period ends immediately at the inception of a replacement policy that covers the loss in whole or in part.

In addition to the difference in coverage triggers (i.e., loss sustained or discovery basis), fidelity bonds may be classified as schedule bonds and blanket bonds. Schedule Bonds cover the person or position that is listed in the policy. When several persons are listed in a single bond, it is called a Name Schedule bond. Under a Position Schedule bond, positions to be covered are listed rather than the individuals. If a person leaves the firm or moves to another position, his or her successor is covered in the scheduled position.

Blanket bonds, in contrast, cover all employees, regardless of position, with new employees covered automatically. Under the portfolio program, blanket bond coverage is provided under the Employee Dishonesty Coverage Form (Form A). The bond limit (penalty) applies on a per-loss basis, regardless of the number of employees that might be involved in a collusive loss. The coverage is subject to a one-year discovery period.

Nonemployee Crime Insurance

Policies designed to cover against loss of money or other property through dishonest acts of persons other than employees are classified according to peril. There are policies to protect against burglary, robbery, theft, forgery, and so on. Only the specified type of criminal activity indicated is covered, and coverage exists only when the loss meets the definition of the particular type of crime covered. For example, burglary consists of stealing property when the premises are not open for business and requires forcible entry into the premises. Insurance policies covering loss by burglary typically require visible evidence of forcible entry into the premises or forcible exit. Robbery, on the other hand, consists of taking property by violence or threat of violence. Theft is much broader in meaning than is either burglary or robbery and includes an illegal taking of property, thus embracing both burglary and robbery.[9] All nonemployee crime forms exclude employee fidelity losses. There are 15 crime coverage forms, designated forms A through N, and form R. Form A covers employee dishonesty, and forms B through N and form R cover the nonemployee crime exposure. We will not attempt to discuss all of the remaining 14 coverages, but will limit our examination to the following seven forms.[10]

Forgery or Alteration Coverage (Form B)

Forgery or alteration crime coverage protects the insured and banks in which the insured carries checking or savings accounts against loss resulting from forgery or alteration, or checks, drafts, promissory notes, and other designated financial instruments that are drawn on the insured's account. Coverage applies to outgoing instruments and does not protect against loss resulting from acceptance of forged checks.

Theft, Disappearance, and Destruction Form (Form C)

The Theft, Disappearance, and Destruction Form covers money and securities for loss by theft, but

goes further and also provides coverage against loss by "disappearance and destruction." In effect, it provides open-peril coverage on money and securities. Separate limits of coverage apply to losses on premises and losses off premises. The insured may select either or both, and separate limits apply to each.

Robbery and Safe Burglary Coverage Form (Form D)

The Robbery and Safe Burglary Policy covers property other than money and securities and may be written to cover three exposures: on-premises robbery, off-premises robbery, and safe burglary. The insured may select any or all of the coverages, and separate amounts of insurance may be written for each coverage.

Robbery is defined in the form as taking property from a person by someone who has caused or threatened to cause that person bodily harm or has committed an obviously unlawful act witnessed by that person. In addition to violence or threat of violence, coverage would be provided if an employee saw a thief grab an item and run out of the store, even though the custodian was not injured or threatened.

Safe burglary means the taking of property from within a locked safe or vault by forcible entry or the removal of the entire safe from the premises. If the burglar opens the safe by manipulation of the dial, there is no coverage; the loss must result from forcible entry into the safe. The policy includes coverage for damage to the safe or other property of the insured during a successful, or attempted, safe burglary. There is no requirement that the premises be entered forcibly.

Premises Burglary Coverage (Form E)

The premises burglary coverage covers loss of merchandise, furniture, fixtures, and equipment because of burglary. It does not cover loss of money or securities. Visible evidence of forcible entry or forcible exit is required, and the policy covers damage caused by burglars. In addition, the policy is extended to cover loss by robbery or

---

[9]Coverage for some nonemployee crime losses is included in the open-peril Causes of Loss Special Form. Property other than money and securities, for example, if not excluded, is covered for loss by burglary, robbery, or theft under the Special Form. The expansion of fire insurance coverages to include crime perils has reduced the demand for monoline crime coverages on property other than money and securities.

[10]The remaining seven forms (H through N) cover losses associated with safe deposit boxes, securities deposited with others, and the property of guests in hotels and motels.

attempted robbery of a watchperson employed exclusively by the insured while on duty within the premises. Losses resulting from employee infidelity are specifically excluded.

Computer Fraud (Form F)

The Computer Fraud Coverage Form covers money, securities, and other property against theft following and directly related to the use of a computer to fraudulently cause a transfer of property from inside the premises or banking premises to a person outside those premises. An example of the type of loss covered by this form is the transfer of money from the insured's bank account to the thief's bank account.

Extortion Coverage (Form G)

The Extortion Coverage Form covers a type of kidnapping loss that involves the surrender of property (usually money) away from the premises as a result of a threat to do injury to an employee or relative who is (or allegedly is) being held captive. Threats to damage property (i.e., a threat to detonate a bomb at the premises if money is not paid) or the threat to tamper with a product of the insured are not covered.

General Liability Insurance

One of the major exposures facing every business or organization is the possibility of legal liability: the chance that the entity or its owners may be sued for injury to persons or damage to the property of others that arises out of the activities of the business. As noted in Chapter 21, liability coverages can be conveniently divided into three classes: Employers Liability and Workers Compensation, Automobile Liability, and General Liability. The *general liability* exposure encompasses the potential liability to members of the general public (as opposed to liability for bodily injury to employees) that does not arise out of automo-

biles. This exposure includes liability arising out of business premises and the activities of employees both on and off your premises. It also includes liability arising out of the firm's products or work performed by the firm or by independent contractors. Finally, it includes liability assumed under contract. While this exposure can be covered under a variety of policies, the preferred approach is the Commercial General Liability (CGL) Coverage Form.

The Commercial General Liability Coverage Form

The Commercial General Liability (CGL) Coverage Form includes coverage for bodily injury or property damage arising out of business premises and operations, products and completed operations, and independent contractors all in a single contract. Premises and operations coverage protects against suits arising out of defects in the premises and activities of employees away from the premises. Products and completed operations insures liability arising out of products manufactured or sold by the insured and work performed by the insured. Unlike the CPL policy we examined in Chapter 21, the CGL automatically includes coverage for personal injury, including libel, slander, defamation, invasion of privacy, and similar torts. In addition, it provides limited coverage for liability assumed by contract (under a lease or hold-harmless agreement, for example).

Like the CPL, the CGL includes a promise to defend the insured and reserves to the insurer the right to settle any claim that it sees fit. Under the contractual liability coverage, the cost of contractually assumed obligations to defend another party is included in the policy limit.[11] Other defense costs are payable in addition to the policy limit.

---

[11]Under some conditions, the insured and the party whose defense costs have been contractually assumed may be defended in the same action, in which case the defense costs of the other party are covered in excess of the policy limits.

Tidbits, Vignettes, and Conundrums 24.1

That Smarts!

One of the attractions at a 1993 fair held in St. Louis was bungee jumping. After signing a release, a participant was lifted in a bungee cage 170 feet above the ground. The "jump master" carefully checked the fastening of the bungee cord around his ankles and "gave him a go." Unfortunately, the other end of the bungee cord had not been attached. The jumper sustained serious injuries, and the jury awarded him $5 million against both the V.P. Fair Foundation and North Star Entertainment, the bungee jump operator. The judgment was upheld on appeal.

Source: Hatch v. V.P. Fair Foundation, Inc., No. E.D. 73279 and E.D. 73280.

Claims-Made and Occurrence Forms

The CGL form offers two approaches to the provision of this coverage: an "occurrence form" and a "claims-made form." The occurrence form covers injuries and damage that occurs during the policy period, regardless of when a claim was made or suit was brought. Under a claims-made form, coverage applies to injury or damage for which claim is made during the policy period or during an "extended reporting period" specified in the contract. Historically, most general liability policies were written on an "occurrence basis"; these are poorly suited to exposures in which there is the possibility of latent injury or damage. ISO introduced a claims-made version of the CGL in 1985 to provide insurers with a standard coverage form for such exposures.[12]

Claims-made forms are generally written with a *retroactive date*, which is, in effect, an exclusion of losses arising out of events prior to a stated date. The use of a retroactive date is a logical approach to eliminating duplication of coverage when an insured changes from an occurrence form to a claims-made form. The retroactive date eliminates coverage for claims arising out of occurrences before inception, since such losses will presumably be covered under the expired occurrence policy that was replaced. If the retroactive date in any renewal of a claims-made policy is advanced or if coverage is changed from a claims-made form to an occurrence form, a gap in coverage is created. The expired claims-made policy will not cover claims that are filed after its expiration, and the new claims-made policy or occurrence will not cover claims arising out of occurrences prior to its retroactive date (inception). Thus, a claim made during the renewal policy arising out of an occurrence during the expired policy would not be covered. The traditional solution to this gap in claims-made policies has been for the insured to purchase an extended reporting date endorsement (commonly called "tail" coverage) for the expiring policy. An "extended reporting period" provision states that any claim reported within the designated extended reporting period will be deemed to have been reported during the policy and will be covered.

CGL Form Exclusions

Although the CGL policy provides extremely broad liability coverage, it is subject to numerous

---

[12]A series of cases in the early 1980s involving asbestosis injury to workers indicated the flaws in the occurrence form where there is the possibility of latent injuries or damage that may not be discovered until long after it occurs. These latent injuries required insurers to pay losses under occurrence policies long expired, because the injury or damage was not discovered until long after it had occurred. Claims-made forms have been used in the field of medical malpractice insurance for many years.

exclusions. Although some exclusions serve to eliminate uninsurable exposures, most are designed to define the scope of the coverage and to require that some exposures be insured under other contracts. Thus, for example, the CGL excludes injury to employees (which is covered under the Workers Compensation Policy), liability arising out of aircraft, vehicles, or watercraft (which are insured under specialized policies covering these exposures), and pollution liability or liability arising out of employment-related practices (such as discrimination in employment), which are covered under separate specialized liability contracts. The CGL also excludes damage to the insured's products or work or to property in the insured's care, custody, and control. Some of these exclusions in the CGL can be deleted or modified by endorsement. Coverage for other excluded exposures may be available under separate specialized contracts.

Liability Insurance for Specialized Exposures

Although the CGL covers a wide range of liability exposures, it does not include coverage for some of the newer exposures that have emerged in recent years. Some of the more important of these exposures are the following.

Liquor Liability Coverage

An exclusion in the CGL that creates a need for specialized coverage for some insureds is the exclusion of liability arising out of the business of manufacture, sale, or serving of alcoholic beverages. Many states have special statutes, called "dram shop" laws that provide a right of action against the seller in the event that the purchaser injures a third party. The laws vary greatly in their detail. Some apply only when the injury results from sale to a minor or intoxicated person, while others have no such qualification. Some laws provide for liability only to those injured by the intoxicated person, while others permit liability for

loss of support by dependents of the intoxicated party or even injuries sustained by the intoxicated person. Even in those states where such laws do not exist, similar liability may be imposed under common law.[13] The CGL excludes liability arising out of the sale of alcoholic beverages, and these activities must be insured under a Dram Shop or Liquor Liability Policy. Coverage is written on both an occurrence and a claims-made basis.

Pollution Liability Insurance Coverage

The current version of the CGL policy excludes virtually all liability arising out of pollution. An endorsement is available under which an insurer can add pollution coverage to the CGL, but most insurers have been unwilling to extend the policy. In addition to the Pollution Liability Endorsement, the ISO introduced two simplified pollution liability forms as a part of the portfolio revision. The two new pollution liability forms are designated Pollution Liability Coverage Form—Designated Sites and Pollution Liability Limited Coverage Form—Designated Sites. The principal difference between the two forms is that the limited form does not provide coverage for "mandated off-site cleanup costs," while coverage for such costs is specifically insured in the standard form.

Employment Practices Liability Coverage

The 1990s witnessed a significant rise in the incidence of claims alleging wrongful employment practices. Suits alleging discrimination in the workplace, wrongful termination, and sexual harassment have grown at a rapid rate for a variety

---

[13]Dram shop liability laws exist in Alabama, Alaska, California, Colorado, Florida, Georgia, Illinois, Iowa, Maine, Michigan, Minnesota, New Mexico, New York, North Carolina, North Dakota, Ohio, Oregon, Pennsylvania, Rhode Island, Utah, Vermont, and Wyoming. Liability has been imposed on sellers of alcoholic beverages under common law in Arizona, Colorado, Hawaii, Idaho, Indiana, Kentucky, Louisiana, Massachusetts, Mississippi, Missouri, New Jersey, New Mexico, North Carolina, South Dakota, Washington, Wisconsin, and Wyoming.

of reasons, but mainly due to the growth in federal legislation that specifically outlaws various types of discrimination in the workplace.[14] Although risk management principles suggest that this exposure should be addressed by loss prevention and control, not all claims can be prevented. The increase in the number of successful suits alleging employment-related practices therefore led to a demand for a new form of insurance to cover the exposure.

A limited number of insurers offer employment practices liability policies, which cover discrimination, sexual harassment, and wrongful termination. Coverage is written on a claims-made basis with a retroactive date and a limited discovery period. Extended reporting coverage is available for an additional premium if coverage is canceled or nonrenewed by the insurer. Fines and criminal penalties are universally excluded.[15] Some insurers include coverage for punitive damages and some do not. In most cases, defense costs are included in the policy limit, rather than "outside" the policy limit as in the case of the CGL and most other liability contracts. Deductibles range upward from a low of $1000 to $25,000. In addition to the deductible, policies also include a coinsurance provision, which functions as a copayment provision. The insured must usually share a percentage of defense and settlement costs, normally ranging from 5 percent to 25 percent, with the most common being 5 percent or 10 percent.[16]

Pension Fiduciary Liability

The enactment of ERISA in 1974 imposed new responsibilities on employers and fiduciaries with respect to pension plans and group life and health insurance programs, holding them liable to beneficiaries for failure to exercise prudence in the supervision of such a plan. Pension fiduciary liability insurance protects against this exposure. The coverage is sometimes written to include employee benefit errors and omissions coverage, which protects against liability arising from errors in advising employees and from other types of mistakes related to a fringe benefit program.

Professional Liability Insurance

The term professional liability refers to liability arising from a failure to use due care and the degree of skill expected of a person in a particular profession. In cases where there is exposure to bodily injury (as with physicians, surgeons, and dentists), professional liability insurance is called *malpractice insurance*. Where the risk involves property damage (including intangible property), the coverage is referred to as *errors and omissions (E&O) insurance*. E&O insurance is applicable to insurance agents, attorneys, accountants, architects, and real estate agents. In virtually all cases, professional liability insurance is written on a claims-made basis.

Directors and Officers Errors and Omissions Insurance

A special form of coverage known as *directors and officers errors and omissions (D&O) insurance* is

---

[14]Title VII of the Civil Rights Law of 1964, The Equal Pay Act, The Age Discrimination in Employment Act of 1967, The Rehabilitation Act of 1973, The Pregnancy Discrimination Act of 1978, The Americans with Disabilities Act of 1990, The Older Workers Benefit Protection Act of 1990, The Civil Rights Act of 1991, and The Family and Medical Leave Act of 1993.

[15]Initially, there was a debate over whether insurance for employment-related practices—which are illegal—violates public policy. The Civil Rights Act of 1964 recognizes two distinct types of discrimination: that of "disparate treatment" and that of "disparate impact." The former is where you treat people differently and it is an intentional act. The latter is where treatment is actually the same, but results in *de facto* discrimination. This may not be an intentional act. In addition, coverage is deemed permissible for the vicarious liability of an employer even when the act committed by an employee is criminal.

[16]In 1997, ISO filed a new standardized Employment Related Practices Liability (ERPL) Form with state regulatory authorities. This means that an increasing number of insurers will likely offer this coverage in the future. Like the existing contracts on the market, the ISO form is written on a claims-made basis, with defense costs included in the policy limit.

available to protect corporate officers and directors from suits alleging mismanagement. Such suits may be brought by stockholders or by persons outside the firm. The coverage is subject to a deductible and the insured is usually required to bear 5 percent of any loss in excess of the deductible. The coverage excludes losses based on alleged personal gain by the insured and losses resulting from failure to purchase proper insurance coverage.[17]

Umbrella Liability Policy

The possibility of a loss in excess of the limits of coverage under the Comprehensive General Liability Policy or the Business Auto Policy and the fact that higher limits of coverage under these policies can be expensive has always been a problem. One solution to the problem is an Umbrella Liability Policy, a form of coverage that we consider essential for all businesses.

As in the case of the personal umbrella, a commercial umbrella policy is a broad form of blanket excess coverage that serves two functions. First, it applies as a form of excess insurance, cov-

---

[17]Variations of this coverage are available to protect elected and appointed public officials. These include a Board of Education Liability Policy and a Public Official Liability Policy. Like the Officers and Directors coverage discussed earlier, there is no standard form for these coverages, and they are usually sold by specialty insurers.

ering all the hazards of the CGL Policy, the Automobile Liability coverage, and the Employers Liability coverage of the Workers Compensation Policy. In addition, the umbrella is broader than the underlying coverages and protects against some exposures that are not covered by either the CGL or automobile liability insurance.

Workers Compensation and Employers Liability

The state workers compensation laws impose absolute liability on an employer for injuries or occupational diseases suffered by employees that arise out of and in the course of their employment. These laws set forth a schedule of benefits for which the employer becomes liable and imposes the obligation for these benefits on the employer regardless of fault or lack thereof. The laws further require the employer purchase workers compensation insurance or qualify as a self-insurer to secure these benefits and imposes severe penalties if the employer fails to purchase such insurance.

The standard approach to insuring the workers compensation exposure is the Workers Compensation and Employers Liability Policy. The policy provides statutory workers compensation benefits for all states in which the employer conducts operations and that are listed in the policy. In addition, the policy may be extended to provide

---

Tidbits, Vignettes, and Conundrums 24.2

Silicone Liability

In 1998, Dow Corning Corp. and attorneys representing women with silicone breast implants reached a $3.2 billion settlement. Reportedly, each woman in the class action suit will receive about $31,000 from the settlement. The litigation dates from the early 1980s, when implant recipients began to complain of illnesses resulting from the implants. Inconclusive scientific evidence was provided by both sides regarding the link between implants and diseases.

Other States Insurance for states where the firm commences operations except the states of North Dakota, Ohio, Washington, West Virginia, and Wyoming. Coverage for workers compensation losses in these states is available only through monopolistic workers compensation funds operated by the states. However, persons employed outside of these "monopolistic" states and covered under the workers compensation law of their home state are exempt from the requirements of the monopolistic fund states.

In general, an injured worker may not sue his or her employer in the event of injury and, if a suit is brought, the legal principles favor the employer. However, there are some instances in which an employee can bring suit and it is possible for someone other than the injured worker (e.g., a spouse or a third party) to bring suit against the employer when an employee is injured. Section B of the Workers Compensation Policy, Employers Liability, provides protection for suits against the firm in connection with injury to an employee. The limit of liability for this coverage is $100,000. This limit may be increased to $500,000 or $1,000,000 for a small premium. If the firm carries an Umbrella Liability Policy, the employers liability exposure is also covered under the Umbrella Liability Policy.

Commercial Auto and Aviation Insurance

Commercial automobile insurance is a major commercial insurance line. Although aviation insurance is a much smaller field in terms of premiums generated, the two have a number of similarities.

Commercial Automobile Insurance

Most business firms own automobiles, but even if they do not, employees often drive their own cars in the course of their employment, and if they injure someone while doing so, the employer can be held liable. Liability arising out of automobiles is excluded under the CGL policy, and it must therefore be insured separately.

The standard form for insuring commercial automobiles is the Business Auto Coverage Form. This form may be used to provide Liability coverage, Medical Payments, Physical Damage coverage, and Uninsured Motorist coverage. It can also be endorsed to provide no-fault benefits in states where such coverage is required. In addition, separate commercial auto forms are available to insure garages (Garage Coverage Form) and truckers (Truckers Coverage Form and Motor Carriers Coverage Form).

The Garage Coverage Form makes provision for losses arising out of the use of customers' autos in the custody of the garage for servicing and repair. Physical Damage coverage (comprehensive and collision) on customers' vehicles is an option and is provided under Garagekeepers Coverage. The Truckers Coverage Form and the Motor Carriers Coverage Form include provisions that recognize custom and practice in the trucking industry, where independent owner-operators lease their vehicles to licensed truckers that are authorized to serve the public over specified routes. Coverage for the vehicles of these owner-operators is provided by the licensed trucker's insurance.

The liability coverage of the four commercial auto forms may be written to include coverage on owned, hired, and non-owned automobiles, with automatic coverage on additional or replacement autos. An important coverage for business firms that does not have an exact counterpart in the personal auto field is "employers' non-ownership liability," which covers the vicarious liability of an employer when the employer is sued because of the use of the employee's auto on behalf of the firm. Although the employer will be covered by the employee's auto if the limits are adequate, most businesses purchase excess coverage for protection in the event the employee's limits are inadequate.

Physical Damage coverage (Comprehensive and Collision) is available under each of the three commercial auto forms, as are Automobile

Medical Payments coverage and Uninsured and Underinsured Motorist coverage.

Aviation Insurance

The importance and rapid growth of the aviation industry make it desirable to include at least a brief discussion of aviation insurance. The most common coverages are aircraft liability insurance and hull coverage.[18]

Aircraft liability coverages are similar to those for automobile liability, with one major difference: the bodily injury liability is divided into two coverages—Passenger Liability and Bodily Injury Excluding Passengers. Some contracts cover bodily injury to passengers, bodily injury excluding passengers, and property damage liability with a single limit to cover all three exposures. When coverage is written to include passenger liability, Medical Payments coverage is also available.

Admitted Liability coverage, also known as Voluntary Settlement coverage, is issued only with passenger legal liability. It is written on a per-seat basis and provides a specified sum for loss of life, limb, or sight by a passenger. When payment is offered under Admitted Liability, a release of liability against the insured is obtained from the passenger. If the injured party refuses to sign the release, the offer of payment is withdrawn and the injured party must bring suit against the insured, who is protected by the Passenger Bodily Injury coverage.

Package Policies for Business Firms

Although the package policy began with the Homeowners contract, the concept was soon applied to the field of commercial insurance. Eventually, two standard bureau package programs designed for businesses and institutions evolved: the Special Multi-Peril (SMP) Program and the Businessowners Policy (BOP). Many insurers also developed their own commercial packages, which usually parallel the ISO forms, but with distinctive coverage features. With the introduction of the new portfolio program, the ISO SMP program was replaced by a new Commercial Package Policy.

Commercial Package Policy

The ISO portfolio program uses the same standardized forms for both monoline policies and for a multiline package policy, called a Commercial Package Policy (CPP). The contents of a monoline policy differs from that of a package policy only in the number of coverage parts included. Because the CPP uses the same forms as the monoline coverages, the coverage is identical with the separate monoline forms. The CPP is a multiline policy in the truest sense of the term, and can provide property and liability insurance in a single contract.

One of the principal features of package policies has been a discount for the packaging. The CPP follows this principle, providing a package modification factor, which in effect discounts the premiums for individual coverages when they are combined in a qualified package. This discount is allowed only if the policy contains both property and liability coverage, applicable to the same premises. Usually, this will consist of coverage on the insured's building and/or contents under the Building and Personal Property Coverage Form, together with General Liability coverage for the insured's premises and operations. If this requirement is met (i.e., coverage for both the property and the liability exposures), most coverages under the policy will be eligible for the package discount.

Businessowners Policy

The *Businessowners Policy* (BOP) is a package policy approach to insurance for business firms simi-

---

[18]There are two basic forms of hull insurance: one provides open-peril coverage both on the ground and in flight and the other provides open-peril coverage on the ground with coverage in flight limited to the perils of fire, lightning, and explosion and excluding crash or collision.

lar to the CPP but designed for smaller firms. The program was introduced in 1976 and extensively revised in 1987 and again in 1997. The 1987 and 1997 versions generally resemble the format of the simplified portfolio program, but the BOP is not a part of the CPP. It is an independent policy, complete with its own separate forms. Like the Homeowners Policy and the SMP policies, the BOP provides property and liability coverage in a single policy. The program was originally available for small and medium apartments, offices, and mercantile and processing firms. The 1997 revision extended eligibility to contractors, certain restaurants (those with limited cooking and fast-food types), convenience stores without gasoline pumps, and laundry or dry cleaning operations. For those firms that are eligible, the program provides an extremely broad package of coverage on a simplified basis.[19]

Property Coverage

Property coverage is provided under one of two forms, the Standard Property Coverage Form and the Special Property Coverage Form. Coverage under the Standard Form includes the perils of fire and extended coverage, vandalism, sprinkler leakage, sinkhole collapse, volcanic action, and transportation. Coverage under the Special Form is on an open-peril basis, subject to the standard open-peril exclusions.

While the Businessowners forms are similar in most respects to the simplified portfolio property forms, they automatically include a number of features that are options under monoline forms. Coverage on both buildings and contents is for replacement cost, and there is no coinsurance provision. Furthermore, coverage on the building automatically increases by 8 percent a year, unless a higher option has been elected. If contents coverage equals 100 percent of the average monthly val-

ues for the preceding 12 months, an automatic 25 percent increase in contents coverage is provided to offset seasonal variations in stock value. Business income and extra expense coverage are automatically included. There are no limits of liability and no coinsurance clause, and the insured may collect for reduced earnings up to 12 months.

Contingent business interruption, employee dishonesty, and mechanical breakdown coverages are available by endorsement to both property forms. Burglary and robbery coverage is an option under the Standard Form (and is automatically included in the Special Form).

Liability Coverage

In general, the liability coverage of the Businessowners Policy is similar to the simplified CGL "occurrence" form. Coverage is provided for premises and operations, products and completed operations, advertising, and personal injury liability, fire legal liability, and medical payments. There are separate limits for medical expenses ($5000), fire legal liability ($50,000), and liability and medical expenses combined ($300,000, which may be increased to $500,000 or $1 million). Firms that do not own automobiles may cover their non-owned automobile exposure under an optional Hired and Non-owned Auto Liability Endorsement.

Farm Coverages

In addition to the Commercial Package Policy and the Businessowners Policy, coverage is also available on a package-policy approach for persons engaged in farming. A program similar to the Homeowners program, the Farmowners-Ranchowners program, was formerly available for farm occupancies, but was replaced in most states in 1987 by new simplified portfolio farm coverage forms. In addition to providing coverage on the residential exposure similar to that under the Homeowners forms, the Portfolio Farm Program also includes coverage on barns and other farm buildings and farm personal property, such as

---

[19]Eligibility is limited to firms with a square footage below specified maximums that vary by type of occupancy and whose revenues do not exceed specified maximums. Eligibility is limited to firms with gross sales of $3 million or less, except for restaurants, when the maximum is $1 million.

agricultural machinery and equipment, livestock, and grain plus liability coverage specifically tailored to the exposures of farming operations.

Summary

Although our discussion of the commercial property and liability coverages in this chapter has been extremely brief, it should serve to illustrate the general nature of the property coverages available to the business firm for the protection of its assets. The contracts discussed in this chapter should serve to illustrate the complexity of the commercial lines field, and the manner in which the industry has developed contracts to meet a wide range of specialized needs.

Important Concepts to Remember

Commercial Property Coverage
Building and Personal Property Coverage Form
coinsurance
Causes of Loss—Basic Form
Causes of Loss—Broad Form
Causes of Loss—Special Form
Causes of Loss—Earthquake Form
blanket insurance
reporting forms
full value reporting clause
Agreed Value Coverage
Builders' Risk Coverage Form
business interruption insurance
contingent business interruption
Extra Expense Coverage Form
Leasehold Interest Coverage Form
boiler and machinery insurance
accounts receivable insurance
valuable papers insurance

ocean marine insurance
inland marine insurance
cargo insurance
hull insurance
freight insurance
protection and indemnity (P&I) insurance
transportation forms
perils of transportation
equipment floaters
processing and storage floaters
consignment and sales floaters
dealers forms
Employee Dishonesty Coverage Form
discovery period
Extortion Coverage Form
Computer Fraud Coverage Form
Robbery and Safe Burglary Coverage Form

Theft, Disappearance and Destruction Form
Premise Burglary Coverage Form
workers compensation coverage
employers liability coverage
Other States Insurance
product liability
Commercial General Liability (CGL) Coverage Form
occurrence form
claims-made form
personal and advertising injury liability
Dram Shop or Liquor Liability Policy
hired automobiles
non-owned automobiles
common carrier
Commercial Umbrella Liability Policy

Questions for Review

1. Identify and briefly describe the seven broad categories into which commercial insurance coverages are classified in the text.

2. Explain the purpose of the Buildings and Personal Property Coverage Form, indicating the type(s) of property it is designed to cover and the perils against which it provides protection.

3. Briefly describe the provisions of a reporting form that apply in the event that the insured (a) is late in filing a report, or (b) underreports the values on hand.

4. Distinguish between business interruption insurance and extra expense insurance and explain the circumstances in which each form of coverage is required.

5. Briefly describe the nature of contingent business interruption insurance, and give two specific examples in which contingent business interruption insurance would be needed.

6. List and briefly distinguish among the four types of coverage that may be written as a part of an ocean marine policy.

7. Identify and briefly describe the six broad classes into which inland marine coverages may be divided.

8. Identify and briefly describe the three broad classes into which business floater policies may be divided and give an example of a floater policy from each class.

9. Describe the coverage "trigger" under a fidelity bond, indicating the time at which a covered loss must have occurred and the time at which it must be discovered and reported to the insurer.

10. Briefly distinguish between "burglary" and "robbery."

11. In what way is boiler and machinery insurance fundamentally different from other forms of property insurance?

12. Why does the Workers Compensation and Employers Liability Policy not contain a specific statement of the benefits that it provides?

13. What is the purpose of the Other States Insurance optionally available under the Workers Compensation and Employers Liability Policy? Why is it needed?

14. What basic forms of general liability insurance are included in the Commercial Liability Policy?

15. Distinguish between a "claims-made" liability policy and an "occurrence" policy. Under what circumstances are "claims-made" policies used?

16. Why is it advisable for an employer to purchase employers' non-ownership automobile liability coverage, even though the firm's employees may carry their own insurance?

17. Identify the four automobile insurance forms that are used in the commercial lines field. Why do you suspect that there is not a single commercial automobile form as there is in the personal lines field?

18. Under what circumstances is a common carrier liable for damage to goods in its custody? How is the liability exposure associated with this exposure insured?

19. In view of a common carrier's broad liability for damage to goods it transports, why might the owner of goods being shipped by common carrier elect to purchase insurance on such goods?

20. The Businessowners Policy is a standard package approach to insuring small businesses. Briefly describe the general nature of the Businessowners Policy program, and identify the coverages that are included on a mandatory basis.

Questions for Discussion

1. With respect to each type of coverage discussed in this chapter, indicate whether the coverage would probably be considered "essential," "important," or "optional" in programming insurance for the largest bookstore on or near your campus.

2. Why might a business firm that purchases fire and extended coverage on its buildings and personal property also need to purchase inland marine insurance?

3. What elements of the employee dishonesty exposure make it difficult to estimate the size of the loss that can occur? In what way does the fidelity exposure differ from other property exposures?

4. The liability exposures of a business firm are far more complex than those of an individual. What characteristics of the business firm make this so?

5. Of the liability exposures discussed in this chapter, which do you suspect are the most frequently overlooked in programming liability insurance for business firms?

Suggestions for Additional Reading

Hillman, Bruce. *Commercial Property Coverage Guide.* Cincinnati, OH: National Underwriter Co., 1997.

Huebner, S. S., Kenneth Black, Jr., and Bernard L. Webb. *Property and Liability Insurance*, 4th ed. Englewood Cliffs, NJ: Prentice Hall, 1995. Chapters 12–22, 25–29, 33.

Krause, George E. *Businessowners Policy Coverage Guide.* Cincinnati, OH: National Underwriter Co., 1997.

Malecki, Donald S., Ronald C. Horn, Eric A. Wiening, and Arthur L. Flitner. *Commercial Liability Insurance and Risk Management*, 4th ed., vol. 1 and vol. 2. Malvern, PA: American Institute for CPCU, 1995, 1996.

Malecki, Donald S., and Arthur L. Flitner. *Commercial General Liability*, 6th ed. Cincinnati, OH: National Underwriter Co., 1997.

Trieschman, James D., Eric A. Wiening, Bob A. Hedges, Jerome Trupin, and Arthur L. Flitner. *Commercial Property Insurance and Risk Management*, 4th ed., vol. 1 and vol. 2. Malvern, PA: American Institute for CPCU, 1994.

Your Guide to the ISO Commercial Line Policies, 3rd ed. Boston: John Liner Organization, 1991.

Websites to Explore

Aviation Association Underwriters: http://www.aau.com/

Best's Review-Property/Casualty Edition: http://www.ambest.com/review/lh/index.html

Business Insurance Magazine: http://www.businessinsurance.com/

Defense Research Institute, Inc.: http://www.dri.org

National Association of Surety Bond Producers: http://www.nasbp.org

National Fire Protection Association: http://www.nfpa.org

RISKWeb: http://www.RISKWeb.com/

Rough Notes Company: http://www.roughnotes.com/

Surety Association of America: http://www.surety.org

CHAPTER 25

Insurance In The Future

We should all be concerned about the future because we will have to spend the rest of our lives there.
—Charles F. Kettering

CHAPTER OBJECTIVES

When you have finished this chapter, you should be able to

- Outline the most likely changes in the future environment of insurance

- Identify the continuing problems of the insurance industry and the possible solutions to those problems

- Discuss career opportunities in insurance and the necessary training to prepare for those opportunities

Since the end of World War II, the insurance industry has experienced remarkable growth. Concurrent with this growth, it has undergone significant change. The multiple-line transition, the introduction of package policies, variable annuities and variable life insurance, universal life, changes in the regulatory framework, adoption of automobile no-fault laws, continued expansion of the Social Security system, and the involvement of government as a provider of private insurance are all a part of the changing environment within which insurance operates. This final chapter examines the implications of future economic and social changes for the insurance industry. Just as the industry has had to adjust in the past to developments in its environment, future changes undoubtedly will be demanded.

Projecting past trends to predict a future environment is always subject to error, for things may not continue to happen in the future as they have in the past. Still, we can gain some insight into the probable future of the insurance industry and the nature of the industry itself by extrapolating some developments of the current environment within which the insurance industry operates.

Social Insurance Programs

The growth of the private insurance sector is influenced by the extent to which the government acts as a source of financial security for citizens. Although some social insurance is sold by private insurers (most notably workers compensation), most social insurance programs in the United States are operated by the government.

The Social Security System

The problems afflicting the Social Security system were discussed in Chapter 10. As noted in that discussion, the system faces long-range financial problems. These problems are likely to come to a head shortly after the turn of the century. The growing imbalance between workers and beneficiaries and the automatic increases in benefits have put the system on a collision course with insolvency. Although several solutions (such as reducing benefits and increasing the retirement age) have been suggested in the past, Congress has seemed unwilling to make the tough decisions that are required. As the 1990s came to a close and the Armageddon for OASDI seemed nearer, Congressional attention became more focused. In addition to the timeworn suggestions for reducing and deferring benefits, serious discussion about the possibility of privatizing Social Security began. Although there are many who favor this approach, there are some legislators who fear even a modest degree of privatization, viewing it as a first step toward full privatization and the loss of Social Security's income redistribution effects.

Medicare

The Medicare system faces problems that mirror those of the OASDI program. With a growing number of beneficiaries and fewer workers per beneficiary, Medicare will reach a crisis stage shortly after the turn of the century. Although it is conceivable that the solution to the nation's general problem of financing health care (discussed next) may address the Medicare problem, most of the proposals for reform of health care financing generally have avoided suggesting changes in Medicare.

Numerous changes in the system have been legislated over the years in attempts to save the system. The most recent change was the addition of Medicare+Choice, which is expected to extend the cost-saving features of managed care to the Medicare system. Although these changes may defer the time at which the imbalance between income from taxpayers and outgo to beneficiaries occurs, financing the Medicare system remains a problem in search of a solution.

Health Insurance

Although health insurance is a private form of insurance, we have witnessed a shift in national attitudes toward the risks associated with medical expenses. Our current philosophy is that the risk of health care costs is a fundamental risk, and that a national policy is needed to define the ways in which this risk will be addressed. The Congress and the nation are engaged in deliberations over how this risk will be managed.

In Chapter 16, we identified problems facing the nation with respect to health care delivery and financing: access to health care and the increasing cost of health care. These problems are among the most troublesome areas facing both the insurance industry and society today. For the insurance industry, the influence of runaway health care costs is pervasive. In addition to the obvious impact on health insurance, the cost of hospital and physicians' services are a significant factor in the cost of automobile insurance, general liability insurance, and workers compensation insurance. Despite the attention focused on the problem, health care financing and health insurance remain problems in search of a solution.

Changes in the Legal Environment

Changes in the laws of society have always had a significant impact on the insurance industry, and this will remain so in the coming decades. To a large extent, the growth of the insurance industry will be determined by the legal environment within which it operates. Legislation in many areas affects the need for security and the manner in which that security is provided.

Changes in the Tort System

The automobile no-fault laws enacted during the 1970s are an example of how legislation can influence the insurance industry. Not only did these laws alter the structure of benefits payable for automobile accidents, they also created a legal requirement for automobile insurance where none had previously existed. Before 1971, only three states had compulsory automobile liability insurance laws. State legislatures have increased this number to 41. During the 1990s, the notion of automobile no-fault legislation was resurrected at the federal level in the form of choice no-fault, discussed in Chapter 23. Congressional response was lukewarm and nothing significant occurred on this front.

In recent years, the debate over tort reform has moved from no-fault auto to other areas. In the 1990s, virtually every state enacted some type of tort reform, usually involving limitations on joint-and-several liability, pain and suffering, and punitive damages. Almost immediately, the constitutionality of these reforms was challenged in court.[1] The challenges to state tort reform statutes intensified the efforts of those who believe that tort reform is required at the federal level. Pressure for federal reform in the tort system will likely focus on product liability and medical malpractice.

In 1996, after a decade of lobbying by manufacturers, doctors, drug companies, and other business groups, Congress finally passed national tort reform legislation, the *Common Sense Product Liability Reform Act of 1996,* only to see President

Clinton veto it. An attempt by the House to override the veto failed. The Act would have created a uniform federal product liability standard; restricting and capping punitive damages would have limited a defendant's liability for noneconomic damages to its degree of negligence. It would also have barred cases against manufacturers of durable goods and workplace goods more than 15 years old. Finally, the bill would also have applied the so-called "loser pays rule," in which the unsuccessful party in a suit pays the attorneys' fees of the prevailing party. In 1998, an effort to enact a more limited version of product liability reform failed to gain passage. No product liability reform activity occurred in Congress in 1999.

The debate over tort reform will continue and changes will undoubtedly continue at the state level. Although public sentiment seems to support national tort reform, plaintiff's lawyers and Ralph Nader's Public Citizen organization have taken the lead in opposing legal reform. According to those who oppose legal reform, the current system gives those who are injured access to the court system to which they might otherwise be denied. The eventual resolution of the debate over the tort system will have an important effect on the price and availability of liability insurance for these exposures.

Pollution and Environmental Impairment Liability

More than a dozen federal statutes establish regulations relating to the environment and pollution, and many states have added their own laws in this area.[2] The Environmental Protection Agency (EPA) has identified 38,000 hazardous waste sites in need of cleanup or containment and estimates that at least 25 percent of the nation's 2.3 million

---

[1]A study of challenges to state tort reform laws conducted by the American Tort Reform Association found that 72 decisions since 1985 overturned the reform laws, while 140 decisions sustained the laws. American Tort Reform Association, *The Reformer* (Winter 1997–1998) vol. 2, no. 4.

[2]These include, for example, the Resource Conservation and Recovery Act, the Clean Water Act, the Clean Air Act, the Safe Drinking Water Act, the Toxic Substances Control Act, and the Comprehensive Environmental Response, Compensation, and Liability Act (Superfund).

Tidbits, Vignettes, and Conundrums 25.1

Medicare Fraud

In a report released March 21, 2000, the Inspector General of the U.S. Health and Human Services highlighted problems in the management of Medicare by the Health Care Financing Administration (HCFA). Government auditors have estimated that Medicare lost $13.5 billion last year because of fraud, waste, and mistakes. That's about 8 percent of the amount Medicare paid directly to medical providers. HCFA responded that the rate of improper payments is decreasing, having been reduced from 14 percent in 1994 to 8 percent in 1998.

---

underground gasoline storage tanks may have leaked into the soil and groundwaters. These and other inactive and abandoned hazardous waste disposal sites are the subject of the Comprehensive Environmental Response, Compensation, and Liability Act (CERCLA, also known as *Superfund*), which was passed in late 1980 and renewed in 1986 and 1991. In those instances in which responsible parties cannot be identified, the cleanup costs are covered by the Superfund. Where the responsible party (an owner and operator, the transporter who selected the site, or the generator of the waste) can be identified, such party is responsible for the cleanup cost.

Almost from the inception of Superfund, insurers have engaged in a debate with both industry and government over the responsibility of polluters under the act and the coverage for pollution cleanup costs under the CGL. In 1986, after several unsuccessful attempts to limit coverage for pollution losses to those that are accidental and unexpected, insurers added a total pollution exclusion to the CGL policy, specifically excluding pollution cleanup costs. Whether cleanup costs are covered under the pre–1986 general liability occurrence forms is unsettled. The Supreme Courts in several states have addressed the question of whether government-mandated cleanup costs constitute damages under the policy and have reached conflicting conclusions.[3] In many instances, however, insurers have been held liable under policies long expired, some dating back to the 1940s.

In the 20 years since Congress created it, Superfund has become the world's most expensive environmental program. Instead of cleaning sites, the bulk of Superfund monies have gone to lawyers, consultants, and administrative expenses. The reason, according to critics, is Superfund's retroactive, strict, joint-and-several liability mechanism, which allows responsibility for cleanup costs to be shifted to any party whose activity involved wastes found at a site. By mandating a system under which liability may be assigned to any potentially responsible party (PRP)—regardless of that party's degree of fault—Congress created a system under which litigation was inevitable. Further, by making liability retroactive in cases involving pre–1980 sites (that were operated under different disposal laws than those now in force), Congress created a liability exposure that is incompatible with the functioning of insurance markets. Insurers for parties held liable under Superfund's retroactive

---

[3]State supreme courts in California, Iowa, Massachusetts, Minnesota, North Carolina, and Washington have ruled that pollution cleanup costs fall within the definition of damages under pre–1986 CGL policies. State supreme courts in Maine and New Hampshire have ruled that they do not.

liability provisions are unable to pass cleanup-related costs on to insurance buyers because the policies under which coverage is provided expired many years ago.

When the companies or people responsible for contamination at Superfund sites cannot be found, or cannot perform or pay for the cleanup work, cleanup costs are paid from the Superfund Trust Fund. Until 1995, the Trust Fund money came mainly from taxes on the chemical and petroleum industries. The authority for levying these taxes expired in 1995 and no revenues from taxes have been collected since that time. In 1991, Congress extended Superfund until 1995, but as of 2000, despite attempts by every Congress since 1994 to pass renewal legislation, Superfund remains in limbo.

The future of Superfund remains an area of significant concern in the insurance industry and in society. Estimates of the industry's ultimate burden from these claims have ranged from $40 billion to $1 trillion, with a large portion of the costs representing legal expenses.[4] In large part, the resolution of the pollution liability problems depends on the provisions Congress includes in any new Superfund legislation.

Workers Compensation Laws

Some observers are questioning the fragmentation of our system for compensating the disabled. Workers compensation laws provide coverage for work-related disability and private health insurance covers other types of disability. Since the need for income is the same for work-related disabilities and other disabilities, some people believe that it would make sense to eliminate the distinction and cover all disabilities under expanded public and private programs. One authority has recommended that the reliance on workers compensation as the primary payer of benefits for work-related injuries be reduced.[5] There is an increased interest in the notion that some form of 24-hour coverage should be adopted as an alternative to separate coverage for occupational disabilities under workers compensation and coverage for other disabilities under health insurance disability policies.

Some impediments to 24-hour coverage are structural in nature. The workers compensation system was accepted by employers because of the exclusive remedy doctrine. Employers and their insurers are reluctant to relinquish the exclusive remedy protection of workers compensation due to a fear that litigation would increase costs. Currently, a few states have enacted enabling legislation that allows employers and their insurers to adopt 24-hour coverage as an alternative to workers compensation. Many observers believe that 24-hour coverage is both desirable and inevitable.

Protection for Catastrophe Exposure

As a result of increased population density and associated capital investment, the concentration of asset values in some areas has increased the potential for catastrophe losses. Simulation studies indicate that the potential for a megacatastrophe—ranging upward to $100 billion or more—exists in several areas on both the East and West Coasts. Insurance companies have become increasingly concerned as the magnitude of catastrophe losses that have occurred has increased. This concern was heightened by the $15.5 billion insured losses of Hurricane Andrew in 1992, followed by the $12.5 billion in losses from the Northridge, California, earthquake in 1994. With the increased concentration of values, it is argued, it is only a matter of time before a megacatastrophe occurs. Every earthquake and hurricane

---

[4]A report published in October 1995 by Standard and Poor's predicted that the cost would be approximately $40 billion, or more than 20 percent of the industry's capital and surplus. See *Standard and Poor's Creditweek*, October 30, 1995, p. 43.

[5]See Michael L. Murray, "Workers Compensation—A Benefit Out of Time," *Benefits Quarterly*, vol. 1, no. 2 (Second Quarter 1985).

that occurs is inevitably followed by dire predictions that "the next one could be worse."

In the wake of these disasters, California, Florida, and Hawaii created state catastrophe funds to provide direct insurance or reinsurance for hurricane and/or earthquake losses. Other states that have considered state catastrophe funding programs include New York, Texas, Louisiana, and North Carolina.

Despite the creation of the state disaster funds, there has been a growing demand for a federal national disaster reinsurance program. The first proposal for a federal reinsurance program came in 1990, the year after the Loma Prieta earthquake in California. National disaster plan initiatives have been introduced in every session of Congress since that time. In 1999, the House Banking Committee passed disaster reinsurance legislation, *Homeowners Insurance Availability Act* (H.R. 21), a hybrid of two bills introduced the previous year. The bill would authorize the Treasury Department to sell up to $25 billion of disaster reinsurance to qualified state insurance programs and indirectly, via an auction process, to insurance companies and financial institutions. The Senate was expected to take up a companion measure early in 2000.

Federal Tax Laws

Provisions of the federal tax laws—especially those relating to the taxation of life and health insurance, annuities, pensions, and other qualified retirement programs—have important implications for the insurance industry and for insurance consumers. In January 1998, in his 1999 budget address, President Clinton proposed several changes in the tax laws that would have decreased the appeal of life insurance and annuities as investments. With respect to annuities, he proposed making exchanges of annuity contracts taxable events. For life insurance, he proposed that the cost of death protection be excluded from the basis in computing the taxable gain on cash value distributions. President Clinton also proposed eliminating the *Crummey rule*, which has been an essential underpinning of irrevocable life insurance trusts for decades. Although none of the recommendations were implemented, they reflect areas of change in the law that could be resurrected as part of any initiative to increase taxes.

In the 106th Congress, estate tax repeal was a high priority among Republicans and many Democrats. Two bills were introduced for the total repeal of the estate tax, and two others proposed its phase-out over a ten-year period.

Changes in the federal tax laws that affect the taxation of insurance products would have an effect on the appeal of the relevant insurance or annuity products as investments.

Possible Changes in Regulation

Although changes in insurance regulation are likely in several areas, two major issues relating to regulation dominate the current environment: proposals to amend or repeal the McCarran–Ferguson Act and the possible erosion of state regulatory authority. Besides these issues, there are several other developments on the horizon whose future depends on the resolution of these first two issues.

Repeal or Modification of McCarran–Ferguson

In the opinion of many observers, the threat to state regulation is greater today than at any time in its history. Changes in the marketplace, including globalization of insurance, electronic commerce, and the convergence in the financial services market, have led many to question the viability of state regulation. Concerns about the inefficiency of state regulation have led some industry members to propose creation of a federal insurance regulator. In response, the NIAC has embarked on an ambitious agenda to modernize state regulation and to create a national system of regulation by increasing the level of coordination among the states.

Erosion of State Regulatory Authority

In addition to the possible repeal of McCarran–Ferguson, there are other developments that have the potential to significantly diminish the states' authority to regulate insurance. These developments involve a type of creeping federal regulation created by Congress and in some instances, by the courts. The erosion of state authority has resulted from legislation that preempts state authority in specific limited areas and court decisions that give federal agencies preeminence in resolving state–federal jurisdiction conflicts.

One area in which the authority of the states to regulate insurance has been significantly eroded is health insurance. As explained in Chapter 16, the enactment of ERISA created a dual regulatory structure in this country for health insurance and health benefits. Although subsequent legislation gives states authority to regulate MEWAs, self-insured, single-employer plans that cover an estimated 48 million persons remain exempt from state regulation under ERISA. Despite the past problems associated with MEWAs, several of the health insurance reform proposals in Congress in recent years would authorize a new variety of MEWA, association health plans (AHPs), which would be exempt from all state mandated laws.

A second area in which the regulatory authority of the states has been diminished is with respect to the insurance-related activities of commercial banks. Prior to 1999, federal banking laws generally prohibited banks from underwriting or selling insurance, although some banks have been permitted to engage in insurance agency activities under a limited exception to the rule separating banking and commerce.[6] During the 1990s, the Office of the Comptroller of Currency (OCC), which regulates national banks, argued that the OCC, not state insurance departments, has the right to regulate the insurance-related activities of banks. The OCC was upheld by the U.S. Supreme Court in the 1996 *Barnett Bank v. Nelson* case.[7] The adverse effect of the decision was compounded by the *Chevron* doctrine, according to which the courts will give deference to the federal regulator when interpreting federal law.[8] In 1999, Congress enacted legislation (discussed later in the chapter) that reconfirmed state authority for the regulation of insurance. This legislation also authorized a significant expansion in the insurance-related activities of commercial banks. With the accelerating convergence of banking and insurance both nationally and internationally, the question of how bank-insurance activities will be regulated is an important one for the future of state regulation.

Other agencies in the federal bureaucracy that have oversight of private insurers and private insurance markets include the Federal Emergency Management Agency (flood insurance) and the Department of Agriculture (federal crop insurance). The proposed U.S. Treasury catastrophe reinsurance program would further involve the federal government in the insurance industry.

Although the future regulation of insurance is uncertain, it appears that if the states' authority to regulate the insurance industry is further diminished, it will be the result of the gradual preemption of that authority by the courts and the Congress, rather than by the repeal of McCarran–Ferguson.

---

[6]In 1916, Congress amended the *National Banking Act* to give banks in towns of fewer than 5000 inhabitants the power to sell insurance. Then, in 1956, in the *Bank Holding Company Act*, Congress authorized insurance agency affiliates of banks through the holding company mechanism, in which a bank holding company is allowed to own both a bank and an insurance agency.

[7]United States Supreme Court—No. 94–1837 *Barnett Bank of Marion County, N. A., Petitioner v. Bill Nelson, Florida Insurance Commissioner, et al.* [March 26, 1996]. *Barnett* was the Supreme Court's second recent opinion upholding the OCC's position on an issue relating to the powers of national banks. In January 1995, the Court held that national banks are permitted to sell annuities as agents without regard to state insurance laws. *NationsBank of North Carolina v. Variable Annuity Life Insurance Co.*, 115 S.Ct. 810 (1995).

[8]*Chevron U.S.A. Inc. v. Natural Resources Defense Council, Inc.*, 467 U.S. 837(1984).

Changes in the Insurance Industry

Not only will the environment within which the insurance industry functions change in the future, but there will undoubtedly also be changes within the industry itself. From the consumer's perspective, the most significant changes within the industry are likely to be shifts in the pattern of distribution and the development of new forms of protection.

Changes in Industry Structure

The number of insurance companies continues to change and will undoubtedly change in the future. During the past decade, there have been a number of mergers, acquisitions, and consolidations that have been defining characteristics in the insurance industry. In the life insurance field, after peaking at 2345 companies in 1988, the number of life insurers dropped to about 1700 by 1998. Although the decrease in the number of property and liability companies was smaller (from 3460 to 3350), a large percentage of property and liability insurers are regional companies that operate in geographically limited markets. Among the major property and liability insurers, there have been more than 500 mergers, acquisitions, and consolidations over the past decade.[9]

Besides the decrease in the number of insurers, a number of insurers have changed their organization structure, either by demutualizing or reorganizations under mutual holding company laws enacted by the state. It is likely that the number of insurers, both in the life insurance field and in the property and liability field, will continue to decline as mergers and consolidations continue.

[9]American Council of Life Insurance, *1997 Life Insurance Fact Book* (Washington, DC: ACLI, 1997); Insurance Services Office, *Insurer Financial Results: 1997* (New York: ISO, 1998).

Changes in Agents' Compensation

Although the practice has been restricted primarily to larger accounts, there is a movement within the industry toward a fee system of compensating agents and brokers for their services in lieu of the traditional commission system. The concept has met serious opposition from some quarters, but for larger accounts it has considerable merit. The traditional commission system ties the agent's compensation to the hazard faced by the insured, which seems illogical. It seems difficult to justify a higher compensation to the agent for handling one account simply because the insured has a frame building, when the work involved is no greater (and may be less) than that done for another account where the insured owns a brick building. The challenges to antirebating laws discussed in Chapter 6 are likely to increase, which may speed the movement toward a net pricing system.

Banks and Insurance

In 1999, after 20 years of debate, Congress repealed the *Glass–Steagall Act of 1933* and replaced it with the *Financial Services Modernization Act* (also known as the *Gramm–Leach–Bliley Act*). This ended the compartmentalization of the financial services industry in the United States that had existed since the Great Depression. The Glass–Steagall Act prohibited banks from owning insurance companies or security brokerage firms. As a result, the financial services industry in the United States has been divided into three broad segments: commercial banking, the insurance industry, and the securities brokerage field. The Financial Services Modernization Act now allows full-scale affiliations among the three industries.

The changes enacted in 1999 have been several decades in the making and occurred against a backdrop of convergence of the three segments of the financial services industry globally. The combination of banking and insurance in Europe has given rise to a phenomenon known as *bancassurance*, the full integration of retail banking and insurance operations.[10] Competition from foreign banks that can freely underwrite and distribute insurance products gave these insurers a competitive advantage over U.S. insurers, which could not offer the same wide mix of insurance, commercial banking, and investment banking services. The Financial Services Modernization Act was as much about international competition as it was about competition in the United States.

With the repeal of Glass–Steagall, the financial services industry will change significantly. In fact, the changes began even before the repeal of Glass–Steagall, as the industry anticipated Congressional Action.[11] From the perspective of the insurance industry, the most significant feature of the Financial Services Modernization Act is the provisions relating to regulation. The law affirms the principle of functional regulation, in which banking activities are regulated by banking authorities (the OCC or state regulator), insurance activities are regulated by the state insurance departments, and security-related activities are regulated by the Securities and Exchange Commission. Equally important, the new law ends the deference that the courts had granted to federal regulators.

Insurance Marketing and the World Wide Web

Another area in which changes in insurance marketing are certain is the World Wide Web (WWW). By the close of the century, most U.S. insurers had established a presence on the Web offering extensive information about their insurance products. A number had actually begun selling insurance online. Given the enormous success in marketing other products over the Web, it seems likely that the potential for marketing insurance via this medium is significant.[12] Regulators are understandably concerned over the implications of Web-based marketing of insurance. In 1998, the NAIC adopted a white paper prepared by the Internet Marketing Issues Group of the Market Conduct and Consumer Affairs Subcommittee that addresses a variety of regulatory issues related to insurance sold over the Internet.

Globalization of Insurance

Although the United States has traditionally dominated the world insurance market, its domination has declined over the past three decades as insurers outside the United States have increased their share of the world premium volume. In 1970, the United States controlled 70 percent of the world premium volume. By 2000, it had fallen to 38 percent.

A part of the growing percentage of world premiums written by foreign insurers is simply a reflection of the growth in the gross national product of foreign countries relative to the United States. As economic activity increases in a nation, the premiums written to protect assets against loss also increase. Thus, a part of the decreased share of world premiums indicated for the United States results not from a decrease in U.S. premiums, but from an increase in premiums in other nations. Individuals and businesses in a particular country tend to purchase their insurance from

---

[10]ING Group, the largest financial services group in the Netherlands, often is cited as a *bancassurance* success story. Although many European banks now sell insurance, ING was the first to implement wholesale mergers between banks and insurers.

[11]In April 1998, Citicorp and the Travelers Group announced plans to merge, a consolidation that was technically illegal at the time it was announced. Had it not been for the repeal of the *Glass–Steagall Act*, after a five-year grace period under the *Bank Holding Company Act*, Travelers would be required to divest itself of the activities that conflicted with the *Glass–Steagall Act*.

[12]Professor James R. Garven reports that insurers marketing via the WWW have a 23 percent cost advantage over insurers that use the traditional agency system. *Insurance Online Marketing Report*, vol. 1, no. 1 (September 1999), p. 2.

domestic insurers, and the growth of other economies has brought a corresponding growth in the insurance premiums in other countries.

Financial Services Trade Barriers

Governments worldwide are deregulating and privatizing, and with deregulation, barriers to trade have also fallen. European countries, in particular, have been working for years to promote competition throughout the continent by removing their various national trade barriers. The leader in this movement is the European Union, whose twelve-member nations have agreed to a phased-in mutual reduction of restrictive laws and regulations.[13] For insurance and other financial services, the European Commission in Brussels has issued a series of twenty-one directives to harmonize insurance regulations in member countries. Since these directives became effective in 1994, an insurer licensed and regulated by one member nation has authorization to operate anywhere in the European Union.

In 1997, a World Trade Organization pact further opened international markets for insurance and financial services generally. The pact is the first multilateral, legally enforceable agreement covering trade and investment in financial services. As such it provides a framework to reduce or eliminate government barriers that prevent financial services from being freely provided across national borders, or that discriminate against firms with foreign ownership.[14] Although the pact creates a framework for the reduction of trade barriers related to insurance, little progress has been made. Whether trade barriers will actually be reduced remains to be seen.

Foreign Insurers in the United States

Coincident with their preparations to capitalize on the opening of European markets, some foreign insurers moved to expand their writings in the United States. Although foreign insurers wrote less than 10 percent of the total premiums in the United States in 1999, many authorities are predicting that the U.S. market will experience major competition from international insurers, including companies from the United Kingdom, France, Germany, and Holland. Companies in these nations are well capitalized, and are seeking areas for expansion. One way in which foreign companies can enter the United States is by acquiring U.S. insurers. Foreign insurers have made a number of significant acquisitions during the 1990s.[15]

Although few Japanese insurers have indicated an inclination to enter the U.S. market, there are signs that this could change. Tokyo Fire and Marine and Nippon Life have both acquired U.S. subsidiaries. With the expansion of Japanese investment in the United States, Japanese insurers will probably increase their presence in the United States to provide coverage for U.S. subsidiaries of Japanese companies they insure in Japan.

U.S. Insurers Abroad

Although less than 5 percent of the U.S. insurance industry's premium writings is generated in foreign countries, there are 60 to 70 U.S. insurers

---

[13]The current member states in the European Union are Belgium, Denmark, France, Germany, Greece, Ireland, Italy, Luxembourg, the Netherlands, Portugal, Spain, and the United Kingdom.

[14]John Jennings, "WTO Agreement: Not Perfect But Good Enough," *National Underwriter, Property & Casualty/Risk Management Edition* (December 22, 1997), p. 1.

[15]These acquisitions include the purchase in 1990 of Fireman's Fund for $3.3 billion by Germany's $54 billion-in-assets Allianz. In addition to this major acquisition, Zurich Insurance of Switzerland acquired Maryland Casualty Insurance Company, Winterthur of Switzerland acquired General Casualty, and Home Insurance Company was acquired by the Trygg-Hansa Group of Sweden and Industrial Mutual of Finland. In 1993, financially troubled Mutual Benefit Life Insurance Company sold its group health, accident, and life business to the Belgium-based N.V. AMEV, through its U.S. subsidiary, AMEV Holdings, Inc.

that have established a significant presence abroad. At the top of this list is the American International Group (AIG). AIG is the largest commercial and industrial insurer in the United States, and over one-half its total operating income comes from foreign sources. Other leading U.S. insurers with a significant presence in the international market include CIGNA, Chubb, Reliance National Insurance Company, and the St. Paul Fire and Marine Insurance Company. One motivation of U.S. insurers that establish an overseas presence is the desire to serve U.S. corporations operating abroad. An equally important goal is to participate in the premium growth that will occur in a number of foreign countries in the near future, which will by far exceed the growth in U.S. premiums.

Major U.S. brokerage firms have also established a presence in many foreign countries, and have contracts with the foreign insurers. In fact, with a few exceptions, such as AIG, U.S. brokers have become international at a faster rate than have U.S. insurers. Even brokers that do not have offices in foreign countries have established working relationships with affiliate agencies abroad,

giving them access to foreign markets and providing a network through which they can serve the foreign insurance needs of their U.S. clients.

The globalization of insurance will undoubtedly accelerate with the changes in the financial services industry and the elimination of restrictions on cross-border insurance sales. The extent to which U.S. insurers will participate in this international market remains to be seen.

Some Persistent Problems

Although the future of the insurance industry appears bright, a number of unresolved problems remain. In general, these problems have existed for a long time, but they have increased somewhat in recent years.

The AIDS Problem

One of the serious problems facing the life and health insurance segments of the industry in the immediate future is the growth of acquired

---

Tidbits, Vignettes, and Conundrums 25.2

Islamic Insurance

Although insurance has found widespread acceptance in the western world, this is not necessarily the case in other cultures. Islamic scholars, for example, disagree on the issue of whether insurance is permitted or is prohibited by the Koran. Some argue that because insurance in the modern sense did not exist during the Prophet's life, it should be permitted. Scholars who argue that insurance is prohibited do so on the ground that it involves prohibited activities that are similar to our concepts of uncertainty in contracts, gambling, and usury (*Gharar, Maisir* and *Riba*), all of

which are prohibited in the Koran. *Takaful*, a mechanism that operates on a basis that is somewhat similar to insurance, has developed as a form of Islamic insurance. The term *Takaful* comes from the Arabic meaning "guarantee each other." *Takaful* is a process of mutual guarantee, in which the participants make contributions to a fund to alleviate the misfortunes of the participants. Participants in a *Takaful* make donations or gifts (*Tabarru*) that represent their contributions to helping all members of the group, including themselves.

immunodeficiency syndrome (AIDS). The most immediate problem arising out of the spread of AIDS is the cost of medical expenses associated with the disease, a problem that has serious implications for the health insurance field. Victims of AIDS who do not have health insurance at the time they contract the disease find it almost impossible to obtain coverage except through state health insurance pools. Even here, however, the cost is sometimes prohibitive.

The spread of AIDS is also a serious problem for the life insurance industry. Because persons infected with AIDS incur abnormally high mortality, they are generally considered uninsurable by private insurers, and underwriting for life insurance has become a focal point in the debate over AIDS and insurance. Given the potential for adverse selection, insurance companies are anxious to preserve their traditional right to evaluate applicants and reject those who have an abnormally high loss potential. The conflicting view is that some precautions are required to ensure that insurers do not unfairly discriminate in their efforts to avoid the AIDS burden. For example, since a large percentage of infected people are male homosexuals, regulators are concerned that insurers will attempt to shortcut the underwriting process and underwrite on the basis of sexual preference, rather than attempting to determine if the applicant is actually infected. In 1987, the NAIC adopted underwriting guidelines that prohibit consideration of a person's sexual preference in underwriting insurance. The guidelines were endorsed by the American Council of Life Insurance and the Health Insurance Association of America, which had hoped that in return for this endorsement the NAIC could be persuaded to recognize the need for insurers to be able to test for infection by the AIDS virus.[16]

AIDS-related claims will remain an important problem for the life and health insurance indus-try as long as the disease itself remains a problem for society, reflecting once again the way in which the problems facing the insurance industry mirror those facing society.

Genetic Testing

In recent years, researchers have made great strides in understanding the structure of human DNA and, in particular, identifying genes that contribute or cause physical conditions. With this increased information, it will become possible for insurers to use genetic testing to identify individuals likely to contract particular diseases. The potential impact on life and health insurance underwriting is enormous.

Some critics argue that insurers should not be permitted to use the information gathered from genetic testing in their underwriting decisions. Their rationale is similar to that used by some states when they attempted to prohibit insurers from testing for the AIDS virus. If insurers have access to information that identifies a genetic disorder, they may charge a higher premium, exclude coverage for the condition, or simply reject the application. In addition to the affordability and availability implications, there are confidentiality concerns when third parties have access to the results of a genetic test.

Where insurers are denied access to this information, of course, significant adverse selection will result. Individuals who have undergone genetic testing and become aware they face a high risk of illness will seek to buy large amounts of insurance. Without access to that same information, the premium charged by insurers would not appropriately reflect the risk being assumed. The result is inadequate pricing and cross-subsidization between those with and without genetic disorders.

Crime and Its Associated Costs

Most Americans today rank crime as a major problem for the nation. Because much of the

---

[16]Insurance departments in California, Massachusetts, New York, and the District of Columbia adopted regulations prohibiting the use of the AIDS antibody test (also known as ELISA, HTLV-III, or the HIV test) as an underwriting tool. The regulations were challenged by the insurance industry and were overturned by the courts.

property that is damaged by vandalism, arson, and looting is covered by insurance, crime is a major concern for the property and liability insurance industry.

Arson and Crimes Against Property

According to the National Fire Protection Association, arson accounts for roughly one out of every seven structural fires (as opposed to vehicle or outdoor fires). Some of these fires were intentionally set to defraud insurers, but others were set by persons with no direct financial interest in the property. In fact, less than 15 percent of arson suspects are motivated by a desire to defraud an insurer. The major cause of arson is vandalism, which is attested to by the fact that the majority of those people arrested for arson are young people. Fires caused by arson cost the insurance industry literally billions of dollars annually.[17]

Other crimes against property—burglary, robbery, and theft—are growing faster than the population. To cite one example, according to the FBI, vehicle theft is the fastest-growing type of crime in the United States. Combined with automobile insurance fraud, it has caused insurance costs to escalate sharply. In addition to the loss of property that is taken or destroyed, many criminal acts also result in bodily injury to the victims of the crime. Damage and theft of property and the attendant bodily injuries inflate insurers' loss ratios and account for a significant part of total insurance claims.

Insurance Fraud

In addition to criminal acts against property such as arson and theft, insurers also suffer losses as a result of fraudulent claims by professional criminals. Insurance fraud has been rampant in the area of health insurance, where unethical physicians collaborate with the criminals to document fictitious claims. Staged automobile accidents are another scam that has been prevalent in some parts of the country.

Although criminal acts are clearly a problem for insurers, they are also a problem for insurance buyers. Based on what the reader has learned about the way in which insurance operates, it should be clear that the increased loss costs that result from criminal activity such as arson, vehicle theft, and crimes against property are passed on to insureds by insurance companies in the form of higher rates. Policyholders pay for losses resulting from these criminal acts in the same way that they pay for the inflated claims by ordinary policyholders who exaggerate their claims. Law-abiding citizens who would never think of stealing sometimes have no qualms about inflating a property damage claim so that the recovery will be sufficient to cover the deductible that would otherwise apply. For insurers and their policyholders, the result is the same as the losses occasioned by arson and other overt criminal acts.

Availability and Affordability of Insurance

Another troublesome issue facing the property and liability insurance industry today is the high cost of insurance for some segments of the insurance-buying public and the response that this high cost has generated among those buyers and among certain other groups. Increasingly, the demand is heard that insurance must be made available to all who want and need it and that it must be made available at affordable rates.

Although the main issue for some people today is still the question of the method we should use to provide the subsidy to those who demand availability and affordability, the entire debate has prompted a reappraisal of the systems that have been used in the past to subsidize some buyers. Increasingly, it is recognized that the distinctions

---

[17]Although insurers rightfully deny payment to arsonists when arson can be proved, the provisions of property policies related to mortgagees that we discussed in Chapter 19 allow the mortgagee or other lender to collect for a loss, even when it is established that the owner torched the property. In addition, as explained in Chapter 19, the NAIC model law aimed at preventing discrimination against domestic abuse victims, requires an insurer to pay claims to an innocent abuse victim for intentional property damage caused by a third party, even when that party is a co-insured under the Homeowners Policy.

Tidbits, Vignettes, and Conundrums 25.3

Insurance Fraud

According to the Washington, D.C.-based Coalition Against Insurance Fraud (CAIF), insurance fraud adds something on the order of $85 billion to the cost of insurance. In a survey conducted by CAIF, when asked why people might commit insurance fraud, about two-thirds of the respondents said that insurance companies make undue profits and that insurance premiums increase regardless of claims. About 6 in 10 agree that people are only looking for a fair return on premiums paid; nearly the same number (56%) agree that rates are based on the assumption that fraud occurs. About one-third of the respondents reported the belief that people are forced to lie to get insurance (33%), or that nobody tells the truth on applications (27%).

---

among the approaches to subsidization are artificial and that in the last analysis it makes little difference if the subsidy is granted through an industry pool, through the tax system, or through the rating system. In each case, one group in society pays a part of the costs that would—absent government interference—fall on a different group. The issue of subsidies in insurance remains a little-understood subject.

Lack of Consumer Sophistication

Another persistent problem facing the insurance industry is the lack of sophistication on the part of consumers. Although many insurance buyers have become more knowledgeable over the past few decades, the majority of consumers misunderstand the purpose of insurance and the way it operates. Much of the dissatisfaction with insurance is based on this misunderstanding. With little notion of the way insurance works or the principles of risk management, many consumers feel that an insurance policy is not worthwhile unless it covers every possible small loss. They find buying insurance a frustrating experience and are frequently disappointed or dissatisfied with their purchase. They complain that the cost of insurance is too high, that deductibles are simply a scheme developed by insurers to get out of paying their just claims, and that the entire insurance mechanism is some sort of "rip-off."

By this time, it is hoped that the reader has gained a sufficient understanding to see just why many criticisms are unjustified. As we have learned, insurance operates on a very simple principle: individuals exposed to loss contribute to a fund, and those who suffer losses are compensated out of this fund. Cutting away the complicated details of the mechanism, it is a system in which the losses of a few are shared by the many. There is nothing magical or mysterious about it, unless one considers the law of averages to be magical or mysterious. When losses are high, rates must also be high. The insurance industry is very much like a conduit or pipe. Money is paid into one end of the conduit and flows out the other. Most of the complaints have focused on the amount of money going in, ignoring the fact that the money going in is a function of the money going out. In a sense, insurance is merely a mirror that reflects the loss experience throughout the economy. Although considerable progress has been made in consumer education, much remains to be done.

Unwarranted Criticism of the Insurance Industry

The insurance industry is a convenient target and criticism of the industry abounds. Industry critics are particularly fond of the charge that because of its exemption from the federal antitrust laws, the industry operates as a cartel, engaging in conspiracies to increase prices. The allegation ignores the obvious fact that if insurers conspire to increase rates, they must also conspire to decrease them. Periods in which insurance prices increase significantly usually follow periods of intense price cutting, when competition drives rates below their actuarial level. When insurance prices decrease below actuarially sound levels, insurers are accused of mismanagement. When premiums increase during the hard phase of the cycle, they are accused of gouging consumers or of conspiracy. There is a much simpler and more believable explanation: that the industry is fiercely competitive and that it therefore exhibits the characteristics of a competitive industry.

The simple fact is that there are some types of insurance that are demonstrably unprofitable for insurers. Given the choice between insuring exposures on which they are virtually guaranteed to lose money and those on which they can reasonably expect to earn money, insurance companies logically choose the latter. One criticism of which some critics are especially fond is that "insurance companies refuse to write some types of insurance simply because those lines are unprofitable." It is a commentary on the complexity of the issues and the confusion in which society finds itself that this criticism goes unanswered.

Those who criticize the reluctance of insurers to write unprofitable classes of business when their overall profitability is satisfactory are, in effect, arguing for cross-subsidies. They would like to make the insurance industry a mechanism for taxing and redistributing wealth. The question is really whether insurers should overcharge buyers of homeowners insurance to subsidize the cost of product liability insurance, or whether premiums for fire and marine insurance should be loaded to cover losses under malpractice insurance. These questions involve complex value judgments that should not be made lightly.

It is undeniable that the insurance industry—like virtually all segments of society—includes some ethically challenged individuals who have few qualms about engaging in dishonest or questionable practices detrimental to consumers. Identifying and eliminating these undesirables is an important responsibility, both for regulators and for other members of the industry. It is of no help, in this respect, when bogus criticism of legitimate business strategies, based on the law of averages, are mischaracterized as a conspiracy to exploit consumers. Unfounded criticism obstructs and interferes with efforts to deal with the real crimes and misdemeanors that may actually occur.

Career Opportunities in Insurance

Economists predict substantial increases in this nation's gross national product and personal income over the next two decades, with corresponding increases in per-capita income. Rising population, housing, businesses, and income will be accompanied by a heightened awareness of the need for financial security. Given the long-range growth expected throughout the economy, with new advances in technology, new products, and higher personal incomes, the continued expansion of the insurance industry seems assured. Regardless of possible inroads by government, the future of the industry seems bright indeed. Increased security needs and the ability to pay for them point to a tremendous growth for the insurance business. This will lead to an increase in the industry's employment needs, and the nation's insurers will be offering thousands of career opportunities to college graduates.

Today's insurers carry on a growing number of activities: rehabilitation of the injured, product safety, industrial hygiene, and medical research. Because the industry serves the needs of consumers in many ways, a broad variety of career positions has been created to provide these services. It would be difficult to find another industry that offers such diversified positions as mathematician, nurse, lawyer, computer analyst, and engineer in addition to the more traditional insurance careers in sales, investments, underwriting, and claims. Regardless of whether the individual's academic work has been in business administration, engineering, economics, mathematics, or computer applications, he or she is likely to find an attractive career in the highly diversified insurance industry.

Broadly speaking, employment opportunities in the insurance field may be divided into two major categories: sales and nonsales. Positions within each of these categories exist in both the property and liability industry and the life and health insurance fields. In addition to jobs within the insurance industry proper, employment opportunities also can be found in the growing field of risk management and corporate insurance buying.

Opportunities in the Insurance Sales Field

Sales positions in the property and liability field exist with direct-writing companies and with independent agencies. Most direct-writing companies recruit on college campuses, seeking sales representatives at the same time they hire other specialists. Although independent agencies have a continuing need for personal lines and commercial lines producers, most agencies do not have sophisticated personnel recruitment programs and so do not recruit on college campuses. Positions with independent agencies therefore must be sought out by the prospective applicant.

Life insurance general agents and district sales managers generally conduct intensive recruiting campaigns on college campuses. Because the turnover rate in life insurance sales is high, there is a constant need for new agents. Many companies have had moderate success in reducing the turnover rate through more intensive selection procedures and better training of new life salespeople.

Sales positions in the insurance field demand a high degree of expertise. Insurance agents do not sell a standard tangible product, but a special kind of financial security that must be tailored to meet the needs of the individual policyholder. In many situations, the role of the agent is far removed from the stereotype of the high-pressure, fast-talking sales type. The professional agent functions as an adviser to his or her clients, filling a role similar to that of the attorney or accountant.

Although the demands on those who enter the field of insurance sales are great, the rewards are also great. Insurance sales positions where the pay is based on a commission rather than salary rank among the highest in the nation in potential earnings.

Nonsales Opportunities in the Insurance Industry

Although many insurance agencies employ nonsales personnel, the person seeking a nonsales position within the insurance industry would be best advised to seek employment with an insurance company.

In the property and liability field, insurance companies recruit actuaries,[18] underwriters, claims personnel, and marketing representatives in addition to the more traditional noninsurance positions found in every business. Underwriters, as the reader will recall, are charged with the responsibility of deciding which of the various applicants for insurance should be accepted. Claims persons handle the delicate problems of loss adjustment. Marketing representatives generally serve as a link between the company and its agency force, although in the case of direct-writing companies, the marketing representative may deal directly with the consumer.

Life insurance companies offer positions similar to those of the property and liability firms. Many life insurance companies have their own staff of actuaries. Special marketing representatives are also employed by the life insurance companies to deal with group programs and pension plans and to as-

---

[18]Larger property and liability insurers have their own staff of actuaries, while smaller companies usually use actuarial consultants.

sist the company's agents in the technical details of more complicated life insurance cases.

Positions with both property and liability insurers and life insurers are challenging and rewarding. Increasingly, the insurance company employee is performing a decision-oriented job, requiring independent judgment and a greater degree of individual responsibility at every level. Executives in the insurance field have traditionally risen from within the industry. This practice of internal promotion is an additional advantage to people choosing the insurance business as a career. Capable people have a greater probability of rapid promotion because of the great expansion the industry foresees during the next 20 years, which is going to result in a shortage of managerial personnel.

Salary levels in both the property and liability field and the life and health insurance field vary with each company and in each region of the country. These positions typically pay less than insurance sales positions, but the U.S. Department of Labor reports that starting salaries for professional workers in the insurance industry are generally comparable with those for similar positions in other industries.

Another important factor to most employees is the industry's stability. Insurance buyers regard insurance as a necessity even during periods of economic recession, and to a large measure the insurance industry is immune to the up-and-down fluctuations of the economy.

Opportunities in the Risk Management Field

Risk management positions are sometimes difficult for the new college graduate to obtain. Many companies seeking to fill staff risk management positions prefer to hire seasoned and experienced personnel from the insurance industry itself. Although occasionally the risk management department of a large corporation will hire a trainee, these positions, like those in independent agencies, must generally be sought out by the applicant.

Concluding Observation

The field of insurance continues to be an exciting one. It constantly faces new problems and challenges, somehow coping with each and surviving to go on to meet new problems. The changing nature of the industry makes it all the more attractive as a field of endeavor. Few industries hold out the opportunity and excitement of a career in insurance today. Besides the challenging and rewarding work itself, the industry also offers many of the intangible factors that young men and women are seeking: the opportunity to render a worthwhile service to society, a socially useful career with high prestige, and greater-than-average personal rewards.

Important Concepts to Remember

Comprehensive Environmental Response, Compensation, and Liability Act (CERCLA)

Superfund
unregulated market
net pricing system

globalization of insurance
European Union

Questions for Review

1. Describe the major problems facing the Old-Age, Survivors, and Disability Program and the Medicare program in the future.

2. Identify and describe the changes in the tort system that may affect the insurance industry during the next decade.

3. Identify the features of the *Comprehensive Environmental Response, Compensation, and Liability Act* (CERCLA) that have made the Superfund program ineffective. What problems does the industry face with respect to environmental losses? What proposals have been made to address these problems?

4. Describe the major features of the proposals for addressing the insurance industry's exposure to catastrophe loss.

5. What are the significant changes that may be expected in the regulation of insurance during the next decade?

6. Describe the proposals for changes in federal tax law discussed in the chapter and explain how each proposal would affect the demand for insurance.

7. Describe the legal impediments to the combination of banking and insurance in the U.S. and explain the legislative proposals to address these impediments.

8. Describe the issues that face the life and health insurance industry as a result of advances in genetic testing.

9. Identify and describe the factors that are contributing to the globalization of insurance.

10. What is the impact of crime and fraud on the insurance industry?

Questions for Discussion

1. Which of the factors discussed in this chapter do you personally believe will have the greatest impact on the insurance industry during the next decade? Why?

2. One of the chronic problems facing the insurance industry is the lack of consumer sophistication and the misconceptions on the part of insurance buyers regarding the purpose of insurance. What, in your opinion, can the insurance industry do to remedy this problem?

3. Do you think that there is a solution to the conflict between capital's need for an adequate return and the public's entitlement to the security of the insurance product? Should insurance companies be permitted to refuse to write those lines of insurance that are unprofitable?

4. What do you think of the employment outlook in the insurance industry? Do you think that it will be better, about the same, or worse than the situation in other fields?

5. What do you think is the most important principle you have learned in this course? Why?

Suggestions for Additional Reading

Brockmeier, Warren G. (ed.). *The Impact of Consumer Activism on the Insurance Industry*. Malvern, PA: Society of CPCU, 1991.

Ensfellner, Karl C., and Mark S. Dorfman. "The Transition to a Single Insurance Market in the European Union." *Risk Management and Insurance Review*, vol. 1, no. 2 (Winter 1998).

Focus on the Future: The Insurance Industry Looks Toward the 21st Century. Malvern, PA: Society of Chartered Property and Casualty Underwriters, 1987.

Huber, Peter. "The Environmental Liability Dilemma." *CPCU Journal*, vol. 40, no. 4 (December 1987).

Hutchin, James W. "Managing Risks in a Global Environment." *The John Liner Letter* (Fall 1995).

Insurance Services Office. *Long-Term Profitability: The Risk-Return Tradeoff*. New York: Insurance Services Office, 1990.

Long, John D. *Ethics, Morality, and Insurance.* Bloomington, IN: Bureau of Business Research, Graduate School of Business, Indiana University, 1971.

Skipper, Harold D. Jr. *International Risk and Insurance: An Environmental-Managerial Approach.* Irwin, NY: McGraw-Hill, 1998.

Slattery, Thomas J. "Globalization a Necessity for Insurers." *National Underwriter Property and Casualty Edition* (June 24, 1991).

Websites to Explore

Coalition Against Insurance Fraud: http://www.insurancefraud.org

Environmental Protection Agency: http://www.epa.gov/

Global Risk Management Network: http://www.grmn.com/pages/welcome.asp

Institute for Global Insurance Education: http://www.igie.org/

Insurance Fraud Bureau: http://www.ifb.org/

Insurance Information Institute—Superfund: http://www.iii.org/media/SUPERFND.HTM

International Association of Insurance Fraud Agencies, Inc.: http://www.iaifa.org

National Disaster Coalition: http://www.naturaldisaster.org

National Insurance Crime Bureau: http://www.nicb.com

Risk World: http://www.riskworld.com/

The Insurance Job Center: http://connectyou.com/talent/

APPENDIX A

Glossary

Absolute Liability A legal doctrine under which one can be held liable even in the absence of negligence having been proven, as in the case of workers compensation.

Acceptance Agreeing to terms by means of which a bargain is concluded and the parties are bound; the binding of an insurance contract by the insurer.

Accident An event or occurrence that is unforeseen and unintended.

Accident Insurance A form of health insurance against loss by accidental bodily injury.

Accidental Bodily Injury Injury to the body of the insured as the result of an accident.

Accidental Death Benefit A provision added to a life insurance policy for payment of an additional benefit in case of death by accidental means; it is often referred to as "double indemnity."

Accumulation Period A specified period of time, such as 90 days, during which the insured person must incur eligible medical expenses at least equal to the deductible amount in order to establish a benefit period under a major medical expense or comprehensive medical expense policy.

Acquisition Cost That portion of an insurance premium that represents the cost of producing the insurance business; it includes the agent's commission, the company field expense, and other related expenses.

Actual Cash Value The limit of indemnification under the Standard Fire Policy and other property contracts; in most cases it is replacement cost minus depreciation.

Actuary Person professionally trained in the technical aspects of insurance and related fields, particularly in the mathematics of insurance such as the calculation of premiums, reserves, and other values.

Additional Living Expense Insurance paying the extra expense involved in living elsewhere during the period of time it is impossible to remain in a dwelling that has been damaged by fire or another insured peril.

Adjustment Bureau An organization that contracts with insurers to provide loss settlement services on behalf of those insurers.

Adjustable Life Insurance A type of life insurance that allows the policyholder to change the plan of insurance, raise or lower the face amount of the policy, increase or decrease the premium, and lengthen or shorten the protection period.

Adjuster One who settles insurance claims; may be a salaried employee or an independent operator.

Administrator A person authorized to administer the estate of a deceased person by the court; his or her duties are to collect assets of the estate, pay its debts, and distribute the residue to those entitled: he or she resembles an executor, who is appointed by the will of the deceased. The administrator is appointed by the court and not by the deceased and therefore must give security for the administration of the estate, called an administration bond.

Admitted Assets Those assets of an insurer which under state law can be taken into account in representing the financial position of the company.

Admitted Company An insurer of another state or country licensed under the laws of a state to do business in that state.

Advance Premium Mutual An insurance company owned by its policyholders that charges an advance premium that is expected to cover losses and expenses; policies may be assessable or nonassessable.

Adverse Selection The tendency of persons with a higher-than-average probability of loss to seek or continue insurance to a greater extent than do persons with an average or below-average probability of loss.

Advisory Organization A cooperative ratemaking body that is supported by member companies; advisory organizations collect loss statistics and publish trended loss costs.

Agent In property and casualty insurance, an individual authorized by an insurance company to create, modify, and terminate contracts of insurance; in life insurance, a sales and service representative who is also called a "life underwriter."

Aggregate The greatest amount recoverable on account of a single loss or during a policy period, or on a single project.

AIDS Acquired immune deficiency syndrome. A fatal, incurable disease caused by a virus that can damage the brain and destroy the bodys ability to fight off illness.

Alien Company An insurance company organized under the laws of a foreign country.

All-Risk A term commonly used by insurance people to describe broad forms of coverage; it is misleading because no property or liability insurance policy is truly an all-risk coverage. There is a concerted effort to eliminate use of this term and to replace it with the term open peril.

Allied Lines A term that has been adopted to refer to the lines of insurance that are allied with property insurance; these coverages provide protection against perils traditionally written by fire companies, such as sprinkler leakage, water damage, and earthquake.

Alternate Delivery Systems Health services provided in other than an inpatient, acute-care hospital, which are designed to provide needed services in a more cost-effective manner.

Ambulatory Care Medical services that are provided on an outpatient (nonhospitalized) basis; services may include diagnosis, treatment, and rehabilitation.

American Agency System The term applied to the system of insurance marketing in which the agent is an independent business operator rather than an employee of the company.

Amortized Value The amount at a given point in time to which the purchase price of a bond purchased at a discount or premium has been increased or decreased.

Annual Statement An insurer's financial report to insurance departments issued at the end of the year. The report is required by the various state insurance departments and is made according to a form agreed upon by the supervising authorities.

Annuitant The person during whose life an annuity is payable, usually the person to receive the annuity.

Annuity A contract that provides an income for a specified period of time, such as a number of years or for life.

Annuity Certain A contract that provides an income for a specified number of years, regardless of life or death, to the insured if living or to his or her beneficiary if deceased.

Apportionment A division according to the interests of the various parties therein, as the apportionment clause in a fire policy.

Appraisal An estimate of value, loss, or damage; see Arbitration.

Arbitration The submitting of a matter in dispute to the judgment of a specified number of disinterested persons called "arbitrators," whose decision, called an "award," is binding upon the parties.

Arson The criminal act of maliciously burning or attempting to burn property.

Assault An intentional, unlawful threat of bodily injury to another by force, or force unlawfully directed toward the person of another, under such circumstances as to create well-founded fear of imminent peril, coupled with apparent present ability to execute the attempt; see also Battery.

Assessable Insurance to which the policyholder may be required to contribute in the event the company becomes unable to pay its losses; confined to certain mutual companies.

Assessment A charge sometimes levied against policyholders by certain types of companies.

Assessment Mutual an insurance company owned by its policyholders that issues policies under which the policyholders may be assessed for losses and expenses.

Assigned Risk An applicant for automobile or workers compensation insurance declined by one or more companies; such a risk may be assigned to designated companies as directed by recognized authority. The operation is called an "assigned risk plan."

Assignment The legal transfer of one person's interest in an insurance policy to another person.

Assured A person who has been insured by an insurance company or underwriter against loss.

Attorney-In-Fact One appointed to act for another; the chief administrative officer of a reciprocal insurance group, who uses his or her power of attorney to commit the members of the group as insurers of each other; also one who executes a surety bond on behalf of the company being represented.

Attractive Nuisance   A dangerous place, condition, or object that is particularly attractive to children; in these cases the courts have frequently held that where "attractiveness" exists, the owner is under a duty to take steps to prevent injury to those who may be attracted and the owner may be held liable for failure to do so.

Automatic Premium Loan   A provision in a life insurance policy authorizing the insurer to pay automatically by means of a policy loan any premium not paid by the end of the grace period.

Automatic Treaty   A reinsurance contract under which risks written by the reinsured are automatically assumed by the reinsurer subject only to the terms and conditions of the treaty.

Automobile Insurance Plan   A state pool in which each automobile insurer in the state accepts a portion of the undesirable automobile insurance applicants; formerly called "assigned risk plans."

Automobile Liability Insurance   A form of liability insurance that is specifically designed to indemnify for loss incurred through legal liability for bodily injury and damage to property of others caused by accident arising out of ownership or operation of an automobile.

Bailee   One who has possession of property belonging to another.

Bailment   A delivery of goods or personal property by one person to another in trust for the execution of a special object upon or in relation to such goods. Bailment may be for the benefit of the bailee, for the benefit of the bailor, or for mutual benefit. In addition, bailment may be gratuitous or may be a bailment for hire.

Bailor   The owner of property that has been delivered to and is in the possession of another.

Battery   Any unlawful beating or other wrongful physical violence or constraint inflicted upon a human being without his or her consent; see Assault.

Beneficiary   One for whose benefit a contract is made; the person to whom a policy of insurance is payable.

Beneficiary, Contingent   The person or persons designated to receive the death benefit if the primary beneficiary dies prior to the death of the insured.

Beneficiary, Irrevocable   A beneficiary that cannot be altered by the insured, the insured having relinquished the right to change the beneficiary designation.

Beneficiary, Primary   The person or persons designated to receive the benefits under the policy.

Betterment   An improvement rendering property better than mere repairs would do.

Bid   A proposal or offer.

Binder   A written agreement (sometimes oral) whereby one party agrees to insure another party pending receipt of, and final action upon, the application.

Binding Receipt   In life insurance, a receipt for a premium that accompanies the application for insurance. It binds the company if issuance is approved, to make the policy effective from the date of the receipt.

Blanket   In property and liability, used to designate insurance that extends to more than one location, or one class of property or one employee.

Blue Cross   An independent, nonprofit membership corporation providing protection against the costs of hospital care in a limited geographical area.

Blue Shield   An independent, nonprofit membership corporation providing protection against the costs of surgery and other items of medical care in a limited geographical area.

Bodily Injury   Physical injury to a person.

Boiler and Machinery Insurance   Coverage for loss arising out of the operation of pressure, mechanical, and electrical equipment; it may cover loss suffered by the boiler and machinery itself and may include damage done to other property, as well as business interruption losses.

Bond   A written agreement of obligation under seal; the person to whom the obligation is owed is called "obligee"; the person liable for the undertaking is called the "obligor" or "principal"; if a third party guarantees performance of the agreement, he or she is called the "surety."

Bottomry   In the early days of marine insurance, a ship owner would borrow money on a mortgage on the ship, and the mortgage would provide that if the ship were lost, the borrower would not have to repay the loan. This was bottomry, which thus combined money lending with insurance. When cargo instead of hull was involved, it was called "respondentia."

Breach of Contract   Failure to comply with the terms or conditions incorporated in a insurance policy, frequently resulting in a restriction of coverage or a voiding of a policy itself.

Broker An individual who arranges and services insurance policies on behalf of the insurance buyer; he or she is the representative of the insured, although the broker receives compensation in the form of a commission from the company.

Bureau See Advisory Organization.

Burglary Felonious abstraction of property from within premises by persons making felonious entry by force of which there are visible marks on the exterior.

Business Interruption Insurance covering the loss of earnings resulting from, and occurring after, destruction of property; also called "use and occupancy insurance."

Business Life Insurance Life insurance purchased by a business enterprise on the life of a member of the firm: it is often bought by partnerships to protect the surviving partners against loss caused by the death of a partner, or by a corporation to reimburse it for loss caused by the death of a key employee.

Businessowners Policy A multiple-line package policy for small businesses that includes property and liability coverages.

Calendar Year Deductible In health insurance, the amount of expense that must be borne by the insured during a calendar year before the health insurance policy makes payment for loss.

Capital Sum A lump sum payable for dismemberment and sight losses.

Capitation A method of payment for health services in which a physician or hospital is paid a fixed, per capita amount for each person served regardless of the actual number of services provided to each person.

Captive Agent An agent who, by contract, represents only one company and its affiliates.

Captive Insurer An insurance company established by a parent firm for the purpose of insuring the parent's exposures.

Cash Surrender Value The amount available in cash upon voluntary termination of a policy before it becomes payable by death or maturity.

Cash Value Accumulation Test One of two tests used in determining if a contract is a life insurance policy for the purpose of the Internal Revenue Code; see Cash Value Corridor Test.

Cash Value Corridor Test One of two tests used in determining if a contract is a life insurance policy for the purpose of the Internal Revenue Code; see Cash Value Accumulation Test.

Casualty Insurance A classification of insurance coverages used in the monoline era consisting of workers compensation, liability, crime, glass, and boiler coverages; used to distinguish such coverages from "fire" or property coverages.

Catastrophe Loss A loss of unusual size; a shock loss; a very large loss.

Ceding Company A company that has placed reinsurance as distinguished from the company that has accepted the reinsurance.

Certified Professional Public Adjuster (CPPA) Professional designation granted to public adjusters who pass a rigorous examination and meet specified eligibility requirements.

Cession The amount of a risk which the insurance company reinsures; the amount passed on to the reinsurer.

Change of Occupation Clause Standard provision in health insurance policies which reduces benefits if the insured changes to a more hazardous occupation.

Chartered Life Underwriter (CLU) Professional designation granted to persons in the life insurance field who pass a series of rigorous examinations and meet specified eligibility requirements.

Chartered Property Casualty Underwriter (CPCU) Professional designation granted to persons in the property and liability insurance field who pass a series of rigorous examinations and meet specified eligibility requirements.

Claim Notification to an insurance company that payment of an amount is due under the terms of a policy.

Claims-Made Form A liability insurance policy under which coverage applies to claims made during the policy period; see Occurrence Form.

Class Rating An approach to ratemaking in which a price per unit of insurance is computed for all applicants with a given set of characteristics. For example, the rate may apply to all persons of a given age and sex, to all buildings of a certain type of construction, or to all businesses of a certain type.

CLU See Chartered Life Underwriter.

Coinsurance In property and casualty insurance, a clause or provision in an insurance policy requiring a specified amount of insurance based on the value of the property insured; normally, there is a premium reduction for purchasing insurance to some percentage of the value of the property—if the insured fails to comply with the clause, he or she will suffer a penalty in the event of partial loss; in health insurance, a policy provision requiring the insured to share a given percentage of the loss.

Collateral Source Rule A legal principle applicable in the area of tort liability, which holds that the plaintiff's measure of damage should not be mitigated by payments received from sources other than the tortfeasor.

Collusion A compact between persons usually to the detriment of other persons or for some improper purpose.

Combined Ratio A rough indication of the profitability of a property and liability insurer's underwriting operations, generally computed by adding the ratio of losses incurred to premiums earned and expenses incurred to premiums written.

Commercial The opposite of personal; of a business nature, usually mercantile or manufacturing.

Commission The fee paid by the insurance companies to agents for the sale of policies.

Common Carrier A firm that offers to transport merchandise for hire and must accept shipments from anyone who wishes to use its services. Different laws and rules govern common carriers than those applicable to private or contract carriers that only transport the goods of those with whom they have made agreements.

Common Law Distinguished from law created by enactment of statutes; common law comprises the body of principles and rules of action, which derive their authority solely from the judgments and decrees of the courts or from usages and customs of immemorial antiquity.

Comparative Negligence A modification of the principle of contributory negligence. In those jurisdictions which follow the principle of comparative negligence, negligence on the part of the injured party will not necessarily defeat the claim, but will be considered in determining the amount of damages.

Compensation Wages, salaries, awards, fees, commissions, or financial returns of any kind.

Completed Operations A commercial liability insurance coverage applicable to liability arising out of work performed by the insured after such work has been finished.

Comprehensive A loosely used term signifying broad or extensive insurance coverage.

Comprehensive General Liability (CGL) A business liability policy that covers a variety of exposures in a single contract.

Comprehensive Major Medical Insurance A policy designed to give the protection offered by both a basic and major medical health insurance policy; it is characterized by a low "deductible" amount, coinsurance feature, and high maximum benefits ($500,000, $1 million or more). Some policies are written without a maximum limit.

Comprehensive Personal Liability Insurance A type of insurance that reimburses the policyholder if he or she becomes liable to pay money for damage or injury he or she has caused to others; this form does not include automobile liability but does include almost every activity of the policyholder except business operations.

Concealment Deliberate failure to reveal material facts that would affect the validity of a policy of insurance.

Concurrent Covering the same kind of property at the same location under the same terms and conditions, with the same types of coverage, as two or more insurance policies.

Concurrent Causation A legal doctrine in property insurance that makes the insurer liable for damage when property is damaged by two causes, one of which is excluded and the other covered.

Conditionally Renewable A continuation provision in health insurance under which the insurer may not cancel the policy during its term but can refuse to renew under specified circumstances.

Conditions Those provisions in insurance contracts that qualify the insurer's promise of indemnity or impose obligations on the insured.

Confining Sickness That which confines an individual to his or her home or a hospital (visits to physicians and hospitals are generally considered as not terminating confinement).

Consequential Loss Loss occurring after, and as a result of, some other loss, as loss of profits resulting from a fire or a loss of frozen foods resulting from electrical failure.

Consideration Price, token, or other matter used as an inducement for the completion of a contract, as an insurance premium.

Constructive Total Loss A loss of sufficient amount to make the cost of salvaging or repairing the property equal to or greater than the value of the property when repaired.

Contingent Conditional; depending upon another happening—a contingent beneficiary is one next in line after the first named.

Contingent Beneficiary In life insurance, a beneficiary who is entitled to receive proceeds if the primary beneficiary has died.

Contract Bond A surety bond issued to support the obligation of one who is engaged to perform under a contract.

Contractual Liability Legal liability assumed under contract.

Contribution A participation, as two insurance policies in the same loss.

Contributory Negligence The lack of ordinary care on the part of an injured person, which combines with the defendant's negligence and contributes to the injury as a proximate cause. In some jurisdictions, contributory negligence on the part of an injured party will defeat his or her claim.

Convention Blank See Annual Statement.

Conversion Wrongful appropriation to one's own use of property belonging to another.

Conversion Privilege Privilege granted in an insurance policy to convert to a different plan of insurance without providing evidence of insurability.

Convertible Term Insurance Term insurance that can be exchanged, at the option of the policyholder and without evidence of insurability, for another plan of insurance.

Coordination of Benefits A group health insurance policy provision designed to eliminate duplicate payments and provide the sequence in which coverage will apply when a person is insured under two contracts.

Corridor Deductible In health insurance, a deductible under a major medical policy that applies after coverage under a base plan is exhausted.

Cost Containment The control or reduction of inefficiencies in the consumption, allocation or production of health care services that contribute to higher than necessary costs.

Coverage The insurance afforded by the policy.

CPCU See Chartered Property Casualty Underwriter.

CPPA See Certified Professional Public Adjuster.

Credit Insurance A form of guarantee to manufacturers and wholesalers against loss resulting from default on the part of debtors.

Credit Life Insurance Term life insurance issued through a lender or lending agency to cover repayment of a specific loan, installment purchase, or other obligation in case of the debtor's death.

Crime A wrong against public laws or customs punishable by fine, imprisonment, or death after trial in a criminal court.

Crop-Hail Insurance Protection for monetary loss resulting from hail damage to growing crops.

Currently Insured Under OASDHI, the status of a worker who has at least six quarters of coverage out of the last thirteen quarters and whose beneficiaries are entitled to "currently insured" benefits.

Damages The amount claimed or allowed as compensation for injuries sustained or property damaged through the wrongful acts or the negligence of another; an award.

Declarations That part of an insurance policy containing the representations of the applicant.

Deductible A provision whereby an insured may be required to pay part of a loss, the insurance being excess over the amount of the deductible.

Deferred Annuity An annuity providing for the income payments to begin at some future date, such as in a specified number of years or at a specified age.

Defined Benefit Plan A pension plan in which the retirement benefit is defined and in which the employer's contribution is a function of that benefit.

Defined Contribution Plan A pension plan under which the payments into the plan are fixed, but the retirement benefit is variable; also called a money purchase plan.

Dental Insurance A type of health insurance that covers dental care expenses.

Dependency Period The period during which children will be dependent on a surviving parent.

Deposit Premium An original premium paid by the insured at the inception date of the policy; estimated premium, subject to later adjustment.

Depreciation The lessening of value through age, deterioration, and obsolescence.

Deviate To file or use a rate which is based upon but which departs from a standard bureau rate.

Diagnosis-Related Groups (DRGs) Standard categories of treatment used in a system that reimburses health care providers fixed amounts for all care given in connection with specific treatments.

Difference In Conditions (DIC) Insurance A broad form of open-peril property insurance written as an adjunct to policies that cover named perils.

Direct Loss Loss resulting directly and immediately from the hazard insured against.

Direct Writer An insurance company that deals directly with the insured through a salaried representative, as opposed to those insurers that use agents; also used to refer to insurers that operate through exclusive agents; in reinsurance, the company that originally writes the business.

Disability Inability to perform all or part of one's occupational duties because of an accident or illness; see Total Disability and Partial Disability.

Disability Benefit A provision added to a life insurance policy for waiver of premium, and sometimes payment of monthly income, if the insured becomes totally and permanently disabled.

Disability Income Insurance A form of health insurance that provides periodic payments to replace lost income when the insured is unable to work because of illness or injury.

Discovery Period The period after termination of an insurance policy or bond, or after the occurrence of a loss, within which the loss must be discovered to be covered.

Dismemberment Accidental loss of limb or sight.

Distress Insurer An insurance company specializing in substandard risk, usually in the field of automobile insurance.

Dividend In insurance contracts, the refund of a part of the premium paid at the beginning of a year which still remains after the company has made deductions for losses, expenses, and additions to reserves.

Dividend Addition An amount of paid-up insurance purchased with a policy dividend and added to the face amount of the policy.

Domestic Insurer A name given to a company in the state of its incorporation, as an Iowa company is domestic in the state of Iowa, foreign as to all other states, and alien as to all other countries.

Double Indemnity A provision under which certain benefits are doubled when an accident is due to specified circumstances, such as public conveyance accidents; in a life insurance policy, a provision that the face amount payable on death will be doubled if the death is a result of an accident.

Dread Disease Policy A limited form of health insurance that pays for treatment of specified diseases such as cancer.

Dram-Shop Law A state statute that imposes liability on sellers of alcoholic beverages in the event that the buyer causes bodily injury to another or in some cases, to himself or herself.

Duplication of Benefits Overlapping or identical coverage of the same insured under two or more health plans, usually the result of contracts of different insurance companies, service organizations, or prepayment plans; also known as multiple coverage.

Earned Premium Premium for which protection has been provided. When a premium is paid in advance for a policy period, the company "earns" a portion of that premium only as time elapses during that period.

Effective Date The date upon which the policy is put in force; the inception date.

Eligibility Period In group insurance, a period during which group members may enroll in the plan without providing evidence of insurability.

Elimination Period See Waiting Period.

Employee Retirement Income Security Act (ERISA) A 1974 federal statute that establishes minimum standards for pension plans.

Employer's Liability Legal liability imposed on an employer making him or her responsible to pay damages to an employee injured by the employer's negligence. Generally, replaced by "workers compensation," which pays the employee whether the employer has been negligent or not.

Endorsement A written amendment affecting the declarations, insuring agreements, exclusions, or conditions of an insurance policy; a rider.

Endowment Insurance Insurance payable to the insured if he or she is living on the maturity date stated in the policy, or to a beneficiary if the insured dies prior to that date.

Environmental Impairment Liability (EIL) Liability arising out of pollution.

Errors and Omissions Insurance Professional liability insurance for individuals in professions such as accounting, insurance, law, or real estate, where the exposure is primarily a property damage one as opposed to bodily injury.

Estate Possessions of a deceased person; possessions of a minor or incompetent person; possessions of a bankrupt person or corporation; worldly goods of anyone.

Estoppel An admission or declaration by which a person is prevented from proving the contrary.

Evidence of Insurability Any statement of proof of a person's physical condition and/or other factual information affecting his or her acceptance for insurance.

Excess That which goes beyond, as excess insurance, over and above a primary amount.

Excess of Loss Reinsurance A form of reinsurance whereby the reinsuring company reimburses the ceding company for the amount of loss the ceding company suffers over and above an agreed aggregate sum in any one loss or in a number of losses arising out of any one event.

Exclusion That which is expressly eliminated from the coverage of an insurance policy.

Exclusive Agency System An insurance marketing system under which the agent represents a single company or company group.

Expected Loss Ratio The percentage of the final rate allocated for the payment of losses.

Expense Ratio The proportionate relationship of an insurer's expenses to premium expressed as a percentage.

Experience Rating An insurance pricing system in which the insured's past experience determines the premium for the current protection.

Expiration The date upon which an insurance policy terminates unless continued or renewed by an additional premium.

Exposure Unit of measurement to which an insurance rate is applied.

Extended Coverage Insurance A standard package of perils usually sold in conjunction with the peril of fire; includes the perils of windstorm, hail, smoke, explosion, riot, riot attending a strike, civil commotion, vehicle, and aircraft.

Extended Term Insurance A form of insurance available as a nonforfeiture option; it provides the original amount of insurance for a limited period of time.

Extended Unemployment Insurance Benefits Additional unemployment benefits under a state-federal program payable during periods of high unemployment to workers who have exhausted their regular benefits.

Extra Expense Insurance A form of indirect loss property insurance that pays for the increased costs of continuing operations following damage to property by an insured peril.

Face Amount The amount stated on the face of a life insurance policy that will be paid in case of death or at the maturity of the contract; it does not include dividend additions, or additional amounts payable under accidental death or other special provisions.

Factory Mutuals A group of mutual companies, principally located in New England, specializing in the insurance of manufacturing properties.

Facultative Reinsurance Reinsurance effected item by item and accepted or declined by the reinsuring company after scrutiny, as opposed to reinsurance effected by treaty.

FAIR Plan Fair Access to Insurance Requirements state pools designed to provide insurance to property owners who are unable to obtain property insurance because of the location of their property or other factors over which they have no control.

Family Income Policy A life insurance policy, combining whole life and decreasing term insurance, under which the beneficiary receives income payments to the end of a specified period if the insured dies prior to the end of the period, and the face amount of the policy either at the end of the period or at the death of the insured.

Family Maintenance Policy Life insurance which pays, in addition to the face of the policy, a monthly income for a period commencing with the insured's death and continuing for the number of years specified; the period is most often 10, 15, or 20 years.

Family Policy A life insurance policy providing insurance on all or several family members in one contract, generally whole life insurance on the wage earner and smaller amounts of term insurance on the spouse and children, including those born after the policy is issued.

Family Purpose Doctrine A legal doctrine that imposes vicarious liability on the head of the family for operation of a family car by family members.

Federal Flood Insurance A federally subsidized flood insurance program enacted in 1968 under which flood insurance is available in areas that meet specific conditions.

Federal Insurance Administration A government office responsible for the supervision of insurance programs such as the Federal Riot Reinsurance Program, Federal Flood Insurance Plan, and Federal Crime Insurance Program.

Fellow Servant One who serves and is controlled by the same employer; also those engaged in the same common pursuit under the same general control.

Fellow Servant Rule Rule that a master is not liable for injuries to a servant caused by the negligence of a fellow servant engaged in the same general business and where the master has exercised due care in the selection of servants.

Fidelity Bond A contract of fidelity insurance; a guarantee of personal honesty of the person furnishing indemnity against defalcation or negligence; a form of insurance or suretyship that protects a party against loss from the dishonesty of employees.

Fiduciary A person or corporation having the duty created by undertaking to act primarily for another's benefit in matters connected with such undertaking, or an agent handling the business of another when the business he or she transacts or the money or property being handled is not his or her own or for his or her own benefit.

Field Supervisor A salaried employee of an insurance company, whose responsibilities are (a) production of new business through existing agents, (b) the appointment of new agents, (c) general supervision of the company's affairs in his or her territory.

File and Use Law A system of rate regulation in which rates may be used immediately by an insurer once they are filed with the state regulatory authority. The supervisory authority may later disapprove and rescind the rates.

Financial Responsibility Law A statute that requires motorists to show evidence of financial responsibility following an accident that involves bodily injury or property damage in excess of some amount; normally, proof of financial responsibility is given through a valid policy of insurance.

Fire As used in insurance contracts, combustion proceeding at a rate rapid enough to generate a flame, glow, or incandescence.

Fire Insurance Coverage for losses caused by fire and lightning, as well as the resultant damage caused by smoke and water.

Fire Legal Liability A form of liability insurance that covers damage to leased or rented property caused by fire or other specified perils.

Fleet A group, as of automobiles.

Floater A marine or fire policy, the coverage of which follows the movement of the property insured.

Flood Overflow of water from its natural boundaries. More specifically defined by the National Flood Act of 1968 as "a general and temporary condition of partial or complete inundation of normally dry land areas from (1) the overflow of inland or tidal waters or (2) the unusual and rapid accumulation or runoff of surface waters from any source."

Foreign Insurer An insurance company that is chartered in another state.

Franchise Insurance A class of life insurance in which individual policies are issued to members of a group, with an employer or other body collecting and/or remitting the premiums.

Fraternal Insurance A form of cooperative life or disability insurance that is available to members of a fraternal organization.

Friendly Fire A fire confined to the place it is supposed to be in (e.g., in a stove or similar place).

Fully Insured Under OASDHI, the status of a worker who has 40 quarters of coverage or one quarter of coverage for each year after 1950 or after age 21, if later, and who is entitled to "fully insured" benefits.

General Damages Amounts awarded in litigation to compensate for pain and suffering and other noneconomic loss.

Grace Period The period of time following the due date of a policy premium during which the payment of the premium will continue the policy and during which the policy is in full force and effect.

Graded Commission A reduced commission justified by the size of the premium.

Graded Expense A reduced expense item for the insurance company justified by the size of the premiums.

Graded Premium Whole Life A whole life contract for which the initial premium is low, but increases yearly until it levels off sometime between the tenth and twentieth years.

Gross Premium The premium for insurance that includes the provision for anticipated losses (the pure premium) and for the anticipated expenses (loading).

Group Annuity A policy providing annuities to a group of persons under a single master contract, with the individual members of the group holding certificates stating their coverage; it is usually issued to an employer for the benefit of employees.

Group Insurance Any insurance plan under which a number of individuals and their dependents are insured under a single policy, issued to a sponsor, with individual certificates given to each insured person; the most commonly written lines are life and accident and health.

Guaranteed Investment Contract (GIC) Investment instruments issued by insurers to pension plans that are similar to the certificates of deposit issued by commercial banks.

Guaranteed Renewable Policy A policy which the insured has the right to continue in force by the timely payment of premiums to a specified age (usually age 50), during which period the insurer has no right to make unilaterally any change in any provision of the policy while the policy is in force, but may make changes in premium rates by policyholder class.

Guest Laws State statutes which limit the right of action of an injured guest passenger in an automobile against the driver to instances of gross negligence or willful and wanton negligence.

Hazard A condition that creates or increases the probability of a loss.

Hazard, Moral The increase in the chance of loss caused by dishonest tendencies on the part of an insured.

Hazard, Morale The increase in the chance of loss or in the amount of loss that results from an attitude of carelessness or indifference simply because the loss will be paid by insurance.

Health Insurance A generic term applying to all types of insurance indemnifying or reimbursing for losses caused by bodily accident or sickness or for expenses of medical treatment necessitated by sickness or accidental bodily injury.

Health Maintenance Organization (HMO) A prepaid medical group practice plan for the provision of health care, in which individual subscribers pay an annual fee in return for entitlement to a wide range of health services. HMOs are both insurers and providers of health care.

Hold-Harmless Agreement A contract usually written whereby one party assumes legal liability on behalf of another party.

Hospital Indemnity A form of health insurance that provides a stipulated daily, weekly, or monthly indemnity during hospital confinement without regard to the actual expense of hospital confinement.

Hostile Fire A fire burning where none is intended.

Hull Insurance In ocean marine and aviation insurance, coverage for physical damage to a vessel or aircraft.

Improvements and Betterments Insurance Insurance that protects a tenant against loss to improvement made by him or her to property in which he or she is a tenant.

Incontestable Clause A provision that prevents the insurer from challenging the coverage because of alleged misstatements by the insured after a stipulated period has passed, usually two or three years.

Incurred Losses Losses actually sustained during a fixed period, usually a year. Incurred losses are customarily computed by the formula: losses paid during the period, plus outstanding losses at the end of the period, less outstanding losses at the beginning of the period.

Indemnity, Principle of A general legal principle related to insurance which holds that the individual recovering under an insurance policy should be restored to the approximate financial position he or she was in prior to the loss.

Independent Adjuster One who adjusts losses on behalf of companies but is not employed by any one. He or she is paid by fee for each loss adjusted.

Independent Agent A person operating under the American Agency System, representing several property and liability insurers, and dividing the policies he or she writes among the various companies represented.

Independent Contractor One who performs work for another in his or her own manner and method, and who is not subject to the control or direction of the party for whom the work is performed; he or she is not an employee of the party for whom the work is performed.

Indeterminate Premium Life Insurance Life insurance in which the premium may be adjusted upward or downward after inception, subject to a maximum premium stated in the policy.

Indirect Contingent; that which happens only after something else has occurred.

Individual Retirement Account (IRA) A tax-sheltered retirement plan established by an individual under which earnings accumulate tax free until distributed. Contributions up to $2250 are deductible for some persons.

Industrial Life Insurance Life insurance issued in small amounts, usually less than $1000, on a single life exclusive of additional benefits, with premiums payable on a monthly or more frequent basis, and generally collected at the insured's home by an agent of the company.

Inherent Vice A characteristic depreciation such as the fading of ink, a cracking of parchment, the graying of hair.

Inland Marine Insurance A broad type of insurance, generally covering articles that may be transported from one place to another; the essential condition is that the insured property be movable, though bridges, tunnels, and similar instrumentalities of transportation are also considered inland marine.

Insolvency Fund State plans created by law to guarantee payment of liabilities of insolvent insurers; also called guaranty funds.

Insurable Interest An interest that might be damaged if the peril insured against occurs; the possibility of a financial loss to an individual that can be protected against through insurance.

Insurance An economic device whereby the individual substitutes a small certain cost (the premium) for a large uncertain financial loss (the contingency insured against) that would exist if it were not for the insurance contract; an economic device for reducing and eliminating risk through the process of combining a sufficient number of homogeneous exposures into a group in order to make the losses predictable for the group as a whole.

Insurance Purchasing Group A group of firms or other organizations that band together under the provisions of the Risk Retention Act of 1986 for the purpose of buying insurance collectively.

Insurance Regulatory Information System (IRIS) A computerized model designed by the National Asso-

ciation of Insurance Commissioners for the detection of potential insurer insolvencies before they occur through analysis of selected audit ratios.

Insurance Services Office (ISO) The principal ratemaking organization for property and liability insurers.

Insured In life insurance, the person on whose life an insurance policy is issued; in property and liability insurance, the person to whom or on whose behalf benefits are payable under the policy.

Integration A coordination of retirement or disability benefits with benefits payable under Social Security, through a specific formula.

Interest-Adjusted Method A means of measuring differences in cost among life insurance policies that considers the time value of money.

Interest-Sensitive Whole Life A participating life insurance policy in which the dividends are geared to current money rates. Some insurers guarantee a particular rate for the first few years of the policy.

Intestate Leaving no will at death.

Invitee A person having an express or implied invitation to enter a given location.

Irrevocable Beneficiary A beneficiary designation that may be changed only with the consent of the beneficiary.

Joint-and-Last Survivor Annuity An annuity issued on two lives under which payments continue in whole or in part until both have died.

Joint-and-Several Liability A judgment obtained against multiple tort feasors that may be enforced against the tort feasors collectively or individually; permits the injured party to recover the entire amount of compensation due for injuries from any tort feasor who is able to pay, regardless of the degree of that party's negligence.

Joint-Life Annuity An annuity issued on two lives under which payments cease at the death of either of the two persons.

Joint Mortgage Protection Policy Decreasing term life insurance written on the lives of two persons, with the insurance payable at the death of the first.

Joint Underwriting Association (JUA) A loss-sharing mechanism used in some states to provide insurance to high-risk drivers.

Judgment The decision of a court or the reason for such decision.

Judgment Rating The process of determining the rate for a coverage without the benefit of extensive loss experience or statistical information.

Jumping Juvenile Insurance Permanent life insurance on children under which the face amount automatically increases to a multiple of the initial amount when the child reaches a specified age.

Keogh Plan A tax-qualified retirement plan for self-insured individuals similar in most respects to qualified corporate pensions.

Key-Persons Insurance A life insurance program designed to cover the key employees of an employer; it may be written on a group or individual policy basis.

Lapse Termination of a policy due to failure by the insured to pay the premium as required.

Lapsed Policy A policy discontinued for nonpayment of premiums; the term is technically limited to a termination occurring before a life insurance policy has a cash or other nonforfeiture value.

Last Clear Chance An exception to the doctrine of contributory negligence that makes a person who has a final opportunity to avoid an accident and fails to do so legally liable.

Law of Large Numbers The theory of probability that is the basis for insurance; the larger the number of exposure units, the more closely will the actual results obtained approach the probable results expected from an infinite number of exposures.

Leasehold Interest An intangible use interest that exists when the provisions of a lease stipulate a rental that is greater or less than the prevailing market price of renting similar facilities.

Legal Reserve Life Insurance Company A life insurance company operating under state insurance laws specifying the minimum basis for the reserves the company must maintain on its policies.

Level Premium Insurance Life insurance for which the cost is distributed evenly over the premium paying period; the premium remains constant from year to year, and is more than the actual cost of protection in the earlier years of the policy and less than the actual cost in the later years; the excess paid in the early years accumulates the reserve.

Liability A debt or responsibility; an obligation that may arise by a contract made or by a tort committed.

Licensee A person on one's property with stated or implied permission but not to further the purposes of the landholder. The property owner is obligated to warn a licensee of any dangers the licensee might not be expected to know about.

Life Annuity A contract that provides an income for the life of the annuitant.

Lifetime Disability Benefit A benefit for loss of income payable as long as the insured is totally disabled, even for life.

Limited Payment Life Insurance A form of whole life insurance on which premiums are payable for a specified number of years less than the period of protection, or until death if death occurs before the end of the specified period.

Limited Policies Those that cover specified accidents or sickness.

Livery In automobile insurance, the carrying of passengers for hire.

Lloyds A voluntary association of individuals organized for the purpose of writing insurance; normally refers to Lloyd's of London, a group of individual underwriters and syndicates that underwrite insurance risks severally, using facilities maintained by the Lloyd's of London Corporation.

Loading That part of an insurance rate designed to cover expenses, profit, and a margin for contingencies; in some instances, an additional amount added to an insurance rate because of some extraordinary hazard or expense.

Long-Term Disability A generally accepted period of time for more than two years—can vary according to company standards.

Loss The unintentional decline in, or disappearance of, value due to a contingency.

Loss Frequency The number of claims on a policy during a premium period.

Loss Ratio The proportionate relationship of incurred losses to earned premiums expressed as a percentage.

Loss Reserves An estimated liability in an insurer's financial statement, indicating the amount the insurer expects to pay for losses that have taken place but which have not yet been paid.

Losses Incurred But Not Reported (IBNR) Losses resulting from accidents that have taken place but on which the company has not yet received notice or report of the loss.

Major Medical Expense Insurance Policies especially designed to help offset the heavy medical expenses resulting from catastrophic or prolonged illness or injury; they provide benefit payments for 75–80 percent of all types of medical treatment by a physician above a certain amount first paid by the insured person and up to the maximum amount provided by the policy—usually $500,000, $1 million, or more. Some policies are written without a maximum limit.

Manual A book of rates, rules, and coverages usually available for each kind of insurance.

Malpractice Alleged professional misconduct or lack of ordinary skill in the performance of a professional act. A practitioner is liable for damage or injuries caused by malpractice.

Marine Pertaining to the sea or to transportation; usually divided as to "ocean marine" and "inland marine"; the insurance covering transportation risks.

Mass Merchandising The sale of group property and liability insurance, generally through an employer.

Material Fact Information about the subject of insurance that if known would change the underwriting basis of the insurance, and which would cause the insurer to refuse the application or charge a higher rate.

Medicaid State programs of public assistance to persons regardless of age whose income and resources are insufficient to pay for health care. Title XIX of the federal Social Security Act provides matching federal funds for financing state Medicaid programs.

Medical Information Bureau (MIB) An organization to which life insurers report health impairments of applicants for life insurance; the information is then available to member companies for underwriting purposes.

Medical Payments An additional coverage included in some liability contracts under which the insurer agrees to reimburse injured persons for medical expenses.

Medicare Hospital and medical expense insurance provided under the Social Security system.

Medigap Private health insurance products that supplement Medicare insurance benefits.

Miscellaneous Hospital Expense A provision for the payment on a blanket basis or schedule basis of hospital services (other than room and board, special nursing care, and doctors fees) up to a stipulated maximum amount.

Misrepresentation A misstatement: if done with intent to mislead, it may void the policy of insurance.

Misstatement of Age Clause In life and health insurance, a policy provision requiring an adjustment in the amount of insurance when the insured has misstated his or her age.

Modified Endowment Contract (MEC) A life insurance contract that does not meet the requirements specified in the Internal Revenue Code and on which a withdrawal of investment earnings by a cash surrender or loan before age $59\frac{1}{2}$ is subject to penalty.

Modified Whole Life A form of whole life insurance with a lower-than-usual initial premium that increases after three to five years.

Moral Hazard A dishonest predisposition on the part of an insured which increases the chance of loss.

Morale Hazard A careless attitude on the part of an insured that increases the chance of loss or causes losses to be greater than would otherwise be the case.

Morbidity The incidence and severity of sickness and accidents in a well-defined class or classes of persons.

Morbidity Table A statistical table showing the probable incidence and duration of disability.

Mortality Table A statistical table showing the probable rate of death at each age, usually expressed as so many per thousand.

Mortgage A written instrument giving one party (the mortgagee), usually a creditor, an interest (lien) in the other party's (mortgagor) property as security for a debt.

Multiple Employer Trust (MET) A legal trust established by a plan sponsor that brings together a number of small, unrelated employers for the purpose of providing group medical coverage on an insured or self-funded basis.

Multiple-Line Insurance Policies that combine many perils previously covered by individual policies of fire and liability companies; the Homeowner's Policy is one example; other examples are the commercial portfolio package policy and the farm coverage program.

Mutual Insurance Company An insurer, without capital stock, that is owned by the policyholders; it may be incorporated or unincorporated.

Named Insured The person designated in the policy as the insured as opposed to someone who may have an interest in a policy but not be named.

Named-Peril Coverage Property insurance that covers losses that result from specifically named causes; see Open-Peril Coverage.

National Association of Insurance Commissioners A national organization of state officials who are charged with the regulation of insurance; although the organization has no official power, it exerts a strong influence through its recommendations.

Nationwide Marine Definition A classification of insurance coverages developed by the National Association of Insurance Commissioners to delineate marine insurance from other lines of insurance.

Negligence Failure to exercise the degree of care that would be expected from a reasonable and prudent person.

Net Payment Cost Index In life insurance, a measure of cost of a life insurance maintained in force until death, with allowance for interest at some rate.

Net Retention The final amount of insurance retained by the insurance company after reinsuring such amounts as it did not wish to retain.

No-Fault Insurance A form of first-party insurance written in conjunction with a no-fault law. Under a no-fault law, the person causing injury is granted immunity from tort action and the person injured must collect for his or her loss from his or her own insurer.

Nonadmitted Insurer An insurer that has not been licensed to write insurance in a given jurisdiction.

Noncancelable or Noncancelable and Guaranteed Renewable Policy A continuous term health insurance policy that guarantees the insured the right to renew for a stated number of years or to a stated age (usually 60 or 65), with the premium at renewal guaranteed.

Nonconcurrency A condition that exists when two or more policies covering the same property are written subject to different provisions.

Nonconfining Sickness A sickness that does not confine the insured to his or her home or a hospital.

Noncontributory Plan A group insurance or pension program under which the employer pays the entire cost.

Nonforfeiture Option Privilege available to the policyholder based upon his or her interest in the contract or once cash value has been created.

Nonoccupational Policy One that does not cover loss resulting from accidents or sickness arising out of or in the course of employment or covered under any workers compensation law.

Nonparticipating Insurance Policy insurance on which the premium is calculated to cover as closely as possible the anticipated cost of the insurance protection and on which no dividends are payable to the insured.

Obligee The person in favor of whom some obligation is contracted, whether such obligation be to pay money, or to do, or not do something; the party to whom a bond is given.

Obligor The person who has engaged to perform some obligation; one who makes a bond; the bonding company.

Occupational Disease A disease or condition of health resulting from performance of an occupation, such as psittacosis, mercury poisoning, dust collection in the lungs, and the like; in most states occupational disease is now covered as part of the workers compensation exposure.

Occupational Safety and Health Act of 1970 (OSHA) A federal statute establishing safe and healthy working conditions on a nationwide basis. The act sets job safety and health standards enforced by Labor Department safety inspectors and also provides for compilation of relevant statistics on work injuries and illness.

Occurrence A happening that occupies some length of time, as an individual catching cold after sitting in a draft in a theater all evening; sometimes a series of accidents; see Accident.

Occurrence Form A liability insurance policy under which coverage applies to injuries or damage sustained during the policy period, regardless of when the claim is made; see Claims-Made Form.

Ocean Marine Insurance Coverage on all types of vessels, including liabilities connected with them, and on their cargoes; the cargo coverage has been expanded to protect the owners from warehouse to warehouse, inclusive of all intermediate transit by rail, truck, or otherwise.

Open Form A continuous policy written on a reporting basis.

Open-Peril Coverage A term used to describe a broad form of property insurance in which coverage applies to loss arising from any fortuitous cause other than those perils or causes specifically excluded. This is in contrast to other policies which name the peril or perils insured against; see All-Risk.

Optionally Renewable In health insurance, a contract in which the insurer reserves the right to terminate coverage at an anniversary or premium-due date.

Ordinary Life Insurance A form of whole life insurance usually issued in amounts of $1000 or more with premiums payable on an annual, semiannual, quarterly, or monthly basis to the death of the insured or to the end of the mortality table employed, whichever occurs first and at which time proceeds (benefits) are due; the term is also used to mean straight life insurance.

Overhead Disability Insurance A type of short-term disability income contract that reimburses the insured person for specified, fixed monthly expenses, normal and customary in the operation and conduct of his or her business or office.

Ownership of Expiration Exclusive right on the part of a property and casualty insurance agent operating under the American Agency System to the records of dates and details of expiring policies.

P&I Insurance See Protection and Indemnity.

Package Policy A combination of the coverages of two or more separate policies into a single contract.

Paid-up Insurance Insurance on which all required premiums have been paid; the term is frequently used to mean the reduced paid-up insurance available as one of the nonforfeiture options.

Parol Evidence Rule When the parties to a contract have purported to embody their contract in writing, that writing is the contract and all of the contract; therefore no evidence is admissible to prove any terms of the contract different from, or in addition to, those set forth in writing.

Partial Disability A provision generally found in accident and occasionally in sickness policies designed to offer some weekly or monthly indemnity benefit if the insured cannot perform all the important daily duties of his occupation.

Participating Insurance Policies that entitle the policyholder to receive dividends reflecting the difference between the premium charged and the actual operating expenses and mortality experience of the company; the premium is calculated to provide some margin over the anticipated cost of the insurance protection.

Particular Average A term meaning an accidental and usually a partial loss suffered by one interest and not chargeable against others; see General Average.

Paul v. Virginia A U.S. Supreme Court decision of 1869 in which the court ruled that insurance was not commerce and therefore not interstate commerce, thereby exempting the industry from federal control. This decision was reversed in the South Eastern Underwriters Association case of 1944.

Penalty The limit of an insurer's or surety's liability under a fidelity or surety bond.

Percentage Participation Clause In health insurance, a provision that requires the insured to bear a percentage of expenses in excess of the deductible; also called coinsurance.

Peril The cause of possible loss; the event insured against.

Permanent Life Insurance A phrase used to cover any form of life insurance except term; generally insurance, such as whole life or endowment, that accrues cash value.

Permissible Loss Ratio The maximum percentage of premium income that can be expended by the company to pay claims without loss of profit.

Personal Auto Policy A simplified language automobile policy designed to insure private passenger automobiles and certain types of trucks owned by an individual or husband and wife.

Personal Injury In law, a term used to embrace a broad range of torts that includes bodily injury, libel, slander, discrimination, and similar offenses. Also a standard insurance coverage that protects against a more limited group of torts (false arrest, detention or imprisonment, malicious prosecution, wrongful entry or eviction, and libel, slander, or defamation).

Personal Producing General Agent (PPGA) Life insurance agent who has established a record of successful production and who is granted a contract that gives him or her greater compensation than he or ahe received as an agent. These agents absorb all their own expenses, including office facilities, clerical staff, and other overhead expenses.

Physical Hazard A condition of the subject of insurance that creates or increases the chance of loss, such as structural defects, occupancy, or similar conditions.

Plaintiff A party to a lawsuit who brings charges against another party called the defendant.

Policy The written contract of insurance that is issued to the policyholder insured by the company insurer.

Policy Dividend A refund of part of the premium on a participating life insurance policy reflecting the difference between the premium charged and actual experience.

Policy Loan A loan made by an insurance company to a policyholder on the security of the cash value of his policy.

Policy Period The term for which insurance remains in force, sometimes definite, sometimes not.

Policy Reserve The amounts that a life insurance company allocates specifically for the fulfillment of its policy obligations; reserves are so calculated that, together with future premiums and interest earnings, they will enable the company to pay all future claims.

Policyholders Surplus Total capital funds as shown in an insurer's annual statement. Consists of capital, if any, unassigned funds (surplus), and any special funds that are not in the nature of liabilities.

Pollution The contamination of the environment that includes air pollution, noise pollution, water pollution, and disposal of waste materials.

Pool A risk-sharing mechanism in which the members of a group agree to be collectively responsible for losses.

Postselection Underwriting An insurer's practice of reevaluating the desirability of insureds at or prior to the renewal of their policies.

Preauthorized Check Plan A plan by which a policyholder arranges with his bank and insurance company to have his premium payments drawn, usually monthly, from his checking account.

Preexisting Condition A physical condition that existed prior to the effective date of the policy.

Preferred Provider Organization (PPO) A health care delivery organization composed of physicians, hospitals, or other health care providers that contracts to provide health care services at a reduced fee.

Premises and Operations A commercial liability coverage that protects against liability arising out of the ownership or maintenance of premises or out of the activities of employees away from the premises.

Premium The payment, or one of the periodic payments, a policyholder agrees to make for an insurance policy.

Premium Loan A policy loan needed for the purpose of paying premiums.

Premium Period The length of time covered by the premium, usually identical with the policy period but frequently not.

Prepaid Group Practice Plan A plan under which a person pays in advance for the right to specified health services performed by participating physicians and institutions.

Primary Basic, fundamental; an insurance policy that pays first with respect to other outstanding policies.

Primary Beneficiary The individual first designated to receive the proceeds of an insurance policy; see Contingent Beneficiary.

Principal The applicant for, or subject of, insurance; the one from whom an agent derives his or her authority.

Principal Sum A term used to refer to the lump sum amount payable for accidental death, dismemberment, or loss of sight.

Prior Approval Law A system of rate regulation in which rates must be filed with the state regulatory authority and approved before they may be used.

Private Insurance Voluntary insurance programs available from private firm or from the government by which an individual may obtain protection against the possibility of loss due to a contingency.

Pro Rata Apportionment A division of loss according to the interest of the various companies providing insurance; thus, if Company A has insured the property involved for $10,000 and Company B has insured the property for $20,000, Company A will pay one-third of any loss and Company B will pay two-thirds.

Pro Rata Cancellation Cancellation with a return of premium charged for the period of time the policy was in force equal to the ratio of the total premium to the total policy period; see Short Rate Cancellation.

Probationary Period (also sometimes called "waiting period") A period of time from the policy date to a specified date, usually 15–30 days, during which no sickness coverage is effective; it is designed to eliminate a sickness actually contracted before the policy went into effect—occurs only at the inception of a policy.

Producer An agent for an insurance company.

Prohibited Risks Those not written by a company because of an unusual occupational exposure or uninsurable physical or moral conditions.

Proof The act of substantiating another act, such as a claim for insurance payment.

Proposal An application for insurance or the facts contained in it; a recommendation.

Prorate Clause In health insurance, an optional policy provision designed to protect the company when an insured changes to a more hazardous occupation and does not have his or her policy amended accordingly; the company may pay only such portion of the indemnities provided as the premium paid would have purchased at the higher classification, subject to the maximum limits fixed by the company for such more hazardous occupation; it also protects the insured when he or she changes to a less hazardous occupation by providing for a return premium.

Protection and Indemnity (P&I) Insurance Liability insurance coverage in an ocean marine policy.

Provisions The terms or conditions of an insurance policy.

Proximate Cause The immediate or actual cause of loss.

Public Adjuster One who represents the policyholder instead of the company.

Public Guarantee Insurance Programs Compulsory quasi-social insurance programs designed to protect lenders, investors, or depositors against loss in connection with the failure of a financial institution or other type of fiduciary; for example, the Federal Deposit insurance Corporation.

Public Law 15 An historic piece of legislation passed by Congress in 1945 whereby insurance was exempted from the operation of federal antitrust laws "to the extent that it is regulated by the various states." Certain other restrictions were added, such as a prohibition of coercion; also known as the "McCarran–Ferguson Act."

Punitive Damages Damages awarded separately and in addition to the compensatory damages, usually on account of malicious or wanton misconduct, to serve as a punishment for the wrongdoer and possibly as a deterrent to others.

Pure Premium That part of the premium that is sufficient to pay losses and loss adjustment expenses but not including other expenses. Also, the premium developed by dividing losses by exposure disregarding any loading for commission, taxes, and expenses.

Pure Risk A condition in which there is the possibility of loss or no loss only.

Quota Share Reinsurance A reinsurance contract that reinsures an agreed fraction of every risk of the kind described in the contract, which the ceding company writes.

Rate The cost of a unit of insurance.

Rated Policy An insurance policy issued at a higher-than-standard premium rate to cover the extra risk involved in certain instances where the insured does not meet the standard underwriting requirements, for example, impaired health or a particularly hazardous occupation.

Rating Bureau See Advisory Organization.

Reasonable and Customary Charge A charge for health care that is consistent with the going rate or charge in a certain geographical area for identical or similar services.

Rebate The improper return of part or all of a premium to a policyholder.

Reciprocal Exchange An association of individuals who agree to exchange insurance risks—each member of the association insures each of the other members and in turn is insured by each of the other members; see Attorney-in-Fact.

Recurring Clause A period of time during which a recurrence of a condition is considered as being a continuation of a prior period of disability or hospital confinement.

Reduced Paid-up Insurance A form of insurance available as a nonforfeiture option; it provides for continuation of the original insurance plan, but for a reduced amount.

Refund Annuity An annuity that provides that the difference between the original cost and payments made to the annuitant will be paid to a beneficiary.

Regular Medical Expense Insurance Coverage for services such as doctor fees for nonsurgical care in the hospital or at home, X-rays, or laboratory tests.

Reimbursement Benefits those for which the insured is reimbursed on an actual expense-incurred basis.

Reinstatement The restoration of a lapsed policy.

Reinsurance Insurance placed by an underwriter in another company to cut down the amount of the risk assumed under the original insurance.

Relation of Earnings to Insurance Clause In disability insurance, a provision that reduces payment to the proportion of policy benefits that the insured's earnings at the time of disability (or average earnings for two years prior to disability) bear to total disability benefits under all policies; also called the average earnings clause.

Renew To continue; to replace, as with a new policy.

Renewable at Insurers Option In health insurance, a continuance provision that reserves to the insurer the right to refuse to renew the contract.

Renewable Term Insurance Term insurance that can be renewed at the end of the term, at the option of the policyholder, and without evidence of insurability, for a limited number of successive terms; the rates increase at each renewal as the age of the insured increases.

Rental Value Insurance Insurance arranging to pay the reasonable rental value of property that has been rendered untenantable by fire or some other peril insured against, for the period of time that would be required to restore the property to tenantable condition.

Replacement Cost Insurance Property insurance that pays for damaged or destroyed property without a deduction for depreciation.

Reporting Form Insurance that depends upon regular reports from the insured to determine the amount of insurance or the premium or both.

Representation Statements made by an applicant in the application that he represents as being substantially true to the best of his or her knowledge and belief, but that are not warranted as exact in every detail.

Res Ipsa Loquitur (the thing speaks for itself) Rebuttable presumption that the defendant was negligent; the presumption arises upon proof that the instrumentality causing the injury was in the defendant's exclusive control, and that the accident is one which ordinarily does not happen in the absence of negligence.

Reserve Liability set up for particular purposes.

Residual Disability Benefit A provision in disability income policies that grants benefits based on a reduction in earnings, as opposed to inability to work full time.

Residual Market Plan A mechanism through which high-risk insureds who cannot obtain insurance through normal market channels are insured.

Respondeat Superior (let the master answer) The principal is liable in certain cases for the wrongful acts of his agent; the doctrine does not apply where

the injury occurs while the servant is acting outside the legitimate scope of his or her authority.

Respondentia An early form of marine insurance on cargo; similar to bottomry, the equivalent on hulls.

Restoration Reinstatement, as the amount of coverage after a loss.

Retention The act of retaining an exposure to loss; also that part of the exposure that is retained.

Retroactive Conversion Conversion of term life insurance into whole life insurance at the insured's original age at issue rather than at the insured's attained age at conversion.

Retrocession The amount of risk that a reinsurance company reinsures; the amount of a cession which the reinsurer passes on.

Retrospective Rating The process of determining the cost of an insurance policy after expiration of the policy, based on the loss experience under the policy while it was in force.

Return Premium An amount due the insured upon cancellation of a policy.

Revocable Beneficiary A beneficiary designation that may be changed by the policyowner without the consent of the existing beneficiary.

Rider A document that amends the policy; it may increase or decrease benefits, waive a condition or coverage, or in any other way amend the original contract—the terms rider and endorsement are often used interchangeably.

Risk In the abstract, used to indicate a condition of the real world in which there is a possibility of loss; also used by insurance practitioners to indicate the property insured or the peril insured against.

Risk Management A scientific approach to the problem of dealing with the pure risks facing an individual or an organization in which insurance is viewed as simply one of several approaches for dealing with such risks.

Risk Retention Act A 1986 federal statute that exempts risk retention groups and insurance purchasing groups from a substantial part of state regulation.

Risk Retention Group Group-owned insurer formed under Risk Retention Act of 1986, whose primary activity consists of assuming and spreading the liability risks of its members.

Robbery The unlawful taking of property by violence or threat of violence.

Salvage Value recoverable after a loss; that which is recovered by an insurance company after paying a loss; see Subrogation.

Schedule A list of coverages or amounts concerning things or persons insured.

Schedule Rating A system of rating in which debits and credits are added and subtracted from a base rate to determine the final rate for a particular insured.

Second-Injury Fund In workers compensation, a state fund that pays the increased benefits when a second work-related injury combined with a previous injury results in greater disability than would be caused by the second injury only.

Second-to-Die Policy A life insurance contract that insures two lives with the promise to pay only at the second death; also called survivorship whole life insurance.

Self-Insurance A risk retention program that incorporates elements of the insurance mechanism.

Senior Professional Public Adjuster (SPPA) Professional designation granted to public adjusters with 10 years' experience who pass a rigorous examination and meet other specified eligibility requirements.

Separate Account Funds held by a life insurer that are segregated from the other assets of the insurer and invested for pension plans.

Settlement Option One of the ways, other than immediate payment in a lump sum, in which the policyholder or beneficiary may choose to have the policy proceeds paid.

Seven-Pay Test A test applied to life insurance contracts under the Internal Revenue Code that is designed to determine if the contract is primarily an investment instrument rather than a life insurance contract. Premiums during the first seven years of the contract may not exceed seven annual net level premiums for a 7-pay policy; see Modified Endowment Contract.

Short Rate Cancellation Cancellation with a less than proportionate return of premium; see Pro Rata Cancellation.

Short-Term Disability A generally accepted period of time for two years or less; can vary according to company standards.

Sickness Insurance A form of health insurance against loss by illness or disease.

Single Premium Whole Life A whole life policy in which the initial premium, together with interest earnings, is sufficient to pay the cost of the policy over its lifetime.

Single Premium Deferred Annuity An annuity under which the initial premium accumulates together with investment income to create a fund that will be paid out to the annuitant at some time in the future.

Social Insurance Compulsory insurance, in which the benefits are prescribed by law and in which the primary emphasis is on social adequacy rather than equity.

South-Eastern Underwriters Association (SEUA) case U.S. Supreme Court decision in 1944 that reversed the decision in *Paul v. Virginia* and held that insurance is interstate commerce.

Special Agent A representative of an insurance company who travels about a given territory dealing with agents and supervising the company's operations there.

Special Damages Amount awarded in litigation to compensate for specific identifiable economic loss.

Speculative Risk A condition in which there is a possibility of loss or gain.

SPPA See Senior Professional Public Adjuster.

Sprinkler Leakage Insurance Insurance against loss from accidental leakage or discharge from a sprinkler system due to some cause other than a hostile fire or certain other specified causes.

Staff Adjuster One who adjusts losses and is paid a salary by one company for all his time.

Standard Provisions (health insurance) A set of policy provisions prescribed by law setting forth certain rights and obligations of both the insured and company; these were originally introduced in 1912 and have now been replaced by the Uniform Provisions.

Standard Risk A person who, according to a company's underwriting standards, is entitled to insurance protection without extra rating or special restrictions.

Statutory Accounting Accounting prescribed by regulatory authorities for insurance companies. Under the statutory accounting system, GAAP (Generally Accepted Accounting Principles) are not followed, but statutory conventions replace GAAP.

Statutory Profit The profit of an insurer computed under the statutory system of accounting.

Stock Insurance Company An insurance company owned by stockholders, usually for the purpose of making a profit.

Straight Life Insurance Whole life insurance on which premiums are payable for life.

✳ **Subrogation** An assignment or substituting of one person for another by which the rights of one are acquired by another in collecting a debt or a claim, as an insurance company stepping into the rights of a policyholder indemnified by the company.

Substandard (impaired risk) Risks that have some physical impairment requiring the use of a waiver, a special policy form, or a higher premium charge.

Suicide Clause Life insurance policy provision that limits the insurer's liability to the return of premiums if the insured commits suicide during the first two years of the policy.

Superfund A federal environmental cleanup fund created principally from taxes on the chemical industry intended for use in cleaning up waste dumps.

Supplementary Contract An agreement between a life insurer and a policyholder or beneficiary by which the insurer retains the proceeds payable under an insurance policy and makes payments in accordance with the settlement option chosen.

Supplementary Medical Insurance (SMI) Optional insurance under the Medicare program that covers physicians' fees and other specified medical services.

Surety A guarantor of a duty or obligation assumed by another.

Surety Bond An agreement providing for monetary compensation should there be a failure to perform certain specified acts within a stated period: the surety company, for example, becomes responsible for fulfillment of a contract if the contractor defaults.

Surgical Expense Insurance Health insurance coverage that provides benefits toward the physician's or surgeon's operating fees, sometimes with a scheduled amount for each surgical procedure.

Surplus Line Commonly used to describe any insurance for which there is no available market to the original agent or broker, and that is placed in a nonadmitted insurer in accordance with the Surplus or Excess Line provisions of state insurance laws.

Surrender Cost Index In life insurance, a measure of the cost of a policy, including interest foregone, if the policy is surrendered for its cash value at the end of a specified period.

Survivorship Whole Life A life insurance contract that insures two lives with the promise to pay only at the second death; also called the "second-to-die" policy.

Term The length of time covered by a policy or a premium.

Term Insurance Insurance payable to a beneficiary at the death of the insured, provided death occurs within a specified period, such as 5 or 10 years, or before a specified age.

Theft The unlawful taking of property of another: the term includes such crimes as burglary, larceny, and robbery.

Third-Party Administration Administration of a group insurance plan by some person or firm other than the insurer or the policyholder.

Third Party Insurance Liability insurance, so called because it undertakes to pay to a third party sums that the insured becomes legally obligated to pay.

Title Insurance Insurance that indemnifies the owner of real estate in the event his clear ownership of property is upset by the discovery of faults in his title: largely written by companies specializing in this class alone.

Tort An injury or wrong committed against an individual.

Total Disability Disability which prevents the insured from performing all the duties of his occupation or any occupation; the exact definition varies among policies.

Travel Accident Policies Those that are limited to paying for loss arising out of accidents occurring while traveling.

Trespasser One who enters property of another without permission. A property owner generally is obligated to avoid intentional injury to trespassers and do so by a full disclosure of all information material to the proposed contract.

Trust Transfer of property right to one person called a "trustee" for the benefit of another called a "beneficiary."

Trust Fund Plan A pension plan administered by a trustee rather than by an insurance company.

Twisting The act of switching insurance policies from one company to another, to the detriment of the insured.

Uberrimae Fidei Literally, of the utmost good faith. The basis of all insurance contracts—both parties to the contract are bound to exercise good faith and do so by a full disclosure of all information material to the proposed contract.

Umbrella Liability Insurance A form of excess liability insurance available to corporations and individuals protecting them against claims in excess of the limits of their primary policies or for claims not covered by their insurance program. This latter coverage requires the insured to pay a self-insured retention.

Underinsured Motorist Coverage A form of automobile coverage that pays for bodily injury to insured persons by a motorist who has insurance that meets the requirements of the financial responsibility law, but is insufficient to cover the loss sustained by the insured.

Underwriter An individual who decides whether the insurance company will issue coverage and, in some cases, the rate at which it will be issued.

Underwriting The process by which an insurance company determines whether and on what basis it will accept an application for insurance.

Unearned Premium That portion of the original premium for which protection has not yet been provided because the policy still has some time to run before expiration. A property and liability insurer must carry unearned premiums as a liability on its financial statement.

Uniform Provisions Statutory policy provisions which specify the rights and obligations of the insured and company.

Uninsured Motorist Coverage A form of automobile insurance that pays for bodily injury to an insured person by a motorist who is uninsured, a hit-and-run driver, or a driver whose insurer becomes insolvent.

Universal Life Insurance A flexible premium life insurance policy under which the policyholder may change the death benefit from time to time (with satisfactory evidence of insurability for increases) and vary the premium payments. Premiums (less expense charges) are credited to a policy account from which mortality charges are deducted and to which interest is credited at rates which may change from time to time.

Unsatisfied Judgment Fund A state fund created to reimburse persons injured in automobile accidents who cannot collect damages awarded to them because the responsible party is either insolvent or uninsured. Such funds are often financed by an addition to the regular automobile registration fee and will only pay unsatisfied judgments up to fixed limits.

Usual, Customary, and Reasonable (UCR) Charges In health insurance, an approach to benefits under which the policy agrees to pay the "usual, customary and reasonable" charges for a procedure, rather than a stipulated dollar amount.

Valued Policy An insurance contract in which the value of the thing insured and the amount to be paid in case of total loss is settled at the time of making the policy.

Valued Policy Law A state statute that specifies that in the event of a total loss, the insured shall receive in payment the full amount of the policy, regardless of the principle of indemnity.

Vanishing Premium Policy A participating whole life policy on which dividends are allowed to accumulate until accumulated dividends plus future dividends are sufficient to pay all future premiums under the policy. The NAIC Model Replacement Regulation prohibits the use of this term in describing a life insurance policy.

Variable Annuity An annuity contract under which the amount of each periodic payment fluctuates according to the investment performance of the insurer.

Variable Life Insurance Life insurance under which the benefits are not fixed but relate to the value of assets behind the contract at the time the benefit is paid.

Variable Universal Life A form of life insurance that combines the flexible premium features of universal life with the investment component of variable life.

Vesting A provision that a participant in a pension plan will, after meeting certain requirements, retain the right to the benefits he or she has accrued.

Vicarious Liability In law, liability arising out of imputed negligence.

Void Of no force or effect; null.

Waiting Period (also sometimes called "elimination period" or "probation period") A provision designed to eliminate disability claims for the first number of days specified for each period of disability; the waiting period may run from three days to as long as one year: this term is also sometimes used to refer to a period of time after policy issuance during which specified conditions are not covered.

Waiver The voluntary relinquishment of a known right.

Waiver of Premium A provision that waives payment of the premium that becomes due during a period of covered total disability that has lasted for a specified period of time, usually, three to six months.

Warranty A statement concerning the condition of the item to be insured which is made for the purpose of permitting the underwriter to evaluate the risk; if found to be false, it provides the basis for voidance of the policy.

Whole Life Insurance Insurance payable to a beneficiary at the death of the insured whenever that occurs; premiums may be payable for a specified number of years (limited-payment life) or for life (straight life).

Workers Compensation A system of providing for the cost of medical care and weekly payments to injured employees or to dependents of those killed in industry in which absolute liability is imposed on the employer, requiring him or her to pay benefits prescribed by law.

Written Premiums The premiums on all policies which a company has issued in some period of time, as opposed to "earned premiums."

APPENDIX B

State Insurance Commissioners

Alabama Davis Parsons, Commissioner of Insurance, Department of Insurance, 201 Monroe Street, Suite 1700, Montgomery, Alabama 36104; tel. 334-269-3550. http://www.aldoi.org/

Alaska Robert A. Lohr, Director of Insurance, Department of Commerce & Economic Development, Division of Insurance, P.O. Box 110805, 333 Willoughby Avenue, 9th Floor, Juneau, Alaska 99801; tel, 907-465-2515.
http://www.commerce.state.ak.us/insurance/

Arizona Charles R. Cohen, Director of Insurance, Department of Insurance, 2910 North 44th Street, Suite 210, Phoenix, Arizona 85018-7256; tel. 602-912-8400.
http://www.state.az.us/id/

Arkansas Mike Pickens, Commissioner of Insurance, Department of Insurance, 1200 W. 3rd Street, Little Rock, Arkansas 72201-1904; tel. 501-371-2600.
http://www.state.ar.us/insurancedept/

California Charles Quackenbush, Commissioner of Insurance, Department of Insurance, 300 Capitol Mall, Suite 1500, Sacramento, California 95814; tel. 916-492-3500.
http:www.insurance.ca.gov/docs/index.html

Colorado William J. Kirven III, Commissioner of Insurance, Division of Insurance, 1560 Broadway, Suite 850, Denver, Colorado 80202; tel. 303-894-7499.
http://www.dora.state.co.us/ insurance/

Connecticut William J. Gilliam, Acting Commissioner of Insurance, Department of Insurance, P.O. Box 816, Hartford, Connecticut 06142-0816; tel. 860-297-3802.
http:www.state.ct.us/cid/

Delaware Donna Lee Williams, Commissioner of Insurance, Department of Insurance, Rodney Building, 841 Silver Lake Boulevard, Dover, Delaware 19904; tel. 302-739-4251.
http://www.state.de.us/govern/elecoffl/inscom.htm.

District of Columbia Patrick Kelly, Acting Commissioner of Insurance, Insurance Administration, District of Columbia Government, 441 4th Street NW, 8th Floor North, Washington, District of Columbia 20001; tel. 202-727-8000.

Florida Bill Nelson, Commissioner of Insurance, Florida Department of Insurance, 200 East Gaines Street, Tallahassee, Florida 32399-0300; tel. 850-922-3100.
http://www.doi.state.fl.us/

Georgia John Oxendine, Commissioner of Insurance, 2 Martin L. King, Jr. Drive, Floyd Memorial Building, 704 West Tower, Atlanta, Georgia 30334; tel. 404-656-2070.
http://www2.state.ga.us/Ga.Ins. Commission/

Guam Joseph T. Duenas, Commissioner of Insurance, Department of Revenue & Taxation, Government of Guam, 378 Chalan San Antonio, Tarnuning, Guam 96911; tel. 011-671-475-1817.

Hawaii Wayne Metcalf, Commissioner of Insurance, Insurance Division, Department of Commerce & Consumer Affairs, 250 S. King Street, 5th Floor, Honolulu, Hawaii 96813; tel. 808-586-2760.
http://www.hawaii. gov/insurance/

Idaho Mary L. Hartung, Director of Insurance, Department of Insurance, 700 West State Street, Third Floor, Boise, Idaho 83720; tel. 208-334-4398.
http://www.doi.state.id.us/

Illinois Nat Shapo, Acting Director of Insurance, Department of Insurance, 320 West Washington Street, 4th Floor, Springfield, Illinois 62767; tel. 217-782-4515.
http://www.state.il.us/ins/default.htm

Indiana Sally McCarty, Commissioner of Insurance, Department of Insurance, 311 West Washington Street, Suite 300, Indianapolis, Indiana 46204-2787; tel. 317-232-2385.
http://www.ai.org/idoi/index.html

Iowa   Terri Vaughan, Commissioner of Insurance, Division of Insurance, 330 E. Maple Street, Des Moines, Iowa 50319; tel. 515-281-5705.

Kansas   Kathleen Sebelius, Commissioner of Insurance, Department of Insurance, State of Kansas, 420 S.W. 9th Street, Topeka, Kansas 66612-1678; tel. 785-296-3071.

http://www.ink.org/public/kid/

Kentucky   George Nichols III, Commissioner of Insurance, Department of Insurance, 215 West Main Street, Frankfort, Kentucky 40602; tel. 502-564-3630.
http://www.state.ky.us/agencies/insur/default.htm

Louisiana   James H. Brown, Commissioner of Insurance, Department of Insurance, P.O. Box 94214, 950 North 5th Street, Baton Rouge, Lousiana 70804-9214; tel. 504-342-5900.
http://wwwldi.state.la.us/

Maine   Alessandro Iuppa, Superintendent of Insurance, Department of Professional & Financial Regulation, Bureau of Insurance, State Office Building, State House, Station 34, Augusta, Maine 04333; tel. 207-624-8475.
http://www.state.me.us/pfr/ins/ inshome2.htm

Maryland   Steven B. Larsen, Commissioner of Insurance, Insurance Administration, 525 St. Paul Place, Baltimore, Maryland 21202-2272; tel. 410-468-2000.
http://www.gacc.com/mia/

Massachusetts   Linda Ruthardt, Commissioner of Insurance, Division of Insurance, Commonwealth of Massachusetts, One South Stations, 5th Floor, Boston, Massachusetts 02210; tel. 617-521-7794.
http://www.magnet.state.ma.us/doi/

Michigan   Frank M. Fitzgerals, Commissioner of Insurance, Insurance Bureau, Department of Commerce, 611 West Ottawa Street, 2nd Floor North, Lansing, Michigan 48933; tel. 517-373-9273.
http://www.cis. state.mi.us/ins/

Minnesota   David B. Gruenes, Commissioner of Insurance, Department of Commerce, 133 East 7th Street, St. Paul, Minnesota 55101; tel. 612-296-6848.
http://www.commerce.state.mn.us/

Mississippi   George Dale, Commissioner of Insurance, Department of Insurance, 1804 Walter Sillers Building, Jackson, Mississippi 39201; tel. 601-359-3569.
http://www.doi.state.ms.us/

Missouri   Keith Wenzel, Director of Insurance, Department of Insurance, 301 West High Street, 6 North, Jefferson City, Missouri 65102-0690; tel. 573-751-4126.
http://services.state.mo.us/insurance/mohmepg.htm

Montana   Mark O'Keefe, Commissioner of Insurance, Department of Insurance, 126 North Sanders, Mitchell Building, Room 270, Helena, Montana 59620; tel. 406-444-2040.
http://www.mt.gov/sao/

Nebraska   Tim Wagner, Director of Insurance, Department of Insurance, Terminal Building, 941 O Street, Suite 400, Lincoln, Nebraska 68508; tel. 402-471-2201.
http://www.nol.org/home/NDOI/

Nevada   Alice Molasky-Arman, Commissioner of Insurance, Division of Insurance, 1665 Hot Springs Road, Suite 152, Carson City, Nevada 89706; tel. 702-687-7650.
http://www.state.nv.us/b&i/id/

New Hampshire   Paula T. Rogers, Commissioner of Insurance, Department of Insurance, 169 Manchester Street, Suite I, Concord, New Hampshire 03301; tel. 603-271-2261.
http://www.state.nh.us/insurance/

New Jersey   Karen L. Suter, Acting Commissioner of Insurance, Department of Insurance, 20 West State Street, P.O. Box 325, Trenton, New Jersey 08625; tel. 609-292-5360.
http://states.naic.org/nj/NJHOMEPG. HTML

New Mexico   D. J. Letherer, Superintendent of Insurance, Department of Insurance, P.O. Box Drawer 1269, Santa Fe, New Mexico 87504-1269; tel. 505-827-4601.
http://www.naic.org/nm/

New York   Neil D. Levin, Superintendent of Insurance, New York Department of Insurance, 25 Beaver Street, New York, New York 10004-2319; tel. 212-480-2289.
http://www.ins.state.ny.us/nyins.htm

North Carolina   Jim Long, Commissioner of Insurance, Department of Insurance, Dobbs Building, 430 North Salisbury Street, Suite 4140, Raleigh, North Carolina 27603; tel. 919-733-7343.
http://www.doi.state.nc.us/

North Dakota   Glenn Pomeroy, Commissioner of Insurance, Department of Insurance, 600 E. Boulevard, Bismarck, North Dakota 58505-0320; tel. 701-328-2440.
http://www.state.nd.us/ndins/

Ohio J. Lee Covington II, Director of Insurance, Department of Insurance, 2100 Stella Court, Columbus, Ohio, 43215; tel. 614-644-2658.
http://www. state.oh.us/ins/

Oklahoma Carroll Fisher, Commissioner of Insurance, Department of Insurance, 3814 N. Santa Fe, Oklahoma City, Oklahoma 73118; tel. 405-521-2686.
http://www.oid.state.ok.us/

Oregon Mary Neidig, Commissioner of Insurance, Department of Consumer & Business Services, 350 Winter Street, N.E., Room 200, Salem, Oregon 97310-0700; tel. 503-947-7980.
http://www.cbs.state.or.us/ external/ins/index.html

Pennsylvania M. Diane Koken, Commissioner of Insurance, Insurance Department, 1326 Strawberry Square, 13th Floor, Harrisburg, Pennsylvania 17120; tel. 717-787-2317.
http://www.state.pa.us/PA_Exec/Insurance/overview.html

Puerto Rico Juan Antonio Garcia, Commissioner of Insurance, Office of the Commissioner of Insurance, Fernandez Juncos Station, 1607 Pone de Leon Ave., Santurce, Puerto Rico 00910; tel. 787-722-8686.

Rhode Island Alfonso E. Mastrostefano, Commissioner of Insurance, Insurance Division, 233 Richmond Street, Suite 233, Providence, Rhode Island 02903-4233; tel. 401-277-2223.

South Carolina Ernest N. Csiszar, Director of Insurance, 1612 Marion Street, P.O. Box 100105, Columbia, South Carolina 29202; tel. 803-737-6150.
http://state.sc.us/doi/

South Dakota Darla L. Lyon, Director of Insurance, Division of Insurance, 118 W. Capitol, Pierre, South Dakota 57501-3940; tel. 605-773-3563.
http://www.state.sd.us/state/executive/dcr/dcr.html

Tennessee Anne Pope, Commissioner of Insurance, Department of Commerce & Insurance, Volunteer Plaza, 500 James Robertson Parkway, Nashville, Tennessee 36243-9565; tel. 615-741-2241.
http://www. state.tn.us/commerce/

Texas Jose Montemayor, Commissioner of Insurance, Department of Insurance, 333 Guadalupe Street, P.O. Box 149104, Austin, Texas 78701; tel. 512-463-6464.
http://www.tdi.state.tx.us/

Utah Merwin U. Stewart, Commissioner of Insurance, Department of Insurance, 3110 State Office Building, Salt Lake City, Utah 84114-1201; tel. 801-535-3800.
http://www.ins-dept.state.ut.us/

Vermont Elizabeth Costle, Commissioner of Insurance, Division of Insurance, Department of Banking, Insurance & Securities, 89 Main Street, Drawer 20, Montpelier, Vermont 05620-3101; tel. 802-828-3301.
http://www.state.vt.us/bis/

Virgin Islands Kenneth E. Mapp, Director of Insurance, Division of Banking & Insurance, 1131 King St., Suite 101, Christiansted, St. Croix, Virgin islands 00802; tel. 809-773-64499.

Virginia Alfred W. Gross, Commissioner of Insurance, State Corporation Commission, Bureau of Insurance, 1300 East Main Street, Richmond, Virginia 23219; tel. 804-371-9741.
http://www.state.va.us/scc/division/boi/index.htm

Washington Deborah Senn, Commissioner of Insurance, Office of Insurance Commissioner, Insurance Building-Capitol Campus, 14th Avenue & Water Street, P.O. Box 40255, Olympia, Washington 98504; tel. 360-753-7301.
http://www.wa.gov/ins/

West Virginia Hanley C. Clark, Commissioner of Insurance, Department of Insurance, 2019 Washington Street East, P.O. Box 50540, Charleston, West Virginia 25305-0540; tel. 304-558-3354.
http://www.state.wv. us/insurance/

Wisconsin Connie L. O'Connell, Acting Commissioner of Insurance, Office of the Commissioner of Insurance, State of Wisconsin, 121 E. Wilson, Madison, Wisconsin 53702; tel. 608-266-3585.
http://badger.state.wi.us/agencies/oci/oci_home.htm

Wyoming John P. McBride, Commissioner of Insurance, Herschler Building, 122 West 25th Street, Cheyenne, Wyoming 82002; tel. 307-777-7401.
http://www.state.wy.us/~insurance/

APPENDIX C

Whole Life Policy

2   WHOLE LIFE POLICY

29-3854-01(1-86) WHOLE LIFE
I/R 4400.00

This is a representative sample of Northwestern Mutual Life's NN series Whole Life Policy. Policy benefits and wording may vary to comply with state regulations. The notations are to guide you through provisions of the policy. They do not modify the policy terms.

Our promise to you. ━━━━━━━━━━━━━━

The Northwestern Mutual Life Insurance Company agrees to pay the benefits provided in this policy, subject to its terms and conditions. Signed at Milwaukee, Wisconsin on the Date of Issue.

PRESIDENT AND C.E.O.   *SECRETARY*

WHOLE LIFE POLICY

Eligible For Annual Dividends.

Insurance payable on death of Insured. Premiums payable for period shown on page 3.

Return the policy ━━━━━━━━━━━━━━
within ten days if you
don't like it, and your
money will be
refunded.

Right to Return Policy — Please read this policy carefully. The policy may be returned by the Owner for any reason within ten days after it was received. The policy may be returned to your agent or to the Home Office of the Company at 720 East Wisconsin Avenue, Milwaukee, WI 53202. If returned, the policy will be considered void from the beginning. Any premium paid will then be refunded.

NN 1

You, as a policyowner, ━━━━━━━━━━━━━━
are also an owner of
this mutual company.

Northwestern
Mutual Life®

WHOLE LIFE POLICY

3

This policy is a legal contract between the Owner and The Northwestern Mutual Life Insurance Company.
Read your policy carefully.

Table of Contents. ————————————————————— **GUIDE TO POLICY PROVISIONS**

NN 1, 4

4   WHOLE LIFE POLICY

                                                    BENEFITS AND PREMIUMS
                                        DATE OF ISSUE   JANUARY 1, 2001

		ANNUAL	PAYABLE
PLAN AND ADDITIONAL BENEFITS	AMOUNT	PREMIUM	FOR
WHOLE LIFE PAID-UP AT 90	$100,000	$1,533.00	55 YEARS

A PREMIUM IS PAYABLE ON JANUARY 1, 2001 AND EVERY JANUARY 1 AFTER THAT.

THE FIRST PREMIUM IS $1,533.00

THE OWNER MAY ELECT THE SPECIFIED RATE OR THE VARIABLE RATE LOAN INTEREST
OPTION. SEE SECTIONS 6.4 THROUGH 6.6 OF THE POLICY. THE VARIABLE RATE
LOAN INTEREST OPTION WAS ELECTED ON THE APPLICATION.

THIS POLICY IS ISSUED IN A SELECT PREMIUM CLASS

DIRECT BENEFICIARY   JANE M DOE, WIFE OF THE INSURED

OWNER   JOHN J DOE, THE INSURED

INSURED   JOHN J DOE   AGE AND SEX   35 MALE

POLICY DATE   JANUARY 1, 2001   POLICY NUMBER   1 000 001

**Type of policy you
bought.**   PLAN ┌─── WHOLE LIFE PAID UP AT 90   AMOUNT $ 100,000

                 NN1

Your policy's "I.D."

                                        PAGE 3

TABLE OF GUARANTEED VALUES PER $1,000 OF FACE AMOUNT

END OF POLICY YEAR	CASH VALUE	PAID-UP INSURANCE	EXTENDED TERM INSURANCE YEARS	DAYS
1	$ 0.00	$ 0.00	0	0
2	10.78	50	3	165
3	22.01	98	6	118
4	33.71	144	8	256
5	45.88	187	10	268
6	58.52	229	12	162
7	71.65	268	14	37
8	85.28	305	15	284
9	99.42	341	17	44
10	114.11	374	18	72
11	129.33	406	19	13
12	145.15	437	19	250
13	161.56	466	20	70
14	178.60	493	20	213
15	196.29	519	20	321
16	214.66	544	21	31
17	233.70	568	21	77
18	253.41	590	21	96
19	273.80	611	21	92
20	294.86	631	21	70
Age 60	383.28	718	19	302
Age 65	475.45	788	18	36
Age 70	567.41	844	16	48

VALUES ARE INCREASED BY PAID-UP ADDITIONS AND DIVIDEND ACCUMULATIONS
AND DECREASED BY POLICY DEBT. VALUES SHOWN AT END OF POLICY YEAR
DO NOT REFLECT ANY PREMIUM DUE ON THAT POLICY ANNIVERSARY.

INSURED	JOHN J DOE	AGE AND SEX	35 MALE
POLICY DATE	JANUARY 1, 2001	POLICY NUMBER	1 000 001
PLAN	WHOLE LIFE PAID UP AT 90	AMOUNT	$ 100,000
NN1			

6   WHOLE LIFE POLICY

SECTION 1. THE CONTRACT

The contract is made up of the policy and the application.

1.1 LIFE INSURANCE BENEFIT

The Northwestern Mutual Life Insurance Company will pay a benefit on the death of the Insured. Subject to the terms and conditions of the policy:

- payment of the death proceeds will be made after proof of the death of the Insured is received at the Home Office; and
- payment will be made to the beneficiary or other payee under Sections 8 and 9.

The company's defense against misrepresentation ends two years after the policy is issued if the insured is still alive.

The amount of the death proceeds when all premiums due have been paid will be:

- the plan Amount shown on page 3; plus
- the amount of any paid-up additions then in force (Section 4.2); plus
- the amount of any dividend accumulations (Section 4.2); plus
- the amount of any premium refund (Section 3.1) and any dividend at death (Section 4.4); less
- the amount of any policy debt (Section 6.3).

The company's defense against suicide ends one year after the policy is issued if the insured is still alive.

These amounts will be determined as of the date of death.

The amount of the death proceeds when the Insured dies during the grace period following the due date of any unpaid premium will be:

- the amount determined above assuming the overdue premium has been paid; less
- the amount of the unpaid premium.

The amount of the death proceeds when the Insured dies while the policy is in force as extended term or paid-up insurance will be determined under Sections 5.2 or 5.3.

1.2 ENTIRE CONTRACT; CHANGES

This policy with the attached application is the entire contract. Statements in the application are representations and not warranties. A change in the policy is valid only if it is approved by an officer of the Company. The Company may require that the policy be sent to it for endorsement to show a change. No agent has the authority to change the policy or to waive any of its terms.

1.3 INCONTESTABILITY

The Company will not contest this policy after it has been in force during the lifetime of the Insured for two years from the Date of Issue. In issuing the policy, the Company has relied on the application. While the policy is contestable, the Company, on the basis of a misstatement in the application, may rescind the policy or deny a claim.

1.4 SUICIDE

If the Insured dies by suicide within one year from the Date of Issue, the amount payable by the Company will be limited to the premiums paid, less the amount of any policy debt.

1.5 DATES

The contestable and suicide periods begin with the Date of Issue. Policy months, years and anniversaries are computed from the Policy Date. Both dates are shown on page 3.

1.6 MISSTATEMENT OF AGE OR SEX

If the age or sex of the Insured has been misstated, the amount payable will be the amount which the premiums paid would have purchased at the correct age and sex.

1.7 PAYMENTS BY THE COMPANY

All payments by the Company under this policy are payable at its Home Office.

SECTION 2. OWNERSHIP

2.1 THE OWNER

The Owner is named on page 3. The Owner, his successor or his transferee may exercise policy rights without the consent of any beneficiary. After the death of the Insured, policy rights may be exercised only as provided in Sections 8 and 9.

The policy can have a new owner.

2.2 TRANSFER OF OWNERSHIP

The Owner may transfer the ownership of this policy. Written proof of transfer satisfactory to the Company must be received at its Home Office. The transfer will then take effect as of the date that it was signed. The Company may require that the policy be sent to it for endorsement to show the transfer.

NN 1,4

2.3 COLLATERAL ASSIGNMENT

The Owner may assign this policy as collateral security. The Company is not responsible for the validity or effect of a collateral assignment. The Company will not be responsible to an assignee for any payment or other action taken by the Company before receipt of the assignment in writing at its Home Office.

The interest of any beneficiary will be subject to any collateral assignment made either before or after the beneficiary is named.

A collateral assignee is not an Owner. A collateral assignment is not a transfer of ownership. Ownership can be transferred only by complying with Section 2.2.

5

The policy may be assigned as security for a loan.

SECTION 3. PREMIUMS AND REINSTATEMENT

3.1 PREMIUM PAYMENT

Payment. All premiums after the first are payable at the Home Office or to an authorized agent. A receipt signed by an officer of the Company will be furnished on request. A premium must be paid on or before its due date. The date when each premium is due and the number of years for which premiums are payable are described on page 3.

Frequency. Premiums may be paid every 3, 6 or 12 months at the published rates of the Company. A change in premium frequency will take effect when the Company accepts a premium on a new frequency. Premiums may be paid on any other frequency approved by the Company.

You have 31 days beyond the due date to pay your premium.

Grace Period. A grace period of 31 days will be allowed to pay a premium that is not paid on its due date. The policy will be in full force during this period. If the Insured dies during the grace period, any overdue premium will be paid from the proceeds of the policy.

If the premium is not paid within the grace period, the policy will terminate as of the due date unless it continues as extended term or paid-up insurance under Section 5.2 or 5.3.

Premium Refund At Death. The Company will refund a portion of a premium paid for the period beyond the date of the Insured's death. The refund will be part of the policy proceeds.

3.2 REINSTATEMENT

The policy may be reinstated within five years after the due date of the overdue premium. All unpaid premiums (and interest as required below) must be received by the Company while the Insured is alive. The policy may not be reinstated if the policy was surrendered for its cash surrender value. Any policy debt on the due date of the overdue premium, with interest from that date, must be repaid or reinstated.

In addition, for the policy to be reinstated more than 31 days after the end of the grace period:

- evidence of insurability must be given that is satisfactory to the Company; and
- all unpaid premiums must be paid with interest from the due date of each premium. Interest is at an annual effective rate of 6%.

How to reinstate your policy.

SECTION 4. DIVIDENDS

You may receive dividends annually.

4.1 ANNUAL DIVIDENDS

This policy will share in the divisible surplus of the Company. This surplus is determined each year. This policy's share will be credited as a dividend on the policy anniversary. The dividend will reflect the mortality, expense and investment experience of the Company and will be affected by any policy debt during the policy year.

4.2 USE OF DIVIDENDS

Annual dividends may be paid in cash or used for one of the following:

This popular way to use dividends provides additional insurance.

- **Paid-up Additions.** Dividends will purchase paid-up additional insurance. Paid-up additions share in the divisible surplus.
- **Dividend Accumulations.** Dividends will accumulate at interest. Interest is credited at an annual effective rate of 3 1/2%. The Company may set a higher rate.

Another popular way to use dividends is to reduce premiums.

- **Premium Payment.** Dividends will be used to reduce premiums. If the balance of a premium is not paid, or if this policy is in force as paid-up insurance, the dividend will purchase paid-up additions.

Other uses of dividends may be made available by the Company.

If no direction is given for the use of dividends, they will purchase paid-up additions.

4.3 ADDITIONS AND ACCUMULATIONS

Paid-up additions and dividend accumulations increase the policy's cash value. They are payable as part of the policy proceeds. Additions may be surrendered and accumulations may be withdrawn unless they are used for a loan, for extended term insurance or for paid-up insurance.

4.4 DIVIDEND AT DEATH

A dividend for the period from the beginning of the policy year to the date of the Insured's death will be payable as part of the policy proceeds.

NN 1,4

6

8   WHOLE LIFE POLICY

The rights you have if
you no longer want to
pay premiums.

SECTION 5. CASH VALUES, EXTENDED TERM INSURANCE AND PAID-UP INSURANCE

5.1 CASH VALUE

The cash value for this policy, when all premiums due have been paid, will be the sum of:

- the cash value from the Table of Guaranteed Values;
- the cash value of any paid-up additions; and
- the amount of any dividend accumulations.

The cash value within three months after the due date of any unpaid premium will be the cash value on that due date reduced by any later surrender of paid-up additions and by any later withdrawal of dividend accumulations. After that, the cash value will be the cash value of the insurance then in force, including any paid-up additions and any dividend accumulations.

The cash value of any extended term insurance, paid-up insurance or paid-up additions will be the net single premium for that insurance at the attained age of the Insured.

You can have term
insurance for a period
of time determined by
the cash surrender
value.

5.2 EXTENDED TERM INSURANCE

If any premium is unpaid at the end of the grace period, this policy will be in force as extended term insurance. The amount of the death proceeds under this term insurance will be:

- the plan Amount shown on page 3; plus
- the amount of any paid-up additions in force (Section 4.2); plus
- the amount of any dividend accumulations (Section 4.2); less
- the amount of any policy debt (Section 6.3).

These amounts will be determined as of the due date of the unpaid premium. The term insurance will start as of the due date of the unpaid premium. The period of term insurance will be determined by using the cash surrender value as a net single premium at the attained age of the Insured. If the term insurance would extend to or beyond age 100, paid-up insurance will be provided instead. Extended term insurance does not share in divisible surplus.

If the extended term insurance is surrendered within 31 days after a policy anniversary, the cash value will not be less than the cash value on that anniversary.

You can take a
dividend paying
policy, good for life,
requiring no further
premium payment, in
an amount
determined by the
cash value.

5.3 PAID-UP INSURANCE

Paid-up insurance may be selected in place of extended term insurance. A written request must be received at the Home Office no later than three months after the due date of an unpaid premium. The amount of insurance will be determined by using the cash value as a net single premium at the attained age of the Insured. Any policy debt will continue. Paid-up insurance will share in divisible surplus.

The amount of the death proceeds when this policy is in force as paid-up insurance will be:

- the amount of paid-up insurance determined above; plus

NN 1

- the amount of any in force paid-up additions purchased by dividends after the policy has become paid-up insurance (Section 4.2); plus
- the amount of any existing dividend accumulations (Section 4.2); plus
- the amount of any dividend at death (Section 4.4); less
- the amount of any policy debt (Section 6.3).

These amounts will be determined as of the date of death.

If paid-up insurance is surrendered within 31 days after a policy anniversary, the cash value will not be less than the cash value on that anniversary reduced by any later surrender of paid-up additions and by any later withdrawal of dividend accumulations.

5.4 CASH SURRENDER

The Owner may surrender this policy for its cash surrender value. The cash surrender value is the cash value less any policy debt. A written surrender of all claims, satisfactory to the Company, will be required. The date of surrender will be the date of receipt at the Home Office of the written surrender. The policy will terminate and the cash surrender value will be determined as of the date of surrender. The Company may require that the policy be sent to it.

5.5 TABLE OF GUARANTEED VALUES

Cash values, paid-up insurance and extended term insurance are shown on page 4 for the end of the policy years indicated. These values assume that all premiums due have been paid for the number of years stated. They do not reflect paid-up additions, dividend accumulations or policy debt. Values during a policy year will reflect any portion of the year's premium paid and the time elapsed in that year.

Values for policy years not shown are calculated on the same basis as those on page 4. A list of these values will be furnished on request. A detailed statement of the method of calculation of all values has been filed with the insurance supervisory official of the state in which this policy is delivered. The Company will furnish this statement at the request of the Owner. All values are at least as great as those required by that state.

5.6 BASIS OF VALUES

The cash value for each policy year not shown on page 4 equals the reserve for that year calculated on the Commissioners Reserve Valuation Method. Net single premiums are based on the Commissioners 1980 Standard Ordinary Mortality Table for the sex of the Insured; except that for extended term insurance, the Commissioners 1980 Extended Term Insurance Table for the sex of the Insured is used for the first 20 policy years. Interest is based on an annual effective rate of 5 1/2% for the first 20 policy years and 4% after that. Calculations assume the continuous payment of premiums and the immediate payment of claims.

7

You can take out all of
your cash value, less
any policy debt.

SECTION 6. LOANS

You can borrow money from the company, the maximum amount to be determined by the loan value.

6.1 POLICY AND PREMIUM LOANS

The Owner may obtain a loan from the Company in an amount that is not more than the loan value.

Policy Loan. The loan may be obtained on written request. No loan will be made if the policy is in force as extended term insurance. The Company may defer making the loan for up to six months unless the loan is to be used to pay premiums due the Company.

Premium Loan. If the premium loan provision is in effect on this policy, a loan will be made to pay an overdue premium. If the loan value is not large enough to pay the overdue premium, a premium will be paid for any other frequency permitted by this policy for which the loan value is large enough. The Owner may elect or revoke the premium loan provision by written request received at the Home Office.

Two important facts about loans: Indebtedness is subtracted at death from the insurance proceeds. Despite the loan, the cash value continues to grow as guaranteed, and the policy continues to be eligible for dividends.

6.2 LOAN VALUE

The loan value is the smaller of a. or b., less any policy debt and any premium then due or billed; a. and b. are defined as:

a. the cash value one year after the date of the loan, assuming all premiums due within that year are paid, less interest to one year from the date of the loan.

b. the cash value on the due date of the first premium not yet billed that is due after the date of the loan, less interest from the date of the loan to that premium due date.

6.3 POLICY DEBT

Policy debt consists of all outstanding loans and accrued interest. It may be paid to the Company at any time. Policy debt affects dividends under Section 4.1. Any policy debt will be deducted from the policy proceeds.

If the policy debt equals or exceeds the cash value, this policy will terminate. Termination occurs 31 days after a notice has been mailed to the Owner and to any assignee on record at the Home Office.

You can choose between a fixed or a variable loan rate and you may be able to change your option once a year.

6.4 LOAN INTEREST

Interest accrues and is payable on a daily basis from the date of the loan on policy loans and from the premium due date on premium loans. Unpaid interest is added to the loan.

The Specified Rate loan interest option or the Variable Rate loan interest option is elected on the application.

The fixed loan rate is 8%. The variable loan rate is based on Moody's Corporate Bond Yield Averages - Monthly Average Corporates.

Change To Variable Rate Loan Interest Option. The Owner may request a change to the Variable Rate loan interest option at any time, with the change to take effect on the January 1st following receipt of a written request at the Company's Home Office.

Change To Specified Rate Loan Interest Option. The Owner may request a change to the Specified Rate loan interest option if the interest rate set by the Company under Section 6.6 for the year beginning on the next January 1st is less than 8%. The written request to change must be received at the Home Office between November 15th and the last business day of the calendar year; the change will take effect on the January 1st following receipt of the request at the Home Office.

6.5 SPECIFIED RATE LOAN INTEREST OPTION

Interest is payable at an annual effective rate of 8%.

6.6 VARIABLE RATE LOAN INTEREST OPTION

Interest is payable at an annual effective rate that is set by the Company annually and applied to new or outstanding policy debt during the year beginning each January 1st. The highest loan interest rate that may be set by the Company is the greater of (i) 6 1/2% for the first 20 policy years and 5% after that or (ii) a rate based on the Moody's Corporate Bond Yield Averages-Monthly Average Corporates for the immediately preceding October. This Average is published by Moody's Investor's Service, Inc. If it is no longer published, the highest loan rate will be based on some other similar average established by the insurance supervisory official of the state in which this policy is delivered.

The loan interest rate set by the Company will not exceed the maximum rate permitted by the laws of the state in which this policy is delivered. The loan interest rate may be increased only if the increase in the annual effective rate is at least 1/2%. The loan interest rate will be decreased if the decrease in the annual effective rate is at least 1/2%.

The Company will give notice:
- of the initial loan interest rate in effect at the time a policy or premium loan is made.
- of an increase in loan interest rate on outstanding policy debt no later than 30 days before the January 1st on which the increase takes effect.

This policy will not terminate during a policy year as the sole result of an increase in the loan interest rate during that policy year.

NN 1,4,9

8

SECTION 7. CHANGE OF POLICY

You can change the ———— 7.1 CHANGE OF PLAN
plan, keeping the
original issue age.

The Owner may change this policy to any permanent life insurance plan agreed to by the Owner and the Company by:

- paying the required costs; and

- meeting any other conditions set by the Company.

You can change the ———— 7.2 CHANGE OF INSURED
policy to insure the
life of another person,
e.g., wife to husband, **Change.** The Owner may change the insured under
one business partner this policy by:
to another.

- paying the required costs; and

- meeting any other conditions set by the Company, including the following:

  a. on the date of change, the new insured's age may not be more than 75;

  b. the new insured must have been born on or before the Policy Date of this policy;

c. the new insured must be insurable; and

d. the Owner must have an insurable interest in the life of the new insured.

Date Of Change. The date of change will be the later of:

- the date of the request to change; or

- the date of the medical examination (or the non-medical application).

Terms Of Policy After Change. The policy will cover the new insured starting on the date of change. When coverage on the new insured starts, coverage on the prior insured will terminate.

The contestable and suicide periods for the new insured start on the date of change.

The amount of insurance on the new insured will be set so that there will be no change in the cash value of the policy at the time of change. If the policy has no cash value, the amount will be set so that premiums do not change.

Any policy debt or assignment will continue after the change.

NN 1,4,9   9

SECTION 8. BENEFICIARIES

8.1 DEFINITION OF BENEFICIARIES

The term "beneficiaries" as used in this policy includes direct beneficiaries, contingent beneficiaries and further payees.

8.2 NAMING AND CHANGE OF BENEFICIARIES

By Owner. The Owner may name and change the beneficiaries of death proceeds:

- while the Insured is living.
- during the first 60 days after the date of death of the Insured, if the Insured just before his death was not the Owner. No one may change this naming of a direct beneficiary during this 60 days.

By Direct Beneficiary. A direct beneficiary may name and change the contingent beneficiaries and further payees of his share of the proceeds:

- if the direct beneficiary is the Owner;
- if, at any time after the death of the Insured, no contingent beneficiary or further payee of that share is living; or
- if, after the death of the Insured, the direct beneficiary elects a payment plan. The interest of any other beneficiary in the share of that direct beneficiary will end.

These direct beneficiary rights are subject to the Owner's rights during the 60 days after the date of death of the Insured.

By Spouse (Marital Deduction Provision).

- **Power To Appoint.** The spouse of the Insured will have the power alone and in all events to appoint all amounts payable to the spouse under the policy if:
  a. the Insured just before his death was the Owner; and
  b. the spouse is a direct beneficiary; and
  c. the spouse survives the Insured.
- **To Whom Spouse Can Appoint.** Under this power, the spouse can appoint:
  a. to the estate of the spouse; or
  b. to any other persons as contingent beneficiaries and further payees.
- **Effect Of Exercise.** As to the amounts appointed, the exercise of this power will:
  a. revoke any other designation of beneficiaries;
  b. revoke any election of payment plan as it applies to them; and
  c. cause any provision to the contrary in Section 8 or 9 of this policy to be of no effect.

NN 1,2,4,6,8,9   10

Effective Date. A naming or change of a beneficiary will be made on receipt at the Home Office of a written request that is acceptable to the Company. The request will then take effect as of the date that it was signed. The Company is not responsible for any payment or other action that is taken by it before the receipt of the request. The Company may require that the policy be sent to it to be endorsed to show the naming or change.

8.3 SUCCESSION IN INTEREST OF BENEFICIARIES

Direct Beneficiaries. The proceeds of this policy will be payable in equal shares to the direct beneficiaries who survive and receive payment. If a direct beneficiary dies before he receives all or part of his full share, the unpaid part of his share will be payable in equal shares to the other direct beneficiaries who survive and receive payment.

Contingent Beneficiaries. At the death of all of the direct beneficiaries, the proceeds, or the present value of any unpaid payments under a payment plan, will be payable in equal shares to the contingent beneficiaries who survive and receive payment. If a contingent beneficiary dies before he receives all or part of his full share, the unpaid part of his share will be payable in equal shares to the other contingent beneficiaries who survive and receive payment.

Further Payees. At the death of all of the direct and contingent beneficiaries, the proceeds, or the present value of any unpaid payments under a payment plan, will be paid in one sum:

- in equal shares to the further payees who survive and receive payment; or
- if no further payees survive and receive payment, to the estate of the last to die of all of the direct and contingent beneficiaries.

Owner Or His Estate. If no beneficiaries are alive when the Insured dies, the proceeds will be paid to the Owner or to his estate.

8.4 GENERAL

Transfer Of Ownership. A transfer of ownership of itself will not change the interest of a beneficiary.

Claims Of Creditors. So far as allowed by law, no amount payable under this policy will be subject to the claims of creditors of a beneficiary.

Succession Under Payment Plans. A direct or contingent beneficiary who succeeds to an interest in a payment plan will continue under the terms of the plan.

As an aid to estate and tax planning, a third-party policyowner can change beneficiaries after the death of the insured.

The marital deduction provision is valuable in cases in which the spouse is the direct beneficiary.

Living successor beneficiaries can be provided for by contract.

This clause may safeguard policy proceeds.

A wide range of payment plans is available.

Interest is paid on policy proceeds from the date of death.

SECTION 9. PAYMENT OF POLICY BENEFITS

9.1 PAYMENT OF PROCEEDS

Death proceeds will be paid under the payment plan that takes effect on the date of death of the Insured. The Interest Income Plan (Option A) will be in effect if no payment plan has been elected. Interest will accumulate from the date of death until a payment plan is elected or the proceeds are withdrawn in cash.

Surrender proceeds will be the cash surrender value as of the date of surrender. These proceeds will be paid in cash or under a payment plan that is elected. The Company may defer paying the surrender proceeds for up to six months from the date of surrender. If payment is deferred for 30 days or more, interest will be paid on the surrender proceeds from the date of surrender to the date of payment. Interest will be at an annual effective rate of 5 1/2% during the first 20 policy years and 4% after that.

9.2 PAYMENT PLANS

Interest Income Plan (Option A). The proceeds will earn interest which may be received each month or accumulated. The first payment is due one month after the date on which the plan takes effect. Interest that has accumulated may be withdrawn at any time. Part or all of the proceeds may be withdrawn at any time.

Beneficiaries, who have the right to withdraw from the chosen payment plan, can change payment plans.

Installment Income Plans. Payments will be made each month on the terms of the plan that is elected. The first payment is due on the date that the plan takes effect.

- **Specified Period (Option B).** The proceeds with interest will be paid over a period of from one to 30 years. The present value of any unpaid installments may be withdrawn at any time.

- **Specified Amount (Option D).** Payments of not less than $10.00 per $1,000 of proceeds will be made until all of the proceeds with interest have been paid. The balance may be withdrawn at any time.

Proceeds under these payment plans continue to earn interest.

Life Income Plans. Payments will be made each month on the terms of the plan that is elected. The first payment is due on the date that the plan takes effect. Proof of the date of birth, acceptable to the Company, must be furnished for each person on whose life the payments are based.

- **Single Life Income (Option C).** Payments will be made for a chosen period and, after that, for the life of the person on whose life the payments are based. The choices for the period are:

  a. zero years;

  b. 10 years;

  c. 20 years; or

  d. a refund period which continues until the sum of the payments that have been made is equal to the proceeds that were placed under the plan.

NN 1,2,4,6,9

- **Joint And Survivor Life Income (Option E).** Payments are based on the lives of two persons. Level payments will be made for a period of 10 years and, after that, for as long as one or both of the persons are living.

- **Other Selections.** The Company may offer other selections under the Life Income Plans.

- **Withdrawal.** The present value of any unpaid payments that are to be made for the chosen period (Option C) or the 10 year period (Option E) may be withdrawn only after the death of all of the persons on whose lives the payments are based.

- **Limitations.** A direct or contingent beneficiary who is a natural person may be paid under a Life Income Plan only if the payments depend on his life. A corporation may be paid under a Life Income Plan only if the payments depend on the life of the Insured or, after the death of the Insured, on the life of his spouse or his dependent.

Payment Frequency. On request, payments will be made once every 3, 6 or 12 months instead of each month.

Transfer Between Payment Plans. A beneficiary who is receiving payment under a plan which includes the right to withdraw may transfer the amount withdrawable to any other plan that is available.

Minimum Payment. The Company may limit the election of a payment plan to one that results in payments of at least $50.

If payments under a payment plan are or become less than $50, the Company may change the frequency of payments. If the payments are being made once every 12 months and are less than $50, the Company may pay the present value or the balance of the payment plan.

9.3 PAYMENT PLAN RATES

Interest Income And Installment Income Plans. Proceeds will earn interest at rates declared each year by the Company. None of these rates will be less than an annual effective rate of 3 1/2%. Interest of more than 3 1/2% will increase the amount of the payments or, for the Specified Amount Plan (Option D), increase the number of payments. The present value of any unpaid installments will be based on the 3 1/2% rate of interest.

The Company may offer guaranteed rates of interest higher than 3 1/2% with conditions on withdrawal.

Life Income Plans. Payments will be based on rates declared by the Company. These rates will provide at least as much income as would the Company's rates, on the date that the payment plan takes effect, for a single premium immediate annuity contract, with no charge for issue expenses. Payments under these rates will not be less than the amounts that are described in Minimum Payment Rates.

11

Life income rates vary with investment conditions, but a minimum rate is guaranteed. Once a payment plan takes effect, that rate is assured thereafter.

Minimum Payment Rates. The minimum payment rates for the Installment Income Plans (Options B and D) and the Life Income Plans (Options C and E) are shown in the Minimum Payment Rate Tables.

The Life Income Plan payment rates in those tables depend on the sex and on the adjusted age of each person on whose life the payments are based. The adjusted age is:

- the age on the birthday that is nearest to the date on which the payment plan takes effect; plus

- the age adjustment shown below for the number of policy years that have elapsed from the Policy Date to the date that the payment plan takes effect. A part of a policy year is counted as a full year.

POLICY YEARS ELAPSED	AGE ADJUSTMENT	POLICY YEARS ELAPSED	AGE ADJUSTMENT
1 to 5	+8	31 to 35	-2
6 to 10	+6	36 to 40	-3
11 to 15	+4	41 to 45	-4
16 to 20	+2	46 to 50	-5
21 to 25	0	51 or more	-6
26 to 30	-1		

9.4 EFFECTIVE DATE FOR PAYMENT PLAN

A payment plan that is elected for death proceeds will take effect on the date of death of the Insured if:

- the plan is elected by the Owner; and

- the election is received at the Home Office while the Insured is living.

In all other cases, a payment plan that is elected will take effect:

- on the date the election is received at the Home Office; or

- on a later date, if requested.

9.5 PAYMENT PLAN ELECTIONS

For Death Proceeds By Owner. The Owner may elect payment plans for death proceeds:

- while the Insured is living.

- during the first 60 days after the date of death of the Insured, if the Insured just before his death was not the Owner. No one may change this election made during those 60 days.

For Death Proceeds By Direct Or Contingent Beneficiary. A direct or contingent beneficiary may elect payment plans for death proceeds payable to him if no payment plan that has been elected is in effect. This right is subject to the Owner's rights during the 60 days after the date of death of the Insured.

For Surrender Proceeds. The Owner may elect payment plans for surrender proceeds. The Owner will be the direct beneficiary.

9.6 INCREASE OF MONTHLY INCOME

A direct beneficiary who is to receive proceeds under a payment plan may increase the amount of the monthly payments. This is done by the payment of an annuity premium to the Company at the time the payment plan elected under Section 9.5 takes effect. The amount that will be applied under the payment plan will be the net premium. The net premium is the annuity premium less a charge of not more than 2% and less any premium tax. The net premium will be applied under the same payment plan and at the same rates as the proceeds. The Company may limit this net premium to an amount that is equal to the direct beneficiary's share of the proceeds payable under this policy.

Beneficiaries can add funds to a payment plan when it takes effect.

Our minimum guarantees for installment income plans.

MINIMUM PAYMENT RATE TABLE
Minimum Monthly Income Payments Per $1,000 Proceeds

INSTALLMENT INCOME PLANS (Options B and D)

PERIOD (YEARS)	MONTHLY PAYMENT	PERIOD (YEARS)	MONTHLY PAYMENT	PERIOD (YEARS)	MONTHLY PAYMENT
1	$84.65	11	$9.09	21	$5.56
2	43.05	12	8.46	22	5.39
3	29.19	13	7.94	23	5.24
4	22.27	14	7.49	24	5.09
5	18.12	15	7.10	25	4.96
6	15.35	16	6.76	26	4.84
7	13.38	17	6.47	27	4.73
8	11.90	18	6.20	28	4.63
9	10.75	19	5.97	29	4.53
10	9.83	20	5.75	30	4.45

NN 1,2,4,6,9

14

WHOLE LIFE POLICY

MINIMUM PAYMENT RATE TABLES
Minimum Monthly Income Payments Per $1,000 Proceeds

Our minimum guarantees for life income plans. ────── LIFE INCOME PLAN (Option C)

MALE ADJUSTED AGE*	SINGLE LIFE MONTHLY PAYMENTS				FEMALE ADJUSTED AGE*				
	CHOSEN PERIOD (YEARS)					CHOSEN PERIOD (YEARS)			
	ZERO	10	20	REFUND		ZERO	10	20	REFUND
55	$ 4.99	$ 4.91	$ 4.66	$ 4.73	55	$ 4.54	$ 4.51	$ 4.38	$ 4.40
56	5.09	5.00	4.72	4.81	56	4.62	4.58	4.44	4.47
57	5.20	5.10	4.78	4.90	57	4.71	4.66	4.51	4.54
58	5.32	5.20	4.85	4.99	58	4.80	4.75	4.57	4.62
59	5.44	5.31	4.91	5.08	59	4.90	4.84	4.64	4.70
60	5.57	5.42	4.97	5.18	60	5.00	4.93	4.70	4.78
61	5.71	5.54	5.04	5.29	61	5.11	5.03	4.77	4.87
62	5.86	5.67	5.10	5.40	62	5.23	5.14	4.84	4.96
63	6.02	5.80	5.16	5.51	63	5.36	5.25	4.91	5.06
64	6.20	5.94	5.22	5.63	64	5.49	5.37	4.98	5.17
65	6.38	6.08	5.28	5.76	65	5.64	5.50	5.05	5.28
66	6.54	6.23	5.33	5.90	66	5.79	5.63	5.12	5.39
67	6.70	6.38	5.38	6.04	67	5.94	5.77	5.19	5.52
68	6.87	6.54	5.43	6.19	68	6.09	5.91	5.25	5.65
69	7.05	6.71	5.48	6.35	69	6.25	6.07	5.32	5.79
70	7.21	6.87	5.52	6.52	70	6.42	6.23	5.37	5.94
71	7.40	7.05	5.55	6.69	71	6.59	6.40	5.43	6.09
72	7.58	7.21	5.59	6.88	72	6.78	6.58	5.48	6.26
73	7.77	7.40	5.62	7.07	73	6.96	6.76	5.52	6.44
74	7.95	7.57	5.64	7.28	74	7.16	6.95	5.57	6.63
75	8.14	7.75	5.66	7.49	75	7.35	7.14	5.60	6.83
76	8.32	7.92	5.68	7.72	76	7.56	7.34	5.63	7.04
77	8.49	8.09	5.70	7.96	77	7.77	7.54	5.66	7.26
78	8.84	8.26	5.71	8.21	78	7.97	7.74	5.68	7.51
79	9.18	8.42	5.72	8.47	79	8.18	7.94	5.70	7.76
80	9.51	8.57	5.73	8.74	80	8.37	8.13	5.71	8.03
81	9.84	8.71	5.74	9.04	81	8.57	8.32	5.72	8.32
82	10.18	8.85	5.74	9.34	82	8.93	8.50	5.73	8.61
83	10.49	8.97	5.75	9.65	83	9.28	8.67	5.74	8.93
84	10.82	9.09	5.75	9.98	84	9.62	8.83	5.74	9.27
85 and over	11.13	9.20	5.75	10.34	85 and over	9.96	8.97	5.75	9.62

LIFE INCOME PLAN (OPTION E)

MALE ADJUSTED AGE*	JOINT AND SURVIVOR MONTHLY PAYMENTS						
	FEMALE ADJUSTED AGE*						
	55	60	65	70	75	80	85 and over
55	$4.16	$4.34	$4.51	$4.65	$4.76	$4.84	$4.88
60	4.26	4.51	4.75	4.98	5.16	5.29	5.37
65	4.35	4.65	4.98	5.31	5.61	5.84	5.98
70	4.41	4.76	5.17	5.62	6.07	6.44	6.68
75	4.46	4.84	5.32	5.88	6.48	7.03	7.42
80	4.48	4.89	5.41	6.05	6.79	7.52	8.07
85 and over	4.5C	4.92	5.46	6.15	6.99	7.85	8.53

*See Section 9.3.

NN 1,2,4,6,8,9   13

It is recommended that you...

read your policy.

notify your Northwestern Mutual agent or the Company at 720 E. Wisconsin Avenue, Milwaukee, Wis. 53202, of an address change.

call your Northwestern Mutual agent for information — particularly on a suggestion to terminate or exchange this policy for another policy or plan.

Please note and vote.

Election of Trustees

The members of The Northwestern Mutual Life Insurance Company are its policyholders of insurance policies and deferred annuity contracts. The members exercise control through a Board of Trustees. Elections to the Board are held each year at the annual meeting of members. Members are entitled to vote in person or by proxy.

WHOLE LIFE POLICY

Eligible For Annual Dividends.

Insurance payable on death of Insured. Premiums payable for period shown on page 3.

NN 1

16   WHOLE LIFE POLICY

WAIVER OF PREMIUM BENEFIT (LIFE & TERM)

1. THE BENEFIT

Disability Before Age 60. If total disability of the Insured starts on or before the policy anniversary nearest his 60th birthday, the Company will waive all premiums that come due on the policy as long as the total disability continues.

Disability After Age 60. If total disability of the Insured starts after the policy anniversary nearest his 60th birthday, the Company will waive those premiums that come due on the policy as long as the total disability continues, but only to the policy anniversary that is nearest his 65th birthday.

Premium Waived On An Annual Basis. Even if premiums have been paid more often than every 12 months, a premium waived on a policy anniversary will be an annual premium.

Refund Of Premium. The Company will refund that portion of a premium paid which applies to a period beyond the policy month in which the total disability began.

Premium For Benefit. The premium for this Benefit is shown on page 3.

2. TOTAL DISABILITY

Definition Of Total Disability. A total disability is one which prevents the Insured from engaging in an occupation. For the first 24 months of total disability, an occupation is the one that the Insured had at the time he became disabled. After 24 months, an occupation is one for which the Insured is qualified by education, training or experience. Due regard will be given to his vocation and earnings before he became disabled.

Disabilities Covered By This Benefit. Premiums are waived for total disability only if:

- the Insured becomes disabled while this Benefit is in force;

- the disability results from an accident or sickness; and

- the disability lasts for at least six months.

Presumptive Total Disability. Even if the Insured is able to work, he will be considered totally disabled if he incurs the total and irrecoverable loss of:

- sight of both eyes;
- use of both hands;
- use of both feet;
- use of one hand and one foot;
- speech; or
- hearing in both ears.

The loss must be the result of an accident that occurs, or from a sickness that first appears, while this Benefit is in force.

3. PROOF OF DISABILITY

Before any premium is waived, proof of total disability must be given to the Company within one year from the start of disability. However, the claim will not be affected if the proof is given as soon as reasonably possible.

4. PROOF THAT DISABILITY HAS CONTINUED

Proof that the total disability has continued may be required once a year. If the proof is not given when it is required, no more premiums will be waived. The Company will not require proof that the disability continues beyond the policy anniversary that is nearest the 65th birthday of the Insured.

5. PAYMENT OF PREMIUM

A premium that comes due while the Insured is disabled, but before the Company has approved the claim, is payable and should be paid. A premium that is paid and later waived will be refunded. A premium that is not paid will be waived if the total disability began before the end of the grace period.

6. TERMINATION OF BENEFIT

This Benefit will terminate on the policy anniversary that is nearest the 65th birthday of the Insured, unless he has been totally disabled since the policy anniversary that is nearest his 60th birthday. It will terminate earlier:

- when the policy terminates.
- when the policy becomes extended term or paid-up insurance.
- when the Owner's written request is received at the Home Office.

I/R 4400.00
29-3855-07 (12-85)

NN 1,2,4,5 WP

SPECIMEN COPY
PROVISIONS MAY VARY SLIGHTLY IN CERTAIN STATES

Secretary
THE NORTHWESTERN MUTUAL LIFE INSURANCE COMPANY

ACCIDENTAL DEATH BENEFIT

1. THE BENEFIT

The Company will pay an Accidental Death Benefit upon receipt of proof that the Insured's death:

- resulted, directly and independently of all other causes, from accidental bodily injury; and
- occurred while this Benefit was in force.

2. PREMIUM AND AMOUNT OF BENEFIT

The premium for and the amount of this Benefit are shown on page 3. The Benefit will be payable as part of the policy proceeds.

3. RISKS NOT ASSUMED

This Benefit will not be payable if the Insured's death resulted from or was contributed to by:

- suicide.
- bodily or mental infirmity or disease.

- an act or incident of war, declared or undeclared.
- riding in any kind of aircraft:
  - a. as a passenger in any aircraft operated by or for the armed forces.
  - b. as a pilot, as a participant in training, or as a crew member. The term "crew member" includes anyone who has any duties at any time on the flight with respect to either the flight or the aircraft.

4. TERMINATION OF BENEFIT

This Benefit will terminate on the policy anniversary that is nearest the 70th birthday of the Insured. It will terminate earlier:

- when the policy terminates.
- when the policy becomes extended term or paid-up insurance.
- when the Owner's written request is received at the Home Office.

SPECIMEN
COPY
PROVISIONS MAY VARY SLIGHTLY
IN CERTAIN STATES

Secretary
THE NORTHWESTERN MUTUAL LIFE
INSURANCE COMPANY

NN 1 Life ADB

I/R 4400.00
29-3855-01 (12-85)

18   WHOLE LIFE POLICY

ADDITIONAL PURCHASE BENEFIT

1. THE BENEFIT

The Company will issue additional permanent life insurance policies on the Insured, with no evidence of insurability, subject to the terms and conditions below.

The term "new policy" means each additional policy issued under this Benefit.

The premium for this Benefit is shown on page 3.

2. PURCHASE DATES

The Owner may purchase a new policy as of each Purchase Date. There is a Purchase Date on each policy anniversary that is nearest the 22nd, 25th, 28th, 31st, 34th, 37th, and 40th birthdays of the Insured.

The Company must receive an application and the first premium for each new policy:

- while the Insured is living; and
- not more than 60 days before, nor more than 30 days after, a Purchase Date.

The Owner of the new policy must have an insurable interest in the life of the Insured.

3. ADVANCE PURCHASE

A new policy may be purchased before a Purchase Date each time one of these events occurs:

- the marriage of the Insured.
- the birth of a child of the Insured.
- the completion, by the Insured, of the legal adoption of a child.

The event must occur while this policy is in force. To make an advance purchase of a new policy, there must be a future Purchase Date that has not been used. An advance purchase of a new policy cancels the next unused Purchase Date.

The Company must receive an application and the first premium for each new policy:

- while the Insured is living; and
- not more than 90 days after the marriage, birth or adoption.

The Company may require proof of the marriage, birth or adoption.

The Owner of the new policy must have an insurable interest in the life of the Insured.

4. AUTOMATIC TERM INSURANCE

The Company will provide term insurance on the life of the Insured during each 90 day period in which the Owner may purchase a new policy. The amount of the term insurance will be the largest amount of insurance which could have been purchased as a new policy under this Benefit. The proceeds of the term insurance are payable on the death of the Insured only if:

- a new policy was not purchased within that period; or
- a new policy purchased within that period is surrendered to the Company for a refund of premiums.

The proceeds of the term insurance will be payable to the beneficiary and subject to the terms of this policy.

5. TERMS OF NEW POLICY

Plan. Each new policy will be on a level premium permanent life insurance plan being issued by the Company on the date of purchase of the new policy. An additional benefit that is made a part of the new policy will contain the provisions of that benefit as it is being issued by the Company on the date of issue of the new policy.

Amount. The minimum amount of each new policy on the Whole Life Paid Up at 90 plan will be $20,000. The amount of each new policy on any other plan must be at least the Company's minimum for policies being issued on that plan at that time. The maximum amount of each policy will be the Amount of the Additional Purchase Benefit shown on page 3. However, in the event of a multiple birth, the maximum amount which may be purchased as an advance purchase will be the Amount of this Benefit multiplied by the number of children of the birth.

Waiver Of Premium Benefit. If the Waiver of Premium Benefit is in force on this policy at the time that the Owner has the right to purchase a new policy:

- a new policy on a plan with a level death benefit on which premiums are payable to age 90 or later may be issued with the Waiver of Premium Benefit. If premiums are being waived for this policy at the time the new policy is purchased, premiums will also be waived for the new policy for as long as they are waived for this policy.
- a new policy on a plan with a nonlevel death benefit or a plan on which all premiums are payable before age 90 may be issued with the Waiver of Premium Benefit only if premiums are not then being waived for this policy. If the Waiver of Premium Benefit is a part of the new policy, it will apply only to a disability that starts after the new policy takes effect.

NN 1 Life APB

I/R 4400.00
29-3855-02 (12-85)   (Continued on reverse side)

Accidental Death Benefit. Each new policy may be issued with the Accidental Death Benefit, provided that:

- the Accidental Death Benefit is a part of this policy when the new policy is issued; and
- the Accidental Death Benefit amount is not more than the amount of the new policy. However, the total amount of Accidental Death Benefit in force with the Company on the life of the Insured may not be more than the Company's published limits.

Provisions. The Suicide and Incontestability provisions in each new policy will be in effect from the Date of Issue of this policy. Each new policy will contain any exclusion provision which is a part of this policy.

Premiums. The premium for each new policy, including any additional benefits, will be determined as of its date of issue based on:

- the Company's premium rates then in effect;
- the plan and amount of the new policy and any additional benefits; and
- the Insured's age on the policy date of the new policy.

If the Insured was age 18 or more on the Policy Date of this policy, the premium for the new policy will be based on the classification of risk of this policy. If the Insured was age 17 or less on the Policy Date of this policy, the premium for the new policy will be based on the classification of risk of this policy adjusted to reflect the Insured's cigarette smoking habits.

Effective Date. Each new policy will take effect on the later of:

- the date the Company receives the application; or
- the date the Company receives the first premium.

6. TERMINATION OF BENEFIT

This Benefit will terminate on the policy anniversary that is nearest the 40th birthday of the Insured. It will terminate earlier:

- when this policy terminates.
- when this policy becomes extended term or paid-up insurance.
- on the use of the final Purchase Date by an advance purchase.
- when the Owner's written request is received at the Home Office.

Secretary
THE NORTHWESTERN MUTUAL LIFE
INSURANCE COMPANY

NN 1 Life APB

APPENDIX D

Universal Life Policy

Fundamental Capital Life Insurance Company

A Stock Company

This is your universal life insurance policy on the life of the insured. It is adjustable insurance because:

- You can vary the amount and frequency of premium payments.

- You can change the specified amount. This results in a change of the death benefit.

We will pay the beneficiary the death benefit proceeds when we receive due proof of the insured's death. Payment will be made only if the policy is in force on the date of the insured's death.

We will pay you the net cash value proceeds of this policy if the policy is in force and the insured is living on the maturity date.

The maturity date is the policy anniversary following the insured's 100th birthday, unless extended. The policy may end prior to the maturity date if premiums and credited interest are insufficient to continue coverage to such date.

Read your policy carefully. This policy is a legal contract between you and us.

Right to Examine Your Policy

We want you to fully understand and be satisfied with your policy. If for any reason, you are not satisfied, return it TO the agent or to our home office within 21 days after receiving it. If you do, the policy will be void from the policy date. We will refund your premium.

_____   _____
    Secretary   President

Universal Life Insurance

Flexible premiums payable until maturity
Adjustable death benefit for the lifetime of the insured
    so long as the policy stays in force
Net cash values, if any, payable at maturity
No dividends
Premiums allocated between a risk premium and an
    accumulation account
Interest rates declarable annually by the company
    subject to the guarantees in the contract.

```
                        SPECIFICATIONS


    POLICY INFORMATION

    POLICY NUMBER                       Sample
    INSURED:                            John Doe
    AGE:                                35

    POLICY DATE                         January 1, 2001
    MATURITY DATE                       January 1, 2065

    FIRST PREMIUM:                      $1000
    AMOUNT OF PLANNED PREMIUM           $1000
    PLANNED PREMIUM PAYABLE             ANNUALLY

    GUIDELINE SINGLE PREMIUM:           $19,652.35
    GUIDELINE ANNUAL PREMIUM:           $1,178.25

    INSURED'S INFORMATION
        INSURED'S UNDERWRITING CLASS    PREFERRED




    *  THE DEATH BENEFIT IS THE LARGER OF THE
       SPECIFIED AMOUNT OF THE ACCOUNT VALUE TIMES
       THE APPLICABLE PERCENTAGE.  SEE PAGE 6.
```

3

Your Contract With Us

Some Terms and Definitions

We identify or define here some of the terms used all through this contract. We explain other terms, not defined here, in other parts of the text.

Account Value: Is equal to the net premiums paid, increased with interest and decreased by the monthly deductions and partial surrenders, if any.

Adjusted Account Value: An amount calculated on each monthly processing day after the first which is used in calculating the monthly cost of insurance.

Applicable Percentage: A factor used in calculating the death benefit. It varies by the attained age of the insured and is contained in the table at the end of the **Death Benefit** section.

Attained Age: For the first policy year is shown on page 3. On each policy anniversary the attained age increases by one and then stays the same for the duration of that policy year.

Beneficiary: The person designated to receive the death benefit proceeds in the event of the insured's death while this policy is in force.

Cash Value: The account value less any applicable surrender charge.

Cumulative Premium Limit: Is the limit on the total premiums that may be paid. It is described fully in the **Premium Payments** section.

Death Benefit: The amount payable on the death of the insured while this policy is in force. It is explained fully in the **Death Benefit** section.

Death Benefit Proceeds: Is the death benefit reduced by any outstanding policy debt.

Full Surrender: Is the surrender of all your rights under the policy accompanied by the payment to you of the net cash value. There may be a surrender charge (see the **Account Value and Cash Value Benefits** section).

Initial Specified Amount: Is the specified amount shown on page 3.

Insured: The person named as the insured on page 3. The insured may be someone other than the owner.

Maturity Date: Is the policy anniversary on or following the insured's 100th birthday, unless extended at your written request.

Monthly Processing Day: The policy date and, in each later month, the same day of the month as the policy date.

Net Account Value: The account value less any outstanding policy debt.

Net Cash Value: The cash value less any outstanding policy debt.

Net Premium: Is the premium paid less any expense charge, and possibly less any premium tax we must pay, explained more fully in the in the **Account Value and Cash Value Benefits** section.

Option: Used in determining the death benefit as defined in the **Death Benefit** section.

Outstanding Policy Debt: The amount required to fully repay all outstanding policy loans.

Partial Surrender: Is a payment to you of some portion of the cash value accompanied by a reduction to the account value and, possibly, to the specified amount. Consequently there may be a reduction to the death benefit. There may be a partial surrender charge (see the **Account Value and Cash Value Benefits** section).

Partial Surrender Factor Remaining (PSFR): Is a factor used in determining the surrender charge for each segment. It is explained fully in the **Account Value and Cash Value Benefits** section.

Policy Date: The effective date of coverage under this policy. Policy months, years and anniversaries are measured from the policy date. It is shown on page 3.

Policy Value for Lapse: Is the amount upon which policy lapse depends. In the first 3 policy years it is the net account value, and thereafter it is the net cash value.

Rating Factor: Is used in determining the cost of insurance rate. It is equal to 1 unless a different rating factor is shown on page 3, in which case it is equal to that number.

Risk Amount: An amount calculated on each monthly processing day, to which the monthly cost of insurance rates apply in calculating the monthly cost of insurance.

Specified Amount Segment (also called **Segment**): The initial specified amount is a segment, as is each increase in specified amount. Each segment will have its own underwriting class and rating factor which may differ from those of other segments. Each segment will also have its own effective date for coverage. For the initial specified amount it is the policy date. For later segments, it is the monthly processing day on or following our approval of any request for increase in specified amount.

Segment Duration: Yearly periods measured from the effective date for each specified amount segment.

Specified Amount: Is an amount used in calculating the death benefit and is equal to the sum of all specified amount segments. It can be changed by a partial surrender and as described in the **Right to Change** section.

Surrender Charge: A charge to the account value in the event of full or partial surrender. There is a surrender charge if full or partial surrender occurs within twelve years following the effective date of the most recent specified amount segment. It is explained further in the **Account Value and Cash Value Benefits** section.

We, Us, Our: First Capital Life Insurance Company.

Written Request: A request in writing signed by you and received by us.

You, Your: The owner of this policy as shown in the application, unless later changed following written request. The owner may be someone other than the insured.

This Policy is a Legal Contract

This policy is a legal contract that you have entered into with us. We promise to provide the

insurance benefits described in this policy. In return, you have submitted a completed application, a copy of which is attached. You also promise to pay the first premium shown on page 3. There is no insurance until the first premium is paid.

The entire contract consists of:

- the basic policy;

- riders, if any, which add benefits to the basic policy;

- endorsements, if any; and

- your application, and any amendments or supplemental applications.

When Coverage Begins

The coverage begins on the policy date provided that the first premium has been paid, and the policy has been delivered while there has been no change in the health of the insured or to the answers to the health questions contained in the application.

Maturity Date

Unless the maturity date is extended at your request, if this policy is in force on the maturity date:

- all insurance benefits end; and

- the net cash value, if any, will be paid as you direct in a lump sum or under a payment plan.

At your written request we will extend the maturity to a date you choose.

The policy may end prior to the maturity date if premium payments are insufficient to

continue coverage to such date. Details are provided in the When This Policy Ends subsection of the **General Terms** section.

Rights of the Owner

As the owner, you can exercise the rights given by this policy. These include:

- the right to apply to change the specified amount according to the **Right to Change** section;

- the right to cash value benefits according to the **Account Value and Cash Value Benefits** section;

- the right to borrow and repay money according to the **Policy Loans** section;

- the right to choose and change the beneficiary according to the **Beneficiary and Proceeds** section;

- the right to choose how proceeds will be paid according to the **Payment Plans** section;

- the right to name, and later rename, a contingent owner who becomes the owner on your death;

- the right to assign ownership or assign the policy as security for an obligation according to the **General Terms** section; and

- the right to reinstate coverage according to the **General Terms** section.

If you die before the insured and have not named a contingent owner, all of these rights belong to your estate.

Premium Payments

Premium payments are flexible. This means you can choose the amount and frequency of

payments. After the first premium has been paid, subsequent premiums can be

paid at any time. The actual amount and frequency of premium payments will affect the cash value and the amount and duration of insurance. Please refer to the **General Terms** section for a detailed explanation of the grace period and of policy lapse.

First Premium

The amount of the first premium is shown on page 3. The first premium is payable when this policy is delivered. There is no insurance until the first premium is paid.

Planned Premium Payments

The amount and the frequency of the planned premiums you selected are shown on page 3. You can request us to change the amount and the frequency subject to the cumulative premium limit.

You can choose to have planned premium payment reminder notices sent at 12, 6, or 3 month intervals. If you desire, we can deduct planned premiums from your bank account monthly. Each monthly payment must be at least $10.

Failure to pay a planned premium will not, in itself, jeopardize coverage under this policy. However, regardless whether a premium was paid when planned or not, the policy will end at the end of the grace period following a monthly processing day on which the

policy value for lapse is insufficient to provide for the monthly deduction (see **General Terms** section).

Unscheduled Additional Premiums

Premiums of any amount may be paid at any time.

Required Premiums to Prevent Lapse.

The first premium together with any subsequent premiums paid and interest credited may not be sufficient to provide insurance to the maturity date. All net premiums are credited to the policy account value. Interest is also credited to account values. The monthly deductions are deducted monthly from the policy account value.

If the policy value for lapse on any monthly processing day is insufficient to cover the monthly deduction due, all policy benefits will end subject to those rights set forth in the Grace Period subsection of the **General Terms** section. In this event additional premium will have to be paid to keep the policy in force.

Cumulative Premium Limit

The maximum amount of premium which may be paid in any policy year is the greater of the minimum amount of premium, if any, required to keep

the policy in force to the end of that policy year, or the net sum of the following:

- the cumulative premium limit for that policy year; less

- the sum of premiums paid in the current policy year and all prior policy years; plus

- the sum of partial surrenders paid in all policy years.

As of the policy date, the cumulative premium limit for each policy year is equal to the larger of a) and b), where a) is the guideline single premium shown on page 3 and b) is the policy year times the guideline annual premium shown on page 3.

A change in the specified amount, an option change, an addition, deletion or change of rider benefits will cause the cumulative premium limit to be adjusted. In the event that an adjustment has been necessary, upon your written request, we will provide you with the current schedule of cumulative premium limits.

Where to Pay

Your payments are to be paid to our home office at the address shown on page 3 unless we notify you of a different address.

Death Benefit

Death Benefit Proceeds

If the insured dies while this policy is in force, we will pay death benefit proceeds equal to the death benefit reduced by any outstanding policy debt upon proof satisfactory to us of the insured's death.

The death benefit proceeds are also subject to the conditions and adjustments defined in the

Beneficiary and Proceeds section.

Death Benefit

The death benefit depends upon the following:

- the option in effect on the date of death; and

- any increases or decreases made to the initial specified

amount shown on page 3 (see the **Right to Change** section).

The death benefit is equal to the larger of a) and b), where:

a) is the specified amount plus, for option 2 only, the account value; and

b) is the account value times the applicable percentage as shown in the table following.

Option

The option is used in determining the death benefit.

There are 2 possible options for this policy, option 1 and option 2. The option at policy inception is shown on page 3. You may later change the option as described in the **Right to Change** section.

APPLICABLE PERCENTAGE

Attained Age	Applicable Percentage	Attained Age	Applicable Percentage	Attained Age	Applicable Percentage
40 or younger	250%	54	157%	68	117%
41	243%	55	150%	69	116%
42	236%	56	146%	70	115%
43	229%	57	142%	71	113%
44	222%	58	138%	72	111%
45	215%	59	134%	73	109%
46	209%	60	130%	74	107%
47	203%	61	128%	75–90	105%
48	197%	62	126%	91	104%
49	191%	63	124%	92	103%
50	185%	64	122%	93	102%
51	178%	65	120%	94	101%
52	171%	66	119%	95 and older	100%
53	164%	67	118%		

Right to Change

You make make a written request to change your policy as provided for in this section. We will not allow any change which would violate the cumulative premium limits as detailed in the **Premium Payments** section.

Increasing the Specified Amount

You must submit a supplemental application, which will become part of this contract, for an increase in specified amount. We also require proof satisfactory to us that the insured is insurable. An increase will go into effect on the monthly processing day on or following our approval of your request.

Each increase in specified amount will be a new specified amount segment.

The policy value for lapse after the increase must be at least enough to cover the next two monthly deductions. If the policy value for lapse would not be at least that amount, you will have to pay, in connection with the increase request, enough additional premium to bring the policy value for lapse to such a minimum level.

Decreasing the Specified Amount

Any decrease will go into effect on the monthly processing day on or following the date we receive the request.

The decrease will first be applied against the most recent specified amount segment. It will then be applied to other specified amount segments in the reverse order in which they occurred.

The specified amount remaining after a decrease may not be less than the minimums we allow. After the tenth policy year, the minimum is $10,000. For the first 10 policy years, the minimums are:

- $25,000 if the insured's age on the policy date is 0–54;

- $20,000 if the insured's age on the policy date is 55–59;

- $15,000 if the insured's age on the policy date is 60–64; and

- $10,000 if the insured's age on the policy date is 65 or older.

Changing the Death Benefit Option

As long as the specified amount times the applicable percentage is less than the specified amount plus, if option 2, the account value, you can request to change the death benefit option you have chosen.

If you request to change from option 2 to option 1, the specified amount will be increased by the amount of the account value. If you request to change from option 1 to option 2, the specified amount will be decreased by the amount of the account value. The change will only be allowed if the resulting specified amount is not less than the minimums described in the preceding subsection. The change will go into effect on the monthly processing day on or following the date we receive the written request.

Account Value and Cash Value Benefits

Cash Value Benefits

Subject to the **Beneficiary and Proceeds** section, you can make a written request to receive a full surrender or a partial surrender from your policy which together constitute the cash value benefits. Subject to the limitations which follow, you can make this request at any time during the insured's life provided this policy is in force. Explanations of terms and methods used to calculate the cash value benefits follow.

Net Premium

The net premium is the premium received less the expense charge, if any. There is no expense charge if the specified amount is at least $100,000. If the specified amount is less than $100,000 the expense charge is 2% of all premiums received for the first 20 policy years only. However, we may waive the charge entirely.

The expense charge applies to all premiums received, including the first premium, any planned premium and any unscheduled additional premium. If there is no expense charge, then the net premium and the premium are the same.

In addition, we reserve the right to deduct from the premium any premium tax which we must pay. In such case, the net premium will be the amount of the premium remaining after we make any such deduction.

Account Value

The account value is calculated daily. The first monthly processing day is the policy date and on that day the account value is equal to the net premium less the monthly deduction as calculated according to the next subsection. Each day after the first monthly processing day, we calculate the account value as follows:

- we start with the account value as of the prior day;

- then, we add the daily interest earned on that account value;

- then, we add any net premium received effective that date (The effective date for crediting net premiums is the business day following our receipt of the premium);

- then, we subtract any partial surrender effective that date (If this is a monthly processing day, the result of this step is the adjusted account value);

- finally, if the calculation is done on a monthly processing day we subtract the monthly deduction as described below.

Monthly Deduction

Each monthly deduction consists of the cost of insurance (see following subsection) plus the cost of additional benefits provided by rider (as described in any such rider) plus, during the first 20 policy years only, a monthly administrative fee, which we may waive, of $6.00 for specified amounts less than $100,000 or $3.50 for specified amounts of $100,000 or more.

Cost of Insurance

In calculating the monthly cost of insurance, we first calculate the risk amount. On the first monthly processing day, the risk amount is equal to the initial death benefit divided by 1.0032737 and the resulting quotient reduced by the premium paid. On any monthly processing day after the first, the risk amount is equal to the death benefit, as of the time the adjusted account value is calculated, divided by 1.0032737 with the resulting quotient reduced by the adjusted account value.

The monthly cost of insurance is calculated on each monthly processing day. It is deducted from the account value on the monthly processing day at the beginning of the policy month for which it applies.

If there is only one specified amount segment, the monthly cost of insurance is equal to the risk amount multiplied by the cost of insurance rate.

If there is more than one specified amount segment, we calculate the monthly cost of insurance as follows:

- first, we allocate a portion of the adjusted account value to each segment in turn, in the same order in which the segments arose, such portion equal to the as yet unallocated adjusted account value, or the segment, if smaller;

- then, we allocate a portion of the risk amount to each segment in turn, in the same order in which the segments arose, such portion being equal to the as yet unallocated risk amount, or, if smaller, the segment reduced by the adjusted account value allocated to the segment.

- then, if after this process there remains any unallocated

risk amount, we allocate it to the most recent segment;

- then, we calculate the cost of insurance for each segment by applying the cost of insurance rate for that segment by the risk amount allocated to that segment;

- finally, we add the cost of insurance for all segments.

Cost of Insurance Rate

The cost of insurance rate is based on the insured's sex, attained age, and on the insured's underwriting class and rating factor for each segment. The rate will differ by segment if the underwriting class or the rating factor is not the same for all segments.

The guaranteed cost of insurance rates are obtained as described in the table of Guaranteed Monthly Cost of Insurance Rates at the end of this contract. We can use cost of insurance rates that are lower than the guaranteed rates.

Interest Rate

Interest on the account value is credited daily. The guaranteed interest rate used in calculating the account value is that rate, which when compounded daily is equivalent to 4% per year. If the net account value is at least $20,000 there is an additional amount of interest credited as described in the next paragraph.

During the first 15 policy years, we will credit on each monthly processing day an additional amount of interest equal to the monthly equivalent of 1/2% per year on any net account value in excess of $20,000. After the 15th policy year, on each monthly processing day on which the net account value is at least $20,000, we will credit an additional amount of interest equal to the monthly equivalent of 1% per year on the entire net account value.

We can use interest rates greater than the guaranteed rates to calculate interest credits for the net account value.

Cash Value

The cash value is equal to the account value reduced by the surrender charge as defined below.

Surrender Charge

Upon full surrender, there is a surrender charge which will not exceed that permitted by applicable state law. After 12 years following the effective date of the most recent specified amount segment, there is no surrender charge. The surrender charge is equal to the sum of the per $1000 of specified amount surrender charge and the percent of account value surrender charge, both as defined below.

The per $1000 of specified amount surrender charge is the sum of the per $1000 of specified amount surrender charge for each segment. The per $1000 surrender charge is calculated separately for each segment and is equal to a) x b) x c) where:

- a) is obtained by first selecting from the Per $1000 of Specified Amount Surrender Charge Table at the end of this contract, the correct rate basis per $1000 of specified amount segment based on the insured's sex and attained age as of the effective date of the segment, then applying it to the original segment amount;

- b) is obtained by selecting, from the same table, the correct percentage for surrender charge rate basis based on the insured's sex and attained age as of the effective date of the segment and on the segment duration; and

- c) is the PSFR for the segment.

The percent of account value surrender charge applies for the first 8 policy years only, and is equal to 4.25% of the account value, but not to exceed the difference between the actual interest credited to the account value for the most recent 12 months and the interest which would have been credited had the minimum guaranteed interest rate been used for that time.

Full Surrender

Subject to the **Beneficiary and Proceeds** section, you can return your policy to us and make a written request for full surrender, in which case your policy will end (see the When This Policy Ends subsection of the **General Terms** section). In such event, we will send you the net cash value as of the date of your request.

Partial Surrender

You can make a written request to receive a partial surrender of a portion of the net cash value, not less than $500, at any time during the insured's life after the first policy year.

The net cash value remaining after a partial surrender must be enough to provide for all monthly deductions and loan interest until the next policy anniversary. This places a maximum limit on the amount of partial surrender available at any point in time.

In the event of a partial surrender, the account value will be reduced by the following amounts:

- the amount of the partial surrender;

- a $25 transaction fee; and

- the applicable partial surrender charge as described in the next subsection.

The reduction to account value may also result in a reduction to the specified amount as follows:

- if the product of the applicable percentage multiplied by the account value before the partial surrender is less than or equal to the specified amount before the partial surrender, then, for option 1 only, the specified amount will be reduced to equal the specified amount before the partial surrender multiplied by the quotient of the account value after the partial surrender divided by the account value before the partial surrender; and

- if the specified amount before the partial surrender is less than the product of the applicable percentage multiplied by the account value before the partial surrender and is greater than the product of the applicable percentage multiplied by the account value after the partial surrender, then, for option 1 only, the specified amount will be reduced to equal the latter product.

Except for the required reductions in specified amount in the event of partial surrender as detailed in this subsection, the specified amount will not be reduced as a result of a partial surrender.

If a reduction in specified amount is necessary due to this provision, it will be applied to reduce the specified amount segments in the same order in which the segments arose. Further, we will not allow any partial surrender which would result in decreasing the specified amount to an amount less than the minimums we allow (see the **Right to Change** section).

Due to this reduction to the account value, and possibly to the specified amount, the death benefit proceeds will also be reduced (see the **Death Benefit** section).

Partial Surrender Charge

The partial surrender charge as of any date is equal to the surrender charge on that date multiplied by the quotient of the partial surrender divided by the cash value just prior to the partial surrender. We call 1 minus such quotient the PSFR reducer.

Partial Surrender Factor Remaining (PSFR)

For each segment there is a PSFR which is a number between 1 and 0. In general, the PSFR represents the portion of a) x b), as shown in the Surrender Charge subsection, which may still be assessed on full or partial surrender. It is 1 if there have been no partial surrenders since the effective date for the segment. Each partial surrender after the effective date of the segment will reduce the PSFR for that segment according to the formula: PSFR after the partial surrender is equal to the PSFR before the partial surrender multiplied by the PSFR reducer as described in the preceding subsection.

Policy Loans

You may borrow money from us any time while this policy is in force. Any outstanding policy debt will reduce any death benefit proceeds or cash value proceeds otherwise payable. The cash value less outstanding policy debt remaining after a loan is taken must be enough to provide for the monthly deductions and interest on the loan until the next policy anniversary.

Loan Interest

Except as provided for in the Preferred Interest Loan subsection below, the loan interest rate is guaranteed not to exceed 6.5% per year. Loan interest will be due on each policy anniversary. We will notify you of the amount of interest due. Interest not paid when due will be added to the loan.

Preferred Interest Loan

Beginning with the twelfth policy month, provided there is sufficient net cash value, you may take a preferred interest loan or combination of loans. The loan interest rate for the preferred interest loan is guaranteed not to exceed 4.25% per year.

The maximum such loan amount each policy year is equal to 10% of the net account value when the loan is taken, provided that such maximum amount may never exceed the total loan available as described in the first paragraph of this section.

The maximum dollar amount of preferred interest loan available for a given policy year is fixed for the year at the time of the first loan request during that year. If the full dollar amount of preferred interest loan is not exercised at that time, the balance may be taken prior to the end of the policy year, but may not be carried over to future policy years.

We May Charge Lower Loan Interest Rates

We may charge loan interest rates lower than the guaranteed rates. Any such lower rate will be determined at the beginning of each policy year and once determined will be guaranteed for the duration of that policy year.

How You Repay a Policy Loan

You can repay all or part of the loan at any time while this policy is in force. Loan repayments will be applied first to loans other than preferred interest loans. A loan that exists at the end of a grace period may not be repaid unless you reinstate this policy.

If you do not repay the loan, the policy will not end unless the policy value for lapse is insufficient to provide for the monthly deduction due on any monthly processing day. However, coverage will not end until we have mailed you, and any assignee of record, 30 days notice at the last known address.

We Can Delay Payment

We can delay loaning you money for up to 6 months, or the period allowed by law, whichever is less, unless the loan is to be used to pay a premium to us.

Security for Your Loan

The only security we require for your loan is the portion of your policy cash value required to repay the loan.

Beneficiary and Proceeds

The **beneficiary** is the person named to receive the death benefit proceeds upon the insured's death. The beneficiary is as named in the application unless later changed. There can be one or more beneficiaries.

You can name any beneficiary to be a **permanent beneficiary**. The interest of such beneficiary cannot be changed without his or her consent. Otherwise, you can change beneficiaries as explained below.

Unless you state otherwise, all rights of a beneficiary, including a permanent beneficiary, will end if he or she dies before the insured.

Changing the Beneficiary

You can change the beneficiary at any time during the insured's life. To do so, send a written request to our home office. The request must be on a form we accept. The change will go into effect when signed subject to any payments we make or other actions we take before we record the change.

A change cancels all prior beneficiary designations; except, it will not cancel any permanent beneficiary designation without such permanent beneficiary's consent.

Proceeds

Proceeds means the amount payable:

- on the maturity date; or

- on full surrender; or

- on the insured's death.

The proceeds on the maturity date, as well as on full surrender, will be the net cash value. The proceeds on the insured's death will be the death benefit less any outstanding policy debt.

All proceeds and partial surrender amounts are subject to the restrictions below.

Payment of Proceeds

Death benefit proceeds or cash value proceeds may be paid in one sum or under our payment plans. Before proceeds are paid, they will be used to pay the interest of anyone to whom this policy has been assigned (see the **General Terms** section on assignments).

Loans and assignments will be paid in one sum.

If there is no beneficiary at the time of the insured's death, we will pay the proceeds to you or your estate.

If the death benefit proceeds are not paid in one sum or applied under a payment plan within 30 days after we receive due proof of the insured's death, we will pay interest. Interest will be paid at the rate of 4% a year from the date we receive such proof of death until paid. If state law requires payment of a greater amount, we will pay that amount.

To the extent allowed by law, all payments under this policy will be free from creditor claims or legal process.

Mistake of Age or Sex

By **age**, we mean the insured's age as of his or her most recent birthday on or prior to the policy date.

If the insured's age or sex is misstated in the application, we will adjust the proceeds to reflect the correct age and sex. In such event, the death benefit we will pay will be equal to the death benefit we would otherwise have paid multiplied by the ratio of the cost of insurance rate most recently charged for the most recent specified amount segment divided by the cost of insurance rate which should have been charged for such segment based on the correct attained age and sex.

Suicide

If the insured commits suicide, while sane or insane, within 2 years from the effective date of any specified amount segment, we will limit the death benefit proceeds associated with that segment to the premium paid for the segment less any policy loans and partial surrenders.

There will be a further deduction from the proceeds for the cost of insurance for any other person insured by rider.

If this policy is reinstated, this provision will be measured from the reinstatement date.

Payment Plans

Death benefit proceeds or cash value proceeds can be left with us and paid under a payment plan.

While the insured is alive, you can choose a plan that will apply to the death benefit proceeds upon the death of the insured. This choice can be changed during the life of the insured.

If you have not chosen a plan prior to the insured's death, a beneficiary can make this choice upon the insured's death. A plan is available only if the amount of proceeds applied is at least $10,000.

To choose a plan send a written request to our home office. We will then send you the proper forms to complete. Your request will go into effect when we record it.

The person named to receive payments under a plan is called a **payee**. If a payee is other than a natural person (such as a corporation), a plan will be available only with our consent.

The minimum interest rate for plans A, B and C is 4% a year, compounded yearly. We may pay a higher rate at our discretion.

Plan A. Interest

The proceeds may be left on deposit with us to earn interest. You can choose when you want to receive payments, subject to our approval.

Plan B. Fixed Installments

Proceeds plus interest will be paid in equal installments. Payments will continue until principal and interest are exhausted. The principal is the amount of proceeds applied to this plan.

This plan can be used only if the total amount paid each year is $60 or more for each $1,000 of proceeds applied.

Plan C. Fixed Period

Proceeds plus interest will be paid in equal installments for the number of years chosen. The period chosen cannot be more than 25 years.

The table below shows the monthly payment for each $1,000 of proceeds applied.

Amount of Each Installment Per $1,000 of Proceeds for Plan C

Fixed Period Years	Monthly Install.	Fixed Period Years	Monthly Install.	Fixed Period Years	Monthly Install.	Fixed Period Years	Monthly Install.	Fixed Period Years	Monthly Install.
1	$84.84	6	$15.56	11	$9.31	16	$7.00	21	$5.81
2	43.29	7	13.59	12	8.69	17	6.71	22	5.64
3	29.40	8	12.12	13	8.17	18	6.44	23	5.49
4	22.47	9	10.97	14	7.72	19	6.21	24	5.35
5	18.32	10	10.06	15	7.34	20	6.00	25	5.22

Plan D. Life Income

Proceeds will be used to provide payments in equal installments for as long as the payee lives. A guaranteed payment period of 10 or 20 years can be chosen. If a guaranteed payment period is chosen, this means that if the payee dies during this period, payments will continue to be made until the end of the period. The table below shows the monthly payment for each $1,000 of proceeds applied.

Plan E. Installment Refund

Proceeds will be used to provide payments in equal installments. Payments will continue until the sum of the payments equal the proceeds applied. If the payee is still living at that time, payments will continue as long as the payee lives. The table below shows the monthly payment for each $1,000 of proceeds applied.

Amount of Each Installment Per $1,000 of Proceeds for Plans D and E

Age of Payee Male	Female	Plan D Guarantee Period 10 Yrs.	20 Yrs.	Plan E Install. Refund	Age of Payee Male	Female	Plan D Guarantee Period 10 Yrs.	20 Yrs.	Plan E Install. Refund	Age of Payee Male	Female	Plan D Guarantee Period 10 Yrs.	20 Yrs.	Plan E Install. Refund
	10*	+	+	$3.14	31	35	$3.61	$3.60	$3.59	56	60	$5.12	$4.81	$4.93
	11	+	$3.15	3.15	32	36	3.64	3.63	3.62	57	61	5.23	4.88	5.03
	12	+	3.16	3.16	33	37	3.68	3.66	3.65	58	62	5.35	4.95	5.13
	13	+	3.17	3.18	34	38	3.71	3.69	3.68	59	63	5.47	5.02	5.24
10*	14	+	3.19	3.19	35	39	3.75	3.73	3.72	60	64	5.60	5.08	5.35
11	15	+	3.20	3.20	36	40	3.78	3.76	3.75	61	65	5.73	5.15	5.46
12	16	+	3.21	3.21	37	41	3.82	3.80	3.79	62	66	5.87	5.21	5.59
13	17	+	3.23	3.23	38	42	3.87	3.84	3.83	63	67	6.01	5.27	5.72
14	18	+	3.24	3.24	39	43	3.91	3.88	3.87	64	68	6.16	5.33	5.86
15	19	+	3.26	3.25	40	44	3.96	3.92	3.91	65	69	6.32	5.39	6.00
16	20	$3.27	3.27	3.27	41	45	4.01	3.96	3.95	66	70	6.48	5.44	6.16
17	21	3.29	3.29	3.29	42	46	4.06	4.01	4.00	67	71	6.65	5.49	6.32
18	22	3.31	3.30	3.30	43	47	4.11	4.05	4.05	68	72	6.83	5.53	6.49
19	23	3.33	3.32	3.32	44	48	4.17	4.10	4.10	69	73	7.01	5.57	6.68
20	24	3.34	3.34	3.34	45	49	4.23	4.15	4.15	70	74	7.19	5.61	6.87
21	25	3.36	3.36	3.36	46	50	4.29	4.20	4.21	71	75	7.38	5.64	7.08
22	26	3.38	3.38	3.37	47	51	4.35	4.26	4.26	72	76	7.57	5.67	7.30
23	27	3.40	3.40	3.39	48	52	4.42	4.31	4.32	73	77	7.76	5.69	7.53
24	28	3.43	3.42	3.42	49	53	4.50	4.37	4.39	74	78	7.95	5.70	7.78
25	29	3.45	3.44	3.44	50	54	4.57	4.43	4.46	75	79	8.14	5.72	8.04
26	30	3.47	3.47	3.46	51	55	4.65	4.49	4.53	76	80#	8.32	5.73	8.32
27	31	3.50	3.49	3.48	52	56	4.74	4.55	4.60	77		8.50	5.74	8.62
28	32	3.52	3.52	3.51	53	57	4.83	4.62	4.68	78		8.68	5.74	8.94
29	33	3.55	3.54	3.54	54	58	4.92	4.68	4.76	79		8.84	5.75	9.28
30	34	3.58	3.57	3.56	55	59	5.02	4.75	4.84	80#		8.99	5.75	9.65

*–Ages 10 and under   #–Ages 80 and over.   +–Not available at this age.

Other Facts About Payment Plans

The first installment under Plans B, C, D and E is payable on the first day the policy proceeds become payable.

A beneficiary cannot assign or commute amounts under a payment plan, unless you permit otherwise. Commute means to receive a discounted cash settlement instead of future guaranteed payments.

A payee who can receive the commuted amount under a plan, can apply that amount under another plan. If transfer is made to Plans D or E, our then current tables and terms of payment will apply.

For Plans D and E we have the right to require proof satisfactory to us that the payee is alive prior to making any payment.

Unless you provide otherwise, if a payee dies, we will make a single payment of the unpaid benefit. The payment will be made to the beneficiary of the payee. If no beneficiary is named, payment will be made to the payee's estate.

The single payment is determined as follows:

- For Plans A and B, the unpaid sum left with us plus any unpaid interest up to the date of the payee's death.

- For Plan C, the commuted value of the remaining unpaid payments.

- For Plans D and E, the commuted value of the remaining unpaid guaranteed payments.

The interest rate used to commute the payments is 4% for C and 3 1/2% for D and E or such higher interest rate that was used to determine the payments.

Unless otherwise provided under Plans C, D and E, the beneficiary of the payee may elect to receive payments over the balance of the period for Plan C or the balance of the guaranteed period for Plans D and E.

General Terms

Assigning Your Policy

During the insured's life, you can:

- assign ownership of this policy to someone else; or

- assign this policy as security for an obligation. (This does not assign ownership.)

A signed copy of the assignment must be sent to our home office on a form we accept. The assignment will go into effect when it is signed subject to any payments we make or other actions we take before we record it. We are not responsible for the validity of any assignment.

If there are permanent beneficiaries, you need their consent before assigning your policy.

Limits on Our Contesting This Policy

We rely on the statements made in the application for the policy. These statements, in the

absence of fraud, are considered representations and not warranties. No statement may be used to contest the validity of this coverage unless it is in an application attached to this policy.

We will not contest the validity of the coverage associated with each specified amount segment after the segment has been in force during the insured's life for 2 years from the effective date for that segment.

If this policy is reinstated, this provision will be measured from the reinstatement date but only for statements made in the reinstatement application.

This subsection does not apply to any provisions for waiver of cost of insurance or accidental death benefits.

Statutory Basis of Minimum Cash Values

The statutory minimum cash values are based on 1980 CSO mortality tables and the guaranteed interest as described

in the Interest Rate subsection of the **Account Value and Cash Value Benefits** section. The cash values are not less than the minimum values required by applicable state law.

Reserves

Reserves are the amount we hold to pay future benefits. They are not less than the minimum required by applicable state law. When required we filed with the state regulatory authorities a statement showing how reserves are calculated.

No Dividends

This policy will not pay dividends. It will not participate in any of our surplus or earnings.

Annual Report

We will send you at least once a year a report which shows the following:

- The current cash value;

- The current interest rate or rates used in accumulating account values;

- The amount of outstanding policy debt;

- Premiums paid since the last report;

- Monthly deductions since the last report; and

- Partial surrenders since the last report.

Illustrative Report

Upon request, we will provide you with an illustrative report showing projected future benefits under your policy. We may charge a reasonable fee for this report.

Payments

All payments of benefits under this policy will be made from our home office.

When This Policy Ends

This policy ends when any of the following occur:

- You request that this policy end;

- You request the full surrender;

- The insured dies;

- The policy reaches its maturity date; or

- At the end of the grace period.

Any deduction we make after this policy ends will be neither a reinstatement nor a waiver of our right to end the policy. Any such deduction will be refunded.

Grace Period

If the policy value for lapse on a monthly processing day is less than the monthly deduction due, this policy will stay in force for 61 days from that monthly processing day. These 61 days are called the grace period.

Policy Lapse

If you do not pay, by the end of the grace period, enough premium (or repay enough loan) to cover the monthly deductions for the grace period plus the month following the grace period, this policy will end. However, coverage will not end until we have mailed you 30 days notice at your last known address. We will also mail such notice to any assignee of record with us. In this event, there will be no death benefit proceeds.

Reinstating the Policy

Reinstatement means to restore the policy when the policy ends at the end of the grace period. We will reinstate this policy if we receive:

- your written request for reinstatement within five years after the end of the grace period and before the maturity date;

- satisfactory proof that the insured is insurable at the original underwriting class and rating factor;

- payment of enough premium or repayment of enough loan to meet the monthly deductions for the grace period and for the month during which reinstatement occurs and for one subsequent month, plus, if lapse occurred prior to the end of policy year 3 and reinstatement is to occur after

the end of policy year 3, an additional amount equal to the surrender charge as of the reinstatement date.

The reinstated policy will be in force from the **reinstatement date** which is the date we approve the reinstatement application. There will be a full monthly deduction for the policy month which includes the reinstatement date.

If a policy loan is reinstated, and likewise if a policy loan is repaid, we will charge no policy loan interest during the period of lapse in coverage nor will we credit any interest for the cash value acting as collateral for the loan. Any cash value in effect at the end of the grace period will also be reinstated.

If a person other than the insured is covered by an attached rider, his or her coverage will be reinstated according to that rider.

Changing the Terms of Your Policy

Any change to your policy for which there is no provision in this contract must be in writing and approved by one of our officers.

An approved change must be endorsed on or attached to your policy. No agent has the authority to make any changes or waive any of the terms of your policy.

To the extent permitted by applicable laws and regulations, we may make changes, without your consent, to the provisions of this policy to comply with any applicable federal or state laws including, but not limited to, requirements for life insurance contracts under the Internal Revenue Code.

PER $1000 OF SPECIFIED AMOUNT SURRENDER CHARGE TABLE

Surrender Charge Rate Basis Per $1000 of Specified Amount Segment

Age*	Male	Female	Age*	Male	Female	Age*	Male	Female
0	4.00	2.68	25	5.42	4.22	50	18.82	13.83
1	2.40	1.80	26	5.70	4.49	51	20.09	14.62
2	2.40	1.82	27	5.92	4.65	52	21.28	15.61
3	2.40	1.84	28	6.13	4.81	53	22.61	16.71
4	2.40	1.86	29	6.29	4.90	54	24.05	17.65
5	2.40	1.88	30	6.70	5.42	55	25.22	18.82
6	2.40	1.90	31	6.98	5.70	56	26.94	20.09
7	2.57	1.92	32	7.32	5.92	57	28.55	21.28
8	2.69	1.95	33	7.65	6.13	58	30.54	22.61
9	2.69	1.98	34	8.21	6.29	59	33.03	24.05
10	2.86	2.00	35	8.64	6.70	60	34.18	25.22
11	2.97	2.10	36	9.09	6.98	61	35.20	26.94
12	3.19	2.25	37	9.51	7.32	62	36.34	28.55
13	3.48	2.40	38	9.88	7.65	63	37.70	30.54
14	3.69	2.54	39	10.25	8.21	64	39.26	33.03
15	3.80	2.70	40	10.78	8.64	65	40.95	34.18
16	3.84	2.81	41	11.25	9.09	66	42.78	35.20
17	4.13	3.02	42	11.85	9.51	67	44.75	36.34
18	4.24	3.29	43	12.50	9.88	68	46.91	37.70
19	4.46	3.49	44	13.18	10.25	69	49.42	39.26
20	4.46	3.59	45	13.83	10.78	70	52.32	40.95
21	4.75	3.63	46	14.62	11.25	71	55.65	42.50
22	4.92	3.90	47	15.61	11.85	72	59.43	42.50
23	5.09	4.01	48	16.71	12.50	73+	60.00	42.50
24	5.18	4.22	49	17.65	13.18			

Percentages for Surrender Charge Rate Basis (Male)

Segment Duration

Age*	1	2	3	4	5	6	7	8	9	10	11	12	13+
0-51	170%	170%	170%	170%	170%	161%	151%	133%	115%	85%	57%	28%	0%
52	170	170	170	170	167	161	151	133	115	85	57	28	0
53	170	170	170	168	164	160	151	133	115	85	57	28	0
54	170	170	168	164	160	156	151	133	115	85	57	28	0
55	170	170	167	163	159	154	150	133	115	85	57	28	0
56	170	167	163	159	154	150	146	133	115	85	57	28	0
57	169	165	160	156	152	147	143	133	115	85	57	28	0
58	165	161	157	152	148	143	139	133	115	85	57	28	0
59-61	160	156	151	147	143	138	134	129	115	85	57	28	0
62	157	155	149	145	140	135	131	126	115	85	57	28	0
63	151	149	144	139	135	130	125	120	115	85	57	28	0
64	145	143	138	133	128	124	119	114	109	85	57	28	0
65	139	137	132	127	122	118	113	108	104	85	57	28	0
66	133	130	125	121	116	112	107	103	98	85	57	28	0
67	127	124	120	115	110	106	101	97	93	85	57	28	0
68	121	118	114	109	105	100	96	92	88	84	57	28	0
69	115	112	107	103	99	94	90	86	82	78	57	28	0
70	109	105	101	97	93	89	85	80	76	72	57	28	0
71	103	99	95	91	87	83	79	75	72	68	57	28	0
72	96	92	88	84	80	77	74	70	67	63	57	28	0
73-75	95	91	87	83	79	75	71	68	64	60	57	28	0
76+	95	90	85	81	76	72	67	62	56	50	43	28	0

Percentages for Surrender Charge Rate Basis (Female)

Segment Duration

Age*	1	2	3	4	5	6	7	8	9	10	11	12	13+
0-29	180%	180%	180%	180%	180%	170%	160%	140%	120%	90%	60%	30%	0%
30-58	170	170	170	170	170	161	151	133	115	85	57	28	0
59	170	170	170	170	166	161	151	133	115	85	57	28	0
60	170	170	170	169	164	159	151	133	115	85	57	28	0
61	170	170	169	165	160	155	150	133	115	85	57	28	0
62	170	170	167	162	157	152	147	133	115	85	57	28	0
63	170	168	163	158	153	148	143	133	115	85	57	28	0
64-65	167	163	158	153	148	143	138	132	115	85	57	28	0
66	162	157	153	149	144	138	133	127	115	85	57	28	0
67	157	152	148	144	138	133	127	122	115	85	57	28	0
68	152	148	143	137	132	126	121	116	110	85	57	28	0
69	146	142	136	131	125	120	115	110	104	85	57	28	0
70	140	135	130	125	119	114	109	104	99	85	57	28	0
71	134	130	125	119	114	109	104	99	94	85	57	28	0
72	134	129	124	118	113	108	103	97	92	85	57	28	0
73-75	134	128	122	116	110	105	99	93	88	83	57	28	0
76+	133	125	117	110	103	96	88	81	73	64	55	28	0

*Attained age as of the effective date of the segment

Guaranteed Monthly Cost of Insurance Rates per $1,000*

	Underwriting Class					Underwriting Class			
	PREFERRED & STANDARD I		STANDARD II			PREFERRED & STANDARD I		STANDARD II	
Age	Male	Female	Male	Female	Age	Male	Female	Male	Female
0	.21921	.15669	.21921	.15669	50	.42768	.36180	.83403	.56449
1	.08584	.07000	.08584	.07000	51	.46688	.38932	.91166	.60537
2	.08251	.06667	.08251	.06667	52	.51193	.42101	.99933	.65209
3	.08084	.06500	.08084	.06500	53	.56365	.45604	1.09871	.70383
4	.07751	.06417	.07751	.06417	54	.62122	.49191	1.20729	.75641
5	.07334	.06250	.07334	.06250	55	.68547	.53028	1.32342	.81066
6	.06917	.06084	.06917	.06084	56	.75557	.56866	1.44626	.86408
7	.06500	.05917	.06500	.05917	57	.82985	.60620	1.57581	.91417
8	.06250	.05834	.06250	.05834	58	.91250	.64375	1.71209	.96343
9	.06167	.05750	.06167	.05750	59	1.00518	.68630	1.85845	1.01603
10	.06250	.05667	.06250	.05667	60	1.10873	.73638	2.02158	1.07866
11	.06750	.05834	.06750	.05834	61	1.22400	.79814	2.20569	1.15717
12	.07667	.06084	.07667	.06084	62	1.35684	.87493	2.41331	1.25825
13	.08917	.06417	.08917	.06417	63	1.50727	.96927	2.64531	1.38107
14	.10334	.06834	.10334	.06834	64	1.67447	1.07532	2.89921	1.51813
15	.11335	.07167	.14669	.08001	65	1.85761	1.18975	3.16834	1.66276
16	.12335	.07501	.16336	.08417	66	2.05588	1.30838	3.45020	1.80994
17	.13085	.07751	.17503	.08834	67	2.26847	1.42954	3.74229	1.95214
18	.13585	.08001	.18420	.09251	68	2.49957	1.55491	4.04883	2.09605
19	.13919	.08251	.19004	.09501	69	2.75591	1.69453	4.38161	2.25256
20	.14002	.08417	.19337	.09751	70	3.04592	1.85845	4.74911	2.43759
21	.13835	.08584	.19337	.09918	71	3.37720	2.05839	5.16235	2.67212
22	.13585	.08667	.19004	.10168	72	3.75992	2.30363	5.62985	2.95957
23	.13252	.08834	.18670	.10418	73	4.19334	2.59756	6.14841	3.30170
24	.12918	.09001	.18170	.10668	74	4.67004	2.93610	6.71732	3.69191
25	.12502	.09168	.17586	.10918	75	5.18003	3.31428	7.32578	4.11856
26	.12252	.09418	.17253	.11335	76	5.71919	3.72382	7.94851	4.57248
27	.12085	.09584	.17086	.11668	77	6.28340	4.16309	8.57456	5.04701
28	.12001	.09834	.17086	.12085	78	6.87612	4.63892	9.20818	5.54895
29	.12001	.10168	.17336	.12585	79	7.51607	5.16656	9.87149	6.09610
30	.12085	.10418	.17753	.13168	80	8.22375	5.76724	10.58674	6.70972
31	.12335	.10751	.18337	.13669	81	9.01810	6.45895	11.37459	7.40696
32	.12668	.11085	.19874	.14252	82	9.91569	7.25729	12.24906	8.20087
33	.13168	.11501	.20087	.15002	83	10.91280	8.15937	13.19603	9.11907
34	.13752	.12001	.21255	.15836	84	11.99040	9.15556	14.18421	10.11631
35	.14419	.12585	.22672	.16753	85	13.12418	10.23537	15.18033	11.17773
36	.15169	.13418	.24339	.18170	86	14.29994	11.39164	16.16034	12.29517
37	.16169	.14419	.26424	.19837	87	15.49991	12.62319	17.16810	13.45788
38	.17253	.15502	.28758	.21755	88	16.71910	13.93142	18.22020	14.67216
39	.18420	.16669	.31427	.23839	89	17.97489	15.32721	19.26842	15.93752
40	.19837	.18087	.34512	.26340	90	19.28574	16.82248	20.32834	17.34402
41	.21338	.19587	.37848	.29008	91	20.68243	18.45266	21.43307	18.86254
42	.22922	.21088	.41517	.31677	92	22.21791	20.28063	22.71710	20.55222
43	.24673	.22588	.45521	.34345	93	24.04369	22.43826	24.36888	22.54368
44	.26590	.24089	.49942	.37014	94	26.50346	25.22305	26.62992	25.22305
45	.28758	.25757	.54613	.39849	95	30.20740	29.24956	30.20740	29.24956
46	.31093	.27508	.59452	.42768	96	36.35803	35.72205	36.35803	35.72205
47	.33595	.29425	.64709	.45771	97	47.21180	46.86829	47.21180	46.86829
48	.36347	.31427	.70383	.49024	98	66.20701	66.09429	66.20701	66.09429
49	.39349	.33678	.76559	.52611	99+	90.90909	90.90909	90.90909	90.90909

*Actual monthly cost of insurance rate is equal to the above attained age rate for the appropriate underwriting class as shown on page 3, multiplied by the rating factor shown on page 3. Any flat extra amount from page 3 must also be added.

Flexible Premium Universal Life Insurance

Flexible premiums payable to maturity
Adjustable death benefit for the lifetime of the
   insured so long as the policy stays in force
Net cash value, if any, payable at maturity
No dividends
Premiums allocated between a risk premium and
   an accumulation account
Interest declarable annually by the company
   subject to the guarantees in the contract

APPENDIX E

Homeowners Policy

HOMEOWNERS POLICY

HOMEOWNERS POLICY		
DECLARATIONS		

Policy Number

Previous Policy Number

COMPANY NAME

Policy Period	From	To	12:01 A.M. Standard time

Named Insured
and mailing address

The **Residence premises** covered by this policy is located at the above address unless otherwise stated:

We will provide the insurance described in this policy in return for the premium and compliance with all applicable policy provisions.

Coverage is provided where a premium or limit of liability is shown for the coverage.

SECTION I COVERAGES	Limit of Liability	Premium	
A Dwelling	$	Basic Policy Premium	$
B Other Structures	$	Additional Premiums	$
C Personal Property	$		$
D Loss of Use	$		$
Premium for endorsement list below			$
		Total Premium	$

SECTION II COVERAGES		
E Personal Liability	$	Each Occurrence
F Medical Payments to Others	$	Each Person

Forms and endorsements made part of this policy
at the time of issue: Numbers and edition dates

Special state Provisions   South Carolina: Valuation Clause
                                Minnesota Insurable Value (Coverage A) $
                                New York: Coinsurance Clause Applies   ____Yes   ____No

Deductible -- Section I $
In case of a loss under Section I, we cover only that part of the loss over the deductible stated.

Section II - Other **Insured Locations**

Mortgagee
(Name and Address

Countersignature of agent/date   Signature/title - company officer

HOMEOWNERS 3 – SPECIAL FORM

AGREEMENT

We will provide the insurance described in this policy in return for the premium and compliance with all applicable provisions of this policy.

DEFINITIONS

A. In this policy, "you" and "your" refer to the "named insured" shown in the Declarations and the spouse if a resident of the same household. "We", "us" and "our" refer to the Company providing this insurance.

B. In addition, certain words and phrases are defined as follows:

1. "Aircraft Liability", "Hovercraft Liability", "Motor Vehicle Liability" and "Watercraft Liability", subject to the provisions in **b.** below, mean the following:

a. Liability for "bodily injury" or "property damage" arising out of the:

(1) Ownership of such vehicle or craft by an "insured";

(2) Maintenance, occupancy, operation, use, loading or unloading of such vehicle or craft by any person;

(3) Entrustment of such vehicle or craft by an "insured" to any person;

(4) Failure to supervise or negligent supervision of any person involving such vehicle or craft by an "insured"; and

(5) Vicarious liability, whether or not imposed by law, for the actions of a child or minor involving such vehicle or craft.

b. For the purpose of this definition:

(1) Aircraft means any contrivance used or designed for flight except model or hobby aircraft not used or designed to carry people or cargo;

(2) Hovercraft means a self-propelled motorized ground effect vehicle and includes, but is not limited to, flarecraft and air cushion vehicles; and

(3) Watercraft means a craft principally designed to be propelled on or in water by wind, engine power or electric motor.

(4) Motor vehicle means a "motor vehicle" as defined in **7.** below.

2. "Bodily injury" means bodily harm, sickness or disease, including required care, loss of services and death that results.

3. "Business" means:

a. A trade, profession or occupation engaged in on a full-time, part-time or occasional basis; or

b. Any other activity engaged in for money or other compensation, except the following:

(1) One or more activities, not described in **(2)** through **(4)** below, for which no "insured" receives more than $2,000 in total compensation for the 12 months before the inception date of the policy;

(2) Volunteer activities for which no money is received other than payment for expenses incurred to perform the activity;

(3) Providing home day care services for which no compensation is received, other than the mutual exchange of such services; or

(4) The rendering of home day care services to a relative of an "insured".

4. "Employee" means an employee of an "insured", or an employee leased to an "insured" by a labor leasing firm under an agreement between an "insured" and the labor leasing firm, whose duties are other than those performed by a "residence employee".

5. "Insured" means:

a. You and residents of your household who are:

(1) Your relatives; or

(2) Other persons under the age of 21 and in the care of any person named above;

b. A student enrolled in school full time, as defined by the school, who was a resident of your household before moving out to attend school, provided the student is under the age of:

(1) 24 and your relative; or

(2) 21 and in your care or the care of a person described in **a.(1)** above; or

c. Under Section II:

(1) With respect to animals or watercraft to which this policy applies, any person or organization legally responsible for these animals or watercraft which are owned by you or any person included in **a.** or **b.** above. "Insured" does not mean a person or organization using or having custody of these animals or watercraft in the course of any "business" or without consent of the owner; or

(2) With respect to a "motor vehicle" to which this policy applies:

(a) Persons while engaged in your employ or that of any person included in **a.** or **b.** above; or

(b) Other persons using the vehicle on an "insured location" with your consent.

Under both Sections I and II, when the word an immediately precedes the word "insured", the words an "insured" together mean one or more "insureds".

6. "Insured location" means:

a. The "residence premises";

b. The part of other premises, other structures and grounds used by you as a residence; and

(1) Which is shown in the Declarations; or

(2) Which is acquired by you during the policy period for your use as a residence;

c. Any premises used by you in connection with a premises described in **a.** and **b.** above;

d. Any part of a premises:

(1) Not owned by an "insured"; and

(2) Where an "insured" is temporarily residing;

e. Vacant land, other than farm land, owned by or rented to an "insured";

f. Land owned by or rented to an "insured" on which a one, two, three or four family dwelling is being built as a residence for an "insured";

g. Individual or family cemetery plots or burial vaults of an "insured"; or

h. Any part of a premises occasionally rented to an "insured" for other than "business" use.

7. "Motor vehicle" means:

a. A self-propelled land or amphibious vehicle; or

b. Any trailer or semitrailer which is being carried on, towed by or hitched for towing by a vehicle described in **a.** above.

8. "Occurrence" means an accident, including continuous or repeated exposure to substantially the same general harmful conditions, which results, during the policy period, in:

a. "Bodily injury"; or

b. "Property damage".

9. "Property damage" means physical injury to, destruction of, or loss of use of tangible property.

10. "Residence employee" means:

a. An employee of an "insured", or an employee leased to an "insured" by a labor leasing firm, under an agreement between an "insured" and the labor leasing firm, whose duties are related to the maintenance or use of the "residence premises", including household or domestic services; or

b. One who performs similar duties elsewhere not related to the "business" of an "insured".

A "residence employee" does not include a temporary employee who is furnished to an "insured" to substitute for a permanent "residence employee" on leave or to meet seasonal or short-term workload conditions.

11. "Residence premises" means:

a. The one family dwelling where you reside;

b. The two, three or four family dwelling where you reside in at least one of the family units; or

c. That part of any other building where you reside;

and which is shown as the "residence premises" in the Declarations.

"Residence premises" also includes other structures and grounds at that location.

DEDUCTIBLE

Unless otherwise noted in this policy, the following deductible provision applies:

Subject to the policy limits that apply, we will pay only that part of the total of all loss payable under Section I that exceeds the deductible amount shown in the Declarations.

SECTION I – PROPERTY COVERAGES

A. Coverage A – Dwelling

1. We cover:

   a. The dwelling on the "residence premises" shown in the Declarations, including structures attached to the dwelling; and

   b. Materials and supplies located on or next to the "residence premises" used to construct, alter or repair the dwelling or other structures on the "residence premises".

2. We do not cover land, including land on which the dwelling is located.

B. Coverage B – Other Structures

1. We cover other structures on the "residence premises" set apart from the dwelling by clear space. This includes structures connected to the dwelling by only a fence, utility line, or similar connection.

2. We do not cover:

   a. Land, including land on which the other structures are located;

   b. Other structures rented or held for rental to any person not a tenant of the dwelling, unless used solely as a private garage;

   c. Other structures from which any "business" is conducted; or

   d. Other structures used to store "business" property. However, we do cover a structure that contains "business" property solely owned by an "insured" or a tenant of the dwelling provided that "business" property does not include gaseous or liquid fuel, other than fuel in a permanently installed fuel tank of a vehicle or craft parked or stored in the structure.

3. The limit of liability for this coverage will not be more than 10% of the limit of liability that applies to Coverage A. Use of this coverage does not reduce the Coverage A limit of liability.

C. Coverage C – Personal Property

1. **Covered Property**

   We cover personal property owned or used by an "insured" while it is anywhere in the world. After a loss and at your request, we will cover personal property owned by:

   a. Others while the property is on the part of the "residence premises" occupied by an "insured"; or

   b. A guest or a "residence employee", while the property is in any residence occupied by an "insured".

2. **Limit For Property At Other Residences**

   Our limit of liability for personal property usually located at an "insured's" residence, other than the "residence premises", is 10% of the limit of liability for Coverage C, or $1,000, whichever is greater. However, this limitation does not apply to personal property:

   a. Moved from the "residence premises" because it is being repaired, renovated or rebuilt and is not fit to live in or store property in; or

   b. In a newly acquired principal residence for 30 days from the time you begin to move the property there.

3. **Special Limits Of Liability**

   The special limit for each category shown below is the total limit for each loss for all property in that category. These special limits do not increase the Coverage C limit of liability.

   a. $200 on money, bank notes, bullion, gold other than goldware, silver other than silverware, platinum other than platinumware, coins, medals, scrip, stored value cards and smart cards.

   b. $1,500 on securities, accounts, deeds, evidences of debt, letters of credit, notes other than bank notes, manuscripts, personal records, passports, tickets and stamps. This dollar limit applies to these categories regardless of the medium (such as paper or computer software) on which the material exists.

   This limit includes the cost to research, replace or restore the information from the lost or damaged material.

Copyright, Insurance Services Office, Inc., 1999

c. $1,500 on watercraft of all types, including their trailers, furnishings, equipment and outboard engines or motors.

d. $1,500 on trailers or semitrailers not used with watercraft of all types.

e. $1,500 for loss by theft of jewelry, watches, furs, precious and semiprecious stones.

f. $2,500 for loss by theft of firearms and related equipment.

g. $2,500 for loss by theft of silverware, silver-plated ware, goldware, gold-plated ware, platinumware, platinum-plated ware and pewterware. This includes flatware, hollow-ware, tea sets, trays and trophies made of or including silver, gold or pewter.

h. $2,500 on property, on the "residence premises", used primarily for "business" purposes.

i. $500 on property, away from the "residence premises", used primarily for "business" purposes. However, this limit does not apply to loss to electronic apparatus and other property described in Categories **j.** and **k.** below.

j. $1,500 on electronic apparatus and accessories, while in or upon a "motor vehicle", but only if the apparatus is equipped to be operated by power from the "motor vehicle's" electrical system while still capable of being operated by other power sources.

Accessories include antennas, tapes, wires, records, discs or other media that can be used with any apparatus described in this Category **j.**

k. $1,500 on electronic apparatus and accessories used primarily for "business" while away from the "residence premises" and not in or upon a "motor vehicle". The apparatus must be equipped to be operated by power from the "motor vehicle's" electrical system while still capable of being operated by other power sources.

Accessories include antennas, tapes, wires, records, discs or other media that can be used with any apparatus described in this Category **k.**

4. Property Not Covered

We do not cover:

a. Articles separately described and specifically insured, regardless of the limit for which they are insured, in this or other insurance;

b. Animals, birds or fish;

c. "Motor vehicles".

(1) This includes:

(a) Their accessories, equipment and parts; or

(b) Electronic apparatus and accessories designed to be operated solely by power from the electrical system of the "motor vehicle", but only while such property is in or upon the "motor vehicle". Accessories include antennas, tapes, wires, records, discs or other media that can be used with any apparatus described above, but only while such property is in or upon the "motor vehicle".

(2) We do cover "motor vehicles" not required to be registered for use on public roads or property which are:

(a) Used solely to service an "insured's" residence; or

(b) Designed to assist the handicapped;

d. Aircraft meaning any contrivance used or designed for flight including any parts whether or not attached to the aircraft;

We do cover model or hobby aircraft not used or designed to carry people or cargo;

e. Hovercraft and parts. Hovercraft means a self-propelled motorized ground effect vehicle and includes, but is not limited to, flare-craft and air cushion vehicles;

f. Property of roomers, boarders and other tenants, except property of roomers and boarders related to an "insured";

g. Property in an apartment regularly rented or held for rental to others by an "insured", except as provided in **E.10.** Landlord's Furnishings under Section I – Property Coverages;

h. Property rented or held for rental to others off the "residence premises";

i. "Business" data, including such data stored in:

(1) Books of account, drawings or other paper records; or

(2) Computers and related equipment.

We do cover the cost of blank recording or storage media, and of prerecorded computer programs available on the retail market;

j. Credit cards, electronic fund transfer cards or access devices used solely for deposit, withdrawal or transfer of funds except as provided in **E.6.** Credit Card, Electronic Fund Transfer Card Or Access Device, Forgery And Counterfeit Money under Section **I** – Property Coverages; or

k. Water or steam.

D. Coverage D – Loss Of Use

The limit of liability for Coverage **D** is the total limit for the coverages in **1.** Additional Living Expense, **2.** Fair Rental Value and **3.** Civil Authority Prohibits Use below.

1. Additional Living Expense

If a loss covered under Section **I** makes that part of the "residence premises" where you reside not fit to live in, we cover any necessary increase in living expenses incurred by you so that your household can maintain its normal standard of living.

Payment will be for the shortest time required to repair or replace the damage or, if you permanently relocate, the shortest time required for your household to settle elsewhere.

2. Fair Rental Value

If a loss covered under Section **I** makes that part of the "residence premises" rented to others or held for rental by you not fit to live in, we cover the fair rental value of such premises less any expenses that do not continue while it is not fit to live in.

Payment will be for the shortest time required to repair or replace that part of the premises rented or held for rental.

3. Civil Authority Prohibits Use

If a civil authority prohibits you from use of the "residence premises" as a result of direct damage to neighboring premises by a Peril Insured Against, we cover the loss as provided in **1.** Additional Living Expense and **2.** Fair Rental Value above for no more than two weeks.

4. Loss Or Expense Not Covered

We do not cover loss or expense due to cancellation of a lease or agreement.

The periods of time under **1.** Additional Living Expense, **2.** Fair Rental Value and **3.** Civil Authority Prohibits Use above are not limited by expiration of this policy.

E. Additional Coverages

1. Debris Removal

a. We will pay your reasonable expense for the removal of:

(1) Debris of covered property if a Peril Insured Against that applies to the damaged property causes the loss; or

(2) Ash, dust or particles from a volcanic eruption that has caused direct loss to a building or property contained in a building.

This expense is included in the limit of liability that applies to the damaged property. If the amount to be paid for the actual damage to the property plus the debris removal expense is more than the limit of liability for the damaged property, an additional 5% of that limit is available for such expense.

b. We will also pay your reasonable expense, up to $1,000, for the removal from the "residence premises" of:

(1) Your tree(s) felled by the peril of Windstorm or Hail or Weight of Ice, Snow or Sleet; or

(2) A neighbor's tree(s) felled by a Peril Insured Against under Coverage **C**;

provided the tree(s):

(3) Damage(s) a covered structure; or

(4) Does not damage a covered structure, but:

(a) Block(s) a driveway on the "residence premises" which prevent(s) a "motor vehicle", that is registered for use on public roads or property, from entering or leaving the "residence premises"; or

(b) Block(s) a ramp or other fixture designed to assist a handicapped person to enter or leave the dwelling building.

The $1,000 limit is the most we will pay in any one loss regardless of the number of fallen trees. No more than $500 of this limit will be paid for the removal of any one tree.

This coverage is additional insurance.

2. Reasonable Repairs

a. We will pay the reasonable cost incurred by you for the necessary measures taken solely to protect covered property that is damaged by a Peril Insured Against from further damage.

b. If the measures taken involve repair to other damaged property, we will only pay if that property is covered under this policy and the damage is caused by a Peril Insured Against. This coverage does not:

(1) Increase the limit of liability that applies to the covered property; or

(2) Relieve you of your duties, in case of a loss to covered property, described in **B.4.** under Section I – Conditions.

3. Trees, Shrubs And Other Plants

We cover trees, shrubs, plants or lawns, on the "residence premises", for loss caused by the following Perils Insured Against:

a. Fire or Lightning;

b. Explosion;

c. Riot or Civil Commotion;

d. Aircraft;

e. Vehicles not owned or operated by a resident of the "residence premises";

f. Vandalism or Malicious Mischief; or

g. Theft.

We will pay up to 5% of the limit of liability that applies to the dwelling for all trees, shrubs, plants or lawns. No more than $500 of this limit will be paid for any one tree, shrub or plant. We do not cover property grown for "business" purposes.

This coverage is additional insurance.

4. Fire Department Service Charge

We will pay up to $500 for your liability assumed by contract or agreement for fire department charges incurred when the fire department is called to save or protect covered property from a Peril Insured Against. We do not cover fire department service charges if the property is located within the limits of the city, municipality or protection district furnishing the fire department response.

This coverage is additional insurance. No deductible applies to this coverage.

5. Property Removed

We insure covered property against direct loss from any cause while being removed from a premises endangered by a Peril Insured Against and for no more than 30 days while removed.

This coverage does not change the limit of liability that applies to the property being removed.

6. Credit Card, Electronic Fund Transfer Card Or Access Device, Forgery And Counterfeit Money

a. We will pay up to $500 for:

(1) The legal obligation of an "insured" to pay because of the theft or unauthorized use of credit cards issued to or registered in an "insured's" name;

(2) Loss resulting from theft or unauthorized use of an electronic fund transfer card or access device used for deposit, withdrawal or transfer of funds, issued to or registered in an "insured's" name;

(3) Loss to an "insured" caused by forgery or alteration of any check or negotiable instrument; and

(4) Loss to an "insured" through acceptance in good faith of counterfeit United States or Canadian paper currency.

All loss resulting from a series of acts committed by any one person or in which any one person is concerned or implicated is considered to be one loss.

This coverage is additional insurance. No deductible applies to this coverage.

b. We do not cover:

(1) Use of a credit card, electronic fund transfer card or access device:

(a) By a resident of your household;

(b) By a person who has been entrusted with either type of card or access device; or

(c) If an "insured" has not complied with all terms and conditions under which the cards are issued or the devices accessed; or

(2) Loss arising out of "business" use or dishonesty of an "insured".

c. If the coverage in **a.** above applies, the following defense provisions also apply:

(1) We may investigate and settle any claim or suit that we decide is appropriate. Our duty to defend a claim or suit ends when the amount we pay for the loss equals our limit of liability.

(2) If a suit is brought against an "insured" for liability under **a.(1)** or **(2)** above, we will provide a defense at our expense by counsel of our choice.

(3) We have the option to defend at our expense an "insured" or an "insured's" bank against any suit for the enforcement of payment under **a.(3)** above.

 HO 00 03 10 00

7. Loss Assessment

a. We will pay up to $1,000 for your share of loss assessment charged during the policy period against you, as owner or tenant of the "residence premises", by a corporation or association of property owners. The assessment must be made as a result of direct loss to property, owned by all members collectively, of the type that would be covered by this policy if owned by you, caused by a Peril Insured Against under Coverage **A**, other than:

(1) Earthquake; or

(2) Land shock waves or tremors before, during or after a volcanic eruption.

The limit of $1,000 is the most we will pay with respect to any one loss, regardless of the number of assessments. We will only apply one deductible, per unit, to the total amount of any one loss to the property described above, regardless of the number of assessments.

b. We do not cover assessments charged against you or a corporation or association of property owners by any governmental body.

c. Paragraph **P.** Policy Period under Section **I** – Conditions does not apply to this coverage.

This coverage is additional insurance.

8. Collapse

a. With respect to this Additional Coverage:

(1) Collapse means an abrupt falling down or caving in of a building or any part of a building with the result that the building or part of the building cannot be occupied for its current intended purpose.

(2) A building or any part of a building that is in danger of falling down or caving in is not considered to be in a state of collapse.

(3) A part of a building that is standing is not considered to be in a state of collapse even if it has separated from another part of the building.

(4) A building or any part of a building that is standing is not considered to be in a state of collapse even if it shows evidence of cracking, bulging, sagging, bending, leaning, settling, shrinkage or expansion.

b. We insure for direct physical loss to covered property involving collapse of a building or any part of a building if the collapse was caused by one or more of the following:

(1) The Perils Insured Against named under Coverage **C**;

(2) Decay that is hidden from view, unless the presence of such decay is known to an "insured" prior to collapse;

(3) Insect or vermin damage that is hidden from view, unless the presence of such damage is known to an "insured" prior to collapse;

(4) Weight of contents, equipment, animals or people;

(5) Weight of rain which collects on a roof; or

(6) Use of defective material or methods in construction, remodeling or renovation if the collapse occurs during the course of the construction, remodeling or renovation.

c. Loss to an awning, fence, patio, deck, pavement, swimming pool, underground pipe, flue, drain, cesspool, septic tank, foundation, retaining wall, bulkhead, pier, wharf or dock is not included under **b.(2)** through **(6)** above, unless the loss is a direct result of the collapse of a building or any part of a building.

d. This coverage does not increase the limit of liability that applies to the damaged covered property.

9. Glass Or Safety Glazing Material

a. We cover:

(1) The breakage of glass or safety glazing material which is part of a covered building, storm door or storm window;

(2) The breakage of glass or safety glazing material which is part of a covered building, storm door or storm window when caused directly by earth movement; and

(3) The direct physical loss to covered property caused solely by the pieces, fragments or splinters of broken glass or safety glazing material which is part of a building, storm door or storm window.

b. This coverage does not include loss:

(1) To covered property which results because the glass or safety glazing material has been broken, except as provided in **a.(3)** above; or

(2) On the "residence premises" if the dwelling has been vacant for more than 60 consecutive days immediately before the loss, except when the breakage results directly from earth movement as provided in **a.(2)** above. A dwelling being constructed is not considered vacant.

c. This coverage does not increase the limit of liability that applies to the damaged property.

10. Landlord's Furnishings

We will pay up to $2,500 for your appliances, carpeting and other household furnishings, in each apartment on the "residence premises" regularly rented or held for rental to others by an "insured", for loss caused by a Peril Insured Against in Coverage **C,** other than Theft.

This limit is the most we will pay in any one loss regardless of the number of appliances, carpeting or other household furnishings involved in the loss.

This coverage does not increase the limit of liability applying to the damaged property.

11. Ordinance Or Law

a. You may use up to 10% of the limit of liability that applies to Coverage **A** for the increased costs you incur due to the enforcement of any ordinance or law which requires or regulates:

(1) The construction, demolition, remodeling, renovation or repair of that part of a covered building or other structure damaged by a Peril Insured Against;

(2) The demolition and reconstruction of the undamaged part of a covered building or other structure, when that building or other structure must be totally demolished because of damage by a Peril Insured Against to another part of that covered building or other structure; or

(3) The remodeling, removal or replacement of the portion of the undamaged part of a covered building or other structure necessary to complete the remodeling, repair or replacement of that part of the covered building or other structure damaged by a Peril Insured Against.

b. You may use all or part of this ordinance or law coverage to pay for the increased costs you incur to remove debris resulting from the construction, demolition, remodeling, renovation, repair or replacement of property as stated in **a.** above.

c. We do not cover:

(1) The loss in value to any covered building or other structure due to the requirements of any ordinance or law; or

(2) The costs to comply with any ordinance or law which requires any "insured" or others to test for, monitor, clean up, remove, contain, treat, detoxify or neutralize, or in any way respond to, or assess the effects of, pollutants in or on any covered building or other structure.

Pollutants means any solid, liquid, gaseous or thermal irritant or contaminant, including smoke, vapor, soot, fumes, acids, alkalis, chemicals and waste. Waste includes materials to be recycled, reconditioned or reclaimed.

This coverage is additional insurance.

12. Grave Markers

We will pay up to $5,000 for grave markers, including mausoleums, on or away from the "residence premises" for loss caused by a Peril Insured Against under Coverage **C.**

This coverage does not increase the limits of liability that apply to the damaged covered property.

SECTION I – PERILS INSURED AGAINST

A. Coverage A – Dwelling And Coverage B – Other Structures

1. We insure against risk of direct physical loss to property described in Coverages **A** and **B.**

2. We do not insure, however, for loss:

a. Excluded under Section I – Exclusions;

b. Involving collapse, except as provided in **E.8. Collapse** under Section I – Property Coverages; and

c. Caused by:

(1) Freezing of a plumbing, heating, air conditioning or automatic fire protective sprinkler system or of a household appliance, or by discharge, leakage or overflow from within the system or appliance caused by freezing. This provision does not apply if you have used reasonable care to:

(a) Maintain heat in the building; or

(b) Shut off the water supply and drain all systems and appliances of water.

However, if the building is protected by an automatic fire protective sprinkler system, you must use reasonable care to continue the water supply and maintain heat in the building for coverage to apply.

For purposes of this provision a plumbing system or household appliance does not include a sump, sump pump or related equipment or a roof drain, gutter, downspout or similar fixtures or equipment;

(2) Freezing, thawing, pressure or weight of water or ice, whether driven by wind or not, to a:

(a) Fence, pavement, patio or swimming pool;

(b) Footing, foundation, bulkhead, wall, or any other structure or device that supports all or part of a building, or other structure;

(c) Retaining wall or bulkhead that does not support all or part of a building or other structure; or

(d) Pier, wharf or dock;

(3) Theft in or to a dwelling under construction, or of materials and supplies for use in the construction until the dwelling is finished and occupied;

(4) Vandalism and malicious mischief, and any ensuing loss caused by any intentional and wrongful act committed in the course of the vandalism or malicious mischief, if the dwelling has been vacant for more than 60 consecutive days immediately before the loss. A dwelling being constructed is not considered vacant;

(5) Mold, fungus or wet rot. However, we do insure for loss caused by mold, fungus or wet rot that is hidden within the walls or ceilings or beneath the floors or above the ceilings of a structure if such loss results from the accidental discharge or overflow of water or steam from within:

(a) A plumbing, heating, air conditioning or automatic fire protective sprinkler system, or a household appliance, on the "residence premises"; or

(b) A storm drain, or water, steam or sewer pipes, off the "residence premises".

For purposes of this provision, a plumbing system or household appliance does not include a sump, sump pump or related equipment or a roof drain, gutter, downspout or similar fixtures or equipment; or

(6) Any of the following:

(a) Wear and tear, marring, deterioration;

(b) Mechanical breakdown, latent defect, inherent vice, or any quality in property that causes it to damage or destroy itself;

(c) Smog, rust or other corrosion, or dry rot;

(d) Smoke from agricultural smudging or industrial operations;

(e) Discharge, dispersal, seepage, migration, release or escape of pollutants unless the discharge, dispersal, seepage, migration, release or escape is itself caused by a Peril Insured Against named under Coverage **C**.

Pollutants means any solid, liquid, gaseous or thermal irritant or contaminant, including smoke, vapor, soot, fumes, acids, alkalis, chemicals and waste. Waste includes materials to be recycled, reconditioned or reclaimed;

(f) Settling, shrinking, bulging or expansion, including resultant cracking, of bulkheads, pavements, patios, footings, foundations, walls, floors, roofs or ceilings;

(g) Birds, vermin, rodents, or insects; or

(h) Animals owned or kept by an "insured".

Exception To c.(6)

Unless the loss is otherwise excluded, we cover loss to property covered under Coverage **A** or **B** resulting from an accidental discharge or overflow of water or steam from within a:

(i) Storm drain, or water, steam or sewer pipe, off the "residence premises"; or

(ii) Plumbing, heating, air conditioning or automatic fire protective sprinkler system or household appliance on the "residence premises". This includes the cost to tear out and replace any part of a building, or other structure, on the "residence premises", but only when necessary to repair the system or appliance. However, such tear out and replacement coverage only applies to other structures if the water or steam causes actual damage to a building on the "residence premises".

We do not cover loss to the system or appliance from which this water or steam escaped.

For purposes of this provision, a plumbing system or household appliance does not include a sump, sump pump or related equipment or a roof drain, gutter, down spout or similar fixtures or equipment.

Section I – Exclusion **A.3.** Water Damage, Paragraphs **a.** and **c.** that apply to surface water and water below the surface of the ground do not apply to loss by water covered under **c.(5)** and **(6)** above.

Under **2.b.** and **c.** above, any ensuing loss to property described in Coverages **A** and **B** not precluded by any other provision in this policy is covered.

B. Coverage C – Personal Property

We insure for direct physical loss to the property described in Coverage **C** caused by any of the following perils unless the loss is excluded in Section I – Exclusions.

1. Fire Or Lightning

2. Windstorm Or Hail

This peril includes loss to watercraft of all types and their trailers, furnishings, equipment, and outboard engines or motors, only while inside a fully enclosed building.

This peril does not include loss to the property contained in a building caused by rain, snow, sleet, sand or dust unless the direct force of wind or hail damages the building causing an opening in a roof or wall and the rain, snow, sleet, sand or dust enters through this opening.

3. Explosion

4. Riot Or Civil Commotion

5. Aircraft

This peril includes self-propelled missiles and spacecraft.

6. Vehicles

7. Smoke

This peril means sudden and accidental damage from smoke, including the emission or puffback of smoke, soot, fumes or vapors from a boiler, furnace or related equipment.

This peril does not include loss caused by smoke from agricultural smudging or industrial operations.

8. Vandalism Or Malicious Mischief

9. Theft

a. This peril includes attempted theft and loss of property from a known place when it is likely that the property has been stolen.

b. This peril does not include loss caused by theft:

(1) Committed by an "insured";

(2) In or to a dwelling under construction, or of materials and supplies for use in the construction until the dwelling is finished and occupied;

(3) From that part of a "residence premises" rented by an "insured" to someone other than another "insured"; or

(4) That occurs off the "residence premises" of:

(a) Trailers, semitrailers and campers;

(b) Watercraft of all types, and their furnishings, equipment and outboard engines or motors; or

(c) Property while at any other residence owned by, rented to, or occupied by an "insured", except while an "insured" is temporarily living there. Property of an "insured" who is a student is covered while at the residence the student occupies to attend school as long as the student has been there at any time during the 60 days immediately before the loss.

10. Falling Objects

This peril does not include loss to property contained in a building unless the roof or an outside wall of the building is first damaged by a falling object. Damage to the falling object itself is not included.

11. Weight Of Ice, Snow Or Sleet

This peril means weight of ice, snow or sleet which causes damage to property contained in a building.

         HO 00 03 10 00

12. Accidental Discharge Or Overflow Of Water Or Steam

a. This peril means accidental discharge or overflow of water or steam from within a plumbing, heating, air conditioning or automatic fire protective sprinkler system or from within a household appliance.

b. This peril does not include loss:

   (1) To the system or appliance from which the water or steam escaped;

   (2) Caused by or resulting from freezing except as provided in Peril Insured Against **14.** Freezing;

   (3) On the "residence premises" caused by accidental discharge or overflow which occurs off the "residence premises"; or

   (4) Caused by mold, fungus or wet rot unless hidden within the walls or ceilings or beneath the floors or above the ceilings of a structure.

c. In this peril, a plumbing system or household appliance does not include a sump, sump pump or related equipment or a roof drain, gutter, downspout or similar fixtures or equipment.

d. Section I – Exclusion **A.3.** Water Damage, Paragraphs **a.** and **c.** that apply to surface water and water below the surface of the ground do not apply to loss by water covered under this peril.

13. Sudden And Accidental Tearing Apart, Cracking, Burning Or Bulging

This peril means sudden and accidental tearing apart, cracking, burning or bulging of a steam or hot water heating system, an air conditioning or automatic fire protective sprinkler system, or an appliance for heating water.

We do not cover loss caused by or resulting from freezing under this peril.

14. Freezing

a. This peril means freezing of a plumbing, heating, air conditioning or automatic fire protective sprinkler system or of a household appliance but only if you have used reasonable care to:

   (1) Maintain heat in the building; or

   (2) Shut off the water supply and drain all systems and appliances of water.

However, if the building is protected by an automatic fire protective sprinkler system, you must use reasonable care to continue the water supply and maintain heat in the building for coverage to apply.

b. In this peril, a plumbing system or household appliance does not include a sump, sump pump or related equipment or a roof drain, gutter, downspout or similar fixtures or equipment.

15. Sudden And Accidental Damage From Artificially Generated Electrical Current

This peril does not include loss to tubes, transistors, electronic components or circuitry that are a part of appliances, fixtures, computers, home entertainment units or other types of electronic apparatus.

16. Volcanic Eruption

This peril does not include loss caused by earthquake, land shock waves or tremors.

SECTION I – EXCLUSIONS

A. We do not insure for loss caused directly or indirectly by any of the following. Such loss is excluded regardless of any other cause or event contributing concurrently or in any sequence to the loss. These exclusions apply whether or not the loss event results in widespread damage or affects a substantial area.

1. Ordinance Or Law

Ordinance Or Law means any ordinance or law:

a. Requiring or regulating the construction, demolition, remodeling, renovation or repair of property, including removal of any resulting debris. This Exclusion **A.1.a.** does not apply to the amount of coverage that may be provided for in **E.11.** Ordinance Or Law under Section I – Property Coverages;

b. The requirements of which result in a loss in value to property; or

c. Requiring any "insured" or others to test for, monitor, clean up, remove, contain, treat, detoxify or neutralize, or in any way respond to, or assess the effects of, pollutants.

Pollutants means any solid, liquid, gaseous or thermal irritant or contaminant, including smoke, vapor, soot, fumes, acids, alkalis, chemicals and waste. Waste includes materials to be recycled, reconditioned or reclaimed.

This Exclusion **1.** applies whether or not the property has been physically damaged.

2. Earth Movement

Earth Movement means:

a. Earthquake, including land shock waves or tremors before, during or after a volcanic eruption;

b. Landslide, mudslide or mudflow;

c. Subsidence or sinkhole; or

d. Any other earth movement including earth sinking, rising or shifting;

caused by or resulting from human or animal forces or any act of nature unless direct loss by fire or explosion ensues and then we will pay only for the ensuing loss.

This Exclusion **2.** does not apply to loss by theft.

3. Water Damage

Water Damage means:

a. Flood, surface water, waves, tidal water, overflow of a body of water, or spray from any of these, whether or not driven by wind;

b. Water or water-borne material which backs up through sewers or drains or which overflows or is discharged from a sump, sump pump or related equipment; or

c. Water or water-borne material below the surface of the ground, including water which exerts pressure on or seeps or leaks through a building, sidewalk, driveway, foundation, swimming pool or other structure;

caused by or resulting from human or animal forces or any act of nature.

Direct loss by fire, explosion or theft resulting from water damage is covered.

4. Power Failure

Power Failure means the failure of power or other utility service if the failure takes place off the "residence premises". But if the failure results in a loss, from a Peril Insured Against on the "residence premises", we will pay for the loss caused by that peril.

5. Neglect

Neglect means neglect of an "insured" to use all reasonable means to save and preserve property at and after the time of a loss.

6. War

War includes the following and any consequence of any of the following:

a. Undeclared war, civil war, insurrection, rebellion or revolution;

b. Warlike act by a military force or military personnel; or

c. Destruction, seizure or use for a military purpose.

Discharge of a nuclear weapon will be deemed a warlike act even if accidental.

7. Nuclear Hazard

This Exclusion **7.** pertains to Nuclear Hazard to the extent set forth in **M.** Nuclear Hazard Clause under Section **I** – Conditions.

8. Intentional Loss

Intentional Loss means any loss arising out of any act an "insured" commits or conspires to commit with the intent to cause a loss.

In the event of such loss, no "insured" is entitled to coverage, even "insureds" who did not commit or conspire to commit the act causing the loss.

9. Governmental Action

Governmental Action means the destruction, confiscation or seizure of property described in Coverage **A, B** or **C** by order of any governmental or public authority.

This exclusion does not apply to such acts ordered by any governmental or public authority that are taken at the time of a fire to prevent its spread, if the loss caused by fire would be covered under this policy.

B. We do not insure for loss to property described in Coverages **A** and **B** caused by any of the following. However, any ensuing loss to property described in Coverages **A** and **B** not precluded by any other provision in this policy is covered.

1. Weather conditions. However, this exclusion only applies if weather conditions contribute in any way with a cause or event excluded in **A.** above to produce the loss.

2. Acts or decisions, including the failure to act or decide, of any person, group, organization or governmental body.

3. Faulty, inadequate or defective:

a. Planning, zoning, development, surveying, siting;

b. Design, specifications, workmanship, repair, construction, renovation, remodeling, grading, compaction;

c. Materials used in repair, construction, renovation or remodeling; or

d. Maintenance;

of part or all of any property whether on or off the "residence premises".

SECTION I – CONDITIONS

A. Insurable Interest And Limit Of Liability

Even if more than one person has an insurable interest in the property covered, we will not be liable in any one loss:

1. To an "insured" for more than the amount of such "insured's" interest at the time of loss; or

2. For more than the applicable limit of liability.

B. Duties After Loss

In case of a loss to covered property, we have no duty to provide coverage under this policy if the failure to comply with the following duties is prejudicial to us. These duties must be performed either by you, an "insured" seeking coverage, or a representative of either:

1. Give prompt notice to us or our agent;

2. Notify the police in case of loss by theft;

3. Notify the credit card or electronic fund transfer card or access device company in case of loss as provided for in **E.6.** Credit Card, Electronic Fund Transfer Card Or Access Device, Forgery And Counterfeit Money under Section I – Property Coverages;

4. Protect the property from further damage. If repairs to the property are required, you must:

   a. Make reasonable and necessary repairs to protect the property; and

   b. Keep an accurate record of repair expenses;

5. Cooperate with us in the investigation of a claim;

6. Prepare an inventory of damaged personal property showing the quantity, description, actual cash value and amount of loss. Attach all bills, receipts and related documents that justify the figures in the inventory;

7. As often as we reasonably require:

   a. Show the damaged property;

   b. Provide us with records and documents we request and permit us to make copies; and

   c. Submit to examination under oath, while not in the presence of another "insured", and sign the same;

8. Send to us, within 60 days after our request, your signed, sworn proof of loss which sets forth, to the best of your knowledge and belief:

   a. The time and cause of loss;

   b. The interests of all "insureds" and all others in the property involved and all liens on the property;

   c. Other insurance which may cover the loss;

   d. Changes in title or occupancy of the property during the term of the policy;

   e. Specifications of damaged buildings and detailed repair estimates;

   f. The inventory of damaged personal property described in **6.** above;

   g. Receipts for additional living expenses incurred and records that support the fair rental value loss; and

   h. Evidence or affidavit that supports a claim under **E.6.** Credit Card, Electronic Fund Transfer Card Or Access Device, Forgery And Counterfeit Money under Section I – Property Coverages, stating the amount and cause of loss.

C. Loss Settlement

In this Condition **C.**, the terms "cost to repair or replace" and "replacement cost" do not include the increased costs incurred to comply with the enforcement of any ordinance or law, except to the extent that coverage for these increased costs is provided in **E.11.** Ordinance Or Law under Section I – Property Coverages. Covered property losses are settled as follows:

1. Property of the following types:

   a. Personal property;

   b. Awnings, carpeting, household appliances, outdoor antennas and outdoor equipment, whether or not attached to buildings;

   c. Structures that are not buildings; and

   d. Grave markers, including mausoleums;

   at actual cash value at the time of loss but not more than the amount required to repair or replace.

2. Buildings covered under Coverage **A** or **B** at replacement cost without deduction for depreciation, subject to the following:

   a. If, at the time of loss, the amount of insurance in this policy on the damaged building is 80% or more of the full replacement cost of the building immediately before the loss, we will pay the cost to repair or replace, after application of any deductible and without deduction for depreciation, but not more than the least of the following amounts:

      (1) The limit of liability under this policy that applies to the building;

      (2) The replacement cost of that part of the building damaged with material of like kind and quality and for like use; or

      (3) The necessary amount actually spent to repair or replace the damaged building.

If the building is rebuilt at a new premises, the cost described in **(2)** above is limited to the cost which would have been incurred if the building had been built at the original premises.

b. If, at the time of loss, the amount of insurance in this policy on the damaged building is less than 80% of the full replacement cost of the building immediately before the loss, we will pay the greater of the following amounts, but not more than the limit of liability under this policy that applies to the building:

  (1) The actual cash value of that part of the building damaged; or

  (2) That proportion of the cost to repair or replace, after application of any deductible and without deduction for depreciation, that part of the building damaged, which the total amount of insurance in this policy on the damaged building bears to 80% of the replacement cost of the building.

c. To determine the amount of insurance required to equal 80% of the full replacement cost of the building immediately before the loss, do not include the value of:

  (1) Excavations, footings, foundations, piers, or any other structures or devices that support all or part of the building, which are below the undersurface of the lowest basement floor;

  (2) Those supports described in **(1)** above which are below the surface of the ground inside the foundation walls, if there is no basement; and

  (3) Underground flues, pipes, wiring and drains.

d. We will pay no more than the actual cash value of the damage until actual repair or replacement is complete. Once actual repair or replacement is complete, we will settle the loss as noted in **2.a.** and **b.** above.

However, if the cost to repair or replace the damage is both:

  (1) Less than 5% of the amount of insurance in this policy on the building; and

  (2) Less than $2,500;

we will settle the loss as noted in **2.a.** and **b.** above whether or not actual repair or replacement is complete.

e. You may disregard the replacement cost loss settlement provisions and make claim under this policy for loss to buildings on an actual cash value basis. You may then make claim for any additional liability according to the provisions of this Condition **C.** Loss Settlement, provided you notify us of your intent to do so within 180 days after the date of loss.

D. Loss To A Pair Or Set

In case of loss to a pair or set we may elect to:

1. Repair or replace any part to restore the pair or set to its value before the loss; or

2. Pay the difference between actual cash value of the property before and after the loss.

E. Appraisal

If you and we fail to agree on the amount of loss, either may demand an appraisal of the loss. In this event, each party will choose a competent and impartial appraiser within 20 days after receiving a written request from the other. The two appraisers will choose an umpire. If they cannot agree upon an umpire within 15 days, you or we may request that the choice be made by a judge of a court of record in the state where the "residence premises" is located. The appraisers will separately set the amount of loss. If the appraisers submit a written report of an agreement to us, the amount agreed upon will be the amount of loss. If they fail to agree, they will submit their differences to the umpire. A decision agreed to by any two will set the amount of loss.

Each party will:

1. Pay its own appraiser; and

2. Bear the other expenses of the appraisal and umpire equally.

F. Other Insurance And Service Agreement

If a loss covered by this policy is also covered by:

1. Other insurance, we will pay only the proportion of the loss that the limit of liability that applies under this policy bears to the total amount of insurance covering the loss; or

2. A service agreement, this insurance is excess over any amounts payable under any such agreement. Service agreement means a service plan, property restoration plan, home warranty or other similar service warranty agreement, even if it is characterized as insurance.

G. Suit Against Us

No action can be brought against us unless there has been full compliance with all of the terms under Section I of this policy and the action is started within two years after the date of loss.

H. Our Option

If we give you written notice within 30 days after we receive your signed, sworn proof of loss, we may repair or replace any part of the damaged property with material or property of like kind and quality.

I. Loss Payment

We will adjust all losses with you. We will pay you unless some other person is named in the policy or is legally entitled to receive payment. Loss will be payable 60 days after we receive your proof of loss and:

1. Reach an agreement with you;

2. There is an entry of a final judgment; or

3. There is a filing of an appraisal award with us.

J. Abandonment Of Property

We need not accept any property abandoned by an "insured".

K. Mortgage Clause

1. If a mortgagee is named in this policy, any loss payable under Coverage **A** or **B** will be paid to the mortgagee and you, as interests appear. If more than one mortgagee is named, the order of payment will be the same as the order of precedence of the mortgages.

2. If we deny your claim, that denial will not apply to a valid claim of the mortgagee, if the mortgagee:

   a. Notifies us of any change in ownership, occupancy or substantial change in risk of which the mortgagee is aware;

   b. Pays any premium due under this policy on demand if you have neglected to pay the premium; and

   c. Submits a signed, sworn statement of loss within 60 days after receiving notice from us of your failure to do so. Paragraphs **E.** Appraisal, **G.** Suit Against Us and **I.** Loss Payment under Section I – Conditions also apply to the mortgagee.

3. If we decide to cancel or not to renew this policy, the mortgagee will be notified at least 10 days before the date cancellation or nonrenewal takes effect.

4. If we pay the mortgagee for any loss and deny payment to you:

   a. We are subrogated to all the rights of the mortgagee granted under the mortgage on the property; or

   b. At our option, we may pay to the mortgagee the whole principal on the mortgage plus any accrued interest. In this event, we will receive a full assignment and transfer of the mortgage and all securities held as collateral to the mortgage debt.

5. Subrogation will not impair the right of the mortgagee to recover the full amount of the mortgagee's claim.

L. No Benefit To Bailee

We will not recognize any assignment or grant any coverage that benefits a person or organization holding, storing or moving property for a fee regardless of any other provision of this policy.

M. Nuclear Hazard Clause

1. "Nuclear Hazard" means any nuclear reaction, radiation, or radioactive contamination, all whether controlled or uncontrolled or however caused, or any consequence of any of these.

2. Loss caused by the nuclear hazard will not be considered loss caused by fire, explosion, or smoke, whether these perils are specifically named in or otherwise included within the Perils Insured Against.

3. This policy does not apply under Section I to loss caused directly or indirectly by nuclear hazard, except that direct loss by fire resulting from the nuclear hazard is covered.

N. Recovered Property

If you or we recover any property for which we have made payment under this policy, you or we will notify the other of the recovery. At your option, the property will be returned to or retained by you or it will become our property. If the recovered property is returned to or retained by you, the loss payment will be adjusted based on the amount you received for the recovered property.

O. Volcanic Eruption Period

One or more volcanic eruptions that occur within a 72 hour period will be considered as one volcanic eruption.

P. Policy Period

This policy applies only to loss which occurs during the policy period.

Q. Concealment Or Fraud

We provide coverage to no "insureds" under this policy if, whether before or after a loss, an "insured" has:

1. Intentionally concealed or misrepresented any material fact or circumstance;

2. Engaged in fraudulent conduct; or

3. Made false statements;

relating to this insurance.

R. Loss Payable Clause

If the Declarations show a loss payee for certain listed insured personal property, the definition of "insured" is changed to include that loss payee with respect to that property.

If we decide to cancel or not renew this policy, that loss payee will be notified in writing.

SECTION II – LIABILITY COVERAGES

A. Coverage E – Personal Liability

If a claim is made or a suit is brought against an "insured" for damages because of "bodily injury" or "property damage" caused by an "occurrence" to which this coverage applies, we will:

1. Pay up to our limit of liability for the damages for which an "insured" is legally liable. Damages include prejudgment interest awarded against an "insured"; and

2. Provide a defense at our expense by counsel of our choice, even if the suit is groundless, false or fraudulent. We may investigate and settle any claim or suit that we decide is appropriate. Our duty to settle or defend ends when our limit of liability for the "occurrence" has been exhausted by payment of a judgment or settlement.

B. Coverage F – Medical Payments To Others

We will pay the necessary medical expenses that are incurred or medically ascertained within three years from the date of an accident causing "bodily injury". Medical expenses means reasonable charges for medical, surgical, x-ray, dental, ambulance, hospital, professional nursing, prosthetic devices and funeral services. This coverage does not apply to you or regular residents of your household except "residence employees". As to others, this coverage applies only:

1. To a person on the "insured location" with the permission of an "insured"; or

2. To a person off the "insured location", if the "bodily injury":

a. Arises out of a condition on the "insured location" or the ways immediately adjoining;

b. Is caused by the activities of an "insured";

c. Is caused by a "residence employee" in the course of the "residence employee's" employment by an "insured"; or

d. Is caused by an animal owned by or in the care of an "insured".

SECTION II – EXCLUSIONS

A. "Motor Vehicle Liability"

1. Coverages **E** and **F** do not apply to any "motor vehicle liability" if, at the time and place of an "occurrence", the involved "motor vehicle":

a. Is registered for use on public roads or property;

b. Is not registered for use on public roads or property, but such registration is required by a law, or regulation issued by a government agency, for it to be used at the place of the "occurrence"; or

c. Is being:

(1) Operated in, or practicing for, any prearranged or organized race, speed contest or other competition;

(2) Rented to others;

(3) Used to carry persons or cargo for a charge; or

(4) Used for any "business" purpose except for a motorized golf cart while on a golfing facility.

2. If Exclusion **A.1.** does not apply, there is still no coverage for "motor vehicle liability" unless the "motor vehicle" is:

a. In dead storage on an "insured location";

b. Used solely to service an "insured's" residence;

c. Designed to assist the handicapped and, at the time of an "occurrence", it is:

(1) Being used to assist a handicapped person; or

(2) Parked on an "insured location";

d. Designed for recreational use off public roads and:

(1) Not owned by an "insured"; or

(2) Owned by an "insured" provided the "occurrence" takes place on an "insured location" as defined in Definitions **B. 6.a., b., d., e.** or **h.**; or

e. A motorized golf cart that is owned by an "insured", designed to carry up to 4 persons, not built or modified after manufacture to exceed a speed of 25 miles per hour on level ground and, at the time of an "occurrence", is within the legal boundaries of:

(1) A golfing facility and is parked or stored there, or being used by an "insured" to:

(a) Play the game of golf or for other recreational or leisure activity allowed by the facility;

Copyright, Insurance Services Office, Inc., 1999

(b) Travel to or from an area where "motor vehicles" or golf carts are parked or stored; or

(c) Cross public roads at designated points to access other parts of the golfing facility; or

(2) A private residential community, including its public roads upon which a motorized golf cart can legally travel, which is subject to the authority of a property owners association and contains an "insured's" residence.

B. "Watercraft Liability"

1. Coverages **E** and **F** do not apply to any "watercraft liability" if, at the time of an "occurrence", the involved watercraft is being:

a. Operated in, or practicing for, any prearranged or organized race, speed contest or other competition. This exclusion does not apply to a sailing vessel or a predicted log cruise;

b. Rented to others;

c. Used to carry persons or cargo for a charge; or

d. Used for any "business" purpose.

2. If Exclusion **B.1.** does not apply, there is still no coverage for "watercraft liability" unless, at the time of the "occurrence", the watercraft:

a. Is stored;

b. Is a sailing vessel, with or without auxiliary power that is:

(1) Less than 26 feet in overall length; or

(2) 26 feet or more in overall length and not owned by or rented to an "insured"; or

c. Is not a sailing vessel and is powered by:

(1) An inboard or inboard-outdrive engine or motor, including those that power a water jet pump, of:

(a) 50 horsepower or less and not owned by an "insured";

(b) More than 50 horsepower and not owned by or rented to an "insured"; or

(2) One or more outboard engines or motors with:

(a) 25 total horsepower or less;

(b) More than 25 horsepower if the outboard engine or motor is not owned by an "insured";

(c) More than 25 horsepower if the outboard engine or motor is owned by an "insured" who acquired it during the policy period; or

(d) More than 25 horsepower if the outboard engine or motor is owned by an "insured" who acquired it before the policy period, but only if:

(i) You declare them at policy inception; or

(ii) Your intent to insure them is reported to us in writing within 45 days after you acquire them.

The coverages in **(c)** and **(d)** above apply for the policy period.

Horsepower means the maximum power rating assigned to the engine or motor by the manufacturer.

C. "Aircraft Liability"

This policy does not cover "aircraft liability".

D. "Hovercraft Liability"

This policy does not cover "hovercraft liability".

E. Coverage E – Personal Liability And Coverage F – Medical Payments To Others

Coverages **E** and **F** do not apply to the following:

1. Expected Or Intended Injury

"Bodily injury" or "property damage" which is expected or intended by an "insured" even if the resulting "bodily injury" or "property damage":

a. Is of a different kind, quality or degree than initially expected or intended; or

b. Is sustained by a different person, entity, real or personal property, than initially expected or intended.

However, this Exclusion **E.1.** does not apply to "bodily injury" resulting from the use of reasonable force by an "insured" to protect persons or property;

2. "Business"

a. "Bodily injury" or "property damage" arising out of or in connection with a "business" conducted from an "insured location" or engaged in by an "insured", whether or not the "business" is owned or operated by an "insured" or employs an "insured".

This Exclusion **E.2.** applies but is not limited to an act or omission, regardless of its nature or circumstance, involving a service or duty rendered, promised, owed, or implied to be provided because of the nature of the "business".

b. This Exclusion **E.2.** does not apply to:

(1) The rental or holding for rental of an "insured location";

(a) On an occasional basis if used only as a residence;

(b) In part for use only as a residence, unless a single family unit is intended for use by the occupying family to lodge more than two roomers or boarders; or

(c) In part, as an office, school, studio or private garage; and

(2) An "insured" under the age of 21 years involved in a part-time or occasional, self-employed "business" with no employees;

3. Professional Services

"Bodily injury" or "property damage" arising out of the rendering of or failure to render professional services;

4. "Insured's" Premises Not An "Insured Location"

"Bodily injury" or "property damage" arising out of a premises:

a. Owned by an "insured";

b. Rented to an "insured"; or

c. Rented to others by an "insured";

that is not an "insured location";

5. War

"Bodily injury" or "property damage" caused directly or indirectly by war, including the following and any consequence of any of the following:

a. Undeclared war, civil war, insurrection, rebellion or revolution;

b. Warlike act by a military force or military personnel; or

c. Destruction, seizure or use for a military purpose.

Discharge of a nuclear weapon will be deemed a warlike act even if accidental;

6. Communicable Disease

"Bodily injury" or "property damage" which arises out of the transmission of a communicable disease by an "insured";

7. Sexual Molestation, Corporal Punishment Or Physical Or Mental Abuse

"Bodily injury" or "property damage" arising out of sexual molestation, corporal punishment or physical or mental abuse; or

8. Controlled Substance

"Bodily injury" or "property damage" arising out of the use, sale, manufacture, delivery, transfer or possession by any person of a Controlled Substance as defined by the Federal Food and Drug Law at 21 U.S.C.A. Sections 811 and 812. Controlled Substances include but are not limited to cocaine, LSD, marijuana and all narcotic drugs. However, this exclusion does not apply to the legitimate use of prescription drugs by a person following the orders of a licensed physician.

Exclusions **A.** "Motor Vehicle Liability", **B.** "Watercraft Liability", **C.** "Aircraft Liability", **D.** "Hovercraft Liability", and **E.4.** "Insured's" Premises Not An "Insured Location" do not apply to "bodily injury" to a "residence employee" arising out of and in the course of the "residence employee's" employment by an "insured".

F. Coverage E – Personal Liability

Coverage **E** does not apply to:

1. Liability:

a. For any loss assessment charged against you as a member of an association, corporation or community of property owners, except as provided in **D.** Loss Assessment under Section II – Additional Coverages;

b. Under any contract or agreement entered into by an "insured". However, this exclusion does not apply to written contracts:

(1) That directly relate to the ownership, maintenance or use of an "insured location"; or

(2) Where the liability of others is assumed by you prior to an "occurrence";

unless excluded in **a.** above or elsewhere in this policy;

2. "Property damage" to property owned by an "insured". This includes costs or expenses incurred by an "insured" or others to repair, replace, enhance, restore or maintain such property to prevent injury to a person or damage to property of others, whether on or away from an "insured location";

3. "Property damage" to property rented to, occupied or used by or in the care of an "insured". This exclusion does not apply to "property damage" caused by fire, smoke or explosion;

4. "Bodily injury" to any person eligible to receive any benefits voluntarily provided or required to be provided by an "insured" under any:

a. Workers' compensation law;

b. Non-occupational disability law; or

c. Occupational disease law;

5. "Bodily injury" or "property damage" for which an "insured" under this policy:

a. Is also an insured under a nuclear energy liability policy issued by the:

(1) Nuclear Energy Liability Insurance Association;

(2) Mutual Atomic Energy Liability Underwriters;

(3) Nuclear Insurance Association of Canada;

or any of their successors; or

b. Would be an insured under such a policy but for the exhaustion of its limit of liability; or

6. "Bodily injury" to you or an "insured" as defined under Definitions **5.a.** or **b.**

This exclusion also applies to any claim made or suit brought against you or an "insured":

(1) To repay; or

(2) Share damages with;

another person who may be obligated to pay damages because of "bodily injury" to an "insured".

G. Coverage F – Medical Payments To Others

Coverage **F** does not apply to "bodily injury":

1. To a "residence employee" if the "bodily injury":

a. Occurs off the "insured location"; and

b. Does not arise out of or in the course of the "residence employee's" employment by an "insured";

2. To any person eligible to receive benefits voluntarily provided or required to be provided under any:

a. Workers' compensation law;

b. Non-occupational disability law; or

c. Occupational disease law;

3. From any:

a. Nuclear reaction;

b. Nuclear radiation; or

c. Radioactive contamination;

all whether controlled or uncontrolled or however caused; or

d. Any consequence of any of these; or

4. To any person, other than a "residence employee" of an "insured", regularly residing on any part of the "insured location".

SECTION II – ADDITIONAL COVERAGES

We cover the following in addition to the limits of liability:

A. Claim Expenses

We pay:

1. Expenses we incur and costs taxed against an "insured" in any suit we defend;

2. Premiums on bonds required in a suit we defend, but not for bond amounts more than the Coverage **E** limit of liability. We need not apply for or furnish any bond;

3. Reasonable expenses incurred by an "insured" at our request, including actual loss of earnings (but not loss of other income) up to $250 per day, for assisting us in the investigation or defense of a claim or suit; and

4. Interest on the entire judgment which accrues after entry of the judgment and before we pay or tender, or deposit in court that part of the judgment which does not exceed the limit of liability that applies.

B. First Aid Expenses

We will pay expenses for first aid to others incurred by an "insured" for "bodily injury" covered under this policy. We will not pay for first aid to an "insured".

C. Damage To Property Of Others

1. We will pay, at replacement cost, up to $1,000 per "occurrence" for "property damage" to property of others caused by an "insured".

2. We will not pay for "property damage":

a. To the extent of any amount recoverable under Section **I**;

b. Caused intentionally by an "insured" who is 13 years of age or older;

c. To property owned by an "insured";

d. To property owned by or rented to a tenant of an "insured" or a resident in your household; or

e. Arising out of:

(1) A "business" engaged in by an "insured";

(2) Any act or omission in connection with a premises owned, rented or controlled by an "insured", other than the "insured location"; or

(3) The ownership, maintenance, occupancy, operation, use, loading or unloading of aircraft, hovercraft, watercraft or "motor vehicles".

This exclusion **e.(3)** does not apply to a "motor vehicle" that:

(a) Is designed for recreational use off public roads;

(b) Is not owned by an "insured"; and

(c) At the time of the "occurrence", is not required by law, or regulation issued by a government agency, to have been registered for it to be used on public roads or property.

D. Loss Assessment

1. We will pay up to $1,000 for your share of loss assessment charged against you, as owner or tenant of the "residence premises", during the policy period by a corporation or association of property owners, when the assessment is made as a result of:

   a. "Bodily injury" or "property damage" not excluded from coverage under Section II – Exclusions; or

   b. Liability for an act of a director, officer or trustee in the capacity as a director, officer or trustee, provided such person:

      (1) Is elected by the members of a corporation or association of property owners; and

      (2) Serves without deriving any income from the exercise of duties which are solely on behalf of a corporation or association of property owners.

2. Paragraph I. Policy Period under Section II – Conditions does not apply to this Loss Assessment Coverage.

3. Regardless of the number of assessments, the limit of $1,000 is the most we will pay for loss arising out of:

   a. One accident, including continuous or repeated exposure to substantially the same general harmful condition; or

   b. A covered act of a director, officer or trustee. An act involving more than one director, officer or trustee is considered to be a single act.

4. We do not cover assessments charged against you or a corporation or association of property owners by any governmental body.

SECTION II – CONDITIONS

A. Limit Of Liability

Our total liability under Coverage **E** for all damages resulting from any one "occurrence" will not be more than the Coverage **E** limit of liability shown in the Declarations. This limit is the same regardless of the number of "insureds", claims made or persons injured. All "bodily injury" and "property damage" resulting from any one accident or from continuous or repeated exposure to substantially the same general harmful conditions shall be considered to be the result of one "occurrence".

Our total liability under Coverage **F** for all medical expense payable for "bodily injury" to one person as the result of one accident will not be more than the Coverage **F** limit of liability shown in the Declarations.

B. Severability Of Insurance

This insurance applies separately to each "insured". This condition will not increase our limit of liability for any one "occurrence".

C. Duties After "Occurrence"

In case of an "occurrence", you or another "insured" will perform the following duties that apply. We have no duty to provide coverage under this policy if your failure to comply with the following duties is prejudicial to us. You will help us by seeing that these duties are performed:

1. Give written notice to us or our agent as soon as is practical, which sets forth:

   a. The identity of the policy and the "named insured" shown in the Declarations;

   b. Reasonably available information on the time, place and circumstances of the "occurrence"; and

   c. Names and addresses of any claimants and witnesses;

2. Cooperate with us in the investigation, settlement or defense of any claim or suit;

3. Promptly forward to us every notice, demand, summons or other process relating to the "occurrence";

4. At our request, help us:

   a. To make settlement;

   b. To enforce any right of contribution or indemnity against any person or organization who may be liable to an "insured";

 HO 00 03 10 00

c. With the conduct of suits and attend hearings and trials; and

d. To secure and give evidence and obtain the attendance of witnesses;

5. With respect to **C.** Damage To Property Of Others under Section **II** – Additional Coverages, submit to us within 60 days after the loss, a sworn statement of loss and show the damaged property, if in an "insured's" control;

6. No "insured" shall, except at such "insured's" own cost, voluntarily make payment, assume obligation or incur expense other than for first aid to others at the time of the "bodily injury".

D. Duties Of An Injured Person – Coverage F – Medical Payments To Others

1. The injured person or someone acting for the injured person will:

a. Give us written proof of claim, under oath if required, as soon as is practical; and

b. Authorize us to obtain copies of medical reports and records.

2. The injured person will submit to a physical exam by a doctor of our choice when and as often as we reasonably require.

E. Payment Of Claim – Coverage F – Medical Payments To Others

Payment under this coverage is not an admission of liability by an "insured" or us.

F. Suit Against Us

1. No action can be brought against us unless there has been full compliance with all of the terms under this Section **II**.

2. No one will have the right to join us as a party to any action against an "insured".

3. Also, no action with respect to Coverage **E** can be brought against us until the obligation of such "insured" has been determined by final judgment or agreement signed by us.

G. Bankruptcy Of An "Insured"

Bankruptcy or insolvency of an "insured" will not relieve us of our obligations under this policy.

H. Other Insurance

This insurance is excess over other valid and collectible insurance except insurance written specifically to cover as excess over the limits of liability that apply in this policy.

I. Policy Period

This policy applies only to "bodily injury" or "property damage" which occurs during the policy period.

J. Concealment Or Fraud

We do not provide coverage to an "insured" who, whether before or after a loss, has:

1. Intentionally concealed or misrepresented any material fact or circumstance;

2. Engaged in fraudulent conduct; or

3. Made false statements;

relating to this insurance.

SECTIONS I AND II – CONDITIONS

A. Liberalization Clause

If we make a change which broadens coverage under this edition of our policy without additional premium charge, that change will automatically apply to your insurance as of the date we implement the change in your state, provided that this implementation date falls within 60 days prior to or during the policy period stated in the Declarations.

This Liberalization Clause does not apply to changes implemented with a general program revision that includes both broadenings and restrictions in coverage, whether that general program revision is implemented through introduction of:

1. A subsequent edition of this policy; or

2. An amendatory endorsement.

B. Waiver Or Change Of Policy Provisions

A waiver or change of a provision of this policy must be in writing by us to be valid. Our request for an appraisal or examination will not waive any of our rights.

C. Cancellation

1. You may cancel this policy at any time by returning it to us or by letting us know in writing of the date cancellation is to take effect.

2. We may cancel this policy only for the reasons stated below by letting you know in writing of the date cancellation takes effect. This cancellation notice may be delivered to you, or mailed to you at your mailing address shown in the Declarations. Proof of mailing will be sufficient proof of notice.

a. When you have not paid the premium, we may cancel at any time by letting you know at least 10 days before the date cancellation takes effect.

b. When this policy has been in effect for less than 60 days and is not a renewal with us, we may cancel for any reason by letting you know at least 10 days before the date cancellation takes effect.

c. When this policy has been in effect for 60 days or more, or at any time if it is a renewal with us, we may cancel:

   (1) If there has been a material misrepresentation of fact which if known to us would have caused us not to issue the policy; or

   (2) If the risk has changed substantially since the policy was issued.

   This can be done by letting you know at least 30 days before the date cancellation takes effect.

d. When this policy is written for a period of more than one year, we may cancel for any reason at anniversary by letting you know at least 30 days before the date cancellation takes effect.

3. When this policy is canceled, the premium for the period from the date of cancellation to the expiration date will be refunded pro rata.

4. If the return premium is not refunded with the notice of cancellation or when this policy is returned to us, we will refund it within a reasonable time after the date cancellation takes effect.

D. Nonrenewal

We may elect not to renew this policy. We may do so by delivering to you, or mailing to you at your mailing address shown in the Declarations, written notice at least 30 days before the expiration date of this policy. Proof of mailing will be sufficient proof of notice.

E. Assignment

Assignment of this policy will not be valid unless we give our written consent.

F. Subrogation

An "insured" may waive in writing before a loss all rights of recovery against any person. If not waived, we may require an assignment of rights of recovery for a loss to the extent that payment is made by us.

If an assignment is sought, an "insured" must sign and deliver all related papers and cooperate with us.

Subrogation does not apply to Coverage **F** or Paragraph **C.** Damage To Property Of Others under Section **II** – Additional Coverages.

G. Death

If any person named in the Declarations or the spouse, if a resident of the same household, dies, the following apply:

1. We insure the legal representative of the deceased but only with respect to the premises and property of the deceased covered under the policy at the time of death; and

2. "Insured" includes:

   a. An "insured" who is a member of your household at the time of your death, but only while a resident of the "residence premises"; and

   b. With respect to your property, the person having proper temporary custody of the property until appointment and qualification of a legal representative.

 HO 00 03 10 00

APPENDIX F

Personal Auto Policy

PERSONAL AUTO POLICY

DECLARATIONS

Policy Number   PA

COMPANY NAME

Previous Policy Number

Policy Period	From	To	12:01 A.M. Standard time

Named Insured
and mailing address

The Auto(s) or Trailer(s) described in this policy is principally garaged at the above address unless otherwise stated:

Number, Street, City, State, ZIP Code

Coverage is provided where a premium or limit of liability is shown for the coverage.

Coverage		Limit of Liability	Auto 1 Premium	Auto 2 Premium
A	Liability	$ each person for bodily injury $ each accident for bodily injury $ each accident for property damage	$ $	$ $
B	Medical Payments	$ each person	$	$
C	Uninsured Motorists	$ each person each accident	$ $	$ $
D	Damage to Your Auto 1. Collision Loss 2. Other than Collision Loss	$ Actual Cash Value minus $ Deductible $ Deductible	 $ $	$ $ $
	Towing and Labor Costs	$ Each disablement	$	$
			$	$
Endorsements made part of this Policy at time of issue:		Endorsement Premium	$	$
		Total Premium Per Auto	$	$
			Total Premium	$

Auto	Year	Trade Name	Model	VIN	Symbol	Age
1 2						

Loss Payee
(Name and Address)

Countersignature of agent/date	Signature/Title - Company Officer

PERSONAL AUTO POLICY

AGREEMENT

In return for payment of the premium and subject to all the terms of this policy, we agree with you as follows:

DEFINITIONS

A. Throughout this policy, "you" and "your" refer to:

1. The "named insured" shown in the Declarations; and

2. The spouse if a resident of the same household.

If the spouse ceases to be a resident of the same household during the policy period or prior to the inception of this policy, the spouse will be considered "you" and "your" under this policy but only until the earlier of:

1. The end of 90 days following the spouse's change of residency;

2. The effective date of another policy listing the spouse as a named insured; or

3. The end of the policy period.

B. "We", "us" and "our" refer to the Company providing this insurance.

C. For purposes of this policy, a private passenger type auto, pickup or van shall be deemed to be owned by a person if leased:

1. Under a written agreement to that person; and

2. For a continuous period of at least 6 months.

Other words and phrases are defined. They are in quotation marks when used.

D. "Bodily injury" means bodily harm, sickness or disease, including death that results.

E. "Business" includes trade, profession or occupation.

F. "Family member" means a person related to you by blood, marriage or adoption who is a resident of your household. This includes a ward or foster child.

G. "Occupying" means in, upon, getting in, on, out or off.

H. "Property damage" means physical injury to, destruction of or loss of use of tangible property.

I. "Trailer" means a vehicle designed to be pulled by a:

1. Private passenger auto; or

2. Pickup or van.

It also means a farm wagon or farm implement while towed by a vehicle listed in **1.** or **2.** above.

J. "Your covered auto" means:

1. Any vehicle shown in the Declarations.

2. A "newly acquired auto".

3. Any "trailer" you own.

4. Any auto or "trailer" you do not own while used as a temporary substitute for any other vehicle described in this definition which is out of normal use because of its:

   a. Breakdown;

   b. Repair;

   c. Servicing;

   d. Loss; or

   e. Destruction.

   This Provision **(J.4.)** does not apply to Coverage For Damage To Your Auto.

K. "Newly acquired auto":

1. "Newly acquired auto" means any of the following types of vehicles you become the owner of during the policy period:

   a. A private passenger auto; or

   b. A pickup or van, for which no other insurance policy provides coverage, that:

   (1) Has a Gross Vehicle Weight of less than 10,000 lbs.; and

   (2) Is not used for the delivery or transportation of goods and materials unless such use is:

   (a) Incidental to your "business" of installing, maintaining or repairing furnishings or equipment; or

   (b) For farming or ranching.

2. Coverage for a "newly acquired auto" is provided as described below. If you ask us to insure a "newly acquired auto" after a specified time period described below has elapsed, any coverage we provide for a "newly acquired auto" will begin at the time you request the coverage.

   a. For any coverage provided in this policy except Coverage For Damage To Your Auto, a "newly acquired auto" will have the broadest coverage we now provide for any vehicle shown in the Declarations. Coverage begins on the date you become the owner. However, for this coverage to apply to a "newly acquired auto" which is in addition to any vehicle shown in the Declarations, you must ask us to insure it within 14 days after you become the owner.

If a "newly acquired auto" replaces a vehicle shown in the Declarations, coverage is provided for this vehicle without your having to ask us to insure it.

b. Collision Coverage for a "newly acquired auto" begins on the date you become the owner. However, for this coverage to apply, you must ask us to insure it within:

(1) 14 days after you become the owner if the Declarations indicate that Collision Coverage applies to at least one auto. In this case, the "newly acquired auto" will have the broadest coverage we now provide for any auto shown in the Declarations.

(2) Four days after you become the owner if the Declarations do not indicate that Collision Coverage applies to at least one auto. If you comply with the 4 day requirement and a loss occurred before you asked us to insure the "newly acquired auto", a Collision deductible of $500 will apply.

c. Other Than Collision Coverage for a "newly acquired auto" begins on the date you become the owner. However, for this coverage to apply, you must ask us to insure it within:

(1) 14 days after you become the owner if the Declarations indicate that Other Than Collision Coverage applies to at least one auto. In this case, the "newly acquired auto" will have the broadest coverage we now provide for any auto shown in the Declarations.

(2) Four days after you become the owner if the Declarations do not indicate that Other Than Collision Coverage applies to at least one auto. If you comply with the 4 day requirement and a loss occurred before you asked us to insure the "newly acquired auto", an Other Than Collision deductible of $500 will apply.

PART A – LIABILITY COVERAGE

INSURING AGREEMENT

A. We will pay damages for "bodily injury" or "property damage" for which any "insured" becomes legally responsible because of an auto accident. Damages include prejudgment interest awarded against the "insured". We will settle or defend, as we consider appropriate, any claim or suit asking for these damages. In addition to our limit of liability, we will pay all defense costs we incur. Our duty to settle or defend ends when our limit of liability for this coverage has been exhausted by payment of judgments or settlements. We have no duty to defend any suit or settle any claim for "bodily injury" or "property damage" not covered under this policy.

B. "Insured" as used in this Part means:

1. You or any "family member" for the ownership, maintenance or use of any auto or "trailer".

2. Any person using "your covered auto".

3. For "your covered auto", any person or organization but only with respect to legal responsibility for acts or omissions of a person for whom coverage is afforded under this Part.

4. For any auto or "trailer", other than "your covered auto", any other person or organization but only with respect to legal responsibility for acts or omissions of you or any "family member" for whom coverage is afforded under this Part. This Provision **(B.4.)** applies only if the person or organization does not own or hire the auto or "trailer".

SUPPLEMENTARY PAYMENTS

In addition to our limit of liability, we will pay on behalf of an "insured":

1. Up to $250 for the cost of bail bonds required because of an accident, including related traffic law violations. The accident must result in "bodily injury" or "property damage" covered under this policy.

2. Premiums on appeal bonds and bonds to release attachments in any suit we defend.

3. Interest accruing after a judgment is entered in any suit we defend. Our duty to pay interest ends when we offer to pay that part of the judgment which does not exceed our limit of liability for this coverage.

4. Up to $200 a day for loss of earnings, but not other income, because of attendance at hearings or trials at our request.

5. Other reasonable expenses incurred at our request.

EXCLUSIONS

A. We do not provide Liability Coverage for any "insured":

1. Who intentionally causes "bodily injury" or "property damage".

2. For "property damage" to property owned or being transported by that "insured".

3. For "property damage" to property:

   a. Rented to;

   b. Used by; or

   c. In the care of;

   that "insured".

   This Exclusion **(A.3.)** does not apply to "property damage" to a residence or private garage.

4. For "bodily injury" to an employee of that "insured" during the course of employment. This Exclusion **(A.4.)** does not apply to "bodily injury" to a domestic employee unless workers' compensation benefits are required or available for that domestic employee.

5. For that "insured's" liability arising out of the ownership or operation of a vehicle while it is being used as a public or livery conveyance. This Exclusion **(A.5.)** does not apply to a share-the-expense car pool.

6. While employed or otherwise engaged in the "business" of:

   a. Selling;

   b. Repairing;

   c. Servicing;

   d. Storing; or

   e. Parking;

   vehicles designed for use mainly on public highways. This includes road testing and delivery. This Exclusion **(A.6.)** does not apply to the ownership, maintenance or use of "your covered auto" by:

   a. You;

   b. Any "family member"; or

   c. Any partner, agent or employee of you or any "family member".

7. Maintaining or using any vehicle while that "insured" is employed or otherwise engaged in any "business" (other than farming or ranching) not described in Exclusion **A.6.**

   This Exclusion **(A.7.)** does not apply to the maintenance or use of a:

   a. Private passenger auto;

   b. Pickup or van; or

   c. "Trailer" used with a vehicle described in **a.** or **b.** above.

8. Using a vehicle without a reasonable belief that that "insured" is entitled to do so. This Exclusion **(A.8.)** does not apply to a "family member" using "your covered auto" which is owned by you.

9. For "bodily injury" or "property damage" for which that "insured":

   a. Is an insured under a nuclear energy liability policy; or

   b. Would be an insured under a nuclear energy liability policy but for its termination upon exhaustion of its limit of liability.

   A nuclear energy liability policy is a policy issued by any of the following or their successors:

   a. Nuclear Energy Liability Insurance Association;

   b. Mutual Atomic Energy Liability Underwriters; or

   c. Nuclear Insurance Association of Canada.

B. We do not provide Liability Coverage for the ownership, maintenance or use of:

1. Any vehicle which:

   a. Has fewer than four wheels; or

   b. Is designed mainly for use off public roads.

   This Exclusion **(B.1.)** does not apply:

   a. While such vehicle is being used by an "insured" in a medical emergency;

   b. To any "trailer"; or

   c. To any non-owned golf cart.

2. Any vehicle, other than "your covered auto", which is:

   a. Owned by you; or

   b. Furnished or available for your regular use.

3. Any vehicle, other than "your covered auto", which is:

   a. Owned by any "family member"; or

   b. Furnished or available for the regular use of any "family member".

   However, this Exclusion **(B.3.)** does not apply to you while you are maintaining or "occupying" any vehicle which is:

   a. Owned by a "family member"; or

   b. Furnished or available for the regular use of a "family member".

4. Any vehicle, located inside a facility designed for racing, for the purpose of:

   a. Competing in; or

   b. Practicing or preparing for;

   any prearranged or organized racing or speed contest.

LIMIT OF LIABILITY

A. The limit of liability shown in the Declarations for each person for Bodily Injury Liability is our maximum limit of liability for all damages, including damages for care, loss of services or death, arising out of "bodily injury" sustained by any one person in any one auto accident. Subject to this limit for each person, the limit of liability shown in the Declarations for each accident for Bodily Injury Liability is our maximum limit of liability for all damages for "bodily injury" resulting from any one auto accident.

The limit of liability shown in the Declarations for each accident for Property Damage Liability is our maximum limit of liability for all "property damage" resulting from any one auto accident.

This is the most we will pay regardless of the number of:

1. "Insureds";
2. Claims made;
3. Vehicles or premiums shown in the Declarations; or
4. Vehicles involved in the auto accident.

B. No one will be entitled to receive duplicate payments for the same elements of loss under this coverage and:

1. Part B or Part C of this policy; or
2. Any Underinsured Motorists Coverage provided by this policy.

OUT OF STATE COVERAGE

If an auto accident to which this policy applies occurs in any state or province other than the one in which "your covered auto" is principally garaged, we will interpret your policy for that accident as follows:

A. If the state or province has:

1. A financial responsibility or similar law specifying limits of liability for "bodily injury" or "property damage" higher than the limit shown in the Declarations, your policy will provide the higher specified limit.

2. A compulsory insurance or similar law requiring a nonresident to maintain insurance whenever the nonresident uses a vehicle in that state or province, your policy will provide at least the required minimum amounts and types of coverage.

B. No one will be entitled to duplicate payments for the same elements of loss.

FINANCIAL RESPONSIBILITY

When this policy is certified as future proof of financial responsibility, this policy shall comply with the law to the extent required.

OTHER INSURANCE

If there is other applicable liability insurance we will pay only our share of the loss. Our share is the proportion that our limit of liability bears to the total of all applicable limits. However, any insurance we provide for a vehicle you do not own shall be excess over any other collectible insurance.

PART B – MEDICAL PAYMENTS COVERAGE

INSURING AGREEMENT

A. We will pay reasonable expenses incurred for necessary medical and funeral services because of "bodily injury":

1. Caused by accident; and
2. Sustained by an "insured".

We will pay only those expenses incurred for services rendered within 3 years from the date of the accident.

B. "Insured" as used in this Part means:

1. You or any "family member":
   a. While "occupying"; or
   b. As a pedestrian when struck by;

   a motor vehicle designed for use mainly on public roads or a trailer of any type.

2. Any other person while "occupying" "your covered auto".

EXCLUSIONS

We do not provide Medical Payments Coverage for any "insured" for "bodily injury":

1. Sustained while "occupying" any motorized vehicle having fewer than four wheels.

2. Sustained while "occupying" "your covered auto" when it is being used as a public or livery conveyance. This Exclusion (2.) does not apply to a share-the-expense car pool.

3. Sustained while "occupying" any vehicle located for use as a residence or premises.

4. Occurring during the course of employment if workers' compensation benefits are required or available for the "bodily injury".

5. Sustained while "occupying", or when struck by, any vehicle (other than "your covered auto") which is:
   a. Owned by you; or
   b. Furnished or available for your regular use.

6. Sustained while "occupying", or when struck by, any vehicle (other than "your covered auto") which is:
   a. Owned by any "family member"; or
   b. Furnished or available for the regular use of any "family member".

   However, this Exclusion (6.) does not apply to you.

 PP 00 01 06 98

7. Sustained while "occupying" a vehicle without a reasonable belief that that "insured" is entitled to do so. This Exclusion **(7.)** does not apply to a "family member" using "your covered auto" which is owned by you.

8. Sustained while "occupying" a vehicle when it is being used in the "business" of an "insured". This Exclusion **(8.)** does not apply to "bodily injury" sustained while "occupying" a:

   a. Private passenger auto;

   b. Pickup or van that you own; or

   c. "Trailer" used with a vehicle described in **a.** or **b.** above.

9. Caused by or as a consequence of:

   a. Discharge of a nuclear weapon (even if accidental);

   b. War (declared or undeclared);

   c. Civil war;

   d. Insurrection; or

   e. Rebellion or revolution.

10. From or as a consequence of the following, whether controlled or uncontrolled or however caused:

    a. Nuclear reaction;

    b. Radiation; or

    c. Radioactive contamination.

11. Sustained while "occupying" any vehicle located inside a facility designed for racing, for the purpose of:

    a. Competing in; or

    b. Practicing or preparing for;

    any prearranged or organized racing or speed contest.

LIMIT OF LIABILITY

A. The limit of liability shown in the Declarations for this coverage is our maximum limit of liability for each person injured in any one accident. This is the most we will pay regardless of the number of:

1. "Insureds";

2. Claims made;

3. Vehicles or premiums shown in the Declarations; or

4. Vehicles involved in the accident.

B. No one will be entitled to receive duplicate payments for the same elements of loss under this coverage and:

1. Part **A** or Part **C** of this policy; or

2. Any Underinsured Motorists Coverage provided by this policy.

OTHER INSURANCE

If there is other applicable auto medical payments insurance we will pay only our share of the loss. Our share is the proportion that our limit of liability bears to the total of all applicable limits. However, any insurance we provide with respect to a vehicle you do not own shall be excess over any other collectible auto insurance providing payments for medical or funeral expenses.

PART C – UNINSURED MOTORISTS COVERAGE

INSURING AGREEMENT

A. We will pay compensatory damages which an "insured" is legally entitled to recover from the owner or operator of an "uninsured motor vehicle" because of "bodily injury":

1. Sustained by an "insured"; and

2. Caused by an accident.

The owner's or operator's liability for these damages must arise out of the ownership, maintenance or use of the "uninsured motor vehicle".

Any judgment for damages arising out of a suit brought without our written consent is not binding on us.

B. "Insured" as used in this Part means:

1. You or any "family member".

2. Any other person "occupying" "your covered auto".

3. Any person for damages that person is entitled to recover because of "bodily injury" to which this coverage applies sustained by a person described in **1.** or **2.** above.

C. "Uninsured motor vehicle" means a land motor vehicle or trailer of any type:

1. To which no bodily injury liability bond or policy applies at the time of the accident.

2. To which a bodily injury liability bond or policy applies at the time of the accident. In this case its limit for bodily injury liability must be less than the minimum limit for bodily injury liability specified by the financial responsibility law of the state in which "your covered auto" is principally garaged.

3. Which is a hit-and-run vehicle whose operator or owner cannot be identified and which hits:

   a. You or any "family member";

   b. A vehicle which you or any "family member" are "occupying"; or

   c. "Your covered auto".

4. To which a bodily injury liability bond or policy applies at the time of the accident but the bonding or insuring company:

   a. Denies coverage; or

   b. Is or becomes insolvent.

However, "uninsured motor vehicle" does not include any vehicle or equipment:

1. Owned by or furnished or available for the regular use of you or any "family member".

2. Owned or operated by a self-insurer under any applicable motor vehicle law, except a self-insurer which is or becomes insolvent.

3. Owned by any governmental unit or agency.

4. Operated on rails or crawler treads.

5. Designed mainly for use off public roads while not on public roads.

6. While located for use as a residence or premises.

EXCLUSIONS

A. We do not provide Uninsured Motorists Coverage for "bodily injury" sustained:

1. By an "insured" while "occupying", or when struck by, any motor vehicle owned by that "insured" which is not insured for this coverage under this policy. This includes a trailer of any type used with that vehicle.

2. By any "family member" while "occupying", or when struck by, any motor vehicle you own which is insured for this coverage on a primary basis under any other policy.

B. We do not provide Uninsured Motorists Coverage for "bodily injury" sustained by any "insured":

1. If that "insured" or the legal representative settles the "bodily injury" claim without our consent.

2. While "occupying" "your covered auto" when it is being used as a public or livery conveyance. This Exclusion (**B.2.**) does not apply to a share-the-expense car pool.

3. Using a vehicle without a reasonable belief that that "insured" is entitled to do so. This Exclusion (**B.3.**) does not apply to a "family member" using "your covered auto" which is owned by you.

C. This coverage shall not apply directly or indirectly to benefit any insurer or self-insurer under any of the following or similar law:

1. Workers' compensation law; or

2. Disability benefits law.

D. We do not provide Uninsured Motorists Coverage for punitive or exemplary damages.

LIMIT OF LIABILITY

A. The limit of liability shown in the Declarations for each person for Uninsured Motorists Coverage is our maximum limit of liability for all damages, including damages for care, loss of services or death, arising out of "bodily injury" sustained by any one person in any one accident. Subject to this limit for each person, the limit of liability shown in the Declarations for each accident for Uninsured Motorists Coverage is our maximum limit of liability for all damages for "bodily injury" resulting from any one accident.

This is the most we will pay regardless of the number of:

1. "Insureds";

2. Claims made;

3. Vehicles or premiums shown in the Declarations; or

4. Vehicles involved in the accident.

B. No one will be entitled to receive duplicate payments for the same elements of loss under this coverage and:

1. Part **A.** or Part **B.** of this policy; or

2. Any Underinsured Motorists Coverage provided by this policy.

C. We will not make a duplicate payment under this coverage for any element of loss for which payment has been made by or on behalf of persons or organizations who may be legally responsible.

D. We will not pay for any element of loss if a person is entitled to receive payment for the same element of loss under any of the following or similar law:

1. Workers' compensation law; or

2. Disability benefits law.

OTHER INSURANCE

If there is other applicable insurance available under one or more policies or provisions of coverage that is similar to the insurance provided under this Part of the policy:

1. Any recovery for damages under all such policies or provisions of coverage may equal but not exceed the highest applicable limit for any one vehicle under any insurance providing coverage on either a primary or excess basis.

2. Any insurance we provide with respect to a vehicle you do not own shall be excess over any collectible insurance providing such coverage on a primary basis.

3. If the coverage under this policy is provided:

   a. On a primary basis, we will pay only our share of the loss that must be paid under insurance providing coverage on a primary basis. Our share is the proportion that our limit of liability bears to the total of all applicable limits of liability for coverage provided on a primary basis.

   b. On an excess basis, we will pay only our share of the loss that must be paid under insurance providing coverage on an excess basis. Our share is the proportion that our limit of liability bears to the total of all applicable limits of liability for coverage provided on an excess basis.

ARBITRATION

A. If we and an "insured" do not agree:

   1. Whether that "insured" is legally entitled to recover damages; or

   2. As to the amount of damages which are recoverable by that "insured";

   from the owner or operator of an "uninsured motor vehicle", then the matter may be arbitrated. However, disputes concerning coverage under this Part may not be arbitrated.

Both parties must agree to arbitration. If so agreed, each party will select an arbitrator. The two arbitrators will select a third. If they cannot agree within 30 days, either may request that selection be made by a judge of a court having jurisdiction.

B. Each party will:

   1. Pay the expenses it incurs; and

   2. Bear the expenses of the third arbitrator equally.

C. Unless both parties agree otherwise, arbitration will take place in the county in which the "insured" lives. Local rules of law as to procedure and evidence will apply. A decision agreed to by two of the arbitrators will be binding as to:

   1. Whether the "insured" is legally entitled to recover damages; and

   2. The amount of damages. This applies only if the amount does not exceed the minimum limit for bodily injury liability specified by the financial responsibility law of the state in which "your covered auto" is principally garaged. If the amount exceeds that limit, either party may demand the right to a trial. This demand must be made within 60 days of the arbitrators' decision. If this demand is not made, the amount of damages agreed to by the arbitrators will be binding.

PART D – COVERAGE FOR DAMAGE TO YOUR AUTO

INSURING AGREEMENT

A. We will pay for direct and accidental loss to "your covered auto" or any "non-owned auto", including their equipment, minus any applicable deductible shown in the Declarations. If loss to more than one "your covered auto" or "non-owned auto" results from the same "collision", only the highest applicable deductible will apply. We will pay for loss to "your covered auto" caused by:

   1. Other than "collision" only if the Declarations indicate that Other Than Collision Coverage is provided for that auto.

   2. "Collision" only if the Declarations indicate that Collision Coverage is provided for that auto.

   If there is a loss to a "non-owned auto", we will provide the broadest coverage applicable to any "your covered auto" shown in the Declarations.

B. "Collision" means the upset of "your covered auto" or a "non-owned auto" or their impact with another vehicle or object.

   Loss caused by the following is considered other than "collision":

   1. Missiles or falling objects;

   2. Fire;

   3. Theft or larceny;

   4. Explosion or earthquake;

   5. Windstorm;

   6. Hail, water or flood;

   7. Malicious mischief or vandalism;

   8. Riot or civil commotion;

   9. Contact with bird or animal; or

   10. Breakage of glass.

   If breakage of glass is caused by a "collision", you may elect to have it considered a loss caused by "collision".

C. "Non-owned auto" means:

   1. Any private passenger auto, pickup, van or "trailer" not owned by or furnished or available for the regular use of you or any "family member" while in the custody of or being operated by you or any "family member"; or

   2. Any auto or "trailer" you do not own while used as a temporary substitute for "your covered auto" which is out of normal use because of its:

      a. Breakdown;

      b. Repair;

      c. Servicing;

      d. Loss; or

      e. Destruction.

TRANSPORTATION EXPENSES

A. In addition, we will pay, without application of a deductible, up to a maximum of $600 for:

1. Temporary transportation expenses not exceeding $20 per day incurred by you in the event of a loss to "your covered auto". We will pay for such expenses if the loss is caused by:

   a. Other than "collision" only if the Declarations indicate that Other Than Collision Coverage is provided for that auto.

   b. "Collision" only if the Declarations indicate that Collision Coverage is provided for that auto.

2. Expenses for which you become legally responsible in the event of loss to a "non-owned auto". We will pay for such expenses if the loss is caused by:

   a. Other than "collision" only if the Declarations indicate that Other Than Collision Coverage is provided for any "your covered auto".

   b. "Collision" only if the Declarations indicate that Collision Coverage is provided for any "your covered auto".

   However, the most we will pay for any expenses for loss of use is $20 per day.

B. If the loss is caused by:

   1. A total theft of "your covered auto" or a "non-owned auto", we will pay only expenses incurred during the period:

      a. Beginning 48 hours after the theft; and

      b. Ending when "your covered auto" or the "non-owned auto" is returned to use or we pay for its loss.

   2. Other than theft of a "your covered auto" or a "non-owned auto", we will pay only expenses beginning when the auto is withdrawn from use for more than 24 hours.

C. Our payment will be limited to that period of time reasonably required to repair or replace the "your covered auto" or the "non-owned auto".

EXCLUSIONS

We will not pay for:

1. Loss to "your covered auto" or any "non-owned auto" which occurs while it is being used as a public or livery conveyance. This Exclusion **(1.)** does not apply to a share-the-expense car pool.

2. Damage due and confined to:

   a. Wear and tear;

   b. Freezing;

   c. Mechanical or electrical breakdown or failure; or

   d. Road damage to tires.

This Exclusion **(2.)** does not apply if the damage results from the total theft of "your covered auto" or any "non-owned auto".

3. Loss due to or as a consequence of:

   a. Radioactive contamination;

   b. Discharge of any nuclear weapon (even if accidental);

   c. War (declared or undeclared);

   d. Civil war;

   e. Insurrection; or

   f. Rebellion or revolution.

4. Loss to any electronic equipment designed for the reproduction of sound and any accessories used with such equipment. This includes but is not limited to:

   a. Radios and stereos;

   b. Tape decks; or

   c. Compact disc players.

This Exclusion **(4.)** does not apply to equipment designed solely for the reproduction of sound and accessories used with such equipment, provided:

   a. The equipment is permanently installed in "your covered auto" or any "non-owned auto"; or

   b. The equipment is:

      (1) Removable from a housing unit which is permanently installed in the auto;

      (2) Designed to be solely operated by use of the power from the auto's electrical system; and

      (3) In or upon "your covered auto" or any "non-owned auto" at the time of loss.

5. Loss to any electronic equipment that receives or transmits audio, visual or data signals and any accessories used with such equipment. This includes but is not limited to:

   a. Citizens band radios;

   b. Telephones;

   c. Two-way mobile radios;

   d. Scanning monitor receivers;

   e. Television monitor receivers;

   f. Video cassette recorders;

   g. Audio cassette recorders; or

   h. Personal computers.

This Exclusion **(5.)** does not apply to:

   a. Any electronic equipment that is necessary for the normal operation of the auto or the monitoring of the auto's operating systems; or

 PP 00 01 06 98

b. A permanently installed telephone designed to be operated by use of the power from the auto's electrical system and any accessories used with the telephone.

6. Loss to tapes, records, discs or other media used with equipment described in Exclusions **4.** and **5.**

7. A total loss to "your covered auto" or any "non-owned auto" due to destruction or confiscation by governmental or civil authorities.

This Exclusion **(7.)** does not apply to the interests of Loss Payees in "your covered auto".

8. Loss to:

a. A "trailer", camper body, or motor home, which is not shown in the Declarations; or

b. Facilities or equipment used with such "trailer", camper body or motor home. Facilities or equipment include but are not limited to:

(1) Cooking, dining, plumbing or refrigeration facilities;

(2) Awnings or cabanas; or

(3) Any other facilities or equipment used with a "trailer", camper body, or motor home.

This Exclusion **(8.)** does not apply to a:

a. "Trailer", and its facilities or equipment, which you do not own; or

b. "Trailer", camper body, or the facilities or equipment in or attached to the "trailer" or camper body, which you:

(1) Acquire during the policy period; and

(2) Ask us to insure within 14 days after you become the owner.

9. Loss to any "non-owned auto" when used by you or any "family member" without a reasonable belief that you or that "family member" are entitled to do so.

10. Loss to equipment designed or used for the detection or location of radar or laser.

11. Loss to any custom furnishings or equipment in or upon any pickup or van. Custom furnishings or equipment include but are not limited to:

a. Special carpeting or insulation;

b. Furniture or bars;

c. Height-extending roofs; or

d. Custom murals, paintings or other decals or graphics.

This Exclusion **(11.)** does not apply to a cap, cover or bedliner in or upon any "your covered auto" which is a pickup.

12. Loss to any "non-owned auto" being maintained or used by any person while employed or otherwise engaged in the "business" of:

a. Selling;

b. Repairing;

c. Servicing;

d. Storing; or

e. Parking;

vehicles designed for use on public highways. This includes road testing and delivery.

13. Loss to "your covered auto" or any "non-owned auto", located inside a facility designed for racing, for the purpose of:

a. Competing in; or

b. Practicing or preparing for;

any prearranged or organized racing or speed contest.

14. Loss to, or loss of use of, a "non-owned auto" rented by:

a. You; or

b. Any "family member";

if a rental vehicle company is precluded from recovering such loss or loss of use, from you or that "family member", pursuant to the provisions of any applicable rental agreement or state law.

LIMIT OF LIABILITY

A. Our limit of liability for loss will be the lesser of the:

1. Actual cash value of the stolen or damaged property; or

2. Amount necessary to repair or replace the property with other property of like kind and quality.

However, the most we will pay for loss to:

1. Any "non-owned auto" which is a trailer is $500.

2. Equipment designed solely for the reproduction of sound, including any accessories used with such equipment, which is installed in locations not used by the auto manufacturer for installation of such equipment or accessories, is $1,000.

B. An adjustment for depreciation and physical condition will be made in determining actual cash value in the event of a total loss.

C. If a repair or replacement results in better than like kind or quality, we will not pay for the amount of the betterment.

PAYMENT OF LOSS

We may pay for loss in money or repair or replace the damaged or stolen property. We may, at our expense, return any stolen property to:

1. You; or
2. The address shown in this policy.

If we return stolen property we will pay for any damage resulting from the theft. We may keep all or part of the property at an agreed or appraised value.

If we pay for loss in money, our payment will include the applicable sales tax for the damaged or stolen property.

NO BENEFIT TO BAILEE

This insurance shall not directly or indirectly benefit any carrier or other bailee for hire.

OTHER SOURCES OF RECOVERY

If other sources of recovery also cover the loss, we will pay only our share of the loss. Our share is the proportion that our limit of liability bears to the total of all applicable limits. However, any insurance we provide with respect to a "non-owned auto" shall be excess over any other collectible source of recovery including, but not limited to:

1. Any coverage provided by the owner of the "non-owned auto";
2. Any other applicable physical damage insurance;
3. Any other source of recovery applicable to the loss.

APPRAISAL

A. If we and you do not agree on the amount of loss, either may demand an appraisal of the loss. In this event, each party will select a competent appraiser. The two appraisers will select an umpire. The appraisers will state separately the actual cash value and the amount of loss. If they fail to agree, they will submit their differences to the umpire. A decision agreed to by any two will be binding. Each party will:

1. Pay its chosen appraiser; and
2. Bear the expenses of the appraisal and umpire equally.

B. We do not waive any of our rights under this policy by agreeing to an appraisal.

PART E – DUTIES AFTER AN ACCIDENT OR LOSS

We have no duty to provide coverage under this policy unless there has been full compliance with the following duties:

A. We must be notified promptly of how, when and where the accident or loss happened. Notice should also include the names and addresses of any injured persons and of any witnesses.

B. A person seeking any coverage must:

1. Cooperate with us in the investigation, settlement or defense of any claim or suit.
2. Promptly send us copies of any notices or legal papers received in connection with the accident or loss.
3. Submit, as often as we reasonably require:
   a. To physical exams by physicians we select. We will pay for these exams.
   b. To examination under oath and subscribe the same.
4. Authorize us to obtain:
   a. Medical reports; and
   b. Other pertinent records.
5. Submit a proof of loss when required by us.

C. A person seeking Uninsured Motorists Coverage must also:

1. Promptly notify the police if a hit-and-run driver is involved.
2. Promptly send us copies of the legal papers if a suit is brought.

D. A person seeking Coverage For Damage To Your Auto must also:

1. Take reasonable steps after loss to protect "your covered auto" or any "non-owned auto" and their equipment from further loss. We will pay reasonable expenses incurred to do this.
2. Promptly notify the police if "your covered auto" or any "non-owned auto" is stolen.
3. Permit us to inspect and appraise the damaged property before its repair or disposal.

PP 00 01 06 98

PART F – GENERAL PROVISIONS

BANKRUPTCY

Bankruptcy or insolvency of the "insured" shall not relieve us of any obligations under this policy.

CHANGES

A. This policy contains all the agreements between you and us. Its terms may not be changed or waived except by endorsement issued by us.

B. If there is a change to the information used to develop the policy premium, we may adjust your premium. Changes during the policy term that may result in a premium increase or decrease include, but are not limited to, changes in:

1. The number, type or use classification of insured vehicles;

2. Operators using insured vehicles;

3. The place of principal garaging of insured vehicles;

4. Coverage, deductible or limits.

If a change resulting from **A.** or **B.** requires a premium adjustment, we will make the premium adjustment in accordance with our manual rules.

C. If we make a change which broadens coverage under this edition of your policy without additional premium charge, that change will automatically apply to your policy as of the date we implement the change in your state. This Paragraph (**C.**) does not apply to changes implemented with a general program revision that includes both broadenings and restrictions in coverage, whether that general program revision is implemented through introduction of:

1. A subsequent edition of your policy; or

2. An Amendatory Endorsement.

FRAUD

We do not provide coverage for any "insured" who has made fraudulent statements or engaged in fraudulent conduct in connection with any accident or loss for which coverage is sought under this policy.

LEGAL ACTION AGAINST US

A. No legal action may be brought against us until there has been full compliance with all the terms of this policy. In addition, under Part **A**, no legal action may be brought against us until:

1. We agree in writing that the "insured" has an obligation to pay; or

2. The amount of that obligation has been finally determined by judgment after trial.

B. No person or organization has any right under this policy to bring us into any action to determine the liability of an "insured".

OUR RIGHT TO RECOVER PAYMENT

A. If we make a payment under this policy and the person to or for whom payment was made has a right to recover damages from another we shall be subrogated to that right. That person shall do:

1. Whatever is necessary to enable us to exercise our rights; and

2. Nothing after loss to prejudice them.

However, our rights in this Paragraph (**A.**) do not apply under Part **D**, against any person using "your covered auto" with a reasonable belief that that person is entitled to do so.

B. If we make a payment under this policy and the person to or for whom payment is made recovers damages from another, that person shall:

1. Hold in trust for us the proceeds of the recovery; and

2. Reimburse us to the extent of our payment.

POLICY PERIOD AND TERRITORY

A. This policy applies only to accidents and losses which occur:

1. During the policy period as shown in the Declarations; and

2. Within the policy territory.

B. The policy territory is:

1. The United States of America, its territories or possessions;

2. Puerto Rico; or

3. Canada.

 No coverage in Mexico

This policy also applies to loss to, or accidents involving, "your covered auto" while being transported between their ports.

TERMINATION

A. Cancellation

This policy may be cancelled during the policy period as follows:

1. The named insured shown in the Declarations may cancel by:

   a. Returning this policy to us; or

   b. Giving us advance written notice of the date cancellation is to take effect.

2. We may cancel by mailing to the named insured shown in the Declarations at the address shown in this policy:

   a. At least 10 days notice:

      (1) If cancellation is for nonpayment of premium; or

(2) If notice is mailed during the first 60 days this policy is in effect and this is not a renewal or continuation policy; or

   b. At least 20 days notice in all other cases.

3. After this policy is in effect for 60 days, or if this is a renewal or continuation policy, we will cancel only:

   a. For nonpayment of premium; or

   b. If your driver's license or that of:

      (1) Any driver who lives with you; or

      (2) Any driver who customarily uses "your covered auto";

      has been suspended or revoked. This must have occurred:

      (1) During the policy period; or

      (2) Since the last anniversary of the original effective date if the policy period is other than 1 year; or

   c. If the policy was obtained through material misrepresentation.

B. Nonrenewal

If we decide not to renew or continue this policy, we will mail notice to the named insured shown in the Declarations at the address shown in this policy. Notice will be mailed at least 20 days before the end of the policy period. Subject to this notice requirement, if the policy period is:

1. Less than 6 months, we will have the right not to renew or continue this policy every 6 months, beginning 6 months after its original effective date.

2. 6 months or longer, but less than one year, we will have the right not to renew or continue this policy at the end of the policy period.

3. 1 year or longer, we will have the right not to renew or continue this policy at each anniversary of its original effective date.

C. Automatic Termination

If we offer to renew or continue and you or your representative do not accept, this policy will automatically terminate at the end of the current policy period. Failure to pay the required renewal or continuation premium when due shall mean that you have not accepted our offer.

If you obtain other insurance on "your covered auto", any similar insurance provided by this policy will terminate as to that auto on the effective date of the other insurance.

D. Other Termination Provisions

1. We may deliver any notice instead of mailing it. Proof of mailing of any notice shall be sufficient proof of notice.

2. If this policy is cancelled, you may be entitled to a premium refund. If so, we will send you the refund. The premium refund, if any, will be computed according to our manuals. However, making or offering to make the refund is not a condition of cancellation.

3. The effective date of cancellation stated in the notice shall become the end of the policy period.

TRANSFER OF YOUR INTEREST IN THIS POLICY

A. Your rights and duties under this policy may not be assigned without our written consent. However, if a named insured shown in the Declarations dies, coverage will be provided for:

1. The surviving spouse if resident in the same household at the time of death. Coverage applies to the spouse as if a named insured shown in the Declarations; and

2. The legal representative of the deceased person as if a named insured shown in the Declarations. This applies only with respect to the representative's legal responsibility to maintain or use "your covered auto".

B. Coverage will only be provided until the end of the policy period.

TWO OR MORE AUTO POLICIES

If this policy and any other auto insurance policy issued to you by us apply to the same accident, the maximum limit of our liability under all the policies shall not exceed the highest applicable limit of liability under any one policy.

POLICY NUMBER:

PERSONAL AUTO
PP 03 11 06 98

THIS ENDORSEMENT CHANGES THE POLICY. PLEASE READ IT CAREFULLY.

UNDERINSURED MOTORISTS COVERAGE

SCHEDULE

Limit Of Liability	Premium		
	Auto 1	Auto 2	Auto 3
$ _____ each person	$ _____	$ _____	$ _____
$ _____ each accident			

With respect to the coverage provided by this endorsement, the provisions of the policy apply unless modified by the endorsement.

INSURING AGREEMENT

A. We will pay compensatory damages which an "insured" is legally entitled to recover from the owner or operator of an "underinsured motor vehicle" because of "bodily injury":

1. Sustained by an "insured"; and

2. Caused by an accident.

The owner's or operator's liability for these damages must arise out of the ownership, maintenance or use of the "underinsured motor vehicle".

We will pay under this coverage only if **1.** or **2.** below applies:

1. The limits of liability under any bodily injury liability bonds or policies applicable to the "underinsured motor vehicle" have been exhausted by payment of judgments or settlements; or

2. A tentative settlement has been made between an "insured" and the insurer of the "underinsured motor vehicle" and we:

a. Have been given prompt written notice of such tentative settlement; and

b. Advance payment to the "insured" in an amount equal to the tentative settlement within 30 days after receipt of notification.

B. "Insured" as used in this endorsement means:

1. You or any "family member".

2. Any other person "occupying" "your covered auto".

3. Any person for damages that person is entitled to recover because of "bodily injury" to which this coverage applies sustained by a person described in **1.** or **2.** above.

C. "Underinsured motor vehicle" means a land motor vehicle or trailer of any type to which a bodily injury liability bond or policy applies at the time of the accident but its limit for bodily injury liability is less than the limit of liability for this coverage.

However, "underinsured motor vehicle" does not include any vehicle or equipment:

1. To which a bodily injury liability bond or policy applies at the time of the accident but its limit for bodily injury liability is less than the minimum limit for bodily injury liability specified by the financial responsibility law of the state in which "your covered auto" is principally garaged.

2. Owned by or furnished or available for the regular use of you or any "family member".

3. Owned by any governmental unit or agency.

4. Operated on rails or crawler treads.

5. Designed mainly for use off public roads while not upon public roads.

6. While located for use as a residence or premises.

7. Owned or operated by a person qualifying as a self-insurer under any applicable motor vehicle law.

8. To which a bodily injury liability bond or policy applies at the time of the accident but the bonding or insuring company:

a. Denies coverage; or

b. Is or becomes insolvent.

EXCLUSIONS

A. We do not provide Underinsured Motorists Coverage for "bodily injury" sustained:

1. By an "insured" while "occupying", or when struck by, any motor vehicle owned by that "insured" which is not insured for this coverage under this policy. This includes a trailer of any type used with that vehicle.

2. By any "family member" while "occupying", or when struck by, any motor vehicle you own which is insured for this coverage on a primary basis under any other policy.

B. We do not provide Underinsured Motorists Coverage for "bodily injury" sustained by any "insured":

1. While "occupying" "your covered auto" when it is being used as a public or livery conveyance. This Exclusion **(B.1.)** does not apply to a share-the-expense car pool.

2. Using a vehicle without a reasonable belief that that "insured" is entitled to do so. This Exclusion **(B.2.)** does not apply to a "family member" using "your covered auto" which is owned by you.

C. This coverage shall not apply directly or indirectly to benefit any insurer or self-insurer under any of the following or similar law:

1. Workers' compensation law; or

2. Disability benefits law.

D. We do not provide Underinsured Motorists Coverage for punitive or exemplary damages.

LIMIT OF LIABILITY

A. The limit of liability shown in the Schedule or in the Declarations for each person for Underinsured Motorists Coverage is our maximum limit of liability for all damages, including damages for care, loss of services or death, arising out of "bodily injury" sustained by any one person in any one accident. Subject to this limit for each person, the limit of liability shown in the Schedule or in the Declarations for each accident for Underinsured Motorists Coverage is our maximum limit of liability for all damages for "bodily injury" resulting from any one accident.

This is the most we will pay regardless of the number of:

1. "Insureds";

2. Claims made;

3. Vehicles or premiums shown in the Schedule or in the Declarations; or

4. Vehicles involved in the accident.

B. The limit of liability shall be reduced by all sums paid because of the "bodily injury" by or on behalf of persons or organizations who may be legally responsible. This includes all sums paid under Part **A** of this policy.

C. No one will be entitled to receive duplicate payments for the same elements of loss under this coverage and Part **A**, Part **B** or Part **C** of this policy.

D. We will not make a duplicate payment under this coverage for any element of loss for which payment has been made by or on behalf of persons or organizations who may be legally responsible.

E. We will not pay for any element of loss if a person is entitled to receive payment for the same element of loss under any of the following or similar law;

1. Workers' compensation law; or

2. Disability benefits law.

OTHER INSURANCE

If there is other applicable insurance available under one or more policies or provisions of coverage that is similar to the insurance provided by this endorsement:

1. Any recovery for damages under all such policies or provisions of coverage may equal but not exceed the highest applicable limit for any one vehicle under any insurance providing coverage on either a primary or excess basis.

2. Any insurance we provide with respect to a vehicle you do not own shall be excess over any collectible insurance providing such coverage on a primary basis.

3. If the coverage under this policy is provided:

a. On a primary basis, we will pay only our share of the loss that must be paid under insurance providing coverage on a primary basis. Our share is the proportion that our limit of liability bears to the total of all applicable limits of liability for coverage provided on a primary basis.

b. On an excess basis, we will pay only our share of the loss that must be paid under insurance providing coverage on an excess basis. Our share is the proportion that our limit of liability bears to the total of all applicable limits of liability for coverage provided on an excess basis.

 PP 03 11 06 98

ARBITRATION

A. If we and an "insured" do not agree:

1. Whether that "insured" is legally entitled to recover damages; or

2. As to the amount of damages which are recoverable by that "insured";

from the owner or operator of an "underinsured motor vehicle", then the matter may be arbitrated. However, disputes concerning coverage under this endorsement may not be arbitrated.

Both parties must agree to arbitration. If so agreed, each party will select an arbitrator. The two arbitrators will select a third. If they cannot agree within 30 days, either may request that selection be made by a judge of a court having jurisdiction.

B. Each party will:

1. Pay the expenses it incurs; and

2. Bear the expenses of the third arbitrator equally.

C. Unless both parties agree otherwise, arbitration will take place in the county in which the "insured" lives. Local rules of law as to procedure and evidence will apply. A decision agreed to by two of the arbitrators will be binding as to:

1. Whether the "insured" is legally entitled to recover damages; and

2. The amount of damages. This applies only if the amount does not exceed the minimum limit for bodily injury liability specified by the financial responsibility law of the state in which "your covered auto" is principally garaged. If the amount exceeds that limit, either party may demand the right to a trial. This demand must be made within 60 days of the arbitrators' decision. If this demand is not made, the amount of damages agreed to by the arbitrators will be binding.

ADDITIONAL DUTIES

A person seeking coverage under this endorsement must also promptly:

1. Send us copies of the legal papers if a suit is brought; and

2. Notify us in writing of a tentative settlement between the "insured" and the insurer of the "underinsured motor vehicle" and allow us 30 days to advance payment to that "insured" in an amount equal to the tentative settlement to preserve our rights against the insurer, owner or operator of such "underinsured motor vehicle".

GENERAL PROVISIONS

The following is added to the **Our Right To Recover Payment** Provision in Part **F:**

OUR RIGHT TO RECOVER PAYMENT

Our rights do not apply under Paragraph **A.** with respect to Underinsured Motorists Coverage if we:

1. Have been given prompt written notice of a tentative settlement between an "insured" and the insurer of an "underinsured motor vehicle", and

2. Fail to advance payment to the "insured" in an amount equal to the tentative settlement within 30 days after receipt of notification.

If we advance payment to the "insured" in an amount equal to the tentative settlement within 30 days after receipt of notification:

1. That payment will be separate from any amount the "insured" is entitled to recover under the provisions of Underinsured Motorists Coverage; and

2. We also have a right to recover the advanced payment.

This endorsement must be attached to the Change Endorsement when issued after the policy is written.

AUTHOR INDEX

SUBJECT INDEX